MW00849974

Live from the Underground

Live from the Underground

A History of College Radio

· ·

KATHERINE RYE JEWELL

The University of North Carolina Press Chapel Hill

This book was published with the assistance of the Anniversary Fund of the University of North Carolina Press.

© 2023 Katherine Rye Jewell
All rights reserved
Set in Charis by Westchester Publishing Services
Manufactured in the United States of America

Library of Congress Cataloging-in-Publication Data
Names: Jewell, Katherine Rye, author.
Title: Live from the underground : a history of college radio /
    Katherine Rye Jewell.
Description: Chapel Hill : The University of North Carolina Press, 2023. |
    Includes bibliographical references and index.
Identifiers: LCCN 2023014311 | ISBN 9781469676203 (cloth ; alk. paper) |
    ISBN 9781469677255 (paperback ; alk. paper) |
    ISBN 9781469676210 (ebook)
Subjects: LCSH: College radio stations—United States—History—
    20th century. | United States—Social life and customs—20th century. |
    BISAC: HISTORY / United States / 20th Century | SOCIAL SCIENCE /
    Ethnic Studies / American / General
Classification: LCC PN1991.67.C64 J49 2023 | DDC 791.44/3—dc23/
    eng/20230422
LC record available at https://lccn.loc.gov/2023014311

Cover illustrations: *Top*, Live message by Bits and Splits/stock.adobe.com;
bottom, record spines.

Chapter 13 was previously published in a different form as "'Specialty'
Listening: Creating Space for Queer Programming on American College Radio
in the Long 1980s," in *Resist, Organize, Build: Feminist and Queer Activism in
Britain and the United States during the Long 1980s*, ed. Sarah Cook and
Charlie Jeffries (Albany: SUNY Press, 2022).

For Caroline and Elizabeth
and the DJs of WRVU 91.1 Nashville

Contents

Figures and Tables

Liner Notes

The first quiz I took in college was on the seven words I can't say on the radio.

In August 1997, I landed at a student activities fair table with the letters WRVU—standing for Radio Vanderbilt University—emblazoned on a make-shift sign. I had always loved music; my tastes had been mostly defined by my dad's record collection and by the radio stations that made it to my hometown in Vermont, including, occasionally at night, the sounds of modern rock alternative WEQX. For me, as for most young people of the 1980s and 1990s, radio (the source of free music before the internet) offered few opportunities for sounds far outside the mainstream of popular music, save those on the left of the FM dial. In the mountains, the only college outlet I could tune into was WFRD out of Dartmouth College, a commercial station that mostly played classic rock (though it did host a Sunday night metal show). Unlike those more tightly formatted stations, as a DJ, WRVU's general manager told me, I could play whatever I wanted.

Picturing myself at the helm of a Sixties-throwback show, I attended the training meeting and took the quiz, gleefully writing down the naughty words. I studied the rules. I learned to operate the board. By the time I took to the airwaves, my musical horizons had expanded, and I became yet another denizen of the 1990s indie-rock scene, worshipping the Pixies, Pavement, Helium, Riot Grrrl bands, and the latest Jon Spencer Blues Explosion or Guided by Voices record (figure 0.1). All-ages venue Lucy's Record Shop closed after my first year, but there were plenty of other small, local clubs for catching a show by Nashville's Lambchop or other touring bands.

My teachers were the host of fellow students who had been sustained in their high school days by college radio and all-ages clubs like Lucy's. These "freaks" in the larger fraternity-dominated culture at Vanderbilt nursed their iconoclasm with postpunk indie rock or soul, funk, and hip-hop (though the majority were middle- and upper-class white kids). Those from the suburbs or exurbs of Nashville, Houston, Washington, D.C., or Atlanta, with famed music scenes or stations at Rice University or Georgia Tech, had been introduced to college radio long before I had been. Such FM

FIGURE 0.1 WUOG hosted a fundraiser in 2003 that auctioned off dates with DJs. The cartoon captures the station's indie-rock and often elitist image compared with the majority of the UGA student body. Mack Williams, *Red and Black*, April 3, 2003.

signals reached the suburbs, linking kids listening on their headphones to underground scenes in nearby cities. They provided a lifeline for those who either didn't fit in or shunned mainstream popular culture, fashion, and other teenage social rituals.

I graduated and became a historian. I returned to college radio to study its historical development when I learned in 2011 that WRVU was being sold. A bastion of opposition to the Vanderbilt fraternity scene drifted online. While station alumni protested its sale, no savior emerged. WRVU's sale yielded another event in the ongoing transformation of popular music amid technological change. I had watched as Napster came and went during my college years, altering expectations for music consumption and channeling music fans' frustration with the gouging prices of CDs. MTV had already been lost to reality TV and glorified gameshows. Yet the technological disruption narrative belied the complexity of college radio culture that existed before mp3s and file sharing.

Radio historians know the long-standing diversity of college radio. Whether through carrier current, AM, FM, digital streaming, or podcasting, it had always been and remains a vibrant and diverse space, with an identity extending far beyond indie rock. This book, while claiming status as a history of college radio, cannot hope to reconstruct this vast historical landscape in its entirety.

But it can explore the origins, meaning, and transformation of this modern college radio culture. In 1985, the Replacements' Paul Westerberg penned an ode to college radio, the stations populating the "left of the dial" on the FM spectrum. Westerberg sang, "Passin' through and it's late, the station started to fade / Picked another one up in the very next state." The song celebrated college radio and its patchwork coverage from college towns to major cities across the country, piecing together a network of like-minded students and musical communities uninterested in the offerings of commercial radio. Road trippers, if not listening to self-made mix tapes, would often turn their dials to the left, exploring what college stations in range offered. Such ritual offered serendipitous musical discovery of local and regional culture that reflected the nation's cultural diversity.

College radio's market power and identity—the sometimes-reviled reputation of elitist indie-rock kids spinning records and manning mics—was a product of historical forces, and it was transient. This book traces the fraught process of college radio's emergence as a cultural and market force, with a recognizable identity, and the ongoing and newly emerging challenges to that identity.

This soundscape's history engages with key developments in the last half of the twentieth century, particularly how Americans considered the nation's cultural diversity and how these debates existed at the nexus of the business of the music industry, politics, media deregulation, and the changing structure and place of higher education within the nation. All reveal shifts in political culture and processes of self-discovery and artistic expression as the business and politics of culture evolved. College radio gave ordinary music fans an entry point to participate in and, maybe, challenge these transformations.

College radio's "modern" history starts when student-run educational stations proliferated on the FM dial in the 1960s. Stations remained distinct and diverse from one another, even as numbers expanded and a collective, though eclectic, musical reputation emerged. By the late 1980s, this network consisted of roughly 1,200 individual stations. Some were on wired, carrier-current signals or were a mere ten watts, enough power to reach the farthest dorm on campus; some projected music with 50,000 watts, airing to potentially millions of listeners. Each offered a unique format to its institutional home or radio market. Some connected to local underground music scenes; some emulated commercial radio as much as possible. Yet these stations offered—and still do—a cross-class, cross-community forum for the clash and, sometimes, resolution of issues meaningful to an array of claimants to public space.

What this book can't do is tell every DJ's story or chronicle each station's history. In recounting the history of a beloved medium like college radio, this and the realities of the historical record present a challenging task for a historian. Some gaps result from archival challenges. Radio continues to be difficult to document. Listeners' experiences are hard to access, meaning this history focuses primarily on DJs and participants at stations or in surrounding campuses. Not all perspectives appear in the archives. At times, reporters or students might not capture elements of a station's history with complete accuracy or detail, and sources are scarce to confirm small details. College radio's collective history remains diffused across institutions of varying organization and degrees of documentation. Most college radio stories remain in the diaries and memories of DJs and listeners, or perhaps on cassette tapes stored in shoeboxes in attics. This book captures some of these. But there are many more stories to tell, voices to highlight, musical and political contributions to assess. College radio stations' relationships with political and activist groups took many forms and deserve elucidation by scholars. Historically black colleges and universities played a significant role in shaping the culture of college and educational radio as well as commercial AM and FM. There remains much radio history yet to uncover.

From archival documents across institutions, debates captured in student newspapers, and oral histories, I reconstruct and complicate college radio's history at the twentieth century's end. It starts in Part I in the 1970s as freeform commercial FM radio settled into album-oriented radio, a narrower format that indicated a fragmenting broadcast (as well as political and cultural) landscape. Within this, college radio emerged as a recognizable—though chaotic—format of its own. Stations collectively developed a national reputation and cultural role but nonetheless remained places of conflict among participants who had divergent expectations for their service. Part II explores college radio's emergence as a national, influential institution caught up in the political and cultural conflagrations of the 1980s that visited both popular culture and higher education, as well as transformed commercial and public broadcasting. College students, even if engaged in amateur, pedagogical radio play, could not escape the culture wars or the scrutiny tuned to popular music in the Reagan years or the shifting financial realities colleges and universities confronted. By Part III as the 1990s dawned, college radio sparked mainstream attention to "alternative" rock and hip-hop as media deregulation and creeping market logics in higher education placed additional expectations and strains on these stations. Service to underground music scenes and networks continued, and students trained for professional careers. Throughout these years, college students and community volunteers took to the airwaves. They came with a variety of expectations, musical interests, and aversions and with a desire to engage in a meaningful activity for their community—however they envisioned it.

Readers might be wondering: isn't college radio's heyday over, thanks to digital streaming and online media? The answer, in short, is no. But the reasons why are complicated, and this book reveals deep connections between musical culture, US politics and policy, and the history of higher education that transcend technological changes at the end of the century.

Live from the Underground

Introduction

. . . .

Two friends looked at the camera and smirked as they poured martinis from a silver shaker. The one in a green turtleneck tried to avoid lapsing into riffs about postmodern subjectivity. The other, wearing a blazer and wire-rimmed glasses, explained that their new punk rock– and college radio–inspired magazine articulated how readers could resist the culture industry. As they escorted a filmmaker through the house serving as their fledgling magazine's headquarters, the two PhD students cued up a seven-inch single by Sabalon Glitz, a local indie band specializing in "space-rock."[1] (One member lived upstairs.) Produced via an independent production and distribution system, the record offered an alternative way of consuming music and captured the vibrancy of Chicago's underground rock scene.[2] These twenty-seven-year-olds in 1993 hoped to awaken young Americans to their saturation in images of pseudo-rebellion. Perhaps they might even resist major record labels that sought to turn them into ordinary consumers. Their magazine would do this by following the model of college radio.

By the early 1990s, this model suggested that defying, or at least opting out of, the culture industry might yet be possible. These students, David Mulcahy and Thomas Frank, were also DJs at the University of Chicago's WHPK. They envisioned their magazine *The Baffler* as extending that station's transgressive mode. Inspired by punk's DIY ethos and existing "outside of" and in "opposition to" conventional modes of cultural production and distribution, the magazine followed college radio's example. Both represented youth taking "cultural production into our own hands," they explained.[3]

Frank's explanation of *The Baffler* while he was a PhD student drew upon the arguments in his dissertation and subsequent book, *The Conquest of Cool*. In it, he challenged many baby boomers' belief that they had rejected midcentury conformity and consumerism through the counterculture. Instead, Frank argued, countercultural types merely bought into hip consumerism to salve the realities of work.[4] For the next generation to defy these alluring trappings, they could look to punk, postpunk, and hardcore rock to challenge an egregious offender: the music industry.[5]

Sure, punk suffered the same fate as the counterculture, with symbols of rebellion co-opted and incorporated into popular culture. But real punks needed no mohawk, dyed hair, or leather jacket. Frank hosted the hardcore show at WHPK in thrifted blazers. Donning some corporatized symbol of rebellion, he told the filmmaker, would be inherently inauthentic. It wasn't enough to buy Nirvana records and wallow in angst; pop culture rebels had to consume in a separate market accessed through actually alternative networks—not corporate-driven radio formats.

College radio offered an ideal venue for these attitudes. It could never overtake commercial radio, remaining scarce and subaltern. Pop culture rejects sought sanctuary at these stations by the 1990s. Protected by institutional homes and noncommercial licenses, these stations operated on the public's airwaves for educational purposes. Such missions offered useful cover for DJs seeking the weird, the unheard, or underappreciated. Such music might never reach, or actively defied, mainstream audiences. Many participants were content with remaining on the outside, in the underground. Stations developed devoted listener bases of engaged music fans and lured college students who didn't quite fit in on campus. Community DJs turned to college radio, too, seeking purchase on the nation's airwaves— or at least however far the usually low-wattage collegiate signal reached.

By the early 1990s college radio had earned a national identity that evoked generational dissatisfaction with pop culture even as it remained deeply conversant with it. These signals did offer alternative voices to willing audiences. Yet college radio's collective status as an alternative, or counterhegemonic, medium is debatable.[6] Virtually all elements of the college radio model—educational mission, anticommercialism, funding mechanisms, organizational structures, professional practices, content, or audience relationships—were contested in one way or another after the 1970s. Some stations explored the furthest fringes of musical expression, but these were missions shaped historically and through conflict. Numerous DJs sought careers in the news, music, and media industries. Not all stations devoted programming to music lacking broad commercial appeal, but these signals and their participants also shaped the nation's landscape of collegiate radio. College radio's status as an alternative medium is thus tenuous, even if in aggregate or individually these stations possessed disruptive potential.[7]

The possibilities and problems inherent in the nation's system of educational radio were apparent at Chicago's WHPK, despite its high marks for experimentation and service. DJs aired new music from across genres, new and old. Shows promoted indie rock and hip-hop and supported local underground music scenes. WHPK reached beyond the campus enclave into the South Side neighborhood, but DJs struggled to make the case for community service to the UChicago students. As graduate students, Frank and other DJs claimed positions in student government to ensure WHPK's funding when the student body president targeted the station for cuts.[8]

They relied on WHPK's history of breaking musical ground to secure university support. In 1984, DJ Ken Wissoker launched what is widely regarded as the first hip-hop show in the Midwest, drawing aspiring artists to the station.[9] He and John "JP Chill" Schauer, DJ of another lauded hip-hop show, received thanks in the liner notes of Public Enemy's 1988 album, *It Takes a Nation of Millions to Hold Us Back*. Common, who went by Common Sense until 1995, was a devoted fan. He camped out on the street outside the studio to get his tapes on air.[10] Serving listeners with new music and maintaining an alternative, community-oriented identity put WHPK at the forefront of musical innovation, including hip-hop. Older listeners, too, tuned in for soul music.

These successes did not protect the station from friction, whether from UChicago students not seeing the point of adventurous radio or from non-affiliated listeners. In one instance WHPK seemingly launched a battle over obscenity and generational differences regarding rap that pitted the station against community members.

At 10:20 P.M. on a Thursday in January 1993, *Chicago Defender* reporter Chinta Strausberg spun past 88.5 on her FM dial, paused, and hit "Record" on her tape player to capture the "garbage" she heard on WHPK.[11] At the next city council meeting, Ninth Ward alderman Robert Shaw played Strausberg's recording. A DJ had aired a twenty-year-old spoken-word piece by comedian and actor Rudy Ray Moore, in which he assumed a sleazy persona replete with irony.[12]

Moore's explicit description of intercourse shocked the room. Perhaps the DJ felt emboldened by a recent Federal Communications Commission (FCC) decision allowing "safe harbor" for indecent material after 10 P.M. Or, perhaps, Chicago's political class saw an opportunity to strike into ongoing culture wars while making an example of a white DJ on a predominantly white station that either presumed to speak for Black audiences or aired what those in power considered harmful representation.[13] Whatever the motivation, the Joint City Council committee decided unanimously to ask the FCC to investigate WHPK for obscenity.

The station found itself caught in Chicago's complex political landscape. WHPK's station manager Greg Lane sent an explanatory letter and did not attend the meeting. Lane likely understood the tenuous position the station occupied: the DJ certainly recognized Moore's irony, but the expression crossed regulatory boundaries. WHPK, moreover, could not arbitrate cultural conversations among Chicago's Black community. The station's governing board sent a supportive statement, but Shaw focused on Lane's "arrogant" letter. Lane, another of *The Baffler*'s founders, defended the broadcast as demonstrating "African American rhythm and blues recordings from the 1960s and 1970s" in the tradition of "Pigmeat Markham, Redd Foxx, Richard Pryor, and Eddie Murphy." Not impressed, Shaw declared the broadcast an "affront" to the community's morality. The *Chicago Tribune* described Lane's defense as "a little too much like a white college kid lecturing them on African American culture."[14] At the center of this incident resided a reality: a predominantly white institution had taken on the responsibility of providing entertainment to a community underserved in many ways, including by media.

Such struggles over the meaning and purpose of college radio transcended any one song, DJ, show, or station. Divergent interests called on stations beyond disgruntled Gen Xers feeling lost in the dreck of commercial radio. Dissonant expectations fueled clashes over content, programming, and allocated airtime, but they also presented the potential for community connection—though they offered surrounding residents no opportunity for media ownership or control.[15]

If or how stations served communal functions depended on governing structures. Their institutional homes determined degrees of independence and perhaps even mission and programming.[16] Students usually set the agenda for signals within these parameters. Radio space existed for white students as a normative part of most universities, while Black and minority students had to actively create opportunities, often remaining marginal within institutional media.[17] Station constitutions might prohibit community listeners from setting schedules or participating as DJs. Communities relied on the goodwill and understanding of individual DJs, leaders, or administrators to operate signals in the public interest and represent their voices. All of this required sufficient funding and institutions allowing signals to operate in their name—which grew tenuous amid declining investment, rising corporate logic within university administrations, and national political conversations that scrutinized university curricula, instructional content, and missions.

College radio stations occupying space on the public airwaves were never separate from larger questions about who controls the airwaves—and national culture. Skirmishes over college radio programming in the 1980s and 1990s signaled problems in the nation's federally regulated media and the potential for disruption. A crowded FM spectrum left fewer spaces for localities to secure representation, compounded by narrow playlists of commercial radio, which grew tighter amid deregulation and consolidation well before the Telecommunications Act of 1996. In that environment, college radio's disruptive potential took on added significance. Embedded within institutional power structures of higher education, federal regulatory bodies, and the corporate culture industry, college radio offered participation in alternative, underground markets and culture while remaining thoroughly a part of the nation's dominant political economy and politics of culture. In sum, these stations embodied the paradoxes of higher education's evolving role in US political and cultural life at the end of the century.

This book explains how college radio got to that point.[18]

The Politics of College Radio

College radio involves more than musical influence or good times in one's undergraduate days. In fact, college radio's evolution illuminates the United States' politics of culture and centrality of universities to these debates since the 1970s. More specifically, this history explains why higher education remains so embattled politically and speaks to the business of culture and the challenges presented by digital disruptions and corporate consolidation. But struggles over the airwaves began long before online streaming. Questions over national identity, democracy, and how citizens confront these questions through media shaped college radio's emergence and its history.

Seventy years of developments in broadcasting technology and regulation gave rise to college radio's left-of-the-dial reputation in the 1980s and 1990s.[19] College stations existed since radio's earliest days, founded by student-led radio clubs, electrical engineering departments, and agricultural extension services at land-grant institutions and expanded to create edifying content for circulation on commercial radio by the 1930s. Thanks to regulatory and legislative decisions, however, commercial national networks crowded out small college broadcasters, which dwindled below fifty signals by the decade's end.[20] College radio continued to reach listeners through syndicated content, carrier-current stations on campus (low-power signals transmitted via wires, or even pipes, able to be picked up over short distances with AM receivers), and occasionally via higher-power AM, until FM emerged as an alternative. The FM frequencies most college radio stations occupied resulted from the FCC setting aside 88.1 to 91.9 FM for noncommercial, educational (NCE) radio in 1945, but adoption lagged.[21]

As college stations appeared on FM, they usually did so under a ten-watt, class D, NCE license with limited range and freedom from advertisers' demands. This license, offered after 1948, provided cheaper access to the airwaves. Lower technology costs and regulatory prodding produced a renaissance in educational broadcasting. By 1967, more than 300 NCE licensed stations existed on FM, most at the low-power class D level.[22] Signals offered classical music, faculty lectures, campus sports, and content to enrich, often with a highbrow reputation. Midwestern institutions provided commodity prices to farmers or educational programs, particularly in Wisconsin, which built one of the few statewide educational FM networks. The network embodied the Wisconsin Idea to lower ivory tower walls and make knowledge and its benefits widely available, an idea that informed many college stations.[23] Religious broadcasts sustained faithful listeners unable to attend services. Meanwhile, student DJs capitalized on universities' promise to provide public service to develop new types of shows.[24] Varied evolutions in governance, curricular functions, and funding meant stations developed with diverse arrangements depending on locality and institution.

These were safe spaces, it seemed. They benefited from educational radio proponents who, in the 1930s, secured the noncommercial, educational FM spectrum allocation: a victory against for-profit corporatized, mass media. College stations, whether on carrier-current, AM, or FM signals, defied commercial pressures to please wide swaths of listeners. Universities appeared as havens for self-expression, focused on liberal arts inquiry and exploration—albeit with their own barriers to entry. Their radio signals, consequently, generated edifying content for nonenrolled listeners; news, sports, and study music aired for students.[25]

College radio was, essentially, a liberal creation of the 1930s.[26] These signals symbolized New Dealers' hopes for radio to enable mass democracy, inspire an enlightened citizenry, and promote cultural pluralism.[27] Elites remained in charge, however, with audiences dependent on how much leeway license holders (usually boards of trustees or university presidents) allowed student-run broadcasters.[28]

Still, stations often operated under a sense of public service, educational mission, and academic freedom—although the latter term rarely came up among participants.[29] Signals debuted on FM in the 1960s and early 1970s during years when, as one historian put it, "the democratic vision of universal mass higher education evaporated."[30] These goals struck a hopeful tone, but college DJs and programmers had several influences.

College stations often took cues from progressive and community radio, which in turn often drew staff from college radio. Progressive radio emerged in 1949, during the deepening Red Scare, from the Pacifica Foundation, which aired dissident voices in defiance of tight Top 40 AM radio playlists that "contained" cultural pluralism.[31] Folk music found its way to collegiate signals alongside jazz and classical shows.[32] Civil rights organizers benefited from coordination provided by Black-owned radio stations and those at historically Black colleges and universities (HBCUs). Students at HBCUs understood radio's uses beyond entertainment.[33] Social and political activists, from civil rights to feminism to gay rights, expanded their pursuits to culture. A number of college stations followed Pacifica in the 1970s, adding programming for queer communities or to aid social causes. Some broadcast Alan Ginsberg's poetry or public service announcements for clinics providing abortion services (as happened at Georgetown University, which among other campus conflicts over the radio station culminated with the university gifting the signal to another college in 1979).[34]

Stations emulated commercial FM as well. Music industry publication *Billboard* in the 1960s noted how college radio programmed more popular rock as students gravitated away from the highbrow fare of classical, jazz, and folk music, making these stations attractive places to market music.[35] But commercial FM and musical culture continued to shift, along with college students' tastes.

Tom Donohue at KMPX-FM in San Francisco began broadcasting "freeform" radio, detailed in a scathing 1967 *Rolling Stone* essay, "AM Radio Is Dead and Its Rotting Corpse Is Stinking Up the Airwaves." "Freeform" meant freedom from format. DJs selected deep cuts (songs not yet hitting the pop charts, or which never would) from rock albums and defied genre boundaries by cuing up blues and electronic music next to reggae, jazz, and classical. Donohue championed rock radio as defiant of the commercialism of pop music, fostering creativity and offering authenticity his listeners craved. AM radio no longer reflected its audience or the quality of recordings from bands like the Beatles, the Byrds, and Bob Dylan.[36] Freeform, such as juxtaposing Muddy Waters with Mozart, assimilated diverse expressions, symbolized the nation's cultural melting-pot idealism, and often drew talent from the ranks of college radio, where DJs felt freer to experiment. College students tuned in, and early freeform FM stations drew talent from the ranks of collegiate DJs.[37]

By the mid-1970s, however, commercial freeform became increasingly standardized into the album-oriented rock (AOR) format, as for-profit radio programmed for continuity to avoid alienating listeners. That left college radio as the spot on the dial more likely to offer freeform hours—even if only in the wee hours of the morning.

These influences produced a national landscape of college radio by the end of the 1970s broadly considered alternative to commercial radio. Jazz, classical, and folk labels enjoyed good relationships with these signals, and mainstream genres developed interest, but these did not wholly define college radio in that decade. Instead, college radio remained shaped by divided schedules and its many services. It remained a profoundly local and pedagogical medium.

College radio's dominant schedule structure facilitated its diverse services. Most stations employed block programming, dividing the day into segments dedicated to certain genres, specialty shows, or freeform hours. Most blocks had no reference to time of day, such as "drive time" in the parlance of "dayparting" in radio programming. This approach accommodated college students, who had erratic schedules that changed each semester and who still had to go to class and take exams. Blocks allowed stations to pursue divergent visions of US culture on a single signal—though they risked, as commercial and public broadcasting professionals warned, serving no one by attempting to serve everyone.[38]

The 1971 entrance of National Public Radio (NPR), funded in part thanks to the Public Broadcasting Act of 1967 through the Corporation for Public Broadcasting (CPB), offered university administrators an alternative to this student-run mix of eclectic programming. In NPR's wake, college radio diverged from public broadcasting. NPR's architects envisioned a network anchored at college stations across the nation, alongside municipal and community broadcasters such as WGBH in Boston or WNYC in New York City. NPR offered attractive and reputable programming to administrators and listeners, whereas student-run radio defied the nationalization of public radio broadcasting.[39] Some signals balanced a few hours of NPR programming per day with student and volunteer-run shows. In several instances, universities shifted student-run signals to NPR affiliates only to see students launch secondary signals in their wake.[40]

Student-run stations, these vaguely alternative, amateur "sandboxes," diverged in sound and mission from nationally syndicated news, information, and cultural programming. Public broadcasting remained solidly in the hands of professionals with no on-air opportunities for students. Limits to these distinctions persisted, however. Although public broadcasting and student-run college radio separated, they existed within a spectrum of non-commercial radio that vied for listeners with countercultural tastes and politics.

College stations' status as countercultural icons in the 1980s and 1990s did not owe to their location at sites of political and cultural upheaval in the 1960s. No straight line can be drawn from the Sixties' counterculture and freeform radio to the breakthrough of "college rock" bands R.E.M., U2, and Nirvana, fostered by the independence and iconoclasm of college radio. Those institutions, particularly elite private and land-grant public colleges and universities, had become "islands of authenticity" after the counterculture's dissolution. But college radio's culture emerged from more than defiance of—or retreat from—the commercial mainstream.[41] That reputation instead emerged as a new generation confronted how to achieve social change and support cultural and individual authenticity.

Instead, competing expectations, goals, and participants, as well as divergent institutional environments, radio markets, and artistic scenes, produced the left of the dial.[42] College radio's narrow reputation as a haven from the pop culture mainstream elevates aspects of its history—particularly its association with mostly white indie rock—above its reality as a diverse, evolving, and contested segment of radio broadcasting that defies identification of any one influence or point of origin.[43]

DJs took their charge to remain independent from commercial influence seriously but nonetheless remained conversant with mainstream popular culture.[44] Despite its noncommercialism, college radio developed powerful market influence.[45] Amateur broadcasters possessed power as cultural arbiters—tastemakers who defined aesthetics that distinguished class status and progressive ideals.[46] College DJs gravitated to underground music, creating a sense that it was good precisely because few people knew about it.

Regulatory and institutional dynamics governing college radio and shaping mass media contribute to blurry boundaries between mainstream and underground in the late twentieth century.[47] DJs spent much time and ink debating the nature of those delineations, particularly as college radio helped give rise to commercial alternative radio formats in the 1980s and 1990s.[48] Increasingly, stations and DJs developed a reputation for abandoning music they helped make popular, contributing to a reputation for musical snobbery. Once their selections became mainstream (*if* they became mainstream, which was often not the case), DJs moved on to something else.

A prevalent ethos of playing "none of the hits, all of the time" owed to stations' homes at institutions of higher education.[49] College radio served communities and offered students training for professional careers while supporting cultural production not bound for the mass market. Such service defied deepening conflicts with surrounding neighborhood residents. Universities encouraged, especially in urban areas, economic development in technology and knowledge economies. As a result, they acted as agents of urban renewal and expanded policing, encouraging gentrification and neighborhood displacement in the 1980s and 1990s.[50]

In other words, college radio's programmers and DJs navigated deep divisions and paradoxes regarding the meaning and value of a college education and institutional benefits to communities and society at large. If college trained students for professions, then stations offered hands-on learning experiences. If higher education was for self-discovery and expression, that protected student-run radio as spaces for exploration.[51] Further, if institutions served community and social functions in a diverse democracy, so too would college radio.

Yet not every station hewed to institutional priorities, with some maintaining structural independence despite affiliation and status as a student activity. Collectively, college stations never simply reflected the intellectual project and cultural and knowledge production of universities: they helped create, via the airwaves, substantive connections to higher education that went beyond professional training and disseminating knowledge.

Moreover, broadcasting beyond campus presented marketing potential, offering an aural bridge between colleges and educated, affluent residents or communities seeking access to institutional resources as public investment contracted. Such competing demands produced struggles for control among communities and campuses. Stations were ripe for conflict when, in addition, student DJs brought their own expectations to radio.

DJs often welcomed the ability to air the explorations of their liberal arts journeys, believing they diversified the nation's sonic profile. Certainly not all DJs held this lofty goal—many focused on developing their professional skills or gaining experience, or on retreating to underground scenes. And some, while believing they generated positive service, nonetheless maintained blinders regarding the cultural representation they provided. But battles over collegiate airwaves had national, political import and connected to questions of power. Even the most iconoclastic DJs seeking refuge from the culture industry benefited from access to their university's cultural capital, whether revolution ensued or not.

Radio stations didn't have to be covering elections or policy questions to be sites of politics, and more was happening in radio in the 1980s and 1990s than the rise of conservative talk formats.[52] Instead, the politics of college radio captures a key turn in US political history that channeled contests over regulation, policy, and power into the realms of media and culture. More than a rejoinder to fights over "bias" in news media or liberal capture of Hollywood, college radio's contested landscape reveals competing visions for how to open the public square and realize the promises of a democratic society. Certainly, media and cultural production always had political connections and import.[53] But participants in college radio, though not all, brought specific expectations regarding that medium's potential public service and political influence and pursued that work through cultural expression and representation.

College radio's history unveils new dimensions of the culture wars that raged after the social revolutions of the 1960s.[54] Red-faced televangelists railing against secularism or pundits lamenting the decline of western civilization tend to define the culture wars in popular imagination. Hand-wringing about images of the occult or the more complicated concerns regarding sexism and violence in music consumed much oxygen. Nor were battles solely about the decline of the New Deal, the disappearance of the working class, and tribalization of American life—or a smokescreen for matters of political economy.[55] These narratives don't capture the culture wars' blurry partisan lines, nor do they offer a complete picture of how these battles visited upon institutions of education and culture.[56] The intensifying cultural battles of the 1980s and 1990s involved more than the coarsening effects of fart jokes on TV and raunchy lyrics on the radio: they were fundamentally about power and who wields it to determine the boundaries of belonging and symbols of American culture.

Colleges offered convenient sites of and targets for politics as industrial work ceased to promise middle-class status and new paradigms for US culture arose. Declining funding and new economic roles prompted institutions of higher education to adopt market-oriented rationales for their continued existence. Philanthropy, federal grants, and patent licensing became more central to funding while curricula shifted to answer specific needs of private industry.[57] During these years, elites lamented fractures in mainstream culture and institutions alongside a fraying sense of "national community" or a "common set of ideals."[58] Multiculturalists, however, rejected the melting-pot ideal of US culture and reimagined bonds of belonging through group identities.[59] Culture-war battles over academic freedom and curricula occurred as the workings of universities grew increasingly politicized in that context—and these battles continue to shape the landscape of higher education to the present.[60]

No one can understand the multifaceted culture wars that continue to rage without understanding the business and politics of institutions on the front lines—especially the politics of college radio. Campus stations were in the crosshairs of government regulators, increasingly diverse sets of affluent Americans, and local communities underserved by media in an era of austerity that was already causing social services, media outlets, and public spaces to contract. The culture wars are, echoing Pat Robertson, a war for the soul of America. The culture wars, revealed by college radio, also involved a war for the *sound* of America. While Americans consumed much national media about these battles, they *participated* in the culture wars through local institutions and their media outlets.[61]

Fighting over radio schedules and student fee allocation might be less sensational than rock stars sniping at Tipper Gore on the Senate floor during 1985's congressional hearings on lyrical content, but the outcomes affected, arguably, more Americans. Programming decisions involved questions over whose voices would shape national culture and how public resources would honor the nation's diversity.[62] College radio repeatedly demonstrates that the pluralistic vision of US culture remains very much alive.

This is not a story of stations merely reflecting and channeling national political and cultural tensions.[63] These stations were, this book argues, crossroads for shifting and often conflicting demands on the nation's media infrastructure, which young people found themselves navigating amid competing conceptions of universities' role in politics, culture, and economic development. Signals existed (for the most part) on public airwaves, which involved student DJs—often unwittingly—in these intensifying battles regarding national identity and its future.

Mass media created passive consumers of culture, or so the story goes.[64] Given college radio's amateurism, where DJs more often identify as cultural consumers than producers or distributors, its influence helped democratize the music industry and offered a participatory entry into media.[65] Audiences and programmers existed in dialogue regarding what sounds best served their interests and represented the breadth of American culture. This openness and exchange made it seem possible to forge a democratic community via the airwaves. But DJs were all too often oblivious to larger structures and realities outside their studios or campuses. And as austerity loomed, fewer constituencies remained to fight for signals' independence if they served no clear market function. By the emergence of online broadcasting and accelerating media consolidation in the late 1990s and early 2000s, existential questions about college radio's purpose had already riven its landscape.

College radio's modern identity emerged through historical processes. It did not always have a reputation for noncommercialism, aesthetic authenticity, and democratic access. Indeed, on closer reflection, college radio stations that functioned as a free-flowing, utopian public sphere were ephemeral, if not apocryphal.[66] College radio circumvented existing gatekeepers in the mainstream music industry in the early 1980s but ended up creating new ones. Still, college radio's modern identity formation was not an inevitable story of corporate co-optation and selling out. Instead, the contested nature of college radio's history is what made the medium so vibrant and cherished among participants and listeners. Through the stories of stations and the DJs taking to the airwaves, this history of college radio investigates how it defied the mainstream to offer a more authentic musical culture while shaping the very mainstream participants purported to detest—all within a rapidly changing and increasingly politicized educational and media landscape.

Part I   **Out of the Alternative 1970s**

· ·

River of shiiiiit / River of shiiiiiit / Flow ooooooooon /
River of shiiiiiiiit

—The Fugs, "Wide, Wide River," *It Crawled into my Hand,
Honest* (1968)

It was winter 1969. Bob Harris held up the beautiful yellow translucent vinyl to the light, placed it on the turntable, cued it to position, and dialed the sound onto the radio. Albert Ayler's "Bells," a "cacophonous saxophone" piece, set the tone for Harris's first show on WRCU, the Colgate University radio station.

Sometime that night Harris pulled out the Fugs' recent, studio-produced album, *It Crawled into My Hand, Honest.* Two songs stood out: "Wide, Wide River," with its hymn-like refrain of "river of shit, roll on," and "Grope Need." Harris cued the latter up.

Somewhere in Hamilton, New York, a few listeners noticed the song's lyrics on WRCU's carrier-current AM signal and penned complaints. Harris packed up his belongings at 2:15 A.M. and walked happily home, unaware of outraged listeners recording their ire on paper, affixing stamps, and directing them to WRCU.

Station manager Ken Bader opened that week's listener mail and could not ignore the complaints. Lyrics such as "sticking my horny candy cane into your existential hole" qualified as obscene, as far as Bader was concerned, and the refrain of "Horny! Horny horny horny!" amounted to sexual content in violation of community standards of decency. Bader, later a respected broadcaster with Public Radio International and National Public Radio, would become known for his exacting professionalism. Horny candy canes would not stand on his watch.[1]

Bader called Harris to his dorm room, inviting his guest to take a seat on the bed. As preppy Colgate sophomores wandered by the bland, unmemorable room, Harris shifted to find a comfortable position and receive his reprimand. He had only DJ'd one show and he was already in trouble.[2]

In the cramped quarters, Bader insisted "existential hole" and "horny candy cane" were explicit sexual references. Harris questioned obscenity's definition—which fluctuated amid ongoing Supreme Court cases and student protests for free speech protections on campus.[3] Bader didn't buy it. Dissidents like Harris threatened WRCU's reputation and pending FM license, which would reach far more listeners, Bader reasoned.

He fired Harris, there in the dorm room.

"There ended my official career in college radio," Harris remembered.

· · · · · ·

College radio, before and long after 1969, enjoyed a reputation for amateurism. Students such as Harris experimented with new sounds to expand listeners' minds and tastes. As college stations moved to FM, it wasn't clear if such amateurism would fly anymore. The previous year, Bader's predecessors shut down broadcasts of political commentary, including anti–Vietnam War editorials amid 1968's Tet Offensive.[4] To satisfy complaining alumni and donors, WRCU's programming softened to "please everybody by playing a little bit of everything."[5]

WRCU's dissidents persisted. They carved out late-night blocks to air "experimental, non-commercial, non-Top 40 rock and roll" defying the "pablum" of mainstream radio.[6] A campus-based station should avoid "teeny bopper music," they argued, and instead educate listeners in the psychedelic rock of Jefferson Airplane and the Mothers of Invention or in John Coltrane and free jazz. In freeform radio, DJs could explore whatever music suited their mood, their trip, or their whims. A Mozart concerto could be followed by Vanilla Fudge, if they so desired. In the mid-1960s, freeform radio formats sprouted at FM stations in San Francisco, New York, Boston, and elsewhere. DJs made overtly political statements, with some stations airing "a non-stop anti-war rally," as one radio historian put it, alongside album cuts and instrumentals for listeners to enjoy on higher-quality FM signals. Drug use was common among DJs, prompting Vice President Spiro Agnew's ire at a White House conference on drugs and the radio industry.[7]

Harris's countercultural tastes fit the freeform ethos. Bob Fass's *Radio Unnameable* on New York City's progressive Pacifica Foundation station WBAI showed him how radio could be as transgressive as film. He joined WRCU to express himself on the airwaves, part of a convergence between freeform and college radio that students across the nation envisioned.[8]

But college stations also trained future broadcast professionals, such as Bader, who used these radio laboratories to hone their skills, learn regulations, build résumés, and provide edifying content for surrounding areas with the debut of new FM signals such as planned at Colgate. The ten-watt, class D license and decreasing technology costs lowered universities' barriers to entry, and they could no longer ignore FM's public relations benefits.

Despite universities' reputation for harboring protesters and fostering countercultural critics of mainstream values, norms, and expression, most college radio stations remained, well, square. Stations depended on supportive campuses and the students who worked the boards, many of whom saw highbrow musical enlightenment as aligned with college radio's educational purpose. Still, students pursued radio for numerous reasons, and universities invested in signals for their own, equally varied, purposes.

Where those conflicting desires would lead college radio, even in the counterculture's peak visibility during 1969 with that summer's Woodstock Festival, remained unclear. Higher education's role in American life was unsettled. Claimants to these new FM stations envisioned them providing professional training, cultural representation, democratic access to the airwaves, and educational programming in the public's interest. As a result, a new idea of "alternative" radio emerged, one strongly associated—although not exclusively—with college radio. The medium during the 1970s established a separate identity from public radio broadcasting.

Whether Harris programmed obscene music remained an open question, but students like Bader, bent on professionalizing college radio, would not prevail. Others followed in Harris's footsteps, cementing college radio on FM as a place for alternative sounds. What that meant for college radio's future remained as vague as the counterculture's legacy.

As radio's popularity shifted from AM to FM, college signals remained diverse—much like the nation's universities themselves. Not all were small, noncommercial ten-watt FM stations, although these were the majority. Commercial college stations, particularly at Ivy League institutions and others in the Northeast, developed an early foothold on FM. These bridged the gap between noncommercial college and commercial radio.

In 1972, WPRB at Princeton University unveiled a new sound that expanded its diverse musical offerings. Leaders announced the format as defining "one of the most progressive radio stations in the entire country." WPRB offered "the sophisticated sound of progressive rock" alongside classical, jazz "that's cool," and soul "that's hot." WPRB relied on advertising revenue, although the institution subsidized rent and electrical service. Programmers targeted community listeners alongside college students.[9] As the program director explained, "We're aiming for a station that you can listen to, as well as have on in the background when you go about your business."[10] DJs sustained an alternative, progressive station offering "a little of everything" while achieving financial viability.[11]

Divisions between college stations and commercial radio were blurry. DJs often graduated to commercial or public radio, thanks to preparation at collegiate stations. And describing "alternative" radio grew more difficult by 1980. One program director defined it as "fluid." It could "cause quite a furor with some people," she explained, "as everyone has his own concept of what 'alternative' programming means." The term "progressive" circulated, too. In the 1970s, progressive rock experimented with classical forms and electronic instruments, exemplifying virtuosity in musicianship. Progressive radio applied to left-leaning organizations such as the Pacifica Foundation and its programming. Yet by the late 1970s, progressive rock meant the sounds emerging after punk—the rise of a "new wave" of synthesizers and experimental music often from Great Britain and Europe. Individual program directors might define what went out over the airwaves under the "alternative" or "progressive" banner.[12]

The mainstream fragmented. Radio programmers segmented audiences by age, gender, and race. Commercial FM diverged into narrower radio formats and genres. Disco supplanted rock music as that genre lost its connection to partying and dancing, with artists seeking to prove their technical prowess with music "for the head rather than the body." Older listeners, a radio consultant explained, looked for the Grateful Dead; a "new generation" clamored for Ted Nugent; and "the mainstream crowd" was "perfectly happy with Heart and Kansas." By the late 1970s, "new wavers" demanded XTC; art-rockers wanted the Talking Heads. American popular music both diversified and stagnated, depending on whom you asked. At major record labels, commercial radio, and stadium-sized concerts, the number of true stars narrowed in the risk-averse industry.[13]

Music and radio scholars identify 1978 as when "college music" emerged as a genre. It included musicians from subcultural bohemian enclaves that would define underground "indie" music in subsequent years as well as cross over to mainstream success.[14] Music, news, and information lacking broad commercial appeal, or that offered specific communities educational or public service content, might be found on college signals. Some took their cue from freeform, operating as the "pipe dream of hippies," as one DJ called the station at the University of Hawaii.

College stations experimented and explored. Reggae and funk were popular. Folk maintained a loyal, if narrow, fan base, before its 1980s pop revival. While most college DJs resisted shouting like Top 40 announcers, many achieved a professional sound. Still, college radio's reputation as an amateur aural "sandbox" was well earned, with untrained students mumbling their way through announcements and playlists. Whatever the case, college radio in the 1970s could be characterized roughly as alternative— leaving it to DJs and programmers to determine what the term meant and how they would define the left of the dial.

1 Redefining College Radio in the Late 1970s

· ·

Music from The Demi-Monde, Oedipus on WTBS (M.I.T.), 1977[1]

The Kinks, "Till the End of the Day"
Flamin' Groovies, "Teenage Head"
The Stranglers, "Hanging Around"
Cheap Trick, "You're All Talk"
The Count Bishops, "Route 66"
AC/DC, "Let There Be Rock"
Ramones, "Suzy Is a Headbanger"
Tweeds, "Shortwave"
Chris Stamey, "The Summer Sun"
The Dictators, "Science Has Gone Too Far"

"It's shitty," a UCLA senior declared.

He meant KLA, the campus carrier-current radio station. By 1974, not only had UCLA failed to join the ranks of institutions with FM signals, but its wired station suffered from technical breakdowns and faulty reception.

Phone lines, not airwaves, carried KLA. Each dorm had a transmitter conveying broadcasts through electrical wires. The station aired an eclectic mix of Latin music, "New Oldies," show tunes, international news, and campus sports, though the decentralized system and shoddy equipment stymied efforts to draw new listeners. Only 6 percent of polled students tuned in to KLA, and those who could tune in reported bad reception and static.[2]

After the FCC reserved space for noncommercial, educational FM signals in the early 1940s, educational radio proponents envisioned a system of college stations on FM.[3] But technical and regulatory barriers slowed FM's growth after World War II, and college radio tended to be found instead on carrier-current stations like KLA's. To promote FM, the FCC lowered impediments and introduced low-watt, class D licenses. As cheaper technology and stereo broadcasting became available in the 1960s, university administrators seemed at last poised to invest in FM. Whereas a mere ten FM signals operated as "educational" radio in 1946, whether owned by colleges and universities, municipalities, or nonprofits, that number surpassed 100 in

1953, and by 1967 there were 326, with 220 owned and operated by colleges and universities.[4]

These signals were no straightforward haven for rebellious programming and music. Administrators did not invest in FM to support radical musical expression or cultivate local music scenes. In the 1950s and 1960s, programming hewed to mainstream tastes or edifying content, including classical or study music, or university concerts and lectures. A few stations incorporated select hours of popular rock or folk revival music in the 1960s, with only a handful dedicating programming entirely to rock music. Some stations' programming benefited from social movements' influence, introducing programming by Black Student Unions or organizations seeking to diversify campuses in the late 1960s—but these shows were not ubiquitous in college radio as stations moved to FM. Students who ran stations often sidelined such programs in favor of what pleased the most students: music that appealed to majority tastes. Jazz labels appreciated college radio's support, which in turn helped signals cultivate a highbrow reputation in line with jazz's developments in those years as well as aligning with higher education's transformations in the post–World War II decades.[5]

Still, college radio's expansion reflected institutions' attempts to widen access, protect students from discrimination, and serve as public goods. It was not an easy road. In the 1970s, higher education faced declining funding as universities assumed duties previously reserved for the state, including workforce development, economic stimulation, urban renewal, and social uplift. Commitments to equal access, whether through affirmative action in admissions or protections linked to Title IX in the Educational Amendment Acts of 1972, marked how institutions of higher education interacted with broader social and cultural developments of the era, supported by policy.

Radio offered inexpensive means of extending institutional access and public service to nearby nonaffiliated residents. Some 56 percent of college radio stations required less than $20,000 in annual operating funds in 1967.[6] (Thirty-four percent operated for between $1,000 and $5,000 per year— roughly half of the national average salary of a university instructor.) Meanwhile, legislators clashed over how to ensure more Americans could access what they viewed as a right: an education.[7]

College radio's expansion was inseparable from these priorities. Radio, though often designed or reserved primarily for campus, burnished institutions' reputations as publicly minded and culturally relevant. Whether operating in the public interest, such as serving agricultural producers in the

Midwest or providing cultural programming, an image of appearing above the normal clamor of pop culture cohered in college radio.[8] Colleges and universities, through radio, supported intellectual and artistic growth in line with liberal arts inquiry while preparing students for careers and serving communities. At their radio stations, liberal arts values of independence, individuality, self-expression, and (sometimes conflicting) commitments to pluralism and multiculturalism mixed with students' desire to gain professional experience. Community listeners could access higher education's experts and knowledge, whether it was science and market information or on-campus lectures from scholars of many fields.

These values and expectations created space for radio experimentation but didn't guarantee it. The laws of physics and broadcasting technology limited signal availability in a single market. At UCLA, as elsewhere, FM promised to ease communication with students and educate and entertain them—or present them with challenging music such as punk, which began to rise up from underground music scenes and capture the attention of aspiring DJs.

But first they had to get on the air.

Claiming the Alternative Spectrum

KLA's technical challenges frustrated both DJs and administrators, who tried every avenue to secure an FM spot. Los Angeles's increasingly crowded spectrum impeded UCLA's hopes. Even at institutions where it seemed natural for a major station to emerge on the FM dial, including UCLA near where a vibrant and generative punk scene would emerge, this did not always happen.

In 1974, Jeff Shanofsky, KLA's sales representative, asked UCLA for legal counsel to obtain an FM signal. Shanofsky set his sights on KROQ, a struggling aspirant to freewheeling progressive rock radio.

While KLA's quest for FM revealed universities' aspirations for their radio stations, KROQ reflected the identity crisis gripping FM radio in the 1970s as the spectrum underwent a "format revolution."[9] Countercultural, freeform rock radio converged on the FM commercial dial in the 1960s. In 1972, Gary Bookasta bought KROQ-AM and KPPC-FM, which operated out of a church basement. After renaming the FM signal KROQ, "The Roqs of Los Angeles" debuted, playing glam rock from the New York Dolls and Ur-metal band Black Sabbath. Listeners dubbed KROQ a "glittering bastard offspring of '60s counterculture and '70s sleaze." As a countercultural icon,

KROQ earned high marks. As a business, it struggled. After a year of no advertising breaks to lure listeners, debts mounted. The station was a "major player," but DJs weren't getting paid. They quit, and the station went off the air in 1974.[10]

Enter UCLA. Shanofsky strategized to secure KROQ's signal. The university could offer to purchase it outright or it could share time. Another alternative: UCLA could sue Bookasta for his FM license, since it was not broadcasting. The share-time option wouldn't give students sufficient experience in running a radio station. Suing for the license could produce "mudslinging," a university lawyer warned, cost over $100,000 in legal fees, and undermine a potential share-time agreement.[11] UCLA opted to offer to purchase.

KROQ rebuffed the offer and withstood its troubles. The FCC warned its owners to resume broadcasting or lose the license. It relaunched in 1976 and went on to originate innovative new wave programming and the "Rock of the 80s" format—music drawn from college radio. KROQ, oddly, given its brief potential association with UCLA, amplified college radio as a launchpad to commercial success for underground artists in the 1980s. Knowing where KROQ headed, it's easy to assume college radio culture sparked punk and new wave revolutions, especially with this early connection between college and commercial rock radio. But punk and new wave had more tenuous connections to college radio, just as these signals had with FM.

Things didn't go as well for KLA. Instead, its history indicates that college radio was more contested and diverse than its popular reputation as an FM haven for underground music suggests. UCLA's radio station remained tethered to deficient technology and impeded by static. By the mid-1970s, FM was the place to be. A survey at one university revealed only twenty-one students had a radio without FM. It would be cheaper to purchase each of these students a pocket FM radio than to maintain the AM signal. Other college stations phased out carrier-current signals in the 1970s and early 1980s, unless, as with KLA, barriers to FM remained or they opted for cable connections, or eventually, the internet. Some kept carrier-current signals to train DJs and engineers before allowing them access to FM.[12] Stations persisting on AM and carrier-current (the total number is difficult to discern) nonetheless remained part of college radio and its culture.[13]

KLA and carrier-current signals participated in the transformation of college radio's "left of the dial" reputation, despite not being located there. That emerging identity transcended technology, station size and reach, and location. KROQ's future as a leader in progressive music demonstrated how college radio was not the only place on the dial interested in breaking new musical ground—though college stations did not have the same commercial pressures.

Much as it was not inevitable for every university to have a noncommercial, educational FM signal, punk had no preordained home on college radio.

College radio's "left of the dial" reputation for airing underground punk, new wave, hardcore, and hip-hop took time to cohere. College radio fostered no straightforward countercultural or punk rock revolution. Neither can a straight line be drawn from the counterculture to punk on college radio to its commercial influence of the 1980s. As with KLA's struggle for FM, college radio's association with "progressive" music in the late 1970s took work and dedication from individual DJs to carve out space for adventurous music.

In fact, punk's first wave had only tenuous connections to college radio. The specific challenges punk presented to the culture industry had yet to take hold and define college radio culture. When it came to participants, the punk scene drew disaffected youth confronting the decade's economic dislocations. Scene insiders earned airtime on some supportive college stations, though haltingly—and the first DJs were not always college students. College stations did not generate these scenes. But they did provide oxygen, introducing sounds—thanks to expanded FM signals—to kids listening in their bedrooms or who might sneak out to a show. Some DJs were uniquely tapped into the exciting music being generated in local scenes across the country, but they had to fight for space amid the many functions college radio had to fulfill in the 1970s.

By mid-decade, the counterculture's prominent symbols for mass political and cultural transformation—particularly festivals such as the Berkeley Folk Festival or Woodstock—had flagged. Participants turned inward to spiritual practices and therapies or to new related pursuits, such as forming activist businesses.[14] Psychedelic musical experimentation gave way to the technical prowess of progressive rock. Rock music, although it became the stuff of mass culture, split into emerging subgenres of metal, glam, country rock, and more. Economic troubles and inflation shifted Americans' focus, although the cultural rebel image remained in vogue, though one increasingly clichéd and corporatized.[15]

FM radio fragmented into specific formats, segmenting audiences into ever smaller pools, targeting and broadcasting to listeners around groups of advertising demographics (a practice referred to as narrowcasting). Music associated with political and cultural movements seemed defanged: a shift captured by the transformation of Jefferson Airplane, critics lamented, into Jefferson Starship, and by the 1980s, Starship. As one critic put it, by the 1980s the band adopted "conformity, conservatism, and a slavish adherence to formula." The re-formed band lacked its previous associations with the 1960s' civil rights movement, anti-war protests, and cultural revolutions.[16]

The underground persisted, though divided aesthetically, geographically, and demographically. In Boston, groups of urban and suburban teenagers looked for alternatives to commercial rock of the Rolling Stones, the Allman Brothers, or Aerosmith. Local-musician-turned-folk-idol James Taylor did not appeal to angry kids seeking sounds with more intensity.[17]

Punk, emerging from England and the United States in 1976, channeled youthful dissatisfaction during the decade's economic malaise, deindustrialization, and urban crises. These musicians, often self-taught, rejected the overwrought solos of rock bands selling out arenas. They adopted simple, four-bar song constructions, punchy lyrics, and straightforward rhyming structures. Punk's confrontational style turned musical conventions upside down. Anyone could do it, signaling a democratic ethos defying the superstar-focused music industry. Local scenes spawned their own institutions and networks to support the music and its fans.

Such energies seemed to revive revolutionary artistic movements and fit with college radio's eclectic music without mainstream appeal. DJs during assigned blocks selected what to play from the station library or bins of new records curated by music or program directors, while others played records from personal collections, adhering to rotations only as station policy required. Stations might dedicate blocks to "specialty" shows of classical, jazz, reggae, or folk. Some relegated the freest of freeform blocks to late night and allocated weekend hours to specialty shows for specific genres.[18] Most served a wide variety of tastes scattered across a weekly schedule.[19]

The majority remained low-watt with a range of only a few miles. Such limits prevented wide reach, but dedicated fans valued these signals for the coverage they provided.

In most radio markets, punk fans were lucky if they could tune in to one show a week, and these were usually late at night, if at all. As punk surfaced from London, New York City, and Los Angeles, it only slowly made its way onto the airwaves.[20]

Oddly, punk's first steps into college radio occurred in Boston, known for its staid, unflashy Brahmins and elite universities. The Hub's wealth of college signals, a growing club scene, and numerous college students offered prime conditions for punk to emerge on college radio.

Oedipus volunteered at commercial rock giant WBCN, writing weekly reports on the music scene. He hosted his show, *The Demi-Monde*, on WTBS at MIT. It was widely regarded as the nation's first punk radio show.[21] At this community-oriented station, thanks to its insulation from MIT in governance, Oedipus showcased punk bands touring in Boston. The Ramones played their first non–New York City show at Cambridge's the Club in 1976, and Oedipus gave the band its first radio interview. He worked days as a photographer, eking by thanks to his dirt-cheap $62.50-a-month room in a six-bedroom brownstone in the then–run down flats of Beacon Hill. His show attracted a following despite the station's meager ten-watt signal. *The Demi-Monde* created so much buzz in Boston that WBCN's program director took notice, and Oedipus began broadcasting at both stations in 1977.

As a scene insider, Oedipus witnessed and facilitated new musical formations. At the brownstone, "punk band DMZ formed in my basement," he remembered. "The Dead Boys, Mink de Ville and touring bands crashed at my house. [Vocalist for the Dead Boys] Stiv Bators slept in the bathtub." Punk gained a notorious reputation in the national press, which aided Oedipus's visibility. WBCN hired Oedipus as a "token purple-haired punk rocker" to showcase bands such as the Talking Heads and Blondie (although Oedipus's hair color was known to vary widely). He emceed concerts and interviewed emerging stars on *The Demi-Monde* and on *Nocturnal Emissions* at WBCN. Oedipus's previous interview with the Damned lured Elvis Costello to his show. The interview promoted Costello's two nights at the Paradise Club. (The British rocker wanted to know why no one was dancing. It was because the tables had been nailed down.)[22]

Oedipus's coverage drew fans like Judy Wilburn, a teenager in the late 1970s. "Dinosaur rock," as she called it, populated AM radio. It was monolithic, boring. Freeform FM radio of "wild-eyed hippies" had been defanged, replaced by rotations of Deep Purple, Jethro Tull, and the technical prowess of prog rock. WBCN muted its history of radical politics and beacon of freeform radio in the 1960s and 1970s. Even Oedipus, as he moved through the ranks at WBCN, began adding more format and structure to programming to compete in the Boston market. WTBS instead captured the local scene's vibrancy and highlighted rising punk bands, particularly with the debut of weekday morning shows *The Late Risers Club* in 1977 and later *Breakfast of Champions*, which focused on new rock music.

For teenagers like Wilburn, progressive rock and radio moved "backwards," with commercial radio becoming "racially segregated" and "apolitical."[23] Top 40 disgusted fledgling punks. One LA punk described the "syrupy garbage on the radio" populated by "the infinitely stupid, effervescent saccharine of the Carpenters and Captain & Tennille." Punks preferred "sonic mayhem" to match their status as "disenfranchised kids."[24] Conflict seethed beneath the decade's seemingly innocuous pop: the sparkly splendor of disco and the bright, polyester suits and dresses of its fans. Disco seemingly papered over young people's struggles with feeling powerless amid stagflation, alienation from elected officials, cultural and demographic shifts, and the disruptions of the turn to a postindustrial economy.[25]

Boston's economy suffered in the 1970s. Whites fled the city after the busing crisis and as white-collar jobs migrated to the I-95 belt, leaving vast expanses of empty warehouses downtown. These offered a perfect spot for youthful mischief. In those spaces, kids hosted their DIY clubs and loft parties. On Washington Street, A Street, down to Fort Point, sites invited art and music students and misfits to congregate.[26] The scene, now supported by college radio, developed its own infrastructure of supporting businesses.

DJs scoured local record shops for releases or traded for imports from England or tapes to play. Kenmore Square's the Rathskeller (the "Rat") connected with CBGB in New York. Boston-based bands traveled to New York, and vice versa. Local agents booked clubs and bands played colleges. Clothing store Hubba Hubba sold S+M gear, leather, records, and self-published zines.

The Cars started playing in small clubs. The Rat hosted the Talking Heads. The Paradise opened down Commonwealth Avenue in 1977 and became another hub for underground artists. Some clubs were big, hosting 1,000 or more, such as when Sun Ra came to play. Screaming Jay Hawkins drew another huge crowd. The venues attracted kids of all ages as well as "dirty old men." This "free range environment" fostered creativity.[27]

Newbury Comics, founded in 1979, built on this trend. The store's stacks of mimeographed "magazines," DIY zines, educated students of the scene. It gave a band, promoter, or record label "a way in" to the scene. The scene had a certain "purity," Wilburn remembered. With AM dominated by Casey Kasem, "awful bands and disco," the local music scene offered authenticity and defied the glitzy commercialism that papered over the nation's economic woes. The music had variety, and the kids were running things.

Boston's scene reportedly consisted of white kids, although at some venues music fans of different backgrounds mixed. Boundaries remained between punk and early hip-hop during these years, without much cross-over between scenes.

Yet this network provided a lifeline for youth who felt on the outs. As a kid who felt she never really fit in, Wilburn found her place in the scene. She played tennis in a loft at the corner of Newbury Street and Mass. Ave., discovering spaces where "you could create yourself, on the fly." Occasionally, local bigwigs would scope it out, like "sight-seers, like they were going to the zoo." Rumors circulated of Senator Ted Kennedy showing up drunk at the Rat, slumming to see what "the exotics are doing."[28]

The art resonated. Graffiti influenced the high art and popular art worlds. But the music—Mission of Burma, other punk bands from the scene—never really became mainstream. Individual college stations in Boston maintained their own identities. WTBS's strong connections with communities garnered a loyal fan base, offering poetry, Haitian music, and Latin sounds as part of its weekly schedule of rock programs. WERS at Emerson College developed a traditional block schedule, along with WZBC at Boston College, which also aired sports. Community DJs offered aural connections with ethnic communities in Boston, and students brought their passions for "music by dead people [classical music]," as Oedipus put it, spoken word, or noise. WTBS's charter required that students hold positions of general manager and program director, but a community-focused mission guided programming. This service translated into cultural work of many types, well beyond airing punk rock.[29]

College radio differed from zine culture, which was profoundly local and DIY. Radio required institutional investment and rationales for its existence that appealed beyond underground punks and had to meet regulatory requirements. College radio offered a place to counter trends, offering fare without wide commercial appeal. In general, these signals championed offering an alternative to mainstream conformity on sale from major labels. But alternative did not solely mean punk. Moreover, even in the late 1970s, Oedipus's punk show, and those following, remained in the minority on college radio.[30] This was even true of stations in proximity to CBGB, the famed punk club in New York City.

Punk Rock Radio in the Suburbs

Certain students matriculated at universities with knowledge of this up-and-coming sound, and they sought out college radio to air their growing music collections. Zines carried news of new bands, and independent record stores carried releases. Punk fans couldn't hear songs they wanted anywhere else on the radio dial. Students seeking to create that space, though, had to navigate station politics to make space for the music they loved.

Marty Byk grew up on hard rock from the Rolling Stones and Led Zeppelin. As a high schooler in New Jersey in the mid-1970s, he picked up on "this punk rock thing." Twenty miles outside Manhattan, he read about bands playing in the East Village in the *Village Voice* and New Jersey publications covering underground clubs. "It was more of a local thing," not like the musicians from England he had grown up on who seemed "untouchable." The Ramones felt within reach. He traveled to the city to see them, but he couldn't hear the music on his radio.[31]

The Runaways debuted at CBGB in 1976 and made quite an impression on Byk. The all-woman quintet from Los Angeles offered a glimpse into a musical world that was forming. He thought, "Wow, this is great." Los Angeles featured its own punk style and hopes. As Exene Cervenka of the band X put it, "I thought punk was gonna end the corporate takeover of America's rock 'n' roll, our real music, and we would never have to give in to the dumbing-down, mass-minded crap of the now-ruined radio."[32]

CBGB was packed—the bathrooms were notoriously disgusting: "any surface could kill you," Byk remembered—and the scene took on a life of its own. Byk felt comfortable, like he knew these people. They were looking for something new, something different, and the scene went "hand-in-hand" with his move into college radio.

CBGB bands' localism and DIY ethos defied the music industry's power and fueled Byk's radio show when he matriculated at Seton Hall to study radio and television. He remembered, "If you [a band], had a record contract, or even if you had put anything out on vinyl, chances are you are associated with some large money corporation." Those labels would spend thousands to produce, distribute, and market records "to make it look like one of these untouchable things." For the bands playing parties and clubs in Manhattan, they made their own, using private presses and selling them to local record stores. "It was a cottage industry," in Byk's words.

The process went something like this. Byk would see a band at a show or read about a new group that sounded interesting. He would discover they had a 45 pressed. "I can buy that," he thought. In time, he realized he'd amassed an impressive collection. With his library of punk 45s, Byk looked to Seton Hall's radio station to "start playing this stuff to a larger audience."

He secured a daytime slot to spin records, but he ran into the powers that be at WSOU.

Seton Hall's station had a powerful signal, and its managers recognized its visibility. In Byk's view, the faculty adviser saw it as a "serious business." He ran WSOU "almost as a professional AM station," with programming run by a rigid time clock, and DJs could only play approved music from certain groups. "You almost had to adhere to a script," Byk remembered. When he secured airtime, he started by playing Led Zeppelin "and that sort of thing," and he slowly introduced songs from his collection and new punk releases.

When Byk spun a punk record one afternoon, the station manager slammed the door open, horrified at the song that broke format. "What do you want me to do?" Byk shrugged. Interrupting the song mid-play would be unprofessional.

After a few such encounters, Byk moved to a nighttime slot, 11 P.M. to 2 A.M. "It was better for everyone," he reflected. Late-night hours allowed him to depart from format. He worked in a local record store, which gave him access to new 45s and LPs at wholesale prices, or to bands that brought their stuff to the store directly. Phone calls and letters poured in, providing him with feedback from local high school kids trying to get access to what was happening downtown. With WSOU's reach in New Jersey, Byk helped disseminate the burgeoning Manhattan punk scene by broadcasting his record collection.

A New Jersey high schooler tuning in to Byk's show would don the moniker Jack Rabid. Like Byk, he owed his musical interest to the Beatles and British rock groups, but punk's raw humor and sound drew him. "You wouldn't hear it in the supermarket or on somebody's car radio," he remembered. "Your classmates had no idea it existed." He might as well have been making it up. "I guess I saw Snotty Jerk Off last week, they were great. And that was followed by the Putrid Morons. That's what it sounded like to them." Other kids looked askance as he started buying punk-styled clothes and listening to Byk's late-night show. One commercial station offered a glimmer of hope for punk's ascendance: WPIX in New York played the Buzzcocks and the Clash, gigs Rabid attended and taped.

He loved emerging new wave bands gracing the airwaves, often achieving mainstream success. But Joe Jackson and Elvis Costello had nowhere "near as supercharged" a sound as the "kick in the ass" provided by the Sex Pistols or the Damned. He remembered listening to the Dead Boys with "my mouth agape that you could say shit like that. Literally shit." Rabid sat in his room, twirling the dial, looking for anything with a "higher octane" sound, the best hope resting with college stations. Few such signals reached Rabid in his suburban home, except for WSOU. On Seton Hall's station, Byk and one other DJ offered what Rabid was looking for. Together, the DJs covered only around five hours of the entire week. Even with those limited hours, Rabid credited Byk with "saving my bacon . . . as a tenth and eleventh grader having the chance to hear so many records I'd only read about, because you just couldn't get them anywhere else." Even if Rabid didn't like a band, he was grateful to know what they sounded like.

• • • • • •

Although punk rock did not define college radio in the 1970s, signals had a similar effect as clubs. As the lore goes, not many people saw the Ramones play in 1976, but each person who did started their own band. A similar adage holds true for punk radio: these shows might have been in the minority in terms of overall programming, but their influence spread. Student DJs used college radio's educational identity to expand programming in alternative and progressive music—which included music influenced by punk rock's golden era as well as bohemian scenes springing up around the country.[33] Nonetheless, punk's association with college radio was by no means inevitable, nor was college radio's association with the left of the dial—as KLA's troubles to secure a signal suggested. For college radio to disrupt the music industry, many barriers remained.

A paradox existed within noncommercial college radio focused on offering an alternative: making music was a business.[34] In scenes supported by college radio, production became more visible than it had in the music industry, but democratizing access remained challenging. The musical undergrounds germinating during the 1970s had the potential to build a respectable middle ground, where artists could maybe make enough to be full-time musicians and live well enough in their towns or cities, supported by local venues, stores, labels and touring. Yet obstacles blunted subcultures' revolutionary potential. They might re-envision society and its core values and structures. More realistically, they provided outlets for those lacking power or to resolve cultural questions without restructuring society. And when it came to radio, it remained an "invisible" medium, taking on different meanings across listeners and communities, helping citizens imagine new communities and identities, or develop and validate subcultures.[35]

College stations in the 1970s were small, often ten-watt affairs offering what mainstream radio considered too unappealing. Space existed on college radio in that decade for many types of music, but that didn't ensure punk rock would have a place. College radio's "alternative" definition left much room for interpretation. And as punk's first wave began to flame out, the new sounds that emerged in its wake, too, as Marty Byk did, had to secure coverage against college radio proponents who wanted to cultivate a professional sound that emulated commercial rock radio, except with a few new cuts thrown in for the youngsters.

2 College Radio's New Wave

· ·

CMJ March 1, 1979 Rock CATS—College Album Tally
Chart Info Based on Airplay of Reporting Stations

1. Elvis Costello, *Armed Forces*, Columbia
2. Blues Brothers, *Briefcase Full of Blues*, Atlantic
3. Dire Straits, *Dire Straits*, Warner Bros.
4. Grateful Dead, *Shakedown Street*, Arista
5. Eddie Money, *Life for the Taking*, Columbia
6. J. Geils Band, *Sanctuary*, EMI
7. Phil Manzanera, *K-Scope*, Polydor
8. Rod Stewart, *Blondes Have More Fun*, Warner Bros.
9. Fabulous Poodles, *Mirror Stars*, Epic
10. Clash, *Give 'Em Enough Rope*, Epic

In the words of one college student, a new wave "crashed into the stagnating pool of rock music" in 1978. This more upbeat music appealed to college-educated listeners more than the no-future sounds of punk, and it began to show commercial appeal.[1] Experimental artists expanded beyond punk instrumentation, exploring electronic sounds and synthesizers, production techniques, and modern art aesthetics. Yet as with new wave's punk predecessor, whether college radio embraced this new sound remained uncertain.

Student DJs insisted their stations existed for their education and to educate others—and they had the right to determine what that meant. Demands fluctuated among reflecting majority tastes, providing professional experience, educating community listeners, and breaking cultural ground. Across college radio in the late 1970s, genre battles, particularly between rock music and "progressive" new wave, emerged out of these competing roles.

Each station's programming depended on local factors, but DJs with differing goals often shared a common belief. Whether they argued for more emphasis on popular rock, progressive and new wave, or even disco, college DJs saw themselves as musical gatekeepers. Although they were amateurs, they had power and responsibility.

The stakes went beyond determining how much KISS or Talking Heads should air. Popular culture was a site of politics, as cultural theorists were arguing simultaneously to these struggles to define educational radio.[2] While working-class Americans supposedly disappeared from pop culture, college radio genre battles cut to questions of representation in media for young people. Disco, by 1977, denied class stratification and masked uncertainties about the nation's economic future.[3] But its expressive styles and diverse practitioners challenged prevalent attitudes regarding race and sexuality as it crossed boundaries and entertained suburbanites.[4] Disco's multiculturalism and assimilation of diverse influences clashed with rock fans' tastes and vision for American culture, the battles between which became the stuff of pop culture spectacle.

In 1979 when Steve Dahl, a Chicago commercial rock DJ, declared "Disco Demolition Nite" among his followers, chaos ensued on the field at a White Sox double header. White working-class youths stormed the field to burn copies of disco records, suggesting antipathy toward the musical genre that grew out of urban nightclub scenes, Black soul, and funk rhythms and embraced nontraditional gender performances, queer identities, and celebrations of ethnic diversity.[5] But disco remained big business at the end of the 1970s, reflected in the mega-selling soundtrack to the disco-themed movie *Saturday Night Fever*.

Educational radio, and especially college radio with its democratic access and structure, offered a platform for young people to shape culture in this context. No longer solely the bastion of "highbrow" culture, college radio's alternative ethos prompted optimism that new voices could be heard through the corporatizing music industry and narrowly formatted commercial radio. New wave appealed to educated listeners, and it connected to underground music and modern art scenes. Punk had disrupted the music industry enough to create space for "obscure freaks" to break through. They offered art rock that provided hope for "a certain breed of hipster" who, despite the doldrums of the decade's economy, hoped for a better future.[6]

At the same time, numerous forces squeezed higher education. Students lacking their parents' opportunity to achieve a middle-class status through stable, unionized industrial work felt pressure to get a degree. Institutions, tasked with training a workforce for a postindustrial economy, acted as economic drivers in surrounding areas. The hospitals, labs, and innovations universities supported—previously thought of as the purview of the state—gained importance amid deindustrialization and urban crises. Higher education's economic possibilities seemed more vital than ever, and institutions could influence culture.

DJs harboring such hopes, however, confronted others who sought the airwaves to gain professional experience to build careers beyond the low-wage, low-prestige service sector. Higher education's economic functions, even at its noncommercial radio stations, were never far from view, and the stakes were getting higher. The New Deal had essentially called these stations into being when reformers pushed for a noncommercial spectrum and educational programming. The pluralist vision New Dealers espoused for American culture persisted at these signals long after the 1930s. These intermingled economic and cultural commitments endured at student-run signals as major-label rock music and commercial radio narrowed.

Corporate consolidation resulted in a handful of record labels controlling over 80 percent of the recording industry by 1980. A small number of multiplatinum artists dominated record sales. KUSF at the University of San Francisco, and those like it, played the newest, freshest music, protected by its nonprofit status and institutional backer. DJs took pride in playlists that defied, one jock explained, "sponsor-manipulation" and "over-age, balding, fat, greedy ogres" in the record industry. KUSF's irreverence and willingness to play anything, regardless of genre, revealed DJs' critique of the corporatization of music while burnishing the station's reputation as cutting edge. Before hitting the mainstream or "selling X million records," Blondie and the Cars graced its airwaves.[7] College radio's reputation as a musical testing ground gained traction in the late 1970s, thanks in large part to these stations' defiance of corporate dictates regarding popular culture.[8]

Corporate consolidation already visited the culture industry, even before major regulatory changes allowed for collecting media control into fewer hands, compounding the paradoxes college-run media faced.[9] Commercial functions existed since college radio's origins, and stations maintained relationships with industry alongside their educational roles. Engineering schools proved instrumental in the development of radio technology, and they launched some of the first college signals.[10] After college FM stations debuted in increasing numbers in the 1960s and 1970s, stations trained future engineers and broadcasting, sales, or journalism majors. Practical experience often meant emulating commercial radio, though with varied sounds and genres. Student DJs served many audiences while earning the professional experience that justified investment in higher education. At one station debuting on FM in 1977, the first week of programming offered "a documentary on the Beach Boys, classical music, sports, basic French, progressive rock, news, community events, Wolfman Jack, jazz and traditional and folk music."[11] DJs tapped new musical trends, and savvy insiders understood the commercial potential in measuring audience engagement. Student DJs might support critiques of the "technological order" and "democratic unfreedom" of industrial life. Programming, too, might disrupt such power by leveraging the cultural capital of host institutions, but they nonetheless remained embedded in and discursive with those power structures.[12]

Other values filtered into these stations, particularly liberals' taste for multiculturalism. KUSF's program director hoped the station would be diverse and expand horizons for listeners with an "open ear and expandable mind." Even though the university owned KUSF, it served San Francisco's communities—a goal in line with the institution's Jesuit mission. This service, DJs asserted, included expanding musical offerings. Without DJs connected to "the people," record companies would "invest in more of the same garbage." Local stations could highlight newcomers and break hits while representing the university's liberal arts purpose.[13]

Barely heard amid these debates were the students on campus who criticized the inch-deep diversity that these visions offered. Nonetheless, a market existed for the music DJs played, and even if the signal was weak, and the playlist hard-fought, their signals generated value. A new publication capitalized on its potential commercial influence, despite the musical identity crisis gripping stations.

Anita Sarko Goes New Wave Too Soon

While many college stations began to "go progressive" in the late 1970s and incorporate new wave, change sometimes came slowly and depended on how hard DJs were willing to fight. Format battles frequently ignited when fans of mainstream rock squared off against new wavers for control of collegiate airwaves.

Punk provided exciting material for DJs and their listeners, but not everyone in college radio embraced these sounds as educational. Even DJs on the pulse of new music that would become big business in the 1980s and define commercial stations such as Los Angeles's KROQ were not always welcomed. Yet the late-night relegation of punk on college radio diminished as more stations offered new and challenging music amid narrowing popular music and radio. Album-oriented radio (AOR) stations relinquished the zaniness of freeform and targeted predominantly young white males, playing few Black artists and focusing on a few progressive rock stars such as Emerson, Lake and Palmer, hard rock from Led Zeppelin, or arena-rockers KISS.[14] For college DJs envisioning a musical counterrevolution, institutional and administrative barriers remained—including those students in charge. Stations earned increasing recognition in the music industry by 1978, but their collective power and influence remained murky.

Uncertainty awaited those seeking alternatives. Popular music seemed locked in a stalemate between disco and rock. New radio formats in country and R&B emerged, but few alternatives existed. Independent labels made up roughly one-tenth of music sales, though they were growing in number.[15] A second British Invasion of new wave artists and punk on both sides of the Atlantic caused waves but didn't displace the mainstream sounds of commercial radio, which remained conservative in programming. Fans from across genres or appreciating many sounds had few places to mingle.[16]

For DJs aspiring to influence popular music, the fuzzy "alternative" of college radio offered some, though limited, opportunities. As AOR formats solidified, college DJs leaned into their stations' alternative identities, seeking deeper album cuts or more obscure music than commercial rock counterparts. Such offerings mixed with public service programming and a range of genres. College radio still had to please students who paid the bills alongside established listeners seeking highbrow fare such as jazz and classical music.

As the FM dial grew more populated, WRAS at Georgia State University (GSU) aired more obscure bands and local music beyond its already-established support, exploring adventurous territory as AOR stations debuted in Atlanta.[17] WRAS faced challenges as enrollments declined, inflation increased costs, and city planners demanded the land on which its current transmitter sat. Moving the antenna cost $6,500. The station expanded power because, a general manager explained to GSU's president, "the rapid physical growth of Atlanta has caused problems with . . . our service to Georgia State students; students are moving farther out of town and more and more high-rise buildings are being built (these severely impede FM radio signals)." A 50 percent price increase in transmitter and studio equipment accompanied rising engineering costs thanks to double-digit inflation that plagued the US economy. To pay for this and other amenities, student fees increased from six to ten dollars per year.[18]

Such financing reflected the decade's shift away from direct federal and state funding of institutions toward reliance on student borrowing or grants, introducing "creative financing" at universities.[19] Institutions passed along the costs of instruction, activities, and facilities to students, who increasingly borrowed for their educations through student loans. Debates over funding college radio stations, and students' demands that these reflect their tastes, grew heated precisely because this shifting funding model burdened students with increased costs—while signals proved to be increasingly valuable to institutions for overcoming divisions between town and gown.

Students gravitated to WRAS for varying reasons, often seeking professional broadcasting experience or to immerse themselves in musical experimentation and progressive rock.[20] WRAS added programming promoting and representing Black culture in the early 1970s. *African Vibrations* defied the station's tendency to program for white college students and confronted a conservative university administration even as the student body grew more diverse.[21] Few Black DJs were included in regular daytime programming not designated as "specialty" offerings. Still, WRAS's programmers conducted ascertainment surveys to assess community needs and expand programming for Atlanta listeners, not only for students and campus affairs. It broadcast public service announcements regarding crime prevention or business workshops and announced a YMCA summer camp and Atlanta Symphony concerts alongside the GSU Physics Department's meeting time.

WRAS, through the *Georgia Music Show,* started by Aubrey Alton and Mike Donnellan, linked with local scenes. The station fostered scene development without being overtly commercial. WRAS provided Georgia bands with a chance to build a fanbase and fill venues. Although shoddy station equipment often chewed through the four-track tapes Alton and Donnellan played on their weekly show, since few bands could afford to press vinyl, they identified the station's educational mission with providing "diversity" on the FM airwaves.[22]

But diversity's definition was subject to contestation. In 1976, a student complained of WRAS's bias against Black students in programming. A first-year student attempted to obtain a show to offer "his own music format," according to the student newspaper. After his first on-air appearance, the student quit. WRAS's general manager explained that the student "did not know the music." The student filed charges claiming Title VI and Title IX violations, and hearings by a special subcommittee of the Committee on Student Communications reviewed policies across student media. It found "no evidence of discrimination" regarding the station's "hiring and personnel policies." Whatever the details of the student's preparation to DJ were, the format privileged mostly white-oriented progressive rock, leaving a few specialty shows for Black listeners' tastes. The committee recommended WRAS survey students to ensure their tastes informed programming.[23]

By 1978, controversy intensified over what WRAS's role should be. With an unprecedented power of 20,000 watts, WRAS faced more pressure than other college stations to fulfill divergent roles in radio. Some listeners wanted the station to be recognized in Atlanta radio for its musical fare, meaning it competed with commercial rock radio. Others wanted music to hew closely to local music scene developments. Still others insisted on a narrow "educational" identity, playing music only for students and offering edifying content. By the late 1970s, dean of Student Affairs H. King Buttermore III identified "a way to compete with top 40" radio while remaining "educational."[24] Most hours would satisfy white college-aged listeners with album-oriented rock with a few deeper cuts mixed in, and educate by giving them access to college events, specialty programming, and public service and information—a pattern repeated at stations that lacked WRAS's visibility.[25]

Buttermore, in charge of the division responsible for the radio station, could influence programming indirectly through selection of staff and student leaders.

Rancor over the format increased as general manager James Tarbox and his program director Doug Jackson, both Georgia State students, streamlined offerings to increase audience continuity in the academic year 1978–79.

One critic, DJ Anita Sarko, announced her objection to WRAS adopting a "commercial approach" on air, during her afternoon show.

Jackson, who was in his car tuning in, turned around, drove back to the station, and fired her.[26]

Sarko was a unique figure at WRAS. A Detroit native and graduate student taking courses in commercial music and recording at Georgia State, she had a passion for punk and new wave and her own extensive record collection. Music called to her, which she consistently returned to after experimenting with careers in teaching and the law. To explore record promotion opportunities, she joined WRAS, where her low-toned voice was a good fit for on-air work, according to the station manager.

But, she admitted, "I was kind of a bad girl on the radio." She invited her friends to sing the sportscast. She cued up Detroit proto-punk band the MC5—something she thought rankled the station's managers. "This was the South," she remembered, "and they didn't like the idea of a woman playing a lot of hard music." Instead, they "wanted women who were either stupid or sounded like they were in heat."[27] Sarko, known for speaking her mind and her progressive music tastes, caused waves.

Jackson charged Sarko with violating a policy to not discuss internal affairs on air. She criticized WRAS for seeking a "uniformity of sound" to create "the broadest appeal possible within a progressive format," Tarbox explained.

Sarko saw the matter differently. She announced, "If they are going to stop playing progressive music, OK. But they shouldn't keep billing themselves as Atlanta's Progressive Alternative." In her view, the general manager fired her because she envisioned WRAS "as a learning center" to "showcase" progressive developments in music, not as a mimic of commercial stations with a few locals thrown in.[28]

Sarko disputed accounts that she departed because Jackson cut her hours. She explained, "The WRAS management," meaning Tarbox and Jackson, "would like the listeners to believe that my resignation was because of my on-the-air time reduction." The real issue, she asserted, was over music. (She refuted that she had been fired, insisting she resigned first.) Jackson and Tarbox preferred rock rather than "progressive" music, meaning punk and new wave music emanating from England, New York, and Los Angeles. "Doug Jackson," she charged, "told me that he did not like my music." In fact, "he told me he knew little about music and hated progressive music." She insisted on "music that is innovative, experimental, and that expands upon new directions." She resigned because she was "tired of fighting" to play what she wanted. She envisioned her protest as more of a swan song than a demand for influence. One fan lamented, "She gave the listener a chance to hear such 'new wave' bands as Television, David Johansen, and Devo when no other disc jockey or station would play them." He valued her dedication to pushing the station away from "conservative" music.[29]

Station leaders and interested administrators worked improve WRAS's visibility within the institution and across Atlanta. A university task force, Tarbox explained, worked on GSU's "overall image," but few campus leaders recognized WRAS's potential to represent the university. "Seven years of neglect" led to resentment. Tarbox emphasized WRAS as a potential draw for the university. "With the format WRAS follows," he asserted, "and with the wide reputation that it has with young people, the station should (and could) be a major force in recruiting new students." Expanding cutting-edge, innovative music such as Sarko offered did not appear on Tarbox's list of actions to improve recruitment. Instead, Tarbox explained, "WRAS stands ready to serve GSU" if only the institution would recognize its asset. Perhaps, with support established, WRAS could branch out into more adventurous territory.

WRAS's student leaders wanted to maintain professionalism and satisfy a wide array of listeners. Tarbox explained, "The disc jockey has to be able to blend songs so the change is smooth; they must also set and keep a certain mood with the cuts played," requiring musical knowledge and understanding of and interaction with audiences. Jackson highlighted how WRAS provided valuable training applicable in careers beyond broadcasting. He defended the format. "For radio to survive," he explained, "it must have listeners."[30]

Jackson understood the station had a unique role as a noncommercial FM signal compared with commercial rock stations. WRAS had to have a format, given its size and reach, but it allowed DJs leeway so long as they supported the rotation and did not violate policy. WRAS's public relations director Jesse Miller linked the station's alternative status with its ability to take risks and air "local talent such as the Razor Boys, Swimming Pool Ques, The Fans, and Glenn Phillips." But Miller set his sights on a career in mainstream broadcasting, given that he also worked part time at a local Top 40 station in nearby Gainesville, Georgia.

Sarko, on the other hand, continued her career in "progressive" music. She packed her bags for New York City, where she became a leading figure in the downtown dance scene. In 1979 she found herself at the Mudd Club, a new wave venue, as an alternate DJ. She liked making people dance, and her success led her to spin records at Danceteria, where she earned a reputation as a DJ "extraordinaire." Her "specialty," she remembered, was breaking new music, unlike other DJs who focused on what was already popular. Her attention to new music helped create links between the hip-hop and punk scenes, as rap artists moved from the Bronx and Brooklyn into downtown clubs. Her work at Danceteria would help launch the careers of groups such as the Beastie Boys, Sonic Youth, and staples of alternative music in the next decade.[31]

For those who wanted to influence the music industry, they went to New York. Sarko had been a bit ahead of her time at WRAS, a fact reflected by her later career (and WRAS's eventual embrace of new wave music). In 1978, as she packed for New York, regional scenes remained atomized, though exciting developments germinated in scenes such as Athens, not far from Atlanta. DIY fanzines and industry tip sheets like CMJ captured what college DJs put into rotation, but Sarko had bigger plans.

It wasn't clear if Sarko was leaving behind a college station that would support progressive music and new sounds beyond mainstream rock. Institutional support and governance structures, administrative priorities, station missions, and student aspirations, as well as the contours of local radio markets, determined whether punk, new wave, or other local music could be found on collegiate airwaves in the 1970s, from Los Angeles, to Boston, to Atlanta, and the college towns in between. Many DJs aimed their musical service toward the commercial radio and major-label industry—and a new publication was there to capitalize on college radio's potential influence.

The CMJ Effect

One college radio alumnus recognized stations' collective power in the music industry. Robert Haber, a graduate of Brandeis University and WBRS-FM, founded CMJ in November 1978 to capture this power. As of the late 1970s, few college stations reported their playlists to *Billboard*. Nevertheless, Haber targeted college radio programmers with his new industry tip sheet, started as supplement to the *Progressive Media Journal* magazine, later CMJ *New Music Report*, usually known by the acronym, CMJ.[32] The biweekly new music tip sheet featured "general news, record reviews, a dialog aimed at a specific issue regarding college radio, a 'free comment' section" to represent the experiences of student DJs and engineers. Boasting an initial staff of ten, Haber's publication targeted those currently involved in the activity and the record business.[33]

Haber noticed how college stations kept tabs on underground music developments and facilitated the exposure of new artists. At Central Connecticut State University in 1979, DJ Mike Parent routinely reported on the most exciting new acts on the college circuit. In October, he wrote about the B-52's recent tour of northeast clubs. "Rock Lobster" enjoyed "substantial airplay in the New York City area where the group has a large following," whereas in Hartford, Parent reported, the cut "52 Girls" was popular.[34] College students monitored the hot new sounds on neighboring stations and area venues. They selected favorite songs from artists making the rounds, with some moving into more mainstream outlets. DJs offered value to record labels: it was expensive to promote new artists, and these stations could create demand and break a band without much investment.

It wasn't the musical offerings of bohemia that defined these stations, as captured by CMJ's charts. In April 1980, CMJ had been collecting college charts from across the country for a year or so. That month, it tallied reports and placed Elvis Costello's *Get Happy!!* At the number one spot on collegiate charts. The Clash followed with its seminal punk album *London*

Calling. With punk artists topping the charts, inspiring emulators to DIY their own music and local scenes, it might seem that by 1980 college radio's association with underground, avant-garde, and politically relevant music had solidified. After all, the Clash's title song featured Joe Strummer's concerns about nuclear fallout and police brutality and referenced the punk movement's recent dissolution and distrust of mainstream music industry pressures and popular appeal.[35]

But dig deeper into the CMJ list in 1980, and a different sound emerges. The number three spot on the list went to Bob Seger and the Silver Bullet Band for *Against the Wind*, followed by Genesis and Billy Joel. Between Warren Zevon and the rapidly rising Boz Scaggs appeared Heart and Journey. These artists, whose work received regular rotation on commercial stations, hardly marked college radio as an outpost for underground misfits and dropouts from mainstream popular culture. Indeed, among the labels with hits—Columbia, EMI, RCA, Polydor, and Atlantic—no small, regionally based independents charted. Even Sire, a successful independent label since 1966 that had launched the Ramones, the Dead Boys, and the Talking Heads, belonged to the Warner Brothers conglomerate. Only Rough Trade, a British label, exemplified the "New Music" CMJ's publishers wanted to highlight.[36]

CMJ's April 1980 chart captured college radio's tendency to emulate commercial rock radio. Common practices and organizations bolstered these tendencies. Conferences and conventions trained student volunteers, disseminated trade news, and provided space for college broadcasters to share new technology and strategies. The Intercollegiate Broadcasting System (IBS) hosted regional annual conventions since 1941, offering best practices and advice for managing stations.[37] In 1981, more than 500 college and high school students attended the Loyola National Radio Conference in Chicago, an annual event in the 1970s and 1980s of "seminars led by professional broadcasters, a video showcase, rock musicians and record company hospitality suites" regarding new music and best practices. Haber attended the National Student Broadcasters convention in Boston to publicize his publication and promote professional practices.[38]

Haber envisioned college radio as a force within the music industry, despite stations' many purposes, missions, and programming structures. He designed CMJ to aggregate college radio's influence. Yet whether college radio would collectively drive trends in new music and force mainstream listeners to tune in to more challenging artists—sonically or politically— remained to be seen. It just wasn't clear if these stations could shape musical culture or how much power individual stations wielded with their playlists.

CMJ tallied the top thirty songs of participating stations, not the specific programming practices across stations, which varied but shared some similar patterns. In 1979, WXCI at Western Connecticut State University reported to CMJ—one of a couple hundred stations (at most) that did then. Although DJs featured many popular artists, the station aimed to expose new bands. "We use what we call an 'X' bin," student managers explained. "In it we put the more major releases that leave the playlist (Pink Floyd, Rush, Utopia, The Knack, etc.). The bin is on a one play per day rotation, so we keep pretty constant exposure of the biggies." Once a week WXCI aired an hour-long "fresh tracks show" to provide exposure for obscure bands, which by 1979 included punk and new wave artists the Cramps, Public Image, Ltd., and the Elevators, as well as local acts.[39] The lists reported to CMJ reflected the top songs aired by DJs across all its block programs. New reggae, if programmed a few hours a week, would not chart (until CMJ debuted a dedicated chart for the genre). DJs might cue up the latest REO Speedwagon in between newer cuts (or vice versa), translating to a chart spot on CMJ. A local artist would have to receive airtime across several college stations in a region to chart, since CMJ eventually aggregated hits into East, West, Midwest, South, and national lists.

But college radio's rising influence, as captured by CMJ, influenced programming structures, rotations, and what bands program directors reported in their biweekly top-thirty lists. This group of stations included Western Connecticut's, which revamped its format after considering the radio market and the sense that college radio offered an alternative format and contribution to the music industry, thanks to CMJ. WXCI's top 100 albums of 1979, with the Cars at number one, featured the Doobie Brothers, Bad Company, Rod Stewart, and Journey, mixed in with Blondie, the Police, Elvis Costello, the Patti Smith Group, and Roxy Music—bands from progressive new wave and underground music scenes gaining exposure.[40] It was in the latter category that DJs envisioned their service to the Danbury market, which already had a beautiful music, two adult contemporary, and one AOR station. The new program director targeted an adult audience with "more refined" tastes. CMJ helped cultivate a cadre of stations with a similar sound.

Individual DJs determined their block's format, by and large, but a specified theme could impose limits. Ted Nugent did not belong in the adult contemporary hour, and DJs carefully considered teenagers' requests.

The program director encouraged DJs to remember they played for the "25–30-year-old person," including women. "This audience is totally different from the seventeen-year-old male who we have been 'rocking out for' in the past." Perhaps the station defied the niche programming trends in FM rock radio, but more likely station leaders simply sought to fill a gap in the Danbury radio market. Adult contemporary radio required DJs to avoid music available anywhere and targeted a wider age range.[41]

The program director rejected freeform as a model. Letting DJs follow their whims would be "ineffective and undesirable," since the station earned listeners "with a structured format." He looked to Lee Abrams's "Superstars" format at a few rock stations around the country that was defining AOR. Nonetheless, the program director acknowledged DJs "dislike having restrictions upon their 'freedom to be creative.'" Instead, he sought an openness to satisfy audiences and DJs and to maintain good relations with record labels. The area seemed "hungry" for what he proposed, he concluded.[42] Audiences and DJs could have it both ways, in sum.

Other stations found themselves caught between two poles of student DJs in the late 1970s. Around 1978, many college stations incorporated progressive new wave and punk music. Often, one or two students took the lead in pushing for format changes to emphasize progressive rock. At the University of Kansas, one student DJ almost single-handedly pushed KJHK away from its commercial emphasis in music, establishing the station as a leader in new music. Steven Greenwood reviewed the top hits in CMJ in December 1978 and hated what he saw. Too many stations remained "slavishly devoted" to the "rarefied pits" of music found on AOR stations. He entreated his fellow music directors to empower their ten-watt "college radio laboratory" to do a real service to audiences, markets, and record companies and "to the many superb artists who are SO deserving of exposure the big AOR stations so shamelessly refuse." Greenwood championed college radio as a place of innovation. In response, Haber encouraged other DJs to weigh in and debate "progressive music." Thanks to Greenwood, KJHK provided oxygen to the local Lawrence music scene. Student DJs who wished to gain professional experience thought they should tightly emulate AOR stations, perhaps with a few newer selections to distinguish college stations from the rest. But Greenwood defied that assessment. Instead, he insisted, "it IS possible to program a 'progressive' station" while gaining "the basic skills" for a job in AOR "if that's what one is foolish enough to want."[43]

But new wave was popular. A DJ at Harvard's station reported a flood of requests in 1978.[44] It's nearly impossible to quantify the number of college stations "going progressive" in the late 1970s due to vagueness of the term and varied programming structures. "Progressive" by the late 1970s translated as "high quality" radio with DJs speaking in a "low-key manner" offering "rock, rock, rock around the clock."[45] CMJ's debut confirmed that college DJs had collective clout in the music industry. Still, what type of music they would promote remained to be determined.

Musical Diversity

At Georgia State's WRAS, commitment to diversity extended only so far, particularly with the station's sparse coverage of Black artists. The station continued to hone its format, generating much controversy under a new general manager with ties to Dean Buttermore. As the new format went into effect, which allowed for new music and experimentation alongside familiar music, by spring 1981 Georgia State students critiqued this new approach—particularly those who felt marginalized by the entire process. Although the administration sought to serve students, it tended to forget minority matriculants.

Black student leaders at Georgia State evaluated their influence across the institution and found it lacking, despite a decade since the Black student movement pushed for campuses to embrace African American history and culture, both in curricula and campus life. Few Black students occupied positions of leadership, particularly in student media.[46]

WRAS's playlist fell under scrutiny. Frank Caudell, president of Georgia State's Black Student Union, found "the time devoted to black programming is eight hours a week," just over 4 percent of airtime. "Yet blacks make up 16 percent of this school," he pointed out. Mathematical equity was not the issue. "But even if there were only 100 black students here," he continued, "they deserve to get something they can relate to." Caudell calculated that during one week of programming, "no more than eight black-oriented acts" appeared in the station's rotation. Sure, a few Black artists made it on air, but WRAS provided scant programming that spoke to Black students.[47]

General manager Mike Garretson invoked the station's format—the format he had implemented—as the reason. Because it was a "progressive-oriented rock" station, meaning it played new wave and mainstream rock acts, "there are few black progressive rock artists" to choose from. WRAS's public relations director Theresa Godwin called Caudell's findings "totally false and ridiculous." She pointed out that in thirty minutes she heard Stevie Wonder and Prince. The Busboys, James Brown, and B. B. King also appeared. She denied that WRAS dedicated only eight hours to "black programming" because Caudell only counted specialty shows, not the Black artists in regular rotation. Godwin contradicted Garretson's assertion that progressive music was a whites-only genre, but she dismissed Caudell's concerns. "ALL people, black and white," she insisted, "have a wide variety of musical tastes, Mr. Caudell, and the programming at WRAS is designed to appeal to all musical tastes, not to judge the music on ethnic aspects, as you have judged our station."[48]

In other words, WRAS emphasized a colorblind, meritocratic basis for judging music, which critics cited as ignoring the social and cultural contexts that produced music. The station aimed for, as Godwin saw it, a pluralistic mélange of music and influences.[49] Caudell hesitated to respond because Godwin appeared "so 'jejune.'" He reiterated Garretson's reliance on a "progressive-oriented rock" format, a euphemism that allowed for the enforcement of a sonic color line while exempting station leaders from responsibility.[50]

Caudell dismissed the Busboys as evidence that WRAS covered Black culture. "One wonders why she did not mention Charley Pride as well; it would have made just as little sense," he argued. Caudell meant that the Busboys, whose rockabilly-style music sounded more like white artists than soul and funk bands, offered little exposure for Black culture. Pride, who resided in the white-dominated country music genre, in Caudell's view reflected similar problems. Caudell did not approach questions regarding these genres' appropriation of Black sounds. "I have nothing against Pride and the 'Busboys' singing in styles generated by other cultures," Caudell explained, "but such acts cannot be termed 'black' in any intelligent attempt to understand and appreciate ethnic diversity." James Brown and B. B. King made the playlist because of "the caucasian love affair with nostalgia," he argued, while WRAS avoided current Black artists from Peabo Bryson to Sara Vaughn. WRAS was not the problem, only a reflection. Instead, he asked "whether those who now exercise hegemony over institutions and resources voluntarily allow others their rightful access to the levers of power, or will extreme force and pressure have to be applied to get people to learn and share?"[51]

Other students observed similar problems. In July 1981, out of a sixty-three-album rotation, a student found only two by Black artists: "That's less than 3.2 percent!" He tuned in for a few hours, counted the Black artists aired, and reported a "token quota" he could count "on one hand." A WRAS defender thought the station "is truly giving us a fair quota," given the number of Black rock artists, the genre of focus on WRAS. "Let more blacks record real rock and roll and I am sure WRAS will play those tunes," he surmised. Although WRAS touted its hard-won format as adding "diversity" to the airwaves, commercial music industry limits remained—and the station's DJ roster remained overwhelmingly white, students observed.[52]

Meanwhile, the station continued to build a strong reputation in Atlanta and within the music industry. WRAS emerged on the radar of record labels and music journalists. By 1982 trade magazines included WRAS among the nation's top college stations. That spring, the station hosted a slogan contest to update its image. History reverberated. One student leader joked that submissions should avoid "WRAS, W.e R.eally A.re S.toned" or "W.e R. really A.re S.igma N.u's," referring to Garretson's perceived tendency to place his fraternity brothers into positions of leadership without any significant radio experience. In all, however, Dean Buttermore's vision for the station seemed to have come to fruition, and the station would evolve and earn high marks and musical influence.[53]

New professional station manager Jeff Walker built on WRAS's success after 1981. "Thousands" of bands sought its promotional access, including "Bruce Springsteen, Frank Zappa, Devo, Mother's Finest, The Dregs, Joan Jett, The Go-Go's, the Talking Heads, and Tom Petty." Gold records hung in the station. Although rumors and innuendo surrounded station history, such as a nighttime DJ conducting a show in the nude or a manager fired for smoking pot, WRAS earned influence along with launching many DJs into careers in commercial broadcasting.[54]

The station's commercial and professional relevance yielded further gains: Buttermore and Walker expanded the station with the construction of a new signal tower. This upgrade allowed WRAS to achieve an output almost unheard of in college radio: 50,000 watts, with the administration shelling out $39,000 for construction.[55]

Walker implemented "dayparting," a programming structure found in commercial radio, such as identifying weekday morning and evening hours as "drive time" that drew different listeners than midday and late night. With WRAS's wide geographical and audience reach, its influence grew and required professional structures. It remained on top of new music trends, championing new wave's crossover to the mainstream as MTV debuted.[56]

By June 1983, New Order topped WRAS's list of most requested bands. After the release of "Blue Monday," New Order proved it could maintain its progressive reputation and garner mainstream appeal. WRAS existed as part of a college radio and commercial FM "progressive network," cementing a popular association between college radio and the first wave of alternative music that would become hugely successful in the 1980s. Atlanta became New Order's "premier stop" that summer, playing to a sold-out venue, inspiring the crowd to "frenzy" levels.[57] WRAS signaled where mainstream popular culture was headed.[58] The student senate also supported expansion. As one proponent argued, WRAS was "the finest radio station in Atlanta" because it "is always first with the upcoming trends—long before the commercially competing stations such as Z-93 and 96-Rock." The Police, Eurythmics, and the Fixx all appeared on its signal before elsewhere in Atlanta, and it promoted local bands.[59]

• • • • • •

It was 1980, and Henry Santoro was doing a shift at WMBR in the basement of the Walker Memorial Building on MIT's campus. The phone rang, and on the other end of the line came an Irish-accented man's voice.

"I have this band here," he explained. "They aren't on tour yet, and their record isn't out, but I'd like to show them a radio station and how it works. Could we arrange a visit?"

"Sure," Santoro replied. Why not?

About an hour later, a group of four teenagers and their manager, the man on the phone, filed into the windowless studio. Whether this visit coincided with the band's visit to WBCN, where DJ Carter Alan promoted them, during a US tour and stop at the Paradise in Boston, remains unclear. In 1980, U2 released its first album, *Boy*, which would produce no hit singles but establish the band's fan base in Ireland and the United Kingdom and on college radio in the United States.

U2 made good use of college radio. In March 1981, to support its release, the band appeared on KFJC in Los Altos Hills, California, after its free show at nearby San Jose State University, co-presented by KFJC. A listener called the band "fresh," and the band recognized that college radio stations such as KFJC played music that was "real." Real rock fans tuned to the left of the dial.[60]

Questions regarding college radio's listenership and service persisted. University administrators grew increasingly interested in how their institution sounded to wider communities, while openings for new types of relevant content emerged. The FCC encouraged college-station license holders to adhere to serve the public—and not use high-power signals as playthings. DJs, even those seeking careers in broadcasting, wanted to play cool music and wield cultural power.

The FCC wasn't very cool, but it influenced college radio's emerging culture and ability to break bands such as U2 to stardom. The FCC could indirectly shape these noncommercial stations, despite their educational purpose and institutional homes. A kerfuffle between rock and disco fans at KOHL at Ohlone College in California revealed these considerations as the station planned a power increase, considering the FCC's new rules regarding ten-watt stations.[61] Some DJs worried higher wattage and a wider listenership would push the station increasingly mainstream and stifle student creativity. Powerful wattage increased the demands placed on college stations, with potentially more radios tuning in whether in metropolitan areas or small college towns.

A diverse landscape of college radio remained populated by many small stations, each doing its own thing, maintaining their own islands of influence, even though coordination and attention emerged. CMJ's debut validated college radio as a decentralized yet powerful network with coherent musical influence. The FCC and public broadcasters occupying real estate on the left of the dial had other ideas for these stations. As college radio's direction and status as gatekeepers and tastemakers solidified and genre battles faded, others looked at these signals with different intentions. The rising popularity of National Public Radio and its proponents, including support at the FCC, began to force college stations to make a decision: they would have to expand, professionalize, or else cease broadcasting on FM altogether.

3 How the FCC Inadvertently Created Modern College Radio

. . . .

I am a student at the university, a staff member at the university and a resident within the listening area of WUOG. On those bases, I feel qualified to suggest that WUOG is not serving the best interests of its listening community by playing rock and roll, however progressively, to the great exclusion of other forms of programming.

—Letters, *Red and Black*, in WUOG clippings, 1981

Two nights of new wave is too much. For that matter, one is too much. If new wave must be played, do it on Friday or Saturday night.

—Handwritten letter, WUOG clippings, 1981

One morning in 1980, *Athens Observer* editor Phil Williams settled down to relax by flipping on University of Georgia (UGA) radio from WUOG for some classical music. The editor probably closed his eyes, maybe enjoyed some eggs or a coffee, and leaned back in his lounger to appreciate a symphony with his newspaper.

Suddenly, a Beatles song "exploded in the air." Startled, Williams reached to turn down the noise, but the song abruptly ended. Silence ensued.

Then it burst onto his radio set again.

This happened four or five times before the familiar lull of classical music resumed.

During another morning's classical rotation, the DJ cued up an odd piece. "Is that music from *Goldfinger*?" Williams asked himself. It certainly was.

Another day, Williams expected to enjoy a Sibelius symphony. Yet the second movement sounded strangely like a Vaughan Williams overture. Or was that Smetana? Williams had enough. He picked up the receiver and called the station, where a DJ fuddled with the controls and fumbled records to the turntable.

When the editor listed his complaints, the supervising DJ explained that a new jock was learning the equipment. Williams pointed out the interjection into Sibelius's oeuvre: the DJ replied, "Hey, that's pretty good that you caught that!" A tape machine was down, and the DJ figured no one would notice the difference as he killed time while rewinding the tape.

Williams, as newspaper editor and longtime resident, had interest in Athens's access to quality music and information. He turned to his typewriter and detailed the experience for WUOG's listener survey and voiced his hopes that the station would improve in his newspaper.[1]

More annoying than the abrupt musical shifts, Williams complained, were the constant interjections of the station's ID, "This is Charles Darwin. When I'm in Athens, I naturally select WUOG." Williams griped, "It was clever the first 8,000 times they used it."[2] Still, he praised WUOG as "nothing short of superb," despite DJs breathing into the microphones occasionally. Professionalism and an increased reliance on National Public Radio programming would "only make it better."[3]

"Unpleasant adventures" in radio broadcasting, as Williams put it, generated pressure for professionalism among student DJs, more rigorous formatting, higher-quality programs from NPR, and greater oversight of noncommercial, educational radio in the 1970s. Jocks-in-training often started by staffing established shows to learn how to use the equipment before being allowed to produce shows of their own—leading to inexperienced and uninitiated classical music DJs blaring the Beatles accidentally or mixing up Finnish and Czech composers. At WUOG, partying in the station and lax oversight led to FCC rule violations, including editorializing, pranks, and obscenities broadcast. DJs engaged in frequent drug use in the studio.[4]

FCC-licensed stations operated under the auspices of the federal regulatory body. To encourage nonprofit and educational institutions to invest in FM, the FCC introduced ten-watt, "entry-level" class D licenses in 1948. The technology for these signals was relatively inexpensive and easy to use, offering just-powerful-enough signals to cover campus and maybe the surrounding community. Reserved specifically for educational radio (although what that meant remained widely malleable), the class D license existed to encourage institutions to populate the noncommercial FM spectrum set aside to fulfill the Communications Act of 1934's promise to use radio to promote the public good.[5] The class D license encouraged college radio's expansion, which accelerated in the 1960s and 1970s alongside FM's growing popularity. Many entrants subsequently expanded power beyond ten watts.[6] With this visibility, more claimants emerged to determine what collegiate broadcasting's collective identity would be.

Greater interest in noncommercial radio in the 1970s culminated in the FCC's 1978 decision to end the entry-level class D license and remove those stations' protections from interference from larger nearby competitors on the same frequency. High-power educational broadcasters, with access to federal funding through the Corporation for Public Broadcasting, viewed small, ten-watt stations as barriers to expansive service. The decision coincided with a "growing belief" that autonomous colleges and universities tasked with contributing public goods "ought to be publicly accountable for their decisions."[7] Such context primed universities to prove they offered benefits beyond the education of young people—a context that further influenced changes in FCC rules regarding college radio.

One could go all the way to Hawai'i and see how the rule change reshaped college radio and put it on the pop culture map, although its effects took different forms across radio markets and institutions. License renewal timelines spread the decision's implications over several years, making it difficult to discern its aggregate effect. But the wide array of outcomes together transformed college radio's cultural power and reputation.

Origins of the Class D Decision

In 1980, Durward Long had a decision to make. Two years prior, the FCC acquiesced to demands from the National Association of Educational Broadcasters (NAEB) and the Corporation for Public Broadcasting (CPB) and phased out the class D, ten-watt license popular at universities and colleges across the nation—including at Long's institution, the University of Hawai'i at Mānoa. Stations could continue to broadcast, but pressure mounted for them to either increase wattage or relinquish signals in case of interference.

In the 1960s, large educational broadcasters mobilized to increase wattage. They succeeded in securing federal support for educational public radio in the Public Broadcasting Act of 1967, which had focused almost exclusively on public television. Radio stations were thus eligible for CPB funding. Efforts accelerated in 1972 thanks to the CPB's desire to "eliminate the tiny school stations" because they were not "an efficient use of spectrum."[8] Reformers' vision for these signals sought a national network of noncommercial, civic-service broadcasters much closer to those in the United Kingdom and western Europe, a lack that extended back to the 1930s when Congress established a commercial broadcasting and regulatory structure.[9]

Momentum in the 1970s produced FCC rule changes that reached deep into the Pacific Ocean and across the continent, forcing administrators like Long to decide what to do with their radio signals. New requirements could be delayed until license renewal or avoided through petition, but eventually, push would come to shove. Campus leaders such as Long had to adapt and reconsider stations' missions. Higher wattages brought greater public relations benefits—and scrutiny. Long trusted his students and coveted this experience for them, but he knew higher wattage brought risks.

The class D decision coincided with a cultural shift taking place at the FCC that prompted increased attention to indecency and obscenity in broadcasting—all in the name of public service. When it came to license regulation, the FCC might limit how many signals an entity could own or who could gain access to the airwaves through additional rules and application approvals. Indirectly, it could shape programming and station management through the threat of action: determining who might be tossed off the air, rather than let on, or driven out of radio by hefty fines for improper content. That mechanism, often referred to as a "chilling effect," prompted stations to implement stricter rules about content before any violation occurred. Regarding indecency, the Supreme Court's *Pacifica v. FCC* decision in 1978 looms large. It empowered the FCC to regulate indecent content, limiting First Amendment protections for broadcasters because of media's unique availability to minors and spectrum scarcity.

The threat of license denial for indecency or obscenity emerged before the *Pacifica* decision, however. Instead, regulatory shifts at the FCC had broader motivations. Regulators encouraged college administrators to professionalize and directly manage their alternative "sandboxes" on the radio so they would offer more edifying, civic-minded content.

Signaling this trend, at the University of Pennsylvania FCC actions forced administrators to scrutinize station programming and management. WXPN, the university's student-run station, aired talk shows with students joking around and crafting prank advertisements, such as for "Stayhard," a supplement to cure "premature ejaculation."[10] A years-long saga began in 1974 when one program, *The Vegetable Report*, broadcast crude commentary. Several listeners issued FCC complaints. When the administration failed to take strong actions regarding station management, regulators disapproved. Commission members charged Penn administrators and trustees with refusing to take "accountability" of the station. The FCC fined WXPN $2,000 and threatened to not renew the license.[11] As WXPN's faculty adviser explained, the FCC was "really steamed up" and had been "looking for a test case for a while." The *Vegetable Report* incident provided that case.[12] After provisional license approval, in 1977 the FCC denied WXPN's license renewal when the administration made no attempt to reorganize the station after the complaints, fines, and warnings. The FCC did not accept Penn's justification that the signal was for students to run. Eventually, after operating on a provisional license, WXPN transformed into a professionally run public broadcaster, while students had access to a carrier-current station.[13]

College broadcasters looked on with horror at the Penn case. The class D decision added to the resonance of these shock waves. Administrators could no longer justify "benign neglect." The FCC clearly wanted institutions to leverage their public resource. Even for stations without a sensational indecency case, the FCC pressured institutions to professionalize—even if stations remained student-run.[14]

University missions influenced and limited college stations' programming, as well. In 1979, Georgetown University gifted—for $1—its progressive and Pacifica Foundation–influenced signal to the University of Washington, D.C. The sale followed years of campus turmoil about programming, such as public service announcements for clinics that provided abortion services or airing sexually charged poetry readings by William S. Burroughs.[15] Whether FCC intervention loomed or not, or whether changes arose from internal campus conflicts or wary license holders, across college radio administrators took seriously the FCC's recommendations to intervene in student-run stations' management and programming.

Sometimes, other students limited adventurous content on collegiate airwaves, demanding stations hew to their tastes instead of unpopular genres. Whatever the cause, the pressures to professionalize were on the rise in college radio in the 1970s despite—or perhaps in conjunction with—the medium's increased value as a cultural gatekeeper.

These pressures reached Hawai'i, where Long pondered his options. The incoming chancellor who controlled the license for ten-watt KTUH-FM debated in what direction to take the student-run station.

KTUH started in 1969 as a lab for the Speech-Communications Department, debuting on air with Otis Redding's rendition of "A Change Is Gonna Come." KTUH offered alternative programming to edify and entertain, with students at the boards. Students freely experimented with new music, offering alternatives to commercial rock radio. In 1976, a student interviewed avant-garde musician Frank Zappa before his concert in Honolulu.[16] Though KTUH was unlikely to run afoul of larger stations in nearby states, given its island home, FCC regulations nonetheless had to be met.[17]

There were two options available. One, Long could pursue a power increase. This avenue meant student broadcasts would reach widely, airing amateur DJs and their experimental tastes in more living rooms and cars.

Two, he could merge KTUH with KHPR, a proposed Hawai'i Public Radio station which had yet to build a studio—a service many Honolulu residents desired. This second option would bring information and news from NPR into affiliation with the university but limit students' on-air opportunities. A deadline loomed as KTUH's license lapsed. Long appreciated public radio's benefits and pedagogical functions. He told the *Honolulu Star-Bulletin*, "I would like to preserve KTUH as a student activity."[18] And so he applied for an increase to 100 watts and turned down NPR affiliation.

Technical matters regarding station mission and wattage usually depended on what goals administrators, public relations officers, boards of trustees, or, in some cases, faculty set. No matter who controlled stations, however, they encountered promoters of nationalized public broadcasting. Moreover, listeners in communities began to expect more of this type of service from campus-affiliated stations.

The 1978 decision that ended the class D license and stymied Chancellor Long did not appear out of the ether. FCC rule changes result from methodical research, process, comment, and hearings—as well as the organization of interests to pursue regulatory changes. The airwaves are a limited public resource: they cross municipal, state, and national borders. Radio reformers had been working for decades for the nationalization of educational radio. The NAEB, which lobbied for access to federal funds for public radio broadcasting, joined with the CPB to expand public radio. These reformers, which included leaders at various colleges and universities, amassed data behind their vision. In 1967, the NAEB commissioned a report to assess the nation's educational signals. The report promoted college radio stations as anchors for a national public broadcasting network to build civic ties. The NAEB lobbied for license changes to support that goal. In April 1967, the FCC issued Docket 14185 for comments, which would subject noncommercial, educational stations to the 100 watts required of commercial stations—thereby increasing the barrier to entry for smaller, undercapitalized stations. The docket remained open until 1976, while another petition proposed reduced interference protections for existing ten-watt stations, asking the FCC to consider "treating these as secondary operations."[19]

Radio's eligibility for federal funding in the Public Broadcasting Act of 1967 accelerated the formation of National Public Radio, which would bring serious news to listeners via educational signals. CPB funding eligibility required five full-time professional staff members, not students. Both the NAEB and CPB saw ten-watt stations as a barrier to public radio. These learning "laboratories" could not act as vehicles for public uplift. Moreover, these small signals potentially limited the range of "full-service" educational broadcasters carrying information and news to the masses.[20]

Many low-power, class D college stations did not even operate year-round, let alone twenty-four hours a day, seven days a week. NPR broadcasts and financial viability depended on securing audience share. As stations at major universities in metropolitan areas—such as the University of Washington's KUOW-FM and Boston University's WBUR—adopted NPR programming, their signals reached widely enough to justify investment. That is, until they ran into smaller, low-wattage stations farther into the hinterlands operating on the same frequency.

Student DJs cuing up Zappa while sparking a joint likely had no idea what was happening. Those who planned careers in broadcasting might have had some insight, but they had little power. Regarding CPB's 1976 petition, defenders emphasized the benefits smaller stations provided, negating the idea that they were wasted signals run by amateurs. Nevertheless, the CPB raised a "serious question" about spectrum use "efficiency" and "breadth of community service" provided by low-watt stations.[21]

Student-run, educational radio and public broadcasting diverged, although overlaps remained. As letters to WUOG demonstrated, many college radio listeners yearned for NPR service and classical music, but they had little desire to stamp out all progressive rock programs or keep students from the airwaves. Few expected all educational broadcasters to be full-service NPR stations (in 1979 there were 200, nationally).[22] At most stations, local programming or syndicated shows supplemented weekly schedules. Stations could invest in local newsrooms, select from a range of syndicated programs such as *Prairie Home Companion*, and save late-night or less popular hours for freeform shows staffed by volunteer community and student DJs. Different visions for these signals created dissonance. High-power, professionally run educational and community stations squared off against low-power, volunteer stations, which would be forced to invest in costly upgrades.[23]

The FCC's 1978 ruling reflected NPR's growing appeal, new programming structure and journalistic practices, and public radio's competitiveness. But the decision produced an unexpected result. Administrators like Durward Long in Hawai'i acquiesced and increased the power of student-run stations without applying for CPB funding or adopting more NPR programming.[24]

Beyond this ironic outcome, college radio remained a relatively unorganized space. A key centralizing organization, the Intercollegiate Broadcasting System (IBS), defined best practices, held conferences, and disseminated information about issues facing college radio. Nonetheless, college radio's atomized nature weakened its collective clout. The IBS filed petitions, along with several individual ten-watt stations, against the new rule and called the CPB "self-serving." The CPB's eligibility limits, including minimum operating hours, professional staff, and 100 watts of power, were discriminatory, they argued. They wanted all noncommercial stations to be eligible for funding.[25] Universities argued that carrier-current stations could not serve commuter populations. Ten-watt stations fulfilled more functions than laboratory training for communications students, and the FCC's rule change threatened to disrupt a functioning system.[26]

Their arguments failed, and the new rule went into effect in 1978.

The FCC offered no new class D assignments and would not protect existing stations from interference from powerful new stations. Commissioners seemed convinced by the argument that existing class D stations prohibited "at last 40–45 new high-power noncommercial FM stations in the top 100 markets" and blocked power increases for at least twenty existing stations. And since class D stations best served small markets, where competition would be less of a factor, the FCC ended their protections, assuming many operations would continue unimpeded without having to upgrade equipment. Ten-watt stations could wait for renewal before acting, or "anticipate the process" and upgrade to 100 watts, or move to a commercial channel, or cease broadcasting.[27]

University of Georgia faculty might not have known that the FCC supported their quest for NPR programming and professionalization in 1980 when they filled out the station survey and clamored for public radio. Professors from psychology, chemistry, and history felt "starved" for classical and jazz programming. WUOG's programs were a "sign of real civilization," even if the station veered too often into rock and disco, which a zoologist considered "worse than muzak." But faculty had no more power than the local pottery studio director who yearned for freeform, or students who wanted music for partying—and maybe studying.[28] Still, rumors circulated of the potential for university-provided NPR service, and changes took hold as administrators recognized that students were at the helm of valuable aural real estate.

Ripple Effects

Administrators supported wattage increases, sometimes with increased oversight, sometimes not. In other cases, stations simply waited to encounter interference or license-renewal deadlines. Other stations gained notoriety as their signals expanded, while others enjoyed already-powerful signals and flirted with adding NPR or public-affairs programming and edifying, diverse music. Some moved to the commercial band to avoid interference. Whatever the case or cause, college radio transformed in the years following the 1978 decision.

Power upgrades were already in the works at some stations as institutions looked to expand public outreach. At the University of California, Santa Cruz, administrators approved a wattage boost in 1980. Unlike at the University of Hawai'i, students pushed for the upgrade without the FCC's initiation. University administrators funded a state-of-the-art studio and wattage increase. In Hawai'i, Long increased KTUH to the new FCC-mandated minimum of 100 watts, but Santa Cruz enlarged its signal from ten to 1,200 watts. The expansion grew out of six years of planning by station manager Robin Lewin and "a band of radio freaks" who "decided to strike out for the comparative big time in radioland." The $100,000 capital investment, funded by student fees (not a tax increase, a local newspaper assured tax-averse California residents), reflected the station's interaction with Santa Cruz's music scene as well as the expertise of a local engineer.

Engineer Don Mussel, known as the "barefoot wonder," helped set up several local FM stations. Lewin envisioned linking UCSC to the community through KZSC, which won over administrators. Mussel proved indispensable: he scoured the area for used equipment to reduce costs. He constructed the operation himself, installed in "3,200 square feet of office and studio space, five studios with live capability in one." The tower would "beam KZSC from Boulder Creek to King City." Its power equaled that of nearby commercial FM stations.[29]

Lewin's inspiration came from experience in community and freeform radio. The resulting station broadcast a steady program of rock music and specialty shows, including "reggae, jazz and latin jazz." A program review board oversaw activities. It included both students and community members to ensure balanced programming for all constituents, making good use of the powerful signal.[30]

For stations set on defying trends in commercial radio, resisting power increases protected their independence. At the University of Chicago, students knew that higher scrutiny accompanying a power increase might jeopardize its "iconoclastic mix of jazz, rock, classical, rhythm and blues, reggae, folk, sports, panel discussions, poetry and foreign-language shows."

Students broadcasting on WHPK-FM since its 1968 debut prided themselves on offering "a distinct alternative to commercial broadcasting." Local commentators agreed that WHPK offered more "refreshing" content "than certain other college stations that attempt to 'play radio,' imitating as closely as possible the lifeless, repetitive formats of stations in the commercial spectrum." It was unclear what station this statement chastised, and student leaders still pursued a power increase.

They faced internal opposition. University administrators hesitated when the station applied for a power increase to 100 watts in 1980. The increase would expand the signal's reach to 3.6 miles, covering the Hyde Park neighborhood.

Student DJs conducted a pledge drive to support the increase, soliciting donations and selling advertisements for the station's program guide. Administrators liked the fundraising, yet they balked at the power increase.[31] Station leaders knew that they might be "forced off the air" while administrators hoped to remain ten watts. DJs feared "eroding the morale" of those fundraising for the expansion. Supporters pointed to the station's musical service to the campus and Hyde Park community, as well as the "practical outlet" it provided for students. Above all, WHPK offered "a needed informational and emotional link with campus" for students "forced to scatter all over Hyde Park." DJs promised to build a "more appreciated, favorable public image" for the university.[32]

The dean of students accepted these arguments, but he knew that increased power came with liability. He tasked station members with improving "quality of programming and continuity of leadership" before he would support the increase. It took him a year to make this offer, coming closer to the FCC's decision on WHPK's application in spring 1981. His ask wasn't easy to meet given the usual turnover of student leadership at college stations. Without support, WHPK's leaders could gamble and stay at ten watts, hoping that they would not face a competing signal or FCC denial of its license renewal.[33]

As students campaigned for the increase, the station programmed new wave and "modern" rock. Summer 1981 saw the Psychedelic Furs, Kraftwerk, and Gang of Four among WHPK's top plays, followed by Magazine, X, and Tom Petty (table 3.1).[34]

The administration finally supported the power increase a year later. The dean of students signed off in January 1982 if WHPK agreed to reinstitute a board of governors and improve the "quality and range of programming." Students and faculty would populate the board. Such oversight would help

TABLE 3.1 WHPK's Top 20, *Chicago Maroon*, August 7, 1981

This Week	Last Week	Record		
1	4	Echo & The Bunnymen	*Heaven Up Here*	WB/Sire
2	2	Stray Cats	*Stray Cats*	Arista (UK)
3	1	Kraftwerk	*Computer World*	Warner
4	10	Various Artists	*Hicks from the Sticks*	Antilles
5	3	Psychedelic Furs	*Talk, Talk, Talk*	CBS
6	6	Undertones	*Positive Touch*	Capitol/ Harvest
7	9	Go-Gos	*Beauty and the Beat*	A&M/IRS
8	5	Gang of Four	*Solid Gold*	Warner
9	–	Ramones	*Pleasant Dreams*	Warner
10	14	Buddy Guy	*Stone Crazy!*	Alligator
11	7	Various Artists	*Taxi*	Mango/ Antilles
12	8	X	*Wild Gift*	Slash
13	12	Neville Brothers	*Fiyo on the Bayou*	A&M
14	19	Tenpole Tudor	*Eddie, Old Bob, Dick and Gary*	Stiff America
15	–	Joe Jackson	*Jumpin Jive*	A&M
16	13	Magazine	*Magic, Murder, Etc.*	A&M/IRS
17	–	Dr. Feelgood	*Case of the Shakes*	Stiff America
18	17	Tom Petty	*Hard Promises*	MCA
19	11	English Beat	*Wha'ppen*	WB/Sire
20	20	Raincoats	*Odyshape*	Rough Trade

with student leadership turnover and stabilize station affairs.[35] The FCC came through with its approval for the power increase.

The increase was a win for the University of Chicago given the city's concentration of ten-watt signals. The physics of radio would not allow every signal to strengthen, and the FCC allowed city leaders some leeway in determining which institutions could power up. Chicago's educational stations did not want their numbers to decrease significantly, and in a series of meetings among radio representatives, a third of which were college-owned stations, an agreement about which would convert to higher power emerged. After FCC-mandated revisions, each station agreed to the city-wide plan and the FCC approved individual proposals.[36]

The station's increased visibility drew detractors. A student newspaper editorial congratulated WHPK on its approval but noted low student listenership compared with stations at Northwestern and the University of Illinois, Chicago. Low listenership, he argued, owed less to the poor signal and more to "programming" that was "frequently just plain dumb." Its inanity would be "embarrassingly magnified with a quantum jump in power." With great investment came great responsibility. College radio had "potential," he argued, particularly to challenge the monotony of FM commercial radio. WBEZ, Chicago's municipal-owned full-service public radio station and charter NPR member, offered a model for valuable radio, the student argued.[37] DJs rejected his advice, emphasizing the station's freedom in content and high-quality jazz programming, evidenced by frequent "requests and praise from some of Chicago's recording artists residing in the South Side."[38]

WBEZ was a praiseworthy station. But, DJs argued, WHPK could not have the same goals as the NPR powerhouse "just as those objectives of the *Chicago Maroon* cannot be the same as those of the *Chicago Tribune* or the *New York Times*." College radio stations like WHPK, though student-run and possessing meager budgets and low wattage, provided high value. Still it was unfair to compare WHPK to Northwestern's station, with its 5,000 watts and institutional home with a robust broadcasting school and financial support. WUIC at the University of Illinois, Chicago, on the other hand, had been silent for a year.[39]

The FCC's rule change overlooked stations' diversity and service they provided. In crowded markets, college stations worked to distinguish themselves from one another. As WHPK expanded its power, added sports coverage, and reviewed programming, it emerged more dedicated to its iconoclastic reputation and to "pushing to the limit of the new sound," unlike the "schlock" found elsewhere, as one DJ put it. By 1985, DJs boasted how WHPK's listeners could discover bands that would, in the future, be reviewed in the *New York Times*. After stations like WHPK "softened up" the public to new music, listeners might accept more "challenging" programming of "rock that will never receive major label distribution and can probably never be adjusted to fit the mainstream." It might be an obscure band cued up next to Throbbing Gristle or hip-hop artists, or, one DJ put it, "as it's called by the middle-aged crowd here on the South Side, that rap shit."[40] WHPK's increase produced an ironic effect: the station pushed further into new and less commercially viable music to distinguish itself from competitors.

WHPK's result was one of many unintended consequences of the FCC's class D rule change.

Some stations took the FCC's option to move to the commercial spectrum. In response to the CPB's 1976 petition, one commenter suggested "it was unlikely that there would be harm in letting Class D's operate in the commercial band." Another commenter envisioned less signal competition in the commercial spectrum because of its stable allocation method. The commercial band might help college stations to avoid costly upgrades in the short term.[41] Despite potentially more open frequencies, however, smaller stations had no protection from higher-wattage competitors on commercial FM.

Such was the fate for WFCS at Central Connecticut State University. In 1980, Connecticut Public Radio set its sights on 90.1 FM, which would override WFCS's low-watt signal.[42] As a result, its host institution pursued several frequency changes over the next decade.

WFCS launched on 90.1 FM in 1972 after beginning on AM. The "left-hand side of the FM dial," students proclaimed, featured "innovators of radio" responsive to listeners, unlike monolithic commercial rock giants.[43] But by 1978 scarcer funding at public institutions threatened radio service while the FCC privileged higher wattages.

To avoid upgrade expenses, administrators opted to move the signal to the commercial band in 1981, hoping to avoid competition. The university funded stereo FM along with a more expansive format, though it remained of limited power and its programs contrasted sharply with those of nearby commercial rock stations. As the student newspaper reported, WFCS would delight those "tired of listening to 'Rapture' more than a dozen times during the day," referring to Blondie's recent hit. Instead, WFCS would mix album-oriented rock with new wave, jazz, and R&B. The formerly "chaotic freeform" format settled on a coherent sound that would establish WFCS as "the new underground station of Greater Hartford."[44]

Central Connecticut's administration bet on the signal while avoiding further costs. Together with an upgrade to stereo, the frequency shift required $25,000 from university funds, a seemingly wise investment compared with a more expensive expansion if remaining at 90.1. WFCS retained noncommercial status, since it lacked the staff to solicit and produce advertising. "Besides the regulations and extra effort" of going fully commercial, the general manager explained, "the station would lose its image as a station that plays noncommercial rock and roll." Advertisers would demand greater audience predictability and a narrower, more rigid program structure, something student DJs wanted no part of. Instead, the station hosted promotional events such as contests for tickets to bluegrass, folk, and rock shows at local clubs—or to win a case of beer.[45]

The class D license's end, rather than immediately yielding a new era in college radio, produced ripple effects for years to come and with a diversity of outcomes. The rule change was not done with WFCS, where commercial competition did emerge, despite the supposed "stability" of commercial spectrum allocation. In 1986, the FCC assigned WFCS's FM spot at 97.9 to a new station out of nearby Enfield. Although WFCS could remain on air, it had no protection if the Enfield station overrode the smaller signal, a near certainty. With WFCS's mere thirty-six watts, below the FCC's threshold of 100 for protection, a student engineer explained, the Enfield outlet would "obliterate our station." WFCS's rotation including the Dead Milkmen and metal and hardcore bands would disappear from 97.9 FM, which sat, serendipitously, between two powerful commercial rock stations, luring listeners as they spun the dial.[46]

WFCS repeatedly adapted and survived with its low wattage and scarce funding. As a third frequency change in six years loomed, only expensive options remained. Moving to another frequency required $33,402 in new equipment, well above a university capital budget surplus allotment of $24,442 that year. Students pleaded for community support and to Connecticut senator Lowell Weicker. More than 1,000 individuals petitioned the student senate for the needed funding. Eventually, the station secured the funds and a location atop a television antenna on Rattlesnake Mountain, which allowed the low-wattage signal to reach Hartford.[47] WFCS moved to 107.7, continuing to broadcast alternative music and heavy metal, competing with Seton Hall's WSOU for status as the nation's top metal college station. The oddities and origination of its commercial signal faded in memory.[48]

Despite the diversity of outcomes, the FCC created a structural shift in licensing college stations and accelerated educational radio's divergence from public broadcasting. Yet the decision produced some ironic protections for college radio's iconoclastic and eclectic reputation. Its musical influence continued to grow alongside stations' relationship with budding music scenes. Pressure to professionalize sound and programming added fuel to stations' defense of their educational role in introducing listeners to music they could not hear elsewhere. A more professional sound and wider geographical reach reinforced those claims, even if regulatory developments created anxiety about the future of student-run radio.

In the 1970s, new music scenes, genres, and labels influenced college radio's emerging culture as ardent music fans introduced new shows and rose to positions of power, such as music director, where they could direct signals and defend stations' "educational" role. From Connecticut, to Illinois, to California, prominent state universities' signals adopted "progressive" programming, hoping to make a mark in radio by playing up-and-coming new wave artists. College radio's professionalization and the proliferation of underground, bohemian scenes operated in tandem to influence popular music. These twin forces shaped college radio's modern culture with its emphasis, though not exclusively, on independent music and discovery fueled by an ethos of noncommercialism.

At Davidson College in North Carolina, students planned a power upgrade for WDAV in 1976, driven by interest in professionalization. Before assuming the general manager position, Carrington Thompson produced a forty-page handbook covering everything from announcing style to FCC rules for logging, "programming theory," and music and audience research techniques.[49] He trained a cohesive and professional-sounding staff before increasing power from ten watts to 18,500. Davidson's administration promised to support the $70,000 upgrade, which the FCC approved in November 1977. The station potentially reached two million listeners with a program of jazz, folk, contemporary and experimental music, and "special services such as story hours for children, foreign language broadcasts," and sports coverage, which commercial stations ignored.[50]

DJs like Thompson saw themselves as professional providers of content for the area. They did not envision breaking new musical acts; rather, they sought to supplement public broadcasting for adult audiences. Davidson's radio director, a drama professor, planned to apply for CPB funding. Rock music might have made up much of WDAV's schedule in 1977, but the director envisioned "increasing classical, verbal, and children's broadcasting," whether syndicated programs or campus-related cultural events. The station would resemble public radio stations such as emerging at WXPN at Penn as it navigated its license troubles.[51]

Distinctions between public and educational—and progressive rock—radio remained fluid. Another Davidson student took to the airwaves in the mid-1970s, playing the station's often "top-name artist" rotation of Steely Dan, Todd Rundgren, and Led Zeppelin.[52]

That student, Bertis Downs, loved music. He worked as a student volunteer at WDAV for two years, as well as on Davidson's concert committee. Downs headed to law school, not a profession in radio. Interest in copyright law took him to the University of Georgia for his JD, where he met Bill Berry, an undergraduate working on the concert committee that Downs joined as a graduate student.

When Berry, Peter Buck, Mike Mills, and Michael Stipe formed R.E.M., Downs joined as their business manager, supporting the band's practices that discerningly avoided commercial endorsements.[53] Moreover, their career became synonymous with the rising visibility and reputation of college radio as they crossed over to mainstream audiences and became emblematic of the Athens, Georgia, music scene linked to WUOG, despite its troubles with professionalization.

WUOG's Professionalization

WUOG in the late 1970s challenged UGA's fraternity-oriented culture. It offered jazz and classical music alongside progressive rock usually programmed later at night. It flirted with country and bluegrass, and in 1974 added bands such as REO Speedwagon, Santana, and Redwing and David Bowie to its rotation.[54] Occasional complaints cropped up regarding the station's unusual selections, with one listener carping, "Should WUOG ignore the more established and proven varieties of rock as characterized by the Beatles, Jethro Tull, Yes, and a host of others?" DJs shunned more mainstream fare, with the listener concluding, "How else can they explain their selection of obscure groups of questionable musical capabilities?"[55] In April 1975, DJs repeated Kraftwerk's *Autobahn* for five hours, punctuated with "taped messages and comments of questionable taste," prompting grumblings from the student communications board that the FCC might levy a fine for obscenity. No fine emerged, but the station developed a reputation for defiance of local cultural norms and for, well, amateurism.[56]

In 1977, the student communications board inquired about increasing WUOG's wattage from 3,200 to 10,000, aiming for a stronger on-air position to attract promotional support from record labels, secure artist interviews, and keep area alumni connected to their alma mater. The power increase stemmed not from the FCC's pending class D decision but rather from a realization that college stations could enhance an institution's image by "educating" the public with music unavailable on commercial radio. The ensuing saga over WUOG's professionalization illustrated the nexus of claims and aspirations transforming college radio culture in the late 1970s, often with students caught in the middle.

Athens's nascent music scene joined promising bohemian underground scenes across the nation. But an oppositional relationship emerged between art students, concert-committee types, and devotees of, as one scene chronicle put it, "frat rock, disco, and rednecks harassing anybody who didn't look like them, shouting (what else?) 'Hey, you, faggot!'"[57] Local band the B-52's offered escape and expression for gender nonconformists and mass culture critics and charted new directions in postpunk music.[58] Sarcastic, excessive, and colorful, "polite, nonthreatening, feminine," the Athens scene yet only promised, rather than delivered, the vibrancy and persistence of regional cultural variations and the patchwork scenes of underground music. Nevertheless, a series of loose affiliations, sometimes involving the radio station, began to cohere.

In May 1979, Kathleen O'Brien met Bill Berry in a dorm. O'Brien, a DJ at WUOG, danced with an informal band calling itself the WUOGerz that offered kazoo songs and new wave covers. Berry joined the group. He accompanied the band as it opened for the Police in 1979, who played for a half-filled venue. The British band with a punk–new wave image invited the WUOGerz to accompany them to Florida for more shows, but band members had classes to attend. Berry continued to work on the concert committee.[59]

A raucous party destination, WUOG created its own controversy. College radio DJs across the nation developed reputations for a lackadaisical sound, love of less popular music, and drug use (figure 3.1). At UGA, student DJs developed an antagonistic relationship with mainstream campus culture; they also rejected commercialism and control. Their ideals of freedom of expression and lack of formatting clashed with attempts to create a more structured format and station identity—both from within the university and from state regulators. Following the 1978 class D ruling, the state of Georgia pursued its own public communications bill to govern the radio training facilities at public institutions such as UGA.[60] Student DJs and advocates of localized educational programming disparaged the bill, which would have given a state-level bureau control over training and programming. Not only was the bill "a crime against the English language, [with] long, vague sentences," one critic charged, the law empowered the Georgia Public Broadcasting Commission with "providing a mechanism to prime the quality and variety of educational experiences for all Georgia citizens" without clearly exempting student-run stations such as WUOG. Critics argued students should be able to pursue "cultural and educational diversity" free of such bureaucratic oversight.[61]

A state takeover did not emerge. Instead, pressure on DJs' laissez-faire attitudes materialized from within Athens.

Fears of micromanagement were merited. The state might not have its sights on WUOG, but university administrators did.[62] Administrative requests to study whom the station served had been proceeding for some time, and spring 1981 saw an acceleration in this trend. A new general manager attempted to reverse "the impression" that WUOG was a "weird jazz"

FIGURE 3.1 College radio DJs had a reputation for amateurism and occasionally unprofessional behavior, such as using drugs while on air and contributing to a zoned-out on-air style, as captured after one such incident at KAOS in Olympia, Washington, in this cartoon printed in the student newspaper, the *Cooper Point Journal*, December 4, 1981.

station, which student newspaper editors explained was "a pedestrian buzz word for music that people can't sing to."[63]

Still, that manager only made changes around the edges as the station engaged in a self-study. He did not move toward the Top 40 fare many students demanded, but he tried to impose order, standardizing musical rotations and programs. The self-study suggested moving the studio to a more "desirable" space to increase visibility among students and recommended an advisory board to offer guidance.[64] Student activities assigned WUOG a new coordinator, graduate student James Weaver, to provide consistent leadership and proper oversight, as well as implement administration-backed reforms.

Weaver worked with WUOG's general manager Jim Forbes to clean up the station—literally and figuratively. The inch-thick dust on tapes strewn about disappeared, and the gum that had "long been stuck under tables" got scraped away.[65]

DJs did not respond positively. Someone took Weaver's picture, published in the student newspaper, and scribbled "Pig!" on it. Emotions ran high. Looking back, one DJ reflected, "In the name of alternative, we were arrogant, elitist, self-indulgent, and excessive." DJs lost touch with "whom we were serving." After station leaders held a meeting in early February 1981 to discuss format changes, recent on-air obscenities, and students broadcasting without credentials, Forbes grew incensed.

Disgusted by staff balking, he called volunteers to the studio and "summarily dismissed every one of us," one DJ remembered, and took the station off the air—immediately.[66] All volunteers had to reapply.[67] The station remained closed for forty-six days.

DJs filed an injunction, declaring their First Amendment rights had been violated, and they formed "FERN: Free Educational Radio Now!" Forbes declared the closure to protect the license, as lax attention to regulations put it at risk. (The local FCC office had no knowledge of the station's troubles.) Forbes insisted that jocks protested changes with "little petty stuff" such as "pretending to be dumb about rules and procedures" and acting "immature and irrational."[68] Working with student affairs administrators, Forbes and Weaver implemented order.

The administration, as license holder, violated no First Amendment rights by implementing changes at a station that represented the institution, not individual students. The student activities director declared he acted in WUOG's best interest. "The old days are gone," he told fired DJs. The closure "saved the license," and "there was no other way to get the donkey's attention than to hit him upside the head." One fired DJ, who went on to a career as a news director in commercial television, complained that the changes set the station back. But he credited Forbes with improving facilities and building a stronger station identity.[69] Musical exposure benefited from stricter structuring.

Forbes reorganized programming and created more identifiable blocks. He took the "'more esoteric stuff'" and relegated it to nighttime shows, leaving popular rock for the daytime hours to cater to a wider cross-section of students. With time, he hoped, listeners would tune in to the hours dedicated to new music and discover up-and-coming and local artists. In preparing the relaunch, WUOG management rebranded the station. Forbes aimed for a "new and cleaner identity" that "stresses professionalism in all endeavors." Since the station had an educational license, it would provide alternative programming while connecting the university with the public.[70]

University administrators lauded WUOG when it resumed broadcasting in April 1981. The student activities director praised Forbes for taking "a bad situation" and making it positive, putting "professional student-operated educational radio back on the air."[71] As one supporter of WUOG's new order stated, "This is not a toy." The station's "[recently boosted] 10,000 watts of power . . . represents the university. Things have gotten kind of loose up here. . . . The philosophy has not been in the interest of trying to be as professional as we should be." Drugs were banned from the control room (or rather, rules were more strictly enforced) and volunteers had to meet minimum professional standards. DJs did not own the station, the new GM explained: "It is owned by the University of Georgia, and president Davison signed the license. . . . It is a privilege to be allowed to represent the university on air."[72]

This deference to educational context and mission yielded a more hierarchical, systematic, and consistent approach to college radio programming—a trend across college stations.[73] Other benefits emerged. Student DJs grumbled about the new rules, but most resumed their positions and enjoyed rising status and influence in the Athens music scene.

Playing the role of tastemaker required rules, policies, hierarchies, and management structures. As scrutiny on college stations grew with greater range and institutional investment, as well as competition for listeners, new imperatives emerged. Stations had to do more than share university news and sporting events or broadcast campus lectures and highbrow musical offerings. Visibility required a stronger identity than the vague alternative to commercial radio that predominated in the 1970s at student-run stations. A coherent college radio reputation emerged, even as diversity missions and programming remained. Music without broad commercial appeal still defined service, as it had in the past, enhanced by a more robust definition of educational radio distinct from public radio. Not all stations fit this profile, but the identity became more nationally coherent, with local variations.

Bolstered by higher wattage and protected under the concept of educational radio, WUOG increasingly mirrored Athens's growing reputation as a haven for bohemian experimentation. Block programs in jazz, blues, and reggae and the diversity of cultural programs remained. The new general manager explained, "We will never be a top-40 station. . . . Why would we spend student money to duplicate what's already been done?" Insularity undermined the station. He explained, "I think in the past that the people in programming just consulted among themselves. They never tried to find out what somebody at a frat house, or a person eating at Belmont Hall or somebody down by Legion Pool might want to hear. We are not eliminating any of the esoteric music. We're just programming it proportionally to the interest in it that exists out there."[74] Even this purportedly more "student oriented approach" did not cater to fraternity and sorority tastes. WUOG maintained its connection to the local, underground music scene and its commitment to airing musical styles not available elsewhere on the dial.

By reining in amateur DJs' excesses and emphasizing professionalism to accompany its increased wattage, WUOG's educational format expanded its connections with Athens's music scene in the 1980s. It gained a reputation for broadcasting the best of Athens, challenging punk's depressing anger with a "happier, freer and apolitical" sound that "doesn't take itself, or anything else, very seriously."[75] It offered an outlet for diverse and minority voices of those on campus who did not enjoy athletics or Greek life. While WUOG implemented a professional image, hierarchical management, and musical rotations, the station developed a powerful alternative voice in the 1980s—putting the college town on the countercultural map, nationally.

· · · · · ·

In January 1981, as forces converged for WUOG's reorganization, UGA's student newspaper featured a new band packing in fans at a local club, naming them the best local band for 1980. A picture of four young-looking men sitting against a wall accompanied the announcement. (It was juxtaposed with singer-songwriter Dan Fogelberg's photo, whose "Longer" received the less-impressive award for year's worst single) (figure 3.2).[76]

The foursome R.E.M. was still more than a year from releasing its *Chronic Town* EP (extended play vinyl record) and not yet close to defining the Athens scene for the nation as it would in coming years.

Buzz about the band coincided almost exactly with WUOG's takeover, which in April 1981 reopened to "prove" itself to the UGA and Athens community.[77] Greater professionalism and wider reach stemming from the FCC's class D decision changed the landscape of college radio, with signals reaching potentially more receivers even if the threat of administrative takeover or conversion to NPR loomed. It is impossible to say if stricter standards and greater professionalism drew more listeners to stations. What is clear is that something was happening in college radio leading up to 1981 that would amplify its collective cultural clout.

The class D rule change took place within a broader transformation of college radio, commercial FM rock radio, and the music industry. By the late 1970s,

FIGURE 3.2 R.E.M. appeared in the UGA student newspaper in April 1981, named best new local band. *Red and Black*, April 10, 1981.

college radio's "alternative" reputation grew increasingly defined by jazz, reggae, folk, and new rock, particularly postpunk and new wave. The record industry took note, hiring staff to service and promote to campus stations, hoping to reach a demographic of eighteen- to twenty-four-year-olds with new music. While the class D decision presented an existential challenge to students' power to run radio stations—threatening the aural "sandbox" of learning radio laboratories—the decision produced unexpected results.

As the class D decision unfolded, financial troubles plagued the music industry. In 1979, several major labels laid off college promotion staff, and executives pondered how to make record service to college stations worthwhile. As one former promoter put it, "It's kind of ironic that all this should happen now when college stations will be going to 100 watts and full broadcasting days," because of the FCC's change.[78] Stations added power and reach, but they had yet to demonstrate their influence.

4 Major Labels and College Radio in Economic Crisis

· ·

Please, as often as possible print people that college stations can get in touch with for service. In particular, Warner Bros., Island, Fantasy, ABC, MCA, Capitol.

—Joe McGinty, WQSU, Selinsgrove, Pennsylvania

What can one do to get service from Casablanca?

—Mitch Katz, WVBU, Lewisburg, Pennsylvania

Why is it so hard to get in touch with some labels? How can we get imports (fast) and get a good selection? (No good import stores in area.)

—Ed Shepherd, WUAG, Greensboro, North Carolina
   CMJ Communication—Record Service, March 1, 1979

In 1981, Tim Sommer, a DJ at WNYU at New York University, played a couple of demos on his weekly *Noise the Show*. The performers were a hardcore band at the time, though they would soon become famous for crossing into another genre. They went by the Beastie Boys. When one of their songs came on Mike Diamond's radio—itself a miraculous feat given the signal barely reached his uptown apartment—he "solo moshed" in his bedroom and "stage-dived" off the bed. It was "extremely limited" exposure, but it was exciting.[1] Both recording the demo and getting some airplay were great feats for the teenagers.

College stations offered a place to test material. Music directors could record the number of plays a record received, listener feedback, and track how rotations influenced sales at local record stores.[2] For upstart bands, airplay might mean a few more fans showed up at their next show.

Student DJs couldn't be lazy if they wanted to be on the cutting edge of new music. College radio was also educational: participation trained students for professional life, whether it was developing a DJ persona, managing schedules, sponsors, or events, or tallying songs played to report to tip sheets. That is, it provided experience if students did the work (even if many conducting such laborious tasks were full-time students and unpaid volunteers—although record label swag provided some incentive). In 1982, Robert Haber of CMJ lamented that of 500 stations subscribing to his new music report, only 150 reported playlists for compilation. This indicated "inertia and apathy" and would not distinguish stations as musical influencers—and DJs might not forge professional networks that would build their careers or influence national culture. CMJ's reporters continued to grow, at least.[3]

An economic recession gripped the nation in 1980 as music industry woes mounted. Inflation and a second gas crisis strained Americans' savings accounts and budgets. Rising revenues in recorded music, which had led to expanded staff, sagged. The downturn, which lasted until the CD's debut, led labels to review departments for cuts. Recently added college promotions staff tended to get slashed, consolidating territory and promotional outreach to fewer employees. College radio, despite stations' insulation from market factors by noncommercial licenses and institutional homes, were not exempt from economic realities.

College stations needed music to play, and most got that music for free thanks to promotional records. As more DJs gravitated toward underground music, imports, and experimental artists, they still had to prove their stations' worth to the music industry. Servicing independent labels or local bands was all well and good and helped create new markets, but stations depended on major-label records.

As Ohlone College's heavy metal DJ warned, "I hate to be a bitch, but . . . if we don't play new stuff the record companies will not send any more."[4]

She was right. College radio had the power to create alternative markets and nurture subcultures, but stations needed records to fill their weekly rotations and service specialty shows. Most music played on college radio came from major labels. Albums were costly, especially to stations dependent on student fees for funding. Although independent labels were rising in number, there was not enough product to fill rotations and music libraries in 1980—and even if there were, it would not guarantee free records.

Major labels joined the FCC in favoring stations with higher wattages and professional practices. This pressure helped to cement college radio's role within the music industry as a tastemaker and as the place on the FM dial to find new music, but it strained stations' ability to fulfill their formal responsibilities to universities, surrounding communities, and as a regulated public resource. The result was tension between college radio's many roles.

They might not all exist within one station, but collectively, pressure mounted.

In 1980, college radio meant one thing at the national, corporate music industry level and another in local music scenes. CMJ existed between these levels, tracking playlists by station and region and compiling a national chart for its front page. Through tip sheets and feedback to labels, student programmers could influence the mainstream. They continued catering to one or many audiences through block scheduling for genres without much commercial coverage.[5] Record labels also had a say. To get albums, stations had to prove they could sell records. With economic troubles gripping the nation and the music industry, it wasn't clear that any national market owed homage to college radio's influence, or if its adventurous sounds could redefine mainstream popular music and commercial radio.

Record Industry Woes

At Wesleyan University's radio station WESU in 1980, DJs held a moment of silence for New York City's WPIX, a "rock champion" focusing on punk and new wave.[6] While many commercial FM rock stations were "confused and even scared" by the sounds emanating from the United Kingdom, WPIX ventured in.[7] But that March, WPIX announced it would seek to be "more mass acceptable." The station associated with Elvis Costello, the Police, Devo, and the Clash abandoned fans for REO Speedwagon, Led Zeppelin, and the Beatles: music targeting the lucrative demographic of sixteen- to twenty-four-year-old males.

The shift reflected narrowing commercial rock radio in the late 1970s as it targeted ever more specific sets of listeners, as well as the music industry's risk aversion in an economic downturn. (WPIX switched formats several times in the early 1980s amid new musical currents, consultants' formulae, and industry consolidation.) WPIX's fans petitioned, hosted "benefit-protest concerts" at local clubs, and demonstrated in front of the East Forty-Second Street studio. Defeated, organizers could only hope another station would provide "obscure" music.[8]

Given recent record labels' treatment of college radio and internal divisions, it remained doubtful whether WESU could emulate WPIX. A simultaneous, familiar contest between mainstream rock fans and proponents for new wave music roiled at WESU. Its reputation as "a stomping ground for egos" did not help matters.[9] Determining musical programming became too much for the general manager and program director to handle, so DJs voted that spring to institute a music director position.[10] Program directors focused on training, production value, and setting the schedule. A music director could work with local record stores and venues, as well as record labels, to manage rotations week-to-week and track playlists, reporting most-requested songs to the public and record stores. They worked with label promotional staff to ensure continued record service to keep rotations fresh and balanced. Sure, some music directors might cook the books to enhance their favorite bands, but most took their role seriously even as conflict emerged.[11]

Genre fights and block programming prompted much rancor. At WESU, "rock slots" allowed DJs freedom, but a series of program directors encouraged new wave, giving prime-time preference to those who did. Some DJs considered this unfair, with mainstream rock fans "relegated" to less popular midday and late-night times because of an "arbitrary decision to concentrate on New Wave." Many DJs played music regardless of these designations, navigating disagreements about how much new material and requests to feature. The music director kept the blocks the same, emphasizing experimentation without becoming a plaything.[12]

A station's entire format did not need to "go progressive" for new music, including ska, synthpop and the experiments of XTC, the Psychedelic Furs, or Lene Lovich to receive exposure.[13] At WESU, students played a healthy rotation of new music amid album-oriented rock (AOR) radio staples and specialty shows. Managers discussed restructuring women's programming and adding Feminist Radio Network broadcasts and "records from women's labels," noting "bad responses from feminists in the past" regarding station coverage. A gospel DJ broadcasted sermons, and a talk show and reggae music rounded out programming changes in spring 1980.[14] Managers requested DJs monitor and respond to requests as well as mix oldies into rotation.

But the issue of mainstream rock versus new wave programming plagued WESU at a problematic time. College stations without a clear musical identity to labels made easy targets for cuts as revenues declined.

For record labels, it made sense to send promotional material to college radio—at least those with sizable listenership and dedicated hours.[15] Some stations divided their schedules between daytime, when more popular fare aired, and freeform and experimental or specialty shows at night, which might receive their own record service in those genres. At Boston College, the weekday nighttime block was programmed with a musical philosophy called "No Commercial Potential."[16]

College stations could drive sales in certain genres, demographics, and markets. Arista Records, for one, enjoyed a good relationship with college stations in the 1970s. Its jazz records, including Gil Scott-Heron's, received play on many college outlets and entered regular rotations.[17] In 1978, the label sent KOHL at Ohlone College in California a recorded interview with jazz artist Ben Sidran, while the station's regular rotation featured Tom Petty and Bruce Springsteen's new album.[18] Numerous artists, including Petty and the band Squeeze, topped both college and commercial rotations. College radio did not drive trends in the industry, but it at least participated in them and defined the boundaries of mainstream radio.[19]

Those good relations gave way to dismay among college DJs in 1979 when Arista and other major labels cut back college promotions. *Billboard* reported in August, "College radio is entering a crucial stage, with many stations in jeopardy of being cut off from free record company service," and labels cut college promotions departments. A&M Records, which for ten years staffed a dedicated college radio promotion team, abruptly axed the wing. RCA, MCA, and Elektra/Asylum all cut staff who focused on promoting to the college crowd.[20]

AOR left behind freeform, and the radio industry adopted data-driven approaches of new formats that made financial sense in hard times.[21] Labels could ill afford to send out records to gather dust on shelves during off months. Bob Frymire, who had led A&M's college division, reduced record service from 500 stations to 150 during the summer months. After all, most students went home for the summer.

Labels' financial woes accounted for layoffs and restructuring, not any shift in perception about college radio. Executives limited service to stations proving they could "make waves in the market," and even the 1978 debut of CMJ did not convince executives to spend money in that market.[22] College radio might have an effect, but in a tighter economic environment, the metrics didn't justify the expense.

Without dedicated staff members, no one was left to advocate for college stations. Commercial stations promised measurable return on investment and a sales team that understood the listener base. At Elektra/Asylum, executives axed its "small network of college reps" and transitioned the former national college coordinator to a "local promotion post, leaving the college department in a shaky situation for now," *Billboard* reported. That summer, although Arista hired a new head of college promotion, it cut the list of stations served by 200, nearly in half. It would continue to review requests from college concert committees, since ticket sales generated rev-

enue. Although CBS, Atlantic, Polydor, and Warner Brothers continued college promotions, the labels reduced free records to stations lacking high
wattage and extensive hours, and they excluded AM carrier-current signals
altogether. College stations had to prove they could break new artists, drive
sales at local record stores, and provide the data to labels to receive
records.

College radio's reputation for amateurism worried promoters. Block formatting segmented audiences and freeform lacked identity. Promoters remembered well the struggles they faced in convincing their bosses to service
freeform FM stations in the late 1960s and early 1970s. As A&M's national
radio promotion director Rich Totoian remembered, FM, and radio in general, had been "mediocre and naive about the music and how to present it,"
making it difficult to convince the higher ups to send them records. The labels came around after Lee Abrams introduced his Superstars format in
the mid-1970s.[23]

But in 1979, radio counted as a no-risk space. College radio might appear
to be just another niche format with a particular demographic appeal, and
stations had to satisfy market rationales. Totoian encouraged promotion directors to work with radio executives and make them realize they "would
all be talk shows or bowling alleys without our music." The situation required cooperation between radio, label, and artist. It was up to the labels
to teach radio what to do with their medium—but that did not extend to all
college stations.[24]

Beneficial relationships continued. Published rotations suggested connections between labels and college stations in early 1980, though cutbacks
loomed. In April 1980, Arista artists Gil Scott-Heron and Hiroshima made
the jazz division's heavy airplay list at WXCI at Western Connecticut State
University. A weekly release of light and heavy rotations thanked Columbia Records for sending Frank Zappa's new twelve-inch. The music director
reported, "I flipped when I read there were only 1,000 copies printed," and
the station possessed one. The music and program directors thanked Warner Brothers for "remembering us—we finally have our communication lines
open again," suggesting improved relations with the label. Gordon Lightfoot's *Dream Street Rose* on Warner received light airplay. Marshall Tucker
Band's *Tenth* and Van Halen's *Women and Children First* received heavy and
moderate airplay, respectively, with Christopher Cross and the Tasmanian
Devils making the moderate list. At WRAS in Atlanta, summer 1980 playlists featured the Grateful Dead, Graham Parker, and the Kinks—all Arista
artists.[25]

As label cutbacks expanded, anxieties spilled into public view. In Massachusetts, MIT's station raised the alarm in November 1979. News reached volunteers that noncommercial, educational stations might need to purchase records rather than receive promotional copies from labels. One DJ called attention to "record manure . . . peepal" and distributors who "cut off the air supply to non-comm. EFFEMME's [FMs]." He suggested DJs contact "those disc heads on high" with the campus perspective. One DJ mentioned his friendship with an EMI promotional manager as a place to start. With the station's recent power increase reaching more listeners in the metro Boston area, record labels' actions seemed foolhardy.[26] But WMBR's low wattage, despite a devoted listenership and recent increase, qualified for cuts. Ironically, at the same moment, the new wave bands that college DJs pushed received wider airplay and label support.

In May 1980, British independent labels Rough Trade and Beggars Banquet churned out new wave and postpunk groups such as Joy Division, the Buzzcocks, and the Raincoats. Miles Copeland III, manager for Squeeze and for his brother's band, the Police, launched I.R.S. Records. He crafted an innovative promotional plan for his label's artists. He secured distribution from Jerry Moss, head of A&M Records (which was known as one of the largest independent labels before PolyGram acquired it in 1989, but its size and relationship with RCA disqualified it and I.R.S. from true "indie" status). With this deal, I.R.S. brought the Buzzcocks to the United States.[27] As WMBR DJs noted, the "small new wave label" signed "many acts broken" by the station. WMBR played Buzzcocks records as well as the Cramps, which had released independent singles produced by Alex Chilton before signing with I.R.S.

When I.R.S. instituted a $25 subscription fee for records sent to noncommercial stations, DJs were baffled. The station seemed a natural fit for I.R.S. with WMBR's location and its DJs with ties to rock giant WBCN in Boston. WMBR's music director told I.R.S. representatives the station would not pay. Not only did he balk at the sum, but he considered it a betrayal. "We feel," he explained, the fee placed an "unjustified burden on a station that has supported them." The music director asked DJs to refrain from playing new I.R.S. records until the label rescinded the charge. He considered boycotting older records, as well, but wanted feedback.[28]

A DJ responded, "Seems like the IRS is indeed living up to their name."[29]

I.R.S. had yet to release its first number-one record, the Go-Go's *Beauty and the Beat* in 1981, which topped many college radio charts on its way to commercial success. Peter Buck still worked at Athens's Wuxtry Records and had only just met Michael Stipe. Their band, R.E.M., would establish I.R.S.'s reputation in the music industry, but in 1980 the future was not clear. WMBR's DJs believed I.R.S. depended on college and noncommercial stations, not vice versa.

College radio helped a few bands such as the Police and Joe Jackson hit the charts. Nonetheless, even record labels with an adventurous roster had commercial ambitions. I.R.S. sought to establish its reputation: if stations had to pay for record service, it would be clear they offered high-quality music.[30] You get what you pay for, right? The label fought to make new wave commercially viable, and so I.R.S. acted like a major label. For the majors, bands featuring synthesizers or experimental sounds seemed like a passing fad. I.R.S. strove to legitimate the music, and college radio helped, but appearing as a major player took precedence to free record service.

Resentment roiled in 1980, particularly at northeast stations that featured bands on the touring circuit and creating buzz in a closely linked network of college broadcasters. And they paraded their resentment. WMBR's famed punk show, the *Late Risers Club*, began a months-long boycott of I.R.S., closing off a primary show on which its artists would appear. While no meaningful larger boycott of I.R.S. emerged, the same was not true for Clive Davis's label, Arista Records.

Arista signed Aretha Franklin in 1980, with a roster featuring Barry Manilow, Dionne Warwick, and the Patti Smith Group, which scored a commercial hit with "Because the Night." Despite these ties, in August 1980, the company announced a $150 subscription fee for college radio stations. In a letter addressed to "college radio programmers," Arista announced, "Certainly, the economic problems of 1979–1980 are no secret to anyone. Arista is not insulated against the economic conditions that are affecting the world business community." Executives felt "forced to take further cost-cutting action in the area of college promotion," following on the cuts made by other labels in 1979. "Not wanting to curtail college service entirely," the letter continued, the subscription fee meant continued record service, with a small cost. Arista's head of promotions considered this a gift to stations since the fee did not cover manufacturing and mailing costs. Titles not covered by the fee would cost $2 each, below the usual list price of $9.98—still a burden to often underfunded college stations.[31]

As students returned to campus, a boycott loomed.

The Northeast Reacts

The Arista boycott started slowly and remained focused in the Northeast. An MIT DJ called for immediate stoppage, "especially that new hit song whatever it might be, and especially that catalog favorite that sells ten every time you play it."[32] Coordination was needed to influence the labels—a difficult feat.

At Wesleyan's WESU, coordinating the Arista boycott sidelined ongoing debates about the station's mix of rock music. Music director Alex Crippen penned a complaint to Arista and sent it to *Variety* and *Billboard*. He enlisted other college stations in the region to join. Crippen, an economics major, bore the labor of confronting the situation, though other board members agreed to help. The board agreed unanimously to not purchase Arista records, "to encourage DJs not to play any back Arista releases," and empowered Crippen to "take appropriate action in furtherance of the boycott, with the objective of protesting the precedent set by Arista's wholesale college discontinuance." The boycott was officially on.[33]

Organizing stations was like herding cats. Plus, murky legalities of boycotting created confusion. Community-oriented WWUH at the University of Hartford received a $300 bill from Arista for various genres' record service. The state attorney general issued a cease-and-desist order against official station participation in the boycott. Individuals could boycott, Arista's lawyers explained, but organizations violated antitrust laws if pursuing such action. University lawyers instructed the station to stop its boycott to avoid a lawsuit.[34] Six other Connecticut stations joined the boycott spearheaded by the outspoken Wesleyan music director. WXCI in Danbury agreed not to play new artists while keeping Arista's back catalog on the air. At the University of Bridgeport, its station received a reprieve from Arista's fee because it operated as a commercial station. Service required proof of pushing album sales and reaching target audiences. Arista's representative told WWUH in a call-in show focusing on the boycott, "There aren't but a handful of college stations that are going to influence sales to any great degree." Stations in the University of California system organized; otherwise, the boycott remained regionally focused, even if word spread.[35]

Crippen admitted he sometimes felt "blasé about the whole deal," but in September 1980 he rallied his allies.[36] WESU compiled a statement of principles regarding Arista's fee and circulated it among college stations for signatures. The statement condemned Arista's discontinuation of free promotional service. Co-signers agreed to forgo new releases from the label and avoid back-catalog records. The boycott extended to promotional activity, including concert ticket giveaways and artist interviews.[37]

College stations knew that if they did not take a stand with Arista, the cost of business could become unsustainable, especially for smaller stations. Although the industry clearly faced financial difficulties, Crippen argued, "the solution is not the wholesale cutoff of college service." Irresponsible stations should have free records suspended, but "to cut a station just because it is associated with a college is unreasonable." College stations could not afford the fees, and "if other labels follow[ed] Arista's lead even the wealthiest station [would] be unable to afford new music." Arista only hurt itself while disincentivizing college stations from adopting professional reporting. Moreover, as commercial FM rock formats narrowed playlists or phased out adventurous programming, as with WPIX's format change, "it is college radio that is willing to take the risks and give airplay to many records that commercial radio is afraid or simply not interested enough to play." New commercial radio DJs often emerged from "the college ranks," and stations provided artists "early exposure with these future decision makers." Boycotters defended college radio's place within the music industry, even if internal debates continued among DJs about the balance of new music with AOR hits.

Fractious discussions took place at boycotting stations. WESU featured new music from Arista jazz artist Gil Scott Heron, who was scheduled to appear at Wesleyan in October. The station promoted the upcoming concert. The problem was, Crippen told the board of directors, "it goes against the general principles of the boycott." He proposed "moderate" promotion. Arista's jazz division contacted WESU and offered, in a friendly tone, to send records on a separate agreement from AOR service. Rumors about indifferent boycott compliance at other stations, including at the University of Hartford and Western Connecticut State University, circulated.[38] The differences in genre service, plus coordinating a boycott across various genres and multiple stations, weakened the boycott.

Optics didn't help. Arista lamented its dire financial position and announced the fee as its earnings increased 69 percent. Summer 1980 earned the label more than 20 percent than it had in years prior, thanks to hits from Air Supply and the Allman Brothers, which it marketed heavily to college students. At the University of Iowa, the student newspaper polled students for the year's top ten albums, and Arista pitched in the Outlaws' new album as a prize for the person whose picks aligned most with the majority's choices.[39] That September, according to label head Clive Davis, Arista's business "skyrocketed," driven by college-age buyers.[40]

Yet in the very same September 1980 *Billboard* issue announcing Arista's revenue, an announcement of the noncommercial service fee appeared. Arista's vice president of AOR promotion, Mike Bone, declared, "Despite hoots and hollers from some college stations," most planned to pay up. Bone insisted "current economic conditions" prompted taking a "hard look at the dollars we are putting into college radio." As Ronald Reagan's aides prepared Reagan to look into the camera and ask Americans, "Are you better off now than you were four years ago," economic hardship drove cutbacks across business sectors, including the music industry. Bone cited the I.R.S. fee as evidence that Arista was not alone.[41]

College radio programmers weren't buying it. Stations had their own financial woes. One station manager called the financial burdens "frightening." He explained, "A college station that operates on a $7,000 a year budget cannot pay the thousands of dollars it would cost if other companies followed Arista's lead." Fees would "virtually eliminate major labels' music from college radio." And since college signals served a wider variety of genres than a typical AOR station, the costs mounted quickly for records covering rock, jazz, R&B, classical, and soul.

WTBU at Boston University, the student-run alternative to the institution's professionally run NPR station, helped organize the multistation boycott—some twenty-five by November. College programmers knew they possessed market power. As WTBU's music director told *Billboard*, "Everybody knows that groups like Blondie, the Police and Joe Jackson broke on college radio," raising stations' importance as commercial stations tightened their rotations. The hits had to start somewhere, and increasingly it seemed that place was college radio.[42]

In November 1980, student broadcasters at the Loyola Radio Conference discussed the fees. Arista's decision coincided with other challenges to promotional support. College department heads at major labels—those with remaining departments—as well as independent promoters told college students to "'sell' your college station to the record companies." They encouraged stations to cultivate "a close relationship with local retail outlets" to ensure record service. Major labels valued support for "newcomer acts," generating "credibility." As PolyGram's East Coast promoter told conferencegoers, "Prove that you have an impact on the market and you'll get records." He would send records where stations could deliver the goods.[43]

IBS also met that month in San Francisco, where 350 attendees discussed the matter. IBS president Jeff Tellis noticed record service "deteriorated." Complaints emerged nationally from "virtually every type of station: closed-circuit, carrier-current, cable, 10-watt FM, and higher-powered FM." Smaller stations suffered the most. Tellis objected to singling out Arista for boycott, given that many labels instituted fees. Declining sales were a reality. Some made reductions "intelligently and trimmed here and there where it was expendable"; others "were not so discriminating," leading to across-the-board fees for service and elimination of college promotions departments.[44] He tried to introduce nuance to the issue, explaining that free jazz mailings continued for "some 200 stations," and regional label representatives remained. Jazz's strong association with noncommercial radio meant labels recognized college radio's value. Moreover, stations that fostered good relationships with the label's regional representatives kept service.[45]

Tellis spared no blame for college stations. He pointed out, "Too many college radio stations had taken their record service for granted" and failed to provide feedback regarding which products listeners liked or were receiving airtime. In other words, stations lacked professionalism and did not take seriously their market function. They might be able to convince administrators to support upgrades in power thanks to FCC license changes, but labels remained unswayed. "We weren't telling our story well enough," Tellis argued, "loud enough, and often enough." Without making their value clear to the industry, when revenues fell college stations got the axe.[46]

That didn't mean college radio lacked usefulness. Some labels failed to realize new artists "simply won't get played within the rigidly formatted playlists of commercial stations" and needed college radio to build buzz. Nonetheless, cuts happened. Tellis explained, "Those stations who had kept in touch, told their story, provided feedback . . . lost the least." Stations that provided sales data from local record stores and proved their influence got free records.[47]

The music industry compounded federal regulatory changes to privilege high-wattage FM stations. Arista's Mike Bone explained that providing free service to a carrier-current station would be "like giving records to some kid's jukebox."[48] CBS served 400 stations but would send more records to those with market research to justify promotional material.

The news was not all bad for freeform, experimental radio. Certain industry sectors hoped colleges would use their FM real estate to diversify radio in ways that benefited independent-label and imprint catalogs. Jay Boberg, appointed by Miles Copeland to run I.R.S. Records, urged stations to differentiate themselves through their playlists. The label still charged $25, and, he added, "as long as your playlist is identical to commercial stations in the same market you're not going to get attention." Elektra/Asylum's college promo director wanted "credibility in the market" for exposing new artists. In other words, in an ironic twist, the record industry, by insisting that college radio support commercial functions, actually helped push programmers further to the fringes of popular music in 1980.

CMJ emphasized professional playlist curation with an emphasis on new music. Robert Haber declared the "best playlists" included "retail information." Professional practices garnered label attention. Atlantic's college department head blamed college stations for not responding to surveys. And an independent promoter put it simply: "Professional AOR stations can see the impact when they sell records. College radio has not proven it can sell records."[49] Clear market segmentation and promotional functions defined commercial radio's business model. College students, on the other hand, knew their station would likely continue even if they didn't push the latest release to the Hot 100 on *Billboard*.

They would survive without free records—but would it be fun?

Boycott participation remained scattered, even in the organized Northeast. Student leaders resented labels' efforts to tell them how to run their stations in addition to the market-based logic at work. They disliked what the fee represented about the music industry's future. At WMBR, the music director suggested Arista signaled what was to come regarding narrowing commercial playlists and pressure to sell, sell, sell. "I am at a total loss as to what we should do about this problem," he told DJs.[50]

MIT DJs debated how to proceed. They could ban all Arista records and those from "sister" labels. They could announce the suspension on all playlists distributed to labels. To work, all DJs and programmers needed to cooperate and inform listeners. Another problem remained. How was the station to secure new records if they boycotted any label with a service fee? Expanding and ongoing boycotts would mean the station had nothing to play.[51] Although *Late Risers' Club* DJs had not yet reduced I.R.S.'s fee, the music director hoped they would prevail. Perhaps Arista would respond to market pressure.[52] But larger stations still received free records, and many paid the fee, so coordination proved difficult.

Arista's logic seemed nonsensical to some. One veteran DJ complained that record service was not nearly as costly as other activities. "If they wanted to save money, why not stop sending promo copies to record stores, where they have a 93% chance of being stolen. No, instead they complain a lot and cut off small radio stations who might actually PLAY them. If they were REALLY that tight for cash, they also might eliminate giving the [W]BCN's, etc., copies to give away." WBCN, the area's former freeform station with many former WMBR DJs on staff, had become a commercial rock powerhouse.[53] Such AOR giants looked to college stations to determine what area audiences wanted to hear and supported protests of record fees. The WBCNs of the world also wanted college radio to orient to the national music industry and create commercial breakthroughs—not what all college DJs had in mind.

Meanwhile, students had stations to run and exams to take. Individual stations managed their own label relations. The matter faded. Fees subsided when the industry's finances improved over the next few years. The boycott was a galling episode, but no existential threat emerged to college radio other than revealing a lack of clarity regarding what college radio could or should be. And by 1981, more stations questioned whether they should play major-label releases at all.

An Industry Player

Although record labels pushed college stations to increase wattage and coordinate with record stores, these signals filled a void in many radio markets. In the San Francisco area, commercial rock radio adopted narrower playlists. When the city's major rock station, KSAN, received the new Bruce Springsteen double album *The River* in October 1980, the artist's first to hit number one in *Billboard*, rock enthusiasts balked when the radio station limited how many songs DJs could play from the album. An arts writer exclaimed, "Eleven cuts! Not too long ago, KSAN DJs would have played every cut, but that was before competition cut into the station's ratings and the dreaded playlist was instigated." Freewheeling commercial FM radio gave way to hits and hit-making.[54]

Freeform FM rock radio disappeared—except on the area's college radio stations. In fact, the writer concluded, "college stations and non-profit outlets" remained to "thrill the passionate rock and radio fan." He cited KUSF at the University of San Francisco as an exemplar. He, like the record label executives, lamented "occasionally inept amateur operation and poor signals." For all these faults, however, amateur signals "offer some startling sounds not heard on the big time local radio stations in years."[55]

Divisions existed in 1980 regarding college radio's position within the industry. Although WESU and others prided themselves on providing alternative radio, what that meant remained unclear. Even stations committed to "alternative radio programming" faced internal disagreements regarding music rotation. Dissension muddied their ability to break new artists, an increasingly valued role. In the previous decade, as IBS's Jeff Tellis explained, college radio simply existed as "cheap imitation of commercial radio."[56] Stations received records simply because they might reach college-aged ears. "Now," he said, "they listen to us for fresh ideas and new music." College radio served decidedly commercial functions, even as it pursued weird, unheard, or experimental music.

Robert Haber of CMJ supported the boycott but suggested stations collectively assert their worth. Though CMJ was only two years old, Haber established his tipsheet as a marker of college radio's influence. He sympathized with outrage at the $150 fee, declaring "United We Stand." Yet the industry had been allowed to assume, he explained, "college radio is dispensable." Arista's fee offered a symptom of that underlying fallacy. College radio, Haber argued, must "seize the moment" and "prove definitively, once and for all that the record industry needs college radio more than college radio needs the record industry." More than 1,000 college stations existed across the country. As commercial radio tightened its playlists and attended to sponsors and ratings, noncommercial stations, with institutional support, "can be more adventurous." Album promotion could make these stations "retail sales-effective." Audiences might be smaller, but a higher percentage of listeners bought music.

College radio audiences weren't passive. Those tuning in constituted "an aware, music-conscious audience that translates into sales," Haber explained. WMBR at MIT, a label executive explained, played up-and-coming artists and deserved free record service because they reached "the most active listeners as well as the opinion-leaders who determine trends in music." Haber sought to preserve college radio's promotional position within the music industry.[57] Music industry sectors were transforming, and college radio had a role to play.

As the Arista boycott fizzled out in early 1981, WESU's directors debated whether to add a prime-time AOR show. Reports that Wesleyan students preferred "an AOR program," the general manager argued, were "unsubstantiated," and he dismissed student tastes in determining programming. The station provided public service and sports coverage, as well as news. Adding AOR would, he concluded, "be a disservice to the listeners of our alternative programs that would be displaced." WESU should not follow in the footsteps of WPIX or kneel to popular demands.[58]

Although Arista's record fee did not end WESU's support of the label's artists, its mission narrowed in 1981. Playlists under a new music director, a dedicated punk and new wave fan, shifted away from major labels such as

Arista.[59] Although divisions persisted regarding the AOR and progressive music balance, and opportunities existed for DJs to "play anything 'from ABBA to ZZ Top,'" music and program directors increasingly pushed the station toward independent labels—a service that grew less controversial as older students graduated and college radio's reputation transitioned.[60]

At Wesleyan, located within the Northeast's dense network of college stations, clubs, and music scenes, DJs could readily share information about new bands by word of mouth. But across even well-connected regions like the Northeast, promotion remained spotty. For an independent release to be played on college radio nationally, DJs needed access to information. Something had to feed the pipeline, and music fans did that work. Dedicated individuals spread the word however they could about exciting new bands far beneath the major—or even independent—labels' attention.

The Arista boycott prompted musicians, critics, and other music aficionados to testify to college radio's importance in spreading that information about up-and-coming music acts. *Village Voice* music critic Robert Christgau told CMJ, "I listen to college radio because I regard it as part of an alternative distribution network. I think it's as important as the press and clubs." Promoters struggled to fit some artists into tightly defined commercial categories of FM rock radio, while labels with an "eclectic" sound found a natural home at college stations. Indeed, as one label executive put it in late 1980, "Maybe it should be called college music," referring to the mix of sounds played on stations across the country.[61]

· · · · · ·

College radio airplay generated real numbers and influence in the early 1980s. Guitarist, composer, and producer Robert Fripp, fresh off collaborations with David Bowie and feminist-folk group the Roches, estimated "between 10% and 15% of sales are generated by college play." Miles Copeland called college radio "an alternative to commercial radio in that it is an end in itself." Free from commercial radio's pressures, "college radio has the rare opportunity to make a significant mark on the radio scene and to influence radio programming trends today." Copeland saw college DJs as a new generation "providing a platform" for "artists to get the exposure they need, and to really be an alternative to commercial radio."[62] The idea implied eclecticism and noncommercialism with market and artistic functions. Artists and producers could experiment, testing out new sounds on serious audiences. Through college radio, labels could monitor commercial appeal by linking exposure to sales at local record stores.

Yet these values suggested stations appreciated a quest for authenticity, of producing art without regard for commercial appeal. Authenticity defied commercial categories, even if music on college radio emerged as its own marketable category of sound. DJs and their listeners preferred songs without an easy pop hook or slick production quality. These sounds signaled a level of taste above the commercial masses but also marked a DJ's status as a tastemaker with insider knowledge.

By 1983, "college music" garnered significant attention in the music press. Journalists chronicled college students' influence in shaping the landscape of popular music. With artists strongly associated with "college music" breaking through to mainstream play, with bands such as R.E.M. and the Replacements forthcoming, college radio contributed to what a member of punk band the Minutemen called the "jamming econ."[63]

New wave gained fans, and college radio would be an important promoter. That was a major-label game, except for independent Rough Trade in the UK. But what of all those seven-inch records that no one paid attention to? Well, no one, that is, but some kids in the Pacific Northwest and other pockets of the nation's nascent music scenes, yet to be discovered. They took issue with college radio's commercial functions. They didn't seem to care if bands broke into commercial FM or MTV. Maybe sustaining local musicians and cultivating a scene featuring good concerts was enough after all.

5 Connecting the Indie Rock Underground in the 1980s

. . . .

Playlist for Monday, February 21, 1983
Steve Kreitzer, Turmoil Radio, *WUSB Stony Brook, New York*

Doug & the Slugs, "If You Don't Come," *Music for the Hard of Thinking*
Channel 3, "Out of Control," *Fear of Life*
Agent Orange, "Too Young to Die," *Living in Darkness*
The Sick, "World War III," on a cart
Angelic Upstarts, "Lust for Glory"
Captain Beefheart, "Moonlight on Vermont," *Trout Mask Replica*
Slapp Happy, "Whipple"
Men without Hats, "Security," 45 rpm
The Waitresses, "It's My Car," *Wasn't Tomorrow Wonderful*
The Bus Boys, "Did You See Me," *Minimum Wage Rock n' Roll*
Jools Holland & the Millionaires, "Bumble Boogie"
The Shaggs, "It's Halloween"
Dead Kennedys, "Halloween," *Plastic Surgery Disaster*
Descendents, "Bikeage," *Milo Goes to College*
Generation X, "Kleenex"
Jack & The Rippers, "Down," on a cart
Ian Hunter, "Life After Death," *You're Never Alone with a Schizophrenic*
Grace Jones, "Demolition Man," *Nightclubbing*
The Replacements, "Kids Don't Follow," *Stink*
Count Floyd, "The Gory Story of Duane and Debbie"
Marshall Crenshaw, "Rave On," twelve-inch
Brian Briggs, "Combat Zone"
It's Immaterial, "A Gigantic Raft in the Philippines," 45 rpm
The Boomtown Rats, "Lookin After #1," 45 rpm
Robert Fripp, "Under Heavy Manners"
The Blockheads, "Take out the Lead," 45 rpm
Dave Davies, "Where Do You Come From," AFLI-3603
Easy Teeth, "Car Noize"
NEWSBREAK

Ten P.M. on a Friday was kind of a "shit slot." That was where the program director at Lafayette College's radio station stuck punk rocker Jack Rabid. With their ten-watts outside Allentown, Pennsylvania, programmers wanted to show labels they broadcast records sent to the station—at least some of the time. Rabid was unlikely to do that, so he got the worst time to air his noisy music.[1]

By the early 1980s, despite the economic recession prompting major-label promotion cutbacks, college radio seemed poised to serve the music industry by testing new product and training future DJs and industry professionals. But college radio also offered a refuge for mainstream culture dropouts, kids who had no desire to emulate pop stars or attend concerts at huge arenas. They wanted music that spoke to their dissatisfaction with politics, celebrity culture, or the materialism of the 1980s. Edgy critiques of elitism, commercialism, corporatism, and conformity in musical culture crescendoed, prompting responses from scholars and media watchdogs as well as punks who sought to DIY their own alternative culture. Even pop culture and mass media could be sites of politics, as both cultural theorists and punk rockers contended.[2]

DJs like Jack Rabid cared more about reaching kids in their bedrooms than in breaking a band to mainstream success. Rabid played his own records or broke the shrink wrap on records at the station, such as the Dickies, a Los Angeles punk band that few DJs would play. "The kids at the campus," well, "weren't interested." Vibrant, local, underground scenes proliferated in garages and tapes and zines circulated, but these sounds were slow to get to college radio.

Many hardcore and punk bands, such as Minor Threat from Washington, D.C., did not have college radio on their radar. It seemed too staid and tied to industry practices and federal regulation of media. Such groups tended to remain limited to circles of followers from California to Texas to Lawrence, Kansas, to the nation's capital. They voiced antiauthoritarian, anti-corporate, antinuclear, and often anti–Ronald Reagan politics, and did so pointedly, which some college radio participants appreciated and saw as a natural fit with noncommercial stations. Band member Ian MacKaye, founder of Dischord Records, disagreed. "Back then," he remembered, "I always thought punk rock and college didn't mix." The band connected with a few stations, but sending out records seemed like a waste. Besides, MacKaye explained, on their first album "I say *fuck* on all but one song." Independent labels had few promotional resources, anyway. And if DJs played their music, they likely had bought the record.[3]

Still, college radio provided some kids a musical lifeline and intersected with underground information networks. Teenage Jeff Tweedy, the future songwriter and member of Uncle Tupelo and Wilco, scoured magazines for bands that sounded interesting. He might pick up an album without having ever heard it or get clued in to records he read about in *Rolling Stone* or his older brother discovered at college.[4] Future musicians in Louisville similarly relied on musical knowledge from older brothers and fanzines. The city didn't have a college station, but future actor and singer-songwriter Will Oldham caught a glimpse through his brother's news from college of the potential for an "exciting, creative life." Britt Walford, later of Squirrel Bait and Slint, scoured *Maximum Rocknroll* for bands that piqued his interest, hoping to secure a copy on tape or an album.[5] Craig Finn, when he was in high school in Minneapolis, long before heading the band the Hold Steady, would hear of a band in a zine or from a friend, call in a request to the local college radio station he could *barely* receive on his bedroom radio, and try to tape the song as it played.[6] Lou Barlow, a teenager in western Massachusetts, discovered music through the several college stations he could pick up before he joined indie rock bands Dinosaur Jr., Sebadoh, and Folk Implosion. The gender dynamics of this were not lost on young women seeking musical inspiration. The overwhelmingly male focus of fanzines and music press inspired the rise of Riot Grrrl in the 1990s, as well as radio programs dedicated to women's music. College radio might not be the impetus stimulating a scene's origination, but it helped kids seeking broader musical horizons to discover something new to defy growing concerns about their waywardness.[7]

In the late 1970s and early 1980s, concerns were growing among adults about rebellious teens, latchkey kids, and pop culture messages that encouraged drug use, promiscuity, and crime—and those concerns targeted young white male music fans like Tweedy, Oldham, Finn, and Barlow. At the same time, fears of child abduction and "stranger danger" made the formerly safe harbor of suburban America seem more threatening.[8] Rules limited young people's access to communal spaces, typified by criminalizing skateboarding in parking lots. Scrutiny by police and mall security made it difficult for hardcore punks to "congregate in public," one historian concluded. Although racist skinheads in Britain and Germany lent legitimacy to some concerns, the overall fixation on youth in the 1980s in the United States had no connection to the rise of "Nazi rock."[9] Fears of directionless teenagers accompanied a moral panic that condemned the nuclear family's decline and culture warriors' demands for public policy to support "family values." These insecurities lurked beneath the celebratory materialism of the 1980s. But young people found a way to express their anger.[10]

Fostering alternative scenes and sounds constituted political activity. Trepidation about punk rockers, reckless skateboarders, or high school dropouts obscured a musical movement taking place in the early 1980s. Scenes developing across communities challenged the corporate culture industry disseminating images of troubled teens that encouraged their surveillance and policing. Anyone paying attention could discover local music and access a network of musical and artistic scenes, marketed through alternative, democratic institutions. These new networks, accompanied by a DIY aesthetic, challenged existing power structures. Those on the outside, marginalized and placed under suspicion, sought to build their own communities and perform locally the political and cultural changes they wished to see. Such scenes, as one historian and participant observed, offered "our answer to what we understood as the failures and limits of our America." New modes of resisting or dropping out of middle-class cultural norms proliferated. A "bohemian diaspora" emerged across the nation, linked by zines and college radio, and independent record stores, labels, and music venues.[11] Scenes offered a vision of social belonging for alienated youth.

Music fans tuning in to college radio might not have been scene insiders, but they nonetheless became extended participants in a musical movement that would accelerate during the 1980s—or which "started back in 1983," as Lou Barlow sang in a 1991 ode to indie rock. A participatory underground formed, fueled by DIY informational networks.[12] College radio served as another outlet where amateurism was the point, supporting similar aesthetics and expression that defied mainstream pop culture. Like zines, college DJs sought to construct and communicate their authentic selves.

Rabid had a zine and a radio show. The two acts were intertwined. Zines linked and often mapped a subterranean culture, creating a network of "disparate individuals" seeking connection in their projects to define themselves outside mainstream societal dictates.[13] Looking for records, discovering new music through zines, calling up to request a song, and recording it took work: it was a participatory culture that built a sense of belonging that 1980s pop culture failed to provide for many teens. A subculture formed, one without many resources but connected across geography and individual scenes. College radio remained a more mediated, regulated, and contested space than zines but created translocal connections. Zines could reflect an individual's tastes, discoveries, and expression without limits; college radio acted as a "cultural node."[14]

This network opposed mainstream culture and the culture industry—and it was there that radio and fanzines diverged. Radio stations had listeners who might stumble across the signal. Administrators interested in the content emanating from campus, when they remembered to check in on them, might interfere. Anyone could start a zine, and the possibilities for individualization were endless, without threat of interference. To access zines, however, one had to be in the network. Radio, too, had barriers to entry, whether it was being a student, passing a test, or securing airtime. But college radio's democratic potential lured participants from the public. Stations might foster bigger communities and networks as well as nascent scenes, despite their institutional limits. For some participants, these signals had revolutionary potential to confront a society that shunned "losers" or weirdos. It offered meaningful, participatory engagement instead of what MTV or the corporate music industry promoted.

These scenes operated adjacent to the islands of authenticity associated with college campuses without depending wholly on them.[15] Yet affinities existed between the emerging culture of college radio and scenes. Student DJs were interested in these growing scenes, and some stations allowed community DJs to feature their sounds. A network emerged to challenge stultifying pop culture and establish alternative markets and durable subcultures. It helped that college enjoyed a reputation as a place for self-exploration, experimentation, and cultural production and intellectual activity that might not have commercial appeal. Often, these had elitist cultural associations of rarefied expressions available only to connoisseurs with specialized skills or knowledge. Hardcore band names might stretch that elitist definition—Vatican Commandos put out a record on Pregnant Nun Records in 1983, for example—but these networks nonetheless similarly created cultural enclaves and community.[16] Fragmented scenes and independent labels grew in number across the nation and generated youthful interest as popular culture felt less relevant and corporatized.[17]

Scene Connections

Jack Rabid started his own band in 1980. He witnessed the underground bands he saw as a teenager "take off," except for Bad Brains, which struggled for a record deal despite selling out shows. Even if major labels felt they gave punk rock a chance, they remained nervous and image conscious, and wary of signing a Black punk act. Apart from I.R.S., which had major-label distribution, only a handful of indie labels served the increasing demand for more challenging rock music, or in the case of Bad Brains, didn't fit the stereotypical white rocker aesthetic labels thought would sell.[18]

Meanwhile, Rabid monitored scenes blooming in Los Angeles, Vancouver, Toronto, and San Francisco, with bands beginning to tour—even though a network of supportive clubs did not exist yet. In Los Angeles, the Screamers booked gigs by telling venues it was a disco band. Other punks ended up in country and western bars in Chicago. The fledgling scene of the mid-1970s began to transition. Drug use took its toll on artists, but a new cohort of artists emerged. They had the ability to explore art through music, entertaining listeners at the same time. "It's modern art, really," Rabid remembered.[19]

This artistic movement inspired emulators and innovators. College radio stations supported a growing infrastructure, cementing a network of venues, publications, and record stores. The "next wave" of artists followed the circuit carved out by the early bands, Rabid observed, "drawing bigger crowds, and the bigger the crowd demonstrated someone ought to be recording this." And "the next thing you know, you finally do have some true indie labels," with bands out on tour. Tours drew college radio, and, Rabid concluded, "it all works in a kind of symbiosis . . . a synchronicity, you know, an ecosystem."

Rabid expanded that national ecosystem beyond his radio show. In June 1980 he started his fanzine, *The Big Takeover*, to chronicle the underground market he saw emerging. He circulated information about the records he discovered, hoping to give kids like him access to bands that would expand their notion of artistic exploration. It started as a newsletter for the Stimulators, describing that band as "fast, tight, loud, powerful and very versatile." The group's authenticity stood out, defying "all that New York art (shit) rock that pseudo-intellectuals rave about in the clubs but can't remember when they exit." Instead, the Stimulators created real excitement. Rabid could not find similar energy except on a few radio shows here and there, scattered across the airwaves of mostly college stations, like the ones that opened his mind as a teenager.[20]

Teenagers, scattered across urban neighborhoods and suburbia, needed to know how to hear records, where to buy them, and where to see the bands play. Fanzines provided information overlooked by larger publications, particularly for bands that put out the music themselves. Rabid directed listeners to WSOU on Monday afternoons for Marty Byk's show (after he graduated to daytime hours), and Saturday nights to Daniel Martin Cooney, who shut down the signal at 2 A.M. with a kazoo rendition of the "Star Spangled Banner." College radio and fanzines provided scene information—even press in New York overlooked key bands like the Stimulators. College stations were the only ones to "have picked up on the greatest single to come out of rock-starved New York," Rabid noted. ("Sound biased? Too bad!" he concluded). Even without traditional publicity, the Stims sold a thousand copies at stores such as Bleeker Bob's, Defiant Pose, Sounds, and Freebeing and in the suburbs.[21]

In a pop music landscape increasingly dominated by synthesizers, kids seeking raw guitar rock had to look hard. By December 1981, Rabid had moved from Lafayette College to NYU, where he was stuck doing a quiz show on WNYU, since station managers had yet to agree to his request for a show featuring his punk and hardcore collection. He kept telling station leaders, "You don't need another person to play" what everyone else aired. He continued to publish his fanzine, which by issue eight was a multipaged publication complete with photographs and even a hand-drawn portrait of the Circle Jerks by one of its members.[22]

An informational network of radio shows, fanzines, clubs, and record stores grew. Publications such as *New York Rocker* picked up on the energy, including "a centerfold-like feature spread on the New York hardcore punk scene with some hot photos of the local bands." With Annabella from Bow Wow Wow on the cover, the writer approached the scene with an open mind. Joining a recent article in *Sounds* and *The Trouser Press*, Rabid declared, "The Big Takeover [of music] is in progress." With zines *Damaged Goods*, *Coast to Coast*, and *Just Another Rag* (to name a few) featuring hardcore bands, he had good reason to be excited.[23]

Rabid regaled hardcore fans who picked up his free magazine at stores such as the Rat Cage with stories from recent shows. He saw Bad Brains appear with some "local talent" such as Reagan Youth, the Undead, the Mob, and Even Worse. Bad Brains, he explained "put on a masterful reggae exhibition at the beginning of the 2nd set, much like lemonade on a parched throat to the musically overheated crowd expecting hot chocolate." The show competed with Siouxsie and the Banshees playing nearby at the Peppermint Lounge, yet Bad Brains sold out CBGB. He traveled to Brooklyn to see the Undead at Zappa's in November, and saw Boston-based S.S. Decontrol, which he called "a cross between Minor Threat and S.O.A., although they steal from neither." He reported they were the first Boston band of this kind to visit the area, although "None of the DC bands ever have."[24]

Zines provided background information on band members, such as explaining how ex-S.O.A. singer Henry Garfield had changed his name to

Henry Rollins. Details included band membership, such as Rollins's move to Black Flag to replace Keith Morris, who had moved to the Circle Jerks, and lineup changes such as the addition of another guitar. News covered the elimination of a staffer at a Morristown, New Jersey, record store who focused on hardcore acquisitions, or radio shows playing hard stuff. Rabid reported a recent sighting of Pete Shelley, formerly of British punk band the Buzzcocks, at Bonaparte Records on Bleecker St. He thanked Jello Biafra for mentioning influential New York City bands in interviews to pique readers' interest. They might request songs on college or community radio or pick up an album on the recommendation of a daring record store clerk.[25]

Cross-scene connections chronicled in the pages of zines spread word of new bands. Rabid traveled to Los Angeles to tour the scene for his readers. He visited in December 1981, lamenting the recent disappearance of venues such as Starwood, lack of support from the Roxy, and the Cuckoo's Nest's outrageous entry fees. Despite the dearth of clubs, he managed to see the Circle Jerks at Al's. After his visit, new venues such as the Hollywood Palladium went back to hosting shows. Even with the club problem, Rabid reported, "There are so many hardcore bands in LA it defies my imagination." Five supportive record stores provided access to albums as well as mail orders from labels.

When it came to radio, college stations offered few outlets in Los Angeles for hardcore music. Instead, Rabid praised commercial KROQ and Rodney Bingenheimer, who "doesn't seem to lose touch with the bands and fans the way so many 'famous' DJs do." The DJ's promotion of LA's music scene prompted thanks from bands in their album liner notes. KNAC in Long Beach, another commercial station, and KPFA, the area's Pacifica network community radio signal, also offered hardcore shows. Those stations did not offer the luxurious eight hours of programming a week found on the ROQ. Bingenheimer interviewed Rabid, who traveled "armed with material— including demos—from NYC bands" to promote on the show. Rabid likened KROQ to WNEW in New York, a commercial station which in 1981 and 1982 took a chance on newer sounds, particularly the local music scene. For a national tour circuit to be successful, and for bands to reach outside home scenes and sell some records, New York had to know what was going on in LA, and vice versa—and LA fans, from Rabid's perspective at the time, seemed to have less exposure to what was going on outside their area.[26]

In San Francisco, another vibrant music scene, Tim Yohannon toiled in 1978 to debut his fanzine, *Maximum Rocknroll*. He began his own radio show on KPFA, collaborating with Jello Biafra of the Dead Kennedys. By early

1982, the show syndicated to Pacifica-affiliated stations, although the New York station dropped it after the first week. Bands could still send their tapes and promote their music through Yohannon's outlet. The scrupulous, outspoken, and devoted music collector amassed records and cassettes that documented the emergence of a national scene. KFJC at Foothill College in Los Altos Hills experienced a revolt among punk rock DJs who jettisoned mainstream rock for adventurous sounds during its rock blocks.[27]

While community radio fueled the hardcore scene, college radio, too, nurtured new music. Back in New York, Rabid tuned to *Noise the Show*, a half hour on Wednesday evenings dedicated to hardcore. Before Rabid secured his own show, Tim Sommer produced *Noise News*, "responsible for just about 80% of the local bands bookings of late," Rabid reported. Drew University's WMNJ sustained New Jersey hardcore fans with Sal Canzonieri's Sunday night show and his newsletters. Sal's little brother aired hardcore tunes at his high school's station. He published Sal's most recent playlist, a handwritten list of sixty-six songs populating his three-hour show. Reflecting the hard and fast—literally fast—music, songs on Sal's show averaged two and a half minutes. By 1982, eastern Pennsylvania residents could hear hardcore from Lafayette College, where a radio DJ represented the hardcore cause for two hours on Monday nights.[28]

Major labels grew less wary of new wave, and bands such as XTC, Psychedelic Furs, and the Go-Go's out of Los Angeles' punk scene began to break onto the mainstream pop charts. Electronic rock inspired by Kraftwerk and Ultravox ceased being a novelty and dominated pop sounds of the 1980s. Synthpop—the next phase of disco to some listeners—became common on commercial radio by 1983. For college radio DJs seeking the local sounds of rock scenes, this bleeding of an art-inspired underground or imported music brought little joy. Synths defined the new sounds of MTV—but for local music scenes to thrive, and for DJs to find cool music from cities and towns scattered across the country, new institutions were required that supported this alternative vision and market for cultural production.

Subterranean Pop

In 1974, Evergreen State students in Washington looked to their student-run station for local music. DJs at the one-year-old station suffered rumors of being run by rampant egos and conducting meetings as "bitch sessions," but detractors could not deny the station defied trends in mainstream—and even college—radio. At the experimental public college, the call letters KAOS seemed to capture the campus atmosphere. Although state legislators hotly debated funding a school that offered progressive education, substituting grades with faculty feedback and eschewing a core curriculum, Evergreen attracted creative thinkers, reflected on its radio station.[29] With an increase to 250 watts in 1975, KAOS expanded its previous range of twelve miles to bring music unavailable elsewhere to Washingtonians. It offered *Jazz and Its Roots*, a prison reform program, "experimental word" and Baroque music, and a Women's Radio Collective feature program. Perhaps programmers hoped to overcome negative sentiments that occasionally imperiled Evergreen's state appropriations. Or maybe they simply focused on issues and music they cared about, letting the culture and public service do the work.[30]

The appropriateness of KAOS's pronunciation would be noted frequently among those chronicling its contributions to musical culture. But the station expanded in an orderly fashion, even if on a shoestring budget. In 1974, students purchased a "rusted and corroded surplus 1949 Air Force transmitter which lay in a pool of water in the basement of Seattle's KRAB-FM" to expand KAOS's range, lovingly disassembled and restored by three students. Although they aspired to "real" radio, meaning reaching beyond students, they shunned the term "professionalism" as "often commercialism." Instead, these students sought to defy AM, which offered "country music for the rednecks and Top 40 for the teenyboppers," as well as commercial FM, fragmenting into hard metal rock, progressive country, classical, or other niche genres. At KAOS, alternative meant creativity. "You can do whatever you always wanted to do with a radio." In the student newspaper, future *Simpsons* cartoon creator Matt Groening reported KAOS staff seeking volunteers to add groundbreaking shows to its diverse list of programs. Nowhere else could listeners find "*in one hour,* salsa music, Cajun music, bluegrass, classical, reggae, jazz, and rock," where radio transcended media and became "an art form: of expression, education, and entertainment."[31] Students at Evergreen, and particularly those who gravitated to KAOS, cared little about influencing mainstream music charts.

Students sought Evergreen State from across the nation for its individualized learning structure and progressive outlook. One of those students came from Chicago and discovered KAOS. When Bruce Pavitt began his radio show, he found a newly remodeled studio complete with reception room. Designers envisioned positioning a potted palm in the lounge area outside the station in the College Activities building, although it's unclear if such luxury awaited DJs headed for their radio shows.[32] Having to fund

55 percent of its operating costs through subscriptions and donations meant KAOS could ill afford plant maintenance.[33]

Pavitt came to Evergreen State in 1979 with a developed appreciation for local scenes and music. Cleveland already demonstrated its ability to foster a creative environment that gave rise to Pere Ubu and fanzine *CLE*. Pavitt watched as networks of "enthusiastic amateurs" kept tabs on what music emerged from such localities and did their best to spread the word. Influenced by the fanzine *OP*, Pavitt delved into this emerging network. His radio show, *Subterranean Pop*, expanded to a fanzine, *Sub Pop*, in May 1980, and later to label Sub Pop Records. It might seem that the future was set: this and similar independent labels would chart a new course in popular music, leading to the supernova success of Sub Pop artist Nirvana and the Seattle music scene's elevation to mainstream prominence in the 1990s.[34]

But in 1980, KAOS was an outlier among college radio stations.[35] Pavitt joined a growing ecosystem that he hoped to support—but it remained nascent.

What was for sure: Pavitt did not like mainstream popular music sucking inspiration increasingly from college radio. What had been a vibrant counterculture, filled with innovative bands such as Devo and the Voidoids and Elvis Costello, had been co-opted. The innovation of 1960s artists from the Beatles to Motown flatulated into arena rock of the 1970s. By 1980, the same seemed to be happening again. As Pavitt observed in the first issue of his zine, "the bland sameness of the pop suprastructure is with us once again." Major labels took what had been exciting and exploratory, turning "once-adventurous bands" into "robot-slaves of a system that is interested in one thing only—money." The idea that college radio should be a farm team of talent for major labels corrupted underlying values supporting truly innovative art. Buying and playing major-label music gave in to corporate-driven schlock, yielding "macho pig-fuck bands whose entire lifestyle revolves around cocaine, sexism, money, and more money." College radio might tap into something unique, but once major labels got hold of it, homogenization would ensue.

"We need," Pavitt argued, "diverse, regionalized, localized approaches to all forms of art, music, and politics." Some bands maintained their authentic links to the underground. Others—Pavitt scorned Patti Smith's recent major-label release, for one—did not.[36]

While student DJs at Wesleyan and across the Northeast boycotted Arista to protest record service fees, Pavitt pursued different sources for music, shunning the majors to support truly vibrant and authentic local music. To that end, Pavitt, along with *OP*, kept tabs on scenes and locals like the Blackouts, the Beakers, and the Debbies, with blurbs describing their sound for music fans. He listed releases from Portland, Oregon, describing its cooperative nature and funding for bands to record performances at a local venue. Including such information about how to build a local infrastructure reinforced *Subterranean Pop*'s goal for scenes to exert "control over [their] own cultural economy."[37]

Pavitt supported cross-scene informational networks. He listed new releases from Chicago, Minneapolis, and Athens, San Francisco, and Los Angeles. He included other localities' zines and venues. Armed with information, music fans could go see a show, buy a 45, or send a SASE to a distant fanzine for more dirt on what the locals were doing—maybe even relocate to participate, if they wanted. *Sub Pop* #2 included a long description of the Cleveland music scene, a report from Calvin Johnson on happenings in Washington, D.C., smatterings of bands from Kansas, Oklahoma, Missouri, Indiana, Iowa, and Houston and Austin. As zines like *Sub Pop* circulated, often hand-to-hand, across scenes, college DJs and other aficionados could seek out the sounds profiled. Fans could request songs from their local college stations, tape them, and play on repeat.

Bands needed support. For support to materialize, people in places of influence—such as on radio stations that might play the music—needed information. For music fans turning to KAOS to hear the latest hardcore band starting up in the mid-Atlantic, however, they had to tune in at specific times. The community station had many voices to cover and audiences to serve. Obscure 45s aired in the rock block after 10 P.M. Kids staying up late to finish their homework or zone out or dedicated fans on late-night shifts could tune in. There was no drive-time feature. New music was for Saturday nights, keeping with grand traditions in rock-and-roll excess and catharsis (figure 5.1).

The block schedule still reigned. It did so at stations across the nation, even if word spread that college radio was the place to find guitars and local music instead of corporate-crafted synths. Some blocks cut across weekdays like a dayparting system. Such blocks ensured listeners could expect certain music at certain times of day, such as classical in the afternoons, as at KAOS. But block scheduling incorporated a public-oriented ethos, making the most of noncommercial radio's possibilities. Within their blocks, DJs could create their own, individualized sound and foster powerful networks to build and sustain local scenes. Their power might remain local or become known to the nation and the world.

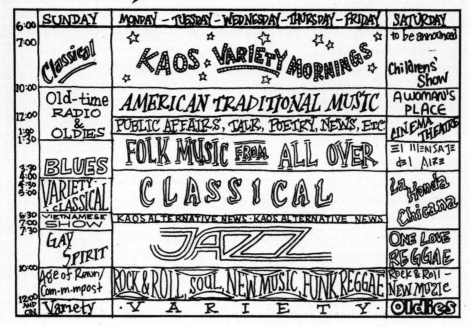

FIGURE 5.1 Block schedule depicted from KAOS at Evergreen State College in Olympia, Washington, printed in the student newspaper, the *Cooper Point Journal*, November 18, 1982.

Pavitt participated in that network eventually via his record label, building a platform for new bands and expression. He wasn't seeking to sell: instead, he hoped to build a local culture and community, a vastly different vision for college radio than a vehicle for professionalization—one more in line with community radio and aligned with the bohemian diaspora in its many forms. Some of that vision owed to KAOS's institutional origins; but it was not only experimental progressive institutions that fostered these connections to far-out music in the 1980s.

Hardcore Stony Brook

If Steve Kreitzer had access to CMJ, he wasn't paying much attention to its charts. He started a show in 1980 that mixed punk and hardcore with popular rock songs. He'd juxtapose Richie Valens's "La Bamba" with Pink Floyd or British punk band the Angelic Upstarts, working-class Londoners the 4-Skins, or the Dead Kennedys from San Francisco. Kreitzer gravitated toward bands that defied punk's commercialization.

He had an impulse to connect, nationally and globally, music that fell far below major labels' radar. By reaching out to bands he read about in zines or heard about from friends, he cultivated a network of labels and bands. His show, *Turmoil Radio*, developed its own music library and earned status as the longest-lasting punk and hardcore show in the nation.

The community DJ relied on his DIY ethos to network. Armed with stamps, postcards, and a form he sent to bands to fill out, he collected biographical information about groups from Arizona to Zagreb, informing them in return about their songs he aired. In 1983, Midland Park, New Jersey, band the Burnt send a cassette of its forthcoming record after Kreitzer requested more information. The band instructed him to "PLAY LOUD," reporting that local college stations liked their *Flintstones* theme cover and songs "Horsemeat" and "Luftwaffe." A band member signed the letter with his moniker, "Arm Pit."[38]

Kreitzer managed local label Slob Records and wrote for fanzines including *Maximum Rocknroll* and *Task*. He coordinated tours for bands from overseas and for Jello Biafra's appearance at Stony Brook University. A nascent network of independent label-releases of seven-inches and cassettes, as well as fanzines and tours, provided oxygen for Kreitzer's show, and he then breathed further life back into the network.

Other DJs with similar shows got in touch. In 1983, a volunteer for KLCC in Oregon, a station licensed to Lane Community College in Eugene, hosted a hardcore show on Friday night and ran a DIY label alongside a "suck ass janitor job" that "pays the rent." The Oregon DJ appreciated Long Island bands Satan's Cheerleaders and Insanity Defense, whose tapes he had sent off for and thoroughly enjoyed. He asked Kreitzer to do a trade for Heart Attack's 1981 seven-inch "God Is Dead," released before its full-length LP on Rat Cage Records. He concluded, "Butthole Surfers are playing here tomorrow, YAHOOOOO."[39]

Kreitzer's informational system expanded. He published his playlists and distributed them to labels and bands, becoming a go-to for up-and-coming labels. Unclean Records of Austin, Texas, placed *Turmoil Radio* first on its list to send records. He'd play tapes for bands yet to release a seven-inch, such as Verbal Assault's self-released cassette in 1984.[40]

Word spread. Jack Talcum of the Dead Milkmen wrote to Kreitzer in August 1984, enclosing a self-produced cassette released before *Big Lizard in My Backyard* appeared from Restless Records in 1985. "Your radio sounds very interesting. Really cool," he wrote. The band's hometown of Philadelphia had WKDU at Drexel University with one good show "every Tuesday night called R.I.O.T. (which Stands for Radically Insane Off the wall Tunes!!!)." That show, formerly linked to zine *Maximum Rocknroll*, occupied the same DIY network as Kreitzer. College stations might not program punk and hardcore around the clock, but shows and DJs appearing a few hours a week fostered a functioning system to disseminate information and music. As Jack Talcum concluded, a "DJ's life must be great. (Is it?)"[41]

It must have been cool. In 1984, Kreitzer received letters from Auckland, New Zealand, Italy, and Blue Island, Illinois. Someone told him that Glenn Danzig would be playing nearby with his band, Samhain, formed after the Misfits dissolved. WBAI, a Pacifica network station in New York, launched its own punk and garage show and solicited record and tape donations, as well as information, from Kreitzer. One New York band reported it received play from stations at SUNY Albany, Siena, and Skidmore, but it had trouble securing distribution to more than a few record stores.

Hardcore and punk shows featuring independent-label releases or self-produced cassettes circumvented the chokehold major labels and distributors had on musical production. Although bands struggled getting product into the hands of consumers, there was hope. The Sluglords' drummer told Kreitzer in 1984, "Glad to hear you have access to the airwaves plus freedom to use it however you please." Although some college stations had formats and rotations, most DJs had leeway within their blocks. Kreitzer cued up the Sluglords' "Trail of Slime," which secured distribution from independent Rough Trade, as well as Dutch–East India and Import East.[42]

By 1983, Kreitzer programmed increasingly independent-label artists, while college radio's roster of new wave artists crossed over to mainstream airplay and major labels. Even champions of college radio's cultural power began to worry that playlists stagnated, particularly as commercial "modern rock" stations emerged, focusing on college radio's fare of new wave and new music in Cincinnati, Chicago, Boston, and elsewhere. If college radio were to sustain and network underground scenes and artists, what happened if their playlists became the domain of established, even if progressive, bands? DJs like Kreitzer and Bruce Pavitt advocated against this, forming powerful informational networks and institutions of their own, but their influence had only just begun to cohere.

Committing to Alternative

When it came to formatting, student music and program directors did not always give industry insiders faith. In 1982, Robert Haber of CMJ and music industry executives presenting at IBS "hinted as tactfully as possible" that college stations focused so much on new wave "that other non-commercial and less popular areas of music might be being ignored." Haber feared college stations resembled "the lily-white airwaves of their commercial peers" catering to young white males.[43] College radio, for all its talk of diversity, failed in aggregate.

Still, changes were afoot. In 1982, Wesleyan program director Douglas Berman received local press coverage for his innovative programming. Berman, who later produced for NPR shows such as *Car Talk* and *Wait, Wait . . . Don't Tell Me*, emphasized service to "various groups of people throughout the area, and not just those at the university." College stations had a responsibility to provide both information and entertainment. Berman balanced programming to satisfy listener tastes from jazz to rock to news.

DJs and music directors at Wesleyan's WESU had strong musical preferences, shaped by directions in the music industry. Bob Nowlan, music director in 1982–1983, noted DJs "have had it with slick and sleepy syntho-pop 'dance music'" dominated by synthesizers and leading to "atrociously sterile, inane, and derivative sounds." Mirroring Pavitt's criticism in *Sub Pop*, biweekly playlists emphasized material received from new labels, such as upstarts Fun Music, M-Raft, Neutra, and Spurtree. Nowlan emphasized college radio as "real" radio. It provided "invaluable assistance" to new music in breaking new artists. Its experimental flexibility enabled college radio to "accommodate diversity and the extreme." Nowlan equated alternative radio with diversity and breaking new music—music that challenged commercialism's corruptive influence and defied dominant trends in the industry.[44]

Nowlan's last statement as music director in February 1983 captured the shift underway at college stations across the country. Many continued to program major-label artists, mixing new and old and expanding specialty shows for soul, reggae, rap, and "diverse" genres, but music directors increasingly emphasized independent-label rock and new releases. A cohort of boosters advanced this thesis within the college radio community. Nowlan insisted "college radio should bend over backwards to assist independent-label music—the source of by far the majority of the most sincere, innovative, and creative music being made today, at least in 'rock.'" College radio was responsive and cheap. Stations could cultivate a devoted listener base "if the station consistently plays and promotes new independent-label music." Then listeners would "count on it as a source of information about which records to buy," just as they trusted zine publishers. Student DJs, although amateurs, had to realize their potential market influence and develop "a sense of purpose." Programmers had to make an "ideological commitment to progressive musical programming." DJs should be open minded, experiment, learn about new music, and advocate for college radio's influence.[45]

In Nowlan's last days as music director, WESU's playlists captured the station's shift. Heavy airplay divided into two lists, one for independent and one for major labels—although the lines between these tended to be blurry, as many independents had major distribution contracts or associations. Soon-to-break-out U2 topped the independent rotation in March 1983 with its album *War*, followed by English Beat (I.R.S.), New Order (Factory), and the Cure (Fiction, part of Universal Music Group). Following these bands which would have mainstream success were influential artists such as Soft Cell (Sire), Bad Brains (Important), and the Dead Kennedys (Alternative Tentacles). Independents did not have ownership of new wave or punk, with major-label-heavy airplay consisting of the Thompson Twins, Siouxsie and the Banshees, Nick Lowe, Falco, and Bow Wow Wow alongside Marshall Crenshaw, Neil Young, and Dire Straits. Prince's *1999* debuted on the major-label-heavy airplay list in March 1983.[46] That April, the music director received over 100 new rock records. Separate listings for major and independent labels disappeared to instead highlight the music played on different shows. Some emphasized new and old, while others focused on "new and eclectic" rock from the Violent Femmes, Echo & the Bunnymen, and Hüsker Dü.[47] Music directors experimented with how college radio curated new music (figure 5.2).

By 1984, as college radio staples such as the Replacements appeared on WESU's heavy rotation, Wesleyan's music director reflected on the changes she witnessed since 1980. "When I was a freshman," she noted, "New Wave was still pretty much only underground—solely the province of college radio." Three years later, while hardcore had not reached mainstream playlists, new wave artists certainly had. Such attention pressured college radio to innovate to keep its alternative status. She insisted, "College radio must look further to provide a true alternative to commercial." WESU

FIGURE 5.2 David Skinner, cartoon depicting the switch in focus in college radio from AOR staples like REO Speedwagon to "college rock" from bands such as R.E.M. "Back to School Comeback Special," CMJ *Progressive Media* 8, no. 11 (1983). Courtesy of Library and Archives, Rock and Roll Hall of Fame and Museum (http://library.rockhall.com).

accomplished this by emphasizing independently produced music, continuing college radio's tradition of looking out for the "new and neglected."[48]

Tensions between commercially viable, major-label music and obscure, independent-label bands and college radio playlists intensified in the 1980s. A Rice University DJ complained in 1982 that "commercial swill" from Men at Work degraded the station. "I do NOT mean to say that anything that sells is bad (eg Stray Cats, etc.), but some of this stuff on playlist—the new Pink

Floyd, for example—URGH!" Another DJ responded, "Some of us like Men at Work." Other targets for ire included Billy Joel. ("Have you taken time to listen before you criticize?" a DJ queried. "YES," the complainer responded.) That year, the stacks filled, and station leaders had to decide what to keep—axing anything "too" commercial.[49] Even Tom Petty and the Heartbreakers was downgraded to light rotation.

Amid these debates, one DJ quit. "Cut the bubblegum," he advised. "You are playing to a sophisticated audience. Act like it."[50]

KTRU and others developed policies about playlists and rotations with more specificity—but vagueness remained. No solid anti-major-label rules emerged. Instead, the idea that college stations privileged indie labels over majors arose out of internal banter and mission statements, rather than universally codified regulations. In 1983, KTRU volunteers hammered out a five-year plan. When it came to music policy, problems emerged in determining terminology: "Pop stations, eclectic, rock n' roll . . . who can tell?" DJs needed someone to manage playlists and answer questions: How long could albums remain on the playlist? How about a "kill date"? Rather than implementing hard rules about major labels, leaders entreated DJs to vary the music and aim for an "alternative" identity.[51]

In the mid-1980s, KTRU volunteers debated the extent of their alternative commitments. Even the classical music show considered programming at other Houston stations. On Saturday afternoons another local station played opera, meaning KTRU would offer "an alternative" and not broadcast vocal music during those hours. Some protested axing Beethoven's Ninth Symphony from the playlist. Others saw a format that worked, and changes would threaten audience loyalty.[52] One DJ feared making the classics show "bland, uniform, and ignorable," luring the same unthinking listeners who tuned in to the area's classic rock station that KTRU DJs chastised as an example of the worst tendencies of commercial radio.

The fight over the classics format raged in pencil scrawling on a sheet of dot-matrix printer paper posted on the station wall. One DJ wrote, "Think about it—would you throw out guitar music because you don't like AC/DC?" Avoiding all vocal music to compete with another station created an arbitrarily large prohibition. Another DJ scrawled, "No, but on the same token, I wouldn't throw the show open to Van Halen, simply because it isn't specifically AC/DC." KTRU did not allow DJs to play whatever they wanted.

Elsewhere on the paper, a staffer scribbled, "Dare to be Silly! Dare to Be Creative! Dare to be Purple!"[53]

Even though the debate took place in jocular terms, DJs took seriously their mission to provide—and define—alternative radio. While the classic format conversation revealed that the 1970s idea of alternative radio continued at college stations, by the mid-1980s the concept narrowed and grew increasingly contested. As one KTRU staffer concluded, "Remember . . . being 'alternative' doesn't mean being every possible alternative. We're alternative in the ways we choose, at the times we choose, to the degrees we choose." The "we" she referred to included the music and program directors. These discussions raised the stakes of elections, in which DJs selected who would define what KTRU's alternative looked like for the next academic year. The classics show offered "boring study music on Saturdays," according to some DJs, and should not simply do the same as other stations. But as another DJ responded—who dared to be purple and use a colorful pen—KTRU should not simply defy, "because we're not all knee-jerk 'alternativists.'" Being alternative meant being deliberate in musical choices, not simply resisting any trend in commercial radio or music.[54]

KTRU held sway in the Texas music scene and sought to expand its influence. In September 1982, the station featured promotions and interviews with the Raybeats, the Roaches, and Wall of Voodoo. The Go-Go's remained a possible interview even though they canceled a Dallas concert because of a sick member. I.R.S. provided records for a contest.[55] A month later, DJs debated increasing power. A willing donor offered to gift a higher-power transmitter, enabling KTRU to keep up with commercial FM competitors. As staff meeting minutes noted, "much discussion!" ensued. Most saw the improvement as a "benefit to community," the meeting secretary noted. They decided to express interest and see if any strings would be attached that might threaten the station's mission.[56] Expanding to 1,000 watts would mean reaching more listeners, and potentially more donations. It also meant "more responsibility" and the potential of losing "our 'lil' ol' station' status."[57] DJs weighed whether they could have round-the-clock programming and maintain quality. Some proposed requiring audition tapes for new DJs. Envisioning the next five years, along with the power increase, DJs determined KTRU's music policy should be more explicit and guided by a music director in charge of the entire rotation.

The station would have to wait another decade for a significant power increase. For the rest of the 1980s, KTRU maintained an atmosphere that led DJs to feel it remained theirs alone. But debates continued about the station's alternative identity—and what that term meant beyond simply challenging expressions. Students seeking to air their favorite music, or who simply felt like a weirdo at Rice, gravitated to KTRU. In January 1984, a DJ requested permission from directors for a dedicated hardcore show. Some wondered if enough hardcore songs existed to make up a show, since most contained expletives or obscenities of some kind.[58] Some DJs used the station's reach to outrage listeners. In 1984, a Monday night DJ "decided to play Satan-related music" before a special show from a local Christian fellowship. "Cute," DJs commented. "Reeeeeeeeeal Cute. Uh-huh." The same DJ could be heard "spouting political propaganda during break," violating Fairness Doctrine and FCC rules regarding editorializing.[59] Such pranks were not alternative or KTRU's mission. Station leaders instituted a new DJ policy manual so no one could claim they "didn't know" about a particular rule, especially regarding "bad words, FCC RULES!!," the emergency broadcasting system, public service announcements (PSAs), and logging requirements.

New policies provided coherence in the station's sound. DJs could not bring records from home without the music director's approval (or have open containers, smoke, or do drugs in the studio—but that didn't always stop them). Reflecting trends toward professionalism, KTRU encouraged DJs to tighten up their delivery, use inflection—it encouraged "less talk, more music"—and avoid dead air. DJs could not joke about PSAs or offer personal messages and call-in dedications. At the same time, KTRU had no "professionalism aesthetic," according to the music director. It was about being alternative, about the music, not about being "career oriented." This varied across stations even if they could be classified under the shifting alternative label. KTRU's music director had final authority over rotations, and DJs should "remember—we are [an] alternative station."[60]

Rice's DJs didn't see themselves as musical evangelizers. They played music they liked for each other, and it seemed impossible that the scene would grow or that hardcore punk would become nationally visible. More listeners increased pressure on stations and their sound, especially since someone might turn them in to the FCC for any content violations, but that pressure had little effect on DJs' aspirations.

· · · · · ·

Back at KUSF in San Francisco, by 1981 the station's link to the city's music scene strengthened with its ability to discover and showcase talents. XTC received "heavy airplay" at many college stations thanks to early exposure on KUSF. Band founder and songwriter Andy Partridge appeared on air. During his interview, he called "American radio fare 'syrup for the masses'" but "KUSF 'sounds O.K. actually.'"[61]

"Thanks Andy!" the station replied.

XTC was not a punk band, nor was it part of the No Wave movement that broke down and expanded rock songs with distortion and experimentation. Neither was XTC insulated from the music industry. Steve Lillywhite produced the band's album *Black Sea* before going on to produce, among others, college radio cornerstone and future megastar U2.

When MTV debuted, student DJs recognized that the cable channel and music videos offered "important promotional tools." XTC's relationship with KUSF and the music industry revealed the looping connections between local-oriented college stations and national touring circuits, promoters, and record labels.

By 1983, students—often white suburbanites with middle-class backgrounds—experienced greater influence in the growing network of "left of the dial" stations capable of breaking new artists to mainstream success. Meanwhile, commercial FM gravitated to new wave, led by stations such as Los Angeles's KROQ.[62] This shift allowed college stations to explore and support local music scenes, knitting together an informational network to support touring bands and build fanbases. But underground, bohemian scenes were not the only beneficiaries of college radio's influence. Public interest obligations linked community DJs and local communities to institutions. Despite the benefits, these links generated conflict between students' self and musical discovery and service to diverse constituents.

Still, by 1983 CMJ's staff members celebrated college radio's emphasis on new music. Five years into the publication's existence, one writer concluded that at last "commercial radio has learned to take its cues from its college cousins."[63] Musical innovation from the ska revival to commercial rap, in addition to synthpop's popularity, defined New Music, CMJ's preferred term for the bands it charted rising through college and community radio, creating a national infrastructure for its promotion. At first, CMJ only reflected what happened at stations reporting their playlists for biweekly charts. By "unifying" reports from stations "which previously had no mouthpiece, no meeting place," CMJ showed how those stations could collectively influence musical culture. "When one college in New Jersey could see that another in Idaho was being adventurous and playing the Adverts or the Residents, it brought them closer." Maybe, at last, many college students would happily tune in to their boundary-pushing stations. Maybe. It remained to be seen if students at hosting institutions would continue funding if they didn't feel they had a say in programming.

6 Students, Communities, Markets, and the Limits of Radio Democracy

· ·

Rotation Adds WRAS Georgia State, Atlanta

July 30–August 5, 1984

Heavy: Hoodoo Gurus, Romeo Void
Medium: A Flock of Seagulls, Silent Running, Torch Song, The Untouchables
Light: Kurtis Blow & Run DMC, Illustrated Man

December 3–9, 1984

Heavy: Bronski Beat, Cabaret Voltaire
Medium: Eurythmics
Light: The Smiths

Adelphi University's radio station WBAU conducted an ascertainment study in 1980 to assess whether it met community and public service obligations. Although the FCC loosened requirements on broadcasters to conduct such incongruously named studies, the station continued the practice to justify its programming. DJs interviewed several leaders of nearby Long Island communities and found demand for coverage of "The Energy Crunch, Minority Concerns, Decline in Educational Standards, [and] Revitalization of Long Island's Downtown Areas," plus issues relating to senior citizens, women, inflation, the environment, and substance abuse. Every Thursday, WBAU aired *The Black Reflection.* A Spanish-language show broadcast weekly, and *Ciaro Scuro Italiano* offered a "celebration for the Italian community on Long Island." *Polka Bandstand* featured news for the area's Slavic community. The station hosted fora for religious discussions, mental health, and women's rights. Another show provided "money and energy saving tips" to help listeners cope with inflation and rising energy costs.[1] WBAU's DJs did their best to serve an array of community needs while allowing students to explore their musical interests.

At the same time, Carlton D. Ridenhour made his way back to classes. The talented graphic design student turned his academic career around, negotiated makeup work for the courses he had ghosted, and began to connect his study to music. Professor Andrei Strobert, a jazz drummer inspired by the Black Arts movement, taught a Black Music and Musicians course that inspired Ridenhour and his friends Bill Stephney, Harry Allen, and Andre Brown in their radio programming.[2]

Ridenhour joined WBAU after meeting Stephney.[3] Stephney, host of the *Mr. Bill Show*, was "the first person to incorporate and orchestrate rap music into college radio," according to Ridenhour, who hosted *Super Spectrum Mixx Hour* on Saturday nights. Stephney matriculated at Adelphi on an Urban League–sponsored scholarship in conjunction with prominent rock station WLIR radio on Long Island. He won the scholarship with an "essay on why more Blacks were needed in the media industry." His facility with media, helped by an internship in commercial radio, inspired his programming at WBAU. There he encountered young performers with "boundless energy." He aired tapes from local artists and conducted interviews. He showed rap could work on radio even before commercial records were widely available.[4] He identified promising artists and defied dominant scenes on campus, a mostly white commuter school. William Drayton hosted a Saturday night show, receiving a ride home from the engineer each week. Soon he joined the group nerding out about music. As hip-hop scholar Jeff Chang described, "They did not fit in with the Black fraternity and sorority scene, full of bougie wannabes who looked down their noses on hip-hop. They mixed more easily with the white, mullet-haired Long Island freaks that hung around the radio station."[5]

College radio stations served as sites of artistic exploration and connection—often in defiance of dominant campus culture. Coverage of musical traditions from Black communities increased alongside enrollments from underrepresented groups, although many stations were slow to respond to changing student demographics. But WBAU's atmosphere proved particularly generative. The friends collaborated, joked, and linked the station further with the growing Long Island music scene. Ridenhour—known as Chuck D—rapped at campus events with William "DJ Flavor Flav" Drayton and Hank "Shocklee" Boxley. Stephney later signed them to Def Jam Records and produced the group: Public Enemy was born.

WBAU offered student DJs self-discovery and expression, a much-touted yet often-derided function of liberal arts education. For Ridenhour, WBAU helped him find his voice and connect with listeners yearning for a sound that resonated. In this regard, WBAU's ascertainment studies and Ridenhour's musical aspirations aligned. As he said, "At that time we felt our community wasn't being talked to at all," and the music provided a platform for him and his cohort to express themselves.[6] WBAU provided a "nest," as Ridenhour described it, to produce and disseminate art with political and social meaning and a platform to speak to communities that media ignored. It had little faculty oversight, but WBAU educated students in a liberal arts tradition of self-discovery and empowerment while facilitating cultural representation and airing music and news unavailable elsewhere.

Students' self-discovery and community representation existed in tenuous equilibrium in college radio. To illustrate, back in 1976, across Long Island Sound at the University of Connecticut, student broadcasters presented a core dilemma. WHUS's program director weighed serving students versus a potential listening audience of three million. "Probably the most debated question at the station," he explained, "is whether WHUS should cater to the campus listening audience or diversify its programs to appeal to the entire potential audience of the broadcasting area." Students frequently wanted stations to satisfy majority tastes. The logic held that progressive rock, and soon new wave or other experimental music shows, neglected students who paid station bills through activity fees. For stations with a community orientation or significant community volunteer involvement or with high wattage such as that at WHUS, student broadcasters understood their obligations to public service—not necessarily to the campus community.[7]

These conflicting demands surfaced differently across universities and intensified as observers predicted enrollment declines and federal funding reductions under Ronald Reagan.[8] Questions regarding whose agenda set stations' tone roiled as they became increasingly important in shaping new directions in music. As cuts loomed, threatening financial aid and increased fees, stations explored creative fundraising and considered what audiences might be willing to contribute their dollars to—potentially undermining programs that supported the self-discovery Chuck D enjoyed at WBAU and also engaged and represented communities.

Existential questions emerged regarding stations' governance, programming, financing, and ultimately whose voices mattered most. DJs, especially nonstudents from surrounding communities, demanded these signals serve democratic purposes. Scrutiny tuned to governance as well as programming for listeners beyond the ivory tower. But college radio's hierarchical structure—even when independent from university administrators and missions—complicated these goals.

Students and Communities: College Radio Democracy

By the 1970s and early 1980s, many prominent institutions looked outward at surrounding communities. Harvard and MIT pursued controversial urban renewal efforts and re-envisioned institutions' role in economic and urban development—with uncertain results. In 1980, the Bayh-Dole Act promoted "collaboration between commercial concerns and nonprofit organizations," effectively allowing universities to reap financial rewards through licensing faculty and research innovation. Rather than having to make research publicly available, private and public institutions alike shifted to an "entrepreneurial, financially risky, and philanthropically" inclined funding model. This shift came with implications for the residents of deindustrializing cities transforming to the service and information economy. Unsurprisingly, working-class neighborhoods suffering the most from these transitions felt residents' voices went unheard in these processes.[9]

At MIT's WMBR, a debate over values and community service intensified. In 1980, disputes over programming prompted DJs to consider the meaning of college radio itself. City residents had blocked MIT's expansion into East Cambridge as the university pursued collaborations in biotech and alignments with private industry to revitalize the area surrounding the university. But the radio station reached into these communities, unimpeded by physical barriers.

In May, the program director established new programs, combining long-standing community-oriented programs with increased opportunities for students. The meeting included representatives from news, folk, classical, jazz, rock, and long-running R&B show *The Ghetto*. Informal discussion provided the program director, Anita, with input for the new schedule. A DJ declared these decisions commenced without a good sense of who the audience was. He advocated for market research to "develop a more concrete idea of who our listeners are, what they listen to" to "better serve our listeners." Invoking only an "abstract" sense of "our listeners" served no one.[10] This DJ wanted data to help serve communities. Such market-based rhetoric reflected universities' community involvement and urban improvements occurring under the umbrella of economic development, which often displaced existing residents who lacked resources and power.[11] Yet DJs and development-minded administrators differed in expected outcome. DJs' desire to serve existing residents clashed with universities that wished to reshape surrounding urban neighborhoods and their inhabitants—though they used similar tools and logics.

A philosophical problem remained when crafting weekly radio schedules. Audiences already put up with "wholesale changes three times a year" as semesters ended, and student schedules shifted: still they tuned in, regardless of block scheduling's limits. Some DJs felt the station's blocks and frequent schedule changes might serve niche tastes but worked against building a listener base. These movable parts could be rearranged or cut as schedules changed; though these blocks didn't appeal widely, long-running shows might develop devoted, if narrow, community supporters. Blocks allowed DJs to stick to their interests, rather than requiring they broaden musical coverage or expose listeners to more than certain sounds. As one DJ put it, "We lost our commitment to diversity some years ago when we instituted block programming." He proposed volunteers "rededicate ourselves to diversity" and recommit to "presenting shows and ideas not heard elsewhere in Boston radio, even if it means breaking up some of the program blocks." WMBR could offer public service and a "real alternative" in news and public affairs.[12]

Programming for varied needs presented no easy task. By June 1980, a movement to remove the program director swelled, motivated by program changes put forward without consulting affected DJs. As one opponent explained, "a great many shows were juggled around with no apparent rationale," while others "were placed in extremely illogical time-slots that were destructive." Twenty-two DJs met, with fourteen voting no confidence in the program director. Four supported her; four abstained. Without a quorum—volunteers exceeded eighty—the gathered did not have the power of removal.

Debate revolved around prioritizing long-standing community-oriented shows versus providing opportunities for new—student—DJs, who were dwindling in number. The program director explained that semester schedule changes dated to "when we were a 10 watt student station with personnel changes at the end and beginning of school terms." With higher wattage reaching more communities, and a host of community volunteers staffing well-established and high-quality shows, some DJs believed it was time for a change. Moreover, as one DJ recalled, the constant shifting did not eliminate "mediocre" programs in favor of new and more innovative offerings. A "spinoff" of the punk rock institution, the *Late Risers Club*, had been ranked as a "'good' show" but faced cancellation. DJs balked at "experimenting" in favor of continuity to encourage listenership. Some questioned changing the schedule from year to year, let alone semester to semester, beyond normal staffing shifts.[13]

WMBR and other student-run, noncommercial stations lacked commercial radio's clear indicators of a program's success. Any change would likely result in a loss of listeners, community DJs complained. But without Arbitron ratings or advertiser feedback, which WMBR did not have—and DJs didn't want—hard data did not exist.

The no-confidence vote, even without a quorum of volunteers, suggested community DJs' dissatisfaction with how student managers made decisions. DJ Dan Gewertz, a future music writer and journalist, explained the vote "was clearly saying" that a good number of DJs were "sick and tired with the arbitrary power the role of program director wields around here." Many student DJs felt the community DJs "siloed" themselves.[14] Each program director might take the station in new directions. DJs had little say in the schedule. The general manager appointed the program director; it was not an elected position.

And therein lay the problem. The system, Gewertz maintained, was undemocratic, and as such, violated core principles of college radio. He proposed a year-round schedule with major changes subject to station-wide discussion. He wrote, "I am in favor of democracy. If we can't have democracy work in an all-volunteer 'people's' radio station, where can it work?" If college radio, the people's media, couldn't collect and incorporate broad opinion into policy, certainly no other media qualified as democratic. The station needed a sense of community. In spring 1980, it felt "un-together," where DJs "just come in and do their show and fail to see the station as a whole," a situation "FOSTERED BY THE MANAGEMENT'S AUTHORITARIANISM [sic.]."[15]

But who, exactly, were the citizens of WMBR with the power to determine its service and sound? The DJs? MIT students, whose facilities housed the studio? Residents of Boston and Cambridge? These dynamics mirrored those among urban development proponents and opponents regarding MIT's expansion. These independent, private institutions occupied and influenced public space. How they answered for their service, however, was complicated, and many of those affected felt marginalized.

No clear resolution emerged. Some pushed for a review before a show's cancellation or for a continuous schedule across the churn of semesters. Finally, the general manager called an all-station meeting and invited DJs to circulate opinions before and during the gathering.[16]

The "boys' club" of college radio exacerbated matters. The program director, one of the few women on the executive staff, faced stronger backlash than did other executives, and her gender factored into responses. One volunteer decried the "annual bloodletting" during programming as "unusually personal" during this cycle. He hoped "our male egos aren't getting in the way." The program director worked with the same system her predecessors had, facing similar scheduling conundrums from DJs' class times and work schedules, but she encountered fierce backlash.[17]

Seniority presented another complicating factor in reaching consensus in scheduling. "I remember," one DJ explained, "when one 'block,' with a lot of 'seniority' wanted more airtime—they got it at the expense of five 'diverse' shows." When it came to democracy, "the perfect example . . . is a lynch mob," and oligarchy and tyranny could easily result from a purportedly democratic system. Another DJ called using democratic practices to shape the program "a cute idea, but extremely inefficient." She continued, "Imagine what would happen if we needed a consensus to get a schedule— we'd be off the air til 1999!"[18]

Other commenters invoked the current political atmosphere. Gewertz objected. "Democracy may be bust in these United States in this Carter-Reagan election year," he argued, "but small groups especially have done quite well by it. What would you prefer . . . a benevolent monarchy?" Another staffer responded, "Democracy works for over 200,000,000 people in America today. It should be able to work for 83 people at MBR. There is no reason for dictatorship ANYWHERE and anyone who believes that will be personally kicked out of here by me." To the idea that democracy functioned well in America, another DJ responded, "Remember this when you go to vote for Ronald (Bomb'em) Reagan or Jimmy or John (two of David Rockefeller's trilateral commissioners)," invoking antinuclear politics. Cynicism regarding US politics influenced the programming debate. Although the minutiae of staffing and decision-making seemed mundane on the surface, matters concerned broad questions about community radio's viability when run through institutions like MIT. DJs confronted how to sustain democratic media as a voice of the people—especially when those people were reeling from deindustrialization and displacement and saw institutions like MIT more as rivals than as allies.[19]

Community DJs might protest, but WMBR existed as a student activity despite its separate license holder. By-laws required the general manager be an enrolled student. Those in favor of continuity from one show to another favored the plan because, as they argued, not enough students volunteered to justify changing the schedule from semester to semester. As a former general manager and student explained, MIT viewed WMBR "first and foremost as an activity provided for MIT students." To maintain physical space and university funding, it had to be student led. "The result," he continued, "seems to be that a democracy at WMBR can be 'advisory only' . . . until a majority of all participants are again students." Until that situation arose, the program director should remain a "centralized" position with preference given to students.[20]

Meanwhile, business continued. A beagle wandered into the studio one day, and a DJ put out a call for its adoption. A DJ reporting on development issues fielded calls from World Bank personnel. Some enterprising members took it upon themselves to reorganize the record library and flushed records that received no airtime. A control knob appeared to be adding audio distortion to a studio device.

The "battle," as one DJ called it, lingered. She called the new program schedule method "screwed" because the same problems reoccurred with each round. Demands on the station simply outgrew the management structure: WMBR served many constituents in a market where media access narrowed. A system developed under a "10 watt mentality" did not transfer well to wattage that reached wider audiences. A class A station required a "more organized" system and cooperation. The controversy grew tiring.

"For what it's worth," she concluded, "I'm sick of this shit."[21]

As managers planned a monthlong shutdown during July to reorganize and clean the studio, tensions resurfaced. One DJ feared "the same few people doing the work while the rest of the station heads for the beach." He suggested correlating required volunteer hours with DJs' airtime to ensure equitable work distribution.[22]

Eventually, one of WMBR's most famous DJs weighed in. Oedipus, by 1980, had joined local rock station WBCN and the board overseeing the MIT station's license. He stated, definitively, "WMBR is a democracy." It was simple. "Station members elect a GM, who, in turn, appoints a PD according to the constitution." DJs should leave Anita alone. "Her position and decisions are not subject to vote." Only voting the GM out would change things DJs disliked.

A disgruntled DJ resented Oedipus for his comments, responding, "Listen slughead if you put more time here at the station especially at station meetings we'd respect your comments." The fact of the matter remained: WMBR's DJs came from various walks of life. Some lived in dorms and could readily volunteer or attend events and meetings; community DJs had day jobs making it hard to pop by to organize the record library during free time. Community DJs tended to host programs with high visibility in the Boston area and offered the most diverse programming to fulfill the station's community mission. College radio might be democratic in its structure, but it relied on volunteers to function—volunteers whose availability and relationship to campus varied.[23]

Another DJ suggested a way to calm tensions. She proposed composing a "musical interpretation of our present problems (and maybe even solutions)." An appropriate song would likely be "an angry, alienated punk piece . . . a turbulent symphony" or freeform jazz. Others suggested an outing for all volunteers, such as *The Ghetto* hosted that summer for its DJs. Even though one DJ reported being attacked by mosquitoes, the respite improved volunteers' morale.[24]

At the next program meeting, again many community DJs who complained about the new program did not attend. Although some carped at the no-shows, clearer guidelines and procedures for handling program objections came together. The guidelines, approved by the nonprofit corporation holding the license, incorporated further input from all DJs.[25]

Even with WMBR's independence from MIT, the station had to prove its worth as a student activity. As one DJ reflected, "I have this feeling of impending disaster on the day that the 'tute [MIT] discovers that student involvement here is nil." The community-oriented mission improved programming: limiting participation to students might damage WMBR's reputation. Requiring all management positions be filled by students might not solve all problems, "but I think we should make an effort to recruit at least 20 new MIT students next year." Incentives included giving students "preferential treatment for time slots," and current DJs would have to create a welcoming environment.[26]

Indeed, WMBR had reason to worry. Rumors circulated that MIT's administration viewed the station with "distress." No one mentioned reasons for this, which could have stemmed from volunteers publishing recommendations in the student newspaper about which new wave clubs carded laxly for beer orders.[27] DJs interpreted the rumors as relating to low student involvement and the station's community orientation. "We need more visibility on campus," a DJ concluded, and to retain newly recruited student DJs. Community DJs tended to stick around for a long time; students came and went.

Few students tuned in, and no significant complaints emerged. Similar tensions between student and community DJs emerged at stations that allowed community or alumni participation. These debates provoked no existential threat regarding MIT radio's content or the mission to cover music left behind by mainstream media. But when students who didn't participate in radio exerted their influence, stations needed to worry.

Students and Other Students

In the 1980s, several student-run stations had their funding put to student vote.[28] Costs stemmed from power upgrades after the FCC's ending of class D licenses, and programs had to justify their worth amid declining federal funding as the Reagan budgets loomed. Governance and funding are not as much fun to talk about as battles between hard rockers and new wavers. But stations need resources, and someone must provide them. Funders tend to have opinions about what they are paying for—at least, when they remember that they foot the bill or can navigate the alphabet soup of overseeing committees and organizations.

Lil Milliken, the new manager at WXYC at the University of North Carolina at Chapel Hill, stewarded its FM debut in January 1977. Its progressive rock format followed college radio trends, offering an alternative to commercial radio amid familiar sounds. It would be "totally oriented toward students," fulfilling FCC license requirements to provide "programs that concern students and that are coordinated with activities on campus." That year, WXYC received 4 percent of the Campus Governing Council's (CGC) budget, which funded student activities out of a $9-per-semester fee.[29]

That support could not sustain a full-time schedule, requiring a governance change to facilitate fundraising. Transferring control from the Media Board, which oversaw all student publications, to a Student Educational Broadcasting (SEB) committee allowed better attention to federally mandated license requirements and the station's business and legal matters.

Things had grown pretty lax. As WXYC's music director explained, Media Board members lacked experience in radio or business to make budget decisions. The time needed to oversee an FCC-licensed station would be too much for the board and would potentially violate the "essence of Student Government," a DJ argued, "which is to let student organizations run themselves except for how much money they'll have to spend." Resources still came from the CGC, which ensured the station remained "accountable" to students.[30]

Emotions ran high as students considered WXYC's management. When the CGC tabled the petition for a separate corporation to govern the station, such as existed at MIT, managers insisted they had no choice but to remove the station from the air to avoid regulatory violations. The FCC required a unitary body to hold a license, and the Media Board's governance improperly divided authority. The Media Board appeared in no public file or federal document, and "politicking" by students threatened the station's achievements. Students, the music director argued, simply did not understand WXYC's importance; it didn't serve only them. The Media Board, a critic charged, operated like a "three-ring circus" where "amateur Richard Nixons" interfered with public communications. Eventually, two managers resigned over debates regarding how the governance issue should be handled.[31]

Finances remained the most glaring issue. Funding trailed other area stations, amounting to one-fifth of the $30,000 allocated to the carrier-current station at East Carolina University. UNC Charlotte's station received $25,000, and it operated only eight hours a day, five days a week. The CGC anticipated securing underwriting grants from local businesses, but this violated a state law, leaving WXYC cash strapped.

Although student managers hotly debated the radio budget and oversight, eventually they secured necessary funding. The CGC recognized that the SEB should govern the station after WXYC leaders' threat to discontinue broadcasting considering the potential illegality of the Media Board's involvement. With the hurdle of appropriate funding and governance cleared, the station could make its mark in the local radio market.[32]

WXYC focused on progressive rock and on developing a reputable image for the university. The music director told the *Daily Tar Heel* that students had plenty of options to hear disco and rock hits. "We want to give them something new, something good," he explained, in addition to news and public affairs. WXYC granted airtime to campus organizations seeking to publicize their activities.

Even with the budget and governance issues solved, WXYC struggled to meet student demands.[33] Some listeners chafed when DJs ignored their musical preferences. In spring 1978, seven complained that a night DJ refused their requests for punk rock. After several calls to different shows, finally one DJ told the callers "there was a 'no play list' including the Allman Brothers, Grateful Dead, Bonnie Raitt, all new wave music, and even an all-American band like Hot Tuna!" The listeners called this "a little bit confusing and extremely fascist." Not all of them liked new wave music, but they believed the station had an obligation to play student requests. Their doggedness exasperated DJs, who took the phone off the hook.[34]

No regime imposed a mainstream AOR approach at WXYC. Managers responded to the complaint, explaining that the list was, in fact, an "Overplay List." It instructed DJs not to play those offerings too much to provide diversity and breadth in on-air content. The list, generated every couple of weeks after a review of playlists, targeted "groups if it appears they are very obviously being played too much, relative to the other groups played." WXYC did not single out punk or new wave, which it did indeed play. As the program director explained, Elvis Costello, Television, and the Ramones could be frequently heard, although the Sex Pistols received an "overwhelmingly negative" response. Requests had to consider the "total 'flow' of the music," and serve "a variety of listeners."[35] Playing the same—even if obscure—band would only replicate Top 40's bad practices.

Most UNC students did not tune in to WXYC, and not because DJs refused to play punk rock. A survey revealed that 81.4 percent of students listened to WXYC "less than 20 percent of the time they listen to the radio," with most never tuning in at all. Not only were students not clamoring for punk rock and new wave, but they didn't appreciate the regular rock rotation. WXYC's general manager blamed the station's newness, having broadcast for only nine months. In response, the CGC increased the station's annual budget from $6,251 to $13,000 to encourage coverage of campus sports, news, and public affairs and lure students who paid for the service.[36]

WXYC offered eclectic coverage of music and campus affairs. Alice Cooper appeared in a live, on-air interview in support of his appearance at the Greensboro Coliseum in June 1978.[37] Programmers added more jazz, the second-most-popular genre among UNC students. Managers increased attempts to collect listener feedback. The station aired university news and featured a listener call-in show to engage students and Chapel Hill residents. WXYC leaders, many of whom were radio, television, and motion pictures (RTVMP) majors, focused on programming consistency and professionalism.[38]

By 1980, WXYC's reputation as "alternative to the alternative" strengthened. Music director Bill Burton explained, "We expose the audience to new music without losing the familiarity to the average rock listener." Noncommercial status allowed for experimentation, and DJs noted commercial stations picked up what WXYC played first. Burton's experience at a commercial outlet in Raleigh shaped his distaste for strict rotations for profit. At WXYC, he aimed to "broaden the whole scope" by playing requests, even if obscure, and to consistently surprise listeners who would be open to all types of music.[39]

Burton lauded listeners' authenticity, which anchored his definition of alternative. They were "real rock music lovers, people who like to listen to music, not just play it in the shower." These listeners had discerning taste; they were not simply seeking a soundtrack for daily life. They wanted music they could connect with and to make new musical discoveries.[40]

Burton hoped to convert more listeners into appreciators of the new and authentic. "Some people won't like it because they never heard it," he explained, "so we give them (stars like) Linda Ronstadt and Bob Seger, then slip in a new Pink Floyd album." As with most other college stations in the 1970s, experimental programs in rock, jazz, and new wave appeared after eleven on weeknights. WXYC reserved Fridays for classical albums. Specialty shows appeared on weekends.

WXYC established a good reputation as an educational station, breaking new bands and offering a true radio alternative. But the format, and status as a student-funded service, continued to produce dissonance. Rather than existing as an independent entity pursuing cultural and musical revolution, student-run radio remained inseparable from larger questions about the purpose of higher education—highlighted by the fact that students often funded stations through activities fees.

WXYC's educational identity continued to face challenges. Questions arose regarding student managers' ability to administer funds properly, leading to the temporary freezing of WXYC's budget in the summer of 1980. In response, the station manager and chief engineer resigned.[41] That fall, DJs publicly disagreed over the format. These troubles led observers to call for a full-time, professional manager to ensure proper handling of station affairs and to make difficult format decisions. The resigning engineer described two factions among DJs. Some championed alternative programming, whereas others thought WXYC should cater directly to majority tastes. Since students paid the bills, the departing station manager suggested a survey of "what the University community wants to hear." He believed students in charge let their personal tastes take precedence over "'public interests,' which is an FCC requirement."[42] The SEB decided it would suggest format changes and provide continuity as students matriculated and graduated.

But the departing general manager did not define educational broadcasting. He chafed at the idea of outside control, fearing it would force WXYC to "imitate commercial stations" and violate its educational status. Educational stations could take risks. "We can be adventurous," he insisted. He also envisioned local connections. "I don't want to be like every college station in the country," he explained. WXYC reached a highly educated audience who appreciated its "alternative style" and strengthened the university's reputation. He agreed a full-time manager would have the time and status to defend what the station should be.[43]

The student broadcasting committee selected Bill Burton as station manager. Burton had been pursuing a graduate RTVMP degree, which he quit to join WXYC's staff. Burton declared, upon assuming the position, "WXYC is not a jukebox." It was not there simply to satisfy student desires. The station's educational function rested in its training of future broadcasting professionals and in educating listeners to new sounds.[44]

WXYC successfully curated an alternative identity, but securing campus support took work. As student DJs pushed to improve their representation on the committee governing the station and assert more control, a faculty committee member resigned in protest. The RTVMP department member insisted that as a licensed public radio station WXYC needed to program "a minimum of 14 hours a week of locally originated, informational, cultural, educational and instruction programming, plus service to area schools." In her assessment, "Very little of this has been achieved." She reminded students that they did not hold the license; the committee did. Student turnover caused "natural instability," requiring institutions to own and administer license obligations. The student broadcasting committee ensured "continuity of promised programming and a stable format based on research." Student board members, the professor insisted, "know little about broadcasting" and were blindly loyal to WXYC rather than to public obligations. She agreed with Burton that the station should not be an "electronic jukebox." Instead, it should focus less on playing music and program more public affairs, news, and culturally and educationally enriching content. If students wanted to have access to alternative sounds, they should have kept a carrier-current station.[45]

Her concerns fell flat, and WXYC continued to broadcast programs that fostered its alternative image. Ironically, the new 1981 schedule included a show titled *Jukebox*, which played old rock and roll on Sunday evenings. Students who signed on as DJs extolled the music they discovered, as well as the fun of "spinning the discs and shooting the breeze." DJs found programming for continuity—at least within their one- or two-hour blocks— an enjoyable challenge. They found it "a good way to get acquainted with a lot of music." Burton's format established a "play" box of records for DJs to select from for most shows. Specialty shows for jazz, new wave, oldies, and bluegrass were exempt from the requirement. Burton considered the station "elitist" in that it programmed "better and more selective" music not "limited by labels" while remaining accessible to the "serious" music listener rather than the passive receiver. As station manager, he could be involved in advising music and program directors, actively shaping the music rotation, selecting DJs, and turning WXYC into "a station I like to listen to."[46]

A war of words broke out in spring 1982. Even with Burton's steady leadership and clear vision for WXYC, students complained that the station was ignoring their tastes. On the heels of a positive, three-part profile in the student newspaper, complaints about the progressive format surfaced. An editorial complained, in response to Burton's goals, "WXYC should not be run so that the great majority of students simply opt not to listen to it." Considering that the station received $11,000 annually in student fees, "it has an obligation to serve students and that includes their musical tastes." Hosting jazz shows, call-in talk shows, and oldies helped but did not go far enough.[47]

As WXYC garnered national attention for quality, its format was recognized as "the most progressive in the state." That format coincided with that of other college stations, nationally, and as they leaned toward independent labels and supporting music scenes, DJs complained that the *Daily Tar Heel* editors seemed uninformed. As one DJ explained, his own musical horizons had expanded beyond his usual fare of "The Who, Yes, Pink Floyd, The Dregs, and such fare." He "put up with this new-wave type stuff" because "WXYC has helped me to appreciate such bands as XTC, the Specials, U2, and the Waitresses." No other radio signal offered these sounds. If students did not tune in or didn't "want to expose themselves to new music," they should not deny others access. He asked, "Is anyone out there clamoring for [the campus art museum] to show nothing but 200 prints of the Mona Lisa? Then why would WXYC play 'Free Bird' 200 times a week?" No media outlet or performer could satisfy everyone, and "to criticize WXYC for failing to satisfy the musical tastes of every student is about as well-founded as Ozzy Osbourne singing 'Bless the Beasts and the Children.'"[48]

Surveying students seemed like a waste of time. One DJ asked, "What should WXYC do with the results? Should programming be changed to reflect by percentage the quantity of students favoring each and every kind of music?" Students, he concluded, should "be proud" WXYC succeeded on its "non-conformist route." The sound that Burton created might not appeal to closed-minded listeners, another DJ admitted. But they failed to appreciate the "delicious diversity" WXYC achieved. If a college radio station could not be creative and embrace an "innovative spirit," what other kind of media could?[49] Besides, WXYC was cheap in comparison. It reached the wider community and cost only $11,000 per year to run, compared with the $360,000 to operate the *Daily Tar Heel*, whose editors criticized the student radio station. WXYC received its appropriation and continued to expand its adventurous musical coverage.

To be sure, WXYC defied the risk-averse commercial FM rock stations elsewhere on the dial. Like other stations across the nation during the early 1980s, however, it faced criticisms for failing students' diversity. While most students might favor mainstream rock hits over Elvis Costello or XTC, other students' musical preferences received short shift. WXYC's claims of diversity fell flat with minority students. Regarding the flak over WXYC, a Black student wrote, "Who can honestly say that there is not something vital missing from WXYC's format? Am I to gather from Burton that today's black music is not progressive? Be real." Black students reported that they might request Parliament or Xavier—two artists largely unavailable on commercial radio—but the station did not own their recent albums.

Black students highlighted how WXYC ignored rap. No Sugar Hill Gang or Grandmaster Flash and the Furious Five appeared in rotation. "Rap music is an all-too-progressive style," a student pointed out, so why not play it on WXYC? The station might be nonconformist, but it largely ignored Black music. The station mirrored institutional failures to recognize Black students. Students continued, "Don't ask me to give up my roots in music just because I am at a predominantly white university." If WXYC wanted to provide exposure to new artists and genres, critics argued, it should seek out Luther Vandross or Atlantic Starr. DJs responded that WXYC was an "equal opportunity station" that played "black progressive music." Meager funds limited the record collection, not student DJs' unwillingness to play Parliament. WXYC covered reggae and ska, but DJs and listeners differed over the balance of representation for white and Black artists.[50] Certainly, in 1982 there were not many rap records to program, and DJs probably had little opportunity to tap into a growing local scene, as Bill Stephney was doing at the same time at Adelphi University on Long Island. Still, a musical philosophy emphasizing an alternative sound tended to focus on white rock artists.

Students repeatedly complained that when they tuned in, they heard unpalatable offerings despite their fees going to support the station. Yet the debate continued to be dominated by a noncommercial-versus-commercial rock divide, with punk, new wave, and avant-garde musical defenders against music fans who wanted to hear hits that could be found on the *Billboard* top 100.

Meanwhile, WXYC's reputation as a top college station continued to grow, as the medium, collectively, became increasingly associated with the format that Burton instituted. Chapel Hill became a stop on the touring circuit of bands seeking to break through via college radio, making their name by publishing records on independent labels and seeking out the college audience. Up-and-coming band R.E.M. appeared there on its first regional tour. Bands, record labels, and music publications took notice of college radio's reputation and musical influence. Chapel Hill's music scene developed alongside that of other college towns and urban centers across the nation. And as funding tightened in the 1980s and scrutiny on university curricula increased, college radio's defenders learned to invoke their identity as educational institutions to protect adventurous radio programming.

Students and the Market

In 1982, at the University of California, Berkeley's station KALX, "a Mecca of the chains and spiked-hair set," caused administrators to fret "about the school's public image." A policy panel formed to shift programming toward "educational" offerings. KALX's program director called the idea an "abuse of the airwaves" motivated by a mistaken assumption that the station cued up profanity-laced songs. Station volunteers considered offering punk and reggae as educational.

Old-fashioned ideas about universities as means of elite acculturation or finishing schools for the upper class had long since fallen away, particularly as the baby boom expanded universities. Institutions were left with slack capacity as the smaller cohort of Gen X students matriculated. In response, colleges shifted to serving more diverse or underserved students. And by the 1980s, student DJs also questioned elitist images of these rarefied institutions. College radio might cultivate middle- and upper-class listeners and an esoteric image, but DJs' aspirations remained compatible with popular perceptions about a liberal arts education's value—although it took work to convince administrators and detractors of college radio's adventurous programming.

Berkeley faced a budget crisis, which heightened scrutiny and reduced support for KALX. California's Proposition 13 in 1978 limited property tax rates and assessments, leading to slashed budgets for education and moving the UC system toward a tuition-based model. The assistant vice chancellor of undergraduate affairs denied KALX volunteers' charge that administrators "don't see any difference between Black Flag and the Beatles" and hated rock music. The issue, the vice chancellor explained, "is financial, not musical," as student fee collection decreased. To confront the crisis, KALX should "'broaden' its programming to attract interest and money from target segments of the community." Having recently boosted its signal from ten to 500 watts, the station raised 60 percent of its own funds and earned independence. But powerful wattage meant "splashing the university's name over the five Bay Area counties," a student explained, which caused administrators to fret that the station did not provide proper community service at a moment when public faith in institutions—and desire to fund them—waned.[51]

KALX had to prove its value, and Berkeley's administrators envisioned a staid format. KALX could air academic events, including lectures, panel discussions, or conferences. News coverage continued to earn high praise and provide meaningful experiences for students.[52] In 1982, a policy board listened to proposals to limit "hard core rock" to weekends and after 9:30 P.M. on weekdays. KALX already broadcast sporting events, public affairs programming, and a syndicated science series. Administrators targeted hardcore and punk, which pushed the line of decency and political expression too far for their liking.[53]

KALX held off the challenge. In 1985, the *San Francisco Examiner* called KALX "the most far-out of the alternative stations" in the Bay Area market. Programmers required students to have breadth. DJs had to include at least one selection each from reggae, hard-core rock, jazz or oldies, and hits list, leaving them free for the remainder of their shows. In 1987, KALX won CMJ's coveted station-of-the-year award as it balanced pedagogical functions while defining noncommercial radio's role in popular culture.[54]

Students played cutting-edge music, even if it drew unwelcome attention. From within, grumblings suggested college radio's power to break new artists might not benefit the medium. One DJ characterized the pressure: "If it doesn't sell, drop it. If it sells, make more of the same. If it's different, don't touch it." This commercial marketing logic might seem distant to college radio, the "music phenomenon of the 1980s," he wrote. "When the 'more of the same' commercialism of the pop music industry was in full control of the air waves in the 70s, alternative music was something you heard in clubs." College stations remained the exception during those dark years—and signals made a name for themselves for playing groups such as Throbbing Gristle, not the latest hit from Donna Summer or Kool and the Gang. "More and more listeners tuned in," he remembered; "more and more college stations joined the fun." He cited the 242 stations listed in CMJ playing an alternative format.[55]

This energy translated into a national alternative scene, but—and here concerns arose—"the alternative music scene has grown into a considerable market," requiring bands to have a marketing strategy. "Unfortunately," he concluded, "the commercialization of music on non-commercial college radio is plainly underway." Other concerned voices chimed in. David Ciaffardini investigated college radio's potential "crumbling" in *Maximum Rocknroll*, including major-label tactics to strong-arm stations into playing new releases. Some label reps refused promotional records that did not "give them airtime," Ciaffardini reported, and they demanded "stations draw up prescriptive playlists" on "promises of future employment to music directors." Such concerns revisited the Arista boycott of 1980, with a twist. Now, reps sought the collegiate airwaves, rather than doubting them, but their directives grew more strident as stations adopted professional practices labels demanded.[56]

Even if record labels failed in pressuring college DJs to cue up latest releases, the KALX DJ remained concerned that alternative music faltered. "It is no longer an alternative," he concluded; "commercial interest" coursed through these noncommercial stations. Artistic merit might continue, but "homogeneity" defined many playlists reported to CMJ, suggesting "those same commercial forces that serialized rock music in the 70s are back for an encore." With such forces aligned to influence college radio's playlists, KALX and others countered by promoting independent-label music and local bands. While in the late 1970s music directors suggested bands such as Chicago and Steely Dan to unite a station's sound across shows, by the mid-1980s that same premise circulated, except synthpop and new wave offered the connective link.

To protect independence, music and program directors emphasized their educational purpose—with a goal of influencing cultural trends. Promoting local bands did not negate college radio's commercial ties. They simply had to figure out the best method to balance obligations. KALX DJs debated the merits of structured versus freeform programming to advance music freedom and accessibility. One DJ worried that structure—such as requiring that DJs play selections from predetermined lists or rotate recognizable tunes between new music—might turn the station into "easy listening" and threaten its "individuality." Yet allowing too loose a structure turned listeners away, limiting exposure to new music.

While leaders debated the merits of programming structures, KALX DJs provided guidance for bands. DJ Marshall Stax hosted the *KALX Demo Tape Show*, starting in spring 1984. Twice a month he aired demos and cassette-only releases. In 1986, he remarked on the higher-quality sound of the average tape, with bands "making direct real-time dubs from their master takes" with air-able quality. He advised bands to avoid putting sound on the first twenty seconds of a tape to avoid distortion. Removing record-protection tabs prevented accidental erasure: "You wouldn't want that, would you?" Money-saving tips included using simple paper around the tape box rather than expensive mailers. Book-rate shipping was cheaper than First-Class postage. Submissions needed a phone number, background information, and upcoming live performances—and "if at all possible," timings for included songs. "A few tapes," Stax explained, "still come in with just the name of the band scrawled on a piece of tape stuck to the cassette shell." Demos had one shot at airplay, given the volume of submissions. For repeat play, bands had to "be 'carted up' (recorded on to a broadcast cartridge)." He added specific instructions about selecting cart length and where to purchase blank carts. In summer 1986, the KALX program guide included a pull-out page bands could fill out with prompted information and use to wrap demo tapes to send to the station.[57]

If a band secured a gig, KALX had advice for that opportunity as well. DJ John Lee explained that good shows took planning from both the band and clubs, and he provided advice from bookers in the area, including at Ruthie's Inn in Berkeley and V.I.S. Club in San Francisco. Coordinating headliner and opening bands made for a coherent sound. Bookers preferred complete shows rather than jumbling random bands onto the same bill. Her advice: bands should go to shows, find out whose sound theirs might mesh well with, and create connections. Listening to college radio to screen bands helped, Lee added.

Gigs developed a fan base, but to get shows, bands needed fans. This "Catch-22 situation" became harder at venues that required bands to sell tickets. And if a band played too many gigs, supporters might burn out.

Promotion mattered. "Word of mouth remains the best of all channels of publicity," Lee advised. KALX and college stations helped with that. "Getting college airplay from fickle DJs definitely helps." Fliers, even if posted illegally, spread the word. Once a band secured a gig with the right headliner, it still had to impress the audience. The booker at local club Berkeley Square explained: "The first gig is real important. They have to do something special to make people want to come back." College radio airplay could help, but bands had to deliver for the buzz to grow. Sending out demos required less effort and time and provided the necessary groundwork for a successful live show.[58]

Stations such as KALX, through personal connections with bands, venues, and publications, provided vital information about local music scenes and access. DJs monitored clubs and record stores for exciting music to bring to listeners. Although DJs dreaded commercialization, college radio developed significant market power by the mid-1980s thanks to their educational identities—which provided some insulation and justification to protect their status as a student activity in need of funding. Even the "most far-out of the 'alternative' stations" in a given market found protection in that identity and market reputation.[59]

• • • • • •

When R.E.M., a band closely associated with college radio, broke through to mainstream audiences in the mid-1980s, college radio seemed to have a clear, recognizable aesthetic (although one mostly consisting of white guitar rockers) balanced with a commitment to public service—at least some of the time. Still, student fees provided funding, in most cases, and administrators needed these signals for institutional purposes. College radio stations depended on fees, or even state funding or philanthropy. As budgets grew more constrained in the 1980s and universities sought expanded sources of revenue, stations had to prove their worth or develop more independence in fundraising, which oriented stations more toward community listeners than campuses.

And as pop culture drew the scrutiny of culture warriors concerned about the effects of dirty lyrics or references to the occult on tender young ears, college radio stations would not be immune. They might be defined as educational radio, but that status did not exempt them from FCC rules regarding obscenity and indecency or from scolding watchdogs. Culture warriors were not alone in setting expectations. News and information from NPR lured educated listeners into closer relationships with institutions providing such programming—appealing to increasingly brand-conscious and cash-strapped universities.

College radio entered the mid-1980s with a national reputation as the best place to hear new music, selected by DJs committed to a meritocratic system of musical selection. But the myriad demands placed on these signals grew increasingly divergent and untenable as college radio's star rose.

Part II National Connections, 1983–1989

··

In 1983, Howie Klein, cofounder of San Francisco's punk and new wave label 415 Records, declared new wave was over. What punk started had led
to "Flashdance, Boy George and English disco—it was watered down." Klein
considered this process to be natural. "It happens all the time," he said. "It's
inevitable—death, taxes, and cultural watering down."[1]

Some worried that college radio, with its strong association with new
wave, might get stale, too. In 1985, zine publisher Jack Rabid typed out an
editorial criticizing college radio. It made him "sick." Stations had grown
"predictable," particularly those with a professional sound. DJs had the luxury of being protected from commercial pressures and ratings but cued up
hits anyway. "The kind of freedom college radio wastes is deplorable and
atrocious," Rabid complained. "How bout those B sides?" he asked. "How
bout playing all the tracks off that LP instead of the same two thirty times?"
He wanted unusual and obscure music: forget professionalism and focus on
education. Radio should be entertaining and fun, intimate, enlightening,
unpredictable, and, he insisted, "GGGOOOOOOOOODD." College radio was
the only option on the dial to "provide the alternative." Independent labels
recorded what major labels wouldn't. But in 1985, he spat, "College radio
now stinks." Too many stations failed to relinquish tested new wave artists
for new, independent releases.[2]

Someone wrote to CMJ to call Rabid's take a "stupid, but ultimately
affecting-self purge." Rabid insisted that he wanted choice in radio—this
was, after all, a democratic value. He wouldn't have a radio show if it weren't
for Marty Byk and Daniel Martin Cooney, whose late-night punk shows encouraged Rabid to get "publicly involved in New Music." He defined alternative music as "a chain, one of people whose basic common ground is
merely the desire for more than what they're being force fed by the media
and societal mores." As Byk put it, "As long as Kenny Loggins is allowed to
keep performing, there will always be a need for alternative."[3]

By 1985, college radio established itself as that alternative. While many
stations, especially those with high wattages in urban areas, maintained a

professional sound and rotation, the medium left space for experimentation. The FCC, pushed by large community broadcasters and the Corporation for Public Broadcasting, encouraged college stations to increase output and professionalize by ending the class D license in 1978—but amateur-run signals and sounds persisted.

The FCC class D decision had an ironic outcome. Student DJs and station managers strengthened educational radio's mission as airing music without commercial appeal. That function drew the music industry's attention, which valued college radio's ability to find an audience and a market for new music, building a fan base large enough for bands to cross over to mainstream, commercial radio—and to MTV. College radio developed a nationally recognizable reputation while remaining a profoundly local medium.

Such attention on college radio led many participants to grow wary of commercial pressure. Even the CMJ's New Music Seminar, an annual event to showcase exciting new acts, seemed to have grown corporate by 1985. Major-label reps at the conference ignored bands like Agent Orange and the Chameleons for Billy Idol and Eurythmics, which already graced MTV.[4] In 1986, David Ciaffardini of *Maximum Rocknroll* entreated "eager beaver" DJs to not buy into CMJ's racket that made it seem like there were rules governing these stations; there weren't. At the Intercollegiate Broadcasting System's annual meeting, a zine publisher passed around flyers entreating DJs to "protest the corruption of non-commercial radio" and avoid major-label recordings.[5]

Such rumblings of discontent revealed how college radio entered a pivotal era in which local stations were swept into national developments—musical, political, regulatory, and in public broadcasting. The culture wars intensified, driven by pundits, politicians, and pop culture figures. Several Washington, D.C., wives, as they were known, including Tipper Gore and Susan Baker, formed the Parents' Music Resource Center in 1985 to confront lyrics in songs corrupting children—including those broadcast on college radio, prompting new regulations regarding indecency.

Pressure on college radio emerged from within the ivory tower, too. Prominent academics and observers of higher education lamented the decline of standards and western civilization at colleges and universities as curricula incorporated content and inquiry drawn from the growth of social and cultural history and ethnic studies.

Students often chastised DJs' pursuit of "nonconformity" for its own sake, regardless of musical quality. One student carped that his campus station provided "a voice for the downtrodden genre of really shitty music."[6] The idea that stations should reflect popular tastes among students wasn't new. But the perception of college radio as the home for the weird, the noisy, and the underappreciated (or unable to be appreciated, depending on the perspective) had become a national reputation alongside the politicization of curricula amid the culture wars. Doubt grew that colleges and universities could support inquiry and exploration without commercial appeal or market function or that education existed for its own sake and not solely for professional advancement. Culture war clashes came in the more invisible form of questions of funding and program control of these quasi-public spaces, a much less flashy venue than censorship battles over obscene or indecent songs.

Media deregulation intensified college radio's oppositional stance to commercialism. DJs saw their work as more than a matter of supporting artistic self-expression. They challenged mainstream record labels' dominance, and college stations became central points of contact between independent-label bands, the "indies," and potential fans—to the annoyance of observers who had other intentions for noncommercial FM radio.

. . . .

Cleveland State University hosted a student-run station in the city known for popularizing rock and roll radio in the 1940s. By the mid-1980s, a roster of DJs catered to punk and hardcore fans. Trent Reznor, who came to the city from rural Pennsylvania, discovered mind-bending sounds on Cleveland's college radio stations that inspired the music he would make with his band Nine Inch Nails. "Just being able to tune in to college radio made my head explode with limitless possibilities," he said when inducting one of those bands, the Cure, into the Rock and Roll Hall of Fame in 2019. Cleveland's collection of college stations provided his "baptism into the world of alternative and underground music."[1]

At Cleveland State's WCJU, the logs DJs filled out listing the songs they played reinforced the station's mission to expose new music of the kind that awoke Reznor's interests. The photocopied form read, "We recommend that you program at least 50% new releases to keep our record collection vital."[2] It's easy to paint college radio's emerging role in the music industry as a top-down phenomenon largely driven by record companies. But Cleveland fans felt the station was *theirs*.

Steve Wainstead, a DJ in 1987, complied with WCJU's rules. He cued up mainstays of punk and hardcore—the Dead Boys, Minor Threat, the Stooges—while adding in new cuts from the Offbeats, the Butthole Surfers, Sisters of Mercy, and the Fall. Occasionally, he devoted an entire show to Frank Zappa or featured listener requests. After one such show, Wainstead noted in his log's margin, "See what happens when listeners run your show?" Requests included classic punk songs such as the Buzzcocks' "What Do I Get" and the Ramones' "Blitzkrieg Bop" in between the Stiff Little Fingers and Flipper. He issued content notifications before songs with testy lyrics, such as "I'm Not a Loser" by the Descendents, which contained phrases such as "you motherfucker," expressing the rage of a self-identified loser.[3] Wainstead mixed major-label and indie plays, but station leaders emphasized the latter. Music log sheets emphasized, "Independent releases keep alternative radio alive" and "Don't let your listeners down," highlighting public service and the station's differences from commercial radio.

College radio had achieved official cool status. At first it was like "a fairy tale come true," as Gina Arnold put it in her book about Nirvana's origins. "The geekiest, most unpopular nerds" turned stations built by engineering students for "newsies, sportifs, and queers" into vehicles for platinum-selling records. Belying this image of independence—of DJs selecting the newest and hottest of unheard acts through a meritocratic system of good taste—college radio developed real power in the music industry and grabbed national attention as the place where new artists could break through to the mainstream. This "college radio effect," as Arnold named it, occurred across small college towns and major metropolitan markets. Conglomerations of "bored and frustrated white kids" built stacks of records that channeled their ennui and anger into market power. Independence, as encouraged by Cleveland State's playlist sheets, ironically encouraged the music industry to further incorporate college stations into its business model.

College radio, label executives recognized, could influence commercial radio airplay and record sales. These stations provided inexpensive exposure, staffed by opinionated and enthusiastic DJs who were much closer to music fans than industry insiders. Even before R.E.M. and the Replacements became major-label darlings by 1988, labels built this pipeline of success.[4] Local ecosystems of radio stations, dive bars and music clubs, independent record stores, labels, and zines created a fan base supporting a cultural *scene*: a community of musicians with similar sounds that offered a testing ground for talent (table 7.1).[5]

But many scene participants resented their new reputation. Even at commercial college stations, DJs valued iconoclasm and freedom in selecting songs. College radio's power to promote major-label contracts and influence pop culture prompted a sense of betrayal—that visibility and the culture industry's capitalist logic would violate these safe, unconventional spaces. Refuges for freaks and geeks had cultural power. For teens like Reznor, who struggled to fit in, college radio made him feel "connected and no longer quite so alone in the world." And as Reznor's musical career would indicate, alternative music could achieve mainstream success—but that meant opening these refuges to outside pressure.

The industry pushed college radio in certain directions. Few labels were interested in the Latin music featured on noncommercial stations, unless the label had a collection of artists to promote. For example, in 1982 three college stations in New York City were "carrying the weight" of covering that genre for the city's listeners, *Billboard* reported.[6] Although stations continued to air diverse genres, college radio's reputation as the place to find the

TABLE 7.1 CMJ New Music Report, November 12, 1984

Top Three

Radio	Clubs	Retail
1. U2	1. David Bowie	1. U2
2. General Public	2. Frankie Goes to Hollywood	2. Prince
3. Let's Active	3. Prince	3. David Bowie

Breakthroughs

Radio	Clubs	Retail
1. Replacements	1. Culture Club	1. Honeydrippers
2. Orchestral Manoeuvres in the Dark	2. Hall and Oates	2. General Public
3. XTC	3. Maria Vidal	3. XTC

next great alternative rock band eclipsed public perception that they provided public service programming, community radio, and diverse genres.

College radio found itself, collectively, in the national spotlight.[7] The limelight aggravated critics of commercial media. Nonetheless, MTV, commercial rock radio, and major labels offered viable career paths for college radio graduates. Many would go on to careers in broadcasting and bring their innovation and taste for new music to the masses—exposing themselves, and bands, to charges of selling out as college radio defenders wielded an increasingly iconoclastic and anticommercial reputation.

The Commercial Impulse

In Champaign-Urbana, the University of Illinois's radio station WPGU operated as a commercial college station, one of a handful across the nation. The 3,000-watt frequency reached forty miles and covered its costs by advertising—a department run by one of the few "grown-ups" working at the station. Yet even this commercial signal felt the pull of new wave music in the late 1970s and early 1980s, reflecting the crossover of "new music" into the mainstream thanks to adoption at college stations.

Jon Ginoli matriculated in fall 1978, seeking out the station. The music director at the time "didn't believe in independent labels." AOR staples like Genesis and Rush anchored rotations. As space opened for new sounds, Ginoli embraced that opportunity.

When Ginoli finally got his own show in spring 1980, he stretched the rules to feature punk and new wave. He liked the Judas Priest single "Breakin' the Law" but picked it mostly because it lasted only two and a half minutes. Listeners might want to hear the five-minute epic cuts from the Scorpions, but Ginoli cued up the one that was two minutes and forty-seven seconds, leaving time on the rest of his show for punk and new wave: the "unexpected" music he wanted to present.

By 1983, when Ginoli graduated, record labels were taking college radio seriously. Radio play could translate into sales if a local record store carried the release. DJs and music directors who maintained a good relationship with staff at these stores could share information regarding which songs received positive listener feedback. Stores collected information about where customers learned about the albums they purchased. WPGU's deep library allowed Ginoli to feature the Velvet Underground and other "oldies," and he picked up 45s at a nearby record store. He played the Only Ones' song "Why Don't You Kill Yourself," from their 1980 album *Baby's Got a Gun*, which became a local hit. A Champaign-based band of local teenagers tuned in and later covered both the Velvet Underground and the Only Ones. It then recorded original music influenced by U2, which WPGU also played.

Ginoli traced the links between his show, local record sales, and music scene development. Few independent releases filled the music library—in fact, CBS Records was the only label to send a sales representative—but Ginoli did what he could. When Joy Division released its twelve-inch with two versions of "Love Will Tear Us Apart," he preferred the B-side, which topped WPGU's charts not long after. He distributed his playlists to local record stores in case listeners sought the records he had played. The town began to draw bands as the independent, underground touring scene grew. The Ramones, the Replacements, and Gang of Four all played locally. Ginoli no longer had to trek to Chicago to see live music. WPGU could break new bands and convince promoters to expand touring networks.

As these relationships developed, internal divisions at WPGU transformed its format. The music scene thrived, but WPGU's tighter rotation raised questions regarding college radio's centrality to these functioning music scenes as well as its service to students. In 1982, as changes took hold, 300 Black students gathered on the university's quadrangle to protest cancellation of a four-hour soul show on Sundays. As budget cuts loomed at the University of Illinois and other campuses, administrators cut academic support services, financial aid, and faculty expansion—all of which fell heaviest on underrepresented students. Concerns about Black music channeled deeper concerns, as one student put it, that Black students had been targeted to be "systematically removed from the campus." For Black students, questions of musical representation were more serious than which band might achieve star status thanks to college radio.[8] Yet by 1983, emphasis on the commercial functions of college radio diminished these other considerations.

Among DJs, aspirations differed. Students seeking careers in journalism, broadcasting, and advertising contrasted with those who gravitated to the station out of a desire to explore and expand musical culture, although groups did overlap. Students building sales experience might not really care what they played so long as they had "real world" experience. A new program emulated commercial alternative trendsetters such as Chicago's WXRT, which by the 1980s was among a handful of commercial rock stations "carrying the torch" for the spirit of 1960s freeform commercial FM.[9] Even this goal bothered Ginoli. By 1984, the music director instructed DJs in what to play, offering mainstream rock hits punctuated by Elvis Costello, "maybe the Buzzcocks," and a few specialty shows. Ginoli stopped listening.[10]

CMJ's chart compilations and the *Gavin Report*'s list launched a new "mature" era of college radio, with offices at major labels dedicated to radio promotion. This shift provided an opportunity for independent music and growing music scenes. Independent labels could use college radio as an extension of their promotional infrastructure and provide an alternative to corporatized pop culture.

Champaign-Urbana's music scene persisted even with WPGU's changes, thanks to this developing promotional network. Underground publications, word-of-mouth, and networks of bohemian scenes across the nation spread the word about new bands. It helped having a college station, but once the momentum was established, new institutions proliferated, and scenes connected.

Fanzines linked scenes and fans. The zine *Better than Nothing* profiled Mattoon, Illinois–based band the Didjits in October 1986. The rural midwestern town had received a new investment: a large bagel factory, making it "the bagel capital of the world." Writer Don Gerard noted, "Most of the residents of Mattoon wouldn't know a bagel if it hit them in the head," but "there are probably a lot more bagel-eaters in Mattoon than there are Didjits fans." In Mattoon, he explained, "Peter Frampton never needed a comeback cuz he never lost popularity." Members honed their sound by listening to the Clash, the Ramones, and Elvis Costello, alongside "dinosaur heavy rock." Comparing them to Chicago-based Big Black, Gerard called their music "good ole shit kicking' rock and roll which they perfected in their practice space—a chicken shed."[11] Zines like this provided vital information for fans seeking something more than Sammy Hagar or to get the Led out. In Louisville, teenager Britt Walford was a Didjits fan as he formed the band Squirrel Bait, and later Slint.[12]

College radio graduates gained useful knowledge. Ginoli's experience in college radio helped him understand how to market his own bands, including, after he moved to San Francisco, an openly gay punk band. He worked in and around the music industry, including as a sales representative for Rough Trade Records, where he promoted the labels' releases to radio. The British label with US distribution followed the emerging business model developing to break underground artists, the roster of which included Depeche Mode and the Smiths. Coverage started with college stations. After tapping into these scenes around the country, and obtaining distribution in local record stores, bands could cross over to mainstream radio airplay and, eventually, MTV. Rough Trade focused on mainstream breakthrough, pushing for its artists to chart in national publications monitoring college radio, unlike smaller independent labels, which maintained stronger local links (although many small labels obtained distribution through Rough Trade).[13]

Distribution, promotion, and radio play were essential for bands to build a fan base. "Unless people can hear a record," Ginoli recognized, "they won't know it exists, they won't know what it sounds like, and they won't know if they want to buy it or not." As former college radio staples such as R.E.M., Hüsker Dü, and the Replacements appeared on commercial playlists, it seemed college radio might be "less progressive," but it remained "the only outlet for non–top 40 music." Bands had to show viability if given a national distribution account or signed with a major label. College radio allowed them to prove they could sell.[14]

The Music Industry Takes Notice

Widespread recognition of college radio's potential to break bands took hold in the mid-1980s. CMJ celebrated its five-year anniversary with a compiled Top 100 list, with the number-one spot going to I.R.S. Records' breakthrough band, the Go-Go's. The all-women punk group from Los Angeles had made it from the underground to MTV.[15] Music and radio industry executives, as well as labels' promotional staff focusing on college radio, looked to cash in. Lee Abrams, the radio consultant who helped formalize the AOR format in the 1970s, predicted increasing fragmentation of commercial radio, with

AOR stations dividing between the twelve- to twenty-year-old audience who preferred Def Leppard and the twenty- to thirty-four-year-olds who tuned in for Genesis.[16] In the context of AOR's loss of iconoclasm, college radio filled a gap. College radio's willingness to play new music pleased industry insiders.

Attention to college radio in national music press in fall 1983 captured the industry's growing interest. A series of articles struck a buoyant tone. *Rolling Stone* trumpeted college radio's "brave new wave" as radical bands featured across these signals crossed into the mainstream. Writer Steve Pond detailed stations' outrageous reputation on some campuses. KXLU at Loyola Marymount in Los Angeles confronted a straitlaced, Jesuit culture, as Pond told it. Yet the station connected to the area's hardcore scene and played Agent Orange, the Beastie Boys, and "oldies" from the Velvet Underground, T. Rex, and the Sex Pistols. Luckily, the powers that be at Loyola didn't seem to be paying much attention, even if the music industry was.[17]

Genre battles and pressures for higher-quality management and sound had not driven the creativity out of college radio. Record labels had pushed stations for more professional practices, particularly in collecting data regarding local hits and corresponding sales at local record stores. Institutions forced students to adopt clearer policies and implemented oversight when higher wattages expanded audiences. Still, the sound remained "naive—and much fresher," according to a promoter who focused on breaking new artists. Without sponsors to worry about, college stations were free to experiment in announcing and with the range of artists played, providing, in some ways, a purer sense of what kids wanted to hear and what they would buy. College DJs' interests and enthusiasm guided programming, which translated into fan energy and credibility for artists.

By 1983, college stations, as CMJ's Robert Haber put it, were "back in the companies' good graces." Labels added promotional staff and record service, focusing on 300 to 400 core stations with formats that supported breaking new artists in large, or targeted, markets. The success of the Jam's latest record, and robust data collection through Haber's *New Music Report* that monitored biweekly college top-thirty lists nationwide, marked college radio's emergence as a collective, reliable market player. Reporters to CMJ expanded from around 250 in 1983 to more than 800 by 1989, adding to the range of stations receiving label notice. *Rockpool* similarly collected college radio charts. The *Gavin Report*, a publication for radio program directors launched an alternative chart in 1982, which in 1985 *Rolling Stone* reported as the "College LP's" list.[18]

Even with influence and chart convergence, college DJs preserved freedom to experiment with new music. Once a struggling station that UCLA administrators eyed for purchase in 1974, Rick Carroll's revamped KROQ in Los Angeles encouraged other stations to pick up on college radio hits. The format Carroll developed there, "the Rock of the Eighties," caught on nationally. Its popularity depended on a tight rotation and specific radio presentation style. KROQ opened its airwaves to new wave bands such as Depeche Mode and UB40, promoted by DJs such as Richard Blade and Swedish Egil, while WXRT helped launch the modern rock radio format in Chicago. Modern rock stations, often with an X in their call letters, focused on "new music," which left college radio to "stay a little more progressive" and focus on new artists.

College radio's defiance of these trends strengthened in the mid-1980s. At Northwestern's WNUR, DJs avoided any act, even former college radio staples such as U2, that could be heard on commercial rock FM. WNUR's music director told *Rolling Stone*, "A guy from RCA keeps calling me about Eurythmics, and I have to tell him that we played that record in February. It's broke now. It's Number Two in the country. What does he need us for? We're more interested in the new Bongo's record." At New York University, DJs reported feeling an "obligation to be alternative." The market—and often labels themselves—demanded it. Although strict "indie only" rules for airplay are often overstated in college radio in the 1980s and 1990s, they nonetheless emerged out of a sense of defiance of mainstream pop culture.[19]

College radio fostered the idea that the "true" spirit of rock and roll and freeform radio persisted despite corporate consolidation in the music industry and the conservative effects of narrow formats in commercial radio. Robert Haber called college radio "the only place left where people play records because they like them," resisting control by consultant- or industry-driven rotations. It was hard to break new artists in a tightly controlled format, which left little room to introduce new artists to listeners and play unfamiliar music frequently enough to construct a fan base. The left of the dial housed the spots on FM to find new and local music, where DJs resisted being seen as testing grounds for new product. While not all stations embraced open formats, and many adopted more hours of NPR programming or offered jazz, folk music, or other genres, a collective alternative identity persisted.

As more commercial stations increased airplay of new wave acts such as Duran Duran and those signed to major labels, college stations could focus on bands yet to break through. "If I wanted to," a KUSF DJ explained, "I could go on the air and play Van Halen into the Sex Pistols into Southern Death Cult." This individualist attempt to "blow minds" through musical exploration produced commercial results. College DJs found themselves, sometimes unwittingly, as gatekeepers and tastemakers within the music industry.[20]

Publications focusing on the business side of the music industry picked up on college radio's influence. *Cash Box* followed *Rolling Stone* in 1983 with coverage of college stations driving retail sales and concert attendance. The industry publication identified "catalysts for new music activity at the club as well as the retail level." College stations, the magazine reported, played imports, particularly British new wave artists, as well as local acts. They developed influence in local markets beyond the confines of campuses. At WNUR in Chicago, with an estimated 1 percent of Northwestern students tuning in, what Chicago residents thought mattered more than student tastes.[21]

College stations drove the retail success of bands at independent record stores. WZBC at Boston College and WUOG at the University of Georgia reportedly kept local record retailers in business. In Athens, commercial stations often overlooked major-label bands such as Aztec Camera, Oingo Boingo, and Lords of the New Church, but the music of those bands could be found on WUOG and at local Wuxtry Records—and labels paid attention.

Label reps took to the pages of CMJ to promote what they wanted college radio to test. Jack Isquith, a recently graduated music director from SUNY Albany's station-turned-independent-promoter, entreated college stations in October 1983 to air more "regional and local" talent. With crossovers like New Order and R.E.M. on commercial radio, college radio's work was done for those artists. Focusing on newer talent could build a station's "identity," rather than cuing up bands already broken through. Plus, working with local bands was "rewarding," he told music directors. "Interviews, contests, and concerts all are at your fingertips if you are willing to work for them." Stations could define themselves in their radio market. For Isquith, that meant promoting the Violent Femmes in the Midwest and Alan Vega in the East. An Elektra Records representative struck a similarly encouraging tone. She praised the "articulate people running the show" and declared college radio's future "looks to be a bright one." Label reps and promoters in CMJ entreated program and music directors to provide feedback on the bands played, what were hits with fans, as well as pleading for airplay.[22]

Music directors embraced this role. One music director in Pittsburgh emphasized college radio as "still the only outlet for exposing innovative music, especially on indie labels" necessitating that they "always be experimenting." Being adventurous translated into real power. "We do have a significant impact on the industry," he remarked, "so why imitate others? Let's just be ourselves—entertaining and always unpredictable."[23]

Label reps praised stations for their close relationship with listeners and noted when college airplay broke an artist. They identified those that "should" be associated with college radio. A representative from Island Records marked Tom Waits as an artist who should be a college radio star. The rep announced in November 1983 in CMJ, "I hereby extend a challenge to college radio: make Tom Waits an artist of national importance!" Filling this commercial function would serve all parties, he argued, justifying institutional support.

Not all college stations played "new music," one music director explained. DJs joined to train for "real world" experience and learned to attend town council meetings, "take notes," and write "a comprehensive and comprehensible news story about it." Others learned the ropes as sports announcers. As he explained, "being at a small station with about 20 broadcasting majors leaves alot [sic] of room for practice and the station has a big enough budget to let me talk to record companies long enough to be turned down." He wanted connections to translate his small-town radio experience into lines on his résumé, but label representatives often ignored small stations. Students at these regional institutions, the music director argued, were there for a practical education. Unlike students at fancy liberal arts colleges or brand-name universities (he cited Temple University in Philadelphia as an example), he did not have the luxury to study abroad and find himself with an "experimester" in England or to play around on the radio. They wanted to learn "concrete things" for job preparation—as well as earn respect from the music industry.[24]

College radio's reputation of playing noncommercial music corresponded with universities' "ivory tower" reputation, often derided as elitist. The music director who emphasized college radio's practical applications read Tolstoy and Camus, but he advised the hot shots in college radio to remember they were there to learn. Another music director agreed. His commercial college station in Pullman, Washington, had to pay its own way without significant funding. Another music director appreciated service from A&M Records and RCA that kept her station afloat, along with the practical experience she gained in production, sales, and on-air techniques.[25]

College radio's growing market power turned up the volume on disapproving murmurs about selling out and the corruptive power of mainstream and major-label success. Media outlets keeping tabs on college radio charts, like CMJ and *Gavin Report*, knit together a national network and commercial relationships that granted cultural power to voices previously left out and nationalized the controversies present in college radio and local music scenes.

MTV may not always have lived up to its countercultural image, but it did provide *120 Minutes*, which debuted in 1986, for alternative music. Like *Rolling Stone*'s "College LP's" chart, the show drew its featured videos from the *Gavin Report*'s alternative chart.[26] This vehicle, along with college radio, propelled bands such as U2 to superstardom. It provided connection between the college radio "farm team" to the commercial music industry and mainstream audiences, solidifying college radio's place within the music industry—even if much of college radio resisted that role as major labels came calling.

The increase in corporate interest could not be ignored. New wave "sold out" to appeal widely, with fans emulating the style and seeking the music for cool credibility. College radio and indie rock aficionados scorned the corporatization of these avant-garde signals, but radio executives understood that new opportunities beckoned. While college radio developed real market influence, student participants developed valuable experience that often led to careers in the music industry. Many label representatives and promoters appearing in the pages of CMJ had been college DJs themselves. In 1983, Jim Cameron, a graduate of Lehigh University's college-station-turned-radio-consultant, explained "old fashioned radio" could compete with MTV for audience if it could "do what MTV can't." On airwaves free from commercial pressures, students could "experiment and evolve."[27] Even college radio's more commercially oriented stations maintained that iconoclasm and love of music for music's sake—and college radio's collective reputation influenced MTV in more ways than shaping the music heard on *120 Minutes* or *Yo! MTV Raps* (1987), hosted by former college DJs Matt Pinfield and Doctor Dré, respectively. But more students than these few DJs forged paths to MTV.

In 1984, Patti Galluzzi served as the general manager of Brown University's WBRU. The commercial station was established among the first collegiate FM signals along with other Ivy League institutions. It was popular, playing an eclectic mix of specialty programs and new wave music, with a good reputation in the community and among artists.

WBRU hit financial problems in the early 1980s. The independently governed station secured a loan from its host institution, hired a salesperson, and revitalized schedules to attract more advertising income. DJs moved from cramped, overcrowded studios to a larger space. They installed brand-new equipment and planned how to pay back the loan. Galluzzi and WBRU's leaders realized that the only way to increase revenue would be to implement greater consistency in programming.

Revamping WBRU was more fun than work. They would meet in Galluzzi's living room, then inevitably move to a local bar or restaurant. "Nobody wanted to leave," she remembered. They frequently stayed until last call, or even after.

This process, based in friendship and informal spaces, was still professional. They hired radio consulting firm Burkhardt and Abrams: with Lee Abrams, the noted radio consultant who had pioneered the album-oriented rock format for FM. Abrams's format developed consistency and music rotations, while keeping in mind that the station wanted to maintain its progressive identity. WBRU blended "cool progressive songs" with oldies from a deeper rotation than a traditional commercial FM station.[28]

Student programmers had to consider what was popular to remain viable and blended popular with cutting-edge music. It was hard, as one Brown University DJ explained: "Instead of finding out the coolest new music from New England, we're learning how to run a commercial radio station." The new format required "less risky new wave music, no urban funk (except on Sunday's *360 Degree Black Experience*), no heavy metal, and no cool oldies," in his view. It targeted a young, white male audience, as other commercial rock stations did.[29] But its reputation for quality and cool music endured, never fully leaving the college radio fold. WBRU promoted bands playing locally, even at smaller clubs, and DJs cued up imports on the show *The Final Frontier*, with its *Star Trek*–inspired promo.[30]

Galluzzi's experiences at WBRU proved invaluable. Galluzzi stayed on after graduation as a paid program director, learning the ropes to help sales with commercial production and client management. She remembered, "I couldn't believe I was making any money" doing something so fun. She watched R.E.M. debut at the station, orchestrating a ticket giveaway and knowing they would be huge, even though no one showed up at that event.

She trained her ear for quality music with wide appeal, seeing how WBRU could "create buzz" around new music. Label representatives gave DJs tickets and backstage passes to shows in Providence and Boston to see what might fit well into rotation. Labels appreciated WBRU playing their artists.

Some bands felt too corporate, in Galluzzi's view, such as Huey Lewis and the News. ("This is not cool," she thought.) Eventually she cued up the catchy songs. Listeners seeking Lewis might discover a new artist, or perhaps hear an old favorite from the Modern Lovers. And when Lewis broke into the Top 40, WBRU no longer felt an obligation to play him, instead focusing on the next breaking artist. Professional, commercially oriented signals to small, freeform stations learned how to identify and navigate their place in local radio markets and national popular culture, depending on their funding, staffing, position within their host institution, and connections to local music scenes.[31]

Galluzzi sensed WBRU's power to shape musical culture—a power that grew from DJs' freedom to play a broad cross-section of music based on their interests. DJs could "direct the way that music went," she remembered. The ear she developed shaped her career. From Brown, she moved to MTV, where she became vice president of music programming. She knew that R.E.M.'s 1990 video for "Losing my Religion" would be a hit, based on the sensibility she developed in walking the tenuous line between experimental and commercially viable at WBRU, while amplifying the local music scene. Many bands crossed over to mainstream success, similar to less-commercially driven college stations across the nation. By the mid-1980s, college radio's crossover reputation was strong—whether students on campus knew about it or not.[32]

The New Music Promotion Machine

Educational radio promised to cultivate an open, diverse, and accepting national culture, but alternative spaces remained valued. Participants wanted educational radio to nurture amateurs and preserve a network of musical creation free from the pressures of commercial success, whether it reshaped national culture or not. By 1983, college radio's dual roles as a farm team for the music industry and as a refuge for music that lacked broad commercial appeal were increasingly at odds.

In October that year, *Billboard* noticed a thriving Athens, Georgia, music scene. The B-52's success gave way to R.E.M., each proving they could headline "major shows" and leading other regional groups to the same success. Love Tractor and Pylon, too, revealed the success of a "new subculture" in development since the mid-1970s. As Love Tractor's guitarist described it, the culture started with a "party scene, in apartments, lofts, and houses," which migrated into venues such as the 40 Watt club. WUOG helped by putting local bands' tapes or EPs on heavy rotation. Bands used funds garnered by local record sales as "gas money for trips to New York." Touring helped launch R.E.M. to success. The band signed a record deal with I.R.S. in 1982. R.E.M.'s first single, "Radio Free Europe," cracked into the *Billboard* top 100 in 1983 at number seventy-eight. The band's first full-length album, *Murmur*, peaked at number two on CMJ's Progressive Radio Top 100 in 1983. *Reckoning*, released in summer 1984, went to number one on CMJ, and the single "South Central Rain" went to eighty-five on *Billboard*. Later albums would follow this crossover pattern, until the band signed with Warner Brothers in 1988 thanks to a national and international fanbase that would take the band into superstar status.

College radio exposed local artists signed to regional labels founded as scenes proliferated, including SST (Long Beach, California, 1978), Twin Tone (Minneapolis, 1977), Dischord (Washington, D.C., 1980), Homestead (Long Island, New York, 1983), and Sub Pop (Seattle, 1986). Labels might offer no promotional support, but word spread anyway. With bands based in regional scenes, college stations such as WUOG increasingly prioritized those bands in playlists and rotations or encouraged students to air only independent-label releases.[33] And with stations fostering the development of musical scenes such as Athens and Olympia, Washington, new artists developed supportive ecosystems and networks to get the word of their new releases to listeners who wanted to hear something new—and to buy it.[34]

Music directors from an array of college radio stations prioritized independent-label artists in the pages of CMJ in 1983 and 1984. At the University of South Carolina, a music director at the school's station considered it "our job to promote all those small starving independent labels just as we support the big ones." He appreciated thrash (a subset of heavy metal music) bands from Boston that generated controversy in the conservative state capitol. He prized their challenging sound and "infamous lyrics," but he wanted to promote small labels. He instructed labels that "don't have enough money to promote their music heavily" to "copy down our address." It was a meritocracy, he argued: "We give everyone a fair shot."[35] Another music director at a Newark, New Jersey, college station considered independent labels as a positive force in music. "Indies," he argued, "put out the best music for the right reasons."[36] This commitment to quality and music that would improve culture lent these sentiments a starry-eyed quality.

Yet it was still hard for independent labels to secure distribution for their albums, or for new bands to receive exposure because of undercapitalized independent labels. I.R.S. Records obtained distribution through major-label A&M for several artists. International holding company Faulty Products allowed I.R.S. to reach the United Kingdom and provided distribution for smaller independent labels. When Faulty Products closed in 1983, as a University of Virginia music director put it, "a gaping hole in the nationwide availability of US underground music" opened.

To bridge this gap in promotion and distribution for independent artists, or artists without record deals, college radio stations released self-made compilation tapes. WTJU in Charlottesville made history as the first station to air releases from hardcore-label Dischord Records. Led by one DJ in 1980, the station began playing tapes from hardcore bands, including those forming in the nearby music scene. By 1983, station leaders gathered bands from Virginia to include on a compilation to provide collective promotion. As WTJU's music director reported, "For some this is their first recorded appearance." Those on the compilation with albums "can't afford to promote them all over the country." WTJU produced the tape for radio stations only. With such tapes, music directors could hear a collection of new artists, complete with "addresses and pertinent info about releases." Charlottesville gained notoriety as a worthy music scene and potential destination for touring bands. Bands on the compilation could spread word cheaply about their releases and build a network of fans at stations airing their music. As WTJU's music director explained, "Awareness is what counts, there's a lot of good music we're all missing because it can't get distribution." College radio might not play all independent-label releases all the time, but their position within music scenes and connection to other stations meant they could disseminate information about local music.[37]

By late 1983, independent labels released more records. College stations could begin to consider featuring more artists without major-label contracts or distribution, as the number of releases increased and informational networks solidified. One music director in New Jersey expressed his station's willingness to "explore and expand the boundaries of a limitless college format" composed of independent-label releases.[38]

As students prepared to go home for Thanksgiving in 1983, college radio music directors considered their role in music culture. With the exposure they could provide, it seemed wasteful to devote airtime to bands that had developed wider popularity. New wave received coverage on MTV, and those artists signed to major labels. As a program director in West Hartford, Connecticut, put it, "Why should college radio stations push bands that are already getting played (make that, OVERplayed) on commercial stations?" He referred to former college radio staples such as the Police, Eurythmics, and Duran Duran. "Sure the music might be okay," he continued, "but shouldn't we be trying to expose people to other, less heard, more adventurous forms of music?" UB40 should receive more airplay, he argued. Another music director reported being "inundated" with new releases, allowing him to be "very selective about choosing adds" for a Pittsburgh station. Such sentiments resembled long-standing preferences in college radio for music not heard elsewhere or avoiding overplaying hits—but the structure of the music industry and college radio's place within it had transformed. College radio's autonomy to make those decisions seemed imperiled.

Music-label representatives wanted college radio to serve new music and create a groundswell of support for their artists, and they, too, promoted selectivity. Independent promoter Jack Isquith advised stations to repeat play for artists to break them. He challenged college radio to make New Order the band of 1984, turning the masses on to a "truly innovative band" as they had with U2 in 1983. College programmers had to "sacrifice" a bit of their freedom to be successful, Isquith advised. No artist would break through to the mainstream with one play a day, he cautioned. Breaking bands would "enhance your station image and industry standing while simultaneously increasing your student and community listenership."[39]

This increased attention on college radio's potential as a proving ground depressed many participants. At CMJ's Music Marathon convention that fall, a panel captured the more cautious trend in radio, as playlists narrowed to focus on generating advertising revenue. Still, as one music director responded, "I will never believe that creativity cannot exist concurrently with profitability in a viable format." College DJs recognized they had power, and they thought long and hard about how to use it. Yet the increasing pressure from media attention and the music industry generated fears of selling out. For DJs, that meant doing what labels told them to do, rather than building rotations and new music collections around what DJs wanted to play, the vibrancy of their local music scenes, and the musical service they wished to provide.

But for bands that began to break through thanks to college radio exposure, the conversation about "crossing over" and selling out proceeded differently.

The Embarrassment to Del Fuegos

The career of Brent "Woody" Giessmann encapsulated the process of crossing over and the controversy that sometimes came when a beloved band reached a mainstream audience. While the term "mainstream" remains fuzzy, it generally marks widely recognizable artists heard on commercial radio and MTV—a long way from the underground scenes that Giessmann navigated in his youth.

Giessmann started a band in high school called the Embarrassment. He had grown up near Wichita, Kansas, and by the early 1980s toured with his band through Texas and Oklahoma, to Kansas City and up to Chicago. The band benefited from the broad network that developed thanks to radio stations like KJHK at the University of Kansas and local music scenes.

Along for the ride were other bands they met on the circuit. The Embos, as their fans called them, cut an ironic sound poking fun at the "artistic party" crowd. They gained a large enough following to earn them the opening spot for Iggy Pop in Chicago and John Cale in Tulsa. Eventually, they opened for the Ramones.[40]

The group hated what its van's stereo picked up on midwestern radio. Band members avoided "Blondie, Donna Summer and Kenny Rogers," who experimented with or represented the dregs of disco on AM, whereas "FM radio is home to REO Speedwagon, Styx and Foreigner," which offered no innovations in rock music. And the diffuse midwestern touring circuit, with long distances between venues and scenes, made for a tough slog.[41]

Occasionally along for the ride was William S. Burroughs, the former Beat and postmodern, satirical author who hailed from Lawrence, Kansas. He had inspired countercultural and punk bands from Bob Dylan to Throbbing Gristle, dabbled in acting, and collaborated with musicians.[42] Burroughs started a small record label, Fresh Sounds of Middle America. That label released the Embos' first recording.

The tape circulated at college radio stations before its vinyl release. Stations provided booking information for gigs. Plus, Giessmann recalled, "they would feed us and they would put us up . . . because we didn't have enough money to pay for hotel rooms." They would "hang up our posters and take us to the record stores where we could leave some of our vinyl on consignment." College DJs provided both information and exposure. "They were our lifeline; it was the most important relationship to have" alongside fledgling record labels that put their music onto cassette or vinyl.

Other than the venues hosting these refugees from mainstream culture, college radio offered Giessmann help. DJs at the University of Kansas supported independent bands like the Embarrassment, he remembered. "They were like our lifeline, for god's sake." Reinforced by college radio and fanzines, news of the band spread after their seven-inch single "Sex Drive" made a "major splash."[43]

News of the Embarrassment spread to Boston—though members had no idea. "College DJs," Giessmann recalled, "would send out their lists" that included the band, "and eventually the Embarrassment had quite a nice little following." They sat in a band member's living room and put together cassettes to take on tour and mail out to college stations. The cassette, an assemblage of garage bands, garnered attention on the West Coast, earning attention from the Dead Kennedys and Black Flag, and "we started connecting with them through college radio and fanzines."

"We were four dorky guys from Kansas that didn't really have a scene," Giessmann remembered. "We had to develop our own. We were like these country bumpkins." It was "kind of like Buddy Holly and the Crickets turned up to sing." They drove hours to get to Kansas City to a record store where they could find hardcore recordings. "What the hell else are you going to do on the weekends in Wichita?" Giessmann recalled getting a bag of marijuana and jumping into a car to make the drive.

Eventually, the Embarrassment discovered new bands, met them on the road, and played shows, and their network expanded to include California's the Gun Club. The Embos received an offer to open for them in Boston. Giessmann explained, "We do this really cool gig with the Gun Club, but the opening act was a really excellent band that I fell in love with." After the set, the guitar player approached Giessmann and said, "Hey man . . . we really love your band and we're really glad that we can do the show together." Giessmann developed a liking for the Gun Club, even though the band sounded a bit untested. It had an "Elvis Presley or the Everly Brothers on LSD" look and sound, to Giessman's ear. The Gun Club's drummer played hubcaps, and was, to be frank, pretty terrible. But the band entertained.

The Embos moved on, occasionally returning to Boston to play.

With bills to pay and members drawn to other interests, the band split. It never attracted wide mainstream appeal, according to one assessment, because of an image that clashed with its sound. The band members were, writer Matt Wall remembered, "former art students concentrating more on sounding good than trying to puff up for the press shots." And "that image, their origins in the middle of the country far away from the hipster scenes on the coasts, and their strangely honest name," Wall explained, "conspired to make them almost unmarketable to a wider audience."[44]

Giessman, after seeing the Boston scene's vibrancy and dedicated fans, grew increasingly restless in Kansas. He was "frustrated as an artist and a musician," and he wearied of "trying to create something that already existed in Boston, which was a very supportive scene." Boston fans loved music, and all Giessmann wanted to do was "live and breathe music."

And so, he remembered, "I went on a two-week binge, and I woke up on an Amtrak train with a one-way ticket to Boston, like 300 bucks and the clothes on my back." He made a beeline to the Rathskeller in Kenmore Square, the venue that hosted touring punk and hardcore acts. A waitress he had met when the Embarrassment played was there.[45]

Lily Denison was "the queen" of the Boston scene. She knew promoters, managers, and all the bands coming through the Rat. She remembered Giessmann from his appearance with the Embos, and asked, "Well, what are you doing here?" Denison took him to a party and that night, where Giessmann played with the band he had admired on a previous trip—the Del Fuegos. The hubcap-playing drummer had taken some bad LSD and left the band. Giessmann was in the right place at the right time.

"Every drummer in town," he remembered, "wanted that gig."

The Del Fuegos, with Giessmann as their drummer, developed a strong sound and good reputation. Giessmann attributed his success to college radio. As he remembered it, "I'm in a position where I'd left this country bumpkin power-pop punk band in Kansas that did one radio single." College radio helped him transition to a new band, and that same network pulled through for the Del Fuegos. These "tastemakers" created a "new, upcoming world of new wave, punk rock, alternative music, whatever you want to call it," Giessmann explained. Community members and students created that network that nurtured the Boston music scene and others like it, from the small, isolated midwestern college towns to the coastal metropolises of Los Angeles, Seattle, Boston, and New York City.[46]

After Giessmann joined the Del Fuegos, the band spent the next few years traveling from city to city, radio station to radio station, recording interviews and performing live on air. Their broken-down, bluesy sound represented Boston's music scene that produced J. Geils, among others, rather than the hardcore of Washington, D.C., or Los Angeles. But they reached a national audience—and found some crossover success with a few singles, alongside contemporaries like the Replacements, R.E.M., and U2. Giessmann recalled a week when U2's *The Joshua Tree* topped every college radio list—save one, which had the Del Fuegos at number one. Although success meant college radio stations paid them less attention, the network had done its work.

"Every local band attached themselves to a local college radio station," Giessmann explained. DJs provided touring musicians a spot to sleep on apartment floors, shared "where to get the best barbecue, and if we're going to Chicago, they would tell us which radio stations to talk to." DJs could tell their friends and spread the word. DJs advised which stations and record stores to send singles to, while fanzines helped build a wider fanbase.[47]

The Del Fuegos signed with Warner Brothers, and a 1984 *Rolling Stone* critics poll named them one of the best new bands that year. In 1986, they returned to Boston to play—this time at a much larger venue than the Rat. *People* magazine noted the occasion. The band "slogged through three hard-scrabble years of playing summer camps, loft parties, beer halls and even a state prison," and succeeded. Their earnings had not followed suit, so the Del Fuegos agreed to let Miller beer use a song in a Super Bowl advertisement. The spot helped members get their first bank account, rather than carrying cash around in duffel bags.

R.E.M.'s Michael Stipe and Giessmann disagreed about the decision. Giessmann remembered, "It was a terrible commercial, but it put a huge check in our bank account so that we could maintain complete control in our lives." They didn't want Warner Brothers telling them what to do, so they considered it a strategic move to protect the band's independence—even if the college radio crowd and Stipe, who decried commercialism, did not agree.[48]

The Embarrassment, a cult favorite, epitomized the college radio scene of the early to mid-1980s. Yet as the decade wore on, the Del Fuegos charted the rise of the network of local scenes, radio stations, fanzines, and record stores and labels that sustained and promoted them. The band generated controversy, but not the kind that drew the scrutiny of culture warriors turning a jaundiced eye toward the lyrics of popular music.

· · · · · ·

Many University of San Francisco students remained unaware that KUSF, alongside other college radio stations, made waves in the music industry. "Some criticize it for not taking a more active role in the University community," a volunteer explained. "Some are not even aware it exists." The music industry recognized KUSF's value, though, named "best college radio station" by "two industry associations." KUSF earned credit for helping promote the 1986 Columbia Records release *A Different Light* by the Bangles and R.E.M.'s *Life's Rich Pageant*. During the station's tenth anniversary celebration in 1987, mayor Dianne Feinstein proclaimed KUSF Day in the city, bestowing a certificate of honor from the San Francisco Board of Supervisors for community service. USF's College of Arts and Sciences dean presented KUSF with the university's first "college service award," even if many students still would not recognize a lot of the music emanating from the signal they funded. KUSF helped Midnight Oil's *Diesel and Dust* reach sales of 500,000 copies, and CBS Records lauded the station for helping promote the album. Tom Simonson, director of college marketing for CBS New York, recognized college radio's "big impact" on music, and he presented KUSF with a gold record commemorating its value.[49]

The hits kept coming, along with gold records. Criticism emerged that college radio focused too heavily on established stars, new wave artists who had crossed over, or a usual roster of labels. Fears included music directors relying on the charts more for rotation adds than what DJs and listeners selected, adopting a self-referential echo chamber that undercut college radio's democratic potential. By 1988, *Billboard* debuted the Modern Rock chart, drawing hits from "new music"–focused commercial rock stations and select college radio stations such as WRAS at Georgia State and WRVU at Vanderbilt University, among others. College radio developed a sound and an association with guitar-driven rock that the industry sought to classify, chart, and award. (College radio charts in CMJ began to include rap and hip-hop as well by the mid-1980s, but the industry was slower to recognize this emerging genre.) By 1990, many music directors did take their cue from the charts, which coincided with major labels investing more in their alternative departments. Despite trends and fears, most bands college radio promoted did not make it to superstardom.[50]

With graduates heading to careers in the music industry and MTV and with stations providing a pipeline to the mainstream for musical acts, cultural observers turned a sharp eye toward college signals. College radio's network—an informational nexus that spread news of the next most important band in the world from scene to scene—garnered mainstream press attention, and the music industry incorporated stations into its business model.

Commercial appeal sharpened the adversarial relationship between college stations valuing their iconoclastic reputation and major-label music, leading to suggestions that DJs avoid any band with a contract other than with an independent. College radio's participants recognized their role in promoting those bands, which often lacked promotional funds or major-label distribution. College radio provided an alternative market and network for their dissemination.

Yet the tussle for control of these stations raised unavoidable questions regarding which groups and communities these local outlets served.

Students at the helm of radio shows during the Reagan years, often with significant freedom to select music and content, proved to be dicey at times. Multiple claimants sought these valuable signals beyond major labels hungry for the next big thing. Media consolidation accompanied governmental deregulation of industries that included media, leading more communities and interests to look to the noncommercial FM spectrum for access to and representation on the public airwaves. These signals were valuable real estate on the electromagnetic spectrum, and the 1980s saw significant national attention turn toward their role—generating controversy as well as praise for cultural service.

High-profile US Senate hearings testified to the controversial nature of music on offer from the mainstream music industry. Powerful stations in the hands of a rebellious college student could produce hefty fines and public outrage, particularly amid the intensifying culture-war battles that raged over cultural expression and indecency. At least, that is what the University of California, Santa Barbara, discovered when a listener sought the help of Tipper Gore and the Parents' Music Resource Center in 1985, sending shock waves reverberating across college stations, many of which could not afford the controversy heaped on KCSB.

8   College Radio in the Political Spotlight

· ·

Nathan Post loved KCSB. Nonetheless, in 1985 and 1986 the thirty-two-year-old continually complained to his alma mater, University of California, Santa Barbara, about his "beloved" station. He stamped letters bound for the studio, UCSB's chancellor, the UC system president, and California's governor requesting that KCSB institute "guidelines" to "maintain a minimum of decency" in its content. Longtime general manager at KCSB Malcolm Gault-Williams repeatedly asserted the station's rules and "good judgement."[1]

Post persisted. He accumulated evidence of KCSB's offensive and socially damaging content on tape. Its 500 watts of power broadcast far, thanks to a tower located on a nearby hill, exposing potentially hundreds of thousands of listeners to its sounds. Post's outrage at one show's content prompted him to send a tape to a newly founded resource for some guidance: the Parents Music Resource Center's (PMRC) headquarters near Washington, D.C.

As a devout Roman Catholic and self-described "environmentalist Republican," Post viewed danger in these filthy songs luring young listeners. Reagan-appointed FCC chair Mark Fowler failed to clean up immorality on publicly accessible media, Post complained. "The airwaves," he protested, "are turning into a sewer under his leadership." Fowler's media deregulation promoted social decline, Post insinuated, echoing concerns of media watchdog organizations such as Morality in Media, a conservative group in New York.[2]

Tipper Gore and the PMRC offered Post the assistance he demanded.[3]

UCSB students paid little attention to what Post flagged for concern. But when Susan Baker, Tipper Gore, and other "Washington wives" formed the PMRC, they took notice. The organization emerged out of National Parent/ Teacher Association concerns regarding sexually explicit lyrics, or references to drug use, the occult, or violence. PMRC members demanded enforcement of pornography laws, contending that some lyrics could be interpreted as distributing sexual material to minors. PTA members contacted politically influential figures, namely, the wives of business moguls and powerful members of the Reagan administration and the US Congress across the partisan aisle. Seventeen well-connected women organized to "inform parents" about rock lyrics in May 1985.[4]

In indecency cases, courts generally deferred to local norms to adjudicate content. Gore's support amplified complaints such as Post's to the FCC's attention, nationalizing the organization's culture-war battle—putting UCSB in the spotlight alongside shock-jock Howard Stern. Gault-Williams remarked, "We (KCSB) could be at the wrong place at the right time in terms of the national political climate." His concerns proved prescient. Scarcity in radio signals, a common rationale to justify regulatory oversight and ensure public service, surfaced regarding indecency in broadcasting. "I would not want to see the station shut down for one minute," Post told the UCSB newspaper. He simply requested that they "clean up the airwaves a little" so the station could continue valuable public service programming.

Prominent debates arose regarding curricula as scholarship expanded to include minorities and women, and the culture wars came for college radio, too. Scholars such as Alan Bloom decried how social changes since the sixties challenged "epistemological foundations" of an older academic order while resisting "vocational" metrics applied to university learning.[5] The "canon wars" at Stanford University grabbed headlines, and PMRC hearings featured prominent rockstars, overshadowing the scrutiny cast on college radio. Post's penchant for letter writing generated waves far beyond the sunny shores of Santa Barbara, California, and complemented these trends.

As college radio's reputation grew in the music industry, and stations sought listeners who might supplement declining funding, the ire of culture-war hawks had damaging implications. College students might not pay much attention to curricula controversies elsewhere, but they did care about matters on their own campuses. For KCSB, Post's complaints were part of a series of "nearly catastrophic" events that threatened the station's identity amid a funding crisis and signaled how academic freedom, media, free speech, and politics intertwined in the 1980s.[6]

The Long History of Policing Obscenity in College Radio

UCSB administrators set a precedent of siding with student media's independence during the free speech movement of the 1960s. Court rulings regarding student media's independence reinforced these interpretations. The idea that student radio constituted protected student speech informed how administrators responded to Post's complaints and the ensuing furor.

College radio was a place of learning, and it showed. KCSB broadcast Black Panther leader Bobby Seale's address to the campus in November 1968. Operators attempted to censor any words deemed offensive. A UCSB student carped that the DJ at the controls "deleted by a fade-out system" key parts of Seale's address. The FCC prohibited certain words, but, the student pointed out, "'penis' and 'vagina' are not on that list but they were nonetheless fade-out victims." Incompetence rather than malice seemed to be the culprit. "Whoever was at the controls must have been a real dunderhead," the complaint continued. "Not only did he delete significant portions which simply could not have been all obscenities, but he let a couple of 'f—ks' and 'bulls—ts' by." Observers concluded that the station was not likely to "buck the FCC's bureaucratic morality," and KCSB could be considered "castrated" like the speech it had butchered.[7] No FCC action emerged, as the body pursued very few obscenity cases, but the tense nature of on-campus protest led to scrutiny on student broadcasts as they reported live from protests and speeches.

Adherence to objectivity and balance extended to coverage of campus politics. KCSB aired the speeches of Senate candidates, interviews with César Chavez amid the Delano grape strike, and a conservative campus group. KCSB's programs ventured into freeform and psychedelic rock, concurrent with trends in 1960s FM rock radio. The station cued up listener requests from Jefferson Airplane and the Velvet Underground, linking the West Coast psychedelic and New York City art world scenes.[8]

Nathan Post's complaints in 1985 were not the first time KCSB clashed with outside attempts to police student radio. In 1969, at a rally KCSB recorded and broadcast, a "four-letter Anglo Saxon word for sexual intercourse" reportedly aired. Two individuals complained, and deputies descended on campus to seize program tapes for evidence of radicals violating obscenity laws. Officers appeared at KCSB's offices and told general manager Michael Bloom "obscenity laws had been violated by one or more speakers at the rally." The station was not in trouble with the FCC; the *speakers* were in trouble with the cops. Deputies demanded the tapes—without a warrant—and word spread across campus of the encounter. Black Student Union (BSU) and Students for a Democratic Society (SDS) representatives, who had organized the event, convened at the station, followed by the vice chancellor and UCSB's manager of safety and security services.

At the studio, campus affiliates squared off with county law enforcement. A deputy indicated that he "coincidentally" arrested BSU leader and poet Vallejo Kennedy for violating probation. Kennedy, a student in the Budd

Schulberg Writers Program, led the rally.[9] In what appeared to be a quid pro quo, deputies demanded the tapes in exchange for Kennedy's release. When Bloom refused, deputies took Kennedy to the local police station to be processed.[10]

The district attorney's office denied any knowledge of complaints and indicated that tapes would not be necessary in an obscenity case. Tensions remained high at UCSB. After police left with Kennedy, BSU, SDS, communications, and administration representatives convened to discuss the incident. All parties supported Bloom's decision to not release the tapes to law enforcement, since the broadcast involved university and student activities.[11]

Lines between civil society and campus remained unclear. The vice chancellor warned students "that the idea of the University campus being inviolate from civil law was a myth."[12] BSU members did not ask for their statements to be aired and taped, and they took place in the campus's free speech zone. Bloom's refusal to release the tapes leveraged legal processes and jurisdiction rather than making a statement defending obscenity as free speech.[13]

UCSB students considered college radio broadcasts to be protected by students' rights to free speech on campus, as with the student newspaper—although that organ replaced curse words with dashes, a difficult blurring to accomplish with live broadcasts.[14] Student radio and the station's campus focus, they believed, should protect the station from external pressure, even from the FCC, while radio participants remained wary.[15]

Questions regarding obscenity tested competing visions of political speech and the boundaries between the university and wider community. At UCSB, the campus maintained its jurisdiction over student reporting, in this case the tapes of a rally. Administrators rejected outside efforts to influence the content and practices of a student activity, even if that activity had an FCC license and broadcast on the public airwaves. As few members of the listening audience complained, no FCC action emerged. As with obscenity law broadly, local preferences took precedence.

Deference to students' free speech and campus protections weakened during the 1970s through a series of cases occurring beyond sunny Santa Barbara. The FCC influenced university administrations to take control of their radio programming beyond eliminating four-letter words from broadcasts. In addition to ending the class D license, a range of methods encouraged or frightened administrations to clean up their stations' schedule, professionalize the airwaves, and exert control over student broadcasting as more signals reached wider audiences.

Student print media received greater protections than radio. Student speech in campus publications received federal court protection with 1970's *Antonelli v. Hammond*, in which Judge Arthur Garrity ruled that a university president could not censor the printing of a student newspaper that contained an Eldridge Cleaver essay and four-letter words.[16] Protections such as *Antonelli* did not extend to FCC-licensed college radio stations—licenses often held by the trustees or university presidents, not the students or the faculty whose voices they amplified.

A year after the *Antonelli* ruling, students at C. W. Post College on Long Island occupied their campus studio for weeks on end. They protested the firing of the general manager, a former Pacifica radio employee, who had taken the station in a progressive direction. Anti–Vietnam War statements, feminist and queer activist causes, and other left-leaning political content as well as countercultural music aired.[17]

Students called on civil-liberties legal icon William Kunstler, who had recently defended the Chicago Seven in their trial after the protests during the 1968 Democratic National Convention. The New York lawyer donated his time to defend the radio station, but the judge threw out the case. Protections for student free speech, such as those being decided in *Antonelli*, did not involve the airwaves, which were regulated by FCC rules.[18]

During the 1970s, when the FCC temporarily revoked the University of Pennsylvania's radio license for allowing students free rein, the FCC had made it clear that universities, as license holders, needed to keep stations in check.[19] Most stations receiving FCC warnings violated logging procedures or technical requirements; no fines or license suspensions for obscenity occurred.

New concerns brought politics and regulators to campuses in the 1980s. Culture warriors took explicit aim at college curricula and scholarship as they feared the decline of teaching of the "canon" of Western civilization. With the attention of concerned Washington wives trained on popular music, college radio would not be exempt from their scrutiny. Amateurism and a commitment to educational radio provided no cover in this new environment. The PMRC drew national attention to lyrical content, while some scholars, such as Bloom, as well as pundits decried the "moral relativism" of university teachings. The culture wars turned attention to all aspects of university education, questioning the civic and social implications for the education on offer—including that broadcast by students over the airwaves.[20]

Making Bacon and the Politics of the Eighties

The tape Nathan Post sent to the PMRC contained a song that raised the hackles of culture warriors. "Making Bacon" by British punk band the Pork Dukes contained "imaginative euphemisms for oral and genital intercourse and the male sexual organ," as reported by the *Los Angeles Times*. Although the song did not contain any of the forbidden "seven dirty words" attributed to the 1978 *Pacifica* Supreme Court ruling that offered guidelines for defining indecency (although the ruling did not specifically prohibit certain words), few critics found any redeemable content in the song. Indeed, one critic called it "the most vulgar, offensive, rude, disgusting, infantile, noxious load of puerile rubbish ever released commercially."[21]

The song might not have been a hit with critics, to say the least, but its devoted fanbase and community were in on the joke. The Pork Dukes resembled hardcore bands that made their own music and scenes in the early 1980s, with signature raunchy humor and satire. They disparaged the cultural politics the PMRC represented. Even if "kids with little power" could not overthrow those they hated, they received a lot of attention, prompting fretting while their network proliferated.[22] In the suburbs, backyard parties featuring skateboarders and hardcore kids dispersed "young male anxiety" beyond private confines, helped along by college radio shows and DJs scattered across the nation. This DIY culture in which kids made their own music and informational network of zines and local radio shows garnered national attention by 1984.[23]

KCSB participated in this network while remaining a community-oriented station reaching from "Ventura to San Luis Obispo."[24] Its news coverage and rock music rotation resembled those of other college stations, punctuated by weekend specialty shows such as *Soul Cell*, a group of DJs seeking "to provide quality music of diverse nations" featuring "the music of Africans in the West" and "Chicano-Latino music." KCSB aired syndicated public affairs programs and featured local politicians and fielded views on community issues.[25] Listener donations and a series of new wave benefits provided vital funding as budgets tightened in the early 1980s.[26] KCSB's schedule left room for rock music commonly associated with college radio. In 1982, a DJ interviewed "band of the 80s" the Pretenders on air.[27]

KCSB navigated the many roles that college stations played in communities and on campuses. UCSB's student government targeted KCSB for funding reductions, as many students demanded a more campus-oriented, rather than community-oriented, signal. Station managers sometimes paid little attention to antics, such as playing the Pork Dukes before 10 P.M., or were lackadaisical when it came to other FCC rules regarding logs, the public file, or equipment. Any violation, not just obscene content, could lead to an FCC fine.[28]

Whether KCSB kept its logs up to date did not concern many students, but national developments regarding pop culture did. They deliberated the PMRC's intentions, with evaluations registering somewhere between inefficacy and hypocrisy. Parents could screen objectionable content, a UCSB student explained, by reading lyrics printed on the album cover. In addition, "The group wants record companies to permanently affix letter-coded labels to the inner jackets of records."[29] Musicians did not "subject" young people to hypersexual or violent content against their will, students argued. No, "rock groups are merely a response to what society wants." Such market-based logic prevailed during Reagan's decade, yet the PMRC debate revealed deeper cultural tensions regarding media and artistic expression percolating to the national level.[30]

Senate Commerce Technology and Transportation Committee hearings investigated PMRC claims that pornography and obscenity threatened America's youth on September 19, 1985. The symbolic hearing—since the committee considered no pending legislation, only recommendations for action—revealed the PMRC's influence. A spectacle emerged. Frank Zappa, Twisted Sister lead Dee Snider, and folk singer John Denver testified, opposing the proposed measures. But Recording Industry Association of America (RIAA) representatives took seriously the PMRC's charge to clean up the industry, eventually yielding the infamous "Parental Advisory" stickers and voluntary cooperation from labels.[31]

Although the group received ridicule as scolding prudes, complicated details produced gray areas. No clear partisan pro- or anti-censorship dividing line emerged, despite the outrage percolating in surrounding public debates. Some college students agreed with labeling and lyric publication, while others insisted the labels relied on subjective judgements.[32] The PMRC paid lip service to voluntarism and individual choice while excoriating expressions they disdained. The PMRC, and Gore in her testimony, did not advocate for outright censorship via law. Instead, Gore invoked consumer choice in pursuit of public goods. As she explained, "We are simply asking that these corporate and artistic rights be exercised with responsibility, with sensitivity, and some measure of self-restraint, especially since young minds are at stake."[33]

Even Dee Snider, avowed defender of freedom of expression and subjective interpretation of lyrics, admitted to the committee's chair, Senator Ernest "Fritz" Hollings, that Congress empowered the FCC to regulate the airwaves. Snider distinguished between content on broadcast media and what individual consumers chose to purchase for private listening. The hearings addressed matters related to album production and sales prohibitions, not the public airwaves.

UCSB students watching all this unfold could not predict how the national conversations around censorship and broadcasting would fall on their institution, knowing nothing of Nathan Post's taping of songs on KCSB. The spectacle of long-haired rocker Dee Snider sparring with senators and Washington wives overshadowed the PMRC's other activities: providing resources for listeners who wanted to complain about offensive songs played on radio.

Nathan Post made the connection. He demanded UCSB act on behalf of public interest and control its radio station. That summer and fall, he wrote many letters citing music he found offensive and obscene, eventually earning the attention of UC's president.

University administrators supported KCSB, allowing it to determine policy and programming without administrative interference, citing decades of court decisions limiting administrators' ability to intervene in the content of student-run media. At first, Post's letters received little attention at the station or from the university, whether from inattention or a laissez-faire attitude about content among station managers. Eventually, the university did respond and insisted student media had independence. University counsel cited the 1970 *Antonelli* ruling prohibiting universities from censoring student media paid for with university funds. In a three-page letter in November 1985, UCSB reiterated the "stringent" definition of obscenity and the FCC's limited power to censor.

"I recognize that this must be disappointing to you," the counsel told Post, but UCSB would not be firing anyone or taking over the station.[34]

Post turned to the PMRC. In July 1986, he contacted Tipper Gore at the organization's Alexandria, Virginia, headquarters and pointed his finger at DJ Eric Stone, who played "what I'll term Raunch," Post explained. Stone included "at least two extremely vulgar, sexually explicit songs" on each Saturday evening show before the start of "safe harbor" hours at 10:00 P.M.

Post found songs "liberally sprinkled with the word 'fuck' or one of a number of variations thereof." Stone felt protected by his show's time slot, but "Making Bacon" aired around 9:30 P.M. Post insisted that listeners "of all ages" could hear it and emphasized that media should "promote sound moral values," arguments that garnered PMRC attention.

Post highlighted excerpts from "Making Bacon" for Gore: "Come here baby, make it quick, kneel down there and suck on my dick. Making bacon is on my mind. Making bacon is on my mind, turn around [baby] let me take you from behind." For good measure, he included the line, "I'm only sucking city boys again."

As Post noted, he had "written the station about these lyrics, the Chancellor, the Governor, the FCC, the President of the University, all to no avail." He concluded, "The FCC is obviously not performing its job." He included his tape and pleaded for help.[35]

The university's vice chancellor took up the task of responding. He wrote to Susan Baker, wife of James A. Baker III, and of the PMRC, who registered her concerns in August 1986 after reading Post's letter. The vice chancellor forwarded Baker the counsel's previous response to Post and asserted that KCSB's bar for obscenities was higher than the FCC's, and he highlighted internal disciplinary mechanisms. This "internal local process" was "much more efficient than reporting alleged violations to the FCC," he argued. Administrators merely passed complaints on to the station. UCSB's administration, in other words, was bowing out.[36]

The same week, however, the FCC announced an investigation into KCSB's programming, thanks to a tip from Tipper Gore. The UC Board of Regents, which held the station's license, had thirty days to "respond to concerns raised by Santa Barbara resident Nathan Post that KCSB aired potentially harmful material."[37] One listener complaint, it seemed, could garner attention of federal regulators and university regents alike.[38]

After reviewing KCSB's bylaws and obscenity definition, as well as the broadcasts' time of day, the advisory board overseeing the campus station declined punishment. DJ Eric Stone agreed to play music such as "Making Bacon" only after 10 P.M. Adhering to the safe harbor regulations should solve the problem: the university's job was not to adjudicate First Amendment protections. As one board member asserted, "The Supreme Court and FCC can't define obscenity. We can't either." The member suggested simply, "Tell programmers not to rebel so much." Another member responded, "This is censorship," while others saw the matter as a tempest in a teapot. They feared jeopardizing their FCC license, but they agreed that the station would receive no fine. Further complaints would mean stricter penalties, however. The meeting concluded with another board member reminding KCSB of station manager and program director responsibilities.

"Why are we here?" he asked.[39] The entire exercise seemed pointless when the station already took steps to curb further infractions.

The UCSB community supported the station. Student newspaper editors scoffed at Post's busy letter writing, though they respected his right to an opinion. One incensed student defended KCSB. If regulated, she argued, KCSB would "become one more generic Santa Barbara radio station that I and other . . . fans find repulsive."[40]

KCSB's business went on as usual as the FCC's bureaucratic wheels slowly turned. Some students objected to the ending of *Gay and Lesbian Perspectives* on KCSB that fall when no personnel could be found for it—raising concerns that the station weakened commitments to alternative programming and voices.[41] Jello Biafra of the Dead Kennedys appeared at a local venue with a spoken-word performance in January 1987. In an interview with the student newspaper, he reflected on the PMRC, chastising complacency. Punk, like society, had grown soft. "That always happens," he argued, "whenever any kind of underground revolt gets widespread enough to become absorbed into consumer culture." Apathy posed a larger problem than federal regulators, as bothersome as they were.[42]

Still, federal regulators could be pretty annoying. That April, FCC commissioner Fowler rendered judgment against four radio stations. KPFK received the harshest punishment for airing the play *Jerker* and its descriptions of sexual acts. The FCC referred the matter to the Justice Department for prosecution under obscenity law.[43] "Shock Jock" Howard Stern earned a Philadelphia station airing his syndicated show a slap on the wrist, though the originating station in New York received no complaints. KCSB received a warning, but no fine.[44]

The rulings accompanied new guidelines: *Indecency Enforcement Standards* (2 F.C.C. Cd.2726 1987) regarding indecent content on the airwaves. After *Pacifica*, the FCC targeted the broadcasting obscenities, such as the "seven dirty words," and recommended indecent content be limited to after 10 P.M. The rules signaled the regulatory agency's more activist position, punishing broadcasts of "explicit, offensive descriptions of sexual or execratory activities" beyond the narrower obscenity focus of the previous decade. Material with a "generic definition of broadcast indecency" might violate rules whose vague language about the malleability of the safe harbor hours opened an interpretive gray area. "Safe harbor" hours allowed edgy content when it was unlikely to reach minors, but it remained unclear what that meant, exactly.[45]

This episode represented one small skirmish in a much broader legislative and judicial conflict regarding government regulation and enforcement of indecency limits—all of which took place, seemingly ironically, in an era moving toward media deregulation. Yet deregulation promoted the corporate ownership of media across format and market, serving to cater content for specific demographics and audiences. Deregulation's proponents, which included members on both sides of the political aisle, saw such changes through the lens of efficiency. Media companies, without burdensome limits on ownership, the idea went, would be able to respond to consumer demand more nimbly catering content to specific tastes. Such logic comported with the PMRC's, which spoke the language of consumer choice and empowerment. Empowering consumers meant giving them what they wanted—including transparent information about the content of their, and their children's, entertainment purchases. Regulation increasingly supported a consumer-oriented and market-oriented rationale. And in the context of the culture wars, that rationale extended to questions of indecency. Album ratings reconciled culture warriors' embrace of the marketplace and consumer choice with their concerns regarding what consumers might elect to buy. In broadcasting, regulatory structures should support what consumers wanted, and thus in an era of increasing concern on both left and right about content, expansion of restrictions in this area matched consumer activism and responded accordingly.

Requirements would fall on noncommercial and commercial broadcasters alike, although questions arose as to whether safe-harbor hours should be more lenient for noncommercial stations. Press outlets widely reported that the FCC had tightened indecency guidelines. A series of court cases and congressional action reaffirmed and expanded the government's "prurient interest" in regulating indecent content to protect children's welfare and "the home against intrusion by offensive broadcasts." Longer-term developments weakened the provisions.[46] But the 1987 rulings produced a chilling effect. Stern and KCSB escaped fines or prosecution, but future enforcement could levy a $2,000 fine for each offense or result in license revocation. College and community radio stations, with limited budgets, feared the hefty fines that could result.

After this ruling, student broadcasters could not count on the rationale administrators used in the KCSB case regarding protected student expression. FCC Mass Media Bureau chief James McKinney asserted, "Students have no First Amendment rights as broadcasters." Only the license holder had those. Gault-Williams saw this as a farce, asking, "How does the licensee one, balance its obligations under federal law as a radio licensee and two, at the same time how does it guarantee students that it does not control student expression," which legal precedent established? The station existed primarily to educate students and to help them discover their voice—a benefit of liberal arts education.

KCSB volunteers feared what would come next. When Fowler, who resisted censorship, left the FCC, DJs feared that his replacement, Dennis Patrick, would not be so lenient. "Over the past six years," one student wrote, "the Reagan administration has provided a comfortable climate for the growth" of watchdog groups like the PMRC that sought "censorship and denial of any material they feel does not conform to . . . rigid views of morality and decency." In the ruling, Patrick made the intent clear, stating, "What we are doing here today is to correct an altogether too narrow interpretation of decency," with chilling enforcement mechanisms put in place.[47]

Members of student media pushed for autonomy and for UC's regents to fight back on behalf of student free speech.[48] The Associated Students Legislative Council, too, defended KCSB, passing a bill opposing censorship and demanding legal action. It wasn't clear how the warning would affect KCSB's programming going forward. A cartoonist for the student newspaper published an image of DJs limiting songs to staid offerings from Pat Boone, Lawrence Welk, and Wayne Newton (figure 8.1).[49]

DJs feared the administration might issue a list of banned records, despite the support KCSB had received throughout the process. Instead, offices charged with oversight reviewed the station's by-laws and procedures—something they had done in response to Post's original complaints in 1985—and found little to alter. Nathan Post thought the warning was fair, though he carped that the FCC "could have done a lot more," especially since the other stations in the ruling received fines and criminal charges.

Eric Stone, the DJ who cued up the Pork Dukes, rolled his eyes. The whole thing had grown way out of proportion. Howard Stern repeatedly uttered four-letter words on air during morning drive time.

"I didn't say anything," Stone said. "I just played a record."[50]

In the next election for student leaders, candidates confronted increasing student involvement and keeping KCSB student-run—not censorship or lists of banned records.[51] Students continued to complain that the station, with its musical fare and community programs, did not do enough to satisfy students' tastes, and funding remained scant as managers sought alternative forms of revenue, such as underwriting.[52]

FIGURE 8.1 This cartoon appeared in the *Daily Nexus*, the student newspaper at the University of California, Santa Barbara, depicting KCSB's future if censors had their way. *Daily Nexus*, April 21, 1987, 8. Regents of the University of California.

Post remained a KCSB fan, occasionally showing up at the station in between his shifts at Florsheim Shoes. "He's really thrown me," Stone told the *Los Angeles Times* in August 1987, when a reporter followed up on the matter. "Recently he's been coming by the station like he's our friend after all of this and talks about getting involved," Stone reported. Post even asked for his own show. He really liked music; he just had concerns about what might reach kids. But his attention annoyed DJs.[53]

The PMRC offered a nationally prominent vehicle for Post's personal crusade.[54] In a way, Post secured involvement in radio, though KCSB rebuffed him. His mission sent chilling shock waves across college radio in the late 1980s, culminating in complicated questions regarding content, coverage, and representation.

The Chilling Effect

College radio participants across the nation took note of KCSB's brush with the PMRC. In November 1986, Intercollegiate Broadcasting System (IBS) president Jeff Tellis addressed the matter in a newsletter. Broadcasting "offensive" language presented "somewhat more of a problem for college radio than traditional commercial broadcasters," as college stations tended to "feature alternative, experimental, and controversial programming." In other words, college radio's iconoclasm and attention to avant-garde and often politically oriented music put it in the crosshairs of culture warriors. Tellis noted loosening of standards on everyday speech while broadcasting faced a higher bar of acceptable expression. Defining that bar proved difficult "as long as people don't think alike."[55] The FCC shied away from direct regulation of content in KCSB's case, but caution grew.

Tellis cautioned against UCSB's rationale that KCSB broadcasts constituted student publications. Instead, based on the WXPN case in the 1970s, the FCC ruled "just the opposite." Control rested in the license holder, usually the trustees or university president. Licensees' ownership was symbolic, with trustees usually having very little do to with station management, but the FCC did not excuse them from their responsibilities. "The FCC," Tellis explained, "has traditionally considered licensee control as one of the foundations of its regulatory philosophy and is unlikely to change this view." The system relied on forcing license holders to ensure robust oversight on what students broadcast on the university's licensed media.

The situation "generated widespread publicity," the IBS observed. Administrators paid attention and sought to avoid negative press coverage. Tellis cautioned, "That's one way it could affect you."[56]

Stations heeded warnings. At WRAS at Georgia State in Atlanta, DJs highlighted Tellis's memo to emphasize licensee control. Broadcasters could no longer assume that the FCC or license holders would exempt material broadcast at 2 A.M.[57]

College stations feared fines and exercised extreme caution. Violations would go into an FCC file, to be reviewed upon license renewal. Such documents could prove "very damaging," Tellis warned, especially with increasing competition for FM signals. Some might feel freer if they were in a radio market without significant numbers of institutions or organizations applying for signals. The Pacifica Foundation appealed the warning it received in 1987 for this reason: it did not want to risk losing the valuable property on the FM spectrum.[58]

Each station weighed its circumstances defensively, and gloom crept across the nation's collegiate broadcasters. In 1988, the future for challenging musical content did not seem bright. Congress eliminated safe harbor rules until a court vacated the law. Republican legislators slipped language requiring indecency enforcement twenty-four hours a day into an appropriations bill, which college students saw as a concerning sign of things to come, even if eventually ruled unconstitutional.[59] For station managers considering do-not-play lists and rules about safe harbor hours or content restrictions, "Obviously," Tellis told them, "you've got to decide that for yourselves." For those pushing musical and content boundaries, "you should use the admittedly fuzzy definitions . . . to try to categorize any material that may be called into question." Regarding indecent material, "it may be aired, but preceded by a cautionary announcement and not at a time of day when there is a reasonable risk that children may be in the audience." Tellis cautioned, "In reality, that may mean not at all."[60]

Few station managers wanted to be the reason their signal received a hefty fine or license revocation. They issued stringent warnings and explicit rules for DJs, pasted on control boards or studio doors. DJs chafed at these rules, while station leaders feared another Steve Post armed with a tape recorder. "All of this," the music director at Rice University's KTRU put it, "is done in the name of protecting our children's tender little ears." While the Senate clashed during the summer of 1987 over the appointment of conservative judge Robert Bork to the Supreme Court, college radio DJs worried that their constitutional protections for free speech and their institutional space to explore experimental music and expression atrophied. National trends in politics seemed allied against them. A Rice student referenced Supreme Court justice William Brennan's dissent in the *Pacifica* decision that echoed an earlier ruling, stating, "One man's profanity is another man's lyric." The student noted this was "a sentiment, by the way, which Supreme Court nominee Robert Bork has publicly ridiculed." But the lever on limiting expression came down to licensee control and tight budgets of noncommercial, educational stations.[61]

Money shaped decisions at stations without strict administrative intervention. Even independent college stations felt pressure. These included WMBR at MIT, where the independent Technology Broadcasting Corporation (TBC) owned the license. In April 1987, a DJ pasted an article from the *Boston Globe* into the log of station communications explaining the FCC's new policy. Underneath the article the DJ wrote, "It might be a good idea if we decide to be a little cautious about what we play until we receive some clarification on this from our lawyers. . . . Stay tuned."[62]

Another DJ responded, "FUCK THAT!"[63]

WMBR's leaders concurred with their oversight board and protected the station's financial interests. The TBC took several months to develop a new obscenity policy. In a memo to volunteers, the program director and general manager explained the new rules. "Because of all this FCC'ing," the pair explained, they unveiled *The Official Station Policy Governing Indecency and Obscenity, etc. etc.* WMBR could not "afford a legal battle with the FCC." They apologized for the vagueness of their public notice, explaining, "Until the FCC makes it more clear what's acceptable and what's not, we're asking everyone to keep things less than radical." DJs should "keep things safe"; in other words, "'safe sex is good sex' or 'no sex is good radio.'"[64]

Concurrently, the TBC explored adding a repeater to WMBR, equipment that would extend its signal to a wider geographic area. On the surface, these two plans had little to do with one another, but directors considered them inextricable. The TBC's lawyer stated that the new obscenity policy would be "one of conservatism." It would be strict "not because we wish to inhibit anyone's right of free speech, but because we cannot afford to defend ourselves. We'd much rather spend the money on new equipment."[65] Outreach to the wider community trumped freedom of expression for DJs, and money ruled all. More coverage meant more listeners—and potentially more outrage.

Station managers deliberated what rules to enact. WMBR management reminded DJs to screen material, and questionable content needed to be cleared by the program director, general manager, or other appointed reviewers.[66] Some stations drafted new obscenity policies earlier—Princeton's station acted in 1985 to protect itself from potential fines—but these accelerated after the KCSB's reprimand. College stations usually reviewed content before airing it, with DJs or music directors affixing labels to the front of albums warning of a swear-word on song 2, side B, or a false stop that might cause a DJ to accidentally cut a song short.

After the FCC's statement, some bands such as the Dead Kennedys or Butthole Surfers, as well as hardcore and rap artists, disappeared from rotations. At WUSB at Stony Brook University on Long Island, the general manager insisted, "Nothing on our rotation is considered questionable." As a result, "the hippest radio station on Long Island" seemed significantly less cool. "College radio is at the forefront of doing things different," WUSB founder and station manager, as well as IBS board chair, Norm Prusslin explained. The resulting "chilling effect" from weighing any potential offense "stifles creativity" and college radio's experimental nature. The program director at the University of Vermont's WRUV limited artists from punk to hip-hop, "and that disturbs me a lot," he noted. An FCC attorney reported petitions from fifteen "broadcasters and media-related organizations" to review the ruling, but the chilling effect remained.[67]

· · · · · ·

KCSB's troubles were not over after the Pork Dukes debacle. As the station added programming to bolster its community appeal and supplement its coffers by attracting more listeners who might donate, a local twenty-seven-year-old house painter and political science student joined as a morning "shock jock." Sean Hannity had taken courses at New York University and Adelphi University, although it is unclear if he sought time on WNYU or WBAU. After moving to California and joining KCSB as a conservative radio host on a campus he decried for its "liberal fascism," Hannity had plenty to say.[68]

In April 1989, he and an anti-gay activist discussed the HIV/AIDS epidemic. Listeners called their rhetoric "dangerous falsehoods about the sexual practices of the gay communities and the means by which AIDS can spread." Hannity reportedly referred to gay people as "disgusting" and their supporters as "brainwashed." According to one account, he "egged on" his guest who suggested gay men transmitted AIDS because they "consumed each other's feces."[69] A local AIDS Community Assistance Program member called the comments "vicious and cruel."[70] Hannity responded that he welcomed "opposing viewpoints" on his shows, including from callers. He called the AIDS epidemic a "loss and tragedy" but expressed disapproval of "bizarre sexual behaviors."[71] KCSB responded by firing him.

Hannity sought the ACLU's help to fight the dismissal as an infringement of his rights. Although ACLU representatives renounced Hannity's views, the organization defended his utterances as protected speech. Hannity had received several warnings, but the station's governing board erred in firing Hannity for content rather than his conduct or the procedures by which he gained access to the airwaves, which would have been within their rights. First Amendment protections didn't apply to raunchy lyrics, but they did to political opinions.

Above all, the incidents with the PMRC and Hannity revealed how college radio's national profile and its expansion had changed matters. In the 1960s, KCSB defended itself against intrusion from external scrutiny by citing student broadcasting as an extension of campus. In the 1980s, student-run radio on the public's airwaves could not deny its external reach and significance. Hannity clearly cut against the station's dominant politics. Months after Hannity's departure, KCSB removed sponsorship from a fraternity event after station leaders accused the frat of homophobic discrimination. But running a federally regulated station meant adhering to considerations beyond dominant local standards of expression.[72]

KCSB offered to reinstate Hannity's eligibility. He had to reapply for his show like every other DJ. Station leaders rejected his application and refused to apologize as Hannity demanded. The programmers insisted Hannity's previous show had been approved via improper methods and did not meet station standards. His proposal had appeared as the Associated Students put KCSB's funding to a student-wide vote. A handful of station leaders sought public affairs programming that would boost ratings and therefore donations. In other words, his application appeared at a moment when leaders redirected programming for funding purposes, a change they came to regret.

Hannity regretted nothing, it seemed. When he received neither the apology nor a doubling of his former airtime as he requested, he left school and advertised his availability for radio work as "the most talked-about college radio host in America."[73]

DJs continued to regard surveillance for indecent content as an attack on free speech, but they did not see Hannity's program through the same lens. Hannity's defense of airing all viewpoints drew derision, as he had been known to hang up on callers with whom he disagreed. As KCSB sought to expand its reach and draw funds through listener support, some allowed that the station may need to compromise its ideals to cultivate a broader listening public. One student newspaper editorial pointed to KCSB's rock show that played "hardcore post-punk, stupid industrial moans or folk," complaining that "only a tiny percentage of people like that garbage" and those who did were too elitist to turn on the radio. The writer suggested KCSB "compromise a little in its idealism" and play some Led Zeppelin or Pink Floyd occasionally, or maybe some jazz. Hannity, the writer offered, was another good bet. The "quasi-Morton-Downey-Wally-George-Geraldo wannabe" offered a show that "wasn't as offensive as it could have been, but Sean was learning." Audiences liked that "he acted like a dick most of the time" because "it was funny." Controversy made listeners tune in. The column was tongue-in-cheek, but station defenders chafed at the ignorance of KCSB's diversity in programming and its responsibilities as an inhabitant of the public's airwaves.[74]

While much ink was spilled debating the relative merits of musical expression, humor, and the nature of free speech protection for student broadcasts, the handwringing over the Pork Dukes hid a deeper battle over whose priorities governed these publicly accessible stations. The concept of educational radio frayed as market-based rationales at work in deregulation and the censorship battles of the 1980s crept into college radio. Modifications in indecency rules emerged over the next few years, thanks to court rulings and congressional wrangling. But the culture wars continued to visit these stations beyond questions of content. KCSB's Pork Dukes troubles reflected more than crusading cultural warriors capturing national attention by targeting dirty lyrics. Hannity's firing suggested something other than liberal censorship. Instead, these cases were among developments in the 1980s that laid bare the often-conflicting demands placed on college stations as multiple voices sought the airwaves, which revealed the wider stakes of the culture wars.

9 The Political Left of the Dial

. . . .

Songs Allowed on KTRU (Rice University) after Relaxation of
Indecency Rules (but not to be announced on air), Fall 1987

Anne Clark, "True Love Tales"
Replacements, "I Don't Know," "Favorite Thing"
Wire, "Mr. Suit"
Concrete Blonde, "Still in Hollywood"
Buzzcocks, "Orgasm Addict"
X, "We're Desperate," "Los Angeles"
Dexy's Midnight Runners, "Burn It Down"

By the 1980s, college stations were known for playing music outside the mainstream and supporting progressive politics, activist groups, and politically charged musicians—often anti-Reagan hardcore punks. At the University of California, Santa Cruz, in 1985, a conservative student group claimed KZSC "blacklisted" their ideas or any rhetoric that was "un-left" after a right-leaning talk show did not receive renewal. Station leaders asserted they evaluated each DJ's individual merits, rather than their professed politics, in scheduling airtime. The host, it seemed, didn't have a radio presence that met KZSC's standards.[1]

But college radio's leftist reputation rested on more than disallowing a few conservative hosts' airtime. While skilled jocks such as Rush Limbaugh capitalized on AM's ill fortunes and revolutionized a previously lackluster radio format, the "left of the dial" indicated the location of noncommercial stations on the FM spectrum and a political identity to counterbalance conservative talk radio (notwithstanding Sean Hannity's short tenure at KCSB).

Key structural differences distinguished college radio as a progressively political space from commercial talk radio. College radio lacked talk radio's syndication and focused partisan pressure. Liberals, critics countered, could rely on their views being aired by National Public Radio's programs, but no viable commercial model emerged. Music critics, too, noted the rebellious image but generally mild sound of hair metal in the 1980s, betokening an "agendaless" popular music that relinquished the fusion of rock and politics that had emerged in the 1960s. Only on "devotedly weird college stations," as one critic put it, was any challenging sound or political content persistent.[2]

Upon closer investigation, no consistent leftist or liberal profile of college radio can be constructed. College stations airing overtly political content, for one, began with specific issues and organizations, whether traditionally political or centered around specific activist causes. They rarely connected to broader ideological or partisan projects.[3] Moreover, these were not simply leftist spaces opposing culture warriors' crusades against indecency. When it came to the culture wars and college radio, incidents such as occurred at Santa Barbara's station with the PMRC were outliers rather than the rule. Policing of popular music emerged from bipartisan sources, not just from the political right. College radio filled a growing gap in political and cultural radio programming—but it did not constitute a left or liberal space to offset conservative talk radio and corporate consolidation.[4] Instead, constraints on college radio's content connected more often with the culture wars through regulatory changes, declining public investment in higher education, and intrainstitutional dynamics as colleges and universities expanded their signals to reach new audiences. Scrutiny on these signals, instead, increased as the business and politics of media transformed.

No one model, and certainly no singular "sound" or political identity, defined college radio in the 1980s and 1990s. Instead of acting as a media property engaging in battles with ideological or cultural foes, these stations served as sites of the complicated culture wars of the era. Those in charge of signals tended to be students navigating complex demands and political contexts. Significant responsibilities rested on the shoulders of young adults still finding their voice and political identities. For DJs expecting freedom to play in their aural "sandbox," the attention of listeners unused to or uninitiated in the sounds and ideas they broadcast caused consternation. Problems emerged when students assumed that their stations acted as extensions of classroom or campus conversations, without explaining esoteric references or understanding their public platform. Questions regarding obligations to objectivity and balanced debate grew all the more complicated with the Fairness Doctrine's repeal, interpreted since 1949 as requiring stations to allow for response from opposing viewpoints to any aired political statement. Above all, these signals became targets for ire when they failed to serve lofty goals for their sound and messaging, and, in particular, regarding how they represented a university's intellectual and cultural life to the public.

Students, communities, and university public relations clashed in ways that even if not meeting the letter of censorship certainly felt like it to participants. Stations' status as laboratories for students, as student activities, or as extensions of university classrooms did not shield college radio participants from questions surrounding musical expression and whom signals served—with constituents interested in policing or accessing media's power for their own cultural preferences.

Killing Camus

Debates in the 1980s about musical content reflected bipartisan culture warriors' concerns about pop culture's influence on Americans' tastes, beliefs, and actions. In 1986, KCSB's reprimand confirmed college radio was included for scrutiny among a "troubling trend" of limits on free speech and musical expression, as Jon Pareles of the *New York Times* put it—himself a graduate of Yale's radio station. San Antonio, Texas, passed ordinances limiting heavy metal concerts. Jello Biafra faced charges of distributing "harmful matter to minors." At Seton Hall's WSOU, fears about pop culture inspiring teenage suicide resulted in furor over the station's emphasis on heavy metal. But college radio revealed more complicated dimensions of the culture wars. Among these, British new wave band the Cure defended its lyrics against charges of racism, an incident that received national press coverage and revealed how amateurism and educational missions would not protect college radio stations in this complex political climate that intertwined with media.[5]

Princeton University's WPRB found itself unwittingly involved in the Cure's struggle to keep its song "Killing an Arab" on its new album. This controversy involved no dirty words or sexual content but nonetheless struck similar chords regarding artistic freedom. In this case, it wasn't the FCC or university administrators pressuring WPRB, a station where student leaders took their obligations to the community and listeners seriously.[6] Instead, the station discovered that pop culture became a closely scrutinized realm for numerous groups to confront expressions they found troubling.

Faris Bouhafa, a former employee of New York music venue Max's Kansas City and of Columbia Records and an American-Arab Anti-Discrimination Committee (ADC) member, saw the track as contributing to racist policy as political tensions rose in the Middle East. It mattered little that lead singer and writer Robert Smith drew the lyrics from existentialist writer Albert

Camus's *The Stranger*. The ADC requested that Elektra Records remove the track and stop sales.[7]

WPRB provided a "turning point" to amplify the song's controversy.

In October 1986, a WPRB DJ cued up the new release. The junior from Alabama, station leaders explained, "assumed" the title referenced Camus. With his accent, the DJ announced the song, reportedly saying, "Here's a song about killing A-Rabs," using an offensive pronunciation one listener reported to the ADC. The DJ was horrified that his diction caused offense, and station leaders immediately issued an explanation.[8]

Efforts against the song were already underway. Bouhafa led a phone campaign to leaders at Warner Brothers, Electra, and Warner-Elektra-Atlantic, which halted distribution of the album in Australia and New Zealand. Smith insisted the song would stay on the album and the Cure continued to perform it, but he understood how "certain reactionary factions of the media, most notably by some particularly brainless DJs," used the song to exacerbate anti-Arab sentiment, and he requested radio stations refrain from airing the song. The WPRB complaint elevated the issue, leading Elektra and the ADC to agree to album stickers denying any racist intent.[9]

That WPRB listener offered the sole complaint cited in the case. The controversy, however, worried WPRB leaders about bad publicity as the story appeared in the *New York Times*, *Village Voice*, and *Rolling Stone*.[10]

College DJs appeared disconnected, possibly elitist, possibly naïve, and as fanning racist flames. Music critic Robert Christgau considered the dissonance between the Cure's "collegiate" audience and listeners who missed "the absurdity-of-ultimate-choices thesis" that rendered racism "immaterial," which was Smith's intention. It was not a protest song or a mockery of racism. It was existentialist commentary and philosophical exploration. But in the political context generating scrutiny on pop music, WPRB had itself a "PMRC-type" incident. Complaints about the DJ's diction and ensuing publicity made it seem "that Howard Sterns all across the land are distorting the song to their own racist ends." Bouhafa's tactics shifted to using the WPRB DJ to show the song's ill effects, which reportedly occurred at other radio stations without Princeton's ivory tower protections.[11]

WPRB issued statements and policy changes to counteract charges of racism. The station "clearly and effectively marked the song as off-limits for airplay" and would suspend any DJ who played it. WPRB's student managers aimed to prove their station was "sensitive to the needs of its listeners."

No FCC fine loomed, but college stations feared bad publicity as much as costly censure.[12]

With public signals, even if campus oriented or operating as student activities, college stations existed within cultural and political currents. Cultural expression had political power, and numerous interests were listening in and seeking to control expression—whether to protect innocent ears or curb racist or sexist sentiments. DJs, often college students, assumed they broadcast to audiences who understood the content or who were in on their jokes, and the DJs largely escaped broader political controversy. But amateurism or educational missions provided no defense against infractions and scandal. That fact grew increasingly clear since the 1970s, after the FCC revoked WXPN's license for lack of institutional oversight. Plus, the media storm surrounding these cases threatened a public relations nightmare even if an FCC fine was not forthcoming. Amid rising financial concerns in the 1980s at colleges and universities, stations could not afford to lose support.

Insiders understood the Cure's reference to existentialist literature. It wasn't really music for the masses, even if the band's pop appeal expanded. No culture warriors or congressional commissions examined whether college stations programmed more of one type of music than another. But more groups looked to these signals to secure representation for their voices, and as they tuned in, conflict over coverage intensified content concerns. While commercial radio adopted narrowcasting to target specific audiences and boost advertising revenue in the 1980s, voices that were shut out looked to noncommercial and community radio to serve niche tastes or music without broad commercial appeal—making it hard for students to adjudicate among demands placed on their stations. College radio's proponents could use learning laboratory functions as a defense, leveraging their educational missions to protect content that lacked commercial appeal, but protections waned regarding decisions made by students covering political events. Twin developments of media deregulation and culture wars, linked to questions about mainstream journalism's objectivity (or liberal media bias, as conservatives charged), provoked deeper questions about the state of democracy and media.

It was a confusing time to be a student DJ trying to figure out what to broadcast and what interests of public import to cover.

The Objectivity Question

College radio stations provided journalistic coverage of campus affairs and wider politics and news. But student journalists, or DJs seeking to support political causes, experienced confusion about their role as objective providers of information and news within complex regulatory and institutional environments. Adding to these confusions, conservatives pushed for the repeal of the Fairness Doctrine, which the FCC did in 1987 after Congress requested a review of the policy. The doctrine, which had been sporadically enforced, required broadcasters to "cover controversial issues of public importance," and if presenting a viewpoint on these issues, to air "the other side." The doctrine's lofty goals never lived up to its promise.[13] (Nor did its repeal solely account for Rush Limbaugh's success.)[14] Yet aspiring journalists on college radio stations took their obligations to objectivity and balance seriously.

Among students' political concerns and conversations, anti-apartheid protests swept across campuses in the mid-1980s. As condemnation of South Africa's racial regime spread, college students demanded that institutions divest the institutions' financial interests linked to the nation's white power structure. Some observers saw the issue as reanimating student protest traditions.

The free speech movement of the 1960s seemed an apt comparison—and college radio covered both movements. UC Berkeley was a key site of protest in both the 1960s and the 1980s. In the 1960s, students rallied in Sproul Plaza against the university's policies regarding student speech as well as its support of the military-industrial complex. Covering the protest constituted objective journalism, airing a newsworthy event on campus.

When anti-apartheid protests occurred in 1987, KALX similarly covered events. Broadcasting remotely from Sproul Plaza required electricity. To power their coverage, student DJs ran an extension cord across the plaza to plug in at the student center. As the gathering grew, UC police began to arrest protesters and unplugged radio equipment, shutting down the broadcast. Police justified their action as avoiding incitement to violence, whereas university officials reported "they were afraid people would trip" over the long extension cord. The protests had their effect, even if the extension cord went amiss. UC's board of regents took up the divestment issue, though the president remained opposed to the move, favoring leveraging stockholder pressure to end apartheid.[15] For radio DJs, practical matters of broadcasting might present impediments as support for anti-apartheid sentiment spread quickly, and no other credible charges of political censorship emerged.

Around the same time, KALX designed a program guide featuring Charles Coypel's 1740 painting *Leda*, depicting "the maiden copulating with the

Greek god Zeus, who has taken the form of a swan." Administrators attempted to cease distribution of the publication but settled for allowing it on campus, with a warning label affixed to any copy sent off-campus.[16] But college radio pursued its political support of anti-apartheid movements unimpeded.

College stations cued up the 1986 single from Artists United Against Apartheid, which featured Joey Ramone and the Velvet Underground's Lou Reed among other artists associated with college radio, as well as reggae artist Peter Tosh's song "Fight Apartheid."[17] At Oberlin College in Ohio in 1987, WOBC recorded a protest for divestment in South African corporations.[18]

Anti-apartheid support offered an issue that drew few requests for "balanced" coverage. It animated student political activity on campuses across the nation, and college radio reflected that trend. Within stations, DJs debated airing political statements and the limits on amplifying activist causes. Although not directly invoked, public debates about broadcasters' responsibility under the Fairness Doctrine seeped into student DJs' logic regarding their role as purveyors of information and opinion about matters of public importance. At Rice University, radio DJs even debated whether an anti-apartheid poster should appear in the studio, as the station had an obligation to objectivity. (Most DJs thought the claim was ridiculous.)[19] Although divestment protests took place within campus confines, for the most part stations operated on the public airwaves. The FCC had been, since 1981, limiting applications of the doctrine, but some students still saw the rule as limiting their freedom to make political statements.[20] Nonetheless, students attempted to cover issues of concern to the campus body.

Heated debates about apartheid and divestment, as well as a resurgent Ku Klux Klan in the 1980s, inspired student broadcasters to cover matters of public importance as well as debunk racist views. Even if the Fairness Doctrine was on its way out, DJs felt it necessary to maintain objectivity in presenting such questions, reflecting higher education's commitment to rigor and debate on campus. But for students without significant supervision or expert advice, such coverage could easily go off the rails. Students who might be accustomed to discussing hot-button issues in classrooms and on campus—outside public view—sometimes failed to consider the implications of extending those debates to the airwaves and emulating the sensational tactics of talk radio.

One such failure occurred at Vanderbilt University's radio station, WRVU, broadcasting in Nashville, Tennessee. Its sounds carried over the barriers between town and Vanderbilt's green campus. Stately magnolia trees and red brick walls separated the university, although it was just a few blocks from Music Row, from the city's musical culture and busy streets. WRVU defied the university's fraternity-dominated culture, connecting more with Nashville's music scene than frat row. In the 1950s, engineering student and music aficionado Ken Berryhill was known for waiting outside the Ryman Auditorium and Grand Ole Opry to record interviews with performers. He aired these on a carrier-current station he rigged up in his dorm.[21] By 1971, Vanderbilt received permission to construct its own FM tower atop the highest dorm on campus.[22]

WRVU DJs took the station's public service mission seriously. They offered news and public affairs coverage of current issues, emulating serious journalists or television and radio's sensational talk shows and call-in programs. In 1979, two weeks of the nightly *Seven O'clock Report* analyzed "the representation of black persons at the university," including interviews with Vanderbilt administrators and call-in segments.[23] When financing proved meager, commitments to public service expanded. In 1980, to fund expanded power and continue offering a unique format in the Nashville market, listeners supported WRVU with donations and attendance at benefit concerts. The Exit/In, a nearby club known for attracting alternative rock acts on tour, hosted concerts to support WRVU, which advertised its events and interviewed acts. Musician Joe Strummer of the Clash visited the station in 1984, granting student DJs an interview (figure 9.1).

In 1987, WRVU needed additional funds. "The old [equipment] is imploding," a representative suggested, but "we're broke."[24] The station engineer and volunteers managed to keep the signal going thanks to community support, yet again.

Listeners saluted WRVU's innovative programming and on-air personalities. In 1987, WRVU announcers earned the most nominations in a newspaper poll for Nashville's "number one Dee-Jay." The newspaper acknowledged that WRVU "probably has more broadcast personalities than any other station in town."[25] Programs such as *George the Bluegrass Show*, hosted by former-student-turned-community-DJ Traci Todd, reflected the city's vibrant music scene. Offering sounds by stars such as Lester Flatt, Roland White, Doug Dillard, and the Nashville Bluegrass Band, Todd connected the Vanderbilt campus to Nashville's historic country and bluegrass community.[26]

WRVU's attempts to reflect campus conversations, however, generated scandal that stemmed from students' problematic interpretation of objectivity and balance in presenting debates about (or, rather, with) racists. In

FIGURE 9.1 Joe Strummer visited the studio of WRVU in March 1984. Photo by E. Thomas Wood.

1988, a call-in show hosted by students included a KKK member as a guest. With the white nationalist organization's membership rising, former Klan national director David Duke announced a bid for president in the Democratic primaries. Duke had appeared on Vanderbilt's campus in 1974, an invitation extended with a similar logic: to "stimulate reaction."[27] That appearance was not broadcast. In 1988, however, WRVU's debate aired across the Nashville area as students emulated television talk show hosts like Phil Donahue or Sally Jessy Raphael.

Criticism emerged first from Vanderbilt's Black Student Union, which rebuked WRVU for the segment. WRVU's general manager insisted that the program aimed "to provide an open forum" and raise awareness. She defended the program as challenging Vanderbilt's culture, such as the Kappa Alpha fraternity's "Old South" parties, which lauded white enslavers as chivalrous and "genteel." The DJs wanted to confront racism on campus. "I think especially students on this campus, which is mostly white and not the subject of the actions of the KKK, really don't understand," the general manager explained. BSU members certainly understood, and they pointed out the broader implications of the broadcast. The KKK member used WRVU's airwaves to decry race suicide from intermarriage and beseeched whites to "maintain their existence." Although some two dozen callers challenged the speaker, the program gave a platform to a racist, terrorist organization.[28]

The incident generated negative press, though the furor remained limited to a brief public relations fiasco rather than producing any meaningful clash between station and campus values. WRVU's leaders vowed to insulate programming from campus controversies by participating with "impartiality." Students wanted to discuss matters of public importance, as well as challenge campus culture. The vague nature of radio's public service obligations and value of "objectivity" muddled matters, particularly when students lacked guidance.

Vanderbilt's student DJs strove for a practiced sound, but most did not envision careers in broadcasting. The station did not coordinate with any communications or journalism curriculum, instead serving more as a link between town and gown and providing a fun student activity. There were established practices, however. In a 1985 handbook dubbed *The Commandments of 91 Rock*, leaders entreated personnel to stick to format. DJs should "NEVER OPEN YOUR MOUTH ON AIR UNLESS YOU HAVE SOMETHING WORTH SAYING." Be "social, not obnoxious," and "talk about familiar things, not inside jokes such as what happened on [dorm floor] Lupton 6 last night," the handbook advised. The troubles arising out of the call-in show featuring the KKK came from bringing campus conversations to the radio and attempting to cause a spectacle. It also violated, by extension, commandment number eight: "The radio station tries to remain politically neutral, so avoid any one-sided political jokes, ethnic slurs, foul language, dirty humor, or anything else that might offend your grandmother."[29] The DJs had good intentions, but their execution failed. The administration did not intervene at WRVU over the KKK appearance, given that the show tried to maintain objectivity.

Programming a radio station had social and political implications, which DJs sometimes struggled to consider. Students' political interests, such as anti-apartheid activism or seeking to (albeit problematically) challenge a resurgent racist movement, extended campus conversations to the wider public. Student DJs understood their station's public significance, but many wanted to keep this purpose tacit, focusing on music and not the underlying values behind constructing a schedule or selecting music for rotation. WRVU's talk show debacle revealed the difficulties inherent in constructing educational radio around student interests. Yet these remained educational signals owned by colleges and universities, staffed by students and volunteers who, for the most part, wanted to play music. Balancing demands on a single station brought dissonance when scheduling to satisfy everyone as well as fulfill political and social goals. Content didn't have to rattle racist sentiments or call for policy change to have political relevance—or to cause questions about how stations should conduct business and manage schedules. Filling socially conscious goals extended to music on specialty shows, but even these served audiences of different mindsets and preferences.

Pleasing "Highbrow" Listeners

Radio offered a useful tool for connecting area alumni and listeners seeking the kind of programs they associated with universities' intellectual and cultural profiles. These ties grew more valuable as college stations faced challenges to their aural profile and audience cultivation amid a tightening financial environment. Other incentives arose to shift audience cultivation. New Corporation for Public Broadcasting funding practices empowered local stations to use funds to select from a range of producers, rather than CPB funding going directly to NPR. Such programming attracted administrators because it added prestige and drew audiences that were "highly educated, socially conscious, and politically aware" to the institution— along with their donations.[30] CPB's staff requirements could be met with or without student participation. Yet community connections occasionally produced friction if programs strayed too far from institutional messaging and desired audiences.

Columbia University's student-run station developed strong community ties. In 1986, as college radio's reputation solidified as a place for independent rock and hip-hop, these priorities clashed with its community commitments both on and off campus. As WKCR's station manager, a rising senior, explained to the student newspaper, "In trying to serve both the New York and Columbia communities, we entered into a quagmire of legal, social, linguistic, administrative, and punitive problems."[31] Trouble started with a question about a community program's political content but developed into a tense conversation about town and gown relations.

Political content on radio shows aimed at nearby ethnic audiences sparked the controversy. The show in question, *L'Heure Haïtienne*, featured leftist political commentary that reportedly drew bomb threats. Administrators and station leaders did not speak Haitian Creole, so they could not monitor the content. Community members complained of Columbia's ungrateful attitude toward nonaffiliated DJs and listeners. Critics labeled the Irish show *Shamrock Shore* as "a two-hour commercial for the IRA." The student station manager banned the broadcast and warned *L'Heure Haïtienne* DJs to avoid libel and cut its hours. All DJs had to sign that they understood the FCC's Personal Attack Rule and (soon to be mothballed) Fairness Doctrine regarding editorializing.[32]

Columbia's administration monitored the situation, involving institutional lawyers and prompting debate about whom the station served. University counsel recommended "monitoring procedures" for all "foreign language programming."[33] The Haitian Students Association called this discrimination and organized a picket of WKCR's jazz festival in protest.[34] The Haitian community, it declared, made *L'Heure Haïtienne* the station's most popular program. As one community member complained, "Haitians— who were listening to the show when most of WKCR's staff was still in elementary school—feel cheated."[35] Students weren't the only ones with claims to the station.

The jazz fest offered a richly symbolic target for protest. The 1960s and 1970s had been "perilous" times for jazz, as corporatization in radio undermined DJs' power and shifted it to program directors and general managers. As demographic research and audience segmentation proceeded, stations implementing "Black Appeal Radio" tended to be owned by whites.[36] The increasing scarcity of Black-owned or Black-focused radio stations left noncommercial college and community radio to cover the expanding genre. Larger public stations focused on maximizing listener donations tended to program more "conservative" or mainstream jazz styles, such as bebop or high-fidelity recordings from the swing era. Smaller noncommercial stations might mix in more progressive styles, including "free or avant-garde jazz, jazz-fusion, instrumental R&B, and low fidelity early recordings."[37] Columbia's station aired a wide range of jazz styles.

DJs Phil Schaap and Sharif Abdus-Salaam earned lauded reputations for jazz programming. Together they expanded WKCR's jazz hours to forty a week in the 1970s.[38] Schaap originated WKCR's annual jazz festival, and he coordinated between the station and his job at Polygram Records after 1984.[39] On noncommercial signals with FM's high fidelity, DJs could play extended selections, such as Miles Davis's "Bitch's Brew," untenable on a station needing to break for commercials.[40] Jazz's long history and numerous discourses, by the 1980s, "had moved to concert halls, to academic institutions, and in close proximity to the classical section of music stores," joining "the cultural aristocracy," as one music scholar put it. The genre continued to innovate, but many listeners associated it more with National Public Radio than with marginalized subcultures, ignoring artistic developments within the genre.[41]

Although not "ideologically homogeneous," jazz as "'serious music' became pervasively dominant in media discourse of the 1980s," suggesting "affluence, sophistication, and a highbrow aesthetic" that resisted classification as "popular music."[42] *L'Heure Haïtienne*'s listeners likely did not aspire to pop status, but they did (even if unintentionally) challenge the dominance of jazz, a Black musical art and form that nonetheless shut out community voices that did not appeal to affluent—and often white— audiences.

To avoid controversy, WKCR's volunteers used their station's student-run status as a shield against complaints about a lack of diversity and unfair treatment. The show was cut, DJs argued, because more room was needed for students to assume on-air responsibilities, not to appeal to highbrow audiences. The license belonged to the university, which leaders used as justification for reducing community DJs and programs.[43] The station continued to air experimental jazz forms, as well as other genres.[44]

Political content sparked the conflagration over *L' Heure Haïtienne*, but questions about which communities the station should serve provided the tinder. Communities without Columbia affiliation placed justifiable demands on WKRC, as at other stations. These were public signals, even if jazz supported signals' collegiate and highbrow identities.

In some cases, university or station missions, rather than controversy, pushed programming in new directions. At Temple University, the long-standing all-jazz format at student-run WRTI, technological "gremlins" plagued reception in 1984. Administrators had to decide whether to invest in new equipment, prompting the transfer of station oversight from the School of Communications' Department of Radio-Television and Film to the university's public relations department. Listeners feared disruption of jazz shows, but officials assured that they simply wanted WRTI to do a "better job" and address the university's "*laissez-faire* attitude toward management and operations." Temple doubled the station's budget and promised improvements, while fans feared "homogenization" of jazz and an increased focus on fusion styles that appealed more to white audiences. Longtime volunteers thought this would "alienate" dedicated listeners. One announcer suggested that as WRTI aired more music "not representative of the jazz tradition," its longtime Black listeners tuned out. General listenership might expand with the new format, fulfilling public relations goals, but existing audiences felt disserved. Even if no "overt acts of censorship" emerged, DJs told reporters that "they have been discouraged from playing the speeches of the Rev. Dr. Martin Luther King Jr., and Malcolm X and the political raps of Gil Scott-Heron and the Last Poets," formerly heard frequently on WRTI.[45]

Again, the student DJ question, as at Columbia, factored into the debate. Some longtime volunteers noted a shift in personnel. White student volunteer rates increased after Temple's administrative takeover. A former student DJ explained that community volunteers without Temple affiliation feared "being phased out." The increase of full-time staff positions also made WRTI eligible for CPB funding.

Meanwhile, coverage of fusion, "crossover," and "new age" jazz expanded. The new general manager considered the shift a natural consequence of adding student volunteers. One jazz fan called the programming "bland, middle-of-the-road music that's perceived as being accessible to a non-jazz audience." Changes justified by increasing the learning lab potential for students served to "broaden" WRTI's audience, facilitated by the expansion of news and information programming. More listeners meant more potential dollars from fundraising and corporate underwriting, even if jazz fans felt slighted. The new general manager justified the changes as giving students opportunities, denying an agenda to sideline avant-garde tastes. Some DJs lost their time slots, but they could be "fill-in" staff, the general manager justified. WRTI's reputation for quality jazz programming continued, along with student involvement, but the struggle over what subgenres aired reflected questions about whether noncommercial radio in the mid- and late 1980s would serve as a pluralistic celebrant of US culture or support "oppositional" voices that highlighted ongoing inequality and challenged established notions of cultural hierarchy.[46]

A shift in national priorities rather than a local dispute over hours of fusion versus avant-garde jazz music exacerbated matters. As NPR pioneer Bill Siemering told the local press, "College and public stations are finding that they have to become commercially viable" to remain on the air, meaning appealing to audiences willing to pledge financial support. Stations could serve "highly educated and socially conscious" listeners who valued diversity and multiculturalism—but they had to keep them tuned in. If each noncommercial station in a market cultivated a "highly specific audience" by focusing on consistency in programming, rather than providing "something-for-everyone," it was likely to garner support.[47] NPR's researchers encouraged stations to adopt continuity in content to ensure a dedicated audience that would donate.[48] Siemering worried that such pressures would force noncommercial stations to become "easy listening" rather than "alternative." With competition for FM space and listeners on the rise, alongside the need for their dollars as already meager federal support for public radio in the Reagan-era fiscal environment seemed in doubt, those seeking to claim public radio space faced greater competition and the need to self-fund.[49]

• • • • • •

College radio's educational musical service bolstered universities' image in an era that put pressure on signals as well as their host institutions to fulfill public obligations previously reserved for the state. Such pressure fell in line with a general trend in governance to turn to market-based or private solutions to social problems or to provide public goods. Federal agencies defaulted to majority tastes and preferences when it came to media regulation, while more options sprang up on cable television and corporate media conglomerates grew. These regulatory and market developments made college stations more valuable, but they also increased pressure to serve multiple audiences—all while university allocations remained stubbornly immovable, except in cases that required capital improvements or repairs. Many stations needed to cultivate listeners who might donate funds, record labels that might provide free record service, and students who often supported stations financially through student fees. These developments occurred alongside the political attention on musical content.

It's impossible to separate the business and politics of higher education from regulatory and cultural debates in the 1980s. Not every station was affected, and results varied, but collectively college radio continued to be swept into national developments. Universities drew culture-wars scrutiny for curricula, the supposed left-leaning politics of the professoriate, and the vision of US culture they supported through teaching and, by extension, their radio stations. Colleges and universities sought to expand awareness for multicultural voices and public service to defend their status as a public good. All of these demands visited college radio stations in addition to their rising musical profile—all of which could not be fulfilled in the number of hours available in the week by a mostly volunteer staff and meager funding. These signals' multiple purposes and divergent audiences explain why they developed no meaningful counterweight to the rise of conservative talk radio in the 1980s.

Conservative forces were at work within college radio, as well, even if they were untethered to any partisan goal or outcome. Fans came to expect a certain sound from college radio, even as musical innovation continued. By 1988, many college stations had placed Public Enemy, Living Color, Herbie Hancock, and more into rotation—an overdue development. A University of San Francisco student expressed "amusement" when the school's station aired Public Enemy, remarking, "Even the merchants of megahipdom who run KUSF get tired of the familiar clangety-clang of 'alternative rock' from time to time," opting for new sounds. Could it be that this haven for "the 10,000 Smithereens and the Young Fresh Lemondrops" might "start busting serious beats"? Unlikely, he concluded, since rap artists received scant respect.

This "discovery" of rap by "croissant-n-coffee listeners" left the student annoyed, even angry. *Spin* magazine ignored Chuck D., "probably the most important black lyricist to emerge in the 80's," for its cover.[50] The student was right to have doubts. A mix of fans came to college radio, including those who wanted music that pushed artistic boundaries and those who wanted more NPR-type programs.

Such conflicting demands proved much more influential on college radio culture than national politics regarding pop culture and obscenity. The PMRC and culture warriors provided useful symbols, but they did not influence the musical philosophy and missions that guided how blocks of time were allocated. Real estate on the radio spectrum, even the noncommercial, educational signals on the left of the FM dial, were hot properties.

The "croissant-n-coffee listeners" challenged the independence of these learning laboratories with power within the music industry. They might welcome a few token rap artists to validate their enlightened, multicultural self-regard, and enough wanted music that indicated a cultured, elite outlook. As administrations sought public relations tools that presented a highbrow, serious reputation to surrounding communities—and attracted donor dollars—pressure mounted for stations to "go NPR." Such pressure threatened, as NPR's Bill Siemering warned, the vibrancy of alternative radio.

It makes more sense to see college stations, rather than championing local politics or progressive causes, as sites of politics. Questions about institutional power, influence, and values played out on the airwaves or in studios. Station leaders navigated conflicting commitments, programming content that might satisfy campus-based listeners and rankle others, or vice versa. Listeners who tuned in to seek identity recognition often brought conflicting expectations regarding politics, commercialism, or artistic innovation. And with declining local media service, college and community radio covered political and social causes. It catered to the audiences left behind in the deregulation and corporatization of media and public broadcasting.

10 Cultivating a Public Radio Alternative in the 1980s

. . . .

Something about the Women (Terri) — July 27, 1985
SAW Records, Playlists Folder, WMFO, Tufts University

Ray Gardner, "Castle in the Mist"

Women's Orchestral Works: Concerto for Harp and Orchestra

Amelia & Jennifer, "Folk with a Bite"

Suzanne Vega, "Straight Lines"

The Guest Stars, "I Know, I Know"

Judy Mowatt, "Mother Africa"

Aretha Franklin, "Freeway of Love"

Lisa-Lisa & Cult Jam, "I Wonder if I Take You Alone"

Romeo Void, "Never Say Never"

Rubber, "The Hardest Thing"

Gloria Gaynor, "I Am What I Am"

Aretha Franklin, "Chain of Fools"

Laura Nyro, "Luckie"

Casselberry-Dupree, "You Don't Need to Move a Mountain"

Big Mama Thornton, "Ball & Chain"

Etta James, "Baby What You Want Me to Do"

Koko Taylor, "Evil"

Etta James, "Wake Up This Morning"

Wendy Grossman, "Athogg Highlanders"

Janet Smith, "If I'd Have Known"

Lily Tomlin, "Lady," "The Pageant"

Suzanne Vega, "Marlene on the Wall"

Tania Maria, "Bela Be Bela"

Elis Regina, "Querelas do Brasil"

Natalie Cole, "Dangerous"

Aretha Franklin, "Push"

Judy Mowatt, "Lovemaking"

Eurythmics, "No Fear, No Hate, No Pain"

The B-52's, "Give Me Back My Man"

Nina Hagen, "My Way"

Mary Wells, "Come On"

The Shirelles, "Baby It's You"
Patti Labelle and the Blue Belles, "C'est La Vie"
Supremes, "Reflections"
Shangri-Las, "Walkin in the Sand"
The Orlons, "Chains"
Angels, "My Boyfriend's Back"
Maria Rodrigues, "The Harder They Come"
Rita Marley, "That's the Way"

"You don't have to be a snot to like classical music," the general manager of an Oklahoma public radio station asserted in 1983. A "renaissance" at such stations lured listeners "tired of the drivel" on commercial radio but who maybe didn't want to hear anti-Reagan hardcore songs or folk music. NPR matured. Well-produced and reputable journalism alongside classical music defined the programming at these stations, which attempted to update their image as serving the broad public, not self-appointed elites ensconced in ivory towers of higher education. This left less room for freeform DJs, who developed an at times uneasy relationship with college radio—and sometimes even with classical music hosts such as praised in Oklahoma.

NPR continued to transform. By the mid-1980s, public broadcasters increased focus on news and information, abandoning many cultural programs or dividing service across different signals.[1] Public sources provided about 60 percent of public radio's budget, requiring listener funding and expanded audiences with money to donate.[2] Stations focused less on "bluegrass or symphonies or local culture" and more on what listener-donors would pay for: professionally produced news and information.[3]

University administrators saw the appeal of adding NPR and syndicated shows at the expense of community and freeform shows. Students and community volunteers often were left without much of a voice in these contests for control of the airwaves, even if student fees provided funding. Noncommercial stations benefited from university ownership, financing, and infrastructure, but many had to generate outside support.

College radio's dominant block structure made balancing these demands difficult. As one NPR insider put it, "Trying to serve many different audiences means not serving any of them well."[4] It was hard to build a listener base with weekly schedules divided into one- or two-hour blocks of time. Instead, "the cardinal rule of radio programming is that a station must focus consistently on the one type of programming that appeals to a particular type of listener." Pursuing various roles and audience segments explains college radio's sometimes-muddled political and cultural identity in the 1980s, contributing to a crisis in progressive media even as they kept radio diverse.

Champions of weird and not-commercially viable music or of service to ethnic, religious, and minority communities opposed implementing syndicated shows or expanding listenership to supplement institutional brands. A middle way emerged in some markets for university-owned stations with a listener-funded model that met communities' cultural needs rather than offering syndicated news and information. (One of these is the professionally run folk-music station at UMass Boston, which received CPB funding alongside public broadcasting giants in the same market.) Sometimes, community members pushed for expanded syndicated content. In other cases, students defended radio as a student activity or as pedagogical laboratories against serving wider community audiences.

Allowing students to control what went out over the airwaves was a risky proposition in the 1980s' political climate. Other concerns than preventing students' on-air antics prompted this sentiment, however. NPR, with a ready-made professional sound and identity signifying education and knowledge, offered universities a public relations boon. Providing public radio service helped smoothe tense town and gown relations. It bolstered university reputations. But it alienated longtime volunteers and friends of freeform. Struggles over freeform versus syndicated programming in the 1980s extended beyond playlist content. Instead, they revisited long-standing, core questions about what college radio would be, and whom it would serve—all of which intensified amid ongoing media deregulation.[5]

Even before Ronald Reagan appointed Mark Fowler to the FCC in 1981, public-service requirements for commercial broadcasters were weak.[6] Media companies consolidated across entertainment sectors, leading to larger and larger corporate conglomerates and metrics-driven programming designed to attract audience share among targeted demographics. As one radio scholar explained, deregulation "denied radio access to a wide variety of groups of individuals who did not fit into a market-based formula." Coverage narrowed for local voices, information, and culture, leaving noncommercial radio stations "to pick up the slack."[7] Competition for coverage intensified in the 1980s as commercial radio narrowed and fewer outlets existed for minority artists and voices. In this environment, locally owned and controlled stations drew audiences that felt shut out of corporate media.[8] The market-based logic behind deregulation similarly influenced how universities evaluated their radio stations.

Amid these developments, college radio continued to solidify its reputation in the music industry for breaking artists—many of whom were white and appealed to middle- and upper-class college and college-educated audiences. Listeners tended to want to participate in an exclusive in-crowd or community of the like-minded or self-identified affinities. Whether that translated into cool cache, party soundtracks, organizing activist communities, finding music to get stoned to, or challenging the power of the conformist, capitalist culture industry depended on the ear and attitude of the listener. But divergent audiences shared an interest in securing representation on the airwaves, taking up public space to assert their personhood, institutional brands, community solidarity, or culture.

Appealing to listeners outside the university community, audiences that a University of San Francisco DJ dubbed the "croissant-and-coffee listeners," meant balancing yuppie tastes with cutting-edge music student DJs wanted, sometimes sidelining community volunteers for professional staff—or favoring student access over community DJs.[9] Volunteers might square off against each other, or against administrations and professionals seeking to control their signals. All of this added up to a deeply contested left of the dial in the 1980s.

A Jesuit Mission

KXLU-FM's rotations "read like playlists for a black mass," a writer noted in 1984. Nonetheless, the student-run radio station at Jesuit-run Loyola Marymount University (LMU) surprised observers with its title of 1984's Best College Radio Station in a nationwide poll. Featuring bands such as Alien Sex Fiend and Screaming Foetus, KXLU defied Top 40 radio that proliferated in Los Angeles's FM market. Student DJs championed "the last alternative on the left," playing "truly original" music, even if offensive. Staffed by students with interest in professional advancement, the station cut an alternative sound to promote unheard acts.[10] A freeform philosophy dominated most hours, alongside *Alma del Barrio*, a long-standing, acclaimed Latin music program. Weeknights featured classical music, a sharp contrast to KXLU's independent-label rock—which produced a struggle for control between two visions for the station's service mission.[11] Market, institution, culture warrior: each wanted to control what went out over collegiate airwaves. Struggles emerged from within institutions, as well, as happened at LMU.

While observers expressed incredulity that a Jesuit institution permitted such programming, LMU's administration supported the station. In 1985, the institution appointed Rev. J. P. Reynolds, S.J., as a full-time adviser. Reynolds explained, "Maybe sometimes we go too far" airing the rage of hardcore bands, "but I'm excited by the fact that we're an alternative station." Controversy was okay with him. "We Jesuits have a history of going into areas where you don't expect to find a priest," he continued. Social consciousness defined Jesuit tradition, even if some, well, tension emerged over content. Certainly, the administration preferred a full slate of classical music. But LA needed a truly alternative station, and KXLU was there to serve.[12]

Visible stations with sizable listenership faced divergent demands on airtime and questions about whom they served first: students, the public, or culture. Often, several needs could be met without rancor, despite a station's prestige. In 1985, KXLU coordinated a national radio and music convention that provided "nation-wide publicity" and attention from major record labels. Positive press for the university and high regard for KXLU benefited, the general manager explained, "students who will be in the work force soon" who could "take advantage of our popularity and good name."[13]

Despite a public image of synchrony between the station's hardcore rock fare and the Jesuit mission, internal tensions developed over KXLU's image and how it would reinforce the university's reputation. Students and community members squared off, but faculty and the administration entered the conversation. Each group—while not monolithic—envisioned different audiences and definitions of "collegiate" content to support the institution's image and educational "brand."

One faculty member took particular interest in KXLU's classical music shows in 1985. As a history professor and choral director, Rev. Richard H. Trame, S.J., supported expanding the roster of classical music staff. He blamed "the lack of interested students" for "why the station has gone over so much to popular music and rock." KXLU should, he argued, be more than a "plaything for the few dedicated uneducated rock enthusiasts who appear to have gained much control."[14] Classical music, he argued, was the answer.

Administrators cared more about providing students with on-air opportunities than seeking wider appeal with their music or curbing rock.[15] This attitude did not mean that students had free rein. But Trame disdained students' leadership and demanded expanding classical service.

From Trame's communications, it was hard to tell if he initiated the movement against rock music or if the classical department resented rock's dominance and enlisted his help. Whatever the case, Eva Gampel advocated robustly for her division. Gampel, a recent volunteer, was not a student. Nevertheless, she represented the classical division with fervent dedication. Gampel's passion for classical, she promised, would elevate KXLU and the institution's reputation alongside professionally run stations in Los Angeles. With Trame's help, she found four interested students who, with existing staff, could cover thirty-eight hours a week. "Alas," she told Trame, "we have only 25."[16]

Trame intervened when he learned station managers denied Gampel's request. He asked LMU's president Rev. James Loughran to dictate an increase in classical hours. "To my mind," Trame argued, "this can only be to the benefit of the University and its public image," which he saw damaged by "the multitudinous programming for rock music." Many stations played rock, and students with a "general level of cultural competence" gravitated to other stations, not KXLU. Trame did not differentiate between hardcore and the rock found on other area stations. Instead, he envisioned an outlet for his choral concerts and support for music he saw as befitting the institution's reputation. In Gampel, he found "a woman who has such classical interests at heart and has to fight for the time she gets from a somewhat incomprehending staff." Gampel, he insinuated, should represent the institution, not dunderheaded rockers with pedestrian tastes.[17]

Trame lamented the publicity garnered by KXLU's focus on hardcore. *California Living* ran a cover feature on the station with the subtitle asking, "What are those ungodly sounds these Catholic kids are broadcasting?" Trame didn't like it. By not elevating a "go-getter" like Gampel, LMU squandered a valuable resource.

The general manager denied her request because accommodation would require reductions or cancellations of other specialty shows, such as popular Latin and Brazilian music shows. No precedent existed for one strong program to displace others. *Alma del Barrio* and rock music "were strong enough to have knocked all the other formats off the air," he explained, but station leaders opted not to. "Just because classical may have achieved a larger listening audience," the program director explained, "it does not necessarily warrant more time." Besides, classical occupied the popular prime-time weekday slot. He offered to replace syndicated classical programs with newly recruited staff. Gampel refused. That would diminish the prestige and connections she sought. She coveted grant-funded programming, but KXLU's decision-makers warned caution, as funders tended to demand influence—a concession station leaders did not wish to make.[18]

Gampel went to Trame, yet again. He was outraged. "I see no reason why the station," he seethed, "has to produce the type of porno and cheap rock programs involved." He lobbied President Loughran again for intervention. Trame doubled down, reasoning, "Although cultural interests can be construed in a broad manner, those programming aspects which best promote the image of the University as a promoter of the Arts and the intellectual should take precedence over others."[19] In his view, classical offered superior status. He made no case that classical would expand KXLU's audience, only *improve* it. He felt the music needed a champion. After all, wasn't that the function of institutions such as LMU and noncommercial, educational radio—to serve this rarefied market?

Gampel claimed discrimination. She complained that "classical recordings have been disappearing in alarming numbers," suggesting a "climate of distrust and lack of respect for station property."[20] Opera recordings, in fact, moved to another office because of lack of space.[21] But she suspected sabotage. She took her fundraising successes in winter 1986 to Loughran, listing her accomplishments and ignoring student leaders. "I believe," she argued, "we have outgrown the 25 hours of programming allotted to Classical Music on KXLU." KXLU could, she argued, generate "the finest public relations for the University" if only Loughran would force station leaders to consider the university's "long range interests."[22] Trame advocated for Gampel to receive "non-salaried faculty status" to "add prestige to her work with students as she trains them in broadcasting" and given her master's degree in music. He wanted classical to receive "autonomy" alongside expanded hours, to protect it from becoming a "political football" subject to the whims of managers "antipathetic" to classical music. Any student manager, despite KXLU being a student activity, would need to be cleared by her.[23]

Trame and Gampel solicited community support. UCLA chemistry professor and future Nobel laureate Paul D. Boyer wrote Gampel directly to commend KXLU's "excellent service" in classical music. This "welcome breath of fresh air dispelling the trash of the radio waves" created "goodwill" for the institution and fulfilled its educational obligations. He requested appropriate dinnertime programs to accompany his weekend meals—avoiding concert halls, too much talk, and cacophonous pieces. "Occasional exposure," Boyer noted, "to more modern or little heard composers that do not get too markedly atonal or discordant" would be "refreshing." Trame and Gampel could not have scripted a more perfect letter of support from the kind of listener they cultivated.[24]

They needed the support. President Loughran warned Trame in February 1986 that it was "not the time to get into a big battle" about KXLU. He cautioned that "feelings are too strong at the moment," and he suggested a cooling-off period and the status quo to be observed.[25] Trame invested deeply in station management, the selection of KXLU's student leaders, and the balance of programming. Passions ran high. And a big battle was definitely in the works.

By May 1986, Gampel suspected a cabal existed to fire her. She experienced annoying pranks. She hadn't made many friends at KXLU, it seemed. Her repeated memos angered station leaders, who resented her enlistment of Trame in seeking more airtime and in demanding a review of KXLU's management by the College of Communications and Fine Arts. Other DJs had a penchant for leaving studio doors open during classical hours, and mics picked up their carousing, Gampel claimed. This travesty, in her view, needed faculty and administrative intercession. Trame's statements criticizing KXLU's "excessive emphasis on Rock music" and consequent "detriment of the University's image" generated concern among DJs. It might be admirably run, but it did not compete with market leaders, who Trame believed boasted superior sounds in announcing and musical fare.[26] As for Gampel, he considered her as facing nothing less than an "inquisition."[27]

Communications broke down regarding a classical music event purportedly run with KXLU's sponsorship. Gampel had arranged the sponsorship without notifying station leaders. General manager Mark Morris gave her the opportunity to resign before he fired her. Trame defended Gampel, but the matter channeled tensions between rock and classical DJs. Trame charged Morris with harassment, insinuating that he lacked "capacity to judge what is truly favorable to the University's public image and general welfare." Trame entreated LMU's administration to overhaul station staff, entirely.[28]

Trame pulled no punches in making his case for "reordering" KXLU. He told Loughran the station offended "people on the outside," meaning alumni and potential donors. Music offerings, he complained, "have been anything but possessed of . . . Christian moral content." He reported alumni complaints about "sexy" broadcasts. In fact, one faculty member reported "some Protestant friends" invited him to dinner "to protest the programming on KXLU." Hardcore music, it seemed, created an interfaith alliance.[29]

The signal reached many potential listeners across Los Angeles and thus required a professional sound and image, Trame argued. KXLU failed public obligations as "an instrument which covers much of Southern California with an audience potential of several millions." Plus, classical service was lucrative. It generated some $60,000 in annual pledges. He extolled Gampel's leadership and connections and decried her treatment by "rock enthusiasts who have on occasion expressed a desire to eliminate classical programming all together!" Student announcers stumbled over pronunciation of city names, rock music dominated weekly hours, and KXLU offered few broadcasts of campus events, particularly its concerts. Trame called for a College of Communications and Fine Arts board to oversee the station while keeping its student-run status.[30]

But he concluded, "If some students resign because of this, so much the better. It would only indicate that they are more interested in their own objectives and not those of the university."[31]

Trame demanded Morris be dismissed. The history professor, a scholar of the counter-Reformation, had institutional reform in mind. He entreated Morris to not punish Gampel for a professor's efforts. "Are you some sort of infallible tyrant who monopolizes the loyalties of those who are under your jurisdiction?" he asked Morris, accusing the student of "Machiavellianism."[32] Trame, it seemed, saw nothing wrong with the power imbalance of faculty and administrators criticizing student managers of a student activity. KXLU's reach across Los Angeles, and representation of the university to the public, he felt, justified his intervention.

Morris confirmed that DJs outside of the classical division didn't like Gampel very much.[33] That summer, rancor convinced administrators that some reorganization was necessary. Although this intervention meant administrators involved themselves in station affairs, they supported its student-run status. Students, they ruled, not community volunteers, would lead the classical division and *Alma del Barrio*. Over Trame's objections, classical received no additional hours. Despite this move in support of students, administrators requested an image shift. They recommended "continuing orientation and monitoring of our rock format" not to censor, but to encourage "cognizance and respect for the moral standards that the University stands for and the station projects to the general public."[34] LMU's administration wanted students to lead KXLU in this endeavor, not community volunteers. Gampel could continue as a host, not as director.

Trame was displeased. Though Gampel received a reprieve, he complained that the vice president for student affairs who crafted the decision "believes in permitting students untrammeled freedom to present their programs without hinderance and permits them to learn from their mistakes."

Students ran amok, trampling "Christian Values." He attempted to involve powerful alumni in influencing station management.[35]

His efforts floundered. Gampel continued to dictate to the classical music department, leading to resentments and the resignation of a student in line for the director position. The rock and classical camps persisted with pranks. When a classical DJ entreated "rock people" hanging out in the lounge to be quiet during announcements, someone "went into the operation room and switched the turntable to 45 rpm." Gampel's presence caused discord, and student directors demanded her dismissal.[36]

Morris had enough, and he fired Gampel.

Trame's anger would not relent. When KXLU lost out on a best college radio station award in 1986, he flamed Morris. Trame again reproached KXLU as a "disgrace" to the university's image and intellectual reputation that "caters to the puerile mind of the rock enthusiast," while lauding winner KCRW out of Santa Monica College for its "superiority," "compared to about 80% of the crud that goes out over KLXU."

A DJ marked up Trame's missive, noting KXLU won a similar award in 1984, before Gampel took over classical management. "Unfortunately," the staffer explained, "they won it for the 'puerile' mixture of programming you decry." "Best wishes and happy letter writing!" she concluded.[37]

Trame appealed to Loughran to reinstate Gampel, but the president refused. Trame had to inform Gampel the decision was final in November 1986.[38] In retaliation, he denied broadcasts of his choral performances on KXLU if Morris remained general manager.[39]

Morris advertised improvements in the classical format and management. KXLU, he celebrated, "transformed from the quiet non-student operation" to a "unique student-operated, community responsive program challenging the passive classical stations in the Los Angeles market." Classical programming aligned with the mission behind the rock shows: to expose listeners to new sounds in a socially conscious, Jesuit-informed manner. His emphasis on student-run status affirmed that students could achieve success without Gampel.[40] Gampel bid farewell, despite letters of support from classical DJs and fans.[41]

At the same time, word circulated regarding KCSB's troubles with the FCC. Morris copied relevant articles and warned DJs to not broadcast obscenities. After the new FCC rules, several stations including KCMU at the University of Washington refused to say the name of alternative band the Butthole Surfers, "because it's an excretory organ." They feared a fine. No such concern plagued KXLU, which continued to "take risks." A DJ explained that even if a song had "shit" in the lyrics, he might play it with a warning. Decency and quality were in the eye of the beholder, he argued. A song might contain no expletives but demean women.[42]

KXLU continued its bold musical programming and won the Best Radio Station in Los Angeles award in 1988 from *L.A. Weekly.*[43] DJs earned academic awards, four joined the Jesuit Honor Society that year, and the station hosted a party and promoted a benefit for Big Mountain Resistance Force to support Navajo nation members in keeping their land.[44]

Trame paid little attention to these accolades and continued to advocate for Gampel. New general manager Matt Kelly was having none of it. Kelly dismissed Trame's concerns about "slovenly and slipshod procedures," reiterating that KXLU was student run and "susceptible, like everyone, to mistakes." It was a unique opportunity to be able to work on a student-run station. Kelly explained, "These universities are too busy trying to sell an image a la National Public Radio and not spending enough time allowing students hands on experience in a real business environment." He was clear with Trame: "Why not add professional journalists to the newspaper staff? We could certainly improve our P.R. with a glossy *Billboard*-style *Loyolan.*"[45]

Student DJs in the late 1980s feared administrative interference and the imposition of more professional staff, reducing student airtime and management responsibilities. KXLU volunteers defended their market position in LA radio, championing the range of voices they offered. That same mission, when programming ran afoul of what a group in power wanted, might alter a station at the expense of community volunteers. Keeping radio in the hands of students prevented the addition of syndicated programs and national news and information, plus the addition of full-time, professional staff, which threatened to demote students to support staff positions. Administrators cared about whom their station reached but allowed for leeway if the station upheld the university's mission—whether training students or serving communities.

At LMU, administrators supported students against meddling faculty and community volunteers with their own aspirations. It was one debacle in an otherwise successful adventure in new music and student expression. Sometimes such battles shielded alternative music from interference, as in LMU's case. But administrators' wariness of community connections could also cut against musical trends and serving underserved communities, particularly if institutional values did not embrace the social consciousness that LMU's Jesuits (with some exceptions) supported.

Women's Programming

Block schedules provided space for community DJs, or those with a unique record collection in rockabilly, reggae, folk, or jazz. Providing coverage of women's voices, however, revisited long-standing questions about how to provide representation to identities lacking widespread coverage, particularly when relegated to "specialty" shows—segregation many DJs found offensive because it reinforced white, male radio programming as normative. DJs considered whether to integrate artists into a continuous flow of music or separate them into "specialty" shows, which provided dedicated service but tended to limit listeners. With the narrowing of radio spaces available to local activists, as well as a risk-averse music industry that only permitted certain styles of "strong" women, college radio became a place where conversations over representation could take place.

Women DJs often noted the traditionally masculine world of radio. Expanding gender representation confronted how to produce schedules that fit within stations' musical profiles or missions, as well as hierarchical management. Occasionally, a woman would rise to a position of leadership or chart careers in broadcasting thanks to a start in college radio. Donna Halper joined Northeastern University's radio station in 1968 as the first female announcer, then worked as a commercial DJ on progressive radio in the 1970s, where she helped break the band Rush.[46] In 1982, Regina Harris assumed the program director position at WJSU at Jackson State University, and she was reportedly the only Black woman in Mississippi to hold that position at a licensed radio station. She planned a career in management because these professionals provided the "backbone" in radio and television. At WJSU, a jazz station, Harris conducted remote broadcasts from community locations to provide DJs with valuable experience as well as creating ties with listeners. Although many college radio members professed commitment to expanding opportunities across genders, the culture often remained, as one DJ put it, "a boys' club."[47]

Gender representation debates were complex. NPR stations moved away from targeting a range of specific listening demographics with specialty programs. Susan Harmon, an architect of NPR programming at WAMU-FM at the University of Maryland, noted the difficulty of designating shows by their listener. Public affairs shows could be staffed by both men and women, and shows targeting women still reached men. Regarding *Kaleidoscope* on WAMU, a "woman's program," she reported as many male as female callers. "What is a woman's program, anyway?" she asked.[48] Segregated programming, other critics argued, gave "regular" programming a pass to ignore women artists or Black musicians. At the same time, these shows appealed to underrepresented groups who might support the station, while providing a place where they could find guaranteed coverage.

College radio stations continued to serve a range of listeners based on identity and interest. Often, they gained independence from fulfilling narrow campus interests. WHUS at the University of Connecticut by the 1980s had shaken off student government oversight, with funding provided by a separate fee rather than being lumped in with the student activities line item, which required elected students to sign off on the station's budget each year. WHUS existed independently under the University Center for Instructional Media and Technology, which provided engineering support. The unit would have no say in WHUS's policies or programming, a position students hoped would strengthen the station's position on campus. Separation from student government oversight did not preclude internal disputes, however, which emerged over balancing programming and resources, particularly women's shows.[49]

Record library organization featured among the most contentious issues at college stations. Keeping extensive and growing libraries accessible and orderly presented a challenge with rotating volunteers. Thefts and accidental removal of records tended to consume much time at station staff meetings, as well as disagreements over responsibility for music library organization. At WHUS, as other places, DJs who took the initiative to organize the library felt ownership because of their labors.

But in summer 1983, the WHUS's Women's Affairs director told the general manager she could no longer find the women's music file in the studio. The file catalogued the women's music section, records for programs staffed by the Women's Radio Collective. The collective maintained its own library section for its affiliated programs. Members had toiled to inventory records and to "upgrade the section, get new jackets, new copies if necessary." Zealous volunteers undid their work and reintegrated the collective's records into the general library and destroyed the catalog.

The director demanded an apology and an explanation for the file's destruction. "Did you ever hear of the golden rule, do unto others as you would want them to do unto you?????" she inquired. "How would you like it if the Rock, Jazz, or Classical card catalogs were destroyed??? How would you feel if your hard work were undone overnight?" Women's Radio Collective members felt "justified wrath," she explained, and she brought the issue to a board meeting.[50]

The decision to incorporate the women's collection emerged out of conversations regarding the balance between diversity and continuity in programming. Some DJs felt that segregating women's shows chopped up musical offerings and alienated listeners who wanted a more cohesive sound. A month before the Women's Collective complained about the library, volunteers discussed the meaning of noncommercial radio with candidates for program director. One candidate described the meaning of noncommercial radio as "diversity," and DJs questioned how he would "achieve a balance of programming." DJs juxtaposed in the schedule might air divergent sounds, whether because of a show's theme or the DJ's taste in music. The candidate promised to "smooth out" the sound, offering grades for elocution. He hoped to encourage DJs to provide natural transitions between shows, rather than jarring listeners with divergent sounds—despite DJs often priding themselves on these discordant segues.

New leaders allowed women's shows to continue. The issue was not that WHUS would eliminate these programs. Instead, specialty program DJs often felt like outsiders, catering to different listeners and separate values than "regular" college radio DJs. They often developed separate lines of organization and reporting within stations, as well, divorcing them from day-to-day business. Moreover, the episode at WHUS revealed how specialty hosts felt they had to continually justify their existence. By fall 1984, the program proposed policies to clarify matters, including adding a director for women's programs who could speak for DJs.[51] The dust settled, and at WHUS, as elsewhere, women's shows depended more on dedicated volunteers than on managers' sanction or sidelining.

Volunteer enthusiasm was essential for specialty programs, especially when they connected to local activist causes. Women's music shows, for example, often coordinated with local feminist organizations. These organizations looked for any radio station that might support them: it didn't have to be college radio. Starting in 1982 in Arizona, Phoenix Women Take Back the Night organized to confront violence against women. The group hosted International Women's Day celebrations, a common event across college and community radio, and distributed informational pamphlets. Members held a 1985 bike ride from Flagstaff to Tucson to raise awareness. The organization sponsored a *Women's Words* radio show, which they first proposed to KJZZ, a public radio station hosted at Rio Salado College. After that station rejected its proposal, the group found coverage elsewhere. In its active years, the Phoenix group broadcast shows that featured issues including women in sports, breast cancer, women with HIV, lesbian culture, and discussions with women of color about their experiences, "out" lesbian professors, and regional musicians.[52] These networks sustained long-standing radio programs in some markets—but in the 1980s, questions arose about what this cultural work achieved.

Networks formed among groups interested in building community through local, alternative radio. At Tufts University in Medford, Massachusetts, women's music anchored a long-running show on WMFO. *Something About the Women* (SAW) featured women's voices representing numerous communities. An outgrowth of second-wave feminism, the program began in 1975 to feature woman-identified musicians and groups, and it claims status as the nation's longest-running women-focused radio show. Alongside annual International Women's Day broadcasts, the Tufts station helped define feminist radio offerings in the Boston market.[53]

In the mid-1980s, SAW emphasized music as a vehicle for activism. Participants engaged in conversations about their role and identity as the media landscape and representative images of women and sexual minorities transformed. Alongside the spaces secured on prominent noncommercial stations, newfound mainstream and commercial exposure led to questions. As audiences tuned in more frequently to a wider array of voices, the term "women's music" needed clarification. At another university, leaders discussed whether "women's music" had grown stagnant. The group's conversation was inconclusive, suggesting it might be "different" from regular programming, but without any resolution.[54]

In 1989, Toni Armstrong Jr., the managing editor and publisher of women's music journal *Hot Wire*, considered it time to respond to the question, "What is women's music?"[55] Recent trends threatened to dilute the idea into a meaningless category. The consolidation of record labels and risk-averse behavior limited women artists. Even the commercially popular alternative, postpunk genre featuring "displays of androgynous masculinity: men who feel and cry," remained dominated by men who embraced femininity without "empowering women," as one scholar explained.[56] Armstrong highlighted the increase in "male musicians, technicians, producers, distributors, and other businesspeople" who structured women's experiences in the music industry alongside growing resistance to identifying music with feminism and lesbianism.[57]

Consumers needed to beware corporate-packaged versions of "strong women" and femininity that lacked social relevance. As mainstream radio and MTV featured more women, pressure seemed to rise on artists to "compromise," Armstrong explained. On college and community stations, DJs generally avoided pop and mainstream artists. Music directors often sold the latest Madonna promotional record to a used-record store, with proceeds going to buy seven-inch records from independent-label artists.[58] This attitude clashed with specialty shows such as SAW, which placed Madonna in playlists alongside the Indigo Girls, Joni Mitchell, and Melissa Etheridge— all of whom had major-label contracts or MTV airplay. At Tufts, in an end-of-year top artist list, Madonna tied with college radio–affiliated Suzanne Vega, who had crossed over to mainstream radio play.

These debates, rather than pushing social change, added to the burden DJs and artists faced. Artists identifying as women increasingly had to adhere to extra standards of authenticity to make the regular playlist on many college stations, meaning women musicians encountered more gatekeepers across all types of media. These pressures highlighted the need to maintain local spaces to air themes and content that spoke explicitly to women and queer people's identities.[59]

SAW, and shows like it, did more than amplify women's voices on radio. The show featured self-identified artists who embraced political or difficult conversations. African musicians, songwriters who included lesbian themes in their music, or adjacent political messages from artists active in anti-nuclear, public health, or anti-apartheid missions all appeared on SAW. Folk artists featured prominently, but SAW featured artists ranging from the Roches to Aretha Franklin to Eurythmics. By 1989, artists such as k.d. lang and Melissa Ethridge, who began their careers within this network, found mainstream success. SAW and similar shows refused to, as Armstrong put it, trade "expansion" with their identity's "invisibility."[60] They programmed music they wanted, paying little attention to continuity with other programs or expanding listener share. Still, equating commercial success with selling out one's identity defined debates about artistic authenticity in the 1980s.

This complicated concept of authenticity went beyond musical expression. Instead, these voices were authentic because they connected to, built, and represented communities and networks. SAW's blend of artists created a sound that evoked identity in ways unsupported by commercial media. Shows could share information about health issues or specific causes, local to national, from women's perspectives. Many college stations were happy to provide these spaces, as these functions fulfilled missions that included serving the public—even if some DJs looked on skeptically when Madonna appeared on the weekly playlist.

These shows contributed to college radio's progressive identity, even if they played major-label artists. It wasn't simply anti-Reagan hardcore bands, or critics of the capitalist culture industry seeking to build local, alternative markets and communities of music. These activist and community groups solidified college radio's connection to progressive causes and appealed to audiences perhaps unaffiliated with universities.

There was such a thing as too progressive or going too far left or too avant-garde. For administrators, easy excuses existed for shutting out these voices, especially given NPR's allure. Because stations navigated constantly shifting market conditions, university leadership, fundraising demands, regulatory changes, and audiences, the reasons for program cuts or limits in hours can be difficult to discern. But it didn't mean listeners and volunteer DJs sidelined in favor of professional staff and programming were any less angry that their voices were not valued in the public sphere.

Serving College Radio's Many Publics

While some NPR stations emerged on community or municipal signals, such as WNYC in New York or WGBH in Boston, in many markets public broadcasting resources came from colleges and universities. Signals at land-grant universities or other publicly funded colleges hosted flagship NPR stations, converting formerly student-run signals into professional providers of syndicated programming. Some made the switch smoothly, shifting students to other signals. The University of Washington transformed KUOW into a charter member of NPR in 1972, excluding students. (Students launched the ten-watt KCMU-FM in 1974.) Other stations split service, adding NPR news in the morning and evening, punctuated during the daytime hours and late at night by freeform, classical, or other community and musical programming staffed by volunteers. Yet as NPR's reputation grew, those stations found themselves caught between competing priorities, with administrators lured by the reputation and audience garnered by NPR programming and professionalization—to the dissent of volunteer community and student DJs.

One of these stations could be found in Santa Fe. At the University of New Mexico (UNM), KUNM-FM debuted in 1966 with a signal capable of reaching the surrounding area. From KUNM's start, debates regarding whom the station served surfaced. When students tuned in, they heard "basically a classical and jazz station" not in line with their tastes. In 1968, students demanded 75 percent of a schedule consist of pop music, decreasing classical programs from 30 percent of airtime to a tenth. The Radio Board overseeing KUNM required it "reflect the University community" and communicate "uniquely" to the student body. The lone dissenting vote, professor of journalism Tony Hillerman, later author of bestselling mystery novels, feared that the station would emulate commercial pop radio—which students could receive for free. Why pay for a sound with student fees when it was already available? Instead, he felt KUNM should offer something different, adopting a long-standing position against college stations existing merely as students' jukeboxes.[61]

The station fulfilled some of Hillerman's vision. KUNM debuted Samba and jazz programs, and "new groovy" rock that "commercial stations were afraid to touch." The United Mexican American Students aired mariachi music during Fiesta week. Weekends featured classical and easy listening. Station leaders got rid of "the canned stuff" to "play music and see what happened." "Elevator music" was out; in was Pacifica programming, liberal-leaning documentaries, and freeform blocks of, well, who knows what? DJs donned "hippie" garb in advertisements, with one staffer "replete with peace symbol necklace and beads standing next to a nude woman (facing away from the camera) smeared with psychedelic body paint designs with the words KUNM 90.1 Stereo highlighted on her derriere."[62]

The station's listening audience drifted from serving students' variable tastes in pop music. Iconoclasm remained: the program director relished defying the administration and the Radio Board if he received "a new album that had the word 'fuck' or 'shit' on it." He'd play it, and "stand by for a ram from the FCC or the folks in town who hated what we were doing." Few students—or any sizable audience—seemed to be tuning in.

As one staffer put it, "Hell, nobody's listening! Let's not worry."[63]

Freeform meant freedom. One DJ aired a Billy Graham crusade with golf tournament–style commentary in the background. DJs wanted to "shock" and "offend," as well as "skewer" the university administration and even station supporters: "the hip, the groovy, granola eating crowd." Irony and sarcasm ruled, with a heavy dose of antiauthoritarianism.

Devoted fans tuned in, but programming alienated listeners around and at UNM. In 1975, the student newspaper editorialized, "No longer can the station be a country club for yahoos who think they know music. It's time for KUNM to stop being just outrageous and start being part of the community."[64] By 1980, scrutiny transformed programming.

The new general manager, Paul Mansfield, implemented standards drawn from information shared by the CPB regarding audience share and how to create successful pledge drives among listeners.[65] DJs knew if Mansfield rose to general manager, "we would become NPR and not look back. He stood for progress, money, and technology."[66] When KIPC, a Pueblo Indian Council station, went bankrupt in 1977, ceasing its NPR service to the area, University of New Mexico's student senate voted to bring NPR to KUNM. The Radio Board expanded staff to levels required for CPB funding. The student senate raised concerns that only 20 percent of volunteers were students, unlike years prior, but changes continued.[67]

Dissonance grew between NPR proponents and students and local volunteers. DJs provided incidents, however innocuous, justifying the changes. The host of Friday night's *Asylum Radio* habitually "feign[ed] drunkenness on the air and play[ed] outrageous Neo-country music." A community member complained when the show aired Kinky Friedman and his Texas Jewboys' "I'm Proud to be an Asshole from El Paso." A complaint made its way to the desk of UNM's president, who had the dean of students intervene. The dean ordered Mansfield to fire the DJ. Radio Board members protested this usurpation of their authority. The DJ remained fired, and the incident channeled rising rancor over the station's community connections and new professional management structure.[68]

In 1978, KUNM began its NPR affiliation, airing twenty hours of news a week, including the evening program *All Things Considered*.[69] Volunteers could stay, but Mansfield emphasized that "air-shifts" did not "belong (like personal property) to the people filling them." His supervision paled compared with limits on "creative freedom" at commercial stations, he reasoned. He reviewed DJs periodically, looking for "sloppy board work" and dead air. Announcers should avoid "mumbling," improve delivery, and adhere to format. Playing personal preferences, avoiding new releases, or not "exploring the total library" would damage KUNM's sound and fail to appeal to listeners across Santa Fe, whom Mansfield actively sought.[70]

Mansfield expanded programming for the Latino community to draw community listeners. Producers of KUNM's *Raices Y Conciencia del Pueblo* belonged to Latinos in Public Radio, a group distributing "Latino public affairs programs to participating stations within the NPR network." These volunteers requested office space to expand Spanish-language shows.[71] The station's prestige grew, and programming expanded, requiring additional resources. A cascading effect ensued, with station leaders adding NPR hours to draw more support. If the station could prove it served a wide array of listeners, CPB funding might expand.

NPR promoted itself well. In April 1980, Mansfield added NPR's *Morning Edition*. He told all DJs, "NPR is spending a good deal of money on a national awareness campaign for the program." Mansfield's market research indicated high demand for morning news, which would "generate new listeners and introduce them to the best of what we do as a station." Despite internal dissent regarding *Morning Edition*, he proceeded.[72] Mansfield saw NPR and professionalism as the way to maintain independence, not as giving in to external control. Good quality would enhance donations, respectability, and KUNM's ability to influence state support for public broadcasting. Plus, the university's administration could not intervene if KUNM boasted a loyal listener base.

Volunteers agreed on the mission to serve "the people." How it served them, and who "they" were, varied, however. Offering the "best radio possible," presenting "music and information that is not available elsewhere" might suffice. Still, this goal did not always support DJs in taking risks, experimenting, training students, or filling the university's educational obligations. Others emphasized the station as a community forum. KUNM offered a "liaison" between town and gown, providing educational content and programs "sensitive to as many points of view as possible." To reach these multiple goals, DJs demanded better coordination between paid and unpaid staff and continued training of students for on-air spots.[73]

Students went further. They demanded KUNM pull back to serving the university first. In spring 1981, student government leaders decried the lack of student input. The student body president brought complaints to the university regents. Regents had an "obligation" to "keep the Radio Board intact," referring to the campus organization that oversaw the station, which included five students. Students insisted administrative "censorship set a dangerous precedent." Student fees paid for equipment and improvements, but the regents held the license, meaning they could implement whatever changes they wanted without violating the First Amendment.[74]

Volunteers for freeform programs capitalized on the turmoil. Because Mansfield made the decision unilaterally, they seized the governance matter to challenge changes and demanded his resignation. Mansfield's defenders applauded the enlarged broadcast area after an equipment and tower upgrade, which justified "tighter administrative control." Everyone would benefit, in their view.[75]

Tensions rose, and Mansfield quietly resigned. In May 1981, UNM's administration proposed a new oversight plan: a compromise in which "the spoils were divided," according to one participant. A University Radio Committee replaced the Radio Board with control over programming and policy, which maintained student representation. The administration selected station management and set funding. Student fees continued to fund the station, but policy changes assigned funding control to the administration instead of the student senate.[76]

Freeform proponents would not get what they wanted despite Mansfield's resignation. Some developments aligned with their goals as KUNM continued its business over the next few years. The new station manager implemented more nationally syndicated programming. She added *A Prairie Home Companion* and shows to address "women's and Third World issues," as the CBP directed funding to individual stations, rather than to NPR directly.[77] A new program director from Pacifica's KPFK added "'bilingual' freeform radio," and an "ethnic coordinator" joined the staff.[78]

Many listeners appreciated the range of programming. In 1987, one audiophile loved hearing "half an hour of Zydeco, followed by Wendy Waldman, Irene Cara, Aretha Franklin, [and] Tom Waits," mixed with classical and NPR news. KUNM's unique blend, it seemed, captured the community's diversity. "It makes me feel that, by virtue of being a member of the community, KUNM is my station, and mine in a way that no other station is or can pretend to be," one listener noted.[79]

Still, prestige remained a goal, much to the consternation of freeform DJs and students. Management aimed for a "high standard of excellence in the jazz field" and professionally produced classical music programs. "In KUNM's case," a manager told volunteers, "the license is held by the University of New Mexico," implying that programming must reflect institutional values of excellence—which he felt freeform did not do.[80] Some listeners might be angry, but if KUNM curbed eclecticism, its listener base would grow and ensure donations and lucrative underwriting deals, thanks to newly standardized practices for public radio fundraising.[81]

To this end, in winter 1986, KUNM hired a new program director and station manager. The new staff members, Pat Conley and Tim Singleton, "were convinced that 'freeform' programming would not work in the 'modern' public radio market," according to a volunteer DJ. Conley and Singleton proposed programming with "predictability" and implemented a gag order on volunteers discussing impending changes.

Rumors about the changes spread among listeners, who voiced concerns on a March 1987 call-in show. Although hosts assured callers that no major plans were in the works, speculation swirled about dramatic changes, and volunteers knew these to be true.

The April fundraiser went ahead without any mention of new programming. In May, daytime freeform DJs and the jazz hosts received notice that their slots would discontinue in August. Students' on-air opportunities dwindled.

Questions emerged even among paid staff whether new syndicated jazz and classical shows would foster more local programs or reach minorities. Some took a colorblind view, arguing "the goal of public radio was to attract the intelligent listener, regardless of ethnic group." The station hosted *Singing Wire* among other programs for Native American communities. Volunteers claimed this service relied on fostering a public radio image first, offering a gateway to local programs, rather than the other way around. It was a centralized approach. Listeners protested, too, but the general manager insisted all relevant views had been considered. Program decisions, leaders insisted, occurred "on merit alone," not to eliminate ornery volunteers on the freeform programs or quirky fans seeking progressive news and Frank Zappa.[82]

Volunteers defied the new format. The station manager ignored their grievances filed that May. An afternoon freeform DJ announced the planned changes on air, demanded Singleton and Conley resign, and asked listeners to withhold donations. A scuffle reportedly broke out when the program director attempted to "forcefully remove" another announcer for violating the gag rule. The station manager held firm to his decision to curtail freeform on KUNM and would hear no objections.

On June 1, 1987, a disgruntled announcer informed listeners of the pending changes. Daytime freeform would end, replaced "by one more hour daily of NPR's *Morning Edition*, 3 hours daily of another NPR satellite program called 'Performance Today,' and 5 hours daily of a jazz program." Twelve volunteer DJs filed grievances.

After two tense staff meetings, Singleton went public with the changes. He declared that NPR's "advantages" outweighed its "drawbacks." The station operated "on behalf of its licensee, the UNM Board of Regents," and volunteers had no say. One listener declared being "flabbergasted" by these statements. Another called KUNM's freeform hours "truly democratic." Several listeners complained they felt their pledge dollars to be misused.[83]

A modified gag order went into effect in June.[84] An amendment allowed announcements regarding new programs, but not cancellations. Volunteer DJs could not issue "commentaries, opinions, correspondence and/or other announcements." No one was to discuss changes, or a pending rally in support of freeform programming. One volunteer penned a protest rap, the "Freeform Shuffle," which managers also banned.[85]

Freeform's defenders persisted. On June 11, volunteers hosted a call-in show, without the program director's approval, to discuss program changes. UNM administrators refused to meet with volunteer DJs. Management suspended any DJ announcing the planned rally in support for freeform.

Four hundred and fifty supporters gathered on UNM's campus in June. They circulated petitions and posted signatures on the door of the administration building. Friends of Freeform, composed of listeners and volunteers opposing changes, declared KUNM "one of the best radio stations in this world," with freeform constituting its "heart and soul." They put their statement into a PSA to be aired on KUNM. A Friends representative asked Singleton to put the PSA into rotation, as it did not "constitute slander, libel, or obscenity." Not doing so would violate the First Amendment, they charged, since KUNM had no specific requirements for PSA content.[86] (Precedent did not support their position, since FCC regulations privileged license holders over individual DJs in determining content.)

Freeform's defenders went beyond public pressure. On June 30, Friends of Freeform filed a class-action lawsuit in Bernalillo County Court, charging KUNM with fraud. Listeners pledged money in April without knowing the station would soon change its programming. The lawsuit claimed the station misrepresented how funds would be used, since many donations came in for freeform shows set to be canceled. Volunteers enlisted the ACLU's help, charging that their civil rights had been violated. The administration terminated all negotiations with volunteers. The judge issued a restraining order to freeze listener contributions.[87] After receiving threats, the station manager shut off service during a Pacifica News broadcast. The station covered Iran Contra hearings but shut down at night, when freeform usually aired. Paid staff took over production of folk, jazz, and specialty programs.

Another rally protested the end of KUNM's freeform hours on August 1, but the new format went into effect on August 3. The fight reached the pages of the *Wall Street Journal*, which chronicled the departure of DJ Hot Lixx, who mixed "golden oldies" with sharp criticism of New Mexico's prison conditions.[88]

More lawsuits emerged that fall.[89] Student groups disputed the changes, soliciting the student senate's support. They demanded a referendum vote on KUNM to establish a "representative radio board" to make the station accountable to students, who paid fees to support it, amounting to a third of the station's budget.[90]

UNM's president appointed a new Radio Advisory Board to investigate and make recommendations. Board members emphasized the multiple audiences served. Eight hours of music every day, another member disagreed, "isn't much variety." Conflict surfaced between members who sought to grow the listening audience, citing the station's dead last position in FM ratings that year, and those who stressed that KUNM need not compete but should seek out and fulfill "unmet needs." The Radio Board resisted allowing students control of musical programming. Because students turned over from year to year, such churn would further alienate audiences. The board had trouble reconciling maintaining audience interest and training students, citing a "fundamental contradiction between largeness and distinctiveness." One member dissented, but the board did not view freeform and students as representing the university well in public.[91]

The Radio Advisory Board, despite its views regarding freeform, indicted KUNM's management practices. Managers used plagiarized research from a Florida station to justify the format change. Administrators manipulated the public about the situation and misrepresented community protests. The board voted no confidence in station managers and recommended a permanent governing board, rather than relying on a single administrator.[92] The president's allowance of the unilateral format change violated the spirit and principle behind educational radio.[93]

All sides claimed to represent the community's best interests and to value quality, diverse programming. Nonetheless, bitterness defined the process, which fizzled without a clear winner. Administrators rejected the board's findings as "biased" and ignored the recommendations, rebuffing student senate and graduate student association requests for representatives. Resignations continued at the station, while a CPB consultant advised managers to "tough it out" until protesting volunteers quit.[94] A former volunteer director and lone staff person of color, who had issued the gag order, left the station amid "hard feelings."[95]

UNM students and Friends of Freeform persisted. Declaring "Freeform Shuffle Strikes Again," a benefit concert with local musical acts supported their crusade.[96] They petitioned the student senate, which called a referendum to establish a governing board consisting of more students and community members. They next took their complaints to the New Mexico legislature. Because KUNM was a station housed at a public institution, the board of regents recognized it as an important community resource.[97]

In April 1988, the UNM Board of Regents dismissed students who tried to address it about KUNM but formed a subcommittee to "study the problem." The subcommittee convened with representatives of involved groups. It instructed university attorneys to draft a settlement and issued a moratorium on lawsuit activity. In May, the regents ended talks and empowered the university's attorney to settle lawsuits. Through the summer, volunteers reapplied to the station, though management insisted no room remained.[98]

In fall 1988, to heal rifts, an interim advisory board proposed to reintegrate former volunteers who quit or were terminated. Students could fill off-air positions for educational experience. The regents established the Community Advisory Board, allowing undergraduates, graduate students, faculty, and community members to advise in station affairs.[99]

As KUNM adopted the new governance structure, volunteers and staff produced more local programs to fulfill the station's revamped mission. Freeform continued in blocks not filled by syndicated or professionally produced local programs.[100] Staff took care to consider balance between national versus local shows. (Although additional cuts to freeform emerged in 1992, indie rock and freeform hours continued to air on KUMN.)[101]

KUMN's format controversies reflected the power exercised by institutional license holders who faced pressure from within and outside regarding radio, particularly amid changing practices regarding audience identity and cultivation from the CPB and NPR. It became harder in the 1980s to reconcile the "character" of college stations operating with freeform principles, and the reputable sounds available through NPR—and to turn down the prestige and funding that came with it.

• • • • • •

More than the lure of slick, nationally produced and recognized news and information tempted stations to adopt NPR and add professional staff. Students often joined radio stations because they wanted to become media professionals and executives, not simply to play the latest hardcore or experimental noise seven-inch record. Their pedagogical function, which originated such signals, never disappeared, despite how many local venues they supported or artists they exposed to potential fans. Even with the growing gap between public and educational radio, student-run radio still presented a valuable learning experience for those interested in careers in broadcasting. But instead of clashing with administrators who wanted to burnish institutional reputations with NPR programming and listening audiences, these students seeking professional experience more often butted heads with other students who saw radio as an activity in line with their liberal arts education rather than providing them with concrete, marketable skills.

Many constituents looked hungrily at the space occupied by these stations that aired students who fumbled with the controls, mispronounced city names, or had little dedication to jazz traditions. College radio's prestige grew with its recognized ability to break independent or obscure artists to mainstream success, anchoring stops on regional touring networks or sustaining countercultural ecosystems. Yet service relied on radio stations founded for pedagogical functions or as a public relations tool for the university. That was a lot of need to fulfill. As public radio grew more distinct in funding mechanisms and programming from student-run stations relying on student activity fees or curricular connections, it became increasingly difficult to make everyone happy. Varying expectations clashed particularly when tastes and aspirations diverged and the business of radio—and of higher education itself—clashed with the sound of music. It was a paradox, and one fraying at many stations across the nation by the end of the 1980s.

11 Saving the Sound Alternative

· ·

One night in October 1978, news staffer Dave Grissom penned a fake news report. The student in the University of Kansas (KU) journalism program earned professional experience at the student-run radio station KJHK. But sometimes the allure of a good prank is too hard to resist.[1]

The "Waterloo incident" started as a joke when Grissom and a friend prepared a "phony story" reporting 15,000 deaths in Waterloo, Iowa, after a nuclear reactor explosion. They "had a good laugh about it," but the report ended up in the pile of newscasts to be read instead of in the trash. The next newscaster read the story and "all hell broke loose." Panic ensued among worried listeners, and the incident sparked national news coverage and an FCC investigation.

KJHK had themselves a "War of the Worlds"–type of event, akin to the 1938 Orson Welles broadcast that scared some listeners into briefly believing an alien invasion was underway.[2]

Grissom recovered, along with KJHK. He received a suspension but became news director the following fall. KJHK provided serious training. The university's prestigious William Allen White School of Journalism expended significant funds for its supervision, including dedicated faculty.[3] The station produced newscasters, reporters, and other radio and television professionals. One, Steve Doocy, would later anchor at cable channel Fox News (figure 11.1).

This practical laboratory for journalism students emerged alongside a reputation for supporting the local music scene and underground rock circuit—and for a few years, the two purposes coexisted. But a former DJ, writing in the spring of 1990, chronicled years of feuding over station control that subjected KJHK to "censorship, a blacklist, the KKK, and a bomb threat." A McCarthy-like atmosphere at the station topped anything involved in the Waterloo incident.[4]

Avant-garde musician Frank Zappa weighed in on the situation.

Zappa referred to faculty and administrators who attempted to take over the station as "Nazis," and he instructed DJs to "Get rid of those f—— mongoloids!"[5]

FIGURE 11.1 Future Fox News anchor Steve Doocy started his career as a DJ at KJHK in the 1970s. Kenneth Spencer Research Library, University of Kansas.

Zappa's targets included KJHK's adviser and faculty in the journalism program. As one student put it, "The faculty appreciates conformity more than imagination, obedience over intelligence, and order over freedom."[6]

Proponents of professional training tussled over control of a college radio station with advocates of musical exploration as an extension of liberal arts education. Fights over format consumed KJHK in the late 1980s and provoked picket lines and tense exchanges. The station, uniquely positioned at the crossroads of fraying paradoxes in college radio, had all the ingredients for a conflagration.

College DJs resolved after the FCC's 1978 class D decision to prove amateurs could provide professional-sounding radio alongside cutting-edge music. They protected iconoclastic programming with the shield of providing educational content. Signals served the functions of liberal arts inquiry and exploration while also preparing graduates for the workforce—prompting an increasingly tenuous balance between college radio's national musical reputation and its pedagogical and economic functions.

With the atrophy of public services since the 1970s, universities supplied urban and economic development, workforce training, and technological and scientific innovation while supporting artistic exploration and intellectual activity that might not have wide commercial appeal. Some student DJs were able to position themselves parasitically (or symbiotically) with the cultural capital universities held to protect iconoclasm, engaging in real possibilities for alternatives to culture industry power or to push universities into even more challenging expression to subvert existing hierarchies of taste and status.[7] Increasingly, by the late 1980s, DJs found themselves caught in the middle of these clashing expectations for higher education, whether they participated to receive credit for a broadcasting degree or because they loved thrash metal.

Increasingly lost in these battles were the communities outside of universities that relied on these signals. As college radio's national star rose, localism faded as a justification for college radio, even as it persisted in shaping programming at individual stations. KU's journalism faculty placed pedagogical goals and market functions above holding a noncommercial, educational license that offered public service and musical exploration. The faculty undervalued college radio, rock critic Dave Marsh argued, "the only outlet for music in America that isn't dependent on making a profit for investors." Much like the pursuit of higher learning, college radio's cultural contributions should not be measured by album sales or salaries earned upon graduation, he argued. College radio supported artists who enriched national and global culture. But it seemed only ratings mattered.

For institutions, serving the market (however they defined it), rather than producing knowledge and an educated citizenry, justified their existence and funding. In KJHK's situation, providing "real world" skills threatened the cultural explorations college students engaged in, rather than these purposes coexisting and reinforcing one another. Culture warriors in the late 1980s and early 1990s targeted curricula in higher education as eroding values of Western civilization. At student-run stations, a war for the soul of college radio revealed different dimensions of how the culture wars undermined liberal arts education and visited upon university curricula.

Professionals in Training

When KJHK launched on FM in 1975, it offered a "realistic broadcast laboratory" for journalism majors superior to a carrier-current signal. It mirrored the professionalism of KU's other noncommercial station KANU, an initial carrier of NPR's *All Things Considered*. This division between professional, outward-facing radio shielded the student-run station's independence. KJHK had less power but could still be heard by some 50,000 listeners in the Lawrence area. Kansas Jayhawk Radio offered something for everyone: news, jazz, Top 40 during the day, and "progressive at night." It would educate, entertain, and train.[8]

In 1978, the station shifted toward progressive music while maintaining its professionalism. Journalism school students gained experience writing news copy, and advertising students solicited underwriting. An experimental spirit took hold, both in musical coverage and among DJs who enjoyed themselves on and off the air. A freewheeling culture made for unique radio experiences: one DJ broadcast sounds of Pop Rocks candy exploding in his mouth.[9] Antics aside, KJHK needed funds to improve its transmitter and increase power to 100 watts after the FCC's class D phaseout. The student senate promised $18,000 in 1980 for the upgrade. KJHK's faculty adviser gushed that the power and new reel-to-reel tape system lived up to KJHK's prestige. "I'd put us definitely in the top three of 10-watt student-run radio stations in the country," he estimated at a time when few press outlets paid attention to college radio rankings, "and I'd have to sit and figure out who the other two are." The station's relationship with a top-rated school of journalism enhanced its reputation, which it maintained even with the progressive turn.[10]

Meanwhile, KJHK developed relationships with local venues. In 1981, DJs partnered with a local cable system to profile bands appearing at the Lawrence Opera House. Acts included XTC, whose "experimental pop" sound marked groups' growing divergence from other punk contemporaries. The songs remained short and punchy, like those of iconic punk bands the Sex Pistols and the Clash. But XTC included synthesizers and melodic hooks, reflecting the artistic experimentation the punk revolution engendered. That revolution reached Kansas, the local music scene, and established KJHK as a player in its development. KJHK became known as "The Sound Alternative," typifying college radio's emerging musical reputation in the 1980s.

Faculty provided guidance and tolerated the new musical focus as rumors circulated that KJHK's aesthetics was not welcome at the journalism school. In 1984, the *University Daily Kansan*, KU's student newspaper, reported changes behind the scenes. The Sound Alternative "may sound the same," but personnel changes were afoot.

A new broadcast division chair in the journalism department, Max Utsler, envisioned KJHK as a laboratory, without the rabble. With the school's television station having "gone belly up" and demand for the broadcasting major increasing, journalism faculty "turned toward the little stone cottage on the edge of the campus" filled with "thrash albums" and covered in "punk-rock posters."[11] As one professor explained, "It wasn't run like a real station." Advertising majors needed "positive sales experiences," students struggled without "programming consistency," and the audience remained paltry, in his view.[12]

Utsler pursued an unapologetic vision for KJHK as a professional training ground with backing from KU's chancellor. "The closer we can come to creating an on-the-job situation," he explained, "the better it will be for the students and their future employers." KU could serve corporate media companies that demanded experienced graduates. The faculty accepted that the station played unconventional music. Funding required a balance between KJHK as a student activity that allowed for musical exploration and its laboratory functions. (It didn't really matter what the product was to sell, or the content being announced, the faculty reasoned, even if they carped about the lack of audience because of niche musical service.) Utsler aimed to improve on-air delivery, training students in the business of radio by securing underwriters, writing shorter, punchier spots, and making frequent news breaks.[13] Competition for shifts increased, but in 1984 it seemed KJHK would remain the Sound Alternative and feature professionalism in underwriting, news, and reporting.[14]

Over the next three years, however, faculty retirements and resignations prompted a newly installed dean to review KJHK's operations more closely.[15]

The Power and Prestige

KJHK served market functions, just not those that the new dean or Utsler valued. In 1978, Steve Greenwood had shaped KJHK's reputation for playing music unavailable elsewhere. It was the first station in the area to play punk music. Known for boasting a "Johnny Ramone haircut and a bag full of records," Greenwood worked at a local record store and devoted himself to finding the best new music. As music director in the late 1970s, he reshaped the signal with "punk-invigorated rock" and championed the local music scene, promoting bands such as the Embarrassment, the Regular Guys, the Mortal Micronotz, the Clean, and the Thumbs.[16]

Local bands broadcast live. A DJ interviewed local writer William S. Burroughs and poet Allen Ginsberg. KJHK lured bands to the Lawrence Opera House, including the Cramps, the Police, and Stevie Ray Vaughan. Bands drove for hours from Wichita or Lincoln, Nebraska, to play the local clubs.

It took a few years for the scene to develop, and members of KJHK were instrumental players. A local production company and DIY clubs such as the Outhouse were "organized and initiated" by a former DJ and "KJHK management" in 1985. "The live progressive rock scene," one columnist remembered, "was very dead from late 1983 through late 1985. No clubs. No local bands. No action. KJHK was the instrumental force in changing all that."[17] The Meat Puppets, among other underground acts, played there, cultivating Lawrence's reputation. By 1986, KJHK published its own biweekly *New Music Reports* to cover upcoming shows, radio shows, and reviews. *Spin* and *Rolling Stone* recognized Lawrence as an influential scene. KJHK's general manager coordinated with a local label to produce a compilation album of area talent—a practice popular with college radio stations to promote local bands and to raise funds.[18]

But the faculty intervened in station affairs by exploiting blind spots in programming. KJHK's inattention to diversity and sometimes offensive content stoked faculty discontent. In 1983, the organization Blacks in Communication at KU asked the student senate to review KJHK's schedule. The group identified only three hours a week dedicated to minority listeners' interests. The senate could exercise its funding power to encourage the station to diversify its sound and please students who paid its bills. Failing to consider minority perspectives weakened KJHK's claims as an alternative for all listeners. As faculty were building the case for intervention, hosts of talk show *Jay-talk 91* invited two local Ku Klux Klan members on air, supposedly to debate them and debunk their views. Reports of the invitation reached Black Lawrence residents, who convinced journalism faculty to cancel the appearance.[19]

School of Journalism dean Mike Kautsch was watching and planning. As a respected journalist, educator, and scholar of media, technology, and law, he knew the station's potential. His vision aligned with Utsler's.[20] In 1986, KJHK's advisory board engaged a consulting firm to measure listenership among KU students. This industry approach signaled the faculty's desire for professionalization. The study, administrators reported, found only 5 percent of students tuned in to KJHK. Faculty concluded: the station ignored students, "our primary target audience." DJs had a "bad attitude," resisted any oversight, and "alienated" listeners. KJHK needed an "identifiable format."[21]

Faculty demanded the "runaway station" heel, levying an "ultimatum" for students to clean up programming. The board would step in and program the station unless volunteers proposed "a format that the faculty on the board can live with." Faculty board members represented the license holder and could issue whatever requirements they chose without violating the station's constitution, they argued. Only student activities funding allocated by the student senate stood in the way because it required the activity be open to all KU students, regardless of major.[22]

DJs questioned the faculty board's motivations and its survey. The faculty, as one DJ told the dean, willfully misinterpreted data. The surveys "indicate that 65% of students surveyed said that they wanted to hear music from the sixties and seventies," he affirmed. "The next highest figure," however, "was 62%, who said they wanted to hear alternative music." A three-point difference did not suggest students demanded complete revision of KJHK's format, the DJs inferred.[23]

A new playlist circulated at KJHK in December 1987. It replaced the previous format, in which DJs could play any song at any time, limited only by the theme of their program. The change added artists such as A-ha, Billy Joel, and John Cougar Mellencamp, whom DJs previously avoided. Yet listeners could still tune in to the Circle Jerks and the Ramones, depending on the DJ. Leaders billed the change as a reorganization of what the station already played, creating clearer categorization and rotation standards. One DJ told the *Daily Kansan* that he welcomed the change. Now he could play the Replacements' *Pleased to Meet Me*, a major-label album from the Minneapolis band first signed by independent Twin Tone Records but that moved to Sire at Warner Brothers. KJHK management previously slated R.E.M., the Cure, and the Replacements as "too commercial." DJs felt freer to play them after the change, which relaxed rules on playing major-label releases.[24]

KJHK's programming dilemmas reflected college radio's growing popularity and the problems that came with it. DJs freed from rotation rules and requirements could play whatever they liked, especially bands lacking commercial support. With college stations reporting to trade press outlets such as CMJ, which tallied top acts and compiled regional and national charts, a rising band in one scene might achieve national recognition. This trend prompted fears college radio would homogenize and shut out artists without the potential to cross over to mainstream audiences. Opponents of KJHK's change feared losing the station's leadership in independent music, adopting a more nationally oriented sound that hewed to whatever hits appeared on the national college charts, thereby ignoring local artists.[25]

DJs chafed at limits to their freedom to select songs and highlight local bands. The station manager insisted KJHK maintained its Sound Alternative identity, with more structure.

Faculty saw all of this as an overreaction. In the proposed format, alternative music still centered KJHK's programming. Instead of looking to *Billboard* and other mainstream charts, the station consulted "college charts, RockPool/CMJ, and homegrown music" and surveys of KU students.[26] No songs heard on commercial radio would air; instead, deeper cuts from albums by popular artists would appear alongside "KJHK Classics," artists the station had helped launch, and "Hot Up & Comers" from the local scene. The popular thrash show remained on the schedule in spring and summer 1988.

But the fight over KJHK had only just begun.

Fuck You, Billy Tubbs

Kansas's basketball team progressed to the national championship game in the NCAA basketball tournament in 1988 and met Big Eight conference rival Oklahoma in the final.

Max Utsler tuned in on his car radio for KJHK's coverage, which featured remote reports and phone-ins. He listened "aglow with pleasure and pride." He called the broadcast "the epitome of community radio," likely picturing KU fans tuning in across the region. As sportscasters ceded the station back to the music staff, excitement continued—to Utsler's horror.

No recordings remain. But, Utsler explained, "lots of people heard the same thing." The student, perhaps a bit incensed by sports preempting his thrash show, transitioned back to music.

"Well, I'm glad that crap is finally over," he told listeners. "Now back to what we're about: Music!" He dedicated the next song to the Sooners' coach, announcing, "This one's for Billy Tubbs," chanting, "Fuck you, Billy Tubbs! Fuck you!! Fuck you!!!"

Such a violation, if reported to the FCC, jeopardized the station's pending power increase. Perhaps ebullience related to the Kansas win could excuse it, but it was clear the thrash DJ didn't really care about basketball.

Utsler's resolve to overhaul KJHK strengthened. He proposed that only graduate students should be allowed in management positions. The board approved making these positions paid, answerable for "job performance," and elevated to a voting board member position. With the pool narrowed to graduate students, and the general manager's power enhanced, students worried. The general manager "did not necessarily have to work his/her way up the ranks through the KHJK staff positions." In fact, the new requirements counteracted any candidate with that pedigree. Faculty contended, "Nothing is wrong with some academic influence and wisdom."

On the surface, logic prevailed. As a station linked to a communications school, KJHK performed pedagogical functions. But DJs saw Utsler as rigging policy to institute wholesale changes at KJHK through his handpicked general manager.

Utsler hadn't finished. With the application for a 1,000-watt license to be submitted to the FCC, he targeted the thrash music that followed the expletive-laced Tubbs dedication. As a KU publication explained, thrash emerged from the Washington, D.C., music scene as "politically oriented American punk rock marked by a hard and very fast sound and by lyrics that often contain violent images." Utsler thought, horrified, "What if the chancellor is listening? What if some downtown businessman is listening?"[27] Utsler harbored concerns about musical content and the station's professional reputation that violating FCC rules threatened. He tolerated a certain amount of iconoclasm, but this simply went too far.

Tensions crystallized in summer 1988, when the station's advisory board installed interim manager Jerry Howard. Howard appeared to be a faculty plant, reportedly telling a DJ seeking a staff position, "If you are not prepared to go 50% mainstream, don't even apply."[28] Faculty hoped that Howard, a graduate student, could provide staid leadership and safeguard the pending power increase and oversee listener expansion.

Late that June, posters disappeared for KJHK-sponsored shows at local clubs. Howard cut the Monday night thrash show. As DJs described the response, "Thrashheads [went] nuts." In protest, someone spray-painted "No Cash in thrash" on the building housing the studio. Howard confiscated all albums "considered thrash" to scan them for obscenities, taking albums donated by DJs. The summer program director marched to Utsler's office after finding empty boxes where new albums were stored and his official stationery removed from his desk.[29]

Utsler refused to relinquish the records and threw the student out. The program director protested, "They took my job by ripping it out from under me." At a July staff meeting, Utsler insisted he did nothing to interfere with programming, despite having rejected student proposals in response to changes that previous winter. DJs challenged Utsler's interference, to which he reportedly replied, "Well, I suppose you could look at it that way if you *wanted* to."

Student representatives on the advisory board felt powerless. As one member testified, "The faculty's response was thrust upon me. I had no vote. I had no say." The idea of the board as a "governing body" seemed a "farce," with the students serving as mere observers, rather than policymakers. Offended DJs left the meeting and met at Yello Sub/Glass Onion, a favorite local gathering spot, along with some 300 outraged supporters.[30]

DJs poured their concerns on coffee-stained sheets of notebook paper, identifying potential allies and enemies and venting their anger. They debated Jerry Howard's complicity. As one community supporter wrote, Howard "is not the real bogeyman in this horror flick." Instead, he was "a tool manipulated by the actual culprit or culprits," meaning Utsler and his allies. Perhaps Howard would wake up and "realize how he's being used and how he is being made ultimately to be the patsy in this situation." DJs felt stuck. One admitted he possessed scant power in the situation, but his anger was palpable. "I'm just a big, loud guy with long hair and a pair of shorts whose pockets hang down below them." He hoped others would rally. "I'm just one guy—shit, there's a mess of people out there who are pissed off—and they won't go away."[31]

Howard cleaned up KJHK's image on air and off. Besides removing potentially offending albums, he removed the studio's tatty punk-rock posters. Punk and metal DJs saw Howard as an administration toady who promoted pop music from the likes of Whitney Houston and Elton John. The board prevented community members and alumni from station participation, effectively ending specialty shows that catered to listeners in the wider Lawrence community.[32] Utsler dismissed concerns that drastic changes were coming, insisting KJHK could never compete with commercial heavyweights in the area's market—he simply wanted greater professionalism. Was that too much to ask, especially if the station's license might be in jeopardy?[33]

The Camps Emerge

As summer gave way to fall semester 1988, KJHK's volunteers who were not broadcasting majors plotted their response. With almost military precision, they categorized enemies "who want a bite of KJHK." Many students were apathetic about the station until they realized their fees funded it—but even then, they cared only a little. The apathetic crowd, according to DJs, were lulled to complacency by mainstream tunes. Other students with an "intelligent ear to music" wanted "an alternative available and recognize what will be missing" if KJHK adopted more mainstream fare. A smaller cohort dedicated to KJHK "tradition" consisted of students "raised" under an "alternative flag" who resisted faculty control vehemently (figure 11.2). They were angry, indeed.[34]

These DJs squared off against ambitious journalism students. Radio and Television majors, DJs scoffed, "have motivation grilled into them" and "support and except [sic] all 'faculty' decisions." "Faculty" appeared in scare quotes to indicate the machinations of a few who privileged the needs of their majors over existing DJs and devoted listeners. DJs accepted academic motivations compared with a dastardly subgroup they identified, which sought KJHK's professionalization "to stop jocks from playing foul music" and claimed to represent "taste."[35]

KJHK's devoted listeners and local businesses that supported the Sound Alternative protested. KJHK attracted patrons to local record stores, restaurants, venues, and other—often countercultural—businesses. KJHK cultivated community "spirit." Yet these were not the businesses that faculty targeted for advertising revenue.[36]

Utsler demanded faculty power to determine programming. Alternative was "too restrictive and not competitive enough with area commercial stations" to provide valuable training. DJs were "out of control, IE: 'too much use of music with 4-letter words offending women, minorities and other groups and glorifying death, teenage suicide, and drugs." These utterances—and potential FCC fines—put the station's license in jeopardy and offended their sensibilities.[37]

"Sound Alternative" DJs were numerous but lacked institutional clout. They proclaimed "students' rights" and enumerated offenses Utsler committed in the name of professionalization, such as seizing records and installing a handpicked general manager. Community supporters joined, including a few local bar owners and Steve Greenwood, the champion of KJHK's progressive sound in the late 1970s. They defended an "eleven-year award winning tradition" that faculty "usurped from student control."[38] DJs understood that shoddy professionalism endangered KJHK's license, but they rallied around preserving "the Sound Alternative flag" above mimicking commercial radio.[39]

At stake was KJHK's status as a community institution. Faculty appeared to be outsiders to Lawrence. As one DJ suggested, "They aren't going to outlast us." Community listeners maintained deep devotion to KJHK as faculty came and went. "We were listening to KJHK a long time before they even came to this town," one Sound Alternative supporter asserted. If the

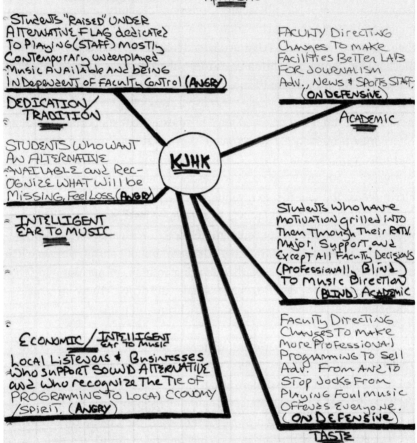

WHO WANTS BITE OF KJHK ?

ABSENT — Students NOT Affiliated w/station Rising-up For Changes at KJHK.
Apathetic

Students "Raised" Under Alternative Flag dedicated To Playing (staff) mostly Contemporary unceaplayed Music Available and being Independent of Faculty Control (ANGRY)

DEDICATION / TRADITION

Students who want An Alternative Available and Recognize what will be Missing, Feel Loss. (ANGRY)

INTELLIGENT EAR TO MUSIC

KJHK

FACULTY Directing Changes To make Facilities Better Lab For Journalism Adv., News & Sports Staff. (ON DEFENSIVE)

ACADEMIC

Students who have Motivation grilled into Them Through Their RTV. Major, Support and Except All Faculty Decisions (Professionally Blind) To Music Direction (BLIND) Academic

ECONOMIC / INTELLIGENT EAR TO MUSIC

Local Listeners & Businesses who support sound Alternative and who recognize The Tie of Programming To Local Economy / Spirit. (ANGRY)

Faculty Directing Changes To make More Professional Programming To Sell Adv. From ANE To Stop Jocks From Playing Foul Music Offends Everyone. (ON DEFENSIVE)

TASTE

FIGURE 11.2 "Who Wants a Bite of KJHK?" detailed by those organized to combat a Top 40 format from being implemented. The sketch details the many expectations that university members and community listeners had for these signals by the end of the 1980s. PP 505 box 1, folder 4, Kenneth Spencer Research Library, University of Kansas.

current students held firm, "we'll be listening to KJHK long after they're gone." But Sound Alternative supporters needed to appear serious, organized, and well informed to convince KU administrators to save the station's identity.

Steve Greenwood campaigned vigorously. He "never graduated" and remained at KU as an employee. His station involvement ended with the new rules, and he felt "personally threatened and intensely angry." He attended public staff meetings, which he taped. After managers banned his attendance, he took to standing outside board meetings, sending letters to Dean Kautsch, and speaking frequently with the press. As reported, "he perceived commercial motives, a corporate invasion, a venal conspiracy to corrupt an ideal"—an ideal he had nurtured. The camps became further entrenched, and "some in the faculty began referring to the alternative music loyalists as 'freakazoids,'" Greenwood chief among them.[40]

Greenwood spared no tactic to save his beloved station. As the format took effect, he taped the new underwriting announcements. In May 1988, before the summer's events regarding thrash programming, Greenwood sent his tapes to the FCC. These thirty-second "donor announcements" went far beyond normal underwriting messages containing "a brief mention that 'This hour of programming has been made possible in part by a donation from so-and-so and such-and-such street address." Greenwood alerted regulators that the spots were "identical" in "form, content and purpose" to commercials, which noncommercial licenses prohibited.

Given Utsler's outrage that a local business might tune in to hear obscenities and thrash metal, it is easy to see how Greenwood connected the underwriting spots to sinister interpretations about the station's recent changes. DJs questioned the rationale of a power increase. The station's 100 watts already reached the surrounding area. More exposure led to higher standards and potentially more underwriting revenue. When the station's engineer reported that faculty pushed for the power increase, DJs asked, "WHY?" As one DJ wrote, "How would taking KJHK into Topeka 'serve the interest of the KU student body?" It only helped sales staff.[41]

The sides grew increasingly entrenched. A new program director, appointed by the board, had only one semester of experience. Protesting DJs received prompt dismissal. Weekly staff meetings were "abolished." The program director attempted to change the station's slogan from the "Sound Alternative," with widespread disapproval.[42]

Toni Shockley, KJHK news director and a senior broadcast journalism major, countered this perspective. Repetitive arguments of disgruntled DJs exhausted her. KJHK, a learning lab, existed as a "teaching tool to give students the opportunity to gain valuable experience they can't get in the classroom." Sure, the station had a public role for KU and Lawrence, but it should serve the students first. "Let's face it," she wrote, "when the station is reaching only 5 percent of the audience, it is not doing anyone, students or listeners, any good." That 5 percent did not rank highly, since those listeners valued music with no appeal outside of narrow circles. Format change "was inevitable," Shockley concluded. "It had to happen." Common sense meant creating radio "for a lot of people" rather than "a token few." Besides, the station still qualified as alternative, only with the addition of "some album-oriented rock and some ethnic music." What was the big deal?[43]

A journalism program graduate and former KJHK music and promotion director wrote to support the change—but not for the reasons Shockley highlighted. Instead, he blamed KJHK's small audience on advertising students. Music DJs did their jobs fine, he argued. Sales staff should produce creative advertising for "one of the nation's most important and innovative college radio stations." Maybe "the remaining 95 percent [of students] are just a bit too thick to appreciate its progressive format. Or someone's not doing their job." How could anyone envision a successful career if they became "button-pushers," lacking creativity and unable to sell alternative music to college students?[44]

Greenwood's tape player kept spinning. He recorded "spots for Rent-A-Center and Duds N' Suds" that fall."[45]

KJHK's debate involved fundamental questions about the purpose of college radio and university education, in general, grounded in the liberal arts. Another former DJ, who worked in promotions for a Chicago NBC affiliate, explained that "a machine" could present a tightly formatted playlist "efficiently and cheaply." If KJHK wanted to train "minimum wage button-pushing radio peons," it violated the purpose of liberal arts education. Radio should reflect the creativity inspired by university education, he argued, advancing culture rather than inculcating mechanization and stultification.[46]

Some observers called KJHK a "disgrace" to a top-flight journalism program. "Announcers talk off-mike, broadcast levels are not consistent," and DJs ignored "the fundamentals of announcing." Editors at the student newspaper concurred but conceded KJHK's "national reputation for promoting progressive music" with "a small but fiercely loyal market-share." Such market-based rationale precluded another Top 40 station, which Lawrence already had.[47]

More groups organized to protect the Sound Alternative. The Committee Representing Students that KJHK Serves formed in September. Between thirty and forty students attended the first meetings, where they strategized to influence station affairs. Community members formed the Committee for the Preservation of Wild Life in Lawrence. A member, former station manager Brad Schwartz, agreed the freeform format required some changes, to "tighten up our sound and become more listenable." Greater visibility would enhance the station's reputation, but not the "mindless intervention" occurring. KJHK's faculty discouraged "learning through experience" (allowing for amateurism) and instead demanded "safety and uniformity." "Instead of encouraging independence" and promoting student leadership, Schwartz argued, faculty "are now supporting conformity." Conformity, he concluded, "leads to failure." The "sacred temple" of KJHK had been invaded and undermined. Education suffered.

Protests stirred in October 1988. KJHK's supporters publicized their arguments, hosted a benefit concert, and picketed and boycotted local businesses.[48] Fourteen sign-carriers marched outside an annual auction to support the station. Their numbers paled in comparison to the 400 or 500 guests in attendance, who together donated $7,000 for station operations. The image of students marching with signs reading "Please Don't Help Sell Out KJHK" and "We Want the Truth" offered a spectacle worthy of feature photographs in local newspapers.[49]

Dissidents petitioned, asking signees to boycott KJHK's underwriters. The petition, with some 300 signatures, appeared in the mailboxes of stores that purchased "donor agreements." A letter to underwriters thanked them for their past financial contributions. But petitioners cited recent "disturbing events" and "certain persons," meaning Utsler and station faculty adviser Sam Elliot, who "acted in a shadowy manner" and "offered consistently murky 'justifications'" for format changes. Underwriters included a local motel, a drive-in theater, a balloon and party goods shop, a tanning salon, an ice cream parlor, and an auto bodywork garage, among other local small businesses. Some ceased support until the format returned to normal.[50]

Kief's Discount Records and Stereo Supply in Lawrence denied its usual support. The manager did not know how the station's changes would affect his business. He chose to "sit tight and see how viable" they were but expressed "hesitancy to being engaged as an advertiser as an adversarial relationship." He decided to wait a semester to see what happened.[51]

Greenwood orchestrated the boycott campaign. Supporters called in song requests and monitored whether they received airplay. Mr. Blues, a former

DJ and special programs co-director until July 1988, refused to sell out to commercial pressures. "Mr. Blues," he wrote, "never programmed music geared towards your head and wallet." He went "right for the jugular, namely your heart and feet. You're talking about my generation, and I'll be damned if I'm going to stand silently and idly by" while faculty undermined KJHK's values and student control. Valuable radio bowed to no commercial influence.[52]

Students feared losing their relevance, commercial or otherwise. Student Mike Mader told the local newspaper that former Dead Kennedy Jello Biafra, who had protested the PMRC's efforts at censorship, spoke at KU. When Mader requested KJHK play a Dead Kennedys song, the on-air DJ told Mader "that they are 'too offensive' to play." The new general manager cited repetition as the reason, since DJs "play . . . the same music over and over again." But DJs felt hamstrung by these rules that would harm the local music scene's vibrancy and connection to national cultural developments.[53]

Jerry Howard ceased KJHK's reports to CMJ. Local venues such as the Outhouse and the Bottleneck "were in danger of not being promoted" because they featured bands no longer "emphasized." As one observer concluded, students failed to receive a proper education without communication between the station and CMJ or local venues. Even though some DJs across college radio stations resented CMJ's power and sought instead to promote locally, the change sparked more outrage.[54]

At the end of the fall semester, a newly appointed general manager stepped in to navigate these tensions. Michael Ulin, a graduate student who had worked at the station between 1979 and 1984, was a "middle-of-the-road" option. Ulin planned to increase listeners while maintaining the station's Sound Alternative identity. Ulin offered to bring partisans together, face-to-face, to quell tensions and return to business.

A station free of controversy would have to wait, with news in January 1989 of the FCC's investigation into underwriting, stemming from Greenwood's complaint. Throughout the boycotts, both sides consistently referred to "advertisers" and "advertisements" instead of underwriters. The "donor statements," as they should have been termed, included wording such as "inexpensive," as in one spot for the airline TWA. The FCC's attorney explained "that the statement might be in violation because 'inexpensive' could be viewed as a qualitative statement." Students writing the spots had to be careful. They could not suggest any action on the part of listeners. The station's sales manager clarified, "We can't even say 'call' and then give a phone number." Violations might be "honest" mistakes, considering the writers were students. But the FCC ruled that KJHK veered into advertising, mistake or not.[55]

The FCC could issue a reprimand, a fine ranging from $100 to $30,000, or even license revocation—an extreme and rare occurrence. Elliot, the faculty adviser, dismissed the potential for a fine. Most likely, the FCC would require increased training for sales staff. He doubted KJHK violated any FCC rule, insisting "the inquiry had been positive because it increased awareness of regulations." The "teaching moment" spin was pretty rosy, given the tensions that led to the FCC's inquiry.[56]

Greenwood saw more nefarious intentions at work. He insisted that the station's power increase proceeded with the intention to lure more donors. He explained, "I am concerned that the journalism school is turning KJHK into an operation for its sales staff to rake in the dough," not train them in fundraising to support community radio. Whatever the case, the FCC's clear rules limited commercials on noncommercial, educational-licensed stations.[57]

With alternative, heavy metal, and rap music taking fire from culture warriors, commercial stations scrutinizing playlists, and record labels instituting voluntary labeling, the shift from alternative to "more mainstream" music at KJHK had fans worried. Supporters encouraged musical risk-taking and "refused to equate selling out with maturity." Staid, safe music represented conformity and apathy—not maturity. Selling out constituted capitulation to commercial pressure, certainly, and implied a lack of commitment to democracy. For KJHK's aggrieved DJs, censorship seemed to lurk behind programming decisions for the sake of some constituents over others.[58]

Institutions that held licenses could direct schedules however they saw fit, so long as they adhered to rules governing educational stations. Censorship continued to be a complicated and emotional issue—and in KJHK's case, no governmental strictures limited programming. The FCC proved to be more an ally than the faculty, at least according to students seeking to maintain control. Even before the FCC investigation, student dissidents claimed a "partial victory."[59]

Details still had to be negotiated regarding student activity funding and representation in governance. The KU student senate renewed KJHK's funding for another year but reviewed the station's hiring practices and initiated a finance committee investigation in spring 1989. Rumors of a hiring blacklist to eliminate "troublemakers" threatened station funding as a student activity, which required open participation. Managers denied its existence, although former DJs testified that they had fallen victim to it. Dean Kautsch defended hiring practices based on station governance. The station belonged to the school of journalism as its laboratory, setting requirements for membership. "I don't see why anyone who is not committed to those goals," he said, referring to broadcasting training, "should be hired." With a field of 200 applicants and 110 spots, managers needed some criteria for participation. In his view, that should be professionalism—even if that meant journalism school majors went to the front of the line.[60]

The senate could not effectively determine if a blacklist existed, or what other violations occurred. Senators supported reorganizing station governance to ensure student DJs had a voice. This ruling limited managers' power and elevated student control, but the journalism school and its pedagogical priorities remained influential.[61]

Hard feelings remained, at least until involved students graduated. For one DJ turned down for renewal, no satisfaction emerged. She was labeled a "troublemaker" by Ulin and the dean, but her supporters claimed that her "true crime" was "that she thought and spoke with an independent mind." KJHK provided little opportunity for creative thought or leadership among students. A journalism major concluded the issue involved not a clash between musical tastes or a "power grab" by faculty. Instead, it was "a struggle for the freedom of education: The freedom of students to decide how students should be educated." By denying students the opportunity to work at KJHK, journalism faculty might provide "practical" experience but not in creativity and expression. Lessons in "politics and self-expression" came from standing against what the faculty had in mind for KJHK.[62]

Mr. Blues responded to the senate resolution, having also been forced to resign. Although the senate offered hope at enhanced student voice, he doubted the station would return to its former glory. "You still won't hear the works of William S. Burroughs, Gil Scott-Heron, or the Dead Kennedys on FM 90.7," he wrote. "Those artists' albums are still (supposedly) locked away . . . along with the rest of the albums that were purged from KJHK in fall 1988." None of the fired or resigned students would return. "The point is lost. The albums are locked away and the truth is in a box over there," he concluded.[63]

The KJHK battle sputtered toward conclusion, despite tense exchanges. When in early June the journalism faculty took control of the station and rebuffed the student senate's recommendations, one student likened an ensuing radio board meeting to "Tiananmen Square minus the tanks," referring to the Chinese government's recent crackdown on student dissidents. Students demanded democratic procedures, which a faculty declared not part of the process of station management.[64] The Senate Executive Committee and KJHK's board compromised a few weeks later. Student leaders accepted the station's laboratory function but rejected that managers be enrolled in the broadcasting major. Removing academic requirements for participation allowed student senate funding to resume without violating student activities rules. Ulin declared he would be happy to step out of the limelight and return to business.[65] Any new show must "be approved by the general manager or members of station management" and be "presented in a professional manner, meeting standards of good quality in content, style, and production characteristics"—a requirement not drastically different from other college stations. A new Programming Advisory Board formed, with most members appointed by the dean.[66]

Even students who had been on board and approved of past changes found fault with faculty interference. Students needed independence, they argued. Sure, the station violated some professional standards. But, as the student newspaper editors concluded, "pulling a certain style of music seems to be a move aimed at discouraging certain people from working at the station." KJHK could have both. "Who said alternative music and professionalism could not go hand in hand?" they asked.[67] Student representatives insisted the station exist as a student activity first, a laboratory for learning second. Only then would the station's true educational function be fulfilled.[68]

Professional standards remained. All music announcers had to complete required training, another common college radio requirement though with some added differences at KU, where the journalism faculty maintained a strong role. Any non–journalism school DJ had to sign a "12-point participation contract affirming support of the station's laboratory function." Term limits on managerial positions ensured that if a manager strayed from the faculty's approved course of action, the manager could be swiftly replaced.[69]

The faculty withdrew its FCC application for a power increase to demonstrate it took seriously the reforms. Dean Kautsch hoped to restore order and reliability. He didn't really care if the senate removed student activities funding. Its rules for open participation hampered professionalization, in his view. The journalism school could provide funding for the academic year. The faculty and the dean would fund the station alone if it meant controlling participation and the station's constitution.[70] But in the end, they opted to keep station participation open.

Meanwhile, the FCC made its decision. Greenwood's complaint resulted in a $2,500 fine to KJHK in September 1989. KJHK paid the fine, and the station continued to broadcast alternative programming. Much to the surprise of the freakazoids, Utsler ended class credit for participation in KJHK in fall 1989.

The following March, the station manager sought to soothe tensions by inviting an FCC official to address DJs on policy regarding indecency and obscenity in broadcasting. The FCC engineer from Kansas City told the students, "The University is not your worst enemy. I am." He reviewed the KJHK situation and concluded, "You've spent an awful lot of time and energy fighting each other, and you're forgetting about me. . . . I can take your license." Claims of censorship and disappearing albums resurfaced in spring 1990. Some students claimed local bands Kill Whitey and Magic Nose had albums disappear, resulting in a benefit concert at the Outhouse to supplement the music library.[71]

Throughout KJHK's troubles, music insiders and press took note of what was happening. The station became the subject of discussion in the heady "Dialogue" section of CMJ's *New Music Report*. Independent record-label founder and frequent commenter Gerard Cosloy heralded Lawrence as "one of the nation's most adventurous outlets for new and unusual rock'n'roll." Cosloy pointed to its top records, including Big Audio Dynamite, the band of former Clash member Mick Jones; the Red Hot Chili Peppers; and Toad the Wet Sprocket, alongside other independent-label mainstays. But the faculty's efforts to create a laboratory and professional environment produced a "chilling effect," mirrored at other stations that abandoned college radio's "artistic endeavor." Collectively stations' role as an inexpensive "research tool for the music profession" threatened creativity. The head of radio promotion at Wax Trax in Chicago warned that a "new conservative regime" took hold in college radio. Fears arose that major-label buyouts and consolidation threatened independent labels, such as with PolyGram's recent purchase of Island Records.[72]

KJHK existed at the "nobler end of the dial" populated by "untrained on-air personnel, weak signals . . . low funding, and lax management." Students dedicated to music offered "imagination, innovation, and the invulnerable feel that this was actually the neatest, weirdest, most human radio station that ever hit the airwaves."

"Freedom," one commenter concluded, "was essential for growth."[73]

· · · · · ·

KJHK's predicaments centered around student versus faculty control. But the battle over acceptable musical fare and over whose tastes and interests should determine a station's programming suggested a broader, national reconsideration of college radio's place in the music industry taking place at the end of the 1980s. In debating college radio's function as a playground or a laboratory, KJHK's partisans were not the first to battle these ideas, nor did KJHK constitute the only station buffeted by divergent expectations.

KJHK had company among college radio stations seeking to set trends in popular music, as well as among those facing criticism from multiple angles. UK students noted how student-run radio came under threat from administrative interference at the University of New Mexico and from the journalism school at the University of Colorado Boulder. Meddling seemed to stem from stations' service to alternative music, in particular.[74] As one music outlet observed, "Nine hundred of the 1300 college radio stations air alternative rock programming almost exclusively." By basing playlists on CMJ and the new *Billboard* alternative modern rock chart, the station "now follows trends instead of setting them."[75] With the growing popularity of commercial alternative formats, concerns grew about college radio's vaunted role in launching local talent to mainstream success and its failure to represent minority voices and less-commercially viable music.

For culture to remain democratic, the structure of college radio needed preservation. No market research firm should ever determine radio programming. That would violate the purpose of higher education—and cultural democracy itself.[76] As rock critic Dave Marsh put it, these stations "educate" listeners "about the cultural past and present. If that isn't an important function of a university, what is?"[77]

By the mid-1980s, college radio both served and defied the music industry and popular trends. Record labels drew talent from "this campus farm system," Marsh argued, and should "kick in some serious bucks" to support stations. After all, they garnered personnel from these schools and should reciprocate, merely functioning as a different form of corporate funding already in place.

As college radio reached the height of its popularity, with bands graduating from the collegiate airwaves to superstar status in the early 1990s, the paradoxes tearing at KJHK and others like it would only grow sharper in the next decade. Alternative increasingly defined the mainstream, promising to revitalize rock's progressive influence in popular culture (even if it left much of rock's roots in Black music behind). College radio's role in launching bands like Nirvana, however, did not mean that these stations were safe harbors for iconoclasm and experimentation. Instead, they were the site of negotiations regarding the boundaries between mainstream and alternative, pop and underground, commercial and freedom from market demands.

Part III The College Radio Paradox, 1989–2003

······································

Musician and producer Steve Albini notoriously captured a revolt against feeding the mainstream music industry with talent in his 1993 essay, "The Problem with Music." Albini compared independent bands competing to sign a major-label contract to a swimming race across a "trench, about four feet wide and five feet deep, maybe sixty yards long, filled with runny, decaying shit." Bands would dive in, seeking the "industry lackey" at the other end offering a contract and potential riches.

It was a vivid image. Albini depicted contenders "wrestling furiously, clawing each other and dunking each other under the shit." The lucky winner then must complete more laps through shit, capitulating to label demands.

The label's "lackey," moreover, likely came from college radio. As Albini put it, "annoying turds who used to staff college radio stations" joined Artist and Repertoire departments at major labels, seeking to discover new bands and "promise them the moon." They lured bands into binding contracts, assuring access to fancy producers and a lucrative advance. By the time bills for recording, fees, promotion, equipment, touring, and buyouts were paid—right down to the catering—band members would receive a pittance, remaining locked in a contract and further debt.

"Some of your friends are probably already this fucked," Albini concluded.[1]

Who wanted to serve that system, selling out local bands to this corruptive and exploitative industry? Profit motives, he argued, came with aesthetic consequences: an extractive business model and coercive production methods watered down sounds to something "palatable" for the masses and stifled creativity.

Albini's screed against the major-label business model excoriated the optimistic "farm team" construction of college radio, painting it as naïve and corrupt. MTV and major labels' distance would shield underground music scenes, for the most part, even if college radio helped a few bands break through to success. That barrier broke in the 1990s, especially after Nirvana's massive 1991 success.[2] Formerly starry-eyed college radio volunteers sold out, Albini charged, and enlisted in a racket that raked in cash for the labels and signed bands to a coercive process that sapped artistry and embroiled them in a legal morass. Scholars noticed a sea-change in youth culture as rock music seemed to prop up existing power structures rather than defy them.[3] Marketers sliced young people's power into consumer groups; corporatized baby boomers marketed and sold prepackaged individuality. It didn't matter that punk infiltrated pop culture and MTV. Even college radio watered down the sound. As one punk put it, challenging sounds could get on MTV, "but there's still gonna be a goddamm [sic] Skittles commercial at the break," weakening the revolution to please the "average viewer" as much as the Milli Vanilli video that might follow. "Wanna be alternative?" he concluded. "Don't play the game."[4]

Corporate co-optation of the underground was not the only story for music or college radio in the late 1980s and 1990s. Narratives about youth crisis permeated popular culture and sensational news stories. Fears regarding a dropout generation of slackers and concerns that America's youth would be unable to compete with counterparts in Germany and Japan circulated widely.[5] Warnings of the dangers from pop music shifted to hip-hop and gangsta rap with its mainstream appeal, growing to influence fashion and style, broadly.[6]

Artistic exploration continued to expand, bringing new voices to light. Women-identified artists and college DJs, often turned off by the hypermasculine world of hardcore punk and college radio, staked their claim. Riot Grrrl, a "confessional" rock style that embraced feminism and empowerment and authentic testimony in the tradition of consciousness-raising groups from the 1970s, offered a movement made up mostly of teen- and college-age white women. It challenged objectification of women in punk, while prominent women artists from Tori Amos to Sheryl Crow challenged male-dominated rock music. Some "mocked conventions of femininity," adopting a baby doll look that quickly became co-opted by the mainstream pop industry and which emphasized "individual rather than collective empowerment." Feminist challenges to male-dominated genres could only make changes at the margins. Even Riot Grrrl "left patriarchal structures . . . untouched."[7]

Some artists who graduated from the college radio scene insisted they could use their power for good. In 1994, upon U2's winning its sixth Grammy, the statue for Best Alternative Music Album for *Zooropa*, Bono pointed to college radio charts as "the most important" for the band's success. U2's global popularity and concert stadiums filled with fans belied the band's underground roots. Bono vowed to "continue to abuse our position and fuck up the mainstream"—an utterance confronting CBS's ten-second broadcast delay to catch any obscenity.[8]

The independent-rock underground of the late 1980s, for all its issues, seemed the only avenue for cultural revolution. Michael Azerrad, who chronicled bands' rise through these scenes, hinged his argument on the idea that participants fulfilled, in a narrow sense, the countercultural goals of the Sixties.[9] While this might have been true for artists, those connections grew more complicated in college radio. Federal regulation limited what could be played on public airwaves at certain times of day. But other, more local demands limited the subcultural and revolutionary possibilities of college radio.

More college students, by the late 1980s, had grown up on "alternative" music and college radio. Yet stations continued to fulfill pedagogical functions, while university administrators harbored different expectations. They tended to see college stations as public relations outlets or as serving narrower pedagogical goals. Community members, both as listeners and as businesses providing underwriting, also had a claim. These signals took up public space that could be used by community signals in these locales, after all.

Selling out, according to one former DJ, simply meant doing something you don't want to do.[10] DJs might want to maintain creative control and act as gatekeepers, curating music they thought would be valuable to listeners and communities. Those prospects grew bleak in the 1990s. Unevenness and contradictions always existed in college radio's identity. But with universities submitting to market logic in governance and promotion, a similar mindset driving deregulation of media at the federal level, college stations found themselves caught among paradoxical expectations. Pedagogical, professional, and public service goals all claimed these airwaves, and in the 1990s the internal paradoxes of college radio frayed and broke. Divergent demands became less tenable even before the Telecommunications Act of 1996 and the internet posed new challenges for radio.

College radio's remarkable cultural influence in the 1990s, reshaping American musical culture and mainstream radio and record labels, belied it as a space where battles for recognition continued to play out—and where universities contended with questions about what their role would be in the market and American culture.

12   The Golden Age of Indie Rock Radio

. . . .

Music Log, KTRU Rice Radio— "Ray's Last Shift" (excerpt), May 4, 1988
KTRU Radio Records, Rice University, Box 27

Joy Division, "Love Will Tear Us Apart"
The Chills, "I Love My Leather Jacket"
Julian Cope, "Kolly Kibber's Birthday"
T. Rex, "20th Century Boy"
Roky Erickson, "Don't Slander Me"
Lime Spiders, "Slave Girl"
David Bowie, "Queen Bitch"
Outnumbered, "Cover Me with Flowers"
Generation X, "Kiss Me Deadly"
Beat Happening, "Bewitched"
The Replacements, "Take Me Down to the Hospital"
The Beatles, "Helter Skelter"
Lou Reed, "The Blue Mask"
Camper Van Beethoven, "Where the Hell Is Bill?"
The Alter Boys, "Piles"
U2, "Out of Control"
Game Theory, "Like a Girl Jesus"
The Flaming Lips, "With You"
Television, "See No Evil"
National Lampoon, "Mr. Roberts"
Lords of The New Church, "New Church"
The Psychedelic Furs, "Flowers"
Sex Pistols, "No Feelings"
The Clash, "Complete Control"
Ramones, "Surfin' Bird"
Buzzcocks, "Orgasm Addict"
Negative Approach, "Tied Down"
Naked Raygun, "Knock Me Down"
Minutemen, "Paranoid Chant"
Motörhead, "Ace of Spades"
T.S.O.L., "Thoughts of Yesterday"
D.O.A., "War"

D.R.I., "I Don't Need Society"

Butthole Surfers, "Sweat Loaf"

Minor Threat, "Salad Days"

Iggy Pop, "I Got a Right"

The Jazz Butcher, "Caroline Wheeler's Birthday Present"

Hüsker Dü, "Eight Miles High"

Dinosaur Jr., "Raisans"

Mission of Burma, "That's When I Reach for My Revolver"

Pere Ubu, "Final Solution"

Peter Gabriel, "Biko"

The Velvet Underground, "Heroin"

Nick Cave & The Bad Seeds, "Tupelo"

The Gun Club, "Sex"

Violent Femmes, "Add It Up"

Jeffrey Lee Pierce, "Sex Killer"

Grateful Dead, "Till the Morning Comes"

Beastie Boys, "Cooky Puss"

Jimi Hendrix, "Fire"

Redd Kross, "Citadel"

That Petrol Emotion, "Mine"

The Dream Syndicate, "Then She Remembers"

Robyn Hitchcock, "Sounds Great When You're Dead"

New Order, "Ceremony"

Miracle Room, "Mother of Destruction"

The Cure, "One Hundred Years"

The Dream Syndicate, "Until Lately"

Fuzzbox, "So Long"

Joy Division, "Transmission"

After graduating from Queens College at CUNY and interning in the music industry wherever she could, Lori Blumenthal landed a job at a tiny desk in a corner of I.R.S. Records. In the mid-1980s it was her job to call up college radio stations and see if they would play the label's releases. She witnessed I.R.S. band R.E.M. cross over into the mainstream, emerging as international superstars from its underground, college radio, independent-label origins.

She developed friendships with stations' volunteers, college students not much younger than herself. Some moved into the industry with her. They grappled with whether they had "sold out," but there seemed a real possibility they could advocate for the music they loved. And by 1990, they were all featured in *Rolling Stone* together.

In an article titled "College Radio Crosses Over," the veteran music magazine chronicled major labels' "serious interest in the college market," hiring cool, young, "hip" promoters to mine college radio to break artists in line with the success of R.E.M, the Cure, and Depeche Mode.[1]

No longer was college radio some "underground medium run free-form style." It had become "streamlined" and friendly to "major-label product." Previously, only bands that had "a weird name, an inaccessible sound and a low-budget independent label distributing its records out of somebody's basement" were considered "alternative." By 1990, this legitimate genre appealed to young, white fans despite its "slightly quirky rock" identity. Of course, this was an overgeneralization of college radio and its history. Certainly, as one DJ-turned-promoter remembered, most DJs paid little attention to charts—and if they did, it was CMJ. Labels had vacillated in how to consider these amateur signals, if at all. What *Rolling Stone* captured, more than any real change in college radio's culture and practices, was the industry's standardized approach to these signals. Corporate giants had figured out how to capitalize on the underground: surprise, surprise.

But maybe, just maybe, amateur DJs could make popular music better and protect iconoclasm. As one promoter explained, "The more records we sell, the more Butthole Surfers we can sign." Promoter Josh Rosenthal lauded freeform heavyweight WFMU, a community station at Upsala College (before it became independent after Upsala closed).[2] Freeform radio seemed to be under assault as promotional material flooded the station and labels were hungry for crossover hits. Signals like WFMU verified the value of independent, freeform programming controlled by amateurs and volunteers in defiance of corporate metrics and influence. Promoters hoped stations would "maintain their integrity," keeping an ear to the underground world of zines and small clubs, imports, and independent-label releases. Once a potential crossover was discovered, they would swoop in and sign the band.

Internal problems, as well as blind spots, persisted in college radio. Many stations focused on alternative rock, keeping other genres "ghettoized," as one DJ put it. Some allowed only one rap show per week or put a few prominent records into rotation. Not all were impervious to the lure of major-label promotions. Student DJs wanted to break the next Sonic Youth. Lori

Blumenthal blamed major labels misguidedly showering cash and attention on these stations. "All the money that's being poured in," she explained, "is somewhat damaging." The only reason majors paid attention to college radio was to discover artists to sign. "There's not much payoff: college radio in itself doesn't sell a lot of records." The money came when those independents received major-label and distribution sales.

The relationships between the major-label music industry and college radio were blurry. Young promoters in this "golden era" had a unique relationship with stations, creating the potential for musical change on a grand scale. They developed personal relationships—in one instance Blumenthal flew to Illinois on her own dime to see a concert with friends she had made at a station there. Optimism circulated that they could forge a new, diverse musical culture. Alternative music was beginning to sell, but late-1980s clashes between college radio stations and major labels occurred over a central question regarding who would get to define what that genre was. College radio was still alternative, purportedly valuing diversity and authenticity. Nonetheless, questions remained about whose voices were allowed to define "alternative."

Indie Labels

Years before he had quotes in *Rolling Stone* as a promoter at Columbia Records, Josh Rosenthal had a pretty good gig. As music director at Syosset High School's station on Long Island, he had access to all the new releases. U2's *War* arrived at the station before it reached stores. Sure, his grades might have suffered, but radio was "the main medium" in the mid-1980s and being music director offered its own education.

Rosenthal talked with other music directors at high school stations. Those contacts became his friends, and his communications with record labels representatives led to an internship at PolyGram Records. "And so," he remembered, "I would take the train a couple times a week to the city to 810 Seventh Avenue." It was unreal. "There I was, like sixteen, seventeen years old or something, working at PolyGram." He watched Tears for Fears debut. Bon Jovi was breaking. John Mellencamp released hits on the label, which also reissued Velvet Underground records.

From there, he moved to a job at CMJ, working for Robert Haber. The office was small, and Rosenthal worked directly with the tip sheet's knowledgeable staff and editors: people like Bill Stephney, freshly graduated from Adelphi University. They talked about music in an analytical manner Rosenthal hadn't encountered before. Like Stephney, who soon joined the executives at Def Jam, Rosenthal was on the path to a career in the music industry while still in high school.[3]

Jack Isquith hired Rosenthal at PolyGram, while advising him that SUNY Albany was a good place to start a career in music. Albany had a good track record of getting students industry jobs, particularly through its radio station. Russ Rieber graduated to manage Modern English and the Replacements. Craig Marks became the music editor at the *Los Angeles Times*. Major-label executive Diarmuid Quinn eventually founded TourDForce productions, managing pop stars Richard Marx and Josh Groban.[4]

Rosenthal entered college radio at Albany as tensions rose over major versus independent labels. Independents existed "in a range of sizes and forms: from multi-million-dollar corporate operations like I.R.S. in the 1980s, to medium-sized labels like Alias, to small labels that concentrate on producing singles rather than full-length albums." The number occupying this last category increased, mostly driven by focusing on specific genres such as the blues, gospel, bluegrass, and punk and hardcore—all of which received coverage on college radio stations in varying degrees. Independent labels expanded available music in an era when it was difficult to record and disseminate music without being a vertically integrated corporation. Music directors at college stations gravitated increasingly toward these small operations, seeing them as in need of their service and committed to musical authenticity.[5]

Most stations divided responsibilities among various music directors by genre. In meetings of those music directors, Rosenthal sometimes faced hostility from those responsible for dealing with indie labels. Rosenthal's background at majors caused suspicion in this atmosphere. "I remember," he said, "sitting in meetings and being completely demonized, because I was like, this major label guy or something." They saw him as "careerist," a cardinal sin, it seemed, that violated musical purity.[6]

Major labels developed a bad reputation among college radio and independent music circles. Not only did independents seem to offer more artistic freedom, but major labels violated DIY ideals and poached talent, alongside their aggressive marketing techniques for undesirable artists.[7] In one case involving CBS Records, the station manager at MIT's WMBR criticized the label's promotional activity. In fall 1985, he wrote in the "Discourse" section of CMJ that CBS offered a new CD player to any station "that presented the best half hour special on 415/CBS Recording artists, and in particular Wire Train." The band signed with Howie Klein's label 415, which focused on signing punk and new wave artists from the San Francisco area. The label had a co-branding deal with CBS's Columbia Records, which provided significant promotional backing to reach a national audience. The label retained artistic control and produced hit acts such as Romeo Void in the 1980s.[8] But when it came to Wire Train, the major label's influence seemed to corrupt the art and the label. Zine publisher Jack Rabid called Wire Train "perhaps the most soul-less, unoriginal, plastic, so-called US New Music band around." An MIT DJ insinuated that CBS's ploy came close to payola. In response to the public complaint, CBS cut WMBR off from record service—symbolizing the kind of hardball tactics that college music directors resented.[9]

These tensions were exacerbated when many indie bands of the moment signed with majors. The Replacements inked a contract with Sire Records on Warner Brothers, and some college DJs panned *Tim* and *Pleased to Meet Me* as "corporate crap." When *Spin*'s first issue covered the Del Fuegos and the Replacements on tour in May 1985, writer Chuck Reece noted that the Minneapolis band notorious for drunken antics and not finishing songs at their shows, by signing with Sire, was "getting straighter." The success of the Replacements "won them new fans," including a spot atop a listener poll of favorite acts on a suburban Boston album-oriented rock (AOR) station, beating out the Cars and J. Geils Band. The vote was remarkable not because the Replacements usurped local favorites. It was a commercial radio station—the kind many college DJs lambasted as old-fart dinosaur rock signals.[10]

Distribution clouded the distinction between indie and major labels, as many indies used major-label distributors to reach consumers outside of narrow geographic confines.[11] Both were in the business of promotion—but few small labels had money to pour into gimmicks to garner airplay. Labels needed capital and a dose of business savvy to win bands exposure. The "typical person who starts an indie label," Corey Rusk, former manager of independent-label Touch and Go, put it, "is someone who loves music and really enjoys working with artists and promoting their music." "But," Rusk qualified, "that same personality type, more often than not, is not that organized, and just can't wrap their head around all the logistical things . . . for their company to function smoothly on the whole sort of nonmusic side of things." Labels had to pump distributors for payments, and it was hard to predict cash flow. Touch and Go, founded out of a zine of the same name in 1979, managed this process well. At some other small labels bands frequently went unpaid, lost out on royalties, or had trouble getting their records into stores.[12] Promotion cost money, and many labels simply didn't have the resources to send out free records, let alone advertise or distribute swag to college stations.

Most indie labels relied on meager promotional budgets, developing a sound and an aesthetic linked to a particular scene or region. Many evoked the DIY ethos of punk and hardcore. Southern California hardcore-label SST "promoted its bands in large part by promoting itself," one scholar argued, such as developing aesthetically consistent packaging—which included a catalog in every album sold, effectively a "form of direct marketing" to fans.[13] Bands and labels grew by word of mouth and through touring. SST expanded beyond bands from southern California by the mid-1980s, signing Hüsker Dü from Minnesota and Sonic Youth from Massachusetts. Some labels such as SST, Touch and Go, and Sub Pop transcended region to develop national presence, but the network of scenes that their bands traversed experienced different levels of development.

Sometimes scenes remained cobbled together on a shoestring, even as connections among them grew. While promoting their album *EVOL* on SST, Sonic Youth played to a small crowd at Houston punk venue Café Mode in June 1986—located, according to the memory of one attendee, in an old basement. The venue, along with Cabaret Voltaire, was a little more established than the previous wave of punk clubs, or rather, club, which had become a kind of "a level underneath dive," with a "frightening-scary-omigod-don't-go-there" vibe.[14] Even at venues that didn't seem like a death wish to attend, communities remained small. Sonic Youth appeared alongside local experimental band Culturcide, Houston's "king of experimental music" at the time. There was a sense that the scene—and the music—would remain obscure.[15]

In the 1980s, scenes struggled to connect and establish infrastructure around narrow genres. Overlapping local scenes relied on one another for oxygen. Punk shows popped up at a gay dance club in Houston. In Seattle, punks and metalheads went to the same shows, helping to generate a sound that would come to define the scene. No sharp lines between groups emerged. As one participant remembered, "There's only twenty people here, you can't really find a group to hate." But momentum was hard to build. In Seattle, an ordinance limiting all-ages shows put a damper on the scene in the mid-1980s.[16] These small communities of entertainment needed each other to survive, and most of the music was "too abrasive and weird" to make it on MTV.[17]

College stations fed off major-label promotions to keep their local sounds on the air. Music directors boxed up free promo records to sell at used record stores, using the proceeds to buy the latest indie releases. Anything that appeared on Top 40 radio was likely to be passed over for rotation. As one DJ described it, "top push means that record promoters are pulling their hair out trying to push mindless music directors at half-ass stations" to play releases—particularly those not doing as well as projected. Even if college stations played the release, most felt they were free to "end our dedication to a band when they achieve such status," as a University of Georgia DJ put it. Besides, there were numerous local bands who needed their help.[18]

Indie labels multiplied, though many collapsed as fast as they launched. Independent labels existed since recording's early days, but since the 1960s they had operated mostly "as research-and-development" for major labels.[19] Fans and artists felt manipulated by corporate major-label executives, and in the 1980s independent labels offered an alternative. Fans, one historian explained, "believed they were making important consumer choices by buying independently produced records," and musicians maintained autonomy. Labels obtained distribution through independents like Dutch East India or Rough Trade. By 1984, influential albums appeared that made it "abundantly clear that the best rock music in the world was being made in this circumscribed little community," as Michael Azerrad explained it.[20]

This growth generated momentum, critical success, and cultural power with national reach. Scenes were connecting across cities and regions. As Rice University's music director noted, 1982 felt very different from 1988, when he programmed his last show for KTRU (figure 12.1).[21]

Everyone still seemed to know each other, but the musical legacy of bands that emerged from that movement obscured how small the scenes and networks were. R.E.M., out of Athens, Georgia, established the formula others wanted to emulate: a viable bohemian scene outside of cities like New York or San Francisco produced unique music that sold well while maintaining an authentic voice and connection to the scene that gave them rise. In Chapel Hill in 1988, members of Superchunk "kick-started" a scene with a show at the club Cat's Cradle.[22] Buzz circulated that this would be the next Athens, though the future remained uncertain. Bands like Dinosaur Jr. on SST released albums that resonated nationally thanks to "little pockets of fans that had been slowly but surely spreading the word."[23]

Fear remained that scenes might collapse, or bands would move to a major and leave the scene behind, or major labels would co-opt a sound, or— as in the case of Dinosaur Jr. after its 1987 release *You're Living All Over*

FIGURE 12.1 Ray Shea served as music director at KTRU in the mid- to late 1980s. During his last shift, he opened his show with Joy Division's "Love Will Tear Us Apart" and closed with the band's "Transmission." He is depicted here with a Joy Division t-shirt, a staple among college radio DJs. Courtesy Woodson Research Center, Fondren Library, Rice University.

Me—success would wreck their creative spirit. College radio's new wave bands suffered in the early 1980s when corporate labels made their own, more marketable, versions. Participants wanted to keep the sense that the music and the scene were theirs.

The real shift came as indies across the nation became more viable. They grew big enough to service stations with albums alongside getting them into stores and the hands of avid fans. Some labels still could be hard to get albums from. (Grumbles circulated about the lack of records from Dischord in Washington, D.C., though the label had good relationships with many DJs.) But enough labels made sure that college stations had the latest releases. For Bruce Pavitt at Sub Pop, the goal was to create an alternative, "decentralized cultural network" in defiance of corporate control of music.[24]

College stations were an integral link in the indie underground business model. They promoted local shows and new releases, and they increasingly resisted major-label pressure.[25] In 1984, the only label representatives that KTRU had regular contact with claiming some independent status was I.R.S., which had distribution through A&M Records (and business with RCA, then MCA, by extension). By 1988 the music director fielded far more calls from independent-label representatives. The pages of CMJ filled with pitches for new releases from small labels across the country.[26]

Resentment grew toward the high-pressure sales tactics of major labels. Sales representatives and promoters could be aggravating—many label reps, Rice's music director remembered, seemed to be passing time in internships on their way to big-time work signing hot pop artists. Plus, their high-pressure sales calls were annoying. As one music director complained, he needed a "frontal lobotomy" after enduring three hours of "hard-core conversations with all our favorites from CBS, RCA, et al." Most DJs were far removed from the "grime and slime of the music industry," with representatives who referred to "sometimes actually good music as lowly product, not even a record or recording or anything but a PRODUCT." Some had good releases, but he found this language "demeaning for a band." He resented receiving six calls a week to push him on "why I haven't added . . . the latest whimper from Gary Newman."[27] College music directors felt empowered enough by 1988 to reject such sales pressure in favor of music they liked and wanted to promote, which didn't have the backing of major-label resources.

Lori Blumenthal at I.R.S. Records felt encouraged about what this movement meant for popular music. She saw the emergence of music to take seriously, with voices previously shut out earning mainstream exposure. I.R.S.'s band the Go-Go's showed that women groups could move from punk scenes to MTV. When Blumenthal joined as a college radio rep for the label in 1984, two people worked in a tiny closet. The label was marginalized at its A&M home, but it was making waves. At I.R.S., she sat at the crossroads of major labels and the indie underground.

She understood how the system could work. Blumenthal knew that college radio would be key to I.R.S.'s success by providing exposure. She threatened to quit to eliminate the record fee levied on college stations. The label's president believed the fee would mean their records would get respect, but she was confident she was right. I.R.S. operated on a different model than the corporate giants. Her phone calls weren't "salesy," she remembered; they were to build relationships and to talk about music. Instead of pressuring stations to put bands into heavy rotation, Blumenthal focused on the background of artists such as Let's Active or the Alarm. Each station had its own "personality." If DJs hated a particular band, they wouldn't play it and there was no point in highlighting it. Stations still might promote a local show for one of her artists. Even at stations unlikely to play I.R.S. bands, she would call up music directors to talk about music. There was, she mused later, a kind of "purity" to these relationships.[28]

Blumenthal made friends. When she started at I.R.S., she lived with her parents and had few expenses. Even without putting it on an expense report, she decided she would try to see R.E.M. play in every city it toured, paying her own way. In retrospect, it might have been naïve, but there was a "sweetness" to it. She would book a plane ticket with a plan to meet up with a college radio volunteer or music director she had only talked to over the phone. She made deep friendships with her contacts, finding like-minded people interested in music and film and excited about life.[29]

It was a magical moment, and it was fleeting. These relationships rode on commonalities of age and outlook, with participants at labels and college radio sharing similar backgrounds and aesthetic preferences. They navigated a deep paradox. This scene, and its national reach, was the best-kept secret, and it was theirs. At the same time, they had an optimism that they could change the world. They were outsiders who wanted to be on the inside of music and culture but hated the idea of being mainstream.

Some apprehensions regarding corruptive major-label influence could be attributed to youthful enthusiasm about a favorite band or sound. But by 1989, as bands at indie labels continued to cross over to mainstream airplay and MTV, these tensions led stations to ponder their role and debate a "philosophy" of college radio.

Indie Rules

Lore has it that sometime in the late 1980s, Mike Mills and Peter Buck of R.E.M. toured college stations to promote *Green*, which would eventually achieve platinum sales. The tour was informal, relying on networks and contacts developed while at I.R.S. At one stop in Illinois, Mills and Buck visited a station without warning.

Upon arriving, they learned that a local band had booked an appearance at the station to promote their upcoming concert.

Rather than crashing their interview and upstaging the local, independent artist, Mills and Buck moved on. Whatever the details, the stars of R.E.M., who had traversed this network on their way to crossover success, appreciated how it functioned and their new place within—or rather, separate from—it. They owed these stations for their success, and in return college radio enjoyed its role in the music industry.[30]

The relationship between independent labels, their artists, college radio, and the mainstream music industry didn't have to be antagonistic or sharply drawn. But by 1989, the lines were growing clearer, both in perception and in reality.

As indie labels grew more viable and distributed records more widely, defining "alternative" music was difficult. The genre, also known as "Modern Rock," gained its own *Billboard* chart in 1988, which drew from the commercial modern rock stations as well as prominent college radio stations. This list distinguished modern rock from the album rock tracks of "traditional rock stations," which would (at that time) play Bon Jovi, Poison, or Van Halen but not UB40, 10,000 Maniacs, or Big Audio Dynamite—bands with connections to college radio.[31] Once they charted, however, stations that had been central to bands' success abandoned them for airplay; they no longer needed college radio's help. Indie-only rules, while more nuanced than in perception and memory, contributed to the sense that college radio operated by different rules than other radio stations, defining its popular reputation.

Athens had already proven its ability to host a vibrant local music scene capable of launching artists to national prominence. The college town's lauded radio station participated in and reinforced that scene. By 1985, WUOG touted noncommercialism and programming practices that made it a destination for bands seeking to be heard and for listeners seeking an alternative to Top 40 pop and rock. WUOG's program director explained, "The rule is . . . if you can hear it on any other stations in town, you can't hear it on our station." This policy, he continued, "means that the residents of this small Southern town, who are used to tuning in to evangelist preachers, easy-listening tunes, or mainstream rock music, are sometimes surprised by bands like the Hoodoo Gurus (the No. 1 college radio band in America), the Drones, or one of Athens's own, Love Tractor."[32]

Unlike commercial radio, where ratings determined ad revenue, student-activities fees funded most campus stations, or they received allocations from the institution—a factor that afforded "stability, allowing stations to be both flexible and innovative."[33] WUOG's noncommercial status protected it and others like it from ratings demands, and student DJs cited educational rationales for exposing listeners to new and obscure musical offerings. Yet WUOG's reputation depended on professionalism. Station hierarchies and an established mission—and the music industry in the mid- to late 1980s—supported and made viable WUOG's anticommercial status.

With educational license and professional standards protecting WUOG and others like it, DJs found themselves free to debate artists' merit and commercial exposure and whether they deserved airplay on their well-respected station. In 1989, DJs engaged in a heated exchange over whether country musician k.d. lang deserved a place in rotation. One DJ complained that "her commercial twang played twice daily is rusting my speakers." Another described her music as "so straight country that the only place it should have on 90.5FM is on [country show] *Dirt Roads and Honky Tonks*." Besides, lang seemed bound for "standard country fare (top 40 kind)." Other DJs countered that "lang's voice and music is completely overlooked and laughed at by commercial radio. . . . Why should we play something as mainstream as the Cure that follows the same 'new wave formula' since 1980?" Lang's fame alone was enough to cut her from rotation, for some. "Don't we usually end our dedication to a band when they achieve such status?" Songs played on the Atlanta commercial station 96 Rock got pulled immediately from rotation. DJs could still play them, but the rotation would not promote them further.

The lang fight ended with a DJ looking at the bigger picture regarding the limitations of a college station. "One lousy record will not make or break WUOG. There have been millions of controversial . . . artists before," he pointed out. Instead, the academic calendar limited WUOG's ability to remain relevant. "If I were going to worry about something, worry about the decline of our reputation as we knock yet another break off the air for several weeks," referring to the station's summer hiatus.

Student volunteers touted their station's reputation as a meritocracy untarnished by commercialism and profit-seeking record promotion. WUOG provided "alternative radio" for the university and surrounding community, as well as professional and leadership experience for student DJs. Commercial radio and MTV offered, as one program director described, "lip-synched techno-pop freeze-dried instant music and 'happy talk' news to lull us. We are taught not to question and not to object, but instead to simply smile and accept what exists, oblivious to the dangers and injustices that surround us." College stations defied such cultural stultification not by programming panels of professors explaining current events, but through music, which could "enlighten, teach, entertain and challenge."[34]

Prominent stations held that if a band reached MTV, college radio's work was done. Occasionally, no-play lists emerged because songs received so many requests after an MTV appearance. Such was the case for the Bauhaus song "Bela Lugosi's Dead" at Rice's KTRU. The sheer number of phone calls from area teenagers clued them in that a band had made it to cable. DJs faced few restrictions on what they could play. Instead, music and program directors understood that they had to "carve out an area on the dial for music that wasn't represented elsewhere," in the words of Dan Osborn from WNUR at Northwestern University (the future founder of Drag City Records). It all went back to college radio's educational and market functions. Major-label artists weren't banned; rather, "if you were going to play something like the Rolling Stones," he explained, "make sure you were not playing the same few dozen songs everyone else was."[35] Osborn encouraged DJs to "mix it up," ensuring the station provided variety in style, including "hardcore, pop, rap, country, folk, experimental, noise, rock, rockabilly, psychedelic, dance, reggae, European avant-garde, African, etc., etc." He wanted DJs to reach back in history. Sixty percent of a rock show should cover new music, but he encouraged DJs to seek out music from the 1940s and before. Regional variation mattered, as did diversifying artists by gender and race. "Just remember," he advised, "you're going to appear an idiot if yr whole show is comprised of music created by middle class white males." And when it came to popularity, he avoided any "Don't play this" rules. Instead, if DJs played a top album from, say, the Beastie Boys, "you should have some reason for it," and "you'd damn well better balance the rest of yr show with more obscure stuff."[36]

In other words, college radio's anticommercialism can be overstated, even if prominent stations such as the University of Chicago's WHPK or Harvard University's WHRB developed deep playlists far from major-label fare. R.E.M. defined college rock and antipathy toward commercialization. Band members took this stance quite literally, refusing to license their songs for commercials. This business decision should not be conflated with college radio, or suggest the band's antipathy toward any commercial endeavor or wide popularity. When they left I.R.S. for Warner, it was largely because its distribution networks could not be replicated by I.R.S., even with A&M's infrastructure, as the band went global.

WUOG's policy for abandoning bands signed with major labels—including R.E.M.—remains more of an urban legend than a hard-and-fast policy. Like many other stations, WUOG DJs collectively avoided music that charted on *Billboard*. When it came to the hometown band, DJs by 1988 avoided songs such as "Orange Crush" heard on commercial rock radio in Atlanta, but music directors entreated DJs to play the "several other really good 'non-REM' sounding material" on *Green*. One DJ refused to play the album only because the Sigma Chi fraternity brothers in the apartment above her, "the closest beings I've ever seen to Neanderthal man," played the album on repeat. With "Stand" and "Orange Crush" receiving play on Top 40, AOR, and heavy metal stations, that DJ declared, "R.E.M. is beyond college radio." Another DJ responded, "Then play their other cuts!" College stations did not exist in a noncommercial vacuum; bands sought college radio to reach listeners and gain attention.[37]

Music directors emphasized diversity. Cultural change was within their grasp, but it might mean avoiding some favorites that had crossed over.[38] Diversity was the goal in programming—even if that goal came with charges of elitism.

Diversity, Elitism, and the Indie Rock Kids

Few strict rules about major-label bands existed in writing, but many college stations encouraged a different sound than commercial signals. At WXYC at the University of North Carolina (UNC) at Chapel Hill, another flagship state university in a quintessential college town, DJs pushed "diversity" and pushed DJs to play "a variety of styles." Outside of specialty shows focused on specific genres such as reggae or broadcasts of women's basketball games, station leaders insisted, "We don't have any music we don't play." But the station developed a notorious reputation for selectivity in staff, with the *Daily Tar Heel* reporting in August 1988 that WXYC turned away nearly 90 percent of applicants.[39]

DJs had to know music and be committed to the music scene around Chapel Hill. The new music director in 1988, Glenn Boothe, brought "enthusiasm about the local music scene," and he was determined to make it viable. Station manager Cheryl Parker emphasized outreach to the UNC student body, many of whom saw the radio crowd as a little freakish in its music sensibilities. Parker merely planned to "make the campus more aware of WXYC," not to change its sound.[40]

WXYC battled more than apathy among UNC students and the appearance of choosiness in selecting DJs. As chief announcer John Sherer explained in spring 1989, "College radio has been stereotyped as the Cure, R.E.M., and the Smiths." These bands were "great in the early 1980s but college radio can get into that rut and get stuck there." Those bands, having achieved success outside of college radio, no longer needed their help. Sherer saw that WXYC and stations like it had a role to play in the music industry by anchoring local scenes and diversifying musical culture. Yet college radio's image remained wedded to bands that made the jump to mainstream success, or perhaps those featured on MTV's *The Cutting Edge* or *120 Minutes*.

The quiz prospective WXYC DJs took was not to recite the top acts on CMJ, but rather to demonstrate originality and "convey more than a superficial musical knowledge." As one DJ remembered, sometimes that meant deep knowledge about Cambodian folk music, or exploring different types of jazz.[41]

The elitist image tended to be sticky. Even students in the university's Radio, Television, and Motion Picture program found it hard to obtain a spot at WXYC. One major complained that these students had a nonexistent chance of becoming a DJ. As for using the station as professional experience, she reported, "I got the message that they offer no support or experience to RTVMP majors." Instead, the quiz for prospective DJs tested "knowledge of groups like Jane's Addiction and The Screaming Blue Messiahs; or is it just Screaming Blue Messiahs without the 'The'?" For that student, his "musical tastes are a little too 'mainstream' for their liking," despite his willingness to take 3 A.M. to 6 A.M. shifts.[42]

DJs who did pass the test remembered it slightly differently. Two friends, Dan Smith and Kevin Kruse, decided to attempt the winter tryouts during their first year at UNC in 1990. As Kruse remembered, "It was kind of legendary how tough this test was." Friends laughed that the pair decided to try this as first-year students, before being immersed in the scene and the station.[43]

"And it was tough," Kruse reflected. Prospective DJs waited together in a room to be called in to be grilled by station managers. Kruse, whose musical knowledge came from bootleg tapes recorded from radio or from friends, had little knowledge of albums. The music director held up the cover of a King Crimson album, and Kruse had no idea what it was. Buckwheat Zydeco was next. Kruse responded, "I've never heard of zydeco." The managers prompted him, pointing to the accordion and crawfish on the cover, to no avail. But he knew blues, rock, and hip-hop, and Smith knew jazz. That was enough. Luckily for him, the managers knew he was from Nashville, so they skipped the country section, assuming he was immersed: "I got off scot free with that." Rumors about the quiz had some merit. But Smith and Kruse passed because they brought a range of knowledge, not answers to specific questions from some secret music snob manual.[44]

Station leaders rejected the notion that there was some kind of "killer questionnaire" and selected DJs for varied taste in music. Instead, Boothe, in his tenure as music director, emphasized devotion to music, whatever its form. He selected DJs who could "entertain but also educate and help promote these new bands." WXYC's motto, proclaimed a student newspaper headline, was "a devotion to everything." Sometimes they weren't very professional: "that's part of the charm."[45] By 1990, the station had added *Backyard Barbecue*, a weekly local music show, as well as a management spot for a local music director. That year WXYC released *Demo-Listen*, a compilation of local bands.[46] WXYC's format might have been mysterious, but scenesters knew that it had a sound and supported local music.[47] A local entrepreneur remembered, "If there was a show of any kind . . . everybody went. All fifty people that were interested in that music."[48] Members of what would become the scene-defining band Superchunk took inspiration from Fugazi and the D.C. scene and released their own collection of seven-inches from bands around town. It was a "gimmick," frontman and guitarist Mac McCaughan remembered, but it worked.[49]

For Boothe at WXYC, upon his arrival at the station no one took seven-inch singles seriously. They were considered "so unimportant that when we got in the first seven-inch by Nirvana, I just gave it away to one of the DJs." But the seven-inch "launched a lot of indie labels." They were easy to mail to radio stations and the music press and sell at shows, and one play could garner the buzz needed to get the band, and their label, going.[50] Radio stations were one piece in promotion. Boothe thought it was silly for Superchunk to release "Slack Motherfucker" as a single, since it couldn't be played on air, but it still sold. Stations helped anchor a scene and promote openness to new music and broadened tastes.

By the late 1980s, WXYC's leaders didn't want students who were seeking that typical college radio sound. Applicants needed to be interested in more bands than Depeche Mode and Suzanne Vega. After 1991, aspirants wanting to play Seattle grunge rock were turned away. Some students might be hip to the Chapel Hill scene because of an article in *Spin* or *Rolling Stone*, and they wanted to be known for playing the next big thing. But that was not necessarily what WXYC leaders wanted.[51] They wanted to play a variety of music to inspire more creativity and to set a tone, to encourage openness to more types of sound and expression.

Listeners might tune in and hear Patsy Cline after the New York Dolls. Fundraisers encouraged listeners to "shake our booty" to seventies music during their annual "Beg-a-Thon" seeking donations to fill coffers. The equipment at WXYC consistently had technical problems, and fundraising would help upgrade its sound.[52] Eventually, after earning $4,000 more than the target goal, the studio secured a new transmitter link and a better reel-to-reel deck and updated the emergency broadcasting system. The student activities constitution required that 4 percent of student fees be allocated to the station, but it fell short for capital expenditures. The station's sponsored nights at local clubs cemented relationships with local venues.[53] Occasionally, gestures helped "dispel the idea of WXYC's out there image," as a Madonna-themed benefit suggested, although it coordinated with a lecture on the pop singer's music and the station's irreverence proved inescapable.[54] It was a "cerebral," tongue-in-cheek event "making fun of ourselves," a DJ explained.[55]

WXYC had a talk show, a sports show, and shows focusing on experimental music. It was eclectic. A freeform ethos guided programming, although there were informal gatekeepers, "people who had been there for a long time, who kind of dictated a lot of how the station was going to work and what kind of things were going to be put into the rotation," a DJ remembered.[56] There was a collection of records to emphasize, and suggestions that DJs play a third from the rotation, a third from standards, and then more obscure hits. "Most," according to one former jock, "went about 95 percent obscure, and maybe a couple standards, that idea you would play hits was just kind of laughed at."[57] DJs had to be students to start working there, but many alumni who stayed in the area could get shifts, even if the first choice of timeslots went to current students. WXYC's most important feature was its relationship to the local community, and many community DJs hosted beloved shows with longevity.

If gatekeepers at WXYC emphasized any type of music, it was local, or any band with a single out that might not get airplay on a commercial alternative station. If that band came to town, DJs knew they could probably go see it for $10 admission at a local club. DJs might even get free tickets as promos, and they gravitated to bands they had the opportunity to see in clubs or record an interview with.

If a band came out on recently launched, local independent-label Merge Records, WXYC was almost guaranteed to play it. "It didn't matter if it was a local band or some other band from Australia," a DJ remembered, "it was gonna be in rotation just to help support" the label. Label staff would often stop by the studio when bands released an album. Some DJs went to work for Merge or another local label, Mammoth Records.

For most DJs, the experience was less about professional development and breaking hits than about musical discovery. As one DJ reflected, "If we saw [local band] Superchunk on *120 Minutes*, that was awesome. But you know, there was nobody ever really, as far as I know, [who] broke through."

DJs liked pulling out an interesting-looking record and "dropping the needle on it." It was part of the learning experience. As another former DJ put it, "it was a constant state of self-education." UNC provided opportunities to "try different things," and WXYC was another example. DJs made their own tapes from the station's music library or brought in their own crates of records to share. Constant curation and musical evaluation were as integral to the experience of doing college radio as being on air. Students could be involved in music without having any actual talent.[58] Nonetheless, they were part of a central institution that was reshaping American mainstream musical culture—whether they wanted to or not, and independent from how many people were actually tuning in.

New Institutions

As music director at UCLA's station in the early 1990s, Eric J. Lawrence felt an odd sense of power. Despite spotty reach into university dorms via its carrier-current signal, KLA was a CMJ reporter. With a listening audience potential the size of UCLA's student body—let alone the number of ears in Los Angeles—KLA garnered the status of a major-market station. CMJ and record labels cultivated relationships with station leaders.

Nobody was listening. "The labels didn't really understand that," Lawrence remembered.

Unreliable equipment, with blown transmitters disrupting broadcasting into the Kerckhoff Coffee House or dorm commons, plagued station leaders. When the signal worked, not all enjoyed the sound. In 1988, a new general manager faced complaints from food vendors that diners did not like "the station's 'late 70s pop/rock.'" She found the sentiment odd, given the station's revamped emphasis on new music and high demand for DJ spots. That fall, 150 students applied for fifty-six DJ positions, even if the station bore a reputation as a "thrash punk outlet." KLA programmed jazz, news, reggae, funk, and a rotation that emphasized heavy, medium, and light playlists. No one got paid, but DJs exhibited an "inexplicable commitment to the station."[59]

UCLA students, if they noticed the absence of a campus FM station, occasionally complained about KLA's reach. One student derided UCLA for not emulating USC, Loyola Marymount, Santa Monica, or Pomona College in Claremont with its own spot on the airwaves. He remarked, "Have you ever tried to run a cable to your car, or to the beach, or to your Walkman so you can hear KLA between classes?" It was annoying that he could not bring the campus and music broadcast by his peers along with him. Competitors boasted strong followings, and commercial alternative pioneer KROQ lured listeners of similar demographics as UCLA students—but students wanted their own powerhouse signal.[60]

If students could tune in to KLA, they would hear artists such as U2, Talk Talk, Tom Waits, Widespread Panic, and Ice-T.[61] In an October 1988 top thirty list, DJs explained, "We bet you thought we only played the music of bands with bizarre sounding names, like They Might Be Giants or Voice of the Beehive! Surprise!"[62] DJs understood they might face resistance from bookstore staff or students who preferred commercial pop. They asserted that KLA was "part of the community" and tried to avoid "the rawest punk" that might "drive everyone away." They took their jobs seriously, even with few listeners. DJs reached a "happy middle ground" where they "didn't fight over philosophy" of playlists and provided DJs freedom.[63]

An ad hoc committee of students and administrators met at the end of 1988 to discuss KLA. According to Lawrence, potential radio participation served as a selling point to incoming students. College radio's visibility and role in shaping popular music convinced administrators to revisit funding and to stop fearing what students might do with a more audible signal. Leaders celebrated the funds that might finally end KLA's "bastard child" status at UCLA.[64] Faculty on the station's board of directors feared granting KLA more money because they had no way of knowing which students would run the station, given frequent turnover. Nonetheless, KLA seemed on the brink of an upgrade.[65]

While UCLA organized to upgrade KLA, the station enjoyed a strong relationship with record labels. They might not have won new fans via the airwaves to bands such as Jane's Addiction, which consistently charted highly, but DJs had "an opportunity to learn and have a degree of influence in the industry." If a band did well on KLA, it had a likelihood of being featured in CMJ. As music director, Lawrence diligently tallied playlists and created a legitimate top thirty. Occasionally, fudging happened because of poor record keeping or a desire to elevate a certain band, but music tip sheets took seriously what college music directors programmed. The sense of being a meritocracy permeated college radio. These were not corporate executives pushing product: that these tastemakers were closer to music fans than industry insiders worked in their favor. What they selected was credible even without audience data or participation—or much of an audience at all.

KLA earned notice among the music industry and nearby labels in Los Angeles. As bands such as Ministry, Skinny Puppy, White Zombie, the Mekons, and George Clinton topped KLA's playlists in early 1990, reflecting the station's emphasis on heavy metal among a variety of sounds, many UCLA students secured opportunities in the record industry. One DJ reported making good contacts during a summer position at Virgin Records.[66] KLA members found positions at major labels, despite few DJs getting involved out of any "careerist" mindset.

As KLA's reputation grew in 1989, a rather smelly bunch of guys emerged from a van near the studio, chomping on Cheetos and "smoking incessantly." One trio member sidled up to the music director and queried if the station had any Swans records. The metal director had invited this new, exciting band and interviewed them. Dave Grohl had not yet joined, but it was clear that this Seattle-based band, Nirvana, was going places.

Nirvana was still signed to independent-label Sub Pop Records during this appearance. Its visit reflected the relationship KLA and other college radio stations had with independent labels as a first stop for promotion and radio appearances, where it would be welcomed. KLA's paltry audience didn't prevent major labels from calling. When MC Hammer hit it big, his label sent KLA a big thank you basket with a bottle of wine and fancy pistachios. "We just barely played this," Lawrence remembered. But the station welcomed promotional materials for British label 4 A.D. band the Pixies, or tickets and t-shirts for bands they were excited about.

Music directors and DJs at KLA never felt pressured or bribed to play certain bands. Some promotional tactics might have been annoying, or they ignored some music. They "never felt obligated" to play certain albums. Still, DJs took pride in their influence—or at least it seemed so.[67]

In 1990, only a few noteworthy crossovers portended the development of an independent-label business model that would elevate the scene associated with the foggy ambiance of the Pacific Northwest.

It was clear Nirvana had the potential to hit it big, with its grinding angst and transgressive style. In October 1990, 500 "screaming teenage punks" packed into an Olympia, Washington, club to see the trio, now with drummer Dave Grohl. As the Evergreen State College newspaper reported, "This band inspires poorly dressed record executives to step from new Lincoln Continentals and wade through underage fans handing out diamond studded business cards." Those fans "shuddered" at rumors of a major-label crossover, but there was a sense that the band had a unique and appealing sound. The band, with its avid following, "could have played 'Free Bird' for two hours" and the crowd would have been rapt.[68]

The writer noted an upcoming appearance by the Dust Devils, from newly founded independent-label Matador Records, where Gerard Cosloy recently joined as a partner. Cosloy was formerly of Homestead Records, home of Dinosaur Jr, Big Black, and Sonic Youth before they signed with Geffen. In 1990, these bands overlapped and reinforced one another as part of the same ecosystem and market, with few plotting or expecting to hit the stratosphere of pop stardom. They simply thought they'd reach a few more fans.

Managing information about new labels and this evolving market presented organizational challenges to college stations. In 1991, WOBC at Oberlin in Ohio, known for its progressive format, penned a new handbook. DJs admitted that managing their music library and many genres was "a mess." A good music director might stay for a few years and establish "many ties with record labels, but we have a hard time determining what they are." Reportedly, "good records" had not been "left by past music directors." It was hard to know whom to contact, or which rep belonged to which label. WOBC enjoyed good record service, and the studio housed a database of some 1,400 record labels. Keeping track was a huge task. Volunteers resolved to see how many promos they received and cultivate relationships. "Many small labels," they noted, "need to see this kind of dedication on our part or they will drop us from their mailing lists." WOBC needed a systematic and transparent procedure for managing label relationships, let alone for tracking what records went into the library and rotation.[69]

Label relationships could fray for several reasons. At Northwestern, sometimes a band would cross over to a major label and then flop. If station leaders did not feature individual bands prominently or the bands failed to resonate with DJs or listeners, relations soured. Major labels would retaliate, cutting off service or criticizing stations in CMJ.[70]

After Nirvana signed to Geffen in 1991—and those Lincoln-driving record executives looked even more hungrily at college stations for the next crossover smash—anti-major-label sentiment in college radio intensified. The personal relationships that Blumenthal and the other promoters featured in *Rolling Stone* in 1990 were less and less possible. The money and attention, as well as the rise of commercial alternative radio, created an adversarial relationship between indie, underground scenes and the mainstream music industry.

· · · · · ·

College DJs, whether or not they envisioned careers in the music industry, felt stations were theirs. They were creating communities and friendships, and they were engaging in musical discovery and exposure with a real sense of influence. DJs provided feedback to music directors and other DJs.[71] Their status as tastemakers or gatekeepers could be rendered positively or negatively, depending on the station or market, or individual tastes involved. Charges of elitism and insider cliquishness certainly appeared, particularly at stations where the sound diverged markedly from prevalent music tastes of students on campus. DJs extended the project of liberal arts education to university airwaves, and that mission shielded them from commercial and protected adventurous programming, with limits.

Market forces always circulated. Hungry major labels threatened what appeared to be a well-functioning, meritocratic system of music discovery and promotion. Good bands would get picked by DJs, or so the logic went. This belief in meritocracy coursed through conversations at college stations about their role in musical culture. DJs focused on expanding coverage of genres lacking commercial airplay, educating listeners about musical history and influences, and ensuring diversity in sound and artists. But commitment to musical diversity often proved more complicated in the details.

When Kevin Kruse, one of the first-year students who risked taking the dreaded test at WXYC, tuned in to the station one day, he was surprised by what he heard. The DJ on air did what was expected: he reached into the rotation, pulled out something unfamiliar, and gave it a play. The DJ read his setlist back for listeners and announced the artist, McSearch. Perhaps he was not thinking, or misread, when he announced not the latest Irish import, but rather hip-hop artist MC Serch.[72] DJs might aspire to play diverse sounds and expose listeners to what they had not heard before—and DJs showed a willingness to be adventurous, playing what the music directors put into the rotation. But having a diverse musical rotation did not always mean all genres received robust coverage from knowledgeable jocks. And when most DJs were young, middle-class white college students, they sometimes missed things.

More than listeners seeking musical discovery tuned in to college radio stations. That public service function gave rise to these stations in the first place, and the demand did not cease with college radio's valuable role in the music industry. Spats with major-label representatives paled in comparison to the sense of betrayal some communities felt when student DJs changed the hours of a long-standing community show or canceled programming altogether. The narrow image of college radio as the domain of white indie rockers obscured its wide service. Yet that service had limits, whether it was airing genres such as hip-hop or fulfilling promises to provide educational and community service.

· ·

In the 1980s, getting a tape or an early demo into even light rotation on college radio might spell success for a band. That hope ballooned for artists and volunteer DJs at KCMU, University of Washington's (UW) radio station in Seattle. It was a classic tale. A groundswell of local bands, clubs, and record labels all found support at the area's college stations. KCMU upgraded its power in 1986 to 404 watts, reaching some fifteen miles around Seattle, extending musical exposure, luring listeners to local shows and dance parties and dollars to local record stores and independent labels. Musicians such as Mark Arm of Mudhoney and Soundgarden guitarist Kim Thayil had shows on KCMU.

The station almost collapsed in 1980 amid university budget cuts and the cessation of UW's broadcasting program. Local donors kept the station on life support until its reputation as a leader in local music cemented its status. A reciprocal relationship emerged. Bands that played benefit concerts for the station began to sign major-label contracts.

Underground artists by the late 1980s—thanks in large part to the alternative musical network that college radio stations supported—achieved stellar commercial success. This was especially true for KCMU artists.

By 1992, Seattle's music scene defined the nation's popular musical culture. Indeed, one artist in particular whose music found a home on KCMU's Sunday night shows made it big, topping MTV and *Billboard* charts and marking a new era for a musical genre.

No, not Nirvana; Anthony L. Neal, otherwise known as Sir Mix-a-Lot.

While alternative rock and hip-hop (particularly gangsta rap) competed for pop commercial status, indie rock often overshadows the relationship between college radio and local hip-hop scenes. In the 1980s, hip-hop networks of DIY-recorded tapes and distribution, radio play, and upstart independent labels grew more viable and commodified, much like what happened in hardcore and indie rock. Hip-hop's relationship to "commercial" was a long-standing and complicated question. Like alternative rock, many artists "crossed over"—"a term," one hip-hop scholar explains, "that, in the world of hip-hop, had become synonymous with selling out," particularly when suburban white teenagers became a lucrative audience in the late 1980s and early 1990s.[1]

"Selling out" remained a difficult term. Many artists chose their path, navigating an often-discriminatory industry as well as culture-war politics regarding Black expression and art. Co-optation narratives similarly crept into hip-hop, as with indie rock, while artists attempted to turn such dynamics to their advantage.

Underground hip-hop artists persisted, taking advantage of noncommercial college and community radio. Even if hip-hop shows remained in the minority, student and community DJs found space on the airwaves to connect listeners to artists and build community.

These negotiations took place amid increasingly fraught questions about whose priorities should control college radio in the 1990s. At colleges and universities, institutional support facilitated community connection. But those institutions retained control. The 1991 recession strained state budgets, prompting fears that college stations would be deemed a "luxury" that institutions could ill afford, forcing them to adopt more mainstream programming and a listener-funded business model and underwriting. As one publication put it in 1994, a struggle raged "for the soul of public radio," pitting listeners and activists against "professionals."[2] Adventurous radio was in danger of falling into the hands of "slack careerists," in which donations went toward "bankrolling the bureaucracy."[3] Listeners might feel like they owned these signals, and they might even contribute their hard-won earnings to support them. Despite the image of facilitating a democratic public sphere, a few unelected officials at universities wielded much power over college radio, in addition to student DJs determining programming schedules.

Many stations remained as they always had: student-run institutions that welcomed volunteer community DJs and covered genres beyond indie rock. Participants still aspired to connect with audiences, building interest for local music and augmenting music scenes. But even the most adventurous DJs might miss out on musical movements or fail to understand how their stations functioned within communities.

Of course, it wasn't always DJs misunderstanding radio's service. Administrators remained in the wings, waiting to intervene if stations caused too much controversy or bad press that damaged institutional image. The balance remained unsteady between public service and providing a learning experience for students. More than corporatization and major-label stultification threatened the diversity of music on the radio.

Culture-war battles regarding rap made for sensational headlines and influenced programming at some stations. Hip-hop shows, like punk in the late 1970s, often received late-night slots, even as more stations began to add albums to regular rotation. But hip-hop fans were one constituency that college radio served, and students running stations, even those dedicated to musical diversity, often lacked the vision or capability to satisfy disparate demands on airtime. Structural limits of universities or colleges and media, and their own individual aspirations, stood in the way.

Hip-Hop Debates

"Why are we so fucking white?"

Jeff Nunnally, program director at KTRU, Rice University's student-run radio station, penned this question in the "Gripes and Groans" book that resided in the station's studio in spring 1987. The station featured Ministry, Howard Jones, and Depeche Mode in its "eclectic" rotation. Nunnally complained, "I could name twenty rap albums that will make any of the white, cheap imitations we have in eclectic wither up." If DJs and listeners valued transgressive sounds, they needed to pay attention to what Black artists were saying, he argued. Fishbone and Run-DMC made the general rotation, along with one Grandmaster Flash song, but, Nunnally pointed out, prominent artists still were disserved. "There is no way," he wrote, "Fishbone should be on light [rotation] while the B-52s are on moderate."[4]

It is possible he referred to a recent incident involving members of Fishbone.

They didn't have much to do the afternoon before their interview at KTRU, but they had some weed. A warm keg of beer from a party the night before sat in the radio station's studio, amusing some DJs. The band visited Houston to promote a new album, as its sound began to transform from ska and funk emphasis of earlier years to incorporate more rock and soul sounds.

No records remain of the appearance, and memories can be fuzzy for reasons beyond consumption of flat beer. A DJ, though buzzed from the beer and relaxed from a contact high, remembered with awe what happened next. One of Fishbone's vocalists began "digging around in the stacks," looking for records to play. DJs let him into the music library, and into "the secondary stacks." There, the DJ remembered, "he was like, 'Where's all your hip-hop? Why is it that you don't have anything?'" KTRU might have been a leader in alternative rock music, but DJs had a blind spot when it came to rap and hip-hop. The singer located some "jazz and old soul records, instrumental stuff," and played the records, keeping the microphone on and rapping over the sounds.[5]

The DJ remembered, "He just basically put on a show himself. Our minds were blown."[6]

College radio enjoyed a prominent position as a tastemaker and gatekeeper for new music. Discerning music enthusiasts scoured import bins at local record stores and dive bar shows for exciting sounds, which they featured on their signals. They highlighted tiny labels trying to make it. College DJs, shielded by a mandate to "educate" listeners and without ratings pressure, could elevate the best music—and even defy the corporate logic of major labels and shape popular culture. Participants knew they often left out innovative artists, particularly from hip-hop. The concept of academic freedom might provide some cover for adventurous artistic exploration, even in radio, but did not guarantee equity in exposure of all voices.

As the Rice DJ reflected later, "We weren't really evangelizing that music: we were doing it for each other. I was never running around trying to convince people what a great band the Wedding Present was." He wasn't in it for outside, external audiences. "College radio was a way for us to evangelize awesome new music just to each other." If others listened in and liked it, great.[7]

Emphasizing educational functions tended to elide the question of college radio's whiteness that Nunnally raised. Some DJs agreed, while others were defensive. One DJ responded, "The fucking whiteness of this station reflects for the most part the fucking whiteness of the record industry." "Blame the culture industry" was his argument. KTRU received few albums from Black artists. For that matter, he continued, "the 'fucking whiteness' of our DJs" could be pinned on "the f'ing whiteness of Rice in general." Nunnally pushed to include more Public Enemy and Boogie Down Productions (BDP) in rotation, with some success.

Black enrollment in colleges and universities, which had increased between 1967 and 1976 by some 247 percent, sagged in the 1980s and accompanied continued questions regarding campus culture.[8] In the 1990s, sociologist Anthony Kwame Harrison found, "students regularly characterized their campus as a *white public space,*" a definition that extended to college radio stations.[9] Black students found little service from college radio, a service that generated what Harrison termed "sonic belonging," meaning Black students, "through their involvement in and around college radio programming, authored their own means of supporting one another and alleviating feelings of isolation."[10] Experiences varied across signals, campuses, and markets. Still, the overwhelming popular image of college radio was one of white, independent-label rock. Although CMJ, which had launched the first chart tracking hip-hop, kept tabs on numerous genres, the bands crossing over to MTV tended to support a narrow image of college radio that ignored minority voices.

These sentiments appeared logical considering conflagrations regarding Black expression in the early 1990s, putting a magnifying glass on rap lyrics. Metal music, produced by mostly white artists, incited concerns about occultism and violence in the 1980s but lacked the implications of the scrutiny placed on rap. Metal, in large part, prompted the Parents Music Resource Center's (PMRC) crusade for warning labels on music albums, signaling a standoff over consumption and parental control regarding how pop music represented and marketed to young people. Black artists, on the other hand, were fighting for a place within US culture and expression, to speak to the experiences inspiring their lyrics and music. This goal paralleled how college students sought to create representative institutions—while possessing significantly less institutional or political power and connection. Regarding college radio, students and artists alike were seeking access to the public airwaves to diversify both campuses and US culture. These debates went beyond questions of genre and sound. They were about institutional access and belonging in public space and national identity.[11]

Culture warriors expanded attention from lyrics to local policing of obscenity, including censoring and arresting members of Miami-based hip-hop group 2 Live Crew in 1990. Picking up where PMRC left off, having secured voluntary labeling of record albums to warn consumers of content not suitable for minors, members of Congress and advocacy groups turned attention to rap lyrics' supposedly deleterious social effects. The National Association for the Advancement of Colored People (NAACP) and the National Political Congress of Black Women condemned violent content and, in 1994, the House of Representatives congressional subcommittee hearing. The politicization of hip-hop lyrics, particularly gangsta rap, channeled questions about the social functions of music within the context of the culture-war battles and in the longer trajectory of civil rights activism. California representative Maxine Waters pushed back, calling it a "foolhardy mistake to single out poets as the cause of America's problems."[12] Scholars such as Tricia Rose, in the years following the hearing, explored the complex dynamics behind early 1990s "hip-hop wars" and beyond.[13]

As these larger conversations unfolded, many college stations ignored Public Enemy's first album, *Yo! Bum Rush the Show*. One DJ at WUOG in Athens at the University of Georgia blamed the station's overwhelmingly "middle class, white bread, conservative restraints" stemming from many DJs' suburban Atlanta roots. "The Cure, Joy Division, and Jesus and Mary Chain are 'alternative' music to them," he argued. Rap only became cool to play when white artists released it. With the Beastie Boys, rap became a trend. "Cool music has no color!" another DJ responded. One DJ resented being chastised for being white and cuing up the Beasties. "Would you prefer that we ignore it?" he asked. The meritocracy reigned, in his mind. "I play it because I like it, not because it's cool," he said, failing to consider how cultural context might shape his tastes. Other DJs simply asked the station to play "alternative" artists across genres—whether it was k.d. lang or Ice-T.[14] Public Enemy did receive good coverage on college stations, eventually, usually in rotations of mostly white rock artists. Specialty shows dedicated to rap and hip-hop proliferated, but the question of how to incorporate the genre and provide it with robust coverage remained an open debate.

Structural problems tied to stations' missions and relationship with record labels presented additional complications. WUOG, for example, lacked relationships with labels releasing Black pop and underground music. The station failed to get in on the ground floor in promoting these artists, some DJs argued. When they received the record, it was "too late." Urban stations had already picked up on the trend, and those artists no longer needed WUOG. Music directors needed to contact these labels and establish their interest in promoting Black music. WUOG's music director brought matters back to the goal of diversity as well as how much exposure the music already received. "In order to provide as diverse a rotation of music as possible," he had to be "very discriminate." That meant a lot of DJs' favorite tunes might not make the cut. Plus, "when things become stale and unfresh," he reminded DJs, "I am failing in my job." WUOG had a reputation of providing high-"caliber" music.[15] Responsibility to diversity and "freshness" constituted a political commitment.[16]

Questions of political content filtered into these discussions as well. At Stanford University, BDP's *Ghetto Music: The Blueprint of Hip-Hop* made its station's top five list in 1989. In 1990, Public Enemy's album *Fear of a Black Planet* sat atop KZSU's list of most played records—although some listeners' favorites were not included. But not all observers understood the difference between censoring music for broadcast and censoring music for sale. KZSU DJs, according to one complaint, "refuse" to play hardcore rap with political and social messages, particularly songs by N.W.A. The station hosted *The Drum*, a long-running hip-hop show, but rap did not penetrate the rotation in large numbers. In December 1989, for example, the only artists close to these genres appearing on KZSU's top thirty submitted to CMJ included a reggae compilation, dub artist Mad Professor, and the Beastie Boys.[17] Most stations, if they hosted dedicated hip-hop shows, reported to CMJ's separate Beat Box list. (Reggae and metal also had separate lists.) In addition to list segmentation, DJs' wariness of controversy stemmed from the chilling effect sweeping across radio thanks to the PMRC, labeling, and the FCC and Congress's waffling on indecency and obscenity rules.

The station's staff blamed the FCC. KSZU's music director responded with incredulity: "Why is it a problem to play 'Fuck the Police' on the radio? Is it too full of 'social commentary,'" as the critic suggested?

"No," he responded. Rather, "if a single person listening made a complaint to the FCC, we could lose our license."[18]

These debates over content, as with the broader conflagrations about hip-hop, obscured deeper issues with scant connection to policing expression. At college stations, underlying questions involved who would control musical coverage. Time allotment and which DJs staffed the boards connected to issues at the heart of the culture wars, even if they sparked no congressional hearings or obscenity fines.

Programming structures presented challenges. A standard practice was to mix hip-hop albums with indie rock, blues, country, bluegrass, and whatever else the music director put into rotation. The goal, as one station manager explained, was to create "a model of diversity." De La Soul might be followed by Doc Watson. DJs' musical horizons expanded with exposure to new music they "wouldn't have otherwise listened to." This prevailing logic of "educational radio" had defended college radio's coverage of genres without mainstream appeal—or without many fans on campus—since the 1970s. "Educational" meant exposure to something new, something challenging, as well as providing public service and coverage of music without commercial radio coverage, often including jazz, classical, reggae, folk, and genres of music from across the world. Aspirant DJs who wanted to focus on hip-hop, or who tuned in and only heard a song or two during an hour that they enjoyed, didn't feel welcome. Leaders hoped introducing more minorities and women as DJs would draw new audiences while pursuing the station's educational mission.[19]

Stations promised opportunities for cultural recognition and community bonding. Many succeeded, creating lasting institutions to provide meaningful service, staffed by students or longtime community volunteers.[20] At predominantly white colleges and universities situated in largely non-white urban areas, the question of town and gown relations shaped conversations about radio. Institutions tasked their radio stations with responsibility for bridging gaps with residents, asking student volunteers armed with some musical background and goodwill to provide meaningful public service and entertainment for communities underserved by commercial media. It was a hefty responsibility, especially when genres such as hip-hop sat in the crosshairs of culture-war skirmishes in the early 1990s and student DJs were left to navigate these waters without much guidance.

A yet broader problem lurked beneath the surface of these expectations. College stations had to fulfill needs that commercial radio failed to, despite their mandate in the Communications Act of 1934 to provide public service. Educational, noncommercial licenses protected college DJs' ability to play the weird and the not commercially viable and to challenge the culture industry's power, if they wanted. But relying on the goodwill of DJs or student leaders at these stations often was not enough to guarantee robust service to the constituents looking to college radio.

Creating Space on College Radio

New York's college scene was important to hip-hop artists' exposure. Hip-hop gained an early foothold at the city's stations and colleges, even before there were numerous commercial recordings available. DJs played self-released tapes or featured in-studio performances. Kurtis Blow and Reggie Wells had radio shows as early as 1979 at City College in New York while they played local clubs. DJ Hollywood and Grandmaster Flash played college parties or nearby clubs with discounted admission for college IDs.

WKCR at Columbia University sat in an ideal location to connect with hip-hop. "Fab Five" Freddy Braithwaite, when asked what college stations mattered to hip-hop, named WKCR. Its signal reached upward through Harlem into the South Bronx, where kids hoped to pick up sounds on their stereos.[21]

But the relationship between Columbia's well-regarded station and hip-hop wasn't inevitable. Pete Nash, who had come to Columbia as a student in 1985, knew this. He had been a basketball player for the college until an injury sidelined him. With time to spare, he would tune in to P Fine's

(Jonathan Finegold) hip-hop show on WNYU, which featured performances and interviews with artists such as Brooklyn's Stetsasonic and L.L. Cool J, among others—including an interview with Public Enemy they sampled on their 1990 album, *Fear of a Black Planet*.[22] What he heard excited Nash, who already participated in hip-hop. The station aired music as well as news about parties and shows to check out. The group Nash had been a part of split when other members left for Syracuse. So he turned his energy to getting a radio show at WKCR.

He secured a spot early in the morning. The new music director was excited to add hip-hop and decided to give Nash a try. After a few weeks of broadcasting, buzz grew about Nash's late-night show.

Nash navigated an odd transition from the experimental music airing before his show, which featured music by avant-garde composers such as John Cage. Nash made it work. He brought on DJ Clark Kent as a partner, who would haul his DJ equipment to perform live on air with the same energy he would in a club. He would "go nuts," Nash remembered. Their innovative show and high-energy presentation earned fans from across the city, including artists such as Large Professor.[23]

Things were going great. Clark got his hands on a test press of Public Enemy's song "Rebel without a Pause" and records from BDP and others, which they were among the first to broadcast. Everything worked, save the jarring transition from the previous show—that is, until one night late in the summer.

Nash started playing basketball again, and an away game conflicted with his show one week. DJ Clark Kent was on tour, so he introduced Nash to his cousin, DJ Richie Rich. The duo asked Rich to fill in.[24]

"Don't do anything stupid, right?" Nash joked. Rich had appeared on the show a few times before, so Nash wasn't worried. Nash would be in Syracuse playing basketball and wouldn't be able to hear the show, but he was excited about it. Clark Kent had secured Biz Markie and his crew from Brooklyn to make an appearance.[25]

They showed, and what aired seemed to go well. After they left, however, reports of missing equipment surfaced, and Nash got the blame. "No shade to Biz," Nash remembered, as no evidence emerged to suggest any culprit.[26]

The music director called Nash into his office. "They looked at us," he remembered, who had "hip-hop heads coming up to the studio, one o'clock in the morning . . . and it was just different." They didn't fit in. "You know," he explained, "we clashed with the John Cage types." The suspicion cast on Nash and his friends, who were all from New York, resembled the problems with Columbia's image in the neighborhood. The Ivy League school was notorious for closing itself off from the streets and residents outside, and suspicion went both ways. But only the university had the power to cut off access to the city's airwaves.[27]

Nash had been busy distributing flyers for his show every week all over Brooklyn and the boroughs, creating good will. Just like that, it was over. Nash took it hard. They had been "rolling," and his firing was "fucked up."[28]

When Stretch and Bobbito secured their show a few years later, Nash was surprised. They invited Nash to visit the show—he had gone on to success at Def Jam and his own crew 3rd Bass with MC Serch—but he refused. "I was like 'fuck no,'" he remembered; "I'm boycotting WKCR whether you're on it or whoever is on it."[29] Nash—as Pete Nice—made two gold records with 3rd Bass. He left his college radio days behind him, but the show had made a mark.

By the 1990s, WKCR connected to the city's hip-hop innovators with shows such as *We Could Do This Show* and *Stretch and Bobbito*, which interviewed many hip-hop superstars before they hit mainstream success. Stretch and Bobbito played tapes from unsigned artists and featured live performances, including future superstars such as Jay Z, who described the show as the "spark" for his career. Nas, who appeared on their show before the release of his album *Illmatic*, called *Stretch and Bobbito* "the most important" hip-hop show in the world. Wu-Tang Clan, Busta Rhymes, Talib Kweli—the list of names that appeared on their show is long and legendary. It was a "rinky dink" college station with an often-malfunctioning board from the 1960s, but it made hip-hop history.[30]

Such successes notwithstanding, Nash was not the only hip-hop DJ on college radio to be scrutinized—far from it. In his case, the station had no proof it was Biz Markie's crew that took equipment, but Nash's association with the New York hip-hop scene was enough to get him blamed and fired. There didn't even have to be on-air obscenities or violations of protocol for the hammer to drop. And when there were on-air problems, as happened a few years later in Nashville, university administrators might blame an entire station and its governance.

As rap and hip-hop thrilled fans across the South, Vanderbilt DJs were there to pick up on the trend. A popular show, *91 Rap*, hosted live acts and featured the latest in regional rap starting in 1989.[31]

One night in spring 1990, in an unclear chain of events, two local high school students ended up on the mics. As the station's supervisor in

Vanderbilt's administration explained, during the show the two young men broadcast a personal insult, and in response the offended party arrived at the studio and "assaulted" those broadcasting. One attacker reportedly "wielded a heavy metal stool."

"A lot of obscenities" aired during the 9 P.M. hour, according to another DJ.[32]

How the event unfolded remained mysterious.[33] Allowing unlicensed students to take to the airwaves, even with supervision, violated the station handbook's commandment number 16: "NO ONE but you should ever speak in the control room while the mike is on—if they do, THROW THEM OUT!" Visitors transgressed commandment number 17: "The more people in the control room with you, the more likely you will become distracted and make mistakes."[34] In 1990, the DJ's absence allowed the guests to assume control. Moreover, though rules existed, it appeared they were laxly followed and positions of authority were unclear.[35]

Confusion regarding how high school students ended up on air spurred the chair of Vanderbilt's Student Communications Inc. (VSC), an offshoot of the student activities group holding the station's license, to action, even if FCC intervention seemed unlikely. The VSC ordered WRVU to cease broadcasting.

DJs understood the real issue. A few told reporters "the altercation had nothing to do with rap music" itself. Instead, "stereotyped allegations that rap music leads to violence" caused the shutdown. As 2 Live Crew's lyrics caused a stir in Broward County, Florida, leading to members' arrest, conversations in American politics and culture shaded events at WRVU in 1990.[36] A few years earlier, administrators barely blinked when WRVU DJs invited a KKK member onto a talk show. But a confused incident that did not place the station's license in jeopardy—let alone give a terrorist organization a city-wide platform—received harsh reprisal. Vanderbilt administrators, already wary of letting college students have access to a powerful radio signal, required reassurance that such an incident would not reoccur. WRVU would need to adhere strictly to its noncommercial license requirements and operate with transparency and clear lines of authority. Its countercultural reputation certainly caused concerns among administrators, but the spark for action came from a show with deep connections to the broader Nashville community, particularly Black residents.[37]

Debates about rap and hip-hop from outside and within Black communities influenced matters across college radio in the 1990s, particularly regarding how stations acted as conduits between universities and communities.

At another school, Grambling State University, a historically Black institution in Louisiana, a different dynamic regarding rap music emerged in 1995. Instead of administrators looking warily at the connections rap music created with the external community, leaders at KGRM consulted their community as concerns about the content of entertainment surfaced regarding the student-run radio station.

In 1995, KGRM officials, including the institution's assistant director for multimedia, instituted a nineteen-day ban on all rap music, which became permanent. The ban commenced on June 19. DJs seemed to embrace the ban, with one student remarking that although she liked groups such as Naughty by Nature, she felt "something has to be done" regarding rising violent and vulgar lyrics. Some DJs and listeners rejected the blanket ban, highlighting positive messages from artists such as Queen Latifah, particularly her recent release, "U.N.I.T.Y." But administrators cited lyrics from artists such as Ice-T and 2Pac as well as R&B "ballads" or new jack swing records as prompting the ban. Talented artists would rightly earn a hit, but afterward, an administrator explained, "artists start copying it and the perversion suddenly becomes the middle of the road in black music."[38]

The issue, administrators insisted, was not rap music per se, but rather obscenity and violence. "If Lawrence Welk put out an offensive album," one dean insisted, "we wouldn't play it." The ban went forward, with hip-hop artists replaced by Boyz II Men, Anita Baker, and vintage jazz and blues. Regarding the banned music, a student complained that he liked the beat more than the lyrics, which were superfluous to the experience. "People still have tapes," a marketing major shrugged, and KGRM would simply lose listeners if it failed to play what students wanted.[39] Although the temperature cooled regarding outright censorship by 1995, with a bill to censor media floundering in the Louisiana legislature, several local and regional politicians praised the ban, which received national press coverage. Senator and presidential aspirant Bob Dole of Kansas commended KGRM on the Senate floor as "transmitting a ripple of hope" in the fight against "those who debase our culture."[40]

Although culture-war hawks looked on with pleasure, Grambling State's confrontation with rap lyrics reflected ongoing conversations within the Black community, and less about FCC rules and censorship. Grambling State's community held a discussion regarding culture and its perceived effects within their families and upon further musical production.

Nuanced discussion at Grambling State was supported by media access, provided by a station where Black students, DJs, and administrators did not have to push for increased hours of airplay or attempt to enact public service of many kinds with limited airtime. The debate's terms signaled a community having a conversation among themselves, despite it taking place on public airwaves and in print. This circumstance was not a departure. When KGRM debuted on FM, it operated as college stations had since the 1960s. But the glee with which external parties looked on and lauded the ban suggested these stations' many functions and wide, recognized influence. Clearly, rap's critics hoped others would follow Grambling State's lead and cut off hip-hop from exposure. For stations balancing multiple and sometimes conflicting demands on their signals, and for student DJs and leaders who wanted to serve communities and promote musical diversity and representation, they had to think carefully about how they proceeded.

Challenging Campus Cultures

At Vanderbilt University, the 1990 closure receded quickly in memory, thanks to student turnover and desire to get back to broadcasting. DJs had business to conduct and genres to break, which they resumed once broadcast relaunched—with some DJs making inroads with certain campus listeners.

Although the rock music WRVU featured tended not to resonate with most Vanderbilt students, student DJ TeRon Lawrence worked to bring the latest in rap and hip-hop innovation to students and community listeners. In 1992, Lawrence's friend Joe Peebles, a football player who had been precluded from other student activities because of athletics participation, returned to his love of DJing. Peebles spun records in high school in nearby Murfreesboro, Tennessee, immersing himself in rap, hip-hop, and R&B. At Vanderbilt, he continued engagement with music through fraternity and football parties, hiring a local DJ with a full kit and records or playing a boombox while Peebles emceed. As he gravitated away from football, the engineering student took to the airwaves on Saturday nights.[41]

WRVU's alternative identity flourished in the early 1990s. It featured hard rock and alternative music on shows such as *Crash*. Peebles's show made sense at the station because rap "was also alternative" at Vanderbilt. For the 212 Black Vanderbilt students—Peebles knew the total because he counted them his senior year—the R&B and hip-hop shows on WRVU existed as part of Black culture and organizations on campus. They felt like outsiders in Vanderbilt's campus culture, but *91 Rap* "fit the mold," as Peebles put it as an increasing number of white students tuned in to the show.

In Nashville, only one commercial FM station allocated time to hip-hop, a meager hour per week. With attention to the genre expanding, Lawrence and Peebles participated in the Nashville rap scene and in nearby Murfreesboro.

Occasionally, touring artists would visit the studio. Sir Mix-a-Lot performed a set live on air. In the early 1990s, few hip-hop artists toured the South. For Peebles, there was a "necessity" for a rap program on Vanderbilt's campus to draw performers by building a fan base. His rotation included Public Enemy and clean versions of N.W.A., mixing in New Edition, Boyz II Men, and R&B artists from Michael Jackson to Keith Sweat.[42]

Members of Vanderbilt's student body helped build *91 Rap*'s playlists. The Posse scholarship brought students to the institution from New York City, giving WRVU DJs a direct line to the New York underground, who could find those students because of the scholarship's visibility. FU-Schnickens (before its Top 40 appearance with Shaquille O'Neal), Kwamé, and artists that mainstream Nashville stations ignored garnered airplay on WRVU thanks to their popularity with Posse students. These interregional links helped establish the station's influence and reputation.[43]

Despite the popularity of *91 Soul* and *91 Rap*, WRVU earned its moniker "Nashville's ultimate alternative radio station" with an emphasis on rock music. The 14,500-watt signal by 1995 defied dominant definitions of "alternative" prevalent elsewhere on the FM dial. With Nirvana, Seattle-grunge bands, and college rock acts filling rotations of commercial FM stations and earning MTV music awards, WRVU emphasized independence.

In the mid-1990s, new general manager Sharon Scott and music director Stacy Hand pushed WRVU's musical diversity.[44] They hoped to redefine alternative music and pursue true diversity, not simply program music that had yet to break to the mainstream. Hand admitted Vanderbilt students rarely tuned in, explaining, "They tend to like classic rock . . . which we don't play very much of." Nonetheless, "someone's out there."[45]

Scott hesitated before selecting Vanderbilt as her college choice, given the institution's staid reputation. She grew up in Atlanta listening to WRAS at Georgia State and Georgia Tech's "weird and different" WREK. Her mother dragged her to Nashville for a campus visit, and when Scott saw the Tower Records across from campus, she changed her mind (or, at least, that is how her mother remembered it). Scott started at WRVU with a 3- to 6-A.M. slot, and she loved how she felt no pressure regarding what she played. WRVU maintained its freeform ethos. "We played anything we wanted," she remembered, "within FCC law. We skirted right on the edge."

It was empowering, sitting at the mic and being able to reach so many potential listeners.

Scott tried out several themes. She hosted a world music show, then launched *91 Bitch* to represent the Riot Grrrl scene. Ideas about a format change floated around the station. The program director agreed it would be a good idea to depart from the "alternative rock" reputation college radio had built in the 1980s. Rotations grew stale. It was great for the bands, "but when college radio was still playing the same thing as alternative commercial stations," listeners "lost the true, alternative source for new, undiscovered music." Scott supported the format change, pushing DJs not to "throw on whatever your friends want to hear," but to "really think about the music that you want to play, to come up with more of a direction for their radio shows, enrich themselves and their knowledge."[46]

By the mid-1990s, DJs at WRVU were "all doing our thing, and people didn't realize how powerful they were." Gwen Stefani came through. But WRVU DJs were more interested in Will Oldham and Slint from Louisville. When Slint's *Spiderland* dropped in 1991, Scott remembered, "you would not believe how much that record got played." Maybe WRVU's constant coverage helped the Louisville scene, which had no visible college radio station, while Seattle eclipsed all in pop visibility. For Oldham, Louisville's lack of a college station was not a detriment. In his view, without youth being exposed early to Nirvana or alternative youth cultures, artists had to search for something else to counter commercial pop and rock. Perhaps the dearth of radio explained the Louisville scene's different, dreamy, mystical, peaceful yet "still rock and rolly" style, as Scott explained it. For WRVU, Scott loved how it received an exciting breadth of material.[47]

Universities often clashed with local communities, particularly in areas where university policing and real estate purchases created a culture of surveillance and pushed out residents unable to afford rising rents. These tensions did not exclude radio. Yet cultural connections and service were in the hands of students. In Vanderbilt's case, DJs wanted diversity for their station, and their outreach developed meaningful relationships between town and gown and sought out marginalized communities.

One WRVU DJ's interest in gay culture and the club scene, along with a revival of dance music in 1990s, created a long-standing gay institution on the airwaves in the city known as the Buckle of the Bible Belt. College station's commitment to providing aural real estate to marginalized voices sometimes led to charges of elitism, or white students pursued diverse programming with significant blinders. But this was not true of the institution built by Ron Slomowicz.[48]

In socially conservative areas such as Nashville, college radio could provide crucial links between activists and individuals while giving voice to a diverse queer community. The 1992 launch of *Out of the Closet* at WRVU exemplified this function. Slomowicz, a first-year student from Orlando, Florida, versed in that city's club scene, had watched *Pump Up the Volume,* a movie starring Christian Slater as a radio DJ. The movie convinced him radio was a medium through which ideas could "infect people's minds." After attending a gay and lesbian student conference, at which a presenter detailed activities in queer radio, Slomowicz knew he had to start his own show. He constructed a character—DJ Ron—who hosted local activists, drag performers, and musicians and featured the nationally syndicated gay news program *This Way Out,* which had launched in 1988 in Los Angeles to confront degrading stereotypes amid the AIDS epidemic.[49]

As a student, Slomowicz experienced hostility for being out. Vanderbilt's LAMBDA organization hosted secret meetings to prevent harassment. For some students who were out on campus, right-wing students researched their homes and revealed their sexual identity in local newspapers. One targeted student's parents disowned him.

With his radio show, Slomowicz connected with and amplified activist connections, providing a lifeline for queer students at Vanderbilt and within the Nashville area. In his first semester, some local right-wing organizations protested his show, but he found WRVU to be a beneficial platform and space. *Out of the Closet* featured political and community activists and transgender allies and showcased Pride events. Slomowicz interviewed Nashville HIV-activist Mark Middleton, who created the character Bianca Page as a drag performance. Slomowicz coordinated events with local dance clubs such as the Underground, which although it was a "straight" club welcomed all. Clubs hosted activists and fundraisers and handed out free condoms or promoted safe sex. They provided meeting spaces for community building, and Slomowicz's radio show linked this network to listeners who might not otherwise have access to Nashville's queer community. His radio show acted as a clearing house of local information—and it helped individuals.

In the Sony Walkman era, kids could listen in to his show on headphones with no one being the wiser, giving them access to gay culture while allowing them to remain in the closet. Occasionally the show provided more direct support. In May 1993, in the show's first year, a teenager called while DJ Ron broadcast. The caller said he was gay, his parents did not know, and he was going to take his own life. Slomowicz contacted a suicide hotline, which reached out to the teen in crisis. Slomowicz, a young student himself, nevertheless had amassed vital resources and connections.

The next Thanksgiving, while doing a fun show during the holiday weekend, the boy's father called. His son had come out after the crisis Slomowicz witnessed. "You talked him down," the father said. While he "still didn't get the gay scene," the father credited DJ Ron and his show with saving his son's life.

This story exemplifies radio's personal nature and the importance of securing space on the airwaves for queer voices. Censorship continued to be a problem in the 1990s, such as when someone cut Philadelphia station WXPN's transmitter signal to a repeater at the Kent County school system during the hours *Amazon Country* and *Gaydreams* aired.[50] The FCC's vague rulings in 1987 had a chilling effect on shows that centered around sexual identity, and it had fined a Pacifica station (a nonprofit community signal linked to the progressive Pacifica Foundation) for airing a play with queer themes and depictions of sexuality.[51] DJ Ron also avoided musical content with explicit drug references to not court trouble.

Music served an important role as more voices emerged in mainstream music and popular culture. The local activist groups' need for an outlet, or for individual service and local networking, did not diminish. Certain affiliations drew extra scrutiny from programmers and administrators, particularly in the case of hip-hop. Student DJs and supportive governance structures could allow for expansion in college radio missions that would create meaningful spaces for both students and community members shut out of coverage or marginalized on the nation's airwaves. College radio could serve community functions if students possessed the vision and community connections. Sometimes, however, service extended to genres that did not fit the progressive political or cultural profile college radio participants expected, despite communities feeling similarly dependent on these stations for service to their cultural heritage.

Polka Magic

Students' self- and musical discovery occasionally overshadowed—or slighted—tastes they did not consider on the cutting edge. In fact, ignorance or failure to understand often-derided musical genres' cultural role led to a sense of betrayal in some communities, even if college radio championed musical diversity. Sometimes DJs didn't see certain music as cool. And even well-intentioned programming changes, driven by a desire to diversify the music aired, slighted beloved content.

WHUS at the University of Connecticut developed an array of public service and cultural programs, with shows catering to specific populations and ethnic communities. Chief among these was *Polka Magic* on Saturday mornings. The show earned esteem as a long-standing institution on WHUS by 1993 when trouble arose.[52]

In this case, tensions between polka hosts and station leaders emerged from poor communication about events. The general manager and program director requested a "Polka Program Policy." They would implement an events calendar and a shared log of programming and cross-promote events. Station leaders requested community DJs attend board meetings and threatened provisional renewal until hosts agreed on the policies.[53]

Station leaders and polka show DJs clashed. In fall 1993, *Polka Magic's* hosts, father-and-son team Walt and Chet Jedziniak, resigned abruptly, shocking devoted fans. The general manager announced that the *International Variety Show*, previously scheduled alongside *Polka Magic*, would take over the slot. He defended the decision as diversifying the ethnic music covered, since the variety show covered more than polka. Accordingly, the hosts resigned before being dismissed, as they told their listeners. Letters poured into the university including to the station and the Office of Student Affairs and reached the president's desk.

Listeners felt a familial bond with *Polka Magic's* hosts, the Jedziniaks, who had been at WHUS for nine years. As one devoted fan explained, "Saturday mornings will never be the same for my family. We always listened . . . as we prepared a big, hot breakfast . . . and as we lounged around the house before commencing our weekend plans." The Jedziniaks provided "wholesome, upbeat, or endearing" banter and music. She declared the change "tragic" and expressed dismay at the hosts' departure. She refused any future donations until negotiators corrected whatever problem led to their resignation.[54] Another listener called their treatment a "darn shame" and withheld their regular donation.[55]

Another listener complained about the new show and host. Previously, the Jedziniaks featured almost continuous music. After the change, "plugs for religious organization dances, Polish clubs and various polka bands" grew numerous. As a Connecticut resident paying taxes, he considered these "advertisements" a violation of public radio's charter and a misuse of state funds.[56]

WHUS's strong signal reached into central Massachusetts and Connecticut, where a second wave of Polish immigrants settled during the 1940s and

1950s, following the first late nineteenth-century wave. Residents had faced discrimination but built strong community institutions and churches throughout the area. Polish-Americans worked in the region's many textile and paper mills, establishing middle-class status in those decades. They left ethnic enclaves around factories, dispersing tight-knit communities over longer distances. Radio programs such as *Polka Magic* connected listeners to a community increasingly severed from the communal rituals of the factory, labor unions, and community groups. The radio show aired every week, filling in the gaps between community events and linking identity to private family time.

Residents as far away as Rhode Island connected with the programming. One listener explained he had "many, many, many friends" from connecting over their love of the show.[57] Although a number of listeners had tuned in to the *International Variety Show* before *Polka Magic*, many felt, as one letter writer explained, it "cannot compare with the excitement and organization of the Polka Magic segment."[58] As another listener pointed out, "FCC licenses are for communities, not institutions."[59] Polish-American residents demanded recognition from a public radio station. A couple wrote, "We're Polish and resent this. . . . Don't the Polish people count anymore? Why should we always be made to feel inferior?" They demanded the station "chuck the general manager" for affronting the Polish community.[60]

The show served functions beyond sustaining Polish-American identity. Other white ethnics reported enjoying the show. One couple testified, "I am Irish and my husband is Italian and we wouldn't miss it each Saturday morning for anything." The host provided "folksy" and "friendly" entertainment unavailable elsewhere.[61] *Polka Magic* "drew senior citizens out of their homes and into society where they made new friends," a listener testified.[62] According to accounts, the show cultivated a cross-ethnic identity rooted in transformations of working-class New Englanders and immigrant communities over the previous half century.

Listeners' threats to discontinue donations suggested they expected the station to provide community service rather than exist simply as an institutional outlet for students. "Is this the way the station serves the community???" one listener asked, "by forcing the best program and money maker it had off the air?"[63] While white ethnic groups, particularly in urban areas, succeeded in linking their cultural and political goals with media in the 1920s and 1930s, by the century's end they depended on educational FM stations for such service, though exhibiting a transactional attitude. Some AM outlets continued to provide programming, but troubles plaguing the spectrum ignited the business model of conservative talk radio—which targeted this group without providing sociocultural linkages.[64]

Such programs smoothed relations between the university and community. One fan considered *Polka Magic* a "shining star amidst the generally immature, inside joking, and generally unpleasant programming" at WHUS, which catered more to the college-student demographic. The polka show and its ilk, he explained, "are very instrumental in making that all important bridge between 'town and gown' bringing community interest into the campus and visa versa [*sic*]." Indeed, the station made listeners feel that the university did not take a radical turn. "Keep in mind," he warned, "that in these times of 'Family Values' used as political slogans but not kept in reality that these two were a father and son team enjoying spending their Saturdays together in a loving partnership." Ending it meant a "slap in the face to those of us in the community" who looked to such shows to sustain cultural connections.[65]

Polka provided a vital connection to cultural heritage for members of New England's Polish-American community, and residents felt a sense of ownership of the signal. That same sense of betrayal when community involvement or service seemed imperiled sounded across many stations in the 1990s. Who controlled the public airwaves, or could demand service of collegiate signals, cut to questions of democracy and the very function of noncommercial radio even before the Telecommunications Act of 1996 brought further corporatization and undermined local media. Beyond the balance of programming, communities looked to influence the governance of these signals.

Cursed

In January 1994, a former volunteer at KCMU at the University of Washington (UW) wished the station would implement an "indie only" policy. "It was really starting to distress me," she wrote, "that major label music was getting more exposure than I really felt it deserved." DJs played more "safe" and "familiar" music, including only an "embarrassingly small" percentage of indie bands. She wanted regular programs for gay and lesbian communities, as well as Asian and African American listeners who lacked radio service despite their large presence in Seattle. KCMU operated as a nonprofit, listener-supported community station, staffed by non-UW-affiliated volunteers—all of which seemed to weaken in the early 1990s. Volunteers organized to save KCMU's identity and governance structure.[66]

Trouble first appeared in fall 1992, when KCMU's station manager Chris Knab announced the addition of *World Café*, a syndicated music show out of WXPN in Philadelphia, the professionally run station at the University of Pennsylvania. It would occupy two hours every weekday morning. Knab celebrated the show's ability to bring live performances to listeners, something KCMU could not. When a blurb announced the show in the *Seattle Post-Intelligencer*, however, the writer sounded less than enthusiastic. "The demo tape of the show I heard," the announcement read, "didn't sound any more exciting nor nearly as hip as KCMU's own musical mix." The musical reports, furthermore, "sounded a bit sophomoric." Not exactly a ringing endorsement. What's more, the addition of *World Café* threatened local control of programming.[67]

Knab displaced nine volunteers for the new programs, and the change proceeded without any input from volunteers or listeners. Dissent appeared in the station's "Programming Ideas" notebook, where volunteers and staff engaged in written discussion over station matters.[68] As rancor grew, critics met outside of the station. Volunteer DJs organized in October 1992 to protest *World Café*, another show's addition, and ending the Wednesday night jazz program—the only one on the schedule. Three full-time staff members determined the schedule. CURSE objected. Their name said it all, which stood for Censorship Undermines Radio Station Ethics. The volunteers wanted "democratic" radio where listeners and volunteers determined the programming through participatory processes and openness. They ignored Knab's attempts to quell concerns.[69]

KCMU's success as a leader in adventurous music seemed under threat. DJs felt hampered to play what they wanted, including what the paid staff called "harsh and abrasive" music from artists such as John Coltrane. A DJ played a thirty-seven-minute cut from the jazz artist, leading program director Don Yates to tell *Rolling Stone*, "Most bad radio is community and college radio." CURSE members resented that their fundraising paid three staff members rather than supporting volunteers in running the station. In a letter to a local magazine in October 1992, CURSE members told listeners, "The dollars you have been donating to KCMU for the last several years are being used to attract a more affluent audience—and will create a new wave of broadcasting: 'commercial' community radio." Knab similarly rejected angry music as having "no hope." CURSE members suggested this was a move toward the mainstream, seeking listeners who would donate so long as they didn't encounter challenging music.[70]

The stakes involved KCMU's constitution and governance structure. CURSE members entreated listeners to cease their financial support to force a negotiation between management and volunteers, resulting in "a multicultural democratic station structure with a small paid staff that appreciates the format and respects the volunteers."[71]

The fight was on. Charges that KCMU "sold out" appeared across Seattle's press, and national music outlets covered the fracas.[72] Coverage of KCMU volunteers' speech resulted in more firings, with the station manager learning of some DJs' comments through news stories.[73]

CURSE capitalized on Seattle's visibility in the music industry to garner headlines. The issue involved much more than a few syndicated programs or what bands received the most coverage. Instead, as *Seattle Weekly* reported, "The real issue is, who really runs the station?" The station's volunteer board of directors and DJs appeared sidelined by professional staff. The reporter saw merit to both visions for KCMU: CURSE wanted to "provide free access to members of the community," while Knab and program director Don Yates thought "a community station should, as professionally as possible, serve the listening needs of its audience." CURSE should stop "shrieking" and Knab and Yates should stop "stonewalling," the reporter advised. He called charges of censorship "overwrought," but resignations rose alongside firings. A board member resigned, citing meetings as a "useless exercise" and merely a "rubber stamp" for what staff wanted. The news director resigned after refusing to comply with new policies limiting CURSE coverage.[74]

By December, picket lines formed outside the studio. Kim Thayil of Soundgarden supported the protests alongside label executives from Sub Pop, C/Z, and Cargo, which ceased record service. Prominent DJs resigned, including a popular dance club DJ. Thayil appeared at a CURSE press conference and explained how trouble brewed since Knab joined the station in 1985. Knab's punk rock bona fides didn't matter. Critics of KCMU's direction identified his hiring years before the 1992 fight as signaling the administration's desire for KCMU to program more "variety" and adopt a public-radio format.[75] UW's director of broadcast services, who oversaw both the flagship NPR station KUOW and KCMU, convened a meeting. No resolution emerged. Administrators felt no inclination to implement participatory democracy at the university-owned station. "It's not within my power or the regents' power to turn over control to a group of volunteers," the director explained.[76]

Volunteers walked out and shut down the station in December as new policies went into effect. Several DJs were fired after announcing their support for CURSE on air or refusing to fundraise "as a matter of conscience." The scheduled fundraiser collected only half the funds KCMU normally raised, purportedly because CURSE supporters jammed the phone lines and mucked up donations, in addition to scaring off donors. No resolution was in sight.[77] After more dismissals occurred in December, *Billboard* picked up the story. CURSE members refused to give in. Knab and Yates expressed confidence that listeners would ultimately decide.[78]

CURSE's strike amplified the fight. Members demanded Yates and Knab's resignation and an "ensured democratic structure" for programming. Despite criticism that the group offered few positive solutions, CURSE wanted KCMU to keep on being "the one place where music is an educational experience, and not soothing background noise," as one supporter put it.[79] By December 1992, some twenty-two volunteers had been fired or resigned, with two more exits pending.

Eleven fired volunteers and three listeners filed suit against UW, KCMU, Knab, and Yates in January 1993, charging the defendants with violating DJs' civil rights.[80] The volunteers cited their firing for speaking about programming changes on air, airing news coverage of CURSE, and discussing the matter with listeners on the phone and over email. (KCMU locked its doors to anyone except "authorized personnel" after CURSE graffiti bombed the station and records disappeared.)[81]

Community members rallied around the station. Musicians participated in benefit concerts for CURSE, resulting in a re-released twelve-inch titled "Media Warrior." This "three-song record of cryptic origin" featured a "hip-hop styled sample-a-thon of Chris Knab espousing his ironic philosophy," which had aired on KCMU.[82] CURSE members distinguished little between NPR and commercial FM rock radio—each fell prey to commercial forces and homogenization, shutting out local voices and sounds for the sake of larger audiences. A *Hype* magazine cartoon forecast KCMU's future of "fully automated" programming by computer, with one DJ slot for a "white and heterosexual with a clean police record" to play only the music a robot selected. "And no curse-ing over the air!! Haw-Haw-Haw!" the cartoon concluded. The article announced that Mudhoney would headline a February 10 fundraiser for CURSE.[83] Rumors circulated that major labels RCA, Mammoth, and Hightone ceased sending KCMU records, a fact Don Yates denied in the *Hard Report*, noting it was "typical of CURSE's strategy of ignoring the facts if they get in the way of good propaganda." As the lawsuit waited for a trial date, the standoff over KCMU's programming and governance remained tense.

UW consolidated its control as protests mounted. Administrators allocated $20,000 in April 1993 to supplement KCMU's declining fundraising. The university ruled that station meetings were not subject to open meeting rules because they qualified as a department staff meeting and not a "board, commission, committee, council, policy or rule making body."[84] The cash infusion came with the requirement that KCMU pay attention to community sentiment, but administrators would not cede control to volunteers.[85] UW administrators valued the station's community presence but wanted in-house control of programs and scheduling, as well as finances.

University of Washington's director of broadcast services responded to the lawsuit with a motion to dismiss and raised the possibility of a counter-suit. CURSE, it seemed, had used the station's mailing list to disseminate announcements and information about its efforts, and UW issued a cease-and-desist order.[86]

The university refused to side with the volunteers, so their hopes hinged on the court case. Finally, in July 1994, the US district court in Seattle sided with the plaintiffs, agreeing that KCMU policies violated their First Amendment rights. Not every plaintiff received the court's support, nor did the ruling support CURSE's claims that their right to association had been damaged by KCMU's refusal to allow announcement of their meetings on air. But the court agreed to plaintiffs' motion for summary judgment regarding the no-criticism policy. KCMU policy barred CURSE's announcements solely on their content, representatives argued. The court found the policy to be suppression of speech and declared unconstitutional the policy's extension to off-air statements. The court ordered reinstatement of six fired volunteers.[87]

The ruling notwithstanding, UW held the power to determine how KCMU would be run. Suspicion swirled about what that would entail. Former DJs suspected KCMU staff, particularly Knab, "would like paid DJs and a generally more obedient staff" that supported "sanitizing the station for broader market appeal." DJs had successfully fundraised for the station, but it seemed as if their efforts resulted in the dismissal of volunteers for more paid staff.[88]

Knab left the station before the lawsuit's decision was announced, which made way for Tom Mara to guide KCMU into new territory. The CURSE episode would stay in his mind, reminding him to keep the community and its concerns close. The station transitioned to more paid DJs, establishing an all-salaried roster by 1997.[89]

Other community-oriented stations watched with interest what happened at KCMU. KAOS's development director at Evergreen State in Olympia expressed being "pretty disheartened" by the changes. He agreed that a program director should provide guidance and on-air talent needed to "have a voice" regarding programming and the station's mission. The director mentioned hearing rumors that KCMU turned down a lesbian/gay show for not having "appeal to a broad enough audience." Diversity seemed to be diminishing, as well as commitment to indie music. KAOS devoted some 80 percent of its playlists to indie labels.

KCMU's former music director wanted this policy. Beyond music rotations, however, the real issue came down to paid professional staff. DJs, she argued, should never be paid, "ever." Station volunteers should determine what management structures worked for them to preserve openness. At KCMU, "very, very few of the volunteers [before Knab's changes] had any interest in pursuing radio as a career." That music director, in fact, had a job at Microsoft.[90]

Techno-optimism abounded in 1990s Seattle. Computers and the internet offered new ways of doing business, even in radio. Spreadsheets could catalog the music library; station communication could take place over email listservs instead of on accounting books kept in the studio for DJs to pen notes about programming or technical problems. Listener requests came in via fax at some stations.[91] Streaming signals online meant potentially reaching worldwide audiences. For some aspirant student DJs, the internet allowed them to bypass terrestrial radio entirely in their desire to reach listeners.[92]

The old way of doing college radio faced numerous pressures in the 1990s as new attitudes entered the mix. The aspirational ethos of technological progress predicted college radio could expand its promise and audience via the internet. College radio, on the forefront of culture and technological innovation thanks to its campus homes, could suddenly reach global audiences. As with the first radio stations in the 1910s, colleges took the lead in implementing new technology. College stations were among the first to have websites and broadcast online, given resident technical expertise at universities.[93] By 1993, internet broadcasting became more viable, and in 1994 WXYC at the University of North Carolina launched its webcast. WREK at Georgia Tech followed soon after with technology produced at the school, then by KJHK at the University of Kansas.[94] Regarding royalties, it seemed nonprofit status protected them from exorbitant fees.[95] For college stations with niche audiences, webcasting seemed a natural expansion to connect far-flung listeners and befitting college radio's cultural optimism.

When college rock hit the alternative mainstream, the realities of the business of radio and culture belied such rosy promises. Commercial FM developed alternative radio formats, co-opted music from college radio, and standardized both, thanks to corporate buyouts. With corporatization, local radio serving numerous genres still mattered in the 1990s. Deregulation intensified existing pressures for these signals to serve local functions. The internet would only lay bare the divergent expectations for college radio stations already strained in an era of increasing budget austerity and market logics that demanded university activities hew to narrowly defined priorities and missions.

Students and Communities Working Together

Student DJs and communities were not always at odds, particularly if institutions left them alone. Meaningful collaborations between student DJs and community volunteers produced new cultural forms, supported musical scenes, and revitalized programming in the 1990s. Graduates launched record labels and produced new music, and stations continued as key sites of cultural connection.

Bobbito García of *Stretch and Bobbito* at Columbia University's WKCR launched his own independent label alongside a growing number from Rawkus to Stones Throw Records to supported underground artists. For García's first imprint launched with Pete Nice (despite being fired from WKCR), Hoppoh Records, one artist achieved his goal of securing a record contract and album before he was old enough to graduate from college. Dwight Farrell, recording as Count Bass D, released his album *Pre-Life Crisis* in 1995. In February 1996, Count Bass D toured France. He came home to no more contract, but he had achieved a goal. "I went and got a job as a dry cleaner," he remembered, and went about "you know, living." He moved to Nashville, got engaged, and frequently visited the used record store near Music Row, the Great Escape, keeping tabs on what records moved and slowly building his record collection.

One day, a young man approached him at the Great Escape as both were searching for beats to sample. Eothen Alapatt introduced himself as Egon, and he was doing a radio show at WRVU at Vanderbilt. Egon explained he had finished his training and secured airtime for spring 1997, and "I was hoping I would run into you at some point." Egon was familiar with Count Bass D. He asked if Farrell was "down" to join him on his show. Farrell thought he was finished with the business, producing music only in private venues. But Egon "just wasn't going to let me [Farrell] quit." Egon convinced Count Bass D that his giving up on music was "bullshit."

91 Rap had grown into a popular venue connecting with area record stores and touring hip-hop artists. Thanks to the show and its DJs, WRVU developed a good relationship with the local hip-hop scene, although the scene remained small.[96]

Hip-hop in New Orleans, Memphis, and Houston gained influence and national exposure. In Nashville, only *91 Rap* was covering these developments. Egon picked up where those predecessors left off and expanded on the hip-hop ties they had built. Twelve-inch LPs began arriving at the station from independent hip-hop labels or secured by Egon as music director.[97] Nashville's hip-hop scene was nascent, and high schoolers tuned in to get word on what was happening across the South and beyond.

Egon lived in the McGill arts and philosophy project dorm at Vanderbilt, not far from the radio station housed in the student center basement and home to many WRVU DJs. He set up a full DJ booth in his room, ferrying crates of records to the studio between philosophy classes and radio shows, while other residents languished in the lounge or smoked cigarettes outside. Together, he and Count Bass D came up with the name for the show, *911 Emergency.* Farrell was starting his family, and Egon was in college, but their show had influence.

The duo joined a station diversifying its programming and implementing new rules about covering genres beyond indie rock in regular rotation. Although WRVU had been shut down for months after the incident involving *91 Rap*, a stable roster of student leaders and community volunteers provided a sense of stability. Vanderbilt's media adviser supported the station, and students leading WRVU had a good working relationship with Vanderbilt Student Communications, which held the license. No sign of administrative interference emerged, despite past troubles.[98]

911 Emergency, building on *91 Rap*'s successes, pushed past the offerings of local commercial hip-hop radio and put WRVU on the hip-hop map. Together, the DJs pushed the station into new territory, acting as historians and collectors as well as practitioners. Their encyclopedic knowledge went beyond the latest hits offered at commercial stations, with narrow playlists and replication of MTV's latest offerings. As WRVU's general manager explained in 1998, *911 Emergency* fulfilled WRVU's mission to "expand the musical horizon of Nashville."[99]

Egon and Count Bass D established the station as a supporter of southern hip-hop, expanding WRVU's already well-established reputation.[100] By the following spring, Egon drew funk and rock musicians to Nashville whose beats inspired hip-hop innovations. In a benefit for WRVU, a gig featured pianist and composer Weldon Irvine, Mr. Dibbs, and DJ Peanut Butter Wolf. Artists came from San Francisco, Cincinnati, Los Angeles, Boston, and Atlanta. Egon sought Irvine, "one of the pioneers of hip-hop," he explained, "not only because his compositions have been sampled by A Tribe Called Quest and KRS-One, but also because he has been rapping since the early '70s."[101] In 2000, Egon brought composer Galt MacDermot, known for *Hair* and his role in developing funk music. Drummer "Pretty" Purdie and bassist Wilbur "Bad" Bascomb worked on an array of funk, soul, and rock records: all set down beats and rhythms sampled by an array of contemporary DJs and hip-hop artists. Peanut Butter Wolf and Mr. Dibbs returned during Egon's senior year.[102] Count Bass D continued his musical innovations, while Egon moved on to a career in hip-hop producing and record collecting.

WRVU's contributions to hip-hop rested on students' vision of establishing its musical reputation, defying its host campus's conservative culture. The station had to avoid negative publicity, which it mostly did. If DJs filed quietly into the basement of Sarratt Student Center, few Vanderbilt students paid attention. Occasionally, irate letters chastising the station would appear in the student newspaper, but administrators (for a while) left the station alone. It continued to receive funding and even benefited from improved studio and office space with Sarratt's 2000 renovation.

This was how business proceeded for most college stations in the 1990s. Ire might be lobbed at commercial rock giants down the spectrum, or students might complain about the freaky music emanating from their institution's airwaves, paid for by student fees. The extreme battles such as those that DJs at the University of Washington faced were outliers. Most conflict arose from small schedule changes rather than wholesale revisions of station mission or governance. College stations continued to provide independent and underground artists with musical exposure, and they provided specialty programs to serve communities lacking coverage on commercial radio. Indie rock had a visible aesthetic and sound, despite the stagnation of mainstream alternative rock and the devolvement of MTV from music television into reality TV and game shows.

· · · · · ·

College radio stations were local outlets, serving campuses and specific communities without mainstream media coverage. They proved crucial links in developing alternative, underground cultural networks and new, independent institutions. Yet they remained shaped by a national media environment, cultural politics, and culture industry. College radio boasted significant influence, but listeners valued stations less for their ability to withstand commercial forces or break artists and more for providing personal and community connection. What emerges from clashes over programming, such as in the case of covering hip-hop or musical culture for area communities, are not culture-war battles over content. Instead, the real tensions and stakes were about media's failure to represent the American people in all their diversity. Space and visibility within the public sphere seemed to be growing harder to access. Music from underground scenes might cross over to the mainstream, but such success came with as many pitfalls as possibilities.

Sometimes, student DJs didn't appreciate the community functions of their stations. These were activities created for students to gain experience and explore music and culture, supporting their educations and self-development. When most participants were white, middle- or upper-class students, this could lead to blind spots about the cultural and political functions of their stations. Students more interested in influencing alternative music might not understand how long-standing, community-volunteer-run shows served area residents—especially if the music in question, such as polka, wasn't very cool.

Despite these limitations, university radio stations remained the best chance for coverage in many markets. What community members and groups wanted was a place to have conversations and enjoy cultural expression without widespread marketability. Universities, with their missions rooted in liberal arts traditions and pursuit of knowledge, seemed natural hosts for radio signals that allowed such space and support. Their resources and missions shielded content, so long as it coincided with the image a university attempted to build for itself.

As indie rock and hip-hop confronted questions about commercialism and mainstream success, institutions of higher education in the 1990s had their own conversations about what their function might be. Administrators evaluated what programming constituted "educational" in line with their institutional image. College grew more expensive, forcing ordinary Americans to take on higher levels of debt to finance college, while wealthier, and mostly white, parents could take advantage of tax incentives. By 1990, "most undergraduates could no longer choose between paying out of pocket, borrowing, or working their way through college" as liberal architects of student lending had envisioned. The gap between what families could pay toward a college education and the actual costs grew, which fell heaviest on underprivileged students.[103] For students and parents taking out unsubsidized federal loans, college needed to guarantee a better-paying job more than ever before.

Such financial imperatives coupled with culture-war scrutiny on what universities were teaching—particularly in their humanities classrooms as curricula incorporated new scholarship in ethnic and gender studies. Students seeking participation in college radio found themselves caught in the middle of these tense developments over the role and purpose of higher education at the end of the twentieth century. The quest for lucrative outcomes also created increased pressure on these stations as the commercial radio industry came calling.

14 College Radio Confronts Selling Out in the 1990s

. . . .

Top Ten Albums of 1994 on WXYC (UNC-Chapel Hill)
Daily Tar Heel, *December 1, 1994, p. 12*

1. Guided by Voices, *Bee Thousand* (Scat)—basement-brand lo-fi pop
2. Polvo, *Celebrate the New Dark Age* (Merge)—artful tunes and twistings by local heroes
3. Esquivel!, *Space Ace Bachelor Pad Music* (Bar/None)— '50s bandleader does swank lounge
4. Beastie Boys, *Ill Communication* (Grand Royal/Capitol)— '70s funk filtered through '90s hip-hop
5. Shu Da, *Voices from the Distant Steppe* (Real World)—Tuvan throat singers
6. Pavement, *Crooked Rain, Crooked Rain* (Matador)— deconstructionalist slacker rock
7. Gravediggaz, *Six Feet Deep* (Gee Street/island)—death metal meets rap
8. Mountain Goats, *Zopilote Machine* (Ajax)—sunny one-man acoustic road songs/(tie) Palace Brothers, *Palace Brothers* (Drag City)—bleak country laments
9. Thinking Fellers Union Local 282, *Strangers from the Universe* (Matador)—San Francisco's squishy layered music
10. Labradford, *Prezision* (Kranky)—mellowness in the Spacemen 3 tradition

"We're going to buy LIVE 105!"

At University of California (UC), Berkeley's KALX in 1997, DJs launched the station's thirtieth anniversary fundraiser with a ludicrous goal. They would raise $30 million to buy the local commercial alternative rock giant. LIVE 105's sale to Infinity Broadcasting in March signaled accelerating acquisitions in media following deregulation under the Telecommunications Act of 1996. Its playlist stagnated, and the station lost much of its local character. KALX's fundraiser, even if spectacularly successful, would be a drop in the bucket of the sale price. But DJs did enjoy mocking the transaction. The music director quipped, "Why not? You never know. Millionaires could be listening. . . . Ted Turner's giving away money these days."[1]

Alternative radio had come a long way from 1979 when Ted Turner secured the call letters from WTBS at MIT for $50,000. While his aspirations were set on cable television, deregulation reshaped the commercial radio ownership landscape and corporate money influenced media, widely. Relaxed rules in the 1980s allowed for multiple station ownership and pushed commercial radio DJs to cut the chatter and adhere even more to consultant-driven, narrow playlists.

More than a decade of media deregulation culminated in the Telecommunications Act of 1996, which removed significant barriers to corporate consolidation in media. FCC rule changes affected college radio previously, particularly with the end of the class D license in 1978 and phasing out operators' licenses (the tests for which lingered, however, as entrance bars well after individual DJs no longer needed a license).[2] The Telecommunications Act changed the radio landscape, with far-reaching effects. Promising to unleash an era of free competition without regulatory impediments to commercial activity, the act unleashed a wave of consolidation and buyouts in commercial broadcasting. In 1996, Clear Channel owned forty radio stations. By 2002, it owned 1,240, and together with Viacom, these two corporations captured nearly half of listeners and revenues in radio. The number of radio stations grew during the decade, but they existed under fewer owners.[3]

Although noncommercial radio stations remained largely outside legislative reach, signals would feel the effects of that. Competition, regulators had long hoped, would produce "diversity" on the nation's airwaves. Radio had grown less profitable in the 1980s, and thus corporate broadcasters argued for removing further restrictions on ownership to foster "economies of scale" and increase the number of stations—and thereby diversity. The reverse happened. In effect, radio became less local, more syndicated, and "bland and formulaic." Formats might look diverse on the surface, but it was a mirage. As one alumnus of college radio put it, "It does not matter if these stations come up with new formats (Rockin' Oldies and Kickin' Country) if they are playing the same old songs with no local content, no local news and no local interest other than in getting advertising."[4] Such developments put further pressure on noncommercial stations to provide local service and content.

When it came to music, a crisis in rock music affected college radio's identity. College DJs began defining themselves increasingly in opposition to commercial alternative giants down the FM dial, which churned out corporatized versions of alternative rock with no underground connections. As the Future of Music Foundation found in 2002, format "oligopolies" made "access to the airwaves far more difficult for musicians, especially local musicians."[5] The result was less musical diversity, the rise of megastars, and musical stagnation in mainstream rock, with the pipeline for talent strangled by corporate metrics.

College DJs saw this coming, and they hated it. When KALX DJs joked about buying LIVE 105, antipathy toward commercial alternative rock radio had been growing for several years. Commitment to vague values such as opposing "selling out" and prioritizing authenticity reached new heights. Those conversations played out differently depending on the station, band, genre, label, or scene. But in general, college DJs tended to scoff at the professionalism and constraints of formatted radio, a growing tendency as college radio (and their community radio counterparts) seemed the last holdout of local radio on the FM dial. College radio stations seemed the antithesis to alternative rock radio, which morphed into a corporate behemoth thanks to broadcasting deregulation.

College radio was no walled-off outpost for authenticity against consolidation, corporatization, and stultification of musical culture. College DJs felt embattled from within and from without. In most markets, there was some alternative giant on the commercial spectrum for college DJs to mock. WRVU DJs at Vanderbilt in Nashville rolled their eyes at alternative rock on WKDF; Georgia State DJs at WRAS in Atlanta lambasted 99X. KALX had LIVE 105. The lines between college and commercial radio were blurry, especially regarding their contributions to musical culture. There was a middle ground of smaller-wattage, modern rock stations that had grown in number since the debut of WXRT in Chicago. In the 1980s and 1990s, these stations often drew talent from college radio alongside their programming ethos. Most hosted local music shows, even.

Alternative rock was a hot commodity by the early 1990s. College students continued to gravitate to radio to pave the way for professional careers in media—with some clamoring for administrators to support the debut of new stations. Alternative rock's prominence justified the existence of college stations on campuses, in some cases. These expectations for professional outcomes rankled participants in college radio who had no desire to push bands into the limelight, leading to charges of elitism and privilege among radio participants who shunned commercial success. Instead, they looked locally or to adventurous culture to revel in music that would never go mainstream. Antipathy grew as the corporate music industry looked to cash in on the same model that had produced Nirvana's stratospheric success after the release of *Nevermind* in 1991.

Alternative rock radio owed much to college radio, more than college DJs admitted—snark was fun, after all. That influence waned amid deregulation as localism diminished in commercial radio, contributing to college DJs' sense of embattlement. Still, these relationships intertwined more than popular narrative of 1990s would have it. And as college students sought participation in radio given its prominence, paradoxes abounded.

College Links to Modern Alternative

When Kurt St. Thomas cued up "Smells Like Teen Spirit" for the first time on radio—"I know there is some dispute about that, but I was definitely the first," he remembered—the phones went "bonkers." It was clear the album was going to be huge, given the feedback he received from Boston-area listeners. The song, with its first guitar chords and booming drum riff, were a perfect fit for radio, and ears perked up at first listen. Nirvana's sound and style defied the glitzy spandex and big hair of rock of the 1980s and proved alternative could sell, and sell big.[6]

"Alternative, ugh, I hate that word," St. Thomas reflected. He had come out of college radio, as had most of the staff on his station, WFNX, a 7,000-watt commercial modern rock "alternative" broadcaster in the Boston market.[7] The question, as alternative rock became an industry obsession, remained: "Alternative to what?" This was not a new question in the realm of underground and noncommercial media. But as the "alternative" network that had launched Nirvana became the target of corporate suits, the term morphed into a corporate brand and radio format that muddied its meaning further.

Commercial alternative rock stations had been around for almost a decade, but they were a minority. Their cohort included Chicago's WXRT, founded by freeform veteran Norm Winer after he left Boston's rock giant WBCN, which had grown, in St. Thomas's words, "old" in sound. WBCN played Aerosmith; WFNX did not. WOXY in Cincinnati, among other precursors of alternative rock radio, launched in 1983 with a "modern rock" format, a sound that shunned the Top 40 direction of album-oriented rock (AOR). Referring to eclectic "progressive" radio, the soundscape influencing the modern rock stations, one AOR program director scoffed, "It's a cute idea," but it would never win advertisers and make money, in his view.

"Strange, bizarre music is out," he concluded. AOR's troubles resided in radio's fragmentation, as formats split into classic rock, soft rock, and now the new modern rock spinoffs, none of which, programmers feared, "galvanized" listeners. Winer countered that AOR rotations missed new trends in music and "failed in their responsibility" as cultural media.[8]

Among the handful of "modern rock" stations debuting in 1983 came WFNX in Boston, which stepped into the rock radio game in a market where WBCN was the main, legendary player. WCOZ had recently switched format from rock to Top 40. Oedipus, now at WBCN, graduated from his punk rock origins at MIT's WMBR in the 1970s. He planned "to stress the concept of lifestyle radio to cement its adult listenership" while remaining first in new music—though not so far ahead as to be "perceived as elitist." No one wanted rock that was too "out there."[9] Did Stephen Mindich, a countercultural media icon and *Boston Phoenix* founder, care about format wars when he purchased WFNX in nearby Lynn? Probably not. He didn't really "know radio," one music director explained, but he liked it.

Instead, Mindich envisioned putting the newspaper on the radio, and he hired Boston broadcasting veterans, including college DJs, to do it. That bizarre idea translated into on-air freedom. Like the newspaper, which readers paged for theater listings and restaurant reviews, juxtaposing what ballet was playing next to the date for a Ministry concert, it wasn't weird to him for the station to play "Barbra Streisand followed by the Replacements."[10]

WFNX maintained links to underground music scenes. Henry Santoro made the jump from MIT's WMBR to commercial FM with WFNX's launch in 1983. When Mindich asked him to put restaurant reviews and alternative news on the radio, Santoro agreed. He kept a grueling schedule. As news director, he had the morning shift of 6 to 10 A.M. He'd get up at 6 P.M., eat, and then head out to the clubs. In Boston, it was possible to jump from club to club and see seven or eight bands a night. After the shows, he'd head to Chinatown and get some food to go, hop in his car, and drive to Lynn. By then he was sober enough to make it to the station and do his show. Then he'd head home, go to bed, and start the process all over again.[11]

WFNX became known as the college station that played commercials (or college radio that paid, or rather, had "bad pay"). With *Phoenix* headquarters in Boston and the studio in Lynn, few executives made the trek to see what was going on at the station. Station managers were free to program what they liked, depending on the bands they thought were the best, or the most "real." But FNX kept its sound fresh with its young talent like Santoro and interns from college radio.

Angie C was one of these interns, who started at the Lynn station while she DJ'd at the Salem State station. She started school seeking to be a journalist in 1987, but an accident of fate found her at the studio her first week in college. After three weeks, she had her own show. After a month she was assistant program director. She knew that to achieve her radio aspirations, she needed to get her foot in the door. Her goal was WFNX. Backstage at a Soul Asylum show, she met Kurt St. Thomas and expressed her desire to work for the station. He told her to call the *Phoenix* offices. She did and secured an internship.

When it came to WFNX's interns, it was a two-way street. The station provided them with experience in commercial radio and production, and employees "listened to their interns." Interns went to shows and listened to and were doing college radio, and staff members "weren't afraid to see what young people were into." There weren't a lot of rules about interning, including about hours and pay, but students—if they hustled—could get on air.[12]

That happened for Angie C, even as she kept one foot in college radio. One night after a Depeche Mode concert, she was riding home with her "alternapals" and listening to WFNX. When she arrived home, her dad met her at the door with a message: Kurt had called. The station needed someone to fill in. By the time her last friend in the car got home, Angie was on WFNX. She took a deep breath before speaking, as she had learned, and it was "pure magic." She stayed on as rap director at Salem State and attended multiple CMJ conferences, where she rode in an elevator with George Clinton and saw panels that included KISS guitarist Ace Freely and Dave Perner of Soul Asylum. She managed to get into a show at CBGB with a drink pass—being only nineteen at the time—where she saw the Goo Goo Dolls and Uncle Tupelo.[13]

Angie C, the Depeche Mode fan with eclectic musical tastes, discovered a guitar rock resurgence, and she preferred songs such as what she heard on *Bleach*, a tape Kurt St. Thomas discovered because he and his girlfriend's son spent time watching skateboarding videos together. One of those videos had a cut from the album, and he mined the credits until he identified the band. The album became a regular feature on WFNX as it made its way through the college radio scene, and the band conducted its first tour.

Salem State's station and WFNX provided Angie C with a radio education. As she moved into full-time work at WFNX in 1993, she grappled with the "selling out" question, saying goodbye to the laissez-faire experimentation college radio allowed—but it didn't provide a paycheck. WFNX had a format, and a rotation, with a card box filled with the heavy, medium, and light airplays. Rules required DJs to keep the rotation current. Sure, some DJs cheated—repeatedly playing songs such as Archers of Loaf's "Web in Front" because it was two minutes long and a great way to close out a block without much time left. DJs could play what they loved, but there were boundaries. Angie C developed a professional voice: it was relatable and not disingenuous. "People can tell" if a DJ faked it, she explained. Most DJs at WFNX who made the jump to commercial dealt with similar qualms, but they valued the prospect of breaking new bands to a wide audience—even if WFNX's 7,000 watts was nowhere near that of rock giant WBCN.

Modern rock radio found itself with significant industry influence. Columbia Records and Atlantic added alternative music departments, following in line with other majors. Audiences needed to be wooed, introducing them slowly to the deep album selections. Stations needed a defined *sound*. College radio's "eclecticism" couldn't hold listeners for long periods of time if blocks shifted drastically by genre every two hours.[14] Labels were eager to sell the new alternative category—and so they relied on college radio to play a range of indie rock, some of which worked its way to "modern rock" stations on the commercial dial. Together, those built a fanbase for bands, proving they could fill venues and sell records in key demographics.

Modern rock stations remained "underdogs" in their markets, a rung above their weirder college radio siblings. *Billboard* reported that few Top 40 stations recognized modern rock stations' role in crossover hits. Instead, one music director pointed to intangible musical merits, rather than exposure, quipping, "Hip albums will be No. 1 or No. 2 in sales without that much airplay." The same was true for WFNX, at least in WBCN music director Carter Alan's view. Alan, a veteran of MIT's WMBR, saw his DJs as already up on alternative trends. They didn't need WFNX or college stations to lay the groundwork. "We'll go in on a song," he insisted, "if we feel it's right, regardless of whether WFNX or the college stations are on it." Modern rock stations tended to play deep into an album, these music directors argued, but didn't spend enough time on building a following by emphasizing the catchiest songs.[15]

It couldn't be both. Either good music would sell no matter what (although the mechanism of spreading the word remained a mystery) or it needed a range of radio support to generate buzz. Commercial radio stations were competitive with one another, and the modern rock format challenged standard rock stations to add more alternative rock. The coverage and breaking new artists question remained: if a local station provided no coverage for a band yet to chart, whether in *Billboard*, CMJ, or *RockPool*, it was hard for fans to discover it.

Nirvana's *Bleach* exemplified these limits. Sub Pop sent out the album; success required stations to play it. Commercial FM stations had to move their rotations. WFNX played *Bleach*, but it fell off charts and out of rotation by the end of 1989, although it remained on charts at Salem State, Framingham State, and Worcester's College of the Holy Cross, as reported to CMJ.[16]

Although WFNX would never have WBCN's market share, with its much smaller wattage, they both drew from a pool of local radio talent, professional staff drawn from rock stations in other markets, and wanted to be the station known for supporting the next big thing. But keeping a sizable listening audience required playing familiar music mixed with new, potential hits (and hyping new music as much as possible).[17]

Carter Alan might have been dismissive of his 7,000-watt neighbor, but WFNX scored a major win in the annals of alternative music success. Angie C was at the Axis club during WFNX's eighth birthday celebration when Nirvana took the stage, the night before *Nevermind*'s release. "Lots of people claim they were there," she explained, "but I have the ticket stub." St. Thomas introduced them as "the fucking coolest band in the world," and the party marked the birth of alternative's pop debut. The appearance (as well as an earlier April 1990 concert at Cambridge club Manray, to some seventy-five attendees) augmented the band's legend, making Nirvana's rise to superstardom and Seattle's heavy rock sound's dominance in the 1990s seem inevitable, although the band's sound had mainstream appeal.[18]

This churn regarding terminology and radio formats repeated a similar pattern from the early 1980s. Then, stations struggled over whether to play new wave or stick with deeper cuts from rock albums, and then again with new wave's mainstream success and corporate co-optation. Comparable debates roiled over the meaning of alternative and stations' role in breaking hits. "College rock" became the prevailing term in the 1980s to describe the breadth of music rising to mainstream attention from college radio's underground connections. Bands such as INXS, Depeche Mode, and the Cure that had strong associations to college radio came to define the modern rock format, which switched to grunge before feeling the pressure of corporate consolidation amid deregulation and the homogenization of "alternative rock" formats. By 1995, modern rock and mainstream rock charts and playlists grew nearly identical—much like how early 1980s "new music" stations converged with MTV and pop charts—even if local playlists offered diverse sounds and weirder music.[19]

In the early 1990s, however, the stakes for individuality and self-expression seemed higher than a decade prior. A loose concept of authenticity bridged the gap between college radio's role in promoting local, underground music scenes and national alternative networks built through touring, festivals, and an emerging AAA (Adult Album Alternative) radio format. Modern rock stations persisted in airing new music and emphasizing musical artistry without neatly fitting corporate metrics for what would score well with the widest audience. During Kurt St. Thomas's tenure as music director at WFNX, he heard in bands such as Nirvana, Beck, and Green Day something "real"; they weren't faking it. This amorphous sensibility anchored a definition of "alternative," which remained variable and personalized even as it influenced corporate radio aesthetics. St. Thomas did not consider Alanis Morrissette for rotation, even though she topped playlists at other commercial stations. (A later program director allowed Kid Rock and Nickelback, with much pushback, as corporate practices crept into the station.) Program meetings were often tense, as DJs debated what would and would not be played.[20]

Even as "alternative" became increasingly standardized at commercial FM stations, some flexibility remained before the late-1990s corporate takeovers.[21] For WFNX, independent ownership provided protection. Stephen Mindich and the *Phoenix* allowed St. Thomas to select music and juxtapose artists unconventionally. WFNX listeners "appreciated art differently" and sought to prove it was possible to push boundaries and be successful. It was more than the music; it was a "lifestyle." WFNX defied the ratings game; Mindich's attitude was "I don't give a shit." It lasted, at least for a little while.

Influential stations need not be in a large metropolitan market. Vermont's WEQX, one of only twenty commercial alternative stations when Jim McGuinn arrived as a program director in 1990, made waves. It reached Burlington, Vermont, and Albany, New York, with its transmitter located atop Mount Equinox in a small town in the Green Mountains. Its diverse rotation of artists and new music produced one often-cited "break" for the Spin Doctors.

McGuinn created a commercial for an upcoming concert in October 1991 that included a selection from "Big Fat Funky Booty." Listeners called in requests for the commercial, and McGuinn added the band's full-length release into rotation. The Spin Doctors, typical of labels' efforts to grow their alternative rock departments, had languished until McGuinn notified Epic of the release's good reception and high sales in the Albany market.

A local newspaper breathlessly declared WEQX achieved the "dream": launching soon-to-be MTV darlings the Spin Doctors as Dewey Phillips had when he cued up "That's All Right" by Elvis Presley in July 1954.[22] The Spin Doctors were not Elvis, but they proved the power of a trusted listener-broadcaster relationship. Staff attended to what resonated with fans, to what bands developed a following through concerts and area colleges. They completed the circle by informing labels when a band had gained traction and needed more publicity. WEQX stood out for its sound and connection, earning it a place atop *Rolling Stone*'s list of top radio stations in 1993, 1995, and 1996.[23]

Nirvana's success changed the formula, adding pressure on modern rock stations like WEQX and WFNX that reached college radio as well. The informational networks created by fanzines, college radio stations, touring bands, and independent record stores became big business, defining a new cool aesthetic for the 1990s. Participants lamented this as corporate co-optation of the underground at its finest.[24]

Still, many listeners were satisfied with the change. Before commercial alternative radio, it took work to find new bands. Many commercial rock stations, even AOR ones, had a local music show, often only a few hours a week. Listeners had to schedule it in their calendars and hearing more required effort. Bands signing to major labels made it easier to access albums at any record store. Listeners could access music they liked and made them feel cool. With sales a sure thing, corporatization loomed. Resistance persisted at modern rock stations such as WOXY in Cincinnati, WFNX in Boston, and WEQX in Vermont—but only the last on the list would survive into the new millennium unscathed by deregulation and the rise of "indie" capitalism, in which a narrow aesthetic of usually white, male-led guitar rock bands could achieve cultural cache and wide success while maintaining a claim to authenticity.[25]

Commercial modern rock stations could not withstand corporatization and deregulation. Owners hired consultants. Even at weird, *Phoenix*-run WFNX, corporate consultants began influencing playlists in the mid- to late 1990s. Stations transformed from mom-and-pop operations—college radio with a paltry paycheck—and became more consultant-driven and homogenous. In 1990 WFNX programmed the Cure, Jane's Addiction, Siouxsie, and Sonic Youth. DJs cued up Creed, Matchbox 20, Limp Bizkit, and Korn. Research and marketing to specific demographics eclipsed the listener connections that inspired DJs like Angie C to get involved in radio. As Kurt St. Thomas put it, by 1998 if the Clash's seminal punk album *London Calling* had debuted and didn't score well in test marketing, it would have been off the station.

For young people repulsed by commercial radio, only college radio remained as a seemingly lone bastion against corporatization and homogenization.

Resisting the Wave

Shifts in mainstream radio and the music industry affected college radio before the 1996 Telecommunications Act. As McGuinn at WEQX saw it, college stations became more elitist, letting go of Nirvana, Jane's Addiction, and bands that formerly constituted most college playlists and topped CMJ's charts. Yet college radio's overwhelming rejection of mainstream labels has been overstated, thanks to adventurous rotations and lax formatting. College radio's reputation grew from not setting hard limits on what DJs could play while encouraging musical exploration and experiments. If a DJ wanted to program a conceptual block populated with Gordon Lightfoot's back catalog, block formatting and a freeform ethos allowed that—though some station managers might prefer that such experiments happen in the wee hours of the morning instead of during drive time.

Radically anticommercial stations existed. Some went far in their opposition to developments in commercial alternative music and radio, perhaps cementing an elitist reputation regarding college DJs, who shunned what satisfied the masses. "Indie," radio scholar Jennifer Waits explained, "represented an aesthetic, carrying cultural cachet and signifying rebellion and convention-breaking." When the aesthetic became increasingly "marketable to the larger consumer culture," with corporate labels co-opting it by "buying or creating small boutique labels," stations balked.

But the image of college radio's defiance of corporate co-optation by refusing to play major-label releases relied on a fallacy, despite the rancor over commercialization. Detractors decried corporations such as Coca-Cola and Pepsi, which co-opted countercultural psychedelia and rebellion in the 1970s to sell more soda. College DJs and listeners tended to see what was happening to alternative rock in the same light, relying on a narrative that belied gray areas beneath the indie-elitist image. As Waits put it, "indie-minded college stations increasingly had to find a new alternative to showcase," making these signals a "crucial site of contested meaning in the larger culture of the 1990s." The battles over authenticity and corporate co-optation were about musical aesthetics and power, less about which labels were allowed. At some stations, even indie labels such as Matador Records, with a distribution deal with Capitol Records, "were off-limits."[26] Such hard-and-fast limits belied a messier reality regarding programming in this tense environment, exacerbated by media deregulation.

In Waits's study of an unnamed college station in California in the 1990s, she found much ambiguity in reported "indie-only" policies regarding music played on the station. Programming policy aimed to create a "uniformly underground aesthetic" except for specialty shows in jazz or classical. Policies functioned to initiate new DJs to the sound station leaders cultivated. Still, it was an overall effect, not a strict rule for every song cued up. New DJs, Waits reported, started with shows on format, meaning highlighting independent-label records. Going off format required deep musical knowledge they generally lacked, and "new DJs in particular tended to rely on music that was familiar-sounding," antithetical to the station's goals.

The music director avoided an explicit mission of breaking bands to commercial success. Such divergences between the local goals of noncommercial radio signals and the music industry's desires created the erroneous image of college stations completely shunning major labels. Some of this image came from the labels themselves, which chastised stations when they abandoned their records. One label, Waits reported, "commented that the station might be 'too cool' for their records," and another complained in CMJ of hypocrisy, adding other labels' releases with similar distribution deals. Charges of elitism swirled, particularly among labels using college radio exposure to build a fan base.[27]

But even at this seemingly radical anti-major-label station, the policy remained unwritten. "Independence," Waits argued, whether from "commercial control," a musical "spirit," or "genre restrictions," remained central to the station's identity. "Indie" was a necessarily vague term, and relationships between noncommercial stations and the commercial industry persisted.[28]

Other California stations exemplified this muddy connection between localism and commercial success that persisted amid a commitment to indie authenticity. UC Irvine's KUCI, despite its strong stance against major labels, helped launch 1990s stoner-rock band Sublime to success. Along with No Doubt, Coolio, and Busta Rhymes, who the *Los Angeles Times* reported all played at KUCI before hitting MTV, the station's "music fiends . . . celebrate and cultivate [Orange] county's many subcultures." Saturday afternoon DJ Tazy Phillips and his well-regarded ska show highlighted artists who would help define popular sounds of the 1990s. Other DJs elevated rockabilly and swing revivals alongside "a dozen or so shows surveying every electronica offshoot to nourish O.C.'s burgeoning underground." Sublime, which signed to a local independent label, appeared on a KUCI-produced compilation organized by Phillips. The compilation included "Date Rape" off the band's second album. The song chronicled a sexual predator's assault, eventual imprisonment, and his own assault in jail and stirred controversy, and some music directors even on commercial stations refused to play it, such as Kurt St. Thomas at Boston's WFNX.

KUCI's compilation brought attention to the song at LA's KROQ, and Sublime careened to success with its third album in the 1990s, released after lead singer Bradley Norwell's death from an overdose. Sublime's success justified KUCI's reputation. The *Los Angeles Times* reported in 1997 that despite its small wattage compared with KROQ, KUCI's influence was clear. Its volunteers committed "to celebrate and cultivate the county's many subcultures."[29] Local scenes with a unique sound could survive thanks to such signals, and the best of these scenes could achieve mainstream success.

As KUCI helped elevate local artists to success, it continued to emphasize its anti-major-label policy. Student programmers exemplified the "indie" rejection of bands with mainstream exposure. The station's influence expanded with a 1991 increase to 200 watts of power, after years of seeking higher wattage, although it remained tiny compared with commercial giants. That quest had threatened the intervention of student government in 1989, which hired a consultant to think about enforcing a single "format," rather than the blocks of rock, jazz, folk, hip-hop, reggae, and classical. As the increase neared fruition, UC's communications staff reassured listeners that no change in format would commence, and student volunteers would continue to guide the station.[30] As a student explained to *Los Angeles Times* music writer and chronicler of Orange County's punk scene Mike Boehm, "Somebody's got to keep pushing the boundaries of music."[31]

Boehm, who watched, chronicled, and championed Los Angeles–area punk, clashed with station leaders, however. A 1990s resurgence in punk, voicing youthful anger and raucous sounds, was gaining mainstream appeal. After the Offspring, a punk band from Garden Grove, California, greeted 2,000 screaming fans at UC Irvine, Boehm had some questions. Was this "the triumph of punk rock" and Orange County's "distinguished, 15-year contribution to it?" Or was it the "death knell" of punk's oppositional stance to the mainstream, the end of "a music of outcasts and misfits shouting warnings, mockery and vilification of the comfy, self-satisfied majority?"

Boehm concluded the Offspring's popular angry sound signaled wide-spread, though overlooked, discontent in the supposedly prosperous and tranquil United States of the mid-1990s. He expressed chagrin at sounding like "narrow-minded, contemptibly clubby college rock tastemakers, who will repudiate good music for the sole reason that it can be appreciated by more than a small coterie of superior elect." After all, mainstream exposure and success seemed to be the point. He couldn't understand why the college radio crowd didn't welcome these local sounds, formerly neglected in favor of Paula Abdul and Vanilla Ice, as positive developments in the music industry. Maybe a new model had emerged, and the college radio set shouldn't worry that its cultural role had been co-opted.

College radio's inhabitants, Boehm suggested, overreacted to the rise of alternative music with elitism and snobbery—a stereotype that channeled and twisted sociologist Pierre Bourdieu's contention that those with cultural capital, including education, determined prevailing tastes. In this rendering, DJs defined new aesthetic expression of class-based tastes for the educated elite who remained fascinated with underground bohemian culture. Participants emphasized their role in diversifying culture, keeping expression vital, challenging, and authentic (perhaps, as Bourdieu's subjects did, incorporating working-class aesthetics).[32] From another perspective, these elitist self-appointed adjudicators of artistic merit ignored class status and marinated in unpalatable, underproduced, morose music. As Alicia Silverstone's character Cher complained in the 1995 movie *Clueless*, "Yuck! Ugh the maudlin music of the university station? Wah wah wah." Of course, the fan of that station was her love interest. But really, she asked, "what was it about college and crybabies?"[33] Boehm might have asked the same jaded question regarding the annoyed response he received from KUCI's student volunteers regarding his column.

KUCI's program director David Mosso rejected Boehm's caricature of clubby college elitists. Mosso, too, had been pondering punk's commodification, but Boehm missed the point of college radio. Mosso disagreed that college rock radio took an arbitrary stance on the fringes for the sake of being self-congratulatory outsiders. Instead, KUCI "strives to give exposure to artists," echoing long-standing defenses of college radio as providing crucial exposure. Because punk and alternative had grown popular, he argued, "college radio is forced by its very nature to look even further underground." Blame the market, not college radio, in other words. The Offspring simply had moved on from its college radio origins, and no longer needed their help.[34] It was a structural, market-based problem—not about aesthetics or elitism. Sublime, which the station had championed, similarly no longer needed its help after KROQ picked the band up.

Mosso made another point, one often overshadowed as major labels looked for talent to be signed and milked for profits. He highlighted college radio's cultural influence in contrast to the pipeline construction. He championed college radio's diversity, as "more accepting of different musical styles and genres than any commercial station on the dial." These stations, along with public radio, "are incredible resources and assets to any community, ones more people should take advantage of and support, not slag on." No one could make the "narrow-minded" tag stick after listening to a few hours of any well-run college station that cared about its community connections. KUCI relied on those listeners to help pay its bills, after all.[35]

So which was it? College radio as a bastion of authenticity and diversity in musical culture, or a testing ground for product that would define the mainstream? It could be both, history had shown, but circling corporate vultures made DJs defensive, particularly because they feared undermining their musical contributions and potential siphoning off of listeners—and donors.

Not all graduates of college radio, not even most, could be classified as suit-wearing sellouts beguiling bands to hawk their artistic souls for corporate profits. Artists need to eat. Bands wanted listeners to hear their music. They also wanted to maintain creative control, which seemed increasingly difficult in the deregulatory and corporatizing environment of commercial radio and the major-label music industry in the 1990s. Many bands that moved into major labels or commercial radio stations chafed at their inability to play the music they wanted or to champion the bands they liked. Yes, DJs like Angie C and many others had the "selling out" conversation with themselves when they moved to commercial stations—but the professional benefits of college radio participation went beyond becoming a radio DJ or promoter at a record label. College students still sought out radio participation for many reasons. Participating in musical culture might draw them in, yet they discovered an activity requiring leadership, professionalism, and creativity that complemented work pursued in classrooms. College radio, in other words, remained a valuable cocurricular activity across campuses in the 1990s, even as DJs committed to authenticity in musical culture.

Late Starts

While former college DJs grappled with whether they had sold out, plenty of undergraduates in the 1990s were trying to buy in. Despite college radio's seeming ubiquity and uniformity, not every university or college hosted an FM radio station allowing DJs to freely explore weird music and express themselves. Students without a signal felt left out—but what they were seeking wasn't always clear. Moreover, those seeking FM real estate confronted entrenched notions of what college radio meant, especially with alternative music commanding significant industry investment.[36] College radio had a large, national profile. When students sought to expand AM signals to FM or launch new ones in the 1990s, aspirants had to make their case in financial and pedagogical terms for universities, where pressure increased to provide skilled workers, not only intellectual exploration. Maybe it was a good way to start a career; maybe it meant being able to participate in a vibrant, youth-oriented musical culture to supplement liberal arts learning. Students navigated this vague divide in securing signals.

At Sacramento State in California, where consultant Rick Carroll started in radio as a student in the 1960s before pioneering the "Roq of the Eighties" format at KROQ, the college shuttered the progressive campus signal in 1978. As college radio's star rose in the 1980s, students lamented not having a radio station. In fall 1989, at the president's "State of the University" address, student Jim Bolt queried why the university had no student-run radio. Students, led by Bolt, mobilized. The Associated Students president contacted university officials and the Communications Studies department chair to investigate the matter.[37]

In spring, buzz grew on campus that the Association Broadcasting Club (ABC), formed by enthusiastic students interested in radio, researched how to launch a station. They envisioned providing "hands-on training for students" with a "loose, multi-cultural format." Students estimated costs, eyed space on campus, and enlisted faculty support. Fifteen years prior, lack of student involvement shuttered the school's previous student-run station. The ABC worked to ensure apathy would not rise again.[38]

It wasn't that the school had no interest in radio. Sacramento State had a professionally run NPR station, which in 1990 sought to expand to 50,000 watts to broadcast both classical and jazz—offering students no on-air experience.[39] Funding, campus officials insisted, was the issue. KXPR, the school's NPR station, rated highly and earned donations from more than 14,000 listeners, raising 75 percent of its own funding. Could a student-run station do that? Observers cited the success of Cal State Northridge's KCSN, with award-winning news broadcasts and placement of students into lucrative careers thanks to their radio experience.[40]

Internships, students argued, were not enough. Proponents for student radio emphasized its uses beyond entertainment, serving as "an education experience for all students of all majors."[41] The new jazz station was nice, but in students' view it did little for the campus.[42]

Administrators, it seemed, did not think the university's image would be supported by student-run radio. According to one student, "the administration sees a student-run station as an 'ego device,' where students use airtime to goof around, say stupid things and play obnoxious music." The reasoning did not hold, he argued. "If that's the administrators [*sic*.] logic," a student concluded, "then classes are ego devices too." Students matriculated to expand their knowledge and experience—what else was college for? To counteract such denigration of liberal arts education and promote adventurous student-run radio, Bolt and his allies emphasized the practical, educational benefits of radio and how broadcasts tied to campus, such as airing theater productions and sporting events.[43]

The university president responded. He asked the Communications Studies department to form a task force to investigate "the relationship between KXPR [Sacramento State's NPR station] to the University's instructional program and to the interest of our students." He amplified internship opportunities "in the off-air operations" at the NPR station.[44] Sacramento State students ignored these offers.

Meanwhile, students in the ABC raised awareness. They hosted a twenty-four-hour Music DJ Marathon in April 1990.[45] Bolt, ABC's president, aimed "to prove to the administration that there are dedicated students, there would definitely be interest, and there wouldn't be a problem with staff." He cited the number of communications studies majors, and he promised a "polished" and as "professional a production as we could get."[46] Students would benefit from professional training and hands-on experience.

With the marathon's success, alongside other pressures, the president softened. The California Broadcaster's Association highlighted the institution's failure to involve students in KXPR, the professionally run station. Carrier-current would suffice, they argued, as a cheap way to get students broadcasting. But the organized students kept their sights set on FM even as the carrier-current station came into being.[47]

Market logic suffused students' efforts to secure a spot on the FM dial. A local reporter highlighted the city's dearth of a typical college radio station where "you're likely to hear intense young DJs playing cutting-edge music from Toad the Wet Sprocket, the Stone Roses, the Posies, and A Tribe Called Quest." Sacramento only had "mellow middle-agers playing Mozart,

Mingus and 'Morning Edition.'"[48] The market, in other words, had space for the format associated with college radio. As the university's second public broadcasting signal came into being, students solicited community support for a "cross-cultural and expressive music that better represents the demographics of their communities."[49]

Radio opportunities grew in response to students' activism. The president added Jim Bolt to KXPR's board of directors. The station instituted student internships. The carrier-current station gained momentum by fall 1990.[50] That was all great, though not enough. Bolt explained, "It's a good start, but I think they (the administration) are underestimating the students."[51]

Meanwhile, Rick Carroll's untimely passing at age forty-two meant the establishment of new scholarships for communications students, though few of the students agitating for a station knew of it or applied. They busily coordinated to launch the station. Some sixty students belonged to ABC by fall 1990. They secured officers, a newsletter, and a fundraising plan and attended radio production classes on Saturdays at a local cable access company. It might be carrier-current, but it was going to be "as slick and professional as possible," according to Bolt.[52]

These student-run radio proponents navigated conflicting expectations for college radio. The administration wanted something that reflected well on the institution; students wanted a signal that fit their aesthetic image of college radio in defiance of commercial trends. A student reporter entreated Bolt not to emulate commercial FM radio. "The beauty of student-run college radio," he argued, "stems from its sheer unprofessionalism." Leave the "slickness" out of it. College radio should challenge broadcasting culture, in other words, not prepare students to join the LIVE 105s of the world. "Fuck the ratings," he argued, and make the administration worry.[53]

Bolt presented his quest as an epic battle with an evil budget-cutting monster. To gain access to radio meant making the best of the carrier-current station to justify expansion to FM. If that meant amplifying professionalism for administrators, so be it.[54]

Upon launch of the carrier-current station in January 1991, some students still complained. A top song list included Fishbone and Devo, Billy Idol and INXS: not cutting-edge or current enough for some. Another student complained, "Bolt seems to lack the musical sensibility and vision necessary for the job."[55] Bolt invited critics to join the station or actually tune in, rather than lambaste top song lists. He defended INXS as a leader in the emergence of "alternative/modern rock" and Billy Idol's career start in Generation X, which the station played.[56] Meanwhile, DJs distributed flyers to local bands soliciting tapes, and the station joined the National Association of Community Broadcasters.[57]

Technical difficulties plagued the station's first semester, but Bolt and his collaborators envisioned great things. A local cable radio station picked up some programs. The Associated Students Board of Directors commended Bolt, his vice president, the program director, and all involved students for launching KEDG.[58] By the fall of 1991, with technical hurdles and bureaucratic red tape cleared, KEDG broadcast to all residence halls and fulfilled student demand for alternative music, "the kind of music most college students listen to," the new music director explained.[59] Its top thirteen song lists in 1991 included alternative stalwarts such as Kate Bush, Primus, Nirvana, and the Meat Puppets, alongside bands from nearby scenes such as Thin White Rope. Students kept their goal for an FM signal central.

They secured the frequency in 1992, changing call letters to KSSU.[60] Bolt's strategizing and promises of professionalism paid off, as the students were able to emphasize the public relations boon for the university and career benefits for participants.

College radio's prominence helped Sacramento State's station, although a reputation for amateurism might have slowed efforts. Administrators had a hard time justifying expenditures on an additional signal if professional opportunities existed at an NPR station, but Bolt and his cohort won them over.

Other colleges and universities found themselves in similar positions as Sacramento State, having let a carrier-current or former FM signal atrophy and disappear, whether though lack of student interest, no departmental home on campus, or neglect. For grateful students, prominent alumni and college radio's reputation gave oxygen to efforts to revive signals in the 1990s.

At Ball State in Indiana, students faced such a situation—but unlike at Sacramento State, these students emphasized competing values to justify their signal. A famous alumnus, late-night comedy icon David Letterman, launched his career in the 1960s as a DJ on a carrier-current station he helped found on campus. After achieving fame, Letterman donated to scholarships and the telecommunications program. The station he helped start went under, so he supported the establishment of WCRD, a new carrier-current AM station in 1986. With additional gifts supporting equipment, it launched in 1988 and headed for an FM expansion by 1994.[61] In 1995, Letterman provided "most of the funding." He had a freewheeling show of fake news stories and weird music as a student—and he wanted Ball State students to have the same opportunity. Instead of emphasizing the professional merits of student-run radio, these students emphasized the value of amateurism and self-discovery, linked to the learning experience. But FM came with the dangers of commercialization and regulation, making students wary.

College radio had come a long way since the 1960s and Letterman's carrier-current signal. WCRD received albums from labels and maintained a freeform format. Moving the signal to a local high school's FM transmitter allowed student DJs to reach beyond campus. Such range came with questions. The pressure to be "an individual" heightened the burden to cut one's own path, listen to different music, to "be our own little unique person," one student complained—but even this seemed to be a conformist stance. "Personally," he wrote, "I'm so sick" of statements such as, "Well, uhhhh, I really liked (insert band here) until they got popular and sold out." It was too much. "Are we all that shallow?" he asked. WCRD, it seemed, was the next to be shunned as selling out for seeking FM. College radio meant rule-breaking, as Letterman's own show had demonstrated. An FM signal came with rules. AM sucked, "but if WCRD gets a frequency to broadcast to the general public and abides by a few FCC rules, then WCRD still sucks. ARRRGH! What the . . . ?!?!?"[62] Students felt frustrated in finding a signal where they could express themselves and their tastes, given the business and politics of college radio and adhering to prevailing aesthetic demands.

An English major objected vehemently to the FM launch. Such a move would, he argued, put DJs under the thumb of "class-act scum-muscles" at the FCC as it monitored obscenity and indecency, and CMJ, which "sets the industry's guidelines for what radio stations are to sell." He scoffed, "Wonder why the 'diversity' in music all sounds exactly the same?" He found it "quite fun to blame the CMJ and the foolish cogs who are under their advisement." Stations seeking popularity and listeners could say goodbye to freedom and authentic artistic exploration. Instead, "hacks" might force volunteer DJs to "follow rules about playing Ministry, Fugazi and Lucy's Fur Coat every hour, so that those fatbacks get scratched and we tune out."[63] WCRD's general manager insisted the station felt no obligation to CMJ, and few programming changes would occur after the upgrade. Instead, the station would be "a place for fun and experience while improving the quality for the listener." AM sounded terrible; FM had high fidelity. Plus, it was no fun broadcasting to yourself, even if changes came with the threat of "selling out."[64]

Alternative music had become mainstream fare by 1994. In response to this trend, Ball State DJs helped the university host a "Ballapalooza" music festival that fall, emulating the alternative music festivals and luring alternative music giants. But the DJs used the event to challenge the narrowness of alternative rock. Instead of Smashing Pumpkins, Ball State students showed up to hear Dead Mr. Sunshine, Dry Rhythm Caustic, and Circle with a Smile. It was a good experience, even if only around 200 fans showed up. Maybe that was a good thing, for those who viewed popularity with suspicion. Commercial FM radio, lucrative festival tours, and major labels seeking to cash in on the work of volunteer DJs cast a shadow over college radio as a place of artistic exploration without careerist pressure.[65] Seeking more listeners didn't mean selling out, but it certainly opened such stations to additional pressures and scrutiny.

David Letterman's career suggested college radio always operated as a ladder for students building careers—even if the vast majority didn't end up on late-night television or even working in entertainment. Freedom from restrictions and formatting allowed for student self-discovery, as Letterman had found. It also served as a platform and a learning experience. And in the 1990s, college radio's visibility and value in the industry offered some exposure and resumé-building activities.

Increasingly, though, DJs felt they could have neither educational self-discovery nor career success. Brand-conscious universities justified their existence by the professional skills they provided students entering the workforce. Culture warriors lambasted university curricula. But it was the increasing price tag of higher education, inflated by the financialization of student debt, devaluing traditional subjects and fields of study as professional preparation. As one historian explained, "when families take on heavy financial burdens, they focus on whether the investment will pay off in narrow financial terms." All around college radio, the commercial and market functions of higher education, as well as institutions' ability to fill in gaps in the nation's increasingly threadbare social safety net, besieged the high-minded rhetoric of postsecondary learning as a public good. Universities tasked with providing public service programming, cultural enrichment, and to "foster stronger moral bonds between citizens and the state" grew increasingly frayed.[66]

As musical culture found itself caught at a crossroads between corporate co-optation and a quest for authenticity, college radio confronted similar tensions regarding the purpose of higher education and cocurricular activities' benefit to students. Like the conflicts students faced over their education—whether it should be a time for personal exploration and enrichment or to gain marketable skills—so, too, did alternative music find itself torn by competing definitions. The business of higher education and cultural production faced stark new questions by the millennium's end.

· · · · · ·

In 1997, as KALX DJs mocked commercial alternative station LIVE 105, music journalists debated "alternative" and its future. Baby boomers choked access for punk rock and new wave on commercial radio, one author wrote, until the industry realized college radio offered a useful promotional tool. Nirvana's meteoric rise birthed "whole new radio formats" as "this new Alternative music edged out the old 'Commercial Alternative' staples like Siouxsie and The Banshees." Alternative rock stations blasted Beck, Pearl Jam, and Smashing Pumpkins in contrast with "classic rock" behemoths that continued rockist homages to Led Zeppelin and Rush. Major labels tried to re-create the Nirvana magic, throwing money at bands and gobbling up indie labels to maintain a veneer of authenticity and credibility. Authenticity had become a brand and entrepreneurship subsumed "indie" into hip capitalism and gentrification.

It wasn't clear who had won the punk wars. Rock music stagnated, as the business model killed the "risk-taking" needed for artistic innovation. Alternative was never a thing, writer Scott Frampton argued; it "was never really a genre or revolution so much as what Wall Street calls a 'market correction' for all the underground rock that never made it to the mainstream because rock radio was still in thrall to Led Zeppelin and Woodstock."[67] Much like the counterculture itself, commercial forces co-opted rock music's revolutionary potential from inception. Extending such logic to college radio, participants perhaps fooled themselves that they facilitated artistic revolution that would alter the nation's social and cultural fabric. Market logic suffused and controlled cultural dissemination, as it did college radio, whatever enthusiasts told themselves.

Writer Douglas Wolk disagreed. He declared, "The Punk wars are over, and we won." Rockers swept away the "glossy sterility" of pop music, from "Kenny G and Celine Dion, to Keith Sweat and Clint Black, to necrophilic duets with dead singers and billions of interchangeable power ballads and the fucking Macarena." What more proof was necessary than the Butthole Surfers selling 500,000 records? Truly challenging musical creation was possible, particularly with production becoming cheaper and accessible. "Don't like the music you hear on the radio?" Wolk asked. "Turn on your computer and make something you do!" An army of bands waited in the wings, and the pressure for new alternatives remained consistent—technological change meant bands could circumvent the suited executives forcing artists to sell their souls. Nirvana and the Smashing Pumpkins claimed all the ground for "minor-key guitar-rock with existentially traumatized lyrics," but the future of music would sound different, as it should.[68]

Wolk was right. The computer provided alternatives for music fans beyond college radio. Radio, and the music industry, were businesses. Jim Bolt, who spearheaded the formation of KSSU at Sacramento State, referred to his endeavor as launching a "start up." The term, popularly associated with Silicon Valley and the tech world, applied to a noncommercial, alternative radio station run by students. In 2013, Wolk would be writing about whether Spotify exploited musicians and writers.[69]

For students unable to secure an FM spot, the internet offered alternatives. At KCR, San Diego State University's radio station, the world wide web offered space FM never provided. The city's crowded spectrum, competing with signals from Mexico, barred access. A cable hookup reached 3,000 subscribers on campus, and expansion to AM brought more listeners. In 1996, as capabilities emerged, KCR ported its "mix of alternative music through the audio portion of the World Wide Web." As the first Southern California college station to expand to the internet, KCR broke through its geographical confines. KCR's web master reported access from Stanford University and Washington, D.C.[70]

KCR detoured around FM entirely. As the station assumed its place on the internet, proponents envisioned a brave new future without the need for terrestrial radio entirely. "There will be no need for radio in the future," a university staff member envisioned. The technician who set up the webcast predicted a promotional boon driven by listeners "working at their desk" able to access the station via computers.[71]

For some stations, it wasn't the internet's allure threatening the existence of their signals or offering a rosy future, or undermining their commitment to punk rock revolution. Expanding to the internet did not solve debates about college radio's promise: it elided confronting college radio's responsibilities to surrounding communities, including providing music lacking presence on commercial radio—whatever the genre. College radio was more than the site for the next big act in alternative rock. Stations populated by genres not suffering from rock's stagnation in the late 1990s persisted. But college administrators had the power to control these signals or shutter them entirely if they did not meet a narrow definition of what constituted the purpose and culture of higher education in the era of the culture wars.

15 Silencing the Harvard of Long Island

● ●

Excerpt from CMJ's Beat Box Chart, February 16, 1996

Fugees—"Fu-Gee-La" (12″)—Ruffhouse/Columbia-CRG

Genius/GZA—"Liquid Swords"—Geffen

Pharcyde—*Labcabincalifornia*—Delicious Vinyl-Capitol

Mic Geronimo—*The Natural*—Blunt-TVT

Fab 5—"Blah" (12″)—Duck Down-Priority

Busta Rhymes—"Woo-Hah!! Got You All in Check" (12″)—Elektra-EEG

2Pac—"California Love" (12″)—Death Row-Interscope

Bahamadia—"Total Wreck" (12″)—Chrysalis-EMI

LL Cool J—*Mr. Smith*—Def Jam/RAL-Island

In 1993, Adelphi University launched an advertising campaign in the *New York Times*. The ad, which ran four times, declared Harvard University "the Adelphi of Massachusetts."[1] Adelphi's president, Peter Diamandopoulos, had studied Classics at Harvard and held big visions for the largely commuter school on Long Island. The ad alluded to Adelphi's (and Harvard's) "lofty" academic goal to "develop the whole man and the whole woman" through liberal arts and engaging with "the 2500-year tradition of Western Civilization." Such an education made students ready for life, not simply to "occupy your mind for the years between high school and post-pubescence." Prospective students could call for a free "Harvard, the Adelphi of Massachusetts" t-shirt.[2]

It was a rosy vision for Adelphi, which faced a troubling decline in enrollments. Diamandopoulos established himself as a traditionalist: he chafed at diversified curricula and expanded coverage of underrepresented texts and voices. Adelphi lacked the resources and endowment of Harvard University. Diamandopoulos laudably decided institutional wealth should not bar students' access to reflecting "sensitively and judiciously on their place and possibility in the world." He thought all students should have access to this kind of learning experience—but his vision remained narrow and paternalistic.[3]

Adelphi was famous for more than its attention-grabbing advertisements. It was home to WBAU, a storied radio station that launched the careers of hip-hop artists Public Enemy and other media figures. The station succeeded beyond most college signals: it linked liberal arts learning with professional experience to produce programming valued by surrounding communities and made significant contributions to American culture. WBAU welcomed community members as DJs and offered Hempstead-area residents exciting new music, including in hip-hop, in keeping with its history. As Bill Stephney explained the station's role, "For Long Island, and especially the African-American communities of Nassau County—it was our local urban station." When Stephney was program director, WBAU not only played up-and-coming hip-hop artists; they visited the studio. "Busta Rhymes used to answer phones on our show with his crew," he remembered. DJs interviewed L.L. Cool J and Grandmaster Flash. Run-DMC hung out at the station regularly."[4]

In the mid-1990s, as Diamandopoulos faced a financial crisis and faculty intransigence against his educational vision, he identified WBAU as a hindrance rather than an opportunity. In his view, it did nothing to further students' engagement with Western civilization. In fact, it damaged the lofty goals he set for his institution.

WBAU's content could not be the overt reason Diamandopoulos axed the station; he knew that much. But eradication was the goal, and WBAU's troubles cut to bigger questions about the place of higher education in US life. The struggle over WBAU's fate in 1995 and 1996 reflected ongoing culture-war battles regarding hip-hop, to be sure. While college radio often aligned with the goals Diamandopoulos laid out—introducing students to content and ideas not readily available in popular culture—WBAU defied the narrow values and texts defining his vision of liberal arts. Other proponents saw college radio as means for professional training, so students could gain marketable skills and careers. This negated Diamandopoulos's vision while simultaneously undermining college radio's independence and iconoclasm. More so, myriad demands placed on these stations grew even more paradoxical.

Stations had to train students for the workforce; offer communities a cultural meeting ground and exemplify the melting pot while providing discrete spaces for genres without commercial coverage that supported multiculturalism; extend liberal arts education to the airwaves without running afoul of culture-war hawks or airing offensive voices; and play edifying music but support artists to mainstream success—to name a few.

They also had to make sure they didn't raise the ire of home campuses to the point that students or administrators demanded change.

WBAU's story demonstrated how these impossible demands tore at the fabric of college radio even before the internet and online music streaming undermined the music industry and offered alternatives to terrestrial radio broadcasting. Adelphi might have presented a dramatic example, but what happened there occurred in less drastic or other forms at many stations for reasons beyond the politicization of culture and the demands for a narrow university curriculum under the guise of protecting Western civilization.

At Adelphi, despite Diamandopoulos's culture-warrior credentials, WBAU's troubles emerged from more than a simple divide between conservative culture warriors targeting avant-garde radio stations and out-of-control students playing free jazz and hip-hop on institutional signals. Nor so did administrators who wanted professional laboratories or institutional brand support clash with students who wanted artistic independence free from administrative oversight. What happened instead revealed these fraying paradoxes of college radio and its many, irreconcilable purposes within a complicated landscape of higher education. Too many partisans looked to these signals for discordant services, and when the going got tough, or administrators had the incentive, they intervened in—and in extreme cases sold—signals that no longer fulfilled the purposes they wanted. Institutions held all the power, no matter how vigorously a station's defenders fought to save it.

Institutional Relevance

In October 1992, WBAU at Adelphi University celebrated its twentieth anniversary with a party. Prominent station alumni attended, including Gary Dell'Abate, a producer for Howard Stern's radio show; Mona Rivera, a reporter for WCBS radio news; Bruce James, a DJ for Power 97 in Philadelphia; and Andre "Doctor Dre" Brown, host of *Yo! MTV Raps*. Some 150 guests included alumni and friends, as well as sixteen students and four administrators. An open bar and hors d'oeuvres watered and fed them as the station played in the background, along with "nostalgic tapes of shows, bits of old productions, and even some videos." WBAU's "intensely loyal" alumni celebrated twenty years of broadcasting.

The station launched in 1972 on FM from an "arts building" that was really a modified Quonset hut, and WBAU grew thanks to individual initiative. Long Island's FM band had been crowded since the 1960s, with numerous institutions and organizations seeking signals. To get a spot, Adelphi split its signal with Nassau Community College. A high school with an unused frequency had been in talks to sell it to Nassau, so a share-time agreement emerged when Adelphi eyed the property. Nassau took the daytime hours, and Adelphi took the evenings. Consulting engineer John Schmidt built the system and managed its expansion, using salvaged parts. Schmidt produced high-quality audio, thanks to his engineering expertise (he had a career at Grumman, building the lunar lander used in the Apollo missions).

Students staffed metal desks and operated the boards. As one alumnus remembered, "At any given moment when you entered the station, you could witness a flashy DJ spinning records, hear a call-in or interview show, or stumble onto a reporter in the back room writing copy for a newscast as the UPI machine clacked . . . spitting out top stories of the day." The station offered public service programs until 8 P.M., followed by music, reaching, depending on the weather, most of Nassau County, Queens, part of Brooklyn, and occasionally Manhattan, Newark, New Jersey, or Bridgeport, Connecticut, and along the Sagtikos Parkway on Long Island to entertain commuters with 350 watts from 150 feet in the air.[5]

In 1986, the station upgraded to 1,100 watts with a new transmitter on the Long Island Marriott Hotel. Administrators and the student group overseeing the station agreed to cover initial costs, and WBAU would repay the institution over time. Each year, the station would conduct a Radiothon, soliciting listeners for donations. All proceeds would go to the university, deposited in "University account # 9050-000 'WBAU Radiothon.'"[6]

But WBAU experienced administrative troubles in 1994, two years after celebrating the station's milestone anniversary. The student turnover problem common at college stations caused issues in standards and consistency. At a board meeting in March, members discussed what to do about allegations of "payola and plugola" regarding one DJ. The station received attractive promotional items from record labels and concert venues, and some DJs seemed to not be able to control their impulse to capitalize on the swag. At a general meeting a few days later, the administrative staff clarified ground rules regarding property and training procedures.[7] Student managers at WBAU addressed this list of common concerns most college stations faced. They had little idea that a much larger issue was looming.

Although station leaders addressed concerns quickly and with appropriate policies, Adelphi University's administrators reviewed the station in early 1995 under the pretense of revisiting these mundane matters.

Rather than citing WBAU for lax management, however, administrators argued it had no institutional relevance. WBAU began as a Department of Communications project, which sought, as many university stations had, a "laboratory" for radio broadcasting students. In 1976 and 1977, students at the station broke with the department as it "abandoned the station and quickly shifted its emphasis from radio to documentary film production." The university recognized WBAU as a student activity, funded by fees. After this break from departmental oversight, WBAU operated independently and with a community focus. DJs felt free to direct programming along the lines they preferred—generating strong links to the region's music scene and valued public service programs. Without any "academic linkages," critics argued, maintaining the station seemed a foolish waste of money.[8]

Adelphi administrators cited diminished student involvement, echoed by student government members who "expressed serious concerns." The station sustained funding from student activities fees but linked amounts to student involvement levels.[9] Without adequately funded supervision, in the form of a professional general manager and engineer, administrators cited "embarrassments for the University." Even though managers demonstrated attention to recent problems, administrators declared WBAU as lacking "adequate training" and "appropriate levels of quality programming." Moreover, outdated equipment required costly upgrades.[10]

A distinct difference emerged between how administrators presented WBAU's troubles and student government assessments. The Student Government Association (SGA) president described WBAU doing "an excellent job." SGA cut the budget only because overall enrollment declined, thereby decreasing funds for all activities. Dean of students Carl Rheins, on the other hand, indicated to reporters as early as May 1995 that the university sought to sell the station. Rheins argued that student-run stations, relics of the 1960s and 1970s, were no longer "viable at a school like Adelphi." News of the sale caused surprise, and it was unclear what "viable" meant in that context or why the station had no value for Adelphi.

John Schmidt, the station's engineer, questioned the administrators' rationale. "The deans aren't happy with the programming," he explained; "I don't think they like hip-hop or heavy metal—[so] they're trying to put words in student government's mouth."[11]

Talking points regarding the station, provided to Adelphi president Peter Diamandopoulos and the board of trustees, took a shocking stance. "WBAU has become," the memo read, "an intellectual embarrassment and its operation can no longer be justified."[12]

Talk of closure surprised community members and students alike. The administration cited few examples beyond a lack of connection to an academic department—not an unusual arrangement for student-run stations. Administrators cherrypicked examples to support their narrative. An anonymous complaint disliked the "cornucopia of lackadaisical and incompetent management of WBAU." The letter's tone indicated a disgruntled DJ penned it. Nothing in the letter suggested the station should be removed from air. Indeed, the author cited the station as a "viable source of information to our community." The author asked the trustees to "investigate" regarding management and "implement rehabilitary measures to save one of Long Island's finest college radio stations."[13]

The author wanted to save the station, not cancel it. That was not what Diamandopoulos wanted, however.

WBAU Goes Silent

In early 1995, as administrators contemplated closing the station, supporters rallied to defend WBAU. Ken Norian, an alumnus with two degrees from Adelphi and part-time general manager at the station, urged caution. WBAU's troubles, he argued, resembled those college radio faced nationally.

Norian described WBAU's past "near death experiences" to highlight the often-cyclical nature of student-radio involvement. He cited the 1970s' "bitter struggle" between the Department of Communications against the student government, which "wanted very much to have control of WBAU." Interest waned in the early 1980s. The station struggled to maintain a full schedule—perhaps explaining Bill Stephney's ability to program so much hip-hop during prime-time slots. But WBAU's past troubles did not spell certain doom in 1995. Although only some two dozen students volunteered at WBAU—none of whom wanted to broadcast sports events, to the dean's disappointment—only a "minuscule fraction of the Adelphi community" attended games. Why subject the radio station to a metric not applied to athletics?[14]

Besides, WBAU performed important public service. WBAU's broadcasts from the Garden City Cathedral "generated a tremendous amount of positive telephone calls," according to station logs. Norian highlighted the station's staid, respectable programming—polka music and children's entertainment—to convince the administration of its viability.[15] In the letter's margins, which circulated among administrators, a glimpse of hope appeared. Rheins penned, "Before we make a final decision we should con-

sider Mr. Norian's letter." But his underlining of the final decision suggested WBAU's fate was sealed.[16]

A personnel change accelerated that fate. After a dean, an active station supporter, retired, Sue Oatey assumed oversight of WBAU as associate dean of student life and development. Under her leadership, Norian found "nearly immediate negative changes in attitude toward and support of WBAU." Oatey lacked a "sense of history" regarding the station and its relationship to the university. Programming for the community and station maintenance fell by the wayside. Instead, "the new administration seemed preoccupied with minutia of detail such as the playing of the Adelphi Alma Mater at sign on and sign off." Any "real" issues, such as the station's aging equipment, received no attention. Instead of moving to preserve the university's asset, Norian argued, "it became increasingly evident" that Oatey and the new administration "abandoned" WBAU.[17]

Administrators had dollar signs in their eyes. In 1995, Dean Rheins "indicated that he thought that WBAU might be worth 'a million dollars.'" Norian tried to correct this impression, given WBAU's limited wattage and noncommercial status. Not to be dissuaded, Rheins saw WBAU as an asset to help the institution's "dire financial situation." Financial concerns indeed seemed pressing. Station managers had a heated dispute with Oatey over a minor telephone bill. Norian "began to get the feeling that a decision had already been made to unload WBAU."[18]

Subsequent events confirmed his suspicion. Administrators sought an excuse to shut down the station—but motivations went beyond financial. WBAU simply did not support the vision administrators had for the school's future. The finances merely provided the ammunition they needed to axe a student activity and community vehicle they considered beneath Diamandopoulos's "Harvard of Long Island" image.[19]

Adelphi's associate director of business affairs later revealed that administrators arrived at the decision to close the station when the SGA linked funding to student involvement in 1994. That December, months before Norian's conversation with the dean, Rheins explored options to sell WBAU. In January 1995, staff tasked with investigating sale options noted that usually, once a sale agreement had been reached, license holders submitted an FCC petition. Subsequently, a public notice would be issued for comments. Administrators thought no such public notice was necessary if modifying a share-time agreement. Stations like WBAU could be dissolved through a private agreement, they determined, without public hearing. By February, Adelphi administrators notified Nassau Community College of their intentions to "cease broadcasting pursuant to the Time Share Agreement" and offered the sale. In March, an appraiser valued the station.[20]

Norian was suspicious, but he remained in the dark about these maneuvers. He described administrative "harassment," including surveillance. "Anonymous" complaints poured into the dean of students' office "about the content of several programs—exclusively the hip-hop shows hosted by black students and members of the local community." Whether popular heavy metal programs received similar attention went unsaid. Oatey admitted "university attorneys" listened to the station during late-night programming. A DJ faced "disciplinary actions" and was fired for broadcasting "obscene and highly inappropriate programming/commentary," although whether the complaint emerged from university surveillance remained unclear.[21]

Oddly, no intervention came from Oatey's office regarding obscenity. This lack of oversight seemed designed to give administrators reason to rid themselves of the station and its potential costs, both financial and reputational.

Meanwhile, rumors indicated administrators invited offers to purchase WBAU. Hofstra University reportedly expressed interest. When pressed, Oatey "admitted with some embarrassment that these negotiations were going on." Norian invited Oatey and Dean Rheins to attend station meetings, hoping to clear up any concerns. They refused.[22]

On August 4, 1995, administrators circulated a closure action plan among themselves. Because selling the license proved more "complex" than the administration originally envisioned—FCC rules would not allow a straight sale to Nassau Community College—Adelphi had to take WBAU "off the air voluntarily" and wait for official license transfer to Nassau. Any funds that exchanged hands would be separate. Oatey noted a "critical juncture" in the sale, emphasizing administrators' expectation of a payout from the license transfer. Station equipment malfunctioning risked an embarrassing loss of signal, and the high cost of replacement, Oatey decided, was prohibitive. Action was required to stave off further costs.[23]

Oatey knew the decision would be controversial. "From a political point of view," she told Rheins, "it would be much easier to go off the air prior to the beginning of school." If they shuttered the station during the semester, "the school newspapers will focus on this as an example of administrative action," and WBAU would be fundraising.[24] So they opted to mute it before anyone could object. The action plan was "excellent," according to Rheins.

Other administrators concurred with the decision. The assistant dean of the College of Arts and Sciences cited "light to non-existent" student involvement. WBAU's "idiosyncratic programming" failed to meet her metric for new equipment investments. Since the Department of Communications had no use for the station as a laboratory—nor would it contribute funds for equipment upgrades—she reported that the dean, her boss, agreed "the liquidation of the radio station would have very little impact on the College of Arts and Sciences."[25]

No obstacles remained. On August 24, 1995, the day before the fall semester's start, Oatey called Ken Norian to inform him she had shut down WBAU. New locks appeared on the door, and a phone message greeted callers informing them of the station's closure. Norian was to stay on as a part-time employee to dispose of WBAU's physical assets. He warned Oatey of potential FCC violations for abruptly ceasing broadcast, but she was unconcerned.[26]

Amid declining enrollments, the administration found an expense it could cut without affecting many students. Rheins's visions of dollar signs did not materialize. As WBAU went silent, Adelphi secured an agreement to transfer the license for $30,000 to Nassau Community College. Norian expressed his disdain: "It might as well have been 30 pieces of silver," he remarked, referring to Judas's price for selling out Jesus.[27]

The Decline of Western Civilization Part III

More than declining enrollments doomed WBAU. Administrators closed WBAU to support institutional rebranding as a prestigious defender of Western civilization and higher learning. The dean of student life linked the decision to the university's "extensive and serious review of its educational priorities and goals in a continuing effort to enhance the intellectual climate of the University." The administration concentrated on programs and student activities in line with a narrower institutional identity.[28] In other words, the station's hip-hop and programming connected with the surrounding Black community and immigrant groups: administrators didn't think these connections supported their "academic" brand.

Administrators moved forward with plans to transfer its FCC license to Nassau Community College. The dean of students planned to transfer WBAU's "extensive record collection" to Adelphi's library and enter circulation.[29]

Students and community members reacted negatively and swiftly. The "political problems" Oatey hoped to avoid materialized—with a vengeance.

"We didn't even have a chance to say goodbye to our listeners," hip-hop DJ Wild Man Steve protested.

A polka show DJ lamented the "devastating" shutdown creating "bitterness and a feeling of betrayal by the community and station memberships."

Administrators struggled to keep their closure justifications clear. While they cited a lack of connection to academics and financial pressure, clearly WBAU's community connections played a role. Dean Rheins told the newspaper this image was "clearly at variance with the university's academic philosophy and mission." Divisions existed on campus regarding the station's programming, but even those who disagreed never demanded closure. The polka DJ admitted, "I also disagreed with some program content." Yet he, Wild Man Steve, and a reggae DJ agreed that station content, not finances or academics, determined administrators' actions.[30]

Negative reactions surged. Administrators, particularly Dean Rheins, grew increasingly concerned after a September 30 *New York Times* article about Adelphi's financial and enrollment troubles.

The article cited numerous crises emerging under Adelphi president Peter Diamandopoulos's watch—despite his hefty annual salary topping half a million dollars. The suburban school's "serenity" belied its dire situation, driven by a 25 percent decline in enrollment over a decade, where "dormitory rooms are vacant, course offerings are dwindling, copy paper is rationed, workers have been laid off, and" significantly for the community, "last month the campus radio station was abruptly closed." Diamandopoulos "preaches passionately to his faculty and students about the need for a 'radical recasting of the academy' and the value of 'frugal spending,'" the report read. Such rhetoric contrasted with his princely salary that made him the second-highest-paid university administrator in the nation behind Boston University's John Silber—who sat on Adelphi's board.[31]

The article probed Diamandopoulos's academic vision for Adelphi. The "blunt and outspoken" president led the institution for ten years and "used his presidency as a bully pulpit to make a case for 'back to the classics' university education"—an ill-fitting vision for "New York's Alternative FM Station."[32]

Administrators scrambled after the *New York Times* article to produce updated talking points regarding the closure. Rheins outlined the steps taken before muting the station, which included an "extensive review" of its "original purpose" and "current status as a 'student club.'" He insisted it no longer served as a laboratory, "nor was the station contributing to the advancement of co-curricular life" since it did not broadcast lectures, athletic events, or theater productions, even though "the station consumed one-fifth of the total student activity budget." Such a situation was not unusual for college radio stations, so he made additional justifications. Rheins cited obscene broadcasts, although the details remained vague, and he made no mention of university surveillance to nab DJs for naughty lyrics. Rheins claimed WBAU fell short of Adelphi's "high standards of demeanor and educational programming." Clearly the administration did not view WBAU's programming as in line with Diamandopoulos's narrow, "classical" view of topics appropriate for higher education.[33]

Amid a curricular culture war regarding the teaching of Western civilization, Diamandopoulos placed himself, and his university, firmly on the side of "tradition"—an arbitrary and loaded standard that WBAU, with its links to African American culture and communities, failed to meet. Culture warriors such as Diamandopoulos instead usually balked at expanding the liberal arts to incorporate history, literature, and artistic traditions outside narrow, Eurocentric, and white constructs.

Public scrutiny intensified regarding presidential compensation, university curricular vision, and finances, in addition to the station's sale. But students and alumni proved particularly outraged regarding WBAU, as Oatey predicted. The *New York Times* noted the swift organization of student and alumni opposition. While faculty organized the Committee to Save Adelphi regarding curricular changes, local attorney and alumnus Thomas Liotti formed Friends of WBAU to coordinate efforts to stop the FCC's approval of the license sale.[34]

Liotti served as copresident of student government in the early 1970s when he campaigned for curricular and academic reform. Among his demands included "abolishment of all mandatory class attendance" and final exams.[35] Liotti's suggestions marked him as a radical among curricular reformers and certainly as a foe of Diamandopoulos's traditionalist view of higher education. Internal memos among Adelphi administrators labeled Liotti a "nemesis of longstanding" to the institution.[36]

Administrators composed responses to the student newspaper's front-page story about the closure and student letters critical of WBAU's sale. Rheins complained when no reporter interviewed him or the legal staff. He reiterated his narrow definition of a student-run station as a "student club" or laboratory for the communications program.[37]

Criticism continued to build. The same day Rheins refuted negative portrayals of the sale, October 14, the *New York Times* published an editorial about Diamandopoulos "plundering" the institution. Under his leadership, the writer found, the commuter university failed to "give students of modest means and modest learning a taste of higher education." As the faculty organized against program cutbacks and Diamandopoulos justified his handsome salary, enrollment declines outstripped those at nearby Hofstra and C. W. Post College. Adelphi's troubles owed to more than demographic changes. Layoffs and WBAU's closure, both symptoms of decline, occurred alongside the library's cessation in book acquisitions while "administrative ranks have continued to grow." Despite a nearly one-third decline in students and similar loss of faculty, administrative staff tripled. Administrators spent lavishly and boasted of being an elite university while cutting courses. The faculty voted 131 to 14 for Diamandopoulos's resignation. As one faculty member put it, "Never, in the 27 years that I've been at Adelphi has this university felt itself weighted down by pessimism and a not so vague sense of moral and social decline."[38]

Students felt demoralized. Faculty had no confidence in the administration's leadership. Community members lost a significant tie to the institution through the radio station. As media attention intensified, Adelphi faculty, staff, and students expressed dismay. Rheins's refutation of a student newspaper article regarding WBAU's closure seemed a petty distraction when it appeared next to letters lamenting the state of the university.[39]

Ken Norian, the recently ousted general manager, and John Schmidt, the part-time engineer at WBAU, refuted Rheins's justifications. They penned an extensive history of WBAU, from its origins as a student activity—not a laboratory for the Communications Department, which did not exist in 1969 when the station started. WBAU "broadcast many informational programs" for the Adelphi community, including shows for young adults or forums regarding substance abuse and recovery, environmental issues, news and public affairs, nursing, and poetry. Plus, "WBAU's music programming," they wrote, "had something of interest to the majority of Adelphi students." Schmidt, for one, remembered days when Run-DMC visited the station after the release of the band's first album. He used to drive William "Flava Flav" Drayton home after his Saturday night DJ shifts. The administration simply failed to realize the station's artistic and cultural value to the students and community.[40]

Norian and Schmidt sharply and publicly criticized the administration's motives, particularly regarding charges that the station aired obscene or "four letter words." Late-night shows enjoyed "safe harbor" according to FCC rules, Norian and Schmidt insisted: late-night hours meant lax rules for content when children were unlikely to be listening. Content could be further restricted by university policy, but administrators never changed guidelines. "It is unreasonable," they explained, "to expect the station staff to adhere to a standard which has never been published."[41]

Norian and Schmidt alleged racist motives. DJs "suspect[ed] that in fact the complaint was with the amount of Black oriented programming, as that was what Dean Rheins and Dr. Oatey complained about." Internal memos indicated Oatey targeted Black DJs for surveillance, despite no FCC complaint ever being filed against the station in its history. Instead, administrators' concerns about programming arose from Diamandopoulos's narrow conception of what constituted proper activities for institutions of higher education: the promotion of Western civilization and culture. Hip-hop, with its voicing of concerns and artistic expression from the Black community and other ethnic groups, did not meet his standard.[42]

The administration's unilateral action appeared more clearly as closure details emerged. The FCC received no documents about the sale or notification regarding intent to sell. When Schmidt queried the FCC, the FCC reported it was unaware the station had ceased broadcast. The cessation itself was a violation. Administrators alone instigated and carried out the closure; student government had no part in it. Rheins and Oatey repeatedly refused to come to meetings or communicate regarding the station, as plans for closure developed in secret.[43]

Administrators repeatedly claimed WBAU failed as a student activity because of low numbers of volunteers. But by closing the station the day before students returned to campus, Norian and Schmidt argued, the administration prevented recruitment to prove the station could rebound. The issue, they had to conclude, was not student participation but a desire to save money and quiet WBAU's voice for the institution.[44]

Friends of WBAU

The license transfer became more complicated than administrators envisioned. Nassau Community College could not broadcast full time, despite the share-time agreement and sale of full-time rights for $30,000. Adelphi's administrators failed to realize the federal body needed to approve the deal. The process could take months, even if no objections emerged in the public comment period.

Friends of WBAU used the delay to organize legal action. Liotti, a defense attorney, filed a complaint in Nassau County Supreme Court. Charges included florid descriptions of fraud and conspiracy, with the board of trustees facilitating "thievery and ravaging" of university resources. The plaintiffs demanded accounting of $36,000 raised at the station's recent Radiothon. If the administration transferred the gifts for purposes other than the donor's intentions, a violation occurred. The plaintiffs demanded return of funds to donors. Additionally, Friends of WBAU demanded a temporary receiver to oversee university assets.[45]

Liotti and Friends of WBAU targeted the entire administrative structure. Remarkably, the lawsuit demanded Liotti be "named receiver and acting President of the University" and for the Supreme Court to appoint a new board of trustees. Although charges included "a range of other forms of 'mismanagement,'" the university's lawyers benefited from these bizarre claims and legal barriers to intervention in nonprofit organizations.[46]

The likelihood of the New York Supreme Court handing Adelphi University over to the plaintiffs' lawyer was a long shot, to say the least. That didn't stop Liotti from pointing out "gross misconduct" and wasteful expenditures. Administrators could not secure a "single positive story about themselves" despite having "hired enumerable public relations experts." He argued, "All they can do is spend huge sums of money on self-laudatory advertising." Alumni's degrees were "a property interest" in the university, in his view, and Diamandopoulos devalued their asset.[47]

WBAU had other champions, especially among students. Contributors to *Afrika Unbound*, a magazine dedicated to Black news and culture on campus, explained the lawsuit's goals for skeptics. It targeted the president and the board for mismanagement, an illegal sale, and misuse of funds. It charged Diamandopoulos with "illegally reimbursing himself and the Board of Trustees for its trip to Greece," and they demanded resignations. For these students, the issue went far beyond WBAU.[48]

Questions remained about misused station donations. Adelphi's legal counsel found the Radiothon funds had not yet been spent and a list of donors existed "in the event these funds are to be returned." No return had been initiated, but the funds had not bankrolled a vacation for trustees. Still, the lawsuit named the institution, Diamandopoulos, and each board member "both individually and in their official capacities" responsible for mismanaging funds.[49] Adelphi's lawyers pushed back by challenging Liotti as not possessing standing to file on behalf of students, given he was an alumnus, not a current student.

Public action accompanied the lawsuit. Friends of WBAU held a press conference on October 20, 1995, to announce the lawsuit. Supporters held picket signs decrying the sale as unfair and demanding resignations from Diamandopoulos and all board members. As students and station members took to the podium, Schmidt reiterated his charge regarding the racist motivations behind WBAU's closure. Some 52 percent of shows were "Black oriented," he told the crowd, and "some of the staff members think it could have been a factor in the University's shutting the station down." He highlighted WBAU's role in promoting hip-hop. Now-famous stars Doctor Dre, Hank Shocklee, William Drayton, and Carlton Ridenhauer counted among station alumni. Speakers attested to the importance of cultural programming for area residents, from polka to Italian news and the Irish show. Doctor Dre's appearance at the press conference highlighted WBAU's association with hip-hop culture and its formidable legacy.[50]

But WBAU's fate edged toward being sealed. In December, the FCC accepted the license modification for Nassau Community College to broadcast full time on the signal. The autumn federal government shutdown further delayed the notice because of furloughed FCC staff. The thirty-day period for comments allowed more time for ire to develop over the closure.[51] Nonetheless, the New York Supreme Court dismissed the lawsuit on December 4.

Friends of WBAU set their sights too high, and technicalities doomed the suit from the start. The judge determined flatly that the plaintiffs had no standing to sue. Plaintiffs circumvented the attorney general's office, claiming a conflict of interest because of ties between the office and Adelphi administrators. This reasoning did not fly with the judge. He declared their "characterization of the office of the Attorney General as 'inept'" as without "basis in fact" and as insufficient for the judge "to ignore the clear statutory language." The Not-for-Profit Corporation Law required that complaints be taken to the attorney general. The judge would not circumvent jurisdiction in this matter.[52] Liotti planned an appeal, but Adelphi's counsel remained unperturbed. University counsel reassured Diamandopoulos, "The appeal is even more frivolous than the underlying action." It would go nowhere.[53]

Afrika Unbound's editorial staff demanded a meeting with Diamandopoulos regarding WBAU's sale and his decisions regarding finances, communication, and curriculum. In response, Diamandopoulos claimed he "too hated to part with the share time in the license," but costs proved "substantial, at a time when no one was stepping forward within the University to take on management of the station." Without a funding source, the station had to close. Eliding that the station had not been housed in the Communications Department for some time, he insisted the faculty had abandoned the station and he had no choice. He denied "pernicious allegations" motivated by the "deep racial suspicion and fear of our sad times" that "the station's historical commitment to hip-hop and other Black musical forms contributed to Adelphi 'getting rid' of WBAU." He insisted, "The truth is more painful and more complex." Although the station achieved "nationally recognized achievement and success, in which I and everyone else who understood the station's history felt deep pride," its "unrelated failures" were "too many and apparently too intransigent to allow its survival." He sidestepped the closure's timing before students came back to campus.[54]

In February, students from *Afrika Unbound* finally met with Diamandopoulos for two and a half hours but came away without reassurance. Afterward, the students told the president, "We gathered from the meeting that there is a breakdown in communication between your deans and yourself. We believe that this is a serious impediment to the ability of your administration to fully address the problems of students at hand." Students raised their lack of input in the shutdown of WBAU and other programs, library funding and staffing, and the administration's lack of support for the Center for African-American Studies. They requested the administration "make a more authentic effort to employ more 'minority' professors" given low representation.[55] These students rejected Diamandopoulos's insistence that he recognized the cultural value of hip-hop, Black expression, or the station's history.

On February 9 at 9:56 A.M., the Office of Student Life and Development received a fax stating in large, bold letters, "Black Radio Programs Kicked off Air by Racist Administration." At 3:51 P.M., another fax arrived. It demanded, "Stop the Sale! Put WBAU Back on the Air."[56]

In the comments, the fax's sender penned, "The real motives come out!"

WBAU's closure originated as a cost-cutting measure by the administration. But financial troubles provided administrators with the cover they needed to silence Black voices, aimed at Black audiences in the area, coinciding with Diamandopoulos's narrow curricular preferences and dismissive attitude toward demands for more diverse course offerings and attention to the needs of Black students.

For the Students

One student undertook an organized and targeted campaign to save WBAU, a centrally important activity to her education. Sophomore, co-assistant editor-in-chief at *Afrika Unbound*, and WBAU volunteer Jackie Parker admitted the station faced administrative and management problems. But, she insisted, "closing it was wrong." In addition to rallying students to demand administrative transparency and recognition of student demands, she pursued direct conversation with Diamandopoulos.

Parker's editorials in *Afrika Unbound* sharply criticized the administration. She spoke as a communications major, first. She selected Adelphi University because it offered the major as well as supplemental activities in radio and newspaper publishing. "After all," she explained, "Adelphi boasted its radio station in the Guide to Undergraduate Life." Tour guides stopped by the studio with groups of prospective students. Parker joined the station and *Afrika Unbound* as a first-year student, and WBAU's closure meant she lost a valuable preparation for her intended career in journalism. As a student interested in technical preparation for the professional world, Parker felt disadvantaged by WBAU's closure. "We focus on liberal learning" at Adelphi, she explained. "You all know what I mean. My astute understanding of the Modern Human Condition will give me all types of insight into the different Modes and Versions of the unemployment line." Without the option of internships or experience in broadcasting, she couldn't compete in the job market.[57] WBAU supported the Adelphi brand and attracted students, but perhaps not the students Diamandopoulos envisioned. Both Parker and Diamandopoulos criticized liberal arts education, albeit from very different perspectives.

When administrators told students they could intern at a commercial station, Parker rejected such platitudes. An internship could not replicate the experience WBAU provided. Parker called WBAU's sale "The Big Lie" and internship offers "insulting." The university's lawyer rebuffed her requests for information, greeting her questions with "silence and blank stares." When he insisted WBAU had not been sold, she thought, "Somebody's lying!" Evidence existed. "To this day," she pointed out, "you can call ext. 6400 and hear, '. . . As of 9 A.M. on August 24, 1995, WBAU-FM ceased broadcasting pending FCC approval of the sale of its broadcast license to WHPC-FM Nassau Community College." Parker did not understand. The lawyer directed her to the court files, and summarily dismissed her.[58] License transfer details aside, her home institution seemed inattentive to transparency in the matter.

The runaround Parker received from administrators amounted to gaslighting. Although the experiences, she reported, "are giving me excellent journalistic experience," time and energy, as well as frustration, could be saved with a simple roundtable of administrators and faculty. She concluded, "Adelphi's administration doesn't want to resolve this." Rather, "they want to drag this out and exhaust all parties who are literally running all over campus." Administrators did not care what students thought, provided student government with no input in decisions, and could shut down any student activity or organization on a whim.[59]

Students demanded the administration recognize them. Among concerns relating to library resources, communication between the administration and students, curricular gaps, and financial problems, WBAU's closure topped the list. Students suggested solutions to their complaints, including reinstatement of WBAU, a survey of students, library renovations, and transparency for policy decisions as well as a more positive marketing plan. A flyer declared, "Students: It's Time to Take a Stand!" Organized students arranged several meetings and rallies to coordinate action.[60]

Students felt slighted and angry. "We pay big bucks to attend Adelphi University," they stated. WBAU's closure, the "phasing out" of important services and programs, such as the Italian cultural center and Rape Crisis Program, added to daily frustrations such as "irrational changing of the St. Paul's Bus Schedule."[61]

At a rally in February 1996, Doctor Dre, a student leader of Friends of WBAU, and Thomas Liotti addressed a crowd gathered to demand WBAU's restoration.[62] The open forum aired grievances about WBAU's closure and concerns about sidelining student voices. "How long," protesters asked, "are Adelphi University students going to stand around and allow the administration to make decisions that affect us, students, without acknowledging our input?" Complacency would lead to more problems. Parker placed WBAU's sale within a larger context of university problems and raised "serious questions" about Adelphi's actions. The sale took place "without student input" and targeted "a lot of minority-based 'alternative' programming."[63]

After the rally, *Afrika Unbound*'s editors presented student government with evidence that the closure violated FCC rules and disregarded student input. The SGA president met with Parker to consider action, but nothing emerged.[64] The editors next attempted to secure more information from Diamandopoulos. They issued questions regarding the costs of management and equipment, requested a listing of administrative efforts to improve WBAU or link it to the Communications Department, and asked for clarification regarding the inconsistent statements regarding its sale.[65]

Beyond asking for clarification, *Afrika Unbound*'s editorial staff acted. The staff members offered a plan to put WBAU back on the air. The station had issues with programming, they knew, including its failure to broadcast sports.[66] If they could relaunch, they would address these concerns. They proposed new rules regarding outside volunteers, security, and professionalism. The editors sketched out fundraising appeals. They suggested WBAU receive a representative in the student government and planned a host of publicity events. Restructuring would enable a return to broadcasting and "shed a ray of hope on the recent flow of negative publicity that Adelphi has been receiving." WBAU's return would "redeem the university's administrators" and affirm their "genuine concern for student issues."[67] In other words, *Afrika Unbound*'s editorial staff tried to make restoring WBAU appealing to administrators who faced a declining public image.

This savvy move also failed. Dean Rheins responded with the same boilerplate talking points circulating since the August 1995 closure. Jackie Parker addressed Rheins's "plethora of justifications," citing Adelphi's intentional lack of support for WBAU.[68] Diamandopoulos met with the students again on February 29 and ignored their proposal for reinstatement. Instead, he planned an open forum. His assistant faxed the editorial staff to convey his appreciation for "the research that you have done and the responsible and civil manner in which you presented your case"—why he expected a group of Black students would behave any other way remained unsaid. He promised to review their findings and act in "students' best interest," but the cursory response indicated his unwillingness to consider their proposal.[69]

Parker made one last appeal to university officials to save the station. She prompted an internal review of the valuation. She hoped the review would yield a higher value and prove the station's worth to the university. Adelphi's associate treasurer told the associate director of business affairs (positions reflecting Adelphi's surfeit of administrators, one could argue) that because the station could not be converted to commercial, its valuation was accurate. Three universities had offered bids. Nassau Community College offered $30,000 plus $50,000 to remove the antenna. Hofstra offered $48,000, and Five Towns College bid $40,000. With these bids and in consultation with an appraiser, the associate treasurer "confirmed that the $50,000 net value to Adelphi" was fair.[70]

Friends of WBAU and *Afrika Unbound*'s editors were out of options by March 1996. They met once more, after which the editorial staff thanked Diamandopoulos for his willingness to address the library's paltry endowment.[71] Parker tried one more time. She requested that Diamandopoulos retract the transfer request and reopen the studio as "an educational laboratory, much like the library," hoping to appeal to his academic aspirations. But the letter conveyed her sense of futility. "I am extremely willing to meet in the near future to discuss the long term fate of the station," she told the president. "I am sure that I will be able to provide you with the substantive information to increase your confidence in a decision to fully reinstate and support WBAU," she closed.[72]

All that was left were grumblings. Nassau's lawyers objected to a petition Friends of WBAU circulated to deny license transfer as a "frivolous pleading." Friends tried to argue that other entities viewed the deal between Adelphi and Nassau as a "scheme to circumvent those provisions of the Communications Act" requiring the FCC hear petitions to deny the action. Five Towns College, which bid on WBAU in summer 1995, objected.[73] "What happened here," the reply stated, "is that Peter Diamandopoulos . . . essentially gave away the College's radio station," amounting to inside dealing. The college requested that the FCC deny the university's request to modify the license, since the administration acted duplicitously to "circumvent possible petitions to deny and/or competing applications" such as from Five Towns College. Friends held a fundraising dance at a local club to raise money for their legal efforts. Doctor Dre DJ'd along with other alumni.[74]

Jackie Parker's absolute last resort was to address an objection directly to the FCC. She requested that commissioners disallow Adelphi's license modification request. She submitted fifteen copies of a report, one for each commissioner, along with supporting documents. She called Adelphi's "give away" of WBAU a "profligate act of President Diamandopoulos" and a result of internal communication problems. "Elusive" negotiations between Nassau and Adelphi elided "the normal closing process." The $30,000 in Radiothon donations remained "in limbo," and the administration violated procedures for eliminating a student activity. She obtained notarized statements from John Schmidt and Ken Norian. The SGA president confirmed the body never voted to close WBAU; it decreased its allocation because of declining enrollment and student volunteers. It had allocated funds for the 1995–96 academic year, but the university overrode them and ended the station.[75]

It wouldn't work.

On June 12, 1996, the FCC approved the license modification. Friends of WBAU petitioned for a review, but the FCC unanimously rejected all petitions filed against the modification, including Parker's. The institution held the license, not the students. As such, the students had no grounds on which to make an appeal. Dean Rheins asked the new SGA president to make this clear to members of her cabinet.[76]

Smooth sailing did not await Diamandopoulos. Charges of mismanagement—and misconduct, misuse of funds, and ethical violations—piled up against the president and his trustees. In July, as the FCC approved the modification to WBAU's license, Adelphi's board of regents began hearings into the institution's affairs. The review found inside brokering, such as the contract for Adelphi's widely mocked advertising campaigns in the *New York Times* in 1990 and 1993 directed by the firm for which the chair of the board served as a director. Charges of intimidation, lack of transparency, and improper contracting with businesses belonging to trustees emerged. As one chronicle of Adelphi's troubles noted, the board included Diamandopoulos's mentor and Boston University's controversial chancellor, John Silber, who notably excluded faculty from decision-making and ranked as the nation's only university president to earn more than Diamandopoulos's hefty salary.[77]

On February 10, 1997, the regents fired Adelphi's trustees, save one.

With Diamandopoulos's branding plan seemingly dead in the water, WBAU's supporters had one last glimmer of hope. John Schmidt, the former station engineer, appraised the new board chair of the debacle. Schmidt requested action before the FCC set the last nail in WBAU's coffin: approval of Diamandopoulos's request to cancel the license once and for all. The share-time agreement had been modified, but Adelphi maintained this one last link to the station. Schmidt offered his services free of charge to resume student broadcasting. He would repair the equipment, connect the studios to a cable modulator, train volunteers, and ensure the station met all FCC regulations. His proposal failed.[78]

When the new board fired Diamandopoulos a few months later, English professor Tom Heffernan asked the new president, James A. Norton, to reconsider WBAU's fate. He argued the station would be an asset, similar to Hofstra's station, which broadcast classical music, or WFUV at Fordham, which functioned as a public broadcasting outlet. "These stations," Heffernan argued, "come near or accede to the quality of National Public Radio," which would augment Adelphi's reputation as an institution of higher education and culture.[79]

In September 1997, a local paper announced it was time to wave goodbye to WBAU. The FCC, it reported, "has officially approved the dissolution of WBAU." Charges lingered that administrators targeted the station because it played hip-hop and "other non-mainstream music," though it graduated nationally recognized radio personalities and musicians.[80] Student pride in a university-owned asset could not prevent its demise. Although Diaman-dopoulos and his corrupt board mismanaged Adelphi's finances and botched responses to enrollment declines, they enjoyed total control of WBAU and the power to destroy it when its programming did not coincide with the administration's vision of higher education.

· · · · · ·

WBAU's story reveals the discordant dynamics troubling college radio by the end of the 1990s. Defunded institutions, the decline of localism in media increasing demands on noncommercial signals, association with genres possessing market appeal, corporate co-optation, and questions about the purpose of liberal arts inquiry—all threatened stations' status. WBAU's closure suggested college radio might have tremendous influence on culture, but influence is not necessarily the same as power. These stations existed to fulfill functions and missions beyond student control. As radio stations on the public airwaves, if they were not carrier-current or wired signals on campus, community members had a claim. But the FCC administered licenses, and institutional license holders in most cases held all the cards. So long as stations benefited institutional image or mission, they could persist. Any shift in administration endangered signals—and once lost, they were irretrievable.

Authenticity and localism in radio seemed endangered in the 1990s, far beyond the loss of the occasional station such as WBAU. Its fate haunted alumni, even though the institution experienced a rebounding reputation after Diamandopoulos's departure. Few outside of Hempstead understood or remarked on its loss. Beyond Adelphi's troubles in the late 1990s, it wasn't clear college radio would always have a place in the radio spectrum given regulatory and cultural developments, though enthusiasts continued to demonstrate its viability and clamored for participation and service.

True, college radio had come a long way since signals debuted on FM in large numbers in the 1960s and 1970s. College radio stations had picked up on musical developments in freeform rock radio and provided an "alternative" to Top 40 as those formerly freeform stations developed tighter formats in the 1970s. Signals' educational functions protected freeform hours on college radio, which often focused on genres lacking commercial exposure or mainstream appeal. That argument reemerged among those who tried to resist against administrative interference as the new millennium dawned. But if administrators were convinced radio signals held little institutional value, there was not much even the most devoted DJs or community members could do to save their aural real estate.

Rising techno-optimism not only overlooked the complicated realities of webcasting such as potentially costly royalties; it played into the hands of administrators who saw their signals as working against the brand of their institution. Administrators found ways to shutter stations that offended them or failed to serve their defined institutional goals. Although WBAU's closure was shocking, it demonstrated how narratives of college radio's decline have deep, complicated roots—and thus rumors of its demise thanks to the digital disruption ignore long-standing realities. Instead, college radio's troubles stem from the nation's inability or unwillingness to support institutions dedicated to cultural and knowledge production regardless of market value or narrow notions of national identity.

College radio's mostly white, indie rock fare dominated the medium's popular image in the 1990s. But throughout the decade, college radio stations continued to be key places to access underground music, including hip-hop and its innovators, though such sounds never defined broad popular conceptions of college radio. Yet for key DJs and shows dedicated to the genre, college radio continued to be a vibrant place to find new sounds— until alternatives broke their position with the music and radio landscape.

Hidden Tracks

· ·

Playlist from hardcore show Rock n Roll Blackbelts, *WRVU,*
Vanderbilt University, Nashville, Tennessee, October 27, 1998.
From the personal collection of Ryan Compton.

Elliott, "Dionysus Burning"
Refused, "Liberation Frequency"
Sunspring, "Love Somebody"
Seven Ten Split, "Come and See"
The Farewell Bend, "On 3"
Texas Is the Reason, "Something to Forget"
Bone, "In Pieces"
Kill Holliday, "Keepsake"
Metroschifter, "All about $"
Avail, "Kiss Off"
Grade, "Weave"
Worlds Collide, "Faces"
Anthrax/Public Enemy, "Bring the Noise"
Refused, "New Noise"
Hot Water Music, "Things on a Dashboard"
Blacktop Cadence, "Cold Night in Virginia"
Split Lip, "Union Town"
Snapcase, "Zombie Prescription"
U.N.K.L.E.
King for a Day, "Hit or Miss You"
Pedro the Lion
Empire State Games, "Armchair General"
Guilt, "Off White"
Sunny Day Real Estate, "Pillars"

By the mid-1990s, even minimally tech-savvy students could disseminate
course papers or dirty videos from computer to computer. Such newfound
skills allowed the first episode of *South Park* to spread across colleges' net-
worked computers like wildfire in 1995, making it one of the internet's first

viral videos. In 1999, Napster connected files, searchable by artist or song title, across potentially millions of computers, and the application proliferated on college students' computers. The service allowed users to share and download mp3s for free. Although Napster would shut down and lawsuits targeted college students for piracy, it was clear internet distribution of music would change the industry—well before the 2004 debut of Apple's iPod.

While students cued up *South Park*'s animated fight between Jesus and Santa Claus and downloaded free music, most of the music industry reacted with horror at the prospect of fans packing their hard drives with digital files ripped from physical media. But indie labels spotted a potentially lucrative way to reach new artists. Matador Records, which had grown into one of New York City's iconic independent labels, embraced the new wave along with other small independents.[1] Matador licensed its music catalog to Napster in 2001 in anticipation of a membership-based file-sharing platform. Label executives seized the internet as a powerful promotional tool, and they wanted to have a say in how their artists would get compensated. Steven Malkmus of the band Pavement saw Napster as an antidote to corporate radio consolidation and narrowing playlists. "With radio and MTV so tightly controlled," he explained, "there are fewer and fewer opportunities for independent artists to get mass exposure for their music." The internet allowed broader reach than college stations with indie rock rotations. Music could reach "millions of people who might otherwise not hear it," and, Malkmus hoped, "making my music available for Napster will enable me to be compensated for that."[2]

Matador and these indie rockers were ahead of their time. Major labels and industry representatives cracked down on Napster. Independent labels or artists tended to not be members of Recording Industry Association of America (RIAA), which sued the download service in 2000.[3] Metal band Metallica notoriously compiled a list of 300,000 Napster users the band claimed illegally distributed song files. Users were allowed by copyright to make copies of songs they owned for their personal use, such as recording songs from vinyl or CD onto a mixtape. But sharing them publicly violated laws. Metallica sought $10 million in damages. Drummer Lars Ulrich said the pirates should instead "just go down to Tower Records" and grab albums "off the shelves." In his view, it was the same thing. He wanted Napster out of business, and he did not hide it.

Chuck D of Public Enemy saw it differently, noticing the power imbalance between superstars and kids trying to find music or up-and-coming artists. He argued, "We should think of it as a new kind of radio—a promotional tool that can help artists who don't have the opportunity to get their music played on mainstream radio or on MTV." Like Pavement's Malkmus, Chuck D evaluated the problems independent labels and artists faced in an era of media deregulation. Bands wanted to make a living. There was no cash prize for remaining underground and niche. To make new music and connect with fans, artists needed fans to find their music.[4] Internet file-sharing might help musical dissemination and discovery. In commercial radio and major record labels, consolidation and corporatization grew from their political power and regulators' faith in markets to foster competition—resulting in less diversity and access to the public sphere.[5]

Little loyalty or love remained for the major-label music industry. Consumers felt gouged, forced to shell out $20 or more for a brand-new CD. Labels cashed in without incentive to lower prices. Some corporate entities, such as Sony and Universal, looked to create their own subscription-based services akin to Napster. RIAA's reported failure to pass along royalty payments to artists increased pressure on the industry giant.[6] Other media entities, particularly newspapers, had already set a standard of making content free on the web, lessening consumers' willingness to pay for content. But memories of labels' fight against home taping in the 1980s echoed, with executives scolding music fans for taking cash out of their favorite artists' pockets. Disregard for the high cost of music, prices rarely affordable to college students seeking to build their music libraries, lowered the moral barrier of entry to Napster.[7]

Yet the fight over Napster seemed distant from the troubles roiling through college signals confronting the digital era. Newly released royalty rates for webcasting, which numerous stations had launched in the 1990s, threatened to be existentially prohibitive to these small stations. At least half of webcasts at colleges and universities ceased broadcast in 2002, according to estimates.[8] WNYU, averaging 100 listeners on its webcast during a month, faced fees of $9,000. Leaders at Rice's KTRU reported that although small, its audience doubled every ten months as high-speed internet proliferated in homes or students streamed from wired dorm rooms. Increases could easily consume, triply so, the station's $5,000 annual budget. Beyond the fees, administrative costs, such as for detailed recordkeeping to comply with reporting requirements, were prohibitive.[9]

Additional challenges to the culture of college radio loomed as music fans found new places to discover music and the fraying promises of higher education put greater scrutiny on maintaining college signals. Convincing administrators and campuses of college radio's value grew increasingly difficult—and not simply because the internet offered an alternative.

Even though college stations were a recognizable feature of US radio and the music industry, they had obligations to their campus homes. A station might raise operating funds and exist independently, but host institutions still provided utilities or cheap studio accommodations. Administrative interference or forcing shutdowns over noncompliant DJs continued as they had before the bullish days of the internet boom.

If a university president encountered a reason to alter the station and its programming, he or she usually had the power. Rice University administrators made several moves to intervene in the station, although students resented the administration attempting to turn KTRU into a "university asset."[10]

Athletics wanted more airtime. The station's manager feared the administration would force coverage, violating "the spirit of a student run radio station."[11] But charges of elitism plagued KTRU. "Don't assume students can recognize Le Tigre as lesbian punk rock," one student complained, "and don't look down upon students if they don't know that Kim Gordon was a member of Sonic Youth." If KTRU leaders didn't justify its campus service, they might lose it.[12]

DJs could not resist demands to air more sports.[13] Basketball broadcasts went ahead, but punk rock DJs in November 2000 weren't having it. The game aired—simultaneously with their show. Listeners heard game announcers intermixed with political songs. An assistant vice president for student affairs noted how the Ramones sang "We Own the Airwaves" over the play-by-plays.[14] The station manager refused to discipline the DJs.

Two days later, the station went silent. A sign on the studio door declared, "No Admittance: Violation subject to Code of Student Conduct."[15] Some 350 students gathered for the meeting between KTRU staff and administrators. Many showed up wearing station bumper stickers over their mouths or on their clothing to demonstrate their support for KTRU. They picketed the president's house (figure HT.1).[16] The student senate condemned the administration's handling of the matter because the station, as a student organization, possessed protection from administrative meddling.[17]

Athletes felt disrespected. Women's basketball supporters doubted the station would have taken the same action if it had been a debate team event or a lecture. KTRU belonged to students, but as one student journalist explained, "KTRU DJs would rather play underground music by artists no one's ever heard of than broadcasting events in which the girl or guy sitting

ROB GADDI/THRESHER

Students silently protest the KTRU shutdown outside President Malcolm Gillis' house last night. Members of Rice's Board of Trustees were arriving for dinner at the president's house during the protest.

FIGURE HT.1 With mouths gagged with station bumper stickers, student DJs and supporters of KTRU protested outside meetings, hearings, and even the university president's house against interference and the imposition of more athletics programs, including a shutdown. Courtesy Woodson Research Center, Fondren Library, Rice University.

next you in class is performing." Athletes were students and paid fees, which funded the station.[18]

Administrators proposed allowing the vice president for student affairs to remove the station manager for not complying with "applicable law or University or station policies."[19] Administrators had been intending, for some time, to take KTRU in hand.

The punk show provided the impetus administrators needed. In the aftermath, the student senate and administrators agreed KTRU would broadcast games and hold student-body-wide elections for station leaders.[20] Students could take a breath and finish up their finals, and the station could resume.

During the frenzied debate, most readers probably overlooked a comment by one letter writer to the student newspaper. The alumnus noted KTRU came to prominence during its coverage of student protests in 1968. He noted those former students' "very proper and civilized conduct" and the Rice community's value of "tolerance and civility." Punk DJs who wanted to play "hard rock and politics" could go to the internet, he suggested. "Let the Athletics Department have the FM transmitter," and DJs could "set up a truly innovative digital Web broadcasting station."[21] The matter seemed settled in 2000, without relegating punks to the web, but KTRU, along with other prominent college stations, was not safe.

In 2003, copyright fee changes for noncommercial stations resolved webcasting costs.[22] Administrators always questioned whether radio served pedagogical functions and if it was worth the risks of letting students have freedom of the airwaves. The internet presented a possible salve to disgruntled DJs when administrators unloaded these signals—as Rice's was in 2010. Administrators sold the FM property to the University of Houston to become a full-time classical station, leaving students to broadcast online and on a lower-powered signal.

Terrestrial radio's appeal waned, pedagogical needs decreased, and institutions of higher education seemed less interested in supporting facilities for students to find their voice—mirroring the decline of support for humanities and liberal arts disciplines in favor of programs training students for the marketplace. Universities engaged in economic development and gentrification of surrounding areas and had little interest in radio that connected with and served existing communities. So long as stations offered a sense of institutional value, they continued undeterred. The FCC suspended only one college radio station's license for obscene content in the history of educational radio, as documented. That was at WXPN at the University of Pennsylvania in the 1970s. Stations that went off the air or ceased student access or community connection did so because administrators no longer saw the point of supporting them.

In the early 2010s, Rice, Vanderbilt, the University of San Francisco, and Georgia State, with prominent stations that had defined college radio, forced broadcasts online, sold stations outright, or converted signals to NPR service. They were not alone. In 2017, Brown University sold its renowned commercial station to a Christian broadcasting network. Stations might maintain college affiliation and a few hours of freeform but offer students internships rather than the experience of hosting their own show, developing programming, or managing marketing or news reporting.

By the 2010s, a popular perception that college radio was dead circulated. One *New York Times* article marked the near-simultaneous disappearance of Rice, Vanderbilt, and USF's signals as "The Day the Music Died."[23] It is difficult to quantify the stations ceasing operations or converting service in some way. The total is small, and stations continue to debut, but the loss of giants in Houston, Nashville (the Music City), and San Francisco cast a pall over radio's future. Despite estimates that some 83 percent of Americans in 2020 tuned in to radio each week, it is hard to escape the sense of irrevocable changes in the business of radio and music.[24]

In the new millennium, questions confront not *who* would make money from popular music, but *if* anyone other than the biggest superstars could make a living as an artist. New pathways for musical discovery created new questions and concerns about college radio and its future.

Still, rumors of college radio's demise are much overstated, even with the loss of such powerful signals and their storied contributions to musical culture from indie rock to reggae to hip-hop. Technological disruptions visited upon college radio alongside the music industry, but connections to higher education, local and national cultural developments, the persistence of signals, and the reopening of opportunities in low-power FM complicate this narrative of decline. Instead, that narrative tends to involve not the closure of stations, which happened throughout college radio's history, but rather the loss of college radio's monopoly as a tastemaker and gatekeeper in the music industry as alternative sources emerged online.

Everyone's a DJ

It was "a shot" to Boston hip-hop when programmers took away "88.9@ Night" on WERS at Emerson College in 2013. The station wanted more commercial music in the prime-time slot, and the hip-hop show featuring local artists, along with a reggae show, got the cut. MC Akrobatik, whose career had launched thanks to Boston's college radio scene's support of local, underground hip-hop in the 1990s, was devastated. The show had been "crucial" for artists like him, and the station's local identity seemed to be shifting.[25]

Akrobatik became a "household name" in Boston for two reasons, as he saw it. His manager promoted shows and got him an audience. "This dude," he remembered, "would plaster his car with posters of a show that's going down at the Middle East in a few weeks, and drive through Cambridge and Boston all month long, bumping our music that was then heard every night on the radio." That was the second ingredient: a hugely popular show on the powerful signal at Emerson College. As Akrobatik explained, "there was no algorithm, or corporation telling you what to like." These DJs formed a trusting relationship with listeners.[26] Long before networks existed online, hip-hop circulated through peer-to-peer networks of cassette recording and exchange, with college radio DJs there to pick up on the buzz from the underground.[27]

With energy and infrastructure growing around Boston's underground hip-hop community, labels tuned in to find talent that could hit it big. Pete Bazile, founder of Detonator Records, put together an event at the Newbury Sound Studio in Boston. He invited top MCs, all the best freestylers in the area covered by WERS, WMBR, or WZBC at Boston College. A DJ from New York was there, "spinning instrumentals all day," and Akrobatik, one of the invited MCs, took turns with the others while Bazile recorded two mixtapes. Bazile reviewed the tapes and decided Akrobatik had what it took. "And so he put out my first single." It became hugely popular on WERS, alongside cuts from Mr. Lif, 7L, and Esoteric.

Akrobatik and scene members felt like they had a home at WERS. "It was a community," he explained. For those "who made hip-hop in Boston" in the 1990s and 2000s, "it was almost like we were an honorary student at Emerson." He made lifelong friends, connecting over language and communications, keeping in touch as students went home to other parts of the country upon graduation. The show *Nightwatch* let listeners know where local artists and DJs would be performing, building a scene.[28]

College radio cultivated a sometimes-unexpected audience for Boston's hip-hop stars. WERS listeners included area college students, who told their friends back home about the new music they were discovering. These signals helped grow the local scene, but it wasn't exactly reaching the mainstream. Instead, Boston's scene remained underground, riding a network of informal ties. For Akrobatik, his twelve-inch "Say Yes, Say Word," released on Detonator Records, reached top twenty-five lists in Canadian college radio. As he remembered, "I'm like, yo, people listen to me in Canada. Next thing I know, I'm on tour in Canada, because of college radio." Without a major-label deal, the only way he would secure international exposure was through alternative networks. Boston's dense population of college students was a benefit, in Akrobatik's view. "So many people come in from around the country and around the world to be part of this place for four years or maybe more," he explained, which "gave us the opportunity to get these fans" who returned home with knowledge of artists from Boston.

Such coverage did reflect divisions, however. Akrobatik drew college listeners—"largely white college audiences"—a fact that "paradoxically reinforced a subtle racial cleavage that had existed in the community for many years," one scholar explained. "Inner-city fans" often didn't tune in, seeking "grittier material and top 40" artists.[29] Boston's commercial radio formats, although they would shift over time, "leaned heavily toward top 40 rap and R&B hits" without picking up on which Boston's underground artists created buzz.[30] Despite these contradictions, college DJs could cultivate audiences and a fan base for underground music and facilitate artistic advancement—and it still does.

College radio remains a viable medium, as is radio generally. But radio, and particularly college radio, is not the only player in musical discovery and community building. Still, something seems lost in the proliferation of online channels, streams, and means of promotion and distribution for artists. While low-power FM community radio has reemerged since the early 2000s, thanks to the FCC's new allowances for low-wattage signals after ending the class D license in 1978, the refrain about the death of radio continues to chime.[31]

As Akrobatik put it, new vehicles for artists to reach potential fans did not have the same kind of connection college radio provided. "Social media is so passive," he explained. People could be "sitting on the throne" scrolling their feeds. But hearing music on the radio, in the car, juxtaposed with an announcement of the artist's next show or other information from a DJ, created a sense of connection and sparked action. Listeners might love a song, Akrobatik explained, "and at the end of the song hear facts" like "you can catch these guys tomorrow night in the Middle East [club]." The listener might turn to their partner and say, "Oh, honey, let's go to the Middle East tomorrow." That word of mouth provided a sense of connection "better than an algorithm." Sure, fans could click a like button, or even share a link to a song. But it wasn't the same.

The individualists won. Everyone can create their own personalized channel, customized to their personality, likes, inside jokes, and associations. You can have a radio station for every occasion. Any lovable weirdo with a niche taste can find others like them.

But communities lose.

Sure, communal experiences can happen around music, at concerts, in online discussions, or in YouTube comments. No more suffering through obnoxious DJs who scream the intros and outros on Top 40, or the mumbling college students learning the boards—not if you don't want to. Stations like KEXP, born from the University of Washington's KCMU, made a hipster aesthetic marketable and valuable. Operating on a listener-funded model similar to NPR, the station turns out shows with global reach thanks to podcasting, internet streaming, and YouTube, like NPR and its popular podcasts and "Tiny Desk Concerts."[32] Now listeners can cultivate their own personal soundscape decoupled from terrestrial radio.

The idea of a college radio aesthetic, or punk and hardcore modes of production, with revolutionary potential has waned. Its history demonstrates that no matter how iconoclastic or rebellious the programming, or how much it challenged the culture industry or offered a retreat, signals by and large depended on institutional and administrative buy-in—no matter the surrounding context of media regulation and politics. Democratization in music production and dissemination occurred, but the business model and communities fractured.

Commercial radio abandoned its commitments to the public square, for all its limits. Podcasting offers alternatives, a form deriving its sense of audience connection from noncommercial radio and its open access to producers. Anyone with a mic and free software can upload a podcast. Listeners can turn to a connected speaker and request that it play a song, or a station from anywhere in the country, or cue up a podcast episode or replay of a radio show—a fundamental change in the listening experience. Podcasting is not radio, as one veteran radio consultant observed. But if that is the case, radio is not radio anymore, either. The ability to "time shift," to tune in to any show, on-demand, or to stream archived episodes, alters a hundred years of radio logic. Broadcasters no longer face licensing requirements or spectrum scarcity, or the troubles of curating a program across a weekly schedule to maximize the public service potential of a radio signal limited by the boundaries of time, physics, and geography.[33]

When everyone is a DJ, radio DJs have less power. As college radio's middle ground position in the music industry weakened, listeners and college DJs haven't lost—but artists have.

Starving artists may have authenticity, but authenticity doesn't pay the bills. File-sharing, webcasting, and eventually streaming indicted and upended the music industry's business model. The industry found ways to make money, but artists' payments did not keep pace, for all the industry's talk of ensuring artist remuneration. College radio stations and independent labels had enabled artists to earn a decent living by cultivating a robust, though perhaps not global or platinum-selling, fanbase that bought records and attended shows. The change in the business model—not the purported disappearance of college radio—is the real detrimental shift for cultural and artistic production.

Institutional investment and infrastructure are required for artistic exploration and its dissemination, whether it's a social safety net, business models that reward artistic creation, or properly funded institutions of higher education. Wealthy patrons used to support artists; some retreated into communal living; philanthropic investments and eventually publicly funded grants sustained artistic production. Bohemian scenes, which emerged with the rise of industrial society, flourished thanks in large part to middle-class consumption of their products.

Discontents of suburban middle-class culture continued producing artistic challengers. Enclaves persisted in zine culture or hardcore shows in basements and backyards. Skaters could drop into an empty swimming pool while playing bootlegged mixtapes. College radio strengthened those networks, getting word to those who yearned for it. That connection is what gave stations power. While the internet did not displace terrestrial radio, it changed the experience and availability of radio in ways that fundamentally altered listening experiences central to how these networks and scenes formed. Even noncommercial signals serving as valuable, public resources had commercial influences.

Freeform continued to exist and define a particular aesthetic. Call it hipster, indie, or bourgeois—it doesn't really matter. Sustaining entire signals with this ethos required a different business model and institutional arrangement than commercial radio. In spite of such divergences, the rise of freeform as a radio format contributed to a sense of fragmentation and audience segmentation saturating broadcast media since the 1970s. Dissident broadcasters cannot escape broader trends, it seems.

One iconic freeform radio station made the internet work, despite the royalty-rate shock (which later agreements relaxed, for noncommercial broadcasters in particular). Run by Ken Freedman, who formed a nonprofit organization to rescue the station's license after an attempted takeover in 1992, the station's mix of block programs and freeform ethos nurtured underground music and defied trends in alternative music in the 1990s. WFMU went independent in 1995, after its host institution Upsala College closed its doors. It was, as one reporter noted, "staffed by a cadre of idiosyncratic obsessives, each possessing extraordinary record collections, encyclopedic knowledge of cultural arcana and a talent for radio as an expressive medium." This iconoclasm and obscurity of music secured devoted listeners, who donated to the station during its legendary fundraising drives (receiving often unparalleled swag that NPR could never hope to replicate, such as small-batch releases of records).[34]

Because the station relied on listener donations, webcasting seemed like a good way to increase audiences, and it developed a robust online presence in 1997. Donors contributed some $750,000 to the station in 1999, developing a community bolstered by discussion boards and blogs offering articles about music and mp3 downloads. The terrestrial signal was a "dinky" 1,250 watts, but more than 300,000 listeners tuned in every month by 1999 thanks to expanded simulcasting and internet broadcasting. In 2007, WFMU reported on a national day of silence among webcasters to protest the US Copyright Office's newest royalty rates. The new rate structure would have forced WFMU to cap the number of streams. With simultaneous news emerging that SoundExchange owed royalty payments to an extensive list of artists, WFMU instead participated in the day of silence by not playing any RIAA/SoundExchange member artists. WFMU supported compensating artists, which is why the station paid up on its royalties in the past.[35] In contrast, the new rules seemed like a "shakedown."

Royalty discussions were exasperating; so too was artists not being properly paid for their work. But WFMU was building a viable model for noncommercial radio to maintain independence even amid a rapidly changing legal and technological context.

Indie rock favorites headlined fundraisers for the station, and its semiannual record fairs drew musicians and music-industry and indie heavyweights, including Sonic Youth's Thurston Moore. WFMU earned top marks from *Rolling Stone*, with critics regularly tuning in and listeners identifying with one another by their bumper stickers—whether they were in Hoboken or Honolulu.

Freeform radio's aurally jarring aesthetic had value, and it prompted an alternative business model. It relied not on the Corporation for Public Broadcasting (WFMU had only four full-time staff members, below the required number, anyway), or on corporate or local business underwriting. Instead, it drew from its devoted fans who appreciated the musical curation and adventures in listening WFMU provided. WFMU DJs represented an ethos circulating in college radio since the 1970s, when it accelerated freeform practices and kept the spirit alive while commercial signals grew increasingly formatted.

The model did not need association with a liberal arts mission or higher education. Iconoclastic radio could find support, particularly at a moment when independent music and musical creation seemed to be embattled from corporatization, co-optation, and technological change. What emerged, as a reporter concluded, was a radio station central in "defining the late-1990's hipster esthetic" that was uncoupled from institutional support and migrated to the internet for dissemination across geography to link like-minded listeners.[36] Community radio could persist.

One of those listeners was Sonic Youth guitarist and record producer Lee Ranaldo. In 2000, he remarked, "There's nothin better late at night . . . than climbing in the car and turning on and tuning in to WFMU cracklin across the river with whatever weird shit they're playing." No matter the DJ, no matter the genre of music, it would be "be brilliant/unusual/interesting as hell and for the most part, surprisingly new." Ranaldo would find himself lost in an aural exploration, driving aimlessly to the musical tangents. The experience was often ephemeral. With most songs, "you'll never hear it again. Ever." But this was "fitting and pure and beautiful," turning music into an "actual experience" that allowed a listener to escape reality, though music was a product to be sold.[37] It wasn't about college radio; it wasn't even about indie rock. It was about radio, in its purest form: a form of listening in that created a different sense of reality and connection, made possible by a freeform ethos. Ranaldo entreated others who appreciated this experience to donate to WFMU to keep it going.

Online broadcasting allowed noncommercial, nonprofit radio signals like WFMU to thrive in the internet age. Streaming offered universities and institutions a cheap, less risky alternative to student-run FM radio signals, which were lucrative assets that could be sold for cash to fill university coffers.

Freeform radio, even WFMU, targets specific audiences with underlying values and self-identification that went beyond the classifications of commercial programmers. Commercial radio metrics studied ratings and market share to sell advertising. Noncommercial radio stations, whether they were National Public Radio, community signals, religious broadcasters, or college outlets, identified their audience by their values and their lifestyle. Block formatting might make it difficult to create a self-supporting radio station from listener donations; that was for institutions of higher education to supplement and for community organizations to support.

In the new millennium, disconnection between artistic exploration and higher education grounded in liberal arts inquiry and knowledge creation, free from market logics, was the real fracture—not of radio audiences—that threatened college radio.

· · · · · ·

That sense of dread is what led me to write this book—a sentiment I have since revised.

I arrived in college in the fall of 1997 as the mp3 began to circulate on students' computers. I remember sitting in my adviser's office as he downloaded hard drive after hard drive of any album he could think of. Savvy students—and faculty, it seemed—sought back catalog albums that were not carried in local music stores or were out of reach because of high sticker prices.[38]

As the music industry transformed as a result, college radio fans developed their own declension narrative. The golden era had long passed. Gatekeeping and providing exposure are no longer necessary. Stations no longer exist as a vital, irreplaceable node in alternative musical markets and networks.[39] A sense of a golden-age-just-passed pervades popular perceptions of college radio. But a continuity defiant of any technological or digital disruption, or death of radio, narrative emerges in the medium's history since the 1970s.

I feel badly for the community members and students who went through the sale of WRVU, the station that gave me my start in college radio. While the details of WRVU's sale and the end of KUSF in San Francisco and Rice's KTRU are different, they all contributed to a sense of college radio's decline (figure HT.2). Signals remained available on the internet, but for participants, the sense of mystery of radio—its magic—seemed lost.[40]

For those of us who experienced WRVU's golden age, we had our fun. Cueing up a song, sliding the level bar into position, and hitting that rubbery button to cue up the record was a physically tactile experience and full of mystery. I had no way of knowing who was tuning in, unless they called the station to make a request (one time, from the kitchen staff at a nearby restaurant for a kids' song we had discovered in a thrift store's "eclectic" record section). One student DJ who experienced the transition reported the disheartening feeling of looking at the monitor and seeing three people tuned in to a webcast—her mom was one. Certainly, before webcasting maybe only your roommate tuned in. But DJs could imagine we were making a real connection—and often, well, sometimes we were. Plus, it's hard to escape the sense of calamity when artists can no longer earn a living making and performing music. Opportunities for connection over the airwaves, however ephemeral to begin with, seem besieged by would-be disruptors and sunshine-y techno-optimism.

College radio's long-standing diversity of services and functions persist—and reveal broader transformations and continuities in higher education and noncommercial media. WRVU is now VandyRadio, dubbed the "soundtrack of campus life." On the surface, the sale appeared to be a wager on digital media surpassing terrestrial radio, rather representing a desire to kill off student-run media, given the institution's investment in studio space and

FIGURE HT.2 Chuck D, whose musical career started at WBAU at Adelphi University—a station closed by that university's president in 1996—appeared in Nashville to support the Save WRVU efforts in 2011. Photo by Chris Nochowicz.

technology. Beneath this, a marked shift in the goal of campus-based media resides. It exists for the benefit of students' skills, career development, and prestige on campus, not as part of a university built for public accessibility. Such functions always existed in college radio from its inception. WRVU's transformation represents, rather than a technological disruption, a return to a narrower purpose for higher education, and with it, college radio. Certainly, the medium is available online, but the streams have fragmented, and the university no longer seeks purchase in the public square. As higher education retreats from offering public goods, radio service follows.

College radio is not dead, however. Stanford University's KZSU celebrated its seventy-fifth anniversary in 2022. KFJC at Foothill College in Los Altos Hills, California, maintains, as one radio insider put it, a "radical to the max" signal, while Georgia Tech's WREK remains "just as weird as ever."[41] The internet, moreover, allowed many stations to continue, with new generations of college students taking to the boards, plotting out a show, reviewing new music, and selecting songs for a set. Many stations still fill community functions and enable musical discovery.

A bright future remains in reach for local, community, and college radio. The recent formation of low-power, freeform community stations unconnected to any institution or university suggests college radio has fallen but its "sensibility" may not be down for the count. Indeed, college radio functions within the larger ecosystem of community radio, historically and to the present, a medium that persists.[42] Community organizers turned the activism against WRVU's sale into the energy to found WXNA, a low-power community station that resurrected the beloved, long-standing community volunteer–run shows of WRVU, as well as welcomed new voices to the airwaves. Sharon Scott, the former WRVU general manager who helped lead the campaign to save the station, followed suit in Louisville, helping to launch WXOX to bring together various communities to air their voices. WXOX offered a vital link for activists and community members seeking news in the summer 2020 uprisings after Breonna Taylor's murder. The end of one college radio signal sparked Scott's participation in the vibrancy of community radio.

The reputation college radio built in the 1980s and 1990s as the place where exciting new music could find an audience, cross over, and shape popular culture and aesthetics became dominant. But it never distinguished college radio in all its complexity. Musical discovery was only one function, though it spawned industry aggregators such as CMJ, the *Billboard* Modern Rock chart, and commercial alternative radio formats.

Musical discovery did not define all of college radio even at the peak of this vaunted reputation in the 1990s. More players entered that game with the emergence of internet streaming and direct-to-fan platforms such as YouTube and Bandcamp, but college radio still has a role to play. In April 2019, musician Julian Casablancas scorned streaming services such as Spotify. He called these impersonal apps the "new MTV," which set themselves up as the new musical gatekeepers. In Casablancas's view, "they're all just ripping everyone off." He craves genuine relationships between artist and audience, facilitated via the underground musical ecosystem. Regarding radio, musical discovery continues. He prefers college and community radio, stating, "I listen to the radio and generally stay below 92."[43]

For participants in those stations, across their many varieties, they act less as tastemakers and more as editors. The endless supply of music on the internet can be overwhelming for music lovers seeking something new. They don't know where to begin, as one KEXP DJ explained it. Rather than acting as a gatekeeper, since anyone can produce music and put it on YouTube, DJs and radio stations curate what is out there. They develop trustful relationships with their listeners.[44]

Radio's magic still exists. And the reach is worldwide, with anyone able to ask their home device to "play [that radio station across the country.]" I regularly tune in to WXNA in Nashville from my home office in Massachusetts. Radio continues to diversify. Podcasting and internet streaming disrupt the terrestrial and time-bound nature of radio, but many maintain that podcasting expanded the definition of radio (and many rely on similar business models, including corporate involvement).[45] It might not have synchronous listening qualities, but communities are nonetheless formed through these productions.

Yes, radio is still relevant. It's just that the definition of radio has expanded.

Identity crises for college stations remain, however, because myriad expectations persist for both radio and higher education while public support declines. Many collegiate signals continue to program as they have for decades, while others innovate. College radio still symbolizes college students' ability to express themselves. Stations might challenge dominant campus culture and stir debate among students—a function in line with college radio's history since the 1970s—or operate in concert with university goals of public service and cultural representation, or provide students with professional experience, among its many divergent roles.

As long as institutions continue to support these signals, they will be there for students to use, to find their voice and amplify others—and maybe, just maybe, provide evidence to the core educational values that underlay liberal arts exploration, beyond providing training and experience with marketable, professional skills. Institutions matter in the process of cultural production, exploration, and dissemination. No wonder higher education remains a prize to be won—or destroyed—among culture warriors. Radio, as the symbol of the public sphere and national voice and supported by higher education's dedication to the pursuit of knowledge, remains a site of struggle over the sound of America.

Acknowledgments

College radio is a collective endeavor, as were the research and writing of this book. I am indebted to countless scholars, colleagues, archivists, college radio participants, journalists, writers, and generous people who helped me locate interviewees or contact information. The outpouring of support and enthusiasm for this subject has been overwhelming and heartening. The college radio network is alive and well, and I benefit greatly from it.

I first pitched this book to Brandon Proia at UNC Press at a conference sometime in 2014, and his wholehearted support of the project pushed it from idea to the page. He could always see the big picture (and the counterhegemonic debates) at the center of this project's big questions, even when I couldn't. I could not envision a press that is a more perfect fit—not only for being housed at an institution with a storied radio station but because many at the press, including Brandon, were college DJs themselves. Many thanks to Dawn Durante for stewarding this project to completion, and to Mark Simpson-Vos for his enthusiasm for this project and for the Cure. Completing the manuscript would not have been possible without the generous support from the University of Connecticut Humanities Institute for a yearlong residential fellowship, during which I wrote the bulk the text. Princeton University Libraries funded a weeklong research trip to that archive—where I found my favorite archival document: meeting minutes at WPRB taken on toilet paper, circa 1985. I'm grateful for all who supported me in securing this funding, from letter writing to their enthusiasm for a project focusing on college radio. Fitchburg State University supported this project through a research course release.

I conducted my first interview for this book with Jack Rabid at his Brooklyn home in January 2015. From there, I followed networks and recommendations, received Twitter messages with leads for contacts and playlists of radio lyrics, and found primary sources. Supporters on social media for this project proved invaluable and sustained my dedication to telling these stories and tracking down new ones. From these leads, I discussed college radio for hours with scores of interviewees. Bertis Downs's enthusiasm fueled the expansion of my subjects as well as informed my arguments. Will Oldham helped me piece together a working definition of "selling out" in our conversation. This book would not have been possible without the labor of those who helped me make these connections and advocated for me. In particular, the support, encouragement, and questions from Jennifer Waits, Paul Riismandel, and Eric Klein at Radio Survivor shaped the argument and larger mission. Waits and Laura Schnitker at the Caucus on College, Community, and Educational Radio at the Radio Preservation Task Force (RPTF) provide vital energy to continue preserving the materials used for research, and their vision for historical scholarship and preservation is the spirit behind this endeavor. RPTF brings together scholars and archivists interested in sound and radio preservation, and I am grateful to Josh Shepperd and Shawn Vancour for their support and encouragement. Shepperd's early enthusiasm for this project helped me see its larger connections to policy and culture, and his support through the editing process encouraged me to aim widely with the book's implications. Above all, future researchers will produce enriching work thanks to RPTF and the Sound Submissions project. Many archivists expressed their excitement that someone was finally accessing these college radio collections, and their support and efforts ensured there would be many stories to tell, accessed thanks to their cataloging, suggestions, scanning, and myriad labors to ensure historians have access to the historical record—including during the COVID-19 pandemic, in some cases. Many thanks to Nick Kennedy for his research assistance at the University of New Mexico.

Thank you to the readers who produced thoughtful and encouraging reports to help shape this project and bring it to fruition. Michael Stamm and Elena Razlogova provided invaluable advice to shape the arguments and hone my writing. Numerous scholars have read the entirety or parts of this book to help hone its arguments, sharpen its prose, strengthen its theoretical underpinnings, or clarify its connections. Drew McKevitt, Caroline Roberts, and Jennifer Waits read the draft manuscript. Sarah Wright stepped in to expertly index at the last minute when my hand was injured. Chapters and passages benefited from the wisdom and encouragement of Patricia Arend, Jim Bolt, Katie Cramer Brownell, Sean Goodlett, Michael Kramer, Kevin Kruse, Ben Lieberman, Tim Lombardo, Kevin McCarthy, David Mislin, James Noble, Eric Perkins, Jack Rabid, Nick Rubin, Seth L. Sanders, Bruce Schulman, Sharon Scott, Josh Shepperd, Jordan Stepp, David Svolba, Sam Tobin, Thom Valicenti, Jeff Warmouth, and Paul Weizer. Friends and colleagues helped troubleshoot problematic sections, writing woes, or archival questions, including Julia Azari, Cari Babitzke, Jonathan Bell, David Bieber, Christine Dee, Dwight Farrell, Josh Hollands, Michael P. Lynch, Austin McCoy, and my cohort at UConn's Humanities Institute. Conversations at panels and in the commentary and informal spaces of numerous conferences and talks helped me hone key arguments, and I'm grateful to Margaret O'Mara, Stephen Petrus, Andrea L. Turpin, and Sherman Dorn for their comments. Writing groups sustained me, including Team Kate, the Dorothy Ross Society for U.S. Intellectual History writing group, and other informal gatherings. My eternal gratitude goes to Cari Babitzke, Seth Blumenthal, Alexis Boylan, Christopher Dingwall, Carlos Figueroa, Kate Grandjean, Heather Hendershot, Brigitte Koenig, Mary Lewis, Micki McElya, Johann Neem, Megan Kate Nelson, Drew McKevitt, Robyn Metcalfe, Jessica Parr, Justin Poche, Arissa Oh, David Onyon, Kirsten Wood, and Ellen Wu for their support through the messy parts of this process. Christine Dee gave me the advice that sparked the idea for this book, and I'm grateful to always have her to talk history and collaborate with. Our Critical Friends group sustains me as we confront myriad crises of higher education and try to do our small part to fight for change. Trivia Church kept me going during the dark days of the pandemic and beyond. Ellie Shermer contributed her insights and expertise to this project and offered her steadfast friendship throughout. Maria da Costa and Monica Vaz provided much-needed support. This project would not have happened without the inspiration and friendship of Elizabeth Cesarini, or the spreadsheet skills and enthusiasm of Caroline Roberts.

My friends and family are the reasons I wrote this book. My parents always encouraged me to find my voice, try new things, and explore, which led me to try college radio to begin with. There I met lifelong friends and collaborators. All of it led me here. Conor Hansen not only has read numerous passages but has listened to me complain, fret, and celebrate and has supported me throughout this entire process while making sure our kids were fed and didn't burn down the house while I was at the archives. And all my love to my future DJs: Leo, Oona, and Niamh.

Notes

Abbreviations

Works frequently cited have been identified by the following abbreviations:

CURSE   Censorship Undermines Radio Station Ethics (CURSE) Records
KEDG   KEDG online archive
KTRU   KTRU Records, Rice University
KUNM   KUNM Records, University of New Mexico
KXLU   KXLU Records, Loyola Marymount University
NFCB   Records of the National Federation of Community Broadcasters (NFCB)
PP505   Committee for the Preservation of Wild Life Records, KJHK, University of Kansas
RRHOF   Rock and Roll Hall of Fame Library and Archives
SAW   Something about the Women Records, WMFO, Tufts University
Turmoil   Turmoil Radio Records, WUSB, SUNY Stony Brook
WBAU   WBAU Records, Adelphi University
WESU   WESU Records, Wesleyan
WHUS   WHUS Records, University of Connecticut
WMBR Book
   Book, Volume, in WMBR Studio, Massachusetts Institute of Technology
WPRB   WPRB Records, Princeton University
WRAS   WRAS Records, Georgia State University
WUOG   WUOG Records, University of Georgia
WXCI   WXCI Records, Western Connecticut State University

Introduction

1. *Chicago Slices Raw: The Baffler Magazine*, Hi 8 mm, 1993, https://mediaburn .org/video/chicago-slices-raw-the-baffler-magazine/; Sabalon Glitz, *Orpheum/ Zoroaster*, vinyl, seven-inch, 33⅓ rpm, Single (Trixie, 1993); Holly Kruse, *Site and Sound: Understanding Independent Music Scenes* (New York: Peter Lang, 2003), 59.

2. Sabalon Glitz's record label, Trixie, had distribution through Chicago's Touch and Go, an independent label with its own distribution arms. Amy Phillips, "Touch and Go Records to Stop Releasing New Music, Shut Down Distribution," Pitchfork, February 18, 2009, https://pitchfork.com/news/34650-touch-and-go-records-to -stop-releasing-new-music-shut-down-distribution/.

3. Michael Azerrad, *Our Band Could Be Your Life: Scenes from the American Indie Underground 1981–1991* (New York: Back Bay Books, 2002), 3–5. Azerrad named this "effective shadow distribution, communications, and promotion network" a "cultural underground railroad." Signing to a major label meant a band lost "an important connection to the underground community" that gave it rise, meaning noncommercial radio, independent labels and record stores, and zines.

4. Thomas Frank, "Commercialization of Dissent: Counterculture and Consumer Culture in the American 1960s" (PhD diss., University of Chicago, 1994); Thomas Frank, *The Conquest of Cool: Business Culture, Counterculture, and the Rise of Hip Consumerism* (Chicago: University of Chicago Press, 1997).

5. Michael Nevin Willard, "Skate and Punk at the Far End of the American Century," in *America in the Seventies*, ed. Beth L. Bailey and David R. Farber (Lawrence: University Press of Kansas, 2004), 182–85. Willard links subcultural growth in the 1970s to "the conditions of an emerging postindustrial society during a time of political and economic decline." Subcultures "developed as a logical way to interact with the material conditions of a postindustrial world," forming "'translocal' microeconomic communities of small-scale craft production and micromedia."

6. Olga Bailey, Bart Cammaerts, and Nico Carpentier, *Understanding Alternative Media* (Maidenhead, Berkshire, UK: McGraw-Hill Education, 2007), 16–20; Brian Fauteux, *Music in Range: The Culture of Canadian Campus Radio*, Film and Media Studies (Waterloo, Ontario: Wilfrid Laurier University Press, 2015), 174. Regarding Canadian college radio, with which US radio shares many characteristics, stations engaged in "specific oppositional practices" reflecting the complexities and contradictions Raymond Williams used to expand on Antonio Gramsci's idea of hegemony. Williams's notions of counterhegemony and alternative hegemony described "oppositional spaces that respond to a given problematic within society and culture."

7. Pure examples occurred, such as KAOS at Evergreen State, where station mission coincided with the institution's experimental and progressive goals. But most college stations' alternative status could be undermined by dominant institutions at any point.

8. Seth Sanders, interview with author, May 23, 2022.

9. "WHPK DJs Organize, Fight Back After Changes Result in Programming Cuts," WTTW News, November 7, 2016, https://news.wttw.com/2016/11/07/whpk-djs-organize-fight-back-after-changes-result-programming-cuts.

10. Moira McCormick, "Rap Central," *Chicago Tribune*, May 14, 2006, www.chicagotribune.com/news/ct-xpm-2006-05-14-0605130264-story.html. Common appeared on WHPK in 1996 in a legendary rap battle with Kanye West. Tomi Obaro, "Pioneering WHPK Keeps Chicago Rap Fresh," AvenueChicago, University of Chicago, https://arts.uchicago.edu/article/pioneering-whpk-keeps-chicago-rap-fresh.

11. "Aldermen Get an Earful of U. of C. Free Speech," *Chicago Tribune*, February 3, 1993.

12. Rudy Ray Moore, *The Rudy Ray Moore Zodiac Album*, vinyl, LP, Kent Sensuous Series, Kent Comedian Series (Comedian International Enterprises, 1972).

13. Public Telecommunications Act of 1992, Pub. L. No. 102-356, 106 Stat. 949 (1992). It is not clear if the station did comply with the rules regarding broadcast times or if this broadcast violated rules. Sanders interview, May 22, 2022.

14. Editorial, *Chicago Tribune*, February 5, 1993; Jaclyn H. Park, "Portrait of an Unzine: The Baffler Challenges the Masses to Get a Clue," *Chicago Magazine*, February 1994.

15. Scenes are distinct from musical communities. The term "community" implies a "population group whose composition is relatively stable," compared with a scene that constitutes a "field of practice" with transient members. Scenes, defined by Kruse, "encompass both the geographical sites of localized musical practice and the social and economic networks that exist within these contexts." Will Straw, "Systems of Articulation, Logics of Change: Communities and Scenes in Popular Music," *Cultural Studies* 5, no. 3 (October 1991): 373; Kruse, *Site and Sound*, 145.

16. Some stations, such as at MIT or the University of Michigan, experienced relative freedom from institutional control, with external bodies holding their licenses. Others were extensions of public relations or academic departments, particularly broadcasting or communications programs. Most were student activities, governed through the student senate or activities board and funded through student fees.

17. Anthony Kwame Harrison, "Black College-Radio on Predominantly White Campuses: A 'Hip-Hop Era' Student-Authored Inclusion Initiative," *Africology: The Journal of Pan African Studies* 9, no. 8 (2016): 136.

18. Numerous scholars have contributed college radio's history and analysis of its practices. Key works include Jennifer C. Waits, "From Wireless Experiments to Streaming: The Secret History and Changing Role of College Radio at Haverford College 1923–2014," *Interactions: Studies in Communication & Culture* 6, no. 1 (March 1, 2015): 65–85, https://doi.org/10.1386/iscc.6.1.65_1; Nicholas Rubin, "Signing On: U.S. College Rock Radio and the Popular Music Industry, 1977–1983," PhD diss., University of Virginia, 2010; Fauteux, *Music in Range*; Jennifer C. Waits, "Does 'Indie' Mean Independence? Freedom and Restraint in a Late 1990s US College Radio Community," *Radio Journal—International Studies in Broadcast and Audio Media* 5, no. 2 & 3 (2007): 83–96; Samuel J. Sauls, "The Role of Alternative Programming in College Radio," *Studies in Popular Culture* 21, no. 1 (1998): 73–81; Sauls, *The Culture of American College Radio* (Ames: Iowa State University Press, 2000); Samuel Brumbeloe, "A Cultural Study of WAPI: One Educational Radio Station and Its Shift to Entertainment," master's thesis, Auburn University, 2002; Rachael Desztich and Steven McClung, "Indie to an Extent? Why Music Gets Added to College Radio Playlists," *Journal of Radio Studies* 14, no. 2 (November 1, 2007): 196–211; Louis M. Bloch, *The Gas Pipe Networks: A History of College Radio, 1936–1946* (Cleveland, OH: Bloch, 1980); Tim Brooks, *College Radio Days: 70 Years of Student Broadcasting at Dartmouth College* (Greenwich, CT: Glenville Press, 2013); Andreas Preuss, "Left of the Dial, Right on the Music: 50 Years of Georgia State FM Radio," master's thesis, Georgia State University, 2021.

19. In the United States, the state "has always been a crucial and necessary player in the formation of media systems," including subsidies, government printing contracts, and in broadcasting regulation, and monopoly rights granted to commercial interests on the radio spectrum: a public property. The commercial structure of US broadcasting was not inevitable. Proponents for nonprofit and

educational broadcasting lobbied for alternatives leading up to and after the Communications Act of 1934, which established the FCC and the regulatory structure governing broadcasting. Robert W. McChesney and Dan Schiller, "The Political Economy of International Communications," United Nations Research Institute for Social Development, Technology, Business and Society, no. 11 (October 2003), 4; Robert W. McChesney, *Telecommunications, Mass Media, and Democracy: The Battle for the Control of U.S. Broadcasting, 1928–1935* (New York: Oxford University Press, 1994).

20. Scholars attribute this eclipse to the FCC's equation of public service with signal clarity, which privileged corporate networks. Still, ongoing tensions remained about the "private use of public airwaves." Michele Hilmes, *Only Connect: A Cultural History of Broadcasting in the United States* (Belmont, CA: Wadsworth/ Thomson Learning, 2002), 68–70; see also Hugh Richard Slotten, *Radio and Television Regulation Broadcast Technology in the United States, 1920–1960* (Baltimore: Johns Hopkins University Press, 2000); Slotten, *Radio's Hidden Voice: The Origins of Public Broadcasting in the United States* (Urbana: University of Illinois Press, 2009).

21. Delays resulted from shifting technology and regulation, such as the FCC's 1945 decision to move the FM spectrum allocation because of television. Slotten, *Radio and Television.*

22. The federal government shaped the policy, technological developments, and regulatory enticements and limits behind the evolution of educational and public broadcasting, including the early years of college radio. McChesney, *Telecommunications*; Ralph Engelman, *Public Radio and Television in America: A Political History* (Thousand Oaks, CA: Sage Publications, 1996); Slotten, *Radio's Hidden Voice*; Slotten, *Radio and Television*; Slotten, "'Rainbow in the Sky': FM Radio, Technical Superiority, and Regulatory Decision-Making," *Technology and Culture* 37, no. 4 (1996): 686–720, https://doi.org/10.2307/3107095; Slotten, "Universities, Public Service Radio and the 'American System' of Commercial Broadcasting, 1921–40, " *Media History* 12, no. 3 (December 2006): 253–72; Josh Shepperd, "The Political Economic Structure of Early Media Reform Before and After the Communications Act of 1934," *Resonance* 1, no. 3 (October 16, 2020): 244–66.

23. The Wisconsin Idea originated at the University if Wisconsin in the late nineteenth century. Chad Alan Goldberg, *Education for Democracy: Renewing the Wisconsin Idea* (Madison: University of Wisconsin Press, 2020), 4; Christopher H. Sterling and Michael C. Keith, *Sounds of Change: A History of FM Broadcasting in America* (Chapel Hill: The University of North Carolina Press, 2008), 94–95.

24. Slotten, *Radio's Hidden Voice*, 41, 240.

25. One chronicler of college radio considered stations' "coming of age" to be when national advertisers bought time. Bloch, *Gas Pipe Networks*, 69; Slotten, *Radio's Hidden Voice*, 41.

26. Radio's localism underwent repeated "pendulum" swings dating to when the federal government implemented the Federal Radio Commission in 1927 to regulate signals. After that decision, college stations fell under federal purview, leading to a decline in signals as national networks grew powerful. Localism in

radio returned as television eclipsed radio in the 1950s, but the pressures on local signals arose again. College radio's expansion in the 1970s and 1980s into a national influence in musical culture interacted with persistent local demands on these signals in a new era. Robert L. Hilliard and Michael C. Keith, *The Quieted Voice: The Rise and Demise of Localism in American Radio* (Carbondale: Southern Illinois University Press, 2005), 1–14; Zachary Joseph Stiegler, "The Policy and Practice of Community Radio: Localism Versus Nationalism in U.S. Broadcasting," PhD thesis, University of Iowa, 2009.

27. Shepperd, "Political Economic Structure," 245. See also Shepperd, *Shadow of the New Deal: The Victory of Public Broadcasting* (Champaign-Urbana: University of Illinois Press, 2023).

28. Tensions over educational radio revisit Jurgen Habermas's discussion of the public sphere as a "deliberative democracy." Yet critics highlighted the existence of multiple public spheres, or counterpublics, and the failures to fulfill the "needs of culturally distinct groups." See discussion in John Allen Hendricks, ed., *Radio's Second Century: Past, Present, and Future Perspectives* (New Brunswick, NJ: Rutgers University Press, 2020), 68–69, https://doi.org/10.2307/j.ctvwcjfxv.

29. Otis L. Graham, *An Encore for Reform: The Old Progressives and the New Deal* (New York: Oxford University Press, 1968), 181.

30. Ellen Schrecker, *The Lost Promise: American Universities in the 1960s* (Chicago: University of Chicago Press, 2021), 7.

31. Eric Weisbard, *Top 40 Democracy: The Rival Mainstreams of American Music* (Chicago: University of Chicago Press, 2014), 6, 22, 166–67.

32. These students extended the quest for the "cult of authenticity" in folk traditions unmarred by modern industrial society, what proved to be a malleable definition. Benjamin Filene, *Romancing the Folk: Public Memory and American Roots Music,* new ed. (Chapel Hill: The University of North Carolina Press, 2000), 49, 77.

33. Brian Ward, *Radio and the Struggle for Civil Rights in the South* (Gainesville: University Press of Florida, 2004), 350–51; Marquita S. Smith and Dorothy Bland, "Preserving and Tuning into Radio Stations at Historically Black Colleges and Universities," *Journal of Radio & Audio Media* (November 16, 2022): 1–23, https://doi.org/10.1080/19376529.2022.2137167. This study by Smith and Bland examines radio at HBCUs and finds a prevalence of outwardly directed signals and programming, as well as efforts to preserve records related to HBCU radio. Sophia Alvarez Boyd, "One Woman's Quest to Preserve the Radio Archives at Historically Black Colleges," *NPR*, February 16, 2020, sec. Education, www.npr.org/2020/02/16/806417287/one-womans-quest-to-preserve-the-radio-archives-at-historically-black-colleges. For the context of Black-owned and Black-oriented radio, as well as college radio at Howard University, see William Barlow, *Voice Over: The Making of Black Radio* (Philadelphia: Temple University Press, 1999), 237, passim.

34. Katherine Rye Jewell, "'Specialty' Listening; Creating Space for Queer Programming on American College Radio in the Long 1980s," in Sarah Crook and Charlie Jeffries, *Resist, Organize, Build: Feminist and Queer Activism in Britain and the United States during the Long 1980s* (Albany: State University of New York Press, 2022), 53–74.

35. Aaron Sternfield, "The College Campus: Record Marketplace, Talent Proving Ground," *Billboard*, March 27, 1965, 7.

36. Tom Donahue, "AM Radio Is Dead and Its Rotting Corpse Is Stinking Up the Airwaves . . . ," *Rolling Stone*, November 23, 1967.

37. Bill Lichtenstein, *WBCN and the American Revolution* (Cambridge, MA: MIT Press, 2021). WBCN in Boston employed a number of area college DJs. Many mainstream DJs and journalists also got their start in college radio, including Charlie Gibson (Princeton), Charles Osgood (Fordham), and numerous NPR hosts, producers, and off-air staff.

38. KMPX, and later WBCN in Boston among others, were populated by many former college radio DJs. Michael J. Kramer, *The Republic of Rock: Music and Citizenship in the Sixties Counterculture* (New York: Oxford University Press, 2013).

39. Sterling and Keith, *Sounds of Change*, 144–46, 170–71.

40. Examples include, among many, the University of Washington and the University of Kansas.

41. New left radicals were "constituting new centers of power in their selves, in individuals and communities," focusing locally, "quietly unhitched from demands for broad social change." Douglas C. Rossinow, *The Politics of Authenticity: Liberalism, Christianity, and the New Left in America* (New York: Columbia University Press, 1998), 344–45; Slotten, *Radio's Hidden Voice*, 41.

42. Oral histories of scenes document their emergence and growing coherence as a sound and an ecosystem. Examples include John Doe and Tom DeSavia, *Under the Big Black Sun: A Personal History of L.A. Punk* (Cambridge, MA: Da Capo, 2016); Jim Fricke, Charlie Ahearn, and Experience Music Project, *Yes Yes Y'all: The Experience Music Project Oral History of Hip-Hop's First Decade* (Cambridge, MA: Da Capo, 2002); Roger Gastman and Corcoran Gallery of Art, *Pump Me Up: DC Subculture of the 1980s* (Los Angeles: R. Rock Enterprises, 2013); Dewar MacLeod, *Kids of the Black Hole: Punk Rock in Postsuburban California* (Norman: University of Oklahoma Press, 2010); Steven Nodine, Eric Beaumont, Clancy Carroll, and David Luhrssen, *Brick through the Window: An Oral History of Punk Rock, New Wave and Noise in Milwaukee, 1964–1984* (Milwaukee, WI: Splunge Communications, 2017); Legs McNeill and Gillian McCain, *Please Kill Me: The Uncensored Oral History of Punk*, repr. ed. (New York: Grove, 2006); Marc Spitz and Brendan Mullen, *We Got the Neutron Bomb: The Untold Story of L.A. Punk* (New York: Three Rivers, 2001); Liz Worth, *Treat Me like Dirt: An Oral History of Punk in Toronto and beyond, 1977–1981* (Toronto: ECW, 2011); Mark Yarm, *Everybody Loves Our Town: An Oral History of Grunge* (New York: Three Rivers Press, 2012).; Lizzy Goodman, *Meet Me in the Bathroom: Rebirth and Rock and Roll in New York City 2001–2011*, repr. ed. (New York: Dey Street Books, 2018).

43. The terms "indie," "college," and "alternative" in relation to music are often used interchangeably. These broad terms usually signify "various guitar-based bands that began and in some cases remained on independent record labels" or that crossed over to mainstream airplay. Kruse, *Site and Sound*, 6–7, 143n73.

44. Alan O'Connor, *Punk Record Labels and the Struggle for Autonomy: The Emergence of D.I.Y.*, Critical Media Studies (Lanham, MD: Lexington Books, 2008), 4.

45. The "DIY universe was a mythic construct" never "independent of mainstream influence." But a DIY aesthetic was "crucial in defining [indie pop/rock music]." Kruse, *Site and Sound*, 11.

46. See Pierre Bourdieu, *Distinction: A Social Critique of the Judgement of Taste*, 11th ed. (Cambridge, MA: Harvard University Press, 2002).

47. I focus on college radio in its most literal sense: stations housed at, affiliated with, or supported by institutions of higher education. For a taxonomy of noncommercial radio stations, see Aaron J. Johnson, "Jazz and Radio in the United States: Mediation, Genre, and Patronage," PhD thesis, Columbia University, 2014, https://doi.org/10.7916/D83T9FCZ, 127–28.

48. These include CMJ, *The Source*, and charts compiled by the *Gavin Report*, *Rockpool*, and numerous chroniclers of rock music in the 1980s and 1990s, from *Spin* magazine to self-produced zines.

49. Variations on this phrase occur frequently in press about college radio. Kate X. Messer, "None of the Hits, All of the Time," *Austin Chronicle*, January 24, 1997, www.austinchronicle.com/music/1997-01-24/527252/; Jaime Wolf, "No Hits, All the Time: WFMU Stays Away from the Latest Trends. Its D.J.'s Would Rather Shape the Next One," *New York Times*, April 11, 1999; Fauteux, *Music in Range*, 29–34.

50. See Roderick A. Ferguson, *We Demand: The University and Student Protests* (Oakland: University of California Press, 2017); Teona Williams, "For 'Peace, Quiet, and Respect': Race, Policing, and Land Grabbing on Chicago's South Side," *Antipode* 53, no. 2 (2021): 497–523, https://doi.org/10.1111/anti.12692; LaDale C. Winling, *Building the Ivory Tower: Universities and Metropolitan Development in the Twentieth Century*, Politics and Culture in Modern America (Philadelphia: University of Pennsylvania Press, 2018), 100–101; Davarian L. Baldwin, *In the Shadow of the Ivory Tower: How Universities Are Plundering Our Cities* (New York: Bold Type Books, 2021), 25, 129. Scholars have established that the modern apparatus of campus policing, though it has long roots, evolved in the student protest era. Dylan Rodríguez, "Beyond 'Police Brutality': Racist State Violence and the University of California," *American Quarterly* 64, no. 2 (2012): 301–13.

51. Zine producers engaged in a process of authentic self-making, "creating an authentic medium of communication, expressing the thoughts and feelings of the authentic individual," creating "a world without any artifice, where they can express what they really feel and who they really are," all while discovering who that self is. Stephen Duncombe, *Notes from Underground: Zines and the Politics of Alternative Culture*, 3rd ed. (Portland: Microcosm Publishing, 1997), 40–41.

52. Recently, historians have analyzed the deep connections between media and politics. Kathryn Cramer Brownell, *Showbiz Politics: Hollywood in American Political Life* (Chapel Hill: The University of North Carolina Press, 2014); Nicole Hemmer, *Messengers of the Right: Conservative Media and the Transformation of American Politics* (Philadelphia: University of Pennsylvania Press, 2018); Brian Rosenwald, *Talk Radio's America: How an Industry Took Over a Political Party That Took Over the United States* (Cambridge, MA: Harvard University Press, 2019);

Heather Hendershot, *What's Fair on the Air? Cold War Right-Wing Broadcasting and the Public Interest* (Chicago: University of Chicago Press, 2011).

53. These developments rest on earlier history, as well, stretching back to the communications revolution of the late nineteenth century. Citizens' sense of self underwent a radical shift: "In a new world of personality and public relations (to say nothing of the new communications), the older republican vision seemed very distant." Technology and communications resided at the center of how Americans confronted politics and social and cultural changes of the twentieth century. Warren Susman, *Culture as History: The Transformation of American Society in the Twentieth Century* (Washington, DC: Smithsonian Books, 2003), xxii–xxiv.

54. Media theorist Stuart Hall stated in 1981, "Popular culture is one of the sites where this struggle for and against a culture of the powerful is engaged: it is also the stake to be won or lost in the struggle." Lawrence Grossberg, *Dancing in Spite of Myself: Essays on Popular Culture* (Durham, NC: Duke University Press, 1997), 7.

55. Steve Fraser and Gary Gerstle, eds., *The Rise and Fall of the New Deal Order, 1930–1980*, repr. ed. (Princeton, NJ: Princeton University Press, 1990); Arthur Meier Schlesinger, *The Disuniting of America: Reflections on a Multicultural Society*, rev. and enl. ed. (New York: W. W. Norton, 1998); Jefferson R. Cowie, *Stayin' Alive: The 1970s and the Last Days of the Working Class* (New York: New Press, 2012); Thomas Frank, *What's the Matter with Kansas?: How Conservatives Won the Heart of America* (New York: Picador, 2005).

56. See chapter 5 in Andrew Hartman, *A War for the Soul of America: A History of the Culture Wars* (Chicago: University of Chicago Press, 2015).

57. The Bayh-Dole Act of 1980 allowed universities to profit from innovations developed with federal grants and rendered "the marketplace rather than the public domain" as "the destination for knowledge." Winling, *Building the Ivory Tower*, 2, 6.

58. Gary Gerstle, *American Crucible: Race and Nation in the Twentieth Century* (Princeton, NJ: Princeton University Press, 2001), 345.

59. Among academics a form of "hard" multiculturalism emerged, one that elevated "cultural hybridity" rather than authentic purity instead seeking to "celebrate the construction of identities that are cosmopolitan, contingent, and fluid." Gerstle, 351.

60. Cody Dodge Ewert, *Making Schools American: Nationalism and the Origin of Modern Educational Politics* (Baltimore: Johns Hopkins University Press, 2022); Natalia Mehlman Petrzela, *Classroom Wars: Language, Sex, and the Making of Modern Political Culture* (New York: Oxford University Press, 2015); Hartman, *War for the Soul of America*, 222–30, 253–58. Battles over schooling and curricula for young people have a long history, developing new dimensions in the culture wars related to sex education, gender, and sexual identity as well as national identity and history.

61. In higher education, particularly the humanities, the "bipartisan neoliberal consensus that emphasizes job training as education's sine qua non" similarly undermined college radio's independence and value to administrators. Andrew Hartman, "The Culture Wars Are Dead: Long Live the Culture Wars!"; Hartman, *War for the Soul of America*.

62. Hilmes argued to see radio and television "as one of our nation's primary sites of cultural negotiation, dispute, confrontation, and consensus." Hilmes, *Only Connect*, 10.

63. Rock served as a central political signifier and concept used on all sides of culture-war battles to debate questions of national identity and culture. See Pekka M. Kolehmainen, "Rock, Freedom, and Ideologies of 'Americanness': U.S. Culture War Debates of the Late Twentieth Century" (doctoral diss., University of Turku, Finland, 2021).

64. Grossberg, *Dancing in Spite of Myself*, 7.

65. Duncombe, *Notes from Underground*, 114–15, 139.

66. Cultural gatekeepers "construct musical cultures and the scenes in which they circulate, establishing which musical forms and styles are in and which are out." Although they focused on "indie" music scenes, they were linked, though in opposition, to "more dominant expressions of musical culture." Fauteux, *Music in Range*, 131.

Part I

1. WBUR in Boston garnered controversy by firing Bader when he refused to read an ungrammatical announcement. Greg Lalas, "Fear on the Air," *Boston*, May 15, 2006, www.bostonmagazine.com/2006/05/15/fear-on-the-air-1/.

2. Robert Harris, undated recording, ca. 2018, author's collection.

3. In 1964 and 1966, the Supreme Court upheld the "community standards" test for obscenity, although expanding local standards to the national level thereby creating more protection for speech. Still, the Court offered few guidelines to define either prevailing community standards or obscenity. In *Jacobellis v. Ohio* (1964), Justice Potter Stewart refused to offer a clear definition and instead stated of obscene, irredeemable speech, "I know it when I see it." Jacobellis v. Ohio, 378 U.S. 184 (1964).

4. Ronald Sternberg, "Loss of Alumni Support Predicted," *Maroon*, May 9, 1968.

5. Joel Gandelman, "WRCU Shows Some Success and a Few Failures," *Maroon*, April 23, 1970.

6. "WRCU Experimenting with Early Morning Radio Slots," *Maroon*, February 15, 1968.

7. Kim Simpson, *Early '70s Radio: The American Format Revolution* (New York: Continuum, 2011), 106–8.

8. Harris, undated recording.

9. Ken Katkin, interview with author, June 25, 2021. The Princeton Bookstore was a reliable advertiser, along with a jewelry store that funded the morning classical music block. Selling ads for rock slots was a bit more challenging. Eventually, WPRB would institute a listener-funded model.

10. "The New Sound," WPRB press release, February 12, 1972, box 11, 1971–72.

11. Andy Pollack, "WPRB: 'Progressive Rock' with a Little of Everything," *Daily Princetonian*, June 3, 1972.

12. "KCSB Live Wire," October 22, 1980, Alexandria Digital Research Library, www.alexandria.ucsb.edu/lib/ark:/48907/f3s75jg4.

13. Bill Brewster, *Last Night a DJ Saved My Life: The History of the Disc Jockey* (New York: Grove, 2014), 70.

14. Nicholas Rubin identifies four "signifiers" for college radio, including highlighting artists with "minimal commercial airplay"; supporting "marginalized" or "challenging" musical styles; focusing musical rotations (the records, usually recent releases, selected for regular airplay) or DJ selections on independent-label releases; and facilitating mainstream success. Rubin, "Signing On: U.S. College Rock Radio and the Popular Music Industry, 1977–1983," PhD diss., University of Virginia, 2010, 4, 6, 9.

Chapter 1

1. Recording on YouTube, August 25, 2020, www.youtube.com/watch?v=BzRuo7_NRNM.

2. John Trezevant, "KLA Audience Claim Probably Only Static," *Daily Bruin*, October 4, 1974.

3. The FCC reserved a few spots for educational signals on AM in 1938. It reserved five spots for noncommercial, educational radio on the FM band in 1941, once the technology moved out of its experimental status and before shifting the FM spectrum to 88 to 108 MHz in 1945, with the included noncommercial setaside between 88 and 92 MHz.

4. Herman W. Land Associates, *The Hidden Medium: A Status Report on Educational Radio in the United States*, prepared for National Educational Radio, a division of the National Association of Educational Broadcasters, April 1967, I–2, I–3.

5. Aaron J. Johnson, "Jazz and Radio in the United States: Mediation, Genre, and Patronage," PhD thesis, Columbia University, 2014, https://doi.org/10.7916/D83T9FCZ.

6. Herman W. Land Associates, *Hidden Medium*, I–4.

7. See Elizabeth Tandy Shermer, *Indentured Students: How Government-Guaranteed Loans Left Generations Drowning in College Debt* (Cambridge, MA: The Belknap Press of Harvard University Press, 2021).

8. The Land report found college stations often were "the only outlet for serious contemporary music" blended with other "fine arts," including radio drama and "genuine culture" reaching "children in urban ghettos, serious students, Indians on reservations, invalids and isolated farmers." Herman W. Land Associates, *Hidden Medium*, I–12.

9. Kim Simpson, *Early '70s Radio: The American Format Revolution* (New York: Continuum, 2011).

10. Kate Sullivan, "KROQ: An Oral History," *Los Angeles Magazine*, November 2001, 91.

11. "KLA Resumes License Search," *Daily Bruin*, September 30, 1974.

12. Clippings, folder 13, box 26, KTRU.

13. Examples include the University of Kansas, with its reputable School of Journalism able to keep both signals populated with students.

14. Bruce J. Schulman, *The Seventies: The Great Shift in American Culture, Society, and Politics* (Cambridge, MA: Da Capo, 2002), 18–21; Joshua Clark Davis, *From Head Shops to Whole Foods: The Rise and Fall of Activist Entrepreneurs* (New York: Columbia University Press, 2017), 5, 34.

15. Thomas Frank, *The Conquest of Cool: Business Culture, Counterculture, and the Rise of Hip Consumerism* (Chicago: University of Chicago Press, 1997), 228.

16. Rob Tannenbaum, "We Built This S#!Tty: An Oral History of the Worst Song of All Time," GQ, August 31, 2016, www.gq.com/story/oral-history-we-built-this -city-worst-song-of-all-time; Bill Lichtenstein, *WBCN and the American Revolution* (Cambridge, MA: MIT Press, 2021). Between 1967 and 1974 is recognized as freeform's golden era, before corporatization and standardization crept in.

17. Oedipus, interview with author, June 11, 2015.

18. Mark Hamilton, interview with author, May 6, 2021. WZBC at Boston College developed this structure by the early 1980s.

19. In the 1970s, college radio stations became "radio's only exclusively freeform alternative music source following the demise of the commercial underground format." Christopher H. Sterling and Michael C. Keith, *Sounds of Change: A History of FM Broadcasting in America* (Chapel Hill: The University of North Carolina Press, 2008), 146, 147.

20. Oedipus interview.

21. Gina Arnold, *Route 666: On the Road to Nirvana* (New York: St. Martin's, 1993).

22. Oedipus interview.

23. Judy Wilburn, interview with author, March 22, 2018; Simpson, *Early '70s Radio*, 111–24.

24. Pleasant Gehrman in John Doe and Tom DeSavia, *Under the Big Black Sun: A Personal History of L.A. Punk* (Cambridge, MA: Da Capo, 2017), 34–35.

25. Michael Nevin Willard, "Skate and Punk at the Far End of the American Century," in *America in the Seventies*, ed. Beth L. Bailey and David R. Farber (Lawrence: University Press of Kansas, 2004), 183.

26. Wilburn interview.

27. Wilburn interview.

28. Wilburn interview.

29. Oedipus interview.

30. Arnold, *Route 666*, 24.

31. Marty Byk, interview with author, March 6, 2015.

32. Doe and DeSavia, *Under the Big Black Sun*, 7.

33. See Grace Elizabeth Hale, *Cool Town: How Athens, Georgia, Launched Alternative Music and Changed American Culture* (Chapel Hill: The University of North Carolina Press, 2020).

34. Popular music became "manufactured, marketed, and purchased like other consumer goods" in the 1890s. Exposing listeners to music, even passively, was an act of promotion. A paradox emerged: music democratized as products saturated American life, but saturation depended on mass production and capital investment.

David Suisman, *Selling Sounds: The Commercial Revolution in American Music* (Cambridge, MA: Harvard University Press, 2012), 7–18, 242.

35. Susan J. Douglas, *Listening In: Radio and the American Imagination* (Minneapolis: University of Minnesota Press, 2004), 5–11.

Chapter 2

1. George Epsilanty, "Music Moves On," *San Francisco Foghorn*, September 20, 1978.

2. Stuart Hall, *Cultural Studies 1983: A Theoretical History*, ed. Jennifer Daryl Slack and Lawrence Grossberg, repr. ed. (Durham, NC: Duke University Press, 2016).

3. Jefferson R. Cowie, *Stayin' Alive: The 1970s and the Last Days of the Working Class* (New York: New Press, 2012), 315.

4. Alice Echols, *Hot Stuff: Disco and the Remaking of American Culture* (New York: W. W. Norton, 2011), 194, 197, 209.

5. Bruce J. Schulman, *The Seventies: The Great Shift in American Culture, Society, and Politics* (Cambridge, MA: Da Capo, 2002), 121.

6. Simon Reynolds, *Rip It Up and Start Again: Post-Punk 1978–84* (London: Faber and Faber, 2006), 1–5.

7. "And Now for Something Completely Irreverent," *San Francisco Foghorn*, September 21, 1979.

8. Jennifer Waits, "Panel Explores Past, Present and Future of KUSF," *Radio Survivor* (blog), August 31, 2013, www.radiosurvivor.com/2013/08/panel-explores -past-present-and-future-of-kusf/; "After Decades, KDNZ Pulls the Plug," *San Francisco Foghorn*, September 10, 2009, https://sffoghorn.com/after-decades-kdnz -pulls-the-plug/.

9. Ben H. Bagdikian, *The New Media Monopoly: A Completely Revised and Updated Edition with Seven New Chapters* (Boston: Beacon, 2004), 28. When Bagdikian's critique of media consolidation appeared in 1983, fifty corporations owned major media outlets. By the re-release of his book in 2004, there were just five companies dominating media ownership in the United States.

10. Determining the "first" college radio station depends on how one defines a radio broadcast. Among the first, Iowa State's WOI emerged from experiments dating to 1911. Jennifer Waits, "Spinning Indie: Where Was the First College Radio Station in the U.S.?," *Spinning Indie* (blog), September 15, 2008, http:// spinningindie.blogspot.com/2008/09/where-was-first-college-radio-station.html; Waits, "College Radio Watch: Who's on First?," *Radio Survivor* (blog), May 6, 2016, www.radiosurvivor.com/2016/05/college-radio-watch-whos-first.

11. Eileen Levy, "WGFR—Educational Radio—Debuts Monday," *Post Star* (Glens Falls, NY), January 14, 1977.

12. Herbert Marcuse and Douglas Kellner, *One-Dimensional Man: Studies in the Ideology of Advanced Industrial Society*, 2nd ed. (Boston: Beacon, 1991), 1.

13. "And Now."

14. Consolidation also occurred internationally. Pekka Gronow, Ilpo Saunio, and Christopher Moseley, *An International History of the Recording Industry* (London: Cassell, 1999), 136.

15. Gronow, Saunio, and Moseley, 136.

16. For examples of playlists where DJs did focus on punk and new wave, and early independent artists, see Charles A. Spoylar's playlists, 1980, Charles A. Spolyar KZSU Playlist Collection (SC1001), Dept. of Special Collections and University Archives, Stanford University Libraries, Stanford, CA.

17. Andreas Preuss, "Left of the Dial, Right on the Music: 50 Years of Georgia State FM Radio," master's thesis, Georgia State University, 2021, 2.

18. Joel Ackerman to Langdale, June 27, 1976, Ackerman folder, box 1, WRAS.

19. Elizabeth Tandy Shermer, *Indentured Students: How Government-Guaranteed Loans Left Generations Drowning in College Debt* (Cambridge, MA: The Belknap Press of Harvard University Press, 2021), 245.

20. Preuss, "Left of the Dial," 11.

21. Preuss, 31–33.

22. Station report on Golob promotion, July 19, 1974, Ackerman folder, box 1, WRAS.

23. "WRAS Checked on Media Bias," *Signal*, January 17, 1976; "No Racial Bias Found in GSU Student Media," *Signal*, February 2, 1976.

24. Undated minutes, Garretson hearings folder, box 2, WRAS.

25. Preuss, "Left of the Dial," 12.

26. Doug Jackson, interview by Andreas Preuss, digital recording, n.d., Preuss's personal collection.

27. Joanne Kaufman, "Outrageous Anita," *Detroit*, March 22, 1987 in clippings, Anita Sarko personal records, care of Erzen Krvica.

28. W. B. Reeves, "Angry Sarko Leaves WRAS," *Signal*, September 25, 1978.

29. Reeves; James Tarbox, "I Stand behind Jackson's Action," *Signal*, October 2, 1978.

30. Tarbox, "I Stand Behind"; "WRAS Harassed: Tarbox's Tire Cut," *Signal*, October 30, 1978.

31. Michael Diamond and Adam Horovitz, *Beastie Boys Book* (New York: Spiegel & Grau, 2018), 124–31.

32. The name varied over time and institutionalized, published by College Media, Inc. For simplicity's sake, I refer to the publication as CMJ across its iterations, identified by the date of publication.

33. Ed Harrison, "Magazine Slants to Programmers," *Billboard*, January 20, 1979.

34. Mike Parent, "Choice Cuts—The B-52's," *Inferno*, October 1, 1979, 17.

35. CMJ Five-Year Anniversary Issue, 1983.

36. CMJ Five-Year Anniversary Issue.

37. Jennifer Waits, "70th Annual IBS College Radio Conference Hits NYC," *Radio Survivor* (blog), March 4, 2010, www.radiosurvivor.com/2010/03/70th-annual-ibs -college-radio-conference-hits-nyc/.

38. Harrison, "Magazine Slants to Programmers."

39. Ed Harrison, "Labels Slashing Back College Radio Support," *Billboard*, August 11, 1979.

40. WXCI's Top 100 Albums of 1979, WXCI 1, 19.

41. Bruce Goldsen to Executive Board, June 4, 1980, WXCI 1, 10.

42. Goldsen to Executive Board.

43. CMJ Communication, *CMJ*, March 1, 1979, 30.

44. "On Campus," *Boston Globe*, December 6, 1978.

45. David Bittan, "For a Smorgasbord of Music, Tune in 103.3 on Your FM Dial," *This Week*, February 27, 1977.

46. Larry Copeland, "GSU Black Leaders Say 'Key Is Involvement,'" *Signal*, March 31, 1981.

47. Copeland.

48. Caudell likely referred to the station's rotation of heavy, medium, and light airplay. Individual DJs might play other artists in between these selections.

49. Letters, *Signal*, April 7, 1981.

50. Jennifer Lynn Stoever, *The Sonic Color Line: Race and the Cultural Politics of Listening*, repr. ed. (New York: NYU Press, 2016), 231.

51. Letters, *Signal*, April 14, 1981.

52. Letters, *Signal*, July 21, 1981; August 4, 1981.

53. Cheryl Lauer, "Dylan to Devo: WRAS Rocks On," *Signal*, February 23, 1982.

54. Lauer; Letters, *Signal*, March 2, 1982.

55. "Student Fee Allocations," *Signal*, May 25, 1982.

56. WRAS playlist, *Signal*, June 28, 1983.

57. WRAS playlist.

58. "Regents to Vote on WRAS Future," *Signal*, October 4, 1983; Letters, *Signal*, October 11, 1983. The FCC approved WRAS's signal expansion across Atlanta's eighteen counties in 1982. The Board of Regents approved the plan in 1983. Tax- and fee-paying students had a right to service, Walker argued.

59. Diana Minardi, "Senators Vote Support for WRAS," *Signal*, October 11, 1983.

60. Henry Santoro, interview with author, March 21, 2021; KFJC cassette, ca. 1981 and Cynthia Lombard, "1981 U2 Interview at KFJC," March 11, 2020, *KFJC History Blog* (blog), https://spidey.kfjc.org/39289/1981-u2-interview-at-kfjc/.

61. KOHL "Graffiti Book," Students: Print, 28.2, Ohlone College Archives, Fremont, CA.

Chapter 3

1. Phil Williams, "A Matter of Balance at WUOG," undated clipping, WUOG 1, 1981.

2. Williams.

3. Phil Williams, letter to WUOG, October 16, 1980, WUOG 4.

4. In 1979, a former DJ "took over" the station on Halloween, causing improper program logging and charges of intimidation. The incident prompted officials to contact the FCC, whereas most incidents remained local scuffles over silly pranks or unprofessional announcing. Chuck Reece, "WUOG Worker May File Charges in Station Takeover," *Red and Black*, November 15, 1979.

5. Paul Riismandel, "Radio by and for the Public: The Death and Resurrection of Low-Power Radio," in Michele Hilmes and Jason Loviglio, eds., *Radio Reader: Essays in the Cultural History of Radio* (New York: Routledge, 2002), 429.

6. Christopher H. Sterling and Michael C. Keith, *Sounds of Change: A History of FM Broadcasting in America* (Chapel Hill: The University of North Carolina Press, 2008), 148.

7. John R. Thelin, *A History of American Higher Education*, 3rd ed. (Baltimore: Johns Hopkins University Press, 2019), 337–43.

8. Sterling and Keith, *Sounds of Change*, 147.

9. Ben H. Bagdikian, *The New Media Monopoly: A Completely Revised and Updated Edition with Seven New Chapters* (Boston: Beacon, 2004), 258–59.

10. Ben Ginsberg, "WXPN Faces Standards Inquiry, Possible U. Controls," *Daily Pennsylvanian*, December 5, 1973.

11. Larry Field, "Trustee Unit to Present Vet Proposal," *Daily Pennsylvanian*, October 2, 1975; Martin Siegel, "Trustee Group Delays Formal WXPN Action," *Daily Pennsylvanian*, October 3, 1975.

12. Martin Siegel, "FCC Fines WXPN $2000," *Daily Pennsylvanian*, December 5, 1975.

13. Jeffrey N. Barker, "FCC Denies WXPN-FM License," *Daily Pennsylvanian*, April 5, 1977. Penn maintained a carrier-current signal that continued until a storm damaged its tower, and it continues online. Jennifer Waits, "Spinning Indie: Radio Station Field Trip 64 - WQHS at University of Pennsylvania," *Spinning Indie* (blog), October 7, 2014, https://spinningindie.blogspot.com/2014/10/radio-station-field -trip-64-wqhs-at.html.

14. At WRAS at Georgia State, for example, administrators consulted the same lawyers as those who advised WXPN, which clearly influenced their attempts to intervene in station affairs. Deborah Matthews, "Mass Firings Cause WRAS Shutdown," *Signal*, September 25, 1979.

15. "GTB Review Panel Confirms Suspension of Two Staffers," *Hoya*, February 19, 1976. Students resumed broadcasting under new call letters in 1982, and they secured the letters WGTB in 1985. "About," WGTB, August 3, 2010, http://georgetownradio.com/about; Guy Raz, "Radio Free Georgetown," *Washington City Paper*, January 29, 1999, http://washingtoncitypaper.com/article/274469/radio-free -georgetown/.

16. David Dugle, "Frank Zappa on Insanity Palace January 1976," Insanity Palace and More (podcast), www.podomatic.com/podcasts/dugledavid/episodes /2015-02-28T22_18_05-08_00.

17. "KTUH Timeline," KTUH, https://ktuh.org/timeline, accessed December 28, 2019.

18. "University's FM Station Applies for Power Boost," *Honolulu Star-Bulletin*, January 3, 1980.

19. Riismandel, "Radio by and for the Public," 432.

20. Riismandel.

21. Riismandel.

22. Michael P. McCauley, *NPR: The Trials and Triumphs of National Public Radio* (New York: Columbia University Press, 2005), 49.

23. Riismandel, "Radio by and for the Public," 435.

24. Sterling and Keith, *Sounds of Change*, 147.

25. Riismandel, "Radio by and for the Public," 432; "Second Report and Order," Pub. L. No. F.C.C. 78-384, Docket No. 20735; RM-1974; RM-2655 (1978) 245–46.

26. "Second Report and Order," 247.

27. "Second Report and Order," 250.

28. Letters, WUOG 4.

29. "Radio KZSC Cranks Up the Juice," *Santa Cruz Sentinel*, May 30, 1980.

30. Matt Speiser, "They used to laugh at KZSC . . . ," *Watsonville Register-Pajaronian*, June 3, 1980.

31. Anna Feldman, "FCC May Approve Boost, but University Hesitates," *Chicago Maroon*, January 23, 1980.

32. Letters, *Chicago Maroon*, January 27, January 30, 1980.

33. Aarne Elias, "Watts Tied to Improvements," *Chicago Maroon*, February 13, 1981.

34. Jeff Makos, "WHPK: Still Spinnin' after All These Years," *University of Chicago Chronicle*, vol. 15, no. 7, December 7, 1995; Eric Zorn, "U. of C. Free-form Station . . ." *Chicago Tribune*, July 11, 1985.

35. Darrell WuDunn, "WHPK Nears Power Increase," *Chicago Maroon*, January 19, 1982.

36. Margo Hablutzel, "WHPK Gets 100 Watt OK," *Chicago Maroon*, May 25, 1982.

37. Editorials, *Chicago Maroon*, November 19, 1982.

38. Letters, *Chicago Maroon*, January 14, 1983.

39. Letters, January 14, 1983.

40. Randy Kelly, "Radio," *Chicago Maroon*, September 28, 1985.

41. "Second Report and Order," 246.

42. "About," *WFCS 107.7 The Edge* (blog), www.wfcsradio.com/about/.

43. "90.1 on Your FM Dial," *Inferno*, February 1, 1979.

44. Larry Roberg, "WFCS Goes FM Stereo," *Inferno*, May 5, 1981.

45. Roberg.

46. Suzanne Sataline, "College Station Needs Power Boost to Avoid Being Tuned Out," *Hartford Courant*, October 10, 1986.

47. Sataline.

48. Suzanne Sataline, "WFCS Will Fight for a New Spot on FM Dial," *Hartford Courant*, November 11, 1986; "About," WFCS.

49. "Thompson Nabs DAV Post," *Davidsonian*, December 9, 1977.

50. "Down in Iredell," *Statesville Record and Landmark*, November 21, 1977.

51. Sheri Gravett, "High Power Coming Soon?," *Davidsonian*, December 16, 1977.

52. Letters, *Davidsonian*, April 9, 1976.

53. Bertis Downs, interview with author, March 27, 2017.

54. "Bluegrass Dumped by WUOG," *Red and Black*, January 16, 1975; "WUOG Additions to Format for This Week," *Red and Black*, October 24, 1974; and "Additions to WUOG Playlist for This Week," October 31, 1974.

55. Letters, *Red and Black*, February 5, 1975.

56. Sandi Martin, "Violations Possible in WUOG 'Joke,'" *Red and Black*, April 5, 1975.

57. Rodger Lyle Brown, *Party Out of Bounds: The B-52's, R.E.M., and the Kids Who Rocked Athens, Georgia* (New York: Plume, 1991), 41.

58. See Grace Elizabeth Hale, *Cool Town: How Athens, Georgia, Launched Alternative Music and Changed American Culture* (Chapel Hill: The University of North Carolina Press, 2020).

59. Brown, *Party Out of Bounds*, 91. Downs, interview with author, July 23, 2020.

60. The state pursued its own public radio station, a decades-long fight that would eventually lead to the takeover of part of Georgia State's broadcast license in 2014.

61. Letters, *Red and Black*, January 30, 1981. The GPBC pursued consolidation because of complicated coverage in the state's public broadcasting, focusing mostly on television service. Sharon J. Salyer, "Conflict, Competition Divide Georgia Public Broadcasting Effort," *Atlanta Constitution*, May 17, 1981, 4-B.

62. David Nelson, "Telecommunications Merger Bill Now Dead, but Idea Remains Alive," *Red and Black*, February 17, 1981.

63. Editorial, *Red and Black*, September 19, 1980.

64. "The WUOG Study," *Red and Black*, November 14, 1980.

65. Bob Keyes, "WUOG Gets Coordinator," *Red and Black*, January 9, 1981.

66. "WUOG Silenced," *Red and Black*, February 19, 1981; Michael Marcotte, "The Turbulent Years," WUOG Reunion, October 1997 in *Airwaves*, Spring 1998, WUOG 4.

67. Keyes, "WUOG Gets Coordinator."

68. Tim Savelle, "Fired Students File for Injunction, Seek Jobs, Return of WUOG to Air," *Red and Black*, February 20, 1981; Salynn Byoles and Tim Savelle, "Powell: WUOG to Be Run as Tight Organization," *Red and Black*, February 27, 1981.

69. Marcotte, "Turbulent Years."

70. Lauren Schad, "WUOG Changes and Management Anger Song Jocks" *Red and Black*, February 5, 1981.

71. Powell to Mike Henry and staff, April 6, 1981, WUOG 1.

72. Conoly Hester, "WUOG Closes to Reorganize," *Banner*, WUOG, 1991 album.

73. "WUOG Closes to Reorganize," *Red and Black*, June 30, 1981.

74. "WUOG," *Red and Black*, February 19, 1981.

75. *Athens Observer*, September 1981, Album 1982, WUOG 1.

76. "1980," *Red and Black*, January 8, 1981.

77. "New Challenges at WUOG," *Red and Black*, April 7, 1981.

78. Boycott materials, box 4, folder 14, Wesleyan Radio Records.

Chapter 4

1. Michael Diamond and Adam Horowitz, *Beastie Boys Book* (New York: Spiegel & Grau, 2018), 58.

2. Bill Holland, "Students Told to Key on Promotion of New Product," *Billboard*, March 20, 1982.

3. Holland.

4. KOHL "Graffiti Book."

5. Lee Abrams in CMJ Five-Year Anniversary issue, 42.

6. Stations in several markets played progressive and new wave music in the late 1970s, including KROQ in Los Angeles and WZIR in Buffalo, NY. Katkin, interview with author, June 18, 2021.

7. Abrams in CMJ Five-Year Anniversary issue.

8. John Rockwell, "The Pop Life," *New York Times*, March 21, 1981.

9. Board Meeting Minutes, October 9 and November 18, 1979, WESU 2:1.

10. Board Meeting Minutes, February 4, 1980, WESU 2:1.

11. Candidates Statements, Spring 1980 Election, WESU 2:1.

12. Wesleyan Broadcast Association Directors, May 7, 1980, WESU 2:1.

13. Jeff Tamarkin, "The Five Year Plan," *CMJ Five-year Anniversary Issue*, 1983, p. 9.

14. Minutes, Board of Directors, March 6, 1980, WESU 2:1.

15. Jack Isquith, interview with author, August 13, 2020.

16. Mark Hamilton, interview with author.

17. Stan Reaves to Perry Cooper, April 11, 1975, folder 1-40, WHCU Department of Black Affairs records, #4904, Division of Rare and Manuscript Collections, Cornell University Library.

18. KOHL "Graffiti Book."

19. Tamarkin, "Five Year Plan."

20. Ed Harrison, "Labels Slashing Back College Radio Support," *Billboard*, August 11, 1979, 1.

21. In the 1970s, radio consultant Lee Abrams recognized FM's failing business model even as listenership rose. His "adult" approach to "progressive, album-oriented" rock radio left the underground behind. Data-driven programming sold well, and he advised stations across the country to bring fans the music they wanted most—without experimental or less-commercially viable cuts. Marc Fisher, *Something in the Air: Radio, Rock, and the Revolution That Shaped a Generation* (New York: Random House, 2007), 195.

22. Harrison, "Labels."

23. Rich Totoian, 178 A&M FM Radio Speech, www.onamrecords.com/audio /TotoianSpeech1978.m4a, accessed November 18, 2018 (site inoperative).

24. Totoian.

25. WRAS Playlists, July 10, 1980, WRAS 3.

26. WMBR Book AA, 46, 47.

27. Michael Azerrad, *Our Band Could Be Your Life: Scenes from the American Indie Underground 1981–1991* (New York: Back Bay Books, 2002), 5.

28. WMBR Book AB, 103.

29. WMBR Book AB, 103.

30. Lori Blumenthal, interview with author.

31. Mike Howe, Arista Records, to College Radio Programmers, August 16, 1980, WMBR Book AB, 214.

32. DJ note, WMBR Book AB, 240.

33. Meeting of the Wesleyan Broadcast Association Board of Directors, September 14, 1980, WESU 2.2.

34. WWUH History, http://www.wwuh.org/history/history5.htm.

35. Colin McEnroe, "College Stations Silence Records in Money Dispute," *Hartford Courant*, September 24, 1980.

36. Meeting of the Wesleyan Broadcast Association Board of Directors, September 28, 1980, WESU 2.2.

37. Statement of Principles, WESU 4.2.

38. Wesleyan Broadcast Association Board of Directors meeting, October 21, 1980, WESU 2.2.

39. Ad, *Daily Iowan*, December 4, 1980.

40. "Arista Revenues Hop 69% Over '79," *Billboard*, September 27, 1980.

41. Doug Hall, "Arista Charging College Stations Fee," *Billboard*, September 27, 1980.

42. "College Station Arista Boycott Gains Strength," *Billboard*, November 15, 1980.

43. Alan Penchansky, "Rx for College Record Cutbacks: 'Sell' Your Stations, Labels Urge," *Billboard*, November 29, 1980.

44. President's Newsletter, IBS, November 1980, WESU 2.14.

45. "350 Collegians Seek Promo Disk Upswing," *Billboard*, November 22, 1980.

46. President's Newsletter.

47. President's Newsletter.

48. Hall, "Arista."

49. Penchansky, "Rx for College Record Cutbacks."

50. WMBR Book AB, 215, WMBR, Walker Memorial Building, Cambridge, MA.

51. WMBR Book AB, 228.

52. WMBR Book AB, 232.

53. WMBR Book AB, 252.

54. Joel Selvin, "Lively Arts," *San Francisco Examiner*, December 7, 1980.

55. Selvin.

56. President's Newsletter.

57. "The Arista Decision: United We Stand," excerpted from CMJ in IBS newsletter, November 1980, WESU 4.14.

58. Jeff Fleming to Board of Directors, February 2, 1981, WESU 2.2.

59. Candidate Statements, February 24, 1981, WESU 2.2.

60. Board of Directors Meeting, February 3, 1981; Candidates Statements, Spring 1981, WESU 2.2.

61. CMJ excerpts in "Arista Decision."

62. "Arista Decision."

63. Azerrad, *Our Band*, 11.

Chapter 5

1. Jack Rabid, interview with author, January 3, 2015.

2. Ben H. Bagdikian, *The New Media Monopoly: A Completely Revised and Updated Edition with Seven New Chapters* (Boston: Beacon, 2004); Susan Krieger, *Hip Capitalism* (Beverley Hills, CA: Sage, 1979). The rise of cultural studies and Stuart

Hall's 1983 lectures presented culture as a site of negotiation and meaning. Stuart Hall, *Cultural Studies 1983: A Theoretical History*, ed. Jennifer Daryl Slack and Lawrence Grossberg, repr. ed. (Durham, NC: Duke University Press, 2016); Hua Hsu, "Stuart Hall and the Rise of Cultural Studies," *New Yorker*, July 17, 2017, www .newyorker.com/books/page-turner/stuart-hall-and-the-rise-of-cultural-studies; Kevin Mattson, *We're Not Here to Entertain: Punk Rock, Ronald Reagan, and the Real Culture War of 1980s America* (New York: Oxford University Press, 2020).

3. Gina Arnold, *Route 666: On the Road to Nirvana* (New York: St. Martin's, 1993), 49.

4. Jeff Tweedy, *Let's Go (So We Can Get Back): A Memoir of Recording and Discording with Wilco, Etc.* (New York: Dutton, 2019), 25.

5. Will Oldham, interview with author, March 22, 2019; Britt Walford, interview with author, June 19, 2021.

6. Craig Finn, interview with author, September 3, 2020.

7. For gender and underground subcultures, see Sara Marcus, *Girls to the Front: The True Story of the Riot Grrrl Revolution* (New York: Harper Perennial, 2010). College DJs weren't always thrilled by requests. As one DJ complained in 1987, he was inundated with phone calls from "12 year old skate punks for the Butthole Surfers because their parents won't buy it for them." "Gripes and Groans" studio notebook, 05, KTRU 26.

8. Curfews and anti-skateboarding ordinances emerged from conceptions of teenagers as prone to "delinquency, violence, or nonconformity." Patsy Eubanks Owens, "No Teens Allowed: The Exclusion of Adolescents from Public Spaces," *Landscape Journal* 21, no. 1 (2002): 156; Hanson O'Haver, "A Crime and a Pastime: The Paranoid Style of American Skateboarding," *Baffler*, no. 40 (2018): 68.

9. Timothy S. Brown, "Subcultures, Pop Music and Politics: Skinheads and 'Nazi Rock' in England and Germany," *Journal of Social History* 38, no. 1 (2004): 157.

10. Kyle Riismandel, *Neighborhood of Fear: The Suburban Crisis in American Culture, 1975–2001* (Baltimore: Johns Hopkins University Press, 2020), 104–7.

11. C. Carr coined the term "bohemian diaspora" in the *Village Voice* to describe the diffusion of cultural rebellion and aesthetics across space in the 1980s. Grace Elizabeth Hale, *Cool Town: How Athens, Georgia, Launched Alternative Music and Changed American Culture* (Chapel Hill: The University of North Carolina Press, 2020), 2, 12.

12. Mary Mancini, "Book Your Own F*ckin' Life (Feat. Bert)," Lucy's Record Shop, www.lucysrecordshop.com/episodes/bert. *Book Your Own Fuckin' Life* zine by *Maximum Rocknroll* emerged later to catalog scenes, telling music fans what stations, venues, and labels and bands to explore from scenes across the country.

13. Stephen Duncombe, *Notes from Underground: Zines and the Politics of Alternative Culture* 3rd ed. (Portland: Microcosm Publishing, 1997, 2017), 36, 57.

14. Brian Fauteux, *Music in Range: The Culture of Canadian Campus Radio*, Film and Media Studies (Waterloo, Ontario: Wilfrid Laurier University Press, 2015), 173.

15. Douglas C. Rossinow, *The Politics of Authenticity: Liberalism, Christianity, and the New Left in America* (New York: Columbia University Press, 1998), 344.

16. Vatican Commandos was from Darien, Connecticut, with the electronic musician Moby as a member.

17. "Indie" emerged as a descriptor of production and distribution and revisited the concept of 1930s concepts of folk less for its business model or market and more for the values and ideas provoked. The DJs and stations explored in this chapter acted as cultural arbiters, some with more power and others more grassroots, occupying a negotiated and transactional role. The goal was a decentralized cultural dissemination so that diverse and regional sources could contribute to a meaningful culture. Benjamin Filene, *Romancing the Folk: Public Memory and American Roots Music*, new ed. (Chapel Hill: The University of North Carolina Press, 2000), 5, 147–48.

18. Rabid interview; *The Big Takeover*, Issue 2.

19. Rabid interview; *The Big Takeover*, Issue 2.

20. *The Big Takeover* Vol. 1, June 14, 1980.

21. *The Big Takeover*, Vol. 1; Rabid interview.

22. *The Big Takeover*, Issue 8.

23. *The Big Takeover*, Issue 6.

24. *The Big Takeover*, Issue 6, Issue 8.

25. *The Big Takeover*, Issue 6, Issue 8.

26. *The Big Takeover*, Issue 8.

27. Cynthia Lombard, "Digging into 1980 Program Guide—KFJC History," *KFJC History Blog* (blog), October 7, 2019, https://spidey.kfjc.org/37844/digging-into-1980-program-guide/.

28. *The Big Takeover*, February 1983.

29. Letters, *Cooper Point Journal*, December 7, 1973; January 21, 1974; June 4, 1974.

30. Millie Brombacher, "KAOS Comes Across," *Cooper Point Journal*, February 27, 1975.

31. Matt Groening, "KAOS: Radio as an Art Form," *Cooper Point Journal*, July 1, 1976.

32. "A Walk through the Future College Activities Building," *Cooper Point Journal*, April 3, 1979.

33. Geoff Kirk, "89 1/3 FM Intense KAOS," *Cooper Point Journal*, November 8, 1979.

34. Bruce Pavitt, interview with author, July 24, 2020.

35. "Welcome to Sub Pop Country," in Bruce Pavitt, Calvin Johnson, Ann Powers, Larry Reid, Gerard Cosloy, and Charles R. Cross, *Sub Pop USA: The Subterraneanan Pop Music Anthology, 1980–1988* (Brooklyn, NY: Bazillion Points, 2014), 7.

36. "New Pop! Manifesto," *Sub Pop #1* in Pavitt, Johnson, Powers, Reid, Cosloy, and Cross, *Sub Pop USA*, 14, 15.

37. "New Pop! Manifesto," 21.

38. Arm Pit to Steve Kreitzer, October 27, 1983, Turmoil, box 3:1983.

39. Malcolm to Kreitzer, no date, Turmoil, box 3: 1983.

40. Letters, Turmoil, box 3:1984.

41. Jack Talcum to Kreitzer, August 14, 1984, Turmoil, box 3: 1984.

42. John Lieb to Kreitzer, March 12, 1984, Turmoil, box 3: 1984.

43. Bill Holland, "Students Told to Key On Promotion of New Product," *Billboard*, March 20, 1982.

44. Playlists, Turmoil box 8: Playlists 1983, 1984.

45. Letters, February 1983, Turmoil, box 3: 1983.

46. Playlist for the Two Weeks Ending March 12, 1983, Turmoil, box 8: Playlists 1983

47. Letters, February 24, 1984, Turmoil, box 3: 1984.

48. Marcy Hirschfeld, Music Director Notes, February 24, 1984, Turmoil, box 3:1984.

49. "Gripes and Groans," 1981; 1982–83.

50. Undated letter, Turmoil, box 2: undated.

51. KTRU directors meeting minutes, 1983, Turmoil, box 2: 1983.

52. Poster, KTRU elections, 1970–1980s, KTRU box 26:1.

53. Poster.

54. Poster.

55. Directors Meeting Minutes, September 29, 1982, KTRU box 26:2.

56. Directors Meeting Minutes, October 13, 1982, KTRU box 26:2.

57. Five-year plan meeting, KTRU box 26:2.

58. Staff Meeting Minutes, January 18, 1984, KTRU box 26:3.

59. DJ Policy Meeting, June 7, 1984.

60. DJ Policy Meeting.

61. "XTC: Live in Concert and at KUSF," *Foghorn*, April 10, 1981.

62. In 1983, some eighty AOR "SuperStars" stations adopted Abrams's model. He explained, "We're cutting way back on acts no longer in existence, like Thin Lizzy. And we've cut way back on Led Zep." Instead, he focused more on new wave artists to draw listeners in the 25-to-34 age bracket. Lee Abrams, "Billboard Meets Signal Changes in AOR Programming" *Billboard,* February 5, 1983.

63. Jeff Tamarkin, "The Five Year Plan," *CMJ Five-year Anniversary Issue*, 1983, 9.

Chapter 6

1. "WBAU Annual Ascertainment Report (for period ending 2/1/80)," WBAU 1:11.

2. Jeff Chang, *Can't Stop, Won't Stop: A History of the Hip-Hop Generation* (New York: St. Martin's, 2005), 240.

3. Chang, 238.

4. "Bill Stephney," The Cipher, April 3, 2017, https://theciphershow.com/episode/195/.

5. "Chuck D '84, '13 (Hon.)," in Chang, *Can't Stop, Won't Stop*, 238.

6. Chuck D, address at Adelphi University, Hempstead, NY, April 16, 2019.

7. Don Mosley, "WHUS," *Connecticut Daily Campus*, April 1, 1977.

8. John A. Centra, "College Enrollment in the 1980s: Projections and Possibilities," *Journal of Higher Education* 51, no. 1 (1980): 18–39.

9. Ladale C. Winling, *Building the Ivory Tower: Universities and Metropolitan Development in the Twentieth Century*, Politics and Culture in Modern America (Philadelphia: University of Pennsylvania Press, 2018), 154–55.

10. WMBR Book AB, 10–11.

11. Winling, *Building the Ivory Tower*, 164, 170, 172.

12. WMBR Book AB, 47, 48.

13. WMBR Book AB, 56, 88.

14. Email from DJ, March 14, 2022.

15. WMBR Book AB, 57, 59.

16. WMBR Book AB, 62, 63.

17. WMBR Book AB, 64, 71.

18. WMBR Book AB, 64, 72.

19. WMBR Book AB, 72, 91, 93.

20. WMBR Book AB, 67.

21. WMBR Book AB, 78, 83.

22. WMBR Book AB, 86.

23. WMBR Book AB, 99.

24. WMBR Book AB, 101.

25. WMBR Book AB, 111–12.

26. WMBR Book AB, 145.

27. "Radio Radio Radio . . . ," *The Tech*, September 26, 1980.

28. "Fee Assessment—KZSU Yes," *Stanford Daily*, October 10, 1978; "Referendum May Decide WJMU's Future," *Decatur Daily Review*, February 20, 1980; "Students to Pull Plug on Station," *Los Angeles Times*, July 21, 1981; "Uconn Radio Links Survival to Fee Hike," *Hartford Courant*, April 9, 1985; "SDSU Council Hold Key to Fate of Campus Radio," *Los Angeles Times*, May 14, 1980.

29. "Milliken Is New Boss at WXYC," *Daily Tar Heel*, October 1, 1976; Leslie Scism, "CGC Committee Chops Already Smaller 'Yack' Request," *Daily Tar Heel*, April 19, 1977.

30. Becky Burcham, "WXYC-FM," *Daily Tar Heel*, August 25, 1977; Bernie Ransbottom, "WXCY Heads Want New Directing Board," *Daily Tar Heel*, September 15, 1977.

31. Letters, *Daily Tar Heel*, September 22, 1977.

32. Howard Troxler, "CGC Abates WXYC Straits, Grants Station over $16,000," *Daily Tar Heel*, September 16, 1977; Bernie Ransbottom, "Board, WXYC Confront Problems," *Daily Tar Heel*, September 19, 1977; Howard Troxler, "CGC Held in Filibuster on Moss Budget," *Daily Tar Heel*, October 20, 1977.

33. "Campus Organizations Offered Access to WXYC Airtime," *Daily Tar Heel*, October 5, 1977.

34. Letters, *Daily Tar Heel*, February 22, 1978.

35. Letters, February 23, 1978.

36. Susan Ladd, "WXYC Listenership Low; Station Manager Undaunted," *Daily Tar Heel*, February 22, 1978.

37. "Radio," *Daily Tar Heel*, June 1, 1978.

38. Cam Johnson, "Media Board, WXYC Relations," August 30, 1978; Roann Bishop, "Board Names New 'XYC Station Manager," *Daily Tar Heel*, March 26, 1979.

39. David Rome, "WXYC Manager Adds His Own Touch," *Daily Tar Heel*, April 14, 1982.

40. Natalie Eason, "WXYC Has Music for All," *Daily Tar Heel*, April 19, 1980.

41. Bill Pschel, "CGC Frees Radio Budget" *Daily Tar Heel*, June 12, 1980.

42. Elaine McClatchey, "'XYC Station Head, Engineer to Resign," *Daily Tar Heel*, October 8, 1980.

43. McClatchey.

44. Elaine McClatchey, 'Station Manager Named," *Daily Tar Heel*, October 16, 1980.

45. Letters, November 17, 1980.

46. Rome, "WXYC Manager."

47. Editorial, *Daily Tar Heel*, April 15, 1982.

48. Letters, *Daily Tar Heel*, April 19, 1982

49. Letters, April 19, 1982.

50. Letters, *Daily Tar Heel*, April 21, 1982; April 22, 1982.

51. Charles Burres, "UC's Rotten Deal for Punks: Radio Station Gets a Dose of Culture," *San Francisco Examiner*, November 7, 1982.

52. Kathleen Newman, interview with author, April 14, 2020.

53. Burres, "UC's Rotten Deal"; "The FM Dial," *San Francisco Examiner*, March 31, 1985.

54. "UC-Run KALX Serves as Mammoth Training Force," *San Francisco Examiner*, June 7, 1987.

55. "UC-Run KALX."

56. Ken Wheeler, "Are the Keane Children Running College Radio?," *KALX Program Guide*, Spring 1986, box 1, folder 19, Josh Gottheil Collection, RRHOF.

57. Insert, *KALX Program Guide*, Summer 1986.

58. John Lee, "Breaking into the Club Scene," *KALX Program Guide*, Spring 1986.

59. "FM Dial."

Part II

1. Mark Bilus, "Music, Radio & the Music Industry: A Look Back, a Look Ahead," CMJ (1978–83 issue).

2. Editorial, *The Big Takeover*, no. 19, December 1985.

3. Opening Statement, *The Big Takeover* no. 20, July 1986.

4. Musician Steve Albini said CMJ "reminded him more of a word-processing software convention than a new music seminar." Jack Rabid, "Into the Pool," *Rockpool*, November 22, 1985.

5. David Ciaffardini, "U.S.: College Radio Crumbling?," *Maximum Rocknroll*, no. 34, March 1986.

6. Letters, *Rice Thresher*, March 12, 1993.

Chapter 7

1. Evan Minsker, "Watch Trent Reznor's Full Speech Inducting the Cure at Rock Hall 2019," Pitchfork, March 29, 2019, https://pitchfork.com/news/read-trent -reznors-speech-inducting-the-cure-at-rock-hall-2019/.

2. Playlists, Steve Wainstead Collection, box 1, folder 12, ARC-0120, Rock and Roll Hall of Fame Library and Archives, Cleveland, OH.

3. Descendents, *Milo Goes to College* (LP liner) (San Pedro, CA: New Alliance Records, 1982).

4. Gina Arnold, *Route 666: On the Road to Nirvana* (New York: St. Martin's, 1993), 26.

5. Alan O'Connor, *Punk Record Labels and the Struggle for Autonomy: The Emergence of D.I.Y.* Critical Media Studies (Lanham, MD: Lexington Books, 2008), 4. See Pierre Bourdieu, *The Field of Cultural Production* (New York: Columbia University Press, 1993).

6. *Billboard* reported that Columbia University, Fordham University, and Seton Hall radio stations, alongside Pacifica station WBAI, had the market share for Latin radio in the city, thanks to shows such as *Alma Latina, Son del Caribe, Nueva Cancion y Demas, Algo Diferente* segments, and *Latin Expressions* that provided a broad range of voices within the multivaried genre, including live performances and artist interviews. Tony Sabournin, "Latin FM Radio: Non-Commercial Outlets Are Carrying the Weight in New York Marketplace," *Billboard*, July 24, 1982, 53.

7. Susan J. Douglas, *Listening In: Radio and the American Imagination* (Minneapolis: University of Minnesota Press, 2004), xvii. Douglas demonstrated how radio was a social construction, resulting from shifting representations of individuals and institutions.

8. Monroe Anderson, "Conservatism, Cutbacks Stir Black Students," *Chicago Tribune*, March 21, 1982. In Urbana, WEFT-FM appeared in 1981 and provided an alternative to the commercially oriented WPGU, operating as a community station with a listener-funded model. Lorri Coey, Bob Paleczny, and Brian Zelip, "History of WEFT," WEFT 90.1 FM, http://new.weft.org/partners/.

9. Bill Wyman, "So Many Records, So Little Time?," *Chicago Reader*, November 15, 1990, www.chicagoreader.com/chicago/wxrt-so-many-records-so-little-time/Content?oid=876653.

10. Jon Ginoli, interview with author, April 19, 2020; Jon Slocum, interview with author, April 17, 2020.

11. Fanzines for Champaign-Urbana, Josh Gottheil Collection, ARC-0150, Box 1, undated folder, RRHOF.

12. Britt Walford, interview with author, June 19, 2021.

13. Holly Kruse, *Site and Sound: Understanding Independent Music Scenes* (New York: Peter Lang, 2003), 52–54.

14. *Better than Nothing*, October 1986, 7, Josh Gottheil Collection, Box 1, Folder 23, RRHOF. .

15. Keaton Bell, "How the Go-Go's Found Their Beat: An Oral History," *Vogue*, August 4, 2020, www.vogue.com/article/go-gos-40th-anniversary-beauty-and-the-beat-oral-history-belinda-carlisle.

16. Lee Abrams, Five Year Anniversary edition, CMJ New Music Report 1983, 42.

17. Steve Pond, "College Radio's Brave New Wave," *Rolling Stone*, September 29, 1983.

18. "College LPs," *Rolling Stone*, November 10, 1983, 32.

19. Pond, "College Radio's Brave New Wave."

20. Pond.

21. Harry Weinger, "College Radio Making Impact at Retail and Concert Level," *Cash Box*, October 1, 1983.

22. CMJ, October 10, 1983.

23. CMJ, October 10, 1983.

24. CMJ, October 24, 1983.

25. CMJ, January 16, 1984.

26. Kruse, *Site and Sound*, 86.

27. Jim Cameron, "New Media, Squeezes Out Old" in *Progressive Media 5th Anniversary Special*.

28. Patti Galluzzi, interview with author, June 19, 2017; David Lavallee, "Ratings Rise at WBRU," *Brown Daily Herald*, January 29, 1985.

29. Lavallee, "Ratings Rise at WBRU."

30. Galluzzi interview.

31. Galluzzi interview.

32. Galluzzi interview; Anthony DeCurtis, "The Taste Makers: College Radio's Growing Clout," *Rolling Stone*, September 25, 1986.

33. Weinger, "College Radio."

34. Russell Shaw, "New Music Thriving in Athens," *Billboard*, October 15, 1983.

35. CMJ, October 24, 1983.

36. CMJ, November 21, 1983.

37. CMJ, October 24, 1983.

38. CMJ, October 24, 1983.

39. CMJ, October 24, 1983; November 7, 1983; November 21, 1983.

40. Brent Giessmann, interview with author, January 6, 2017.

41. Tom King, "The Greatest Band You Never Heard," *Street Level* (podcast), Lawrence.com, August 11, 2006, www.lawrence.com/podcasts/street_level/2006/aug/11/john_nichols_embarrassment/.

42. A biographer called Burroughs "a clandestine agent in the development of rock'n'roll—a spectral figure who haunted the cultural underground and helped usher it into the mainstream." Casey Rae, *William S. Burroughs and the Cult of Rock n Roll* (Austin: University of Texas Press, 2019), 3.

43. Brent Giessman, interview with author, January 6, 2017.

44. Matt Wall, "A Quick History of the Embarrassment," The Embarrassment, www.embos.org/history.htm, accessed November 22, 2–22.

45. Giessmann interview.

46. Giessmann interview.

47. Giessmann interview.

48. Michelle Green, "Boston's Hard Rocking Del Fuegos Are Unspoiled by Money, but Hope to Change That Soon," *People*, March 3, 1986, https://people.com/archive/bostons-hard-rocking-del-fuegos-are-unspoiled-by-money-but-hope-to-change-that-soon-vol-25-no-9/.

49. Meg Dixit, "KUSF Awarded Gold Album," *San Francisco Foghorn*, September 28, 1988.

50. Kruse, *Site and Sound*, 86–88.

Chapter 8

1. Post, Records of the NFCB, 12:11.

2. Dennis McDougal, "A Campus Crusader Marches On," *Los Angeles Times*, August 29, 1987.

3. Post, Records of the NFCB, 12:11.

4. The PMRC purported to act informatively, not to censor, so parents could assert authority and record labels would face incentives to act responsibly. Claude Chastagner, "The Parents' Music Resource Center: From Information to Censorship," *Popular Music* 18, no. 2 (May 1999): 181.

5. Andrew Hartman, *A War for the Soul of America: A History of the Culture Wars* (Chicago: University of Chicago Press, 2015), 230–31.

6. Nicola Krest, interview with author, June 3, 2022.

7. David Heidelberger, "KCSB Radio: Irrelevant," *El Gaucho*, November 25, 1968.

8. Letters, *El Gaucho*, January 17, 1968.

9. "Unruh Breaks Up College Fist Fight," *San Francisco Examiner*, January 16, 1969.

10. Steve Plevin, "KCSB Keeps BSU Rally Tapes; Sheriff Deputies Denied Access," *El Gaucho*, January 15, 1969.

11. Plevin.

12. Plevin.

13. Editorial, *El Gaucho*, January 16, 1969.

14. Steven M. Plevin, "Obscenity Rally Draws 1500; Harassment of Blacks Charged," *El Gaucho*, January 16, 1969.

15. Ronald Weissman, "Fascist Left," *El Gaucho*, January 24, 1969.

16. Antonelli v. Hammond, US District Court for the District of Massachusetts, 308 F. Supp. 1329 (D. Mass. 1970), February 5, 1970.

17. Bill Moser, interview with author, December 20, 2018; Kathe Kirchmeier, "Mates Closes WCWP, Fires Post," *Pioneer*, December 3, 1970.

18. "Kunstler Offers to Assist Post College Sit-In Group," *Daily News*, December 4, 1970.

19. Jeffrey N. Barker, "FCC Denies WXPN-FM License," *Daily Pennsylvanian*, April 5, 1977.

20. Allan Bloom, *The Closing of the American Mind: How Higher Education Has Failed Democracy and Impoverished the Souls of Today's Students* (New York: Simon & Schuster, 1987).

21. Dennis McDougall, "He's Crusader against Indecency," *Los Angeles Times*, August 20, 1987.

22. Kevin Mattson, *We're Not Here to Entertain: Punk Rock, Ronald Reagan, and the Real Culture War of 1980s America* (New York: Oxford University Press, 2020), 291.

23. Mattson, 175.

24. Marcie Morris, "KCSB General Manager Proposes Fund-Raising," *Daily Nexus*, April 17, 1981.

25. "KCSB Livewire," Fall 1980.

26. "KCSB Livewire," Spring 1980.

27. "Pretenders Interviewed on KCSB," *Daily Nexus*, February 19, 1982.

28. Krest interview.

29. The PMRC originally proposed an "X" rating for albums with explicit lyrics. Albums with songs pertaining to drug and alcohol use ("D/A"), occult themes ("O"), and violence ("V") also earned the PMRC's scrutiny. Gary Raskin, "Record Rating: What's Next?," *Daily Nexus*, October 31, 1985.

30. Raskin.

31. Chastagner, "Parents' Music Resource Center," 184.

32. Richard Rifkin, "The Beauty of Freedom," *Nexus*, November 7, 1985.

33. Frank Zappa considered the spectacle a distraction from tax policies being proposed. Dee Snider and John Denver, "Record Labeling: Hearing before the Committee on Commerce, Science, and Transportation," United States Senate, Ninety-ninth Congress, First Session on Contents of Music and the Lyrics of Records, September 19, 1985, (Washington, D.C.: U.S. Government Printing Office, 1985).

34. Gary Morrison to Nathan Post, November 15, 1985, NFCB 12:11.

35. Nathan Post to Mrs. Albert Gore, July 29, 1986, NFCB 12:11.

36. Edward E. Burch to Mrs. James A. Baker, III, September 17, 1986, NFCB 12:11.

37. James C. McKinney to Regents of the University of California, September 22, 1986, NFCB 12:11; Heidi Soltesz, "FCC Inquires into KCSB's Practices after Complaints," *Daily Nexus*, October 9, 1986.

38. The letter arrived "by accident" to KCSB first, though it was "intended for Regental response."

39. Stuart Wolfe to Tamara Scott, October 22, 1986, NFCB, 12:11.

40. Editorial and letters, *Nexus*, October 1, 1986.

41. Letters, *Nexus*, October 23, 1986.

42. "So You Wanna Be a Punk, Eh?," *Nexus*, January 29, 1987.

43. Memorandum Opinion and Order, April 16, 1987, FCC 87-138.

44. "FCC Will Issue a Warning to KCSB," *Nexus*, April 17, 1987.

45. FCC v. Pacifica Foundation, 438 U.S. 726 (1978).

46. In 1988, the D.C. Circuit Court of Appeals required the FCC to clarify its safe harbor hours, but Congress passed a stringent law requiring regulating indecent content during all hours. This law, passed in an appropriations bill, was overturned in 1991. Congress established 6 A.M. to midnight as hours when children might be watching in 1993 in the Public Telecommunications Act, which the D.C. Circuit also overturned. In 1995, the FCC limited the ban on indecency in broadcasting to between 6 A.M. and 10 P.M. The Telecommunications Act of 1996 put in place the rating system for content, though this had less relevance for radio broadcasters. David Crook and Penny Pagano, "FCC Cracking Down on Radio 'Indecency,'" *Los Angeles Times*, April 17, 1987; Sydney Shaw, "FCC Tightens Rules on Obscenity," UPI archives, April 16, 1987, www.upi.com/Archives/1987/04/16/FCC

-tightens-rules-on-obscenity/6012545544000/; "Ideas & Trends" *New York Times*, April 18, 1977; Action for Children's Television v. FCC, 852 F.2d 1332, 1339 (D.C.Cir. 1988) ("ACT I"); Action for Children's Television v. FCC, 932 F.2d 1504, 1508 (D.C. Cir. 1991), cert. denied, 112 S. Ct. 1282 (1992) ("ACT II"); Action for Children's Television v. FCC, 58 F.3d 654, 657 (D.C. Cir. 1995), cert. denied, 116 S. Ct. 701 (1996) ("ACT III").

47. Caroline E. Mayer, "FCC Curbs Radio, TV Language," *Washington Post*, April 17, 1987.

48. Editorial, *Nexus*, April 21, 1987.

49. Cartoon, *Nexus*, April 21, 1987; Anne Claridy, "Council Opposes FCC Decision on Obscenity Issue," *Nexus*, April 24, 1987.

50. "KCSB Changes Little One Month after FCC Warning," *Nexus*, May 13, 1987.

51. Steven Elzer, "New KCSB Manager Aims for Student Control, Involvement," *Nexus*, May 29, 1987.

52. Krest interview. The Associated States put KCSB's funding, along with other activities fees, to a vote in 1988 and 1989. Ben Sullivan, "Measure Asks for Fee Hike," *Nexus*, April 19, 1988; "Yes on KCSB," *Nexus*, April 24, 1989.

53. Dennis McDougal, "A Campus Crusader Marches On," *Los Angeles Times*, August 29, 1987.

54. Heidi Solteaz, "FCC Inquires Into KCSB's Practices After Complaints," *Nexus*, October 9, 1986.

55. "President's Newsletter," November 1986, Intercollegiate Broadcasting System, in WESU 2:12.

56. "President's Newsletter," WRAS 2, Watts folder.

57. "President's Newsletter."

58. "President's Newsletter."

59. *Making Appropriations for the Departments of Commerce, Justice, and State, the Judiciary and Related Agencies for the Fiscal Year Ending September 30, 1989, and for Other Purposes*, Pub. L. No. 100-459, Sec. 608, 102 Stat. 2186, 2228 (1988).

60. "President's Newsletter," WRAS 2, Watts folder.

61. Ray Shea, "Radio Stations and PMRC Spar over Freedom of Speech," *Thresher*, July 21, 1987, 3.

62. Caroline Mayer, "Obscenity: FCC Expands Its Vocabulary," *Boston Globe*, April 17, 1987.

63. MAM, WMBR Book AF, WMBR, 154.

64. Station Policy Governing Broadcast of Indecent or Obscene Material, WMBR Book AN.

65. The Technology Broadcasting Corporation, Meeting Minutes, June 11, 1987, WMBR Book AO.

66. Technology Broadcasting Corporation.

67. Connie Cunningham, "WRAS Not Affected by FCC Indecency Rules," *Signal*, November 17, 1987.

68. Marc Fisher, "The Making of Sean Hannity: How a Long Island Kid Learned to Channel Red-State Rage," *Washington Post*, October 10, 2017, sec. Style, www .washingtonpost.com/lifestyle/style/the-making-of-sean-hannity-how-a-long

-island-kid-learned-to-channel-red-state-rage/2017/10/09/540cfc38-8821-11e7
-961d-2f373b3977ee_story.html.

69. Fisher.

70. Valerie Hamilton, "How Sean Hannity Began His Path to Punditry on Santa Barbara Community Radio," April 21, 2018, www.kqed.org/news/11664214/how -sean-hannity-began-his-path-to-punditry-on-santa-barbara-community-radio.

71. Adam Moss, "Program's Validity Faces Challenge," *Nexus*, May 25, 1989; Adam Moss, "Controversial Radio Show Not Renewed," *Nexus*, June 26, 1989; Adam Moss, "Ex-KCSB Radio Talk Show Host Reinstated," *Nexus*, November 20, 1989.

72. Stacy Sullivan, "KCSB, Fraternity Break Ties over Alleged Prejudice," *Nexus*, October 15, 1990.

73. Krest interview; "Ex-KCSB Talk Show Host Reinstated"; Fisher, "Making of Sean Hannity."

74. Editorial, *Nexus*, June 28, 1989; letters, *Nexus*, July 5, 1989.

Chapter 9

1. Heron Marquez Estrada, "Conservative Voice Makes Itself Heard on Campus," *Santa Cruz Sentinel*, November 17, 1985.

2. Kelefa Sanneh, *Major Labels: A History of Popular Music in Seven Genres* (New York: Penguin, 2021), 29, 54–55.

3. Brian Rosenwald, *Talk Radio's America: How an Industry Took Over a Political Party That Took Over the United States* (Cambridge, MA: Harvard University Press, 2019), 18.

4. Alan Brinkley, *Voices of Protest: Huey Long, Father Coughlin, & the Great Depression* (New York: Vintage, 1983); Nicole Hemmer, *Messengers of the Right: Conservative Media and the Transformation of American Politics* (Philadelphia: University of Pennsylvania Press, 2018); Heather Hendershot, *What's Fair on the Air? Cold War Right-Wing Broadcasting and the Public Interest* (Chicago: University of Chicago Press, 2011); Rosenwald, *Talk Radio's America*, 24. The Pacifica Foundation, which had provided pacifist, progressive radio programming since the 1940s and shaped community radio, also underwent a process of centralization. Jeffrey Land, *Active Radio: Pacifica's Brash Experiment* (Minneapolis: University of Minnesota Press, 1999), 10, 144–46.

5. Jon Pareles, "A Case against Censoring Rock Lyrics," *New York Times*, May 3, 1987.

6. Program director Ken Katkin produced new programs that would be useful for area residents, including a talk show to provide a venue for high school students to share their thoughts and connect with one another. Ken Katkin, interview with author, June 25, 2021.

7. Robert Christgau, "Creative Censorship," *Village Voice*, February 3, 1987.

8. Chris Mohr, interview with author, October 30, 2020; John Swenson, "The Cure Asks Radio Stations Not to Play 'Killing an Arab,'" UPI Archives, January 29, 1987, www.upi.com/Archives/1987/01/20/The-Cure-asks-radio-stations-not-to-play -Killing-an-Arab/5488538117200/.

9. "The Cure Asks."

10. "The Cure Asks"; Christgau, "Creative Censorship"; Anthony DeCurtis, "Cure, Arab Group Reach Accord on Song," *Rolling Stone*, 494, February 26, 1987; Jon Pareles, "College Radio Rocks the Top 40 Boat," *New York Times*, February 13, 1988.

11. Christgau, "Creative Censorship"; DeCurtis, "Cure, Arab Group Reach Accord."

12. Minutes, WPRB 6; Mohr interview.

13. Hendershot, *What's Fair*, 18–19.

14. Rosenwald, *Talk Radio's America*, 2.

15. Barbara Lynne Harris, "UC President Gardener Says He Still Opposes Divestment," *Tribune*, May 1, 1987.

16. J. Rodgers in "The Full and Unabridged History of KALX," KALX 90.7FM Berkeley, www.kalx.berkeley.edu/full-and-unabridged-history-kalx.

17. Cesar Padilla, *Daily Nexus*, January 23, 1986; Airplay September 9, Turmoil: box 6: 1987.

18. Subgroup 2, WOBC Oberlin Papers, University Archives, Oberlin College, OH.

19. Gripes and Groans books, 5 and 6, KTRU.

20. Peter J. Boyer, "Fairness Doctrine: F.C.C. Struggled with Itself Six Years before Reversing a Policy It Opposed," *New York Times*, August 6, 1987; see also Donald J. Jung, *The Federal Communications Commission, the Broadcast Industry, and the Fairness Doctrine, 1981–1987* (Lanham, MD: University Press of America, 1996).

21. "VU Radio Gets Control Panel," *Tennessean*, April 3, 1966.

22. "VU to Get FM Station," *Tennessean*, February 2, 1971.

23. "WRVU-FM Series of Focus on Blacks at VU," *Tennessean*, September 9, 1979.

24. Robert K. Oermann, "Rock Show to Help Keep WRVU on Air," *Tennessean*, April 3, 1987.

25. "WRVU Has Top Number of DJ Vote-Getters," *Tennessean*, November 17, 1987.

26. "A Program Named Sue, or 'George,'" *Tennessean*, March 23, 1989.

27. Margaret Deckbar, "Klansman's VU Speech Part of 'Open Forum," *Tennessean*, October 7, 1974.

28. Cynthia Floyd, "VU Radio Blasted for Klansman Guest," *Tennessean*, April 18, 1988.

29. WRVU E-Staff, "The Commandments of 91 Rock" (Fall 1985), Nick Archer, personal collection.

30. Michael P. McCauley, *NPR: The Trials and Triumphs of National Public Radio* (New York: Columbia University Press, 2005), 2, 9–10.

31. Spencer Harrington, "WKCR Haitian Program Draws Fire," *Columbia Spectator*, April 4, 1986.

32. Spencer Harrington, "WKCR Ethnic Shows under Attack," *Columbia Spectator*, September 12, 1986.

33. Harrington.

34. Scott Susin, "Haitians Protest at WKCR Jazz Fest," *Columbia Spectator*, November 24, 1986.

35. Letters, *Columbia Spectator*, December 4, 1986.

36. Aaron J. Johnson, "Jazz and Radio in the United States: Mediation, Genre, and Patronage," PhD thesis, Columbia University, 2014, https://doi.org/10.7916/D83T9FCZ, 46.

37. Johnson, 47.

38. Johnson, 121.

39. "'Dean of Jazz' Celebrates 25th Year on WKCR," *Columbia University Record*, February 10, 1995.

40. Jazz's "adoption on noncommercial radio increased at a pace with the ouster of the music from commercial radio and the growing recognition of jazz as an art form in U. S. educational institutions," although its place there has grown more tenuous. Johnson, "Jazz and Radio," 54.

41. Justin A. Williams, *Rhymin' and Stealin: Musical Borrowing in Hip Hop* (Ann Arbor: University of Michigan Press, 2013), 49.

42. Williams, 51–52.

43. Letters, *Columbia Spectator*, December 4, 1986.

44. Johnson, "Jazz and Radio," 121.

45. Francis Davis, "A Note of Discord Over Jazz at Temple Station," *Philadelphia Enquirer*, April 14, 1985.

46. Johnson, "Jazz and Radio," 53.

47. Louise E. Chernonsky, "Imagining Listeners through American Experimental Music: NPR's RadioVisions," in *Tomorrow Is the Question: New Directions in Experimental Music Studies*, ed. Benjamin Piekut (Ann Arbor: University of Michigan Press, 2014), https://doi.org/10.3998/mpub.5242620, 229, 247.

48. The key study was David Giovannoni's "Cheap 90" in 1985. A later study, "Audience 88," segmented public radio's listening audience, yielding the educated and socially conscious profile, and led to the "gradual abandonment of the checkerboard programming" of block schedules that promoted diversity but "tended to drive listeners away." McCauley, *NPR*, 79–80; Jack W. Mitchell, *Listener Supported: The Culture and History of Public Radio* (Westport, CT: Praeger, 2005), 121.

49. Francis Davis, "At WRTI, Dissension over Jazz Continues," *Philadelphia Inquirer*, January 3, 1986. Another clash emerged ten years later, when WRTI implemented cut jazz programming again and alienating listeners. Kevin L. Carter, "Laments, Suspicions for WRTI," *Philadelphia Inquirer*, September 16, 1997.

50. Patrick Muñoz, "Spinning Disks," *Foghorn*, September 14, 1988.

Chapter 10

1. Louise E. Chernonsky, "Imagining Listeners through American Experimental Music: NPR's RadioVisions," in *Tomorrow Is the Question: New Directions in Experimental Music Studies*, edited by Benjamin Piekut (Ann Arbor: University of Michigan Press, 2014), https://doi.org/10.3998/mpub.5242620, 26.

2. Jack W. Mitchell, *Listener Supported: The Culture and History of Public Radio* (Westport, CT: Praeger, 2005), 121.

3. Scholars have noted how NPR cultivated a "white public space" and cultural logic. See Christopher Chávez, *The Sound of Exclusion: NPR and the Latinx Public*

(Tucson: University of Arizona Press, 2021). Matthew Lasar, *Uneasy Listening: Pacifica Radio's Civil War* (Cambridge, UK: Black Apollo, 2006), 90.

4. David Giovannoni, interview with author, December 11, 2021.

5. Numerous examples of administrative takeovers, reprogramming of stations, or the implementation of professional staff occur throughout college radio history, but they accelerated in the 1980s. "Entire Student Management Staff of SU's WAER Now Departed," *Syracuse Herald-Journal*, April 25, 1983. See WAER Collection, University Archives, Special Collections Research Center, Syracuse University Libraries, Syracuse University, NY.

6. Lasar, *Uneasy Listening*, 182; Jeremy Tunstall, *Communications Deregulation: The Unleashing of America's Communications Industry* (New York: B. Blackwell, 1986), 150.

7. Lasar, *Uneasy Listening*, 183–84.

8. "Structural convergence" in the entertainment industry accelerated in the 1980s from relaxed antitrust regulation and applying "principles of individual freedom to practicalities of market freedom." Jennifer Holt, *Empires of Entertainment: Media Industries and the Politics of Deregulation, 1980–1996* (New Brunswick, NJ: Rutgers University Press, 2011), 9–11, 54, 58.

9. Patrik Munoz, "Spinning Disks," *Foghorn*, September 14, 1988.

10. Steve Pond, "College Radio's Brave New Wave," *Rolling Stone,* September 29, 1983. Tony Wikicki to Rev. James N. Loughran S.J. November 19, 1984. KXLU 1: 10.

11. Ralph Rugoff, "The Only Alternative Left," *Los Angeles Herald*, May 5, 1985.

12. Rugoff.

13. Wikicki to Loughran, March 15, 1985, KXLU 1:10.

14. Rev. Richard H. Trame to Walter Arlen, June [2]8, 1985, KXLU 1:10.

15. Some students blended NPR-syndicated news programs with local coverage. Occasionally, students produced the content, such as in Manhattan, Kansas, where Kansas State University students and staff produced *AM Manhattan* in 1986. The station's operations manager explained, "We realize we can't match the quality of 'Morning Edition,' but we're hoping that NPR listeners will give us a chance." Weekends remained for students to explore new music, including *Metal Head* and a bluegrass show. "KSDB Changes Programming," *Manhattan Mercury*, February 5, 1986.

16. Eva Gampel to Trame, August 2, 1985, KXLU 1:10.

17. Trame to Loughran, August 6, 1985, KXLU 1:10.

18. Lisa Kos to Gampel, October 29, 1985, KXLU 1:10.

19. Trame to Gampel, November 5, 1985, KXLU 1:10.

20. Gampel to Mark Morris, January 2, 1986, KXLU 1:10.

21. Mark Morris to Gampel, March 3, 1986, KXLU 1:10.

22. Gampel to Loughran, January 21, 1986, KXLU 1:10.

23. Trame to Loughran, February 6, 1986, KXLU 1:10.

24. Paul D. Boyer to Gampel, undated, KXLU 1:10.

25. Loughran to Trame, February 17, 1986, KXLU 1:10.

26. Trame, Statement, March 1, 1986, KXLU 1:10.

27. Trame to Gampel, March 1, 1986, KXLU 1:10.

28. Trame to Judy Puckett, May 20, 1986, KXLU 1:10.

29. Trame to Loughran, May 20, 1986, KXLU 1:10.

30. Trame to Loughran.

31. Trame to Loughran.

32. Trame to Morris, May 21, 1986. Trame to Morris, May 29, 1986.

33. Petition, May 20, 1986, KXLU 1:10.

34. Hank Durand, Summary of KXLU Meeting, June 5, 1986, KXLU 1:10.

35. Trame to Henry Bodkin Jr., October 24, 1986, KXLU 1:10.

36. Trame to Bodkin, November 20, 1986, KXLU 1:10.

37. Trame to Morris, November 17, 1986, with marginalia, KXLU 1:10.

38. Trame to Angus Hawkins, November 22, 1986, KXLU 1:10.

39. Trame to Morris and Durand, December 8, 1986, KXLU 1:10.

40. Morris to Durand, November 23, 1986, KXLU 1:10.

41. Gampel to Classical Music Listeners, December 1, 1986.

42. Lori Pike, "College Radio Stations Critical of FCC Edict," *Los Angeles Times*, August 20, 1987.

43. Clipping from *L.A. Weekly*, April 13, 1988, KXLU 1:10.

44. Report, May 5, 1988, KXLU 1:12.

45. Matt Kelly to Trame, September 28, 1989, KXLU 1:12.

46. Donna Halper, interview with author, June 15, 2021.

47. Theresa King, "Regina Harris Steps to the Front as WJSU-FM Program Director," *Clarion-Ledger* (Jackson, MS), November 17, 1982.

48. "Profile: Susan Harmon," from WAMU Archives, box 1, folder 6, Special Collections and University Archives, Hornbake Library, University of Maryland.

49. December 2, 1982, Staff Minutes, WHUS 2017-0056_1: Communication about TVI.

50. Beth Lazar to Dave Ponak, July 7, 1983, WHUS 2017-0056_1: Communication about TVI.

51. Staff meeting, September 19, 1984. WHUS 2017-0056_1: Unnamed.

52. Articles of Incorporation, box 1, folder 1; audio tapes of Women's Words, boxes 2 and 3, Phoenix Women Take Back the Night and Women's Words Radio Show Collection, Photos and Documents (MS 243), Library and Archives, Arizona Historical Society, Central Arizona Division, Tempe, AZ.

53. "Show Info: Something About the Women," https://spinitron.com/radio/playlist.php?station=wmfo&showid=413#here. For an example of IWD programming, see "Take the Noise Away from the Boys: Rock against Sexism," Side 1, Program 4, Boston Women's Community Radio Records, 1972–93 (inclusive), 1980–89 (bulk), (#T-317.1–T-317.80), Schlesinger Library on the History of Women in America, Harvard University, Cambridge, MA.

54. Directors Meeting Minutes, January 17, 1985, SAW 26:3.

55. Toni Armstrong Jr., "What Is Women's Music? An Endangered Species: Women's Music by, and about Women," *Hot Wire*, September 1989, 17, SAW.

56. Lauren Goodlad in Susan Merrill Squier et al., *Communities of the Air: Radio Century, Radio Culture* (Durham: Duke University Press, 2003), 138.

57. Armstrong Jr., "What Is Women's Music?," 17.

58. "Gripes and Groans," 1986, KTRU Records.

59. Gripes and Groans, 1987. SAW, Top Lists: 8. Armstrong Jr., "What Is Women's Music?," 19.

60. Armstrong Jr., "What Is Women's Music?," 19.

61. KUNM History, KUNM:4.

62. KUNM History.

63. KUNM History.

64. KUNM History.

65. Michael P. McCauley, *NPR: The Trials and Triumphs of National Public Radio* (New York: Columbia University Press, 2005), 78.

66. KUMN History.

67. KUMN History.

68. KUNM History.

69. Paul Mansfield to All Staff, April 21, 1978, KUNM, 4: Interoffice Memos 1978–83.

70. Paul Mansfield to All Staff, April 21, 1978.

71. "Raices" staff to Paul Mansfield, January 26, 1980, KUNM, 4: Interoffice Memos 1978–83.

72. Paul Mansfield to All Staff, April 23, 1980, KUNM, 4: Interoffice Memos 1978–83.

73. Paul Mansfield to Everybody, May 6, 1980, KUNM, 4: Interoffice Memos 1978–83.

74. Barton Bond to Jon Cooper, April 21, 1981, KUNM, 4: Interoffice Memos 1978–83.

75. KUNM History.

76. KUNM History.

77. McCauley, *NPR*, 9.

78. KUNM History.

79. Listener comments, KUNM 1: Announcements on Air 1987, 1988.

80. Patsy Catlett to KUNM Staff and Volunteers, June 22, 1987, KUNM 1: Announcements on Air 1987, 1988.

81. McCauley, *NPR*, 78–80.

82. KUNM Staff Meeting, May 21, 1987, KUNM 8: Meetings 1987.

83. On-Air Statement, June 1, 1987, KUNM 1: Announcements on Air 1987, 1988.

84. Bernadette Chato to KUNM DJs/Board Operators, June 1, 1987, KUNM 1: Announcements on Air 1987, 1988.

85. KUNM History, 25. Appendix, "Chronology of Current KUNM Management Crisis," KUNM 4.

86. Richard Jennings to Tim Singleton, June 15, 1987; press release, Friends of Freeform, undated, KUNM 1: Announcements on Air 1987, 1988.

87. Appendix, "Chronology."

88. Carmella M. Padilla, "If They'd Just Play More Madonna, Maybe the Tempest Would Abate," *Wall Street Journal*, August 4, 1987.

89. KUNM History.

90. Harry Norton to student senators, October 2, 1987, box 1, ASUMN, GSA; Students for KUNM to Students, March 21, 1988.

91. Radio Advisory Board, 1988, KUNM 7.

92. Board of Regents Meeting April 12, 1988; Chronology of KUMN Management Crisis, KUNM 1.

93. Radio Advisory Board, 1988, KUNM 7.

94. Chronology of KUMN Management Crisis.

95. "Key Issues in the Current Crisis," KUNM, 1: Format Changes Responses.

96. Benefit, 1988, KUNM 1.

97. ASUMN, GSA, State, KUNM 1.

98. Resolution Regarding Radio Station KUNM, Board of Regents, April 12, 1988, Board of Regents April 12 Meeting, KUNM 7:1988.

99. KUNM Advisory Board, 1988.

100. Radio Advisory Board meeting, September 12, 1989, Radio Advisory Board, KUNM 7:1989.

101. "KUNM Schedule," www.kunm.org/kunm-radio-schedule.

Chapter 11

1. "Bogus Story Becomes Bombshell," *Kansas City Times*, October 7, 1978.

2. "War of the Worlds II," *Wichita Eagle*, October 10, 1978.

3. Dave Grissom, "30 Years of KHJK: Dave Grissom," Lawrence.com, October 10, 2005, www.lawrence.com/news/2005/oct/10/dave_grissom/.

4. George Gurley, "McCarthyism in the Land of Oz?," CV, April 1990, PP505 1:28.

5. Gurley.

6. Gurley.

7. Pierre Bourdieu, *Distinction: A Social Critique of the Judgement of Taste*, 11th ed. (Cambridge, MA: Harvard University Press, 2002), 170, 338.

8. Betty Pallanich, "KJHK: A New Sound from KU," *JayPlay*, Fall 1975, PP505 1:36.

9. Jan Smith, "KJHK: Emphasis on Music, not Money," unidentified publication Spring 1979, PP505 1:36.

10. Smith.

11. Carolyn Coleman, "Broadcast Head Plans Changes in Radio Station," *Daily Kansan*, June 8, 1985; Joe Popper, "Learning Radio," *Star Magazine*, May 28, 1990, PP505 1:36.

12. Popper.

13. Coleman, "Broadcast Head Plans."

14. Coleman; "KJHK Radio: Goals and Objectives, 1987–1988," memo July 1987, PP505 1:36.

15. Jill Casey, "Changes at KJHK Draw Renewed Criticism," *Lawrence Journal-World* September 1, 1988, PP505 1:36.

16. Jim Schwada, "30 Years of KJHK: Redux by Jim Schwada," Lawrence.com, October 10, 2005, www.lawrence.com/news/2005/oct/10/jim_schwada/?print.

17. Robert Klotz, UDK, March 9, 1990, PP505 1: 36.

18. Lipsitz later founded Bar/None Records, an independent record label in Hoboken, NJ.

19. "Brief History," PP505 1:3.

20. "Mike Kautsch to Retire after 40 Years at KU," *KU Law Blog* (blog), May 9, 2019, https://bloglaw.ku.edu/faculty/mike-kautsch-to-retire-after-40-years-at-ku/.

21. Letters, *Daily Kansan*, December 7, 1987, PP505 1:36.

22. "Goals and Objectives," July 1987.

23. "Brief History," PP505 1:3.

24. "Brief History."

25. "Brief History."

26. "Brief History."

27. Popper, "Learning Radio."

28. "Brief History," PP505 1:3.

29. "Rough Reception," *Jayhawk Journalist Magazine*, Fall 1988, PP505 1:36; Notes, PP505 1:3.

30. "Brief History," PP505 1:3.

31. "Who Wants a Bite of KJHK?" PP505 1:4.

32. Lisa Sheikh, "KJHK Format Change Draws Complaint," June 8, 1988, PP505 1:36.

33. Jill Casey, "KJHK Format Plans Prompt 'No Change' Message," *Lawrence Journal-World*, July 28, 1988, Clippings, PP505 1:36.

34. "Who Wants a Bite of KJHK?," PP505 1:4.

35. Clippings, PP505 1:36; "Who Wants a Bite?,"

36. Clippings, PP505 1:36.

37. Clippings.

38. Jill Casey, "Station Heralded New Music 11 Years Ago," *Lawrence Journal-World*, August 21, 1988, PP505 1:36.

39. Jill Casey, "KJHK Group Boycotts Area Businesses," *Lawrence Journal-World*, October 9, 1988, PP505 1:36.

40. Popper, "Learning Radio."

41. Lisa Sheikh, "KJHK Files Request to Increase Power," *Daily Kansan*, June 28, 1988; handwritten note, Clippings, PP505 1:36.

42. Clippings.

43. Letters, *Daily Kansan*, September 8, 1988.

44. Letters, *Daily Kansan*, September 15, 1988.

45. "Brief History."

46. Letters, *Daily Kansan*, September 20, 1988.

47. Clippings, PP505 1:36.

48. Concert Agenda, October 30, 1988, in Clippings, PP505 1:36.

49. Mark C. McCormick, "Auction Draws Protesters," *Daily Kansan*, October 19, 1988.

50. Clippings; Matthew Moore, "Sound Changes," *Daily Kansan*, September 8, 1988.

51. McCormick, "Auction Draws Protesters"; Jill Casey, "KJHK Group Boycotts Area Businesses," *Lawrence Journal-World*, October 9, 1988.

52. McCormick, "Auction Draws Protesters."

53. Mike Mader, "College Radio," *The Note*, March 1989, PP505 1:36.

54. Mader.

55. Candy Niemann, "FCC Conducting Investigation of KJHK," *Daily Kansan*, January 30, 1989, Clippings, PP505 1:36.

56. Greenwood to FCC, January 28, 1989, Clippings PP505 1:36.

57. Greenwood.

58. Greenwood; Steve Greenwood to Ronald Holberg, Feburary 18, 1989, Clippings PP505 1:36.

59. Greenwood to Holberg.

60. Stan Diel, "Hiring Procedures at KJHK Could Put Its Funding at Risk," *Daily Kansan*, March 3, 1989.

61. Stan Diel, "Finance Committee Starts Investigation of Hiring at KJHK," *Daily Kansan*, March 6, 1989.

62. Stan Diel, "KJHK Manager Rejects Charges of Unfair Hiring," *Daily Kansan*, April 11, 1989.

63. Letters, *Daily Kansan,* April 28, 1989.

64. Tim Carpenter, "Dean issues New Rules for KU Station," *Lawrence Journal-World,* June 14, 1989.

65. Charles Higginson, "KJHK Board, StudEx Compromise," *Daily Kansan,* June 28, 1989.

66. "Agreement OK'd on Funds for KU Station," *Lawrence Journal-World*, June 27, 1989.

67. Editorial, *Daily Kansan*, June 21, 1989.

68. Editorial, *Daily Kansan,* April 21, 1989; Letters, *Daily Kansan*, June 21, 1989; Higginson, "KJHK Board, StudEx Compromise."

69. Robert Klotz letter, Clippings, PP505 1:36.

70. Mike Kautsch to Journalism Faculty, May 17, 1989, Clippings, PP505 1:36.

71. Clippings.

72. "Death Knell Sounds Again for Independent Labels," Clippings, PP505 1:36.

73. Guest column, *Daily Kansan*, March 9, 1990.

74. Charles Higginson, "KU Not Alone in Radio Woes," *Daily Kansan*, June 28, 1989.

75. Popper, "Learning Radio."

76. Dave Marsh, *Rock and Roll Confidential*, July 1989, in Clippings, PP505 1:36.

77. Marsh.

Part III

1. Steve Albini, "The Problem with Music," *The Baffler*, December 1993, https://thebaffler.com/salvos/the-problem-with-music.

2. Dan Ozzi, *Sellout: The Major Label Feeding Frenzy That Swept Punk, Emo, and Hardcore (1994–2007)* (Boston: Houghton Mifflin Harcourt, 2021), xii.

3. Colin Harrison, "Music and Radio," in *American Culture in the 1990s* (Edinburgh: Edinburgh University Press, 2010), 76; see "Is Anybody Listening? Does

Anybody Care? On 'the State of Rock'" in Lawrence Grossberg, *Dancing in Spite of Myself: Essays on Popular Culture* (Durham, NC: Duke University Press, 1997).

4. Ben Weasel, Editorial, *Maximum Rocknroll* (87), August 1990.

5. Joan Didion, "Trouble in Lakewood," *New Yorker*, July 19, 1993.

6. Tricia Rose, *Black Noise: Rap Music and Black Culture in Contemporary America* (Hanover, NH: University Press of New England, 1994); Rose, *The Hip Hop Wars: What We Talk about When We Talk About Hip Hop—and Why It Matters* (New York: Civitas Books, 2008).

7. In music, tensions between civic nationalism critiques of assimilationist tendencies and normative white, heterosexual, and patriarchal values continued. Harrison, "Music and Radio," 80–81.

8. Howard Rosenberg, "From Eloquent to Embarrassing: An Evening of Firsts," *Los Angeles Times*, March 2, 1994.

9. Michael Azerrad, *Our Band Could Be Your Life: Scenes from the American Indie Underground 1981–1991* (New York: Back Bay Books, 2002).

10. Hugh Foley, interview with author, March 6, 2015.

Chapter 13

1. Felicia Angeja Viator, *To Live and Defy in L.A.: How Gangsta Rap Changed America* (Cambridge, MA: Harvard University Press, 2020).

2. David Kirsch, "The Struggle for the Soul of Public Radio," *Extra!*, April/May 1993, 27.

3. Opinion, "90.3's Watery Broth of Mediocrity," *Rocket*, December 1992.

4. "Gripes and Groans," 1987, KTRU 26.

5. "Gripes and Groans."

6. Ray Shea, interview with author.

7. Shea.

8. Figures cited in Anthony Kwame Harrison, "Black College-Radio on Predominantly White Campuses: A 'Hip-Hop Era' Student-Authored Inclusion Initiative," *Africology: The Journal of Pan African Studies* 9, no. 8 (2016): 136.

9. Harrison, 142.

10. Harrison, 143.

11. See Kier-La Janisse and Paul Corupe, *Satanic Panic: Pop-Cultural Paranoia in the 1980s* (Toronto: Spectacular Optical Publications, 2019); "The Devilish History of the 1980s Parental Advisory Sticker: When Heavy Metal & Satanic Lyrics Collided with the Religious Right," *Open Culture*, April 2019, www.openculture.com/2019/04 /the-devilish-history-of-the-1980s-parental-advisory-sticker.html; Gabby Riches, Dave Snell, Bryan Bardine, and Brenda Gardenour Walter, *Heavy Metal Studies and Popular Culture* (Springer, 2016); Robert Walser, *Running with the Devil: Power, Gender, and Madness in Heavy Metal Music* (Hanover, NH: University Press of New England, 1993).

12. Maxine Waters, in Chuck Philips, "Rap Finds a Supporter in Rep. Maxine Waters," *Los Angeles Times*, February 15, 1994.

13. Tricia Rose, *The Hip Hop Wars: What We Talk About When We Talk about Hip Hop—and Why It Matters* (New York: Civitas Books, 2008).

14. Fall 1988 Book, WUOG 5.

15. Fall 1988 Book.

16. Fall 1988 Book.

17. KZSU, CMJ *New Music Report*, December 1, 1989.

18. Letters, *Stanford Daily*, May 6, 1991.

19. Erika Helm, "Student Radio Station Seeks More Minorities," *Daily Tar Heel*, November 22, 1993.

20. Harrison, "Black College Radio," 142.

21. Author's conversation with Freddy Braithwaite, March 2019, Hip Hop Archive, Harvard University, Cambridge, MA.

22. P Fine, *Rap This (P Fine on WNYU): 1986*, Internet Archive, 1986, http://archive .org/details/RapThis-PFine-1986; "Jonathan Finegold, Founder/Owner, Fine Gold Music," *SyncSummit* (blog), June 7, 2017, http://syncsummit.com/finegold/.

23. Pete Nash, interview with author, October 22, 2021.

24. Nash.

25. Nash.

26. Nash.

27. Nash.

28. Nash.

29. Nash.

30. Bobbito García, *Stretch and Bobbito: Radio That Changed Lives* (Saboteur Media, 2015).

31. Joe Helm, interview with author, May 2, 2022.

32. Rob Bingham, "VU Radio Station Silenced," *Tennessean*, April 13, 1990.

33. Bingham.

34. WRVU E-Staff, "The Commandments of 91 Rock" (Fall 1985), Nick Archer, personal collection.

35. Helm interview.

36. Bingham, "VU Radio Station Silenced."

37. Helm interview.

38. "Bum Rap," *Times* (Shreveport, LA), July 7, 1995.

39. "GSU Radio Plans 19-Day Protest of Rap Music's Obscenity, Profanity," *Times* (Shreveport, LA), June 14, 1995.

40. Robert Dole, *Congressional Record*, 104th Cong., 1st Sess., Vol. 141, No. 99, (Senate), June 16, 1995, S8526.

41. Joe Peebles, interview with author, February 25, 2019.

42. With *Yo! MTV Raps* on air, Peebles capitalized on its success to offer his own campus cable show in addition to radio. He wrote to record labels, and in return received four to five videos a day in his campus mailbox that he played on VUTV. Peebles.

43. TeRon Lawrence, interview with author.

44. Jeff Pearlman, "Hello, Out There!," *Tennessean*, March 7, 1995.

45. Pearlman.

46. Sharon Scott, interview with author, March 4, 2019.

47. Scott.

48. Katherine Rye Jewell, "'Specialty' Listening: Creating Space for Queer Programming on American College Radio in the Long 1980s," in *Resist, Organize, Build: Feminist and Queer Activism in Britain and the United States during the Long 1980s*, ed. Sarah Crook and Charlie Jeffries (Albany: State University of New York Press, 2022), 53–74.

49. Ron Slomowicz, interview with author, January 30, 2017; "About TWO—This Way Out," This Way Out, http://thiswayout.org/about-two/.

50. "WXPN Gay Show Cut," *Philadelphia Daily News*, March 8, 1994.

51. See chapter 8.

52. Staff Meeting minutes, January 27, 1993, WHUS box 2017-0055_2, Board Minutes folder.

53. Operations Board Meeting, February 8, 1993, WHUS, Board Minutes folder.

54. Paula Newman to Harry Hartley, October 28, 1993, WHUS box 2017-0055_2, Polka Letters folder.

55. Mr. and Mrs. Harry Hewko to Board of Trustees, October 23, 1993, WHUS, Polka Letters.

56. George Fabian to Harry Hartley, October 30, 1993, WHUS, Polka Letters.

57. Laura Duhaime, October 9, 1993, WHUS, Polka Letters.

58. Donna Andrychowski to Hartley, October 11, 1993, WHUS, Polka Letters.

59. Walter Dolde to Hartley, October 9, 1993, WHUS, Polka Letters.

60. Eleanor and Henry Leonard to Hartley and Board of Trustees, October 9, 1993, WHUS, Polka Letters.

61. Eleanor Fiore to Hartley, October 10, 1993, WHUS, Polka Letters.

62. Katherine Postemski to Board of Trustees, October 11, 1993, WHUS, Polka Letters.

63. Jack and Betty Colody to Hartley-UConn, October 15, 1993, WHUS, Polka Letters.

64. Brian Rosenwald, *Talk Radio's America: How an Industry Took Over a Political Party That Took Over the United States* (Cambridge, MA: Harvard University Press, 2019).

65. Jeffrey Brooks to Hartley, October 10, 1993, WHUS, Polka Letters.

66. Kathy Fennessey to Tom Freeman, January 25, 1994, email, CURSE 1: Internal Correspondence & Memos, 1992–94.

67. "World Radio," *Seattle Post-Intelligencer*, October 23, 1992.

68. Aldrich v. Knab, 858 F. Supp. 1480, No. C93-3Z (United States District Court, W.D. Washington, at Seattle July 19, 1994).

69. Robert Penn, "KCMU Program Changes Protested," *Seattle Post-Intelligencer*, October 31, 1992; B. Morris, "Range Wars," *Rolling Stone*, March 24, 1994, 55–57.

70. Letters, *Hype Magazine*, October 1992.

71. Letters, *Hype Magazine*. Letters also appeared in *The Stranger*, November 2–8, 1992.

72. *The Hard Report*, December 4, 1992.

73. Aldrich v. Knab, 858 F. Supp. 1480.

74. Glen Hirschberg, "CURSE on KCMU," *Seattle Weekly*, November 25, 1992; Irv Pollack to Knab, November 16, 1992, CURSE 1: Internal Memos.

75. Brian Less, "The Power and the Passion," *Urban Spelunker*, November 1992.

76. "Picket Line to Go Up in KCMU Fight," *Seattle Post-Intelligencer*, December 6, 1992; Paula Yoo, "Several Protesters Picket KCMU-FM," *Seattle Times*, December 16, 1992.

77. Yoo, "Several Protesters Picket KCMU-FM"; "KCMU Shutdown," *Seattle Times*, December 24, 1992.

78. Eric Boehlert, "Seattle Station Staffers Quit in P'gramming Row," *Billboard*, December 19, 1992.

79. Rosie Black, "A CURSE Progress Report," CURSE 1: Internal Memos; Letters, *The Stranger*, December 21–January 10, 1993.

80. Aldrich v. Knab, U.S. District Court for the Western District of Washington, January 4, 1993; Chris Moonshadow Martin, "Former KCMU Staffers File Suit against Station," *UW Daily*, January 6, 1993; Paula Yoo, "Ex-KCMU Staffers Sue Station, UW," *Seattle Times*, January 7, 1993.

81. "KCMU in Midst of Full-Court Press," *Billboard*, January 30, 1993.

82. Amie Prentice, "New Grooves; Ambient Grunge," *Stranger*, February 1–7, 1993; Media Warrior, "Turn Down Your Radio" "Music That Matters" / "543 - KCMU" Erika, no. 40778, February 1, 1993 (1988), Northwest Music Archives, http://nwmusicarchives.com/record/turn-down-your-radio-music-that-matters-543-kcmu/.

83. "CURSE Update," *Hype*, February 1993; "Blah Blah Blah," *Hard Report*, March 26, 1993. Some articles attributed local concerts as support for CURSE, including a performance by Ween. This surprised the band, which had no opinion on the matter. Letters, *Hard Report*, April 2, 1993. Clark Humphrey, "Misc.," *Stranger*, April 26–May 2, 1993.

84. Emily Hill to Christopher Knab, January 29, 1993, CURSE 1: Internal Memos.

85. Dana Winter, "A Word from Our Listeners: How Program Change Rocked KCMU," *KCMU-FM* 1 (2020): 11.

86. Todd Maybrown to Nancy Thygesen Day, January 4, 1993, CURSE 1: Internal Memos; "College Radio," *Pulse*, April 1993.

87. Aldrich v. Knab, 858 F. Supp. 1480 (W.D. Wash. 1994), July 19, 1994.

88. Allan Posewitz to Mr. Humphries, February 7, 1994, CURSE 1: Internal Memos.

89. Winter, "Word from Our Listeners," 12.

90. Tom Freeman to Julie Carter, January 20, 1994; Kathy Fennessy to Freeman, January 25, 1994, CURSE 1: Internal Memos.

91. Playlists, Wainstead Collection, RRHOF.

92. For college radio origins of online broadcasting, with case studies at streaming leaders WXYC, WREK, and KJHK, see chapter 1, Andrew Bottomley, *Sound Streams: A Cultural History of Radio-Internet Convergence* (Ann Arbor: University of Michigan Press, 2020).

93. Steven McClung, "College Radio Station Web Sites: Perceptions of Value and Use," *Journalism & Mass Communication Educator* 56, no. 1 (March 2001): 62–73, https://doi.org/10.1177/107769580105600106." College radio stations adopted

websites early on, even if station managers remained unclear about how to use them.

94. "Simulcast—WXYC 89.3 FM," WXYC.org, https://wxyc.org/simulcast/.

95. Julianne Basinger, "Station at UNC a First on Internet," *Charlotte Observer*, December 23, 1994.

96. C. Wiz, interview with author, March 6, 2021.

97. Dwight Farrell, interview with author, August 3, 2020.

98. James Noble, personal correspondence, May 27, 2020.

99. Corwin A. Thomas, "Egon and Count Bass-D Put the Groove in WRVU," *Tennessean*, January 2, 1998.

100. Thomas.

101. "Now This Is the Real Hip-hop," *Tennessean*, April 1, 1999.

102. "Hip-hop to the Beat at WRVU Benefit," *Tennessean*, April 6, 2000.

103. Elizabeth Tandy Shermer, *Indentured Students: How Government-Guaranteed Loans Left Generations Drowning in College Debt* (Cambridge, MA: The Belknap Press of Harvard University Press, 2021), 253–54.

Chapter 14

1. "The Full and Unabridged History of KALX," KALX 90.7FM Berkeley, www.kalx.berkeley.edu/full-and-unabridged-history-kalx.

2. Few, if any, references to the end of the required FCC operators' license occurred in the archives, although occasionally examples of the tests or submission forms remain. Its end occurred largely without comment, at least any that are documented.

3. Peter DiCola and Kristin Thomson, "Radio Deregulation: Has It Served Citizens and Musicians? A Report on the Effects of Radio Ownership Consolidation Following the 1996 Telecommunications Act" (Washington, D.C.: The Future of Music Coalition, November 18, 2002), 8, 11–24.

4. "ECFS Filing Detail Regarding MM Docket 99-25, the FCC Rulemaking on Low Power FM Radio," Federal Communications Commission, April 15, 1999, www.fcc.gov/ecfs/filing/5001904325.

5. "Radio Deregulation," 40.

6. Kurt St. Thomas, interview with author, March 8, 2021.

7. St. Thomas.

8. Leo Sacks, "AOR Stations at Crossroads," *Billboard*, November 5, 1983, 1, 16.

9. Sacks.

10. St. Thomas interview.

11. Henry Santoro, interview with author, February 18, 2021.

12. Angie Shaw, interview with author, March 9, 2021.

13. Shaw.

14. "Modern Rock: Label Expansion Outstrips Radio," *Billboard*, July 22, 1989, 12.

15. "Modern Rock."

16. CMJ, November 3, 1989.

17. *Billboard*, July 22, 1989.

18. Michael Azerrad, *Come as You Are: The Story of Nirvana* (New York: Doubleday, 1994), 103; Michael O'Connor, "Listen to Nirvana's Full Live Set at Axis on September 23, 1991," Vanayaland, September 23, 2013, https://vanyaland.com/2013/09/23/listen-to-nirvanas-full-live-set-at-axis-on-september-23-1991-at-the-wfnx-8th-birthday-party/.

19. Theo Cateforis, *Are We Not New Wave?: Modern Pop at the Turn of the 1980s* (Ann Arbor: University of Michigan Press, 2011), 65; Robin James, unpublished presentation, "What Was the Modern Rock 500," March 2, 2020.

20. Mike Gioscia, interview with author, March 11, 2021.

21. Santoro interview.

22. Mike Curtin, "WEQX and a Radio Station's Dream-Come-True," *Post-Star* (Glenns Falls, NY), February 7, 1993.

23. Yvonne Daley, "With WEQX," *Rutland Daily Herald* (Rutland, VT), March 11, 1993.

24. Venues and zines criticized bands that signed to major labels, such as seen with the Bay Area's Green Day, rejected by the scene that gave them rise. Dan Ozzi, *Sellout: The Major Label Feeding Frenzy That Swept Punk, Emo, and Hardcore (1994–2007)* (Boston: Houghton Mifflin Harcourt, 2021), 18, 23–25.

25. James, "What Was the Modern Rock 500"; Keith Harris, "Did New York Kill Indie Rock?," *Journal of Popular Music Studies* 24, no. 3 (2012): 276–79, https://doi.org/10.1111/j.1533-1598.2012.01334.x.

26. Jennifer C. Waits, "Does 'Indie' Mean Independence? Freedom and Restraint in a Late 1990s US College Radio Community," *Radio Journal—International Studies in Broadcast and Audio Media* 5, no. 2 & 3 (2007), 90.

27. Waits, 90, 91.

28. Waits, 92.

29. Rose Apodaca Jones, "Spheres of Influence," *Los Angeles Times*, November 1, 1997.

30. Mike Boehm, "UCI Radio Staff Turned Off Over Threat to Autonomy," *Los Angeles Times*, October 5, 1988; Mike Boehm, "Student-run KUCI to Boost Power," *Los Angeles Times*, May 21, 1991.

31. Mike Boehm, "KUCI: Alternative Rock Format Won't Change," *Los Angeles Times*, October 10, 1991. KUCI had to eventually pay its own way, starting with fundraisers for $75,000 to cover equipment costs. After cash infusions from UCI, it would be financially self-supporting by 1995.

32. Pierre Bourdieu, *Distinction: A Social Critique of the Judgement of Taste*, 11th ed. (Cambridge, MA: Harvard University Press, 2002).

33. Amy Heckerling (dir.), *Clueless*, Paramount Pictures, 1995.

34. David Mosso, Letters, *Los Angeles Times*, September 3, 1994.

35. Mosso.

36. One late start on FM included the University of Texas station WVRX, which moved from its former carrier-current signal in 1994 and launched related bands such as Spoon. Jason Cohen, "How Did Spoon Become One of the Most Enduring Indie-Rock Bands? It All Started at the University of Texas," *The Alcalde* (blog),

March 1, 2022, https://alcalde.texasexes.org/2022/03/spoon-band-lucifer-on-the-sofa-austin-ut/.

37. Steven T. Lawrence to Robert Jones, October 26, 1989 KEDG online archive, https://kedg.weebly.com/media.html; Lawrence to David Martin, November 2, 1989, KEDG.

38. Paul Riismandel, "The College Radio Station 'That Shouldn't Exist,'" *Radio Survivor* (blog), November 19, 2019, www.radiosurvivor.com/2019/11/podcast-220-the-college-radio-station-that-shouldnt-exist/; Carol Fuccillo, "Student Radio at CSUS? Maybe," *Hornet*, Spring 1990, KEDG.

39. Mark Larson, "New Public Radio Station Will Play Traditional Jazz," *Business Journal* (Sacramento, CA), March 26, 1990, KEDG online archive.

40. Russ Buettner, "KXPR 2, Students 0," *Hornet*, March 23, 1990, in KEDG.

41. "ASI Backs Student Radio," *Hornet*, March 30, 1990, KEDG.

42. Letters, *Hornet*, March 30, 1990, KEDG.

43. Opinions, *Hornet*, April 3, 1990, KEDG.

44. Donald R. Gerth to Dean William Sullivan, April 17, 1990, KEDG.

45. Announcement, April 18, 1990; Campus Organization Office Registration Form; Student Activities Advisor to James Bolt, May 14, 1990, KEDG.

46. Russ Buettner, "Student-Run Radio Tunes Hit the Lawn," *Hornet*, April 27, 1990, KEDG.

47. Russ Buettner, "CSUS under Pressure for Student Radio," *Hornet*, May 1990, KEDG.

48. Tim Grieve, "CSUS Students Want a Radio Station to Call Their Own," *Sacramento Bee*, May 10, 1990, KEDG.

49. Sample form letter for supporters, undated, KEDG.

50. Donald R. Gerth to Jim Bolt, August 17, 1990, KEDG.

51. Rachel Orvino, "Long-awaited Station Falls Short of Student Needs," *Hornet*, September 11, 1990, KEDG.

52. Rachel Orvino, "New Semester Brings Campus Radio to CSUS," *Hornet*, December 1990. Jim Bolt, personal correspondence, March 20, 2022.

53. Opinion, *Hornet*, December 14, 1990, KEDG.

54. Jim Bolt, "Behold, the Land of Music," *Hornet*, December 14, 1990, KEDG

55. Letters, February 1, February 22, 1991, *Hornet*, KEDG.

56. Opinion, *Hornet*, February 22, 1991, KEDG.

57. Board of Directors, Meeting Minutes, February 27, 1991, KEDG.

58. Kent W. Leslie, "KEDG Is Broadcasting on Cable Radio," *Hornet*, May 3, 1991; ASI certificate, May 14, 1991, KEDG.

59. Michael Pipe Jr., "Student Radio No Longer Myth as KEDG Hits Airwaves," *Hornet*, September 20, 1990, KEDG.

60. "About KSSU: Timeline," KSSU.org, www.kssu.com/about.

61. "Station History," WCRD.net, http://wcrd.net/station-history/; Paul Allor, "Riddle Me This . . . Dave," *Ball State Daily News*, vol. 81, no. 13, Ball State University Student Newspaper Collection, Ball State University Digital Media Repository, University Libraries, Muncie, IN.

62. Editorial, *Ball State Daily News*, September 6, 1994.

63. Editorial, *Ball State Daily News*, September 2, 1994.

64. Letters, *Ball State Daily News*, September 8, 1994.

65. Jason LaMar, "Ballapalooza," *Ball State Daily News*, November 9, 1994.

66. Elizabeth Tandy Shermer, *Indentured Students: How Government-Guaranteed Loans Left Generations Drowning in College Debt* (Cambridge, MA: The Belknap Press of Harvard University Press, 2021), 295.

67. Scott Frampton, "The Future of Music: Alternative Is Dead," *CMJ: New Music*, February 1997, 19–20.

68. Douglas Wolk, "The Future of Music: No It's Not," *CMJ: New Music*, February 1997, 19–20.

69. Douglas Wolk, "How Ashamed Should You Feel about Using Spotify?," *Slate*, August 21, 2013, https://slate.com/business/2013/08/spotify-and-pandora-artist-payments-not-as-exploitative-as-theyre-made-out-to-be.html.

70. Bob Findle, "KCR Rocks Out in Cyberspace," *Daily Aztec*, April 16, 1996.

71. Dana Bushee, "KCR Celebrates New Signal at Monty's," *Daily Aztec*, October 27, 1997.

Chapter 15

1. "Display Ad 46," *New York Times*, June 4, 1993, sec. The Arts, 46.

2. "Display Ad 80," *New York Times*, September 6, 1990, sec. Auction Sales, 80.

3. While there were large numbers of elementary-age students in the pipeline, and rising matriculation among students of color increased, the late 1980s and early 1990s had fewer traditional-aged college students than in the past. One report showed a drop in the proportion of school-aged children in the nation from 26 percent in the 1960s to 18 percent in 1991. Thomas D. Snyder, *120 Years of American Education: A Statistical Portrait* (Washington, D.C.: U.S. Department of Education, National Center for Education Statistics, January 1993).

4. Charity Shumway, "Radio Days," *Adelphi University* (blog), November 14, 2013, www.adelphi.edu/news/radio-days/.

5. Chris Kretz, "WBAU Radio at Adelphi University," *LIRTVHS.Org* (blog), July 13, 2021, https://lirtvhs.org/wbau-radio-at-adelphi-university/; "Dr. Jeffrey Palmer '76," https://adelphi.smugmug.com/Alumni/Stories-from-WBAU-Alumni/n-T2P7XQ/i-5jnzRBG; "Linda J. Stewart '82," https://adelphi.smugmug.com/Alumni/Stories-from-WBAU-Alumni/n-T2P7XQ/i-HNHSBZb; "WBAU-FM 20th Anniversary Reunion" invitation; Bill Kahn to Carl J. Rheins, "WBAU/FM Radio Anniversary Party," memo, October 21, 1992, WBAU 1.16.

6. Contract regarding WBAU Radiothon, March 5, 1986, WBAU 1.16.

7. Admin-Board Minutes WBAU, March 13, 1994, WBAU General Station Meeting, March 15, 1994; "A Brief History of Radio Station WBAU at Adelphi University," WBAU 1.15.

8. "Brief History of Radio Station WBAU."

9. David Hinckley, "WBAU Isn't Making the Grade with Adelphi Students," *Daily News*, May 9, 1995.

10. "Discussion Points for President Diamandopoulos and the Board of Trustees," memorandum, August 14, 1995, WBAU 1:17.

11. David Hinckley, "Who Is Unhappy with WBAU: Students or Deans?," *Daily News*, May 15, 1995.

12. Hinckley.

13. "WBAU Seeks Help," clipping, *Delphian*, April 12, 1989, WBAU 2:12.

14. Ken Norian to Carl Rheins, May 9, 1995, WBAU 2:15.

15. Norian to Rheins.

16. Norian to Rheins.

17. Ken Norian, "WBAU Statement," March 22, 1996, Document D in Jackie Parker, WBAU 2:13.

18. Norian, Document D.

19. Norian, Document D.

20. Michael O'Brien to File, "Events Preceding the Sale of WBAU," October 5, 1995, WBAU 2:15.

21. Rheins to Diamandopoulos, October 3, 1995, WBAU 2:13.

22. Norian, "WBAU Statement."

23. Sue Oatey to Carl J. Rheins, "WBAU Action Plan," August 4, 1995, WBAU 2:15.

24. Oatey to Rheins.

25. Joyce E. Jesionowski to Catherine Hennessy, August 9, 1995, WBAU 2.15.

26. Norian, "WBAU Statement."

27. Norian, Document D.

28. Carl J. Rheins to Tara Kaufmann, President, The Student Government Association, "The Cessation of WBAU-FM and Its Impact on the Student Activity Fee," August 24, 1995, WBAU 2:1.

29. Rheins to Kaufmann.

30. Statements, WBAU 1:13.

31. Doreen Carvajal, "President's Pay Rankles Some at Adelphii," *New York Times*, September 30, 1995.

32. Carvajal, "President's Pay."

33. Rheins to Diamandopoulos, October 3, 1995, WBAU 2:15.

34. Carvajal, "President's Pay."

35. William Weng, "Liotti Calls for Immediate Action," *Delphian*, April 15, 1979.

36. Richard J. Schure to Peter Diamandopoulos and Board of Trustees, "Friends of WBAU vs. Adelphi University," October 19, 1995, WBAU 2:15.

37. Rheins to Heather Tilberg, October 12, 1995, WBAU 2.11.

38. Letter, "The Plundering of Adelphi," *New York Times*, October 14, 1995.

39. Letters, *Delphian*, October 18, 1995.

40. Ken Norian and John Schmidt, Letters to the Editor, Editorial, *Delphian*, October 25, 1995.

41. Norian and Schmidt.

42. Norian and Schmidt.

43. Norian and Schmidt.

44. Norian and Schmidt.

45. Richard J. Schure to Peter Diamandopoulos and Catherine Hennessy, "Friends of WBAU vs. Adelphi University," October 18, 1995, WBAU 2:15.

46. Affirmation in Opposition, Friends of WBAU, Inc., et al., against Peter Diamandopoulos, Individually and as president of Adelphi University; The Board of Trustees of Adelphi Diversity, et al.; Index No. 308779/95; press release, "Lawsuit against Adelphi President and Board of Trustees Is Dismissed," December 18, 1995, WBAU 1.14; Jack Sirica, "Adelphi Head Strikes at Faculty Union," *Newsday*, December 2, 1995.

47. Thomas Liotti, Reply, *Friends of WBAU, Inc. et al. vs. Peter Diamandopoulos, et al.*, December 8, 1995, Garden City, NY, in WBAU 2:14.

48. Jean Edouard Jasmin, "Pursuing Onward," *Afrika Unbound*, November 1995.

49. Schure, October 18, 1995.

50. Jason Wright, "Friends of WBAU; Press Conference," *Afrika Unbound*, November 1995.

51. Margaret L. Miller to Anna Marie Mascolo, "WHPC," December 8, 1995, WBAU 2:14.

52. Hon. Gabriel S. Kohn, December 4, 1995, in WBAU 2:14.

53. Richard J. Schure to Peter Diamandopoulos, "Liotti, Friends of WBAU, et al., vs. Adelphi University," January 4, 1996, WBAU 2:14.

54. Peter Diamandopoulos to *Afrika Unbound* Editorial Board and other students, undated, WBAU 2:18.

55. Deborah Bazemore to Diamandopoulos, February 26, 1996, WBAU 2:8.

56. Fax, February 9, 1996, WBAU 2:11.

57. Jackie Parker, "A Communications Major Speaks Out," editorial, *Afrika Unbound*, February 1996.

58. Jackie Parker, "The Big Lie: WBAU," *Afrika Unbound*, February 1996.

59. Parker, "Big Lie."

60. "Problems/Solutions," flyer, undated, WBAU 2:12.

61. A Friend in Need to the President of Adelphi University, February 16, 1996, WBAU 2:11.

62. Fax, "No More Complaining . . . It's Time to Act," February 23, 1996, WBAU 2:11.

63. David Hinckley, "Adelphi Students Try to Save WBAU," *Daily News*, February 26, 1996, in WBAU 2:11.

64. "Student Government Meeting, February 27th, 1996" in *Delphian*, March 13, 1996.

65. Afrika Unbound Editorial Board to Diamandopoulos, February 27, 1996, WBAU 2:12.

66. Afrika Unbound Editorial Board to Diamandopoulos, "Proposal to Reinstate WBAU," February 27, 1996, WBAU 2:12.

67. Afrika Unbound Editorial Board to Diamandopoulos, "Proposal."

68. Jackie Parker to Rheins, "Student Statement in Objection to the Closure of WBAU and Subsequent Request for Its Reinstatement" March 1, 1996, WBAU 2:11.

69. Amy Harrison to Deborah Bazemore et al., March 5, 1996, WBAU 2:15.

70. Michael J. O'Brien to Timothy P. Burton, March 6, 1996, "Chronology of Efforts to Value WBAU," WBAU 2:14.

71. Afrika Unbound to Diamandopoulos, March 6, 1996, WBAU 2:8.

72. Jackie Parker to Diamandopoulos, March 11, 1996, WBAU 2:8.

73. Friends of WBAU, Inc., "Reply to 'Opposition to Informal Objection,' Styled as 'Petition to Deny,'" to Chief, Mass Media bureau, File No. BMLED-951024KA, March 28, 1996, WBAU 2:14.

74. "WBAU Staff Presses On," *Daily News*, May 7, 1996.

75. Parker to Diamandopoulos.

76. Dean Carl Rheins to Laura Harding, July 19, 1996, WBAU 2:14.

77. A. S. Zaidi, "At Adelphi: The Lengthening View," WBAU 2:14.

78. John Schmidt to Steven Isenberg, April 18, 1997, WBAU 2:15.

79. Tom Heffernan to James A. Norton, June 18, 1997, WBAU 2:15.

80. David Hinckley, "FCC Waves Goodby as WBAU Vanishes into Thin Air," *Daily News*, September 6, 1997.

Hidden Tracks

1. "Matador Bullish on Napster," *Hits Daily Double*, December 6, 2001.

2. Lance Fiasco, "Matador Records Licenses Full Catalog to Napster," *Idobi*, December 7, 2001, https://idobi.com/news/matador-records-licenses-full-catalog-to-napster.

3. "RIAA Legal War Continues against Napster," CMJ, May 22, 2000.

4. Glen Sansone, ed., "Metallica: Taking Names, Kicking Nap,'" CMJ, May 22, 2000.

5. Local activists would challenge this trend, but by the late 1990s consumers witnessed "how Big Media companies parlayed bold political entrepreneurialism and the federal government's blind faith in the power of markets and technology to win historic concessions from Congress and the Federal Communications Commission, which they used to dominate local markets from coast to coast." Eric Klinenberg, *Fighting for Air: The Battle to Control America's Media* (New York: Henry Holt, 2008), 14–15.

6. Sansone, "Metallica."

7. "Sony, Universal, MP3 Subscribe to New Idea," CMJ, May 22, 2000.

8. Allison Neumer, "Stations Seek Fee Break," *Chicago Tribune*, November 23, 2002.

9. "Fees Hit College Internet Radio Hard," *Associated Press*, August 26, 2002.

10. Opinions, *Rice Thresher*, October 27, 2000.

11. Olivia Allison and Elizabeth Jardina, "Athletics Ask for More Time on KTRU," *Rice Thresher*, October 13, 2000.

12. Opinions, *Rice Thresher*, October 27, 2000.

13. Olivia Allison, "KTRU Committee to Make Recommendations Today," *Rice Thresher*, November 17, 2000.

14. Juan Saldaña, "'Bumper Stickers over Their Mouths': A Podcast on the 2000 KTRU Shutdown," *Rice Thresher*, May 8, 2018.

15. Elizabeth Jardina, "KTRU off the Air Indefinitely," *Rice Thresher*, November 30, 2000.

16. Hutchinson in Saldaña. Special Issue, *Rice Thresher*, December 5, 2000.

17. Olivia Allison, "Senate Passes KTRU Resolution Unanimously," *Rice Thresher*, December 1, 2000.

18. Letters, *Rice Thresher*, December 1, 2000.

19. "Senate Must Not Act Sunday," *Rice Thresher*, December 2, 2000.

20. Olivia Allison, "KTRU Back on the Air," *Rice Thresher*, December 8, 2000.

21. Letters, *Rice Thresher*, December 1, 2000.

22. Laura Newsome, "FCC Forces WUOG's Audio Webcast off Net," *Red and Black*, November 8, 2002.

23. John Vorwald, "Waning Support for College Radio Sets Off Debate," *New York Times*, December 5, 2010; Freddie O'Connell, "The Day the Music Died," *New York Times*, June 11, 2011.

24. "Public Broadcasting Fact Sheet," *Pew Research Center's Journalism Project* (blog), June 29, 2021, www.pewresearch.org/journalism/fact-sheet/public-broadcasting/; "Audio and Podcasting Fact Sheet," *Pew Research Center's Journalism Project* (blog), June 29, 2021. www.pewresearch.org/journalism/fact-sheet/audio-and-podcasting/. Although most listeners tuned in for talk and news programming, NPR's listenership dipped from 2019, although the number of NPR stations rose slightly.

25. Jared Bridgeman, interview with author, August 6, 2020.

26. Bridgeman.

27. Pacey Foster and Wayne Marshall, "Tales of the Tape: Cassette Culture, Community Radio, and the Birth of Rap Music in Boston," *Creative Industries Journal* 8, no. 2 (July 3, 2015): 164–76, https://doi.org/10.1080/17510694.2015.1090229.

28. Bridgeman interview.

29. Foster and Marshall, "Tales of the Tape, 218.

30. Foster and Marshall, 212.

31. Creation of Low Power Radio Service, FCC, *Federal Register*, vol. 65, no. 31 47 CFR pts. 11, 73 and 74, February 15, 2000, 7615–49.

32. National Public Radio, "Tiny Desk Concerts," https://podcasts.apple.com/us/podcast/tiny-desk-concerts-audio/id657476401.

33. Andrew Bottomley, *Sound Streams: A Cultural History of Radio-Internet Convergence* (Ann Arbor: University of Michigan Press, 2020), 15–17.

34. Elena Razlogova, "The Past and Future of Music Listening: From Freeform DJs to Recommendation Algorithms," in Jason Loviglio and Michele Hilmes, eds., *Radio's New Wave: Global Sound in the Digital Era* (New York: Routledge, 2013), 62–74; Jamie Wolf, "No Hits, All the Time," *New York Times*, April 11, 1999.

35. Liz Berg, "Radio News You Can't Use," *WFMU's Beware of the Blog* (blog), August 6, 2007, https://blog.wfmu.org/freeform/2007/08/radio-news-you-.html.

36. Wolf, "No Hits."

37. Lee Ranaldo—02/00, Sonic Youth, http://sonicyouth.com/dotsonics/lee/prose/wfmu.html.

38. Stephen Witt, *How Music Got Free: The End of an Industry, the Turn of the Century, and the Patient Zero of Piracy* (New York: Penguin, 2015), 95.

39. Freddie O'Connell, "The Day the Music Died," *New York Times*, 2011, sec. Review; Kevin Lozano, "Does College Radio Even Matter Anymore?," *Pitchfork*, February 8, 2017, http://pitchfork.com/features/article/10018-does-college-radio-even-matter-anymore/.

40. Sharon Scott, interview with author, March 4, 2019.

41. Sharon Scott, email, January 12, 2022.

42. "WRVU Group Granted Low-Power FM License," *Nashville Scene*, December 4, 2014, www.nashvillescene.com/nashvillecream/archives/2014/12/04/wrvu-group-granted-low-power-fm-license; Will Mullany, "Student Radio Station WXTJ to Begin Broadcasting on FM," *UVA Today*, June 30, 2015, https://news.virginia.edu/content/student-radio-station-wxtj-begin-broadcasting-fm.

43. Ariel LeBeau, "Julian Casablancas on Music Industry Frustrations, Running a Label & Ignoring Spotify," *Billboard*, April 10, 2019, www.billboard.com/articles/columns/rock/8506486/julian-casablancas-interview.

44. Darek Mazzone, interview with author, September 28, 2020.

45. Bill Rosenblatt, interview with author, July 17, 2020.

Selected Bibliography

Primary Sources

Archives

The following collections are those consulted in researching the history of college radio and inform the chronologies and contexts of this work.

Albuquerque, NM
  Center for Southwest Research, University Libraries, University of New Mexico
    KUNM Records
Amherst, MA
  Amherst College Archives and Special Collections, Amherst College Library
    WAMH/WAMF Records, 1955–2015.
  Special Collections and University Archives, University Libraries, University of
      Massachusetts Amherst
    Black Mass Communications Project, ca. 1970–1985
    Massachusetts Daily Collegian
    University of Massachusetts Amherst, Student Organizations Records
Athens, GA
  Georgia Historic Newspapers Archive, Digital Library of Georgia
    The Red and Black (Athens, Ga.) 1893–current
  Hagrett Rare Book and Manuscript Library, The University of Georgia
      Libraries
    University of Georgia Archives, WUOG records
Atlanta, GA
  University Library, Georgia State University
    Digital Collections: Georgia State University *Signal*
    Special Collections and Archives, WRAS Documents
Auburn, AL
  Auburn University Libraries
    WEGL Records
Boston, MA
  Archives and Special Collections, University Libraries, Northeastern University
    WRBB-FM, 1966–2006.
  Iwasaki Library, Emerson College
    WERS Records
Brookville, NY
  Archives and Special Collections, Long Island University
    Archives of the LIU Post WCWP Radio Station
    Pioneer (student newspaper)

Cambridge, MA
  Pusey Library, Harvard University
    Records of the Harvard Radio Broadcasting Co., Inc., and WHRB
  Schlesinger Library, Radcliffe Institute, Harvard University
    Boston Women's Community Radio Records
  WMBR, Massachusetts Institute of Technology
    "The Book," WMBR studio, Walker Memorial Building
Chapel Hill, NC
  DigitalNC, UNC–Chapel Hill University Library
    Black Ink (Black Student Movement, The University of North Carolina at Chapel Hill)
    Daily Tar Heel (Chapel Hill, NC)
    Lambda (Carolina Gay and Lesbian Association, The University of North Carolina at Chapel Hill)
    North Carolina Newspapers
  The Wilson Library, The University of North Carolina at Chapel Hill
    Southern Folklife Collection, Merge Records Collection
    WXYC Radio records, 1970–2018
Cleveland, OH
  KSSU/KEDG online archive, https://kedg.weebly.com
  Rock and Roll Hall of Fame Library and Archives
    Greg Kot Papers
    Josh Gottheil Collection, (University of Illinois/Champaign-Urbana Fanzines)
    Mike Kole (Cleveland State)
    Rolling Stone Magazine Records
    Steve Wainstead Collection, (Cleveland State)
College Park, MD
  Special Collections and University Archives, Hornbake Library, University of Maryland
    National Federation of Community Broadcasters (NFCB) records
    Susan Stamberg Papers
    WAMU Archives
    WMUC Records
Danbury, CT
  Western Connecticut State University Archives and Special Collections
    WXCI Records, 1972–2009
Davidson, NC
  E. H. Little Library, Davidson College
    The Davidsonian
Fort Collins, CO
  Mountain Scholar Home, University Archive, Colorado State University Libraries, Colorado State University
    Student Unrest Collection

Fremont, CA
    Ohlone College Archives
        KOHL "Graffiti Book"
Hamilton, NY
    Special Collections and University Archives, Colgate University Libraries
        Office of the Provost and Dean of the Faculty records, WRCU
        WRCU Records
Hempstead, NY
    University Archives and Special Collections, Adelphi University
        Afrika Unbound
        The Delphian
        Other Organizations and Clubs, WBAU
Houston, TX
    Woodson Research Center, Fondren Library, Rice University
        Rice University KTRU Radio Records
Ithaca, NY
    DigitalCommons, Ithaca College
        The Ithacan Collection
    Division of Rare and Manuscript Collections, Cornell University Library
        WHCU Department of Black Affairs records
        WVBR records, 1946–2000s
    Keith R. Johnson '56 Archive, Cornell University Library
        The Cornell Daily Sun
Lawrence, KS
    Kenneth Spencer Research Library, University of Kansas Libraries
        Committee for the Preservation of Wild Life in Lawrence Collection, Kansas
            Collection
Los Angeles, CA
    Department of Archives and Special Collections, William H. Hannon Library,
            Loyola Marymount University
        Loyola Marymount University Archives KXLU Records
    Doheney Memorial Library, University of Southern California University
            Archives
        University of Southern California History Collection, *The Daily Trojan, 1912–*
    UCLA Library, hosted by archive.org, University of California, Los Angeles
        Daily Bruin, https://archive.dailybruin.com
Medford, MA
    Digital Collections and Archives, Tufts University
        Freeform Magazine
        Something About the Women Radio Show Records, 1983–1995,Activities
            and Organizations Records, Series 1, WMFO 1971–1985
Middletown, CT
    Special Collections & Archives, Wesleyan University Library
        WESU Records

New Haven, CT
    Manuscripts and Archives, Yale University Library
        WYBC, Yale University, Records
New York, NY
    Department of Archives and Special Collections, Fordham University Libraries
        WFUV-FM Collection
    New York University Archives, New York University Libraries
        Records of WNYU (Radio Station: New York, NY)
    Rare Book & Manuscript Library, Columbia University
        Central Files, 1890–1984, Series I: Central Files, 1895–1971
        Historical Subject Files, Series XIX: Student Life
Northampton, MA
    Smith College Archives
        Radio Club and Student Radio Stations records
Oberlin, OH
    Oberlin College Archives
        Student Life: WOBC Radio Station Records, 1942, 1949–2000, 2002–2011
Olympia, WA
    The Evergreen State College Archives and Special Collections
        The Cooper Point Journal
        KAOS Records
Philadelphia, PA
    University of Pennsylvania Libraries
        The Daily Pennsylvanian digital archives
Princeton, NJ
    Princeton University Archives and Special Collections, Seely G. Mudd
            Manuscript Library
        WPRB Records
Providence, RI
    John Hay Library, Brown University Library
        Brown Alumni Magazine
        Brown Daily Herald, Digital Archive, https://library.brown.edu/cds/dbdh/
San Diego, CA
    San Diego State University Library and Information Access
        SDSU Student Newspapers: *Daily Aztec*
San Francisco, CA
    Gleeson Library Digital Collections, University of San Francisco
        The Foghorn
Santa Barbara, CA
    Department of Special Research Collections, Alexandria Digital Research
            Library, UC Santa Barbara Library
        Santa Barbara *Daily Nexus* and antecedent newspapers
Seattle, WA
    University Libraries, University of Washington
        Censorship Undermines Radio Station Ethics (CURSE) Records

Digital Collections, UW Yearbooks and Documents
KCMU records
The Seattle Civil Rights and Labor History Project, The Black Student Union
    at UW (http://depts.washington.edu/civilr/BSU_news.htm)
University of Washington Department of Radio Education/KUOW records,
    1947–1991
University of Washington President, KEXP-KUOW
South Orange, NJ
Monsignor Noe Field Archives & Special Collections Center, Seton Hall
    University
WSOU Records
Stanford, CA
Department of Special Collections and University Archives, Stanford
    University Libraries
Charles A. Spolyar KZSU playlist collection, 1980–1983
Stanford University, KZSU, records
Stanford Digital Stacks
    KZSU (1981–1983)
The Stanford Daily Archive, stanforddailyarchive.com
Stony Brook, NY
Special Collections, SUNY Stony Brook Libraries
Turmoil Radio Collection
WUSB 90.1 FM: Abbie Kearse Collection
Storrs, CT
Archives and Special Collections, University of Connecticut Library Repository
WHUS Records
Teaneck, NJ
Fairleigh Dickinson University Digital Archives
FDU Teaneck Student Newspapers
Washington, DC
Digital Howard @ Howard University Library
The Hilltop Digital Archive
Georgetown University Archives, Booth Family Center for Special Collections
DigitalGeorgetown, The Hoya Archives
Old Archives: Georgetown University Radio–T.V.

Interviews

Nick Archer	Jared Bridgman	Dwight Farrell
Larry Azrin	Marty Byk	Craig Finn
Jon Bernhardt	Thomas Callahan	Hugh Foley
Monica Black	Jason Cohen	Jon Fox
Lori Blumenthal	DJ C-Wiz	Mitchell J. Frank
Jim Bolt	Adam Devore	Ernest Freeberg
Glenn Boothe	Bertis Downs	Patti Galluzzi

Brent Giessmann   Tom Mara   Bruce Pavitt
John Ginoli   Darek Mazzone   Joe Peebles
Mike Gioscia   Jim McGuinn   Doc Pelzel
David Giovannoni   Dan Miele   Jack Rabid
Donna Halper   Jeremy Mills   Bill Rosenblatt
Mark Hamilton   Mike Mills   Josh Rosenthal
Robert Harris   Kendall Minter   Kurt St. Thomas
Joe Helm   Chris Mohr   Seth L. Sanders
Dave Hughes   Pat Monteith   Henry Santoro
Jack Isquith   Bill Moser   John Schmidt
Mark Kates   Pete Nash   Sharon Scott
Ken Katkin   Una Natterman   Angie C Shaw
Julie Kramer   Kathleen Newman   Ray Shea
Steve Kreitzer   Jamie Noble   Ron Slomowicz
Nicola Krest   Oedipus   Dan Smith
Kevin M. Kruse   Will Oldham   Britt Walford
Eric J. Lawrence   Shachar Oren   Judy Wilburn
TeRon Lawrence   Ted Ownby   Bekah Zeitz
Mike Lupica

Selected Secondary Sources

Alan, Carter, and Steven Tyler. *Radio Free Boston: The Rise and Fall of WBCN.* Boston: University Press of New England, 2013.

Albini, Steve. "The Problem with Music." *The Baffler*, December 1993. https://thebaffler.com/salvos/the-problem-with-music.

Arnold, Gina. *Route 666: On the Road to Nirvana.* New York: St. Martin's, 1993.

Azerrad, Michael. *Come as You Are: The Story of Nirvana.* New York: Doubleday, 1994.

———. *Our Band Could Be Your Life: Scenes from the American Indie Underground 1981–1991.* New York: Back Bay Books, 2002.

Bagdikian, Ben H. *The New Media Monopoly: A Completely Revised and Updated Edition with Seven New Chapters.* Boston: Beacon, 2004.

Bailey, Olga, Bart Cammaerts, and Nico Carpentier. *Understanding Alternative Media.* Maidenhead, Berkshire, UK: McGraw-Hill Education, 2007.

Baldwin, Davarian L. *In the Shadow of the Ivory Tower: How Universities Are Plundering Our Cities.* New York: Bold Type Books, 2021.

Barlow, William. *Voice Over: The Making of Black Radio.* Philadelphia: Temple University Press, 1999.

Bloch, Louis M. *The Gas Pipe Networks: A History of College Radio, 1936–1946.* Cleveland, OH: Bloch, 1980.

Bloom, Allan. *The Closing of the American Mind: How Higher Education Has Failed Democracy and Impoverished the Souls of Today's Students.* New York: Simon & Schuster, 1987.

Bottomley, Andrew. *Sound Streams: A Cultural History of Radio-Internet Convergence.* Ann Arbor: University of Michigan Press, 2020.

Bourdieu, Pierre. *Distinction: A Social Critique of the Judgement of Taste*. 11th ed. Cambridge, MA: Harvard University Press, 2002.

——. *The Field of Cultural Production*. New York: Columbia University Press, 1993.

Brewster, Bill. *Last Night a DJ Saved My Life: The History of the Disc Jockey*. New York: Grove, 2014.

Brinkley, Alan. *Voices of Protest: Huey Long, Father Coughlin, & the Great Depression*. New York: Vintage, 1983.

Brooks, Tim. *College Radio Days: 70 Years of Student Broadcasting at Dartmouth College*. Greenwich, CT: Glenville Press, 2013.

Brown, Rodger Lyle. *Party out of Bounds: The B-52's, R.E.M., and the Kids Who Rocked Athens, Georgia*. New York: Plume, 1991.

Brown, Timothy S. "Subcultures, Pop Music and Politics: Skinheads and 'Nazi Rock' in England and Germany." *Journal of Social History* 38, no. 1 (2004): 157–78.

Brownell, Kathryn Cramer. *Showbiz Politics: Hollywood in American Political Life*. Chapel Hill: The University of North Carolina Press, 2014.

Brumbeloe, Samuel. "A Cultural Study of WAPI: One Educational Radio Station and Its Shift to Entertainment." Master's thesis, Auburn University, 2002.

Cateforis, Theo. *Are We Not New Wave?: Modern Pop at the Turn of the 1980s*. Ann Arbor: University of Michigan Press, 2011.

Chang, Jeff. *Can't Stop, Won't Stop: A History of the Hip-Hop Generation*. New York: St. Martin's, 2005.

Chastagner, Claude. "The Parents' Music Resource Center: From Information to Censorship." *Popular Music* 18, no. 2 (May 1999): 179–92.

Chávez, Christopher. *The Sound of Exclusion: NPR and the Latinx Public*. Tucson: University of Arizona Press, 2021.

Chernonsky, Louise E. "Imagining Listeners through American Experimental Music: NPR's RadioVisions." In *Tomorrow Is the Question: New Directions in Experimental Music Studies*, edited by Benjamin Piekut, 26. Ann Arbor: University of Michigan Press, 2014. https://doi.org/10.3998/mpub.5242620.

Cook, John, Mac McCaughan, and Laura Ballance. *Our Noise: The Story of Merge Records, the Indie Label That Got Big and Stayed Small*. Chapel Hill, NC: Algonquin Books, 2009.

Cowie, Jefferson R. *Stayin' Alive: The 1970s and the Last Days of the Working Class*. New York: New Press, 2012.

Davis, Joshua Clark. *From Head Shops to Whole Foods: The Rise and Fall of Activist Entrepreneurs*. New York: Columbia University Press, 2017.

Desztich, Rachael, and Steven McClung. "Indie to an Extent? Why Music Gets Added to College Radio Playlists." *Journal of Radio Studies* 14, no. 2 (November 1, 2007): 196–211.

Diamond, Michael, and Adam Horovitz. *Beastie Boys Book*. New York: Spiegel & Grau, 2018.

Doe, John, and Tom DeSavia. *Under the Big Black Sun: A Personal History of L.A Punk*. Cambridge, MA: Da Capo, 2016.

Douglas, Susan J. *Listening In: Radio and the American Imagination*. Minneapolis: University of Minnesota Press, 2004.

Duncombe, Stephen. *Notes from Underground: Zines and the Politics of Alternative Culture*. 3rd ed. Portland: Microcosm Publishing, 1997, 2017.

Echols, Alice. *Hot Stuff: Disco and the Remaking of American Culture*. New York: W. W. Norton, 2011.

Engelman, Ralph. *Public Radio and Television in America: A Political History*. Thousand Oaks, CA: Sage Publications, 1996.

Ewert, Cody Dodge. *Making Schools American: Nationalism and the Origin of Modern Educational Politics*. Baltimore: Johns Hopkins University Press, 2022.

Fauteux, Brian. *Music in Range: The Culture of Canadian Campus Radio*. Film and Media Studies. Waterloo, Ontario: Wilfrid Laurier University Press, 2015.

Ferguson, Roderick A. *We Demand: The University and Student Protests*. Oakland: University of California Press, 2017.

Filene, Benjamin. *Romancing the Folk: Public Memory and American Roots Music*. New ed. Chapel Hill: The University of North Carolina Press, 2000.

Fisher, Marc. *Something in the Air: Radio, Rock, and the Revolution That Shaped a Generation*. New York: Random House, 2007.

Foster, Pacey, and Wayne Marshall. "Tales of the Tape: Cassette Culture, Community Radio, and the Birth of Rap Music in Boston." *Creative Industries Journal* 8, no. 2 (July 3, 2015): 164–76. https://doi.org/10.1080/17510694.2015.1090229.

Frank, Thomas. *The Conquest of Cool: Business Culture, Counterculture, and the Rise of Hip Consumerism*. Chicago: University of Chicago Press, 1997.

———. *What's the Matter with Kansas? How Conservatives Won the Heart of America*. New York: Picador, 2005.

Fraser, Steve, and Gary Gerstle, eds. *The Rise and Fall of the New Deal Order, 1930–1980*. Repr. Ed. Princeton, NJ: Princeton University Press, 1990.

Fricke, Jim, Charlie Ahearn, and Experience Music Project. *Yes Yes Y'all: The Experience Music Project Oral History of Hip-Hop's First Decade*. Cambridge, MA: Da Capo, 2002.

Gastman, Roger, and Corcoran Gallery of Art. *Pump Me Up: DC Subculture of the 1980s*. Los Angeles: R. Rock Enterprises, 2013.

Gerstle, Gary. *American Crucible: Race and Nation in the Twentieth Century*. Princeton, NJ: Princeton University Press, 2001.

Goldberg, Chad Alan. *Education for Democracy: Renewing the Wisconsin Idea*. Madison: University of Wisconsin Pres, 2020.

Goodman, Lizzy. *Meet Me in the Bathroom: Rebirth and Rock and Roll in New York City 2001–2011*. Repr. Ed. New York: Dey Street Books, 2018.

Graham, Otis L. *An Encore for Reform: The Old Progressives and the New Deal*. New York: Oxford University Press, 1968.

Gronow, Pekka, Ilpo Saunio, and Christopher Moseley. *An International History of the Recording Industry*. London: Cassell, 1999.

Grossberg, Lawrence. *Dancing in Spite of Myself: Essays on Popular Culture*. Durham, NC: Duke University Press, 1997.

Hale, Grace Elizabeth. *Cool Town: How Athens, Georgia, Launched Alternative Music and Changed American Culture.* Chapel Hill: The University of North Carolina Press, 2020.

Hall, Stuart. *Cultural Studies 1983: A Theoretical History.* Edited by Jennifer Daryl Slack and Lawrence Grossberg. Repr. ed. Durham, NC: Duke University Press, 2016.

Harris, Keith. "Did New York Kill Indie Rock?" *Journal of Popular Music Studies* 24, no. 3 (2012): 276–79. https://doi.org/10.1111/j.1533-1598.2012.01334.x.

Harrison, Anthony Kwame. "Black College-Radio on Predominantly White Campuses: A 'Hip-Hop Era' Student-Authored Inclusion Initiative." *Africology: The Journal of Pan African Studies* 9, no. 8 (2016): 135–54.

Harrison, Colin. "Music and Radio." In *American Culture in the 1990s,* 65–96. Edinburgh: Edinburgh University Press, 2010.

Hartman, Andrew. "The Culture Wars Are Dead: Long Live the Culture Wars!" *The Baffler,* no. 39 (2018): 48–55.

———. *A War for the Soul of America: A History of the Culture Wars.* Chicago: University of Chicago Press, 2015.

Hemmer, Nicole. *Messengers of the Right: Conservative Media and the Transformation of American Politics.* Philadelphia: University of Pennsylvania Press, 2018.

Hendershot, Heather. *What's Fair on the Air? Cold War Right-Wing Broadcasting and the Public Interest.* Chicago: University of Chicago Press, 2011.

Hendricks, John Allen, ed. *Radio's Second Century: Past, Present, and Future Perspectives.* New Brunswick, NJ: Rutgers University Press, 2020. https://doi .org/10.2307/j.ctvwcjfxv.

Hilliard, Robert L., and Michael C. Keith. *The Quieted Voice: The Rise and Demise of Localism in American Radio.* Carbondale: Southern Illinois University Press, 2005.

Hilmes, Michele. *Only Connect: A Cultural History of Broadcasting in the United States.* Belmont, CA: Wadsworth/Thomson Learning, 2002.

Hilmes, Michele, and Jason Loviglio, eds. *Radio Reader: Essays in the Cultural History of Radio.* New York: Routledge, 2002.

Holt, Jennifer. *Empires of Entertainment: Media Industries and the Politics of Deregulation, 1980–1996.* New Brunswick, NJ: Rutgers University Press, 2011.

Janisse, Kier-La, and Paul Corupe. *Satanic Panic: Pop-Cultural Paranoia in the 1980s.* Toronto: Spectacular Optical Publications, 2019.

Johnson, Aaron J. "Jazz and Radio in the United States: Mediation, Genre, and Patronage." PhD thesis, Columbia University, 2014. https://doi.org/10.7916 /D83T9FCZ

Jung, Donald J. *The Federal Communications Commission, the Broadcast Industry, and the Fairness Doctrine, 1981–1987.* Lanham, MD: University Press of America, 1996.

Klinenberg, Eric. *Fighting for Air: The Battle to Control America's Media.* New York: Henry Holt, 2008.

Kolehmainen, Pekka M. "Rock, Freedom, and Ideologies of 'Americanness:' U.S. Culture War Debates of the Late Twentieth Century." Doctoral diss., University of Turku, 2021.

Kramer, Michael J. *The Republic of Rock: Music and Citizenship in the Sixties Counterculture*. New York: Oxford University Press, 2013.

Krieger, Susan. *Hip Capitalism*. Beverley Hills, CA: Sage, 1979.

Kruse, Holly. *Site and Sound: Understanding Independent Music Scenes*. New York: Peter Lang, 2003.

Land, Jeffrey. *Active Radio: Pacifica's Brash Experiment*. Minneapolis: University of Minnesota Press, 1999.

Lasar, Matthew. *Pacifica Radio: The Rise of an Alternative Network*. Philadelphia: Temple University Press, 2000.

———. *Uneasy Listening: Pacifica Radio's Civil War*. Cambridge, UK: Black Apollo, 2006.

Lichtenstein, Bill. *WBCN and the American Revolution*. Cambridge, MA: MIT Press, 2021.

Loviglio, Jason, and Michele Hilmes, eds. *Radio's New Wave: Global Sound in the Digital Era*. New York: Routledge, 2013.

MacLeod, Dewar. *Kids of the Black Hole: Punk Rock in Postsuburban California*. Norman: University of Oklahoma Press, 2010.

Marcus, Sara. *Girls to the Front: The True Story of the Riot Grrrl Revolution*. New York: Harper Perennial, 2010.

Marcuse, Herbert, and Douglas Kellner. *One-Dimensional Man: Studies in the Ideology of Advanced Industrial Society*. 2nd ed. Boston: Beacon, 1991.

Martin, Bradford. *The Other Eighties: A Secret History of America in the Age of Reagan*. New York: Farrar, Straus and Giroux, 2011.

Mattson, Kevin. *We're Not Here to Entertain: Punk Rock, Ronald Reagan, and the Real Culture War of 1980s America*. New York: Oxford University Press, 2020.

McCauley, Michael P. *NPR: The Trials and Triumphs of National Public Radio*. New York: Columbia University Press, 2005.

McChesney, Robert W. *Telecommunications, Mass Media, and Democracy: The Battle for the Control of U.S. Broadcasting, 1928–1935*. New York: Oxford University Press, 1994.

McChesney, Robert W., and Dan Schiller. "The Political Economy of International Communications." United Nations Research Institute for Social Development, Technology, Business and Society, no. 11 (October 2003).

McClung, Steven. "College Radio Station Web Sites: Perceptions of Value and Use." *Journalism & Mass Communication Educator* 56, no. 1 (March 2001): 62–73. https://doi.org/10.1177/107769580105600106.

McNeil, Legs, and Gillian McCain. *Please Kill Me: The Uncensored Oral History of Punk*. Repr. ed. New York: Grove, 2006.

Mitchell, Jack W. *Listener Supported: The Culture and History of Public Radio*. Westport, CT: Praeger, 2005.

Nodine, Steven, Eric Beaumont, Clancy Carroll, and David Luhrssen. *Brick through the Window: An Oral History of Punk Rock, New Wave and Noise in Milwaukee, 1964–1984*. Milwaukee, WI: Splunge Communications, 2017.

O'Connor, Alan. *Punk Record Labels and the Struggle for Autonomy: The Emergence of D.I.Y.* Critical Media Studies. Lanham, MD: Lexington Books, 2008.

O'Haver, Hanson. "A Crime and a Pastime: The Paranoid Style of American Skateboarding." *The Baffler*, no. 40 (2018): 66–72.

Owens, Patsy Eubanks. "No Teens Allowed: The Exclusion of Adolescents from Public Spaces." *Landscape Journal* 21, no. 1 (2002): 156–63.

Ozzi, Dan. *Sellout: The Major Label Feeding Frenzy That Swept Punk, Emo, and Hardcore (1994–2007)*. Boston: Houghton Mifflin Harcourt, 2021.

Pavitt, Bruce, Calvin Johnson, Ann Powers, Larry Reid, Gerard Cosloy, and Charles R. Cross. *Sub Pop USA: The Subterraneanan Pop Music Anthology, 1980–1988*. Brooklyn, NY: Bazillion Points, 2014.

Petrzela, Natalia Mehlman. *Classroom Wars: Language, Sex, and the Making of Modern Political Culture*. New York: Oxford University Press, 2015.

Preuss, Andreas. "Left of the Dial, Right on the Music: 50 Years of Georgia State FM Radio." Master's thesis, Georgia State University, 2021.

Crook, Sarah, and Charlie Jeffries, eds. *Resist, Organize, Build: Feminist and Queer Activism in Britain and the United States during the Long 1980s*. Albany: State University of New York Press, 2022.

Rae, Casey, *William S. Burroughs and the Cult of Rock 'n' Roll*. Austin: University of Texas Press, 2019.

Reynolds, Simon. *Rip It Up and Start Again: Post-Punk 1978–84*. London: Faber and Faber, 2006.

Riches, Gabby, Dave Snell, Bryan Bardine, and Brenda Gardenour Walter. *Heavy Metal Studies and Popular Culture*. London: Palgrave MacMillan, 2016.

Riismandel, Kyle. *Neighborhood of Fear: The Suburban Crisis in American Culture, 1975–2001*. Baltimore: Johns Hopkins University Press, 2020.

Rodríguez, Dylan. "Beyond 'Police Brutality': Racist State Violence and the University of California." *American Quarterly* 64, no. 2 (2012): 301–13.

Rose, Tricia. *Black Noise: Rap Music and Black Culture in Contemporary America*. Hanover, NH: University Press of New England, 1994.

———. *The Hip Hop Wars: What We Talk About When We Talk about Hip Hop—and Why It Matters*. New York: Civitas Books, 2008.

Rosenwald, Brian. *Talk Radio's America: How an Industry Took Over a Political Party That Took Over the United States*. Cambridge, MA: Harvard University Press, 2019.

Rossinow, Douglas C. *The Politics of Authenticity: Liberalism, Christianity, and the New Left in America*. New York: Columbia University Press, 1998.

Rubin, Nicholas. "Signing On: U.S. College Rock Radio and the Popular Music Industry, 1977–1983." PhD diss., University of Virginia, 2010.

Sanneh, Kelefa. *Major Labels: A History of Popular Music in Seven Genres*. New York: Penguin, 2021.

Sauls, Samuel J. *The Culture of American College Radio*. Ames: Iowa State University Press, 2000.

———. "The Role of Alternative Programming in College Radio." *Studies in Popular Culture* 21, no. 1 (1998): 73–81.

Schlesinger, Arthur Meier. *The Disuniting of America: Reflections on a Multicultural Society*. Rev. and enl. ed. New York: W. W. Norton, 1998.

Schrecker, Ellen. *The Lost Promise: American Universities in the 1960s*. Chicago: University of Chicago Press, 2021.

Schulman, Bruce J. *The Seventies: The Great Shift in American Culture, Society, and Politics*. Cambridge, MA: Da Capo, 2002.

Schulman, Bruce J., and Julian E. Zelizer, eds. *Media Nation: The Political History of News in Modern America*. Philadelphia: University of Pennsylvania Press, 2017.

Shepperd, Josh. "The Political Economic Structure of Early Media Reform Before and After the Communications Act of 1934." *Resonance* 1, no. 3 (October 16, 2020): 244–66.

——. *Shadow of the New Deal: The Victory of Public Broadcasting*. Urbana: University of Illinois Press, 2023.

Shermer, Elizabeth Tandy. *Indentured Students: How Government-Guaranteed Loans Left Generations Drowning in College Debt*. Cambridge, MA: The Belknap Press of Harvard University Press, 2021.

Simpson, Kim. *Early '70s Radio: The American Format Revolution*. New York: Continuum, 2011.

Slotten, Hugh Richard. *Radio and Television Regulation Broadcast Technology in the United States, 1920–1960*. Baltimore: Johns Hopkins University Press, 2000.

——. *Radio's Hidden Voice: The Origins of Public Broadcasting in the United States*. Urbana: University of Illinois Press, 2009.

——. "'Rainbow in the Sky': FM Radio, Technical Superiority, and Regulatory Decision-Making." *Technology and Culture* 37, no. 4 (1996): 686–720. https://doi.org/10.2307/3107095.

——. "Universities, Public Service Radio and the 'American System' of Commercial Broadcasting, 1921–40." *Media History* 12, no. 3 (December 2006): 253–72.

Smith, Marquita S., and Dorothy M. Bland. "Preserving and Tuning into Radio Stations at Historically Black Colleges and Universities." *Journal of Radio & Audio Media*, November 16, 2022, 1–23. https://doi.org/10.1080/19376529.2022.2137167.

Spitz, Marc, and Brendan Mullen. *We Got the Neutron Bomb: The Untold Story of L.A. Punk*. New York: Three Rivers, 2001.

Squier, Susan Merrill, Steven Wurtzler, Bruce B. Campbell, Nina Huntemann, and Laurence A. Breiner. *Communities of the Air: Radio Century, Radio Culture*. Durham: Duke University Press, 2003.

Sterling, Christopher H., and Michael C. Keith. *Sounds of Change: A History of FM Broadcasting in America*. Chapel Hill: The University of North Carolina Press, 2008.

Sterling, Christopher H., and John M. Kittross. *Stay Tuned: A History of American Broadcasting*. 3rd ed. LEA's Communication Series. Mahwah, NJ: Lawrence Erlbaum Associates, 2002.

Stiegler, Zachary Joseph. "The Policy and Practice of Community Radio: Localism Versus Nationalism in U.S. Broadcasting." PhD thesis, University of Iowa, 2009.

Stoever, Jennifer Lynn. *The Sonic Color Line: Race and the Cultural Politics of Listening*. Repr. ed. New York: NYU Press, 2016.

Suisman, David. *Selling Sounds: The Commercial Revolution in American Music.* Cambridge, MA: Harvard University Press, 2012.

Susman, Warren. *Culture as History: The Transformation of American Society in the Twentieth Century.* Washington, DC: Smithsonian Books, 2003.

Thelin, John R. *A History of American Higher Education.* 3rd ed. Baltimore: Johns Hopkins University Press, 2019.

Tunstall, Jeremy. *Communications Deregulation: The Unleashing of America's Communications Industry.* Oxford, UK: B. Blackwell, 1986.

Tweedy, Jeff. *Let's Go (So We Can Get Back): A Memoir of Recording and Discording with Wilco, Etc.* New York: Dutton, 2019.

Viator, Felicia Angeja. *To Live and Defy in LA: How Gangsta Rap Changed America.* Cambridge, MA: Harvard University Press, 2020.

Waits, Jennifer C. "Does 'Indie' Mean Independence? Freedom and Restraint in a Late 1990s US College Radio Community." *Radio Journal—International Studies in Broadcast and Audio Media* 5, no. 2 & 3 (2007): 83–96.

———. "From Wireless Experiments to Streaming: The Secret History and Changing Role of College Radio at Haverford College 1923-2014." *Interactions: Studies in Communication & Culture* 6, no. 1 (March 1, 2015): 65–85. https://doi.org/10.1386/iscc.6.1.65_1.

Waksman, Steve. *This Ain't the Summer of Love: Conflict and Crossover in Heavy Metal and Punk.* Berkeley: University of California Press, 2009.

Walser, Robert. *Running with the Devil: Power, Gender, and Madness in Heavy Metal Music.* Hanover, NH: University Press of New England, 1993.

Ward, Brian. *Radio and the Struggle for Civil Rights in the South.* Gainesville: University Press of Florida, 2004.

Weisbard, Eric. *Top 40 Democracy: The Rival Mainstreams of American Music.* Chicago: University of Chicago Press, 2014.

Willard, Michael Nevin. "Skate and Punk at the Far End of the American Century." In *America in the Seventies,* edited by Beth L. Bailey and David R. Farber, 181–207. Lawrence: University Press of Kansas, 2004.

Williams, Justin A. *Rhymin' and Stealin: Musical Borrowing in Hip Hop.* Ann Arbor: University of Michigan Press, 2013.

Williams, Teona. "For 'Peace, Quiet, and Respect': Race, Policing, and Land Grabbing on Chicago's South Side." *Antipode* 53, no. 2 (2021): 497–523. https://doi.org/10.1111/anti.12692.

Winling, LaDale C. *Building the Ivory Tower: Universities and Metropolitan Development in the Twentieth Century.* Politics and Culture in Modern America. Philadelphia: University of Pennsylvania Press, 2018.

Witt, Stephen. *How Music Got Free: The End of an Industry, the Turn of the Century, and the Patient Zero of Piracy.* New York: Penguin, 2015.

Worth, Liz. *Treat Me like Dirt: An Oral History of Punk in Toronto and beyond, 1977–1981.* Toronto: ECW, 2011.

Yarm, Mark. *Everybody Loves Our Town: An Oral History of Grunge.* New York: Three Rivers Press, 2012.

Index

class D licensing, 54, 63; college radio governance, 220; eligibility, 8, 214, 221; funding, 54, 57–58, 66, 190, 193, 199, 215; resistance to regulations, 59

Cosloy, Gerard, 242, 270

Costello, Elvis, 27, 43, 143

counterculture: college radio, 9, 16–17, 72, 155, 247, 282, 306; co-optation of, 109, 312, 323; decline of, 25; media, 149; networks, 222, 233

country music: association with whiteness, 48, 100; college stations, 67, 187, 215, 261, 288; programming, 262; radio format, 38, 303; versus punk, 96; versus rock, 25

Cramps, 80

Crippen, Alex, 82–83

crossover, 29, 49, 141, 147, 151–52, 157, 193, 251, 259, 269–70, 308

cultural pluralism, 6–7, 12, 23, 36, 193

culture wars: censorship, 3, 278; curricular debates, 12, 137, 165, 194, 225, 301, 322, 324, 335, 365; hip-hop, 239, 273–74, 276, 279, 283, 300, 326; KCSB (see KCSB); market forces, 171, 182, 195, 200; metal music, 239; moral panic, 93; politics of higher education, 181, 200, 365; punk, 166; shaped by college radio, 11–12, 133, 136, 160, 162, 174, 179, 182, 279, 326–27, 365; WBAU (see WBAU)

Cure (band), 182–83

CURSE (Censorship Undermines Radio Station Ethics), 292–95. See also KCMU

C.W. Post College, 165, 336

Davidson College. See WDAV

Dead Kennedys, 98, 177, 238

Def Jam Records, 114, 253

Del Fuegos, 154, 157–58

deindustrialization, 26, 35, 119

democracy: airwave access, 12, 17, 35, 95, 118; higher education, 7; music industry, 12, 32, 94, 358; program-

ming, 159, 218, 273, 292; politics of punk, 26; station governance, 115, 119, 241, 243, 273, 292–94; visions of, 11, 119–20, 292

demographic shifts, 28, 114, 336

demo tapes, 74, 131–32, 272, 292

Depeche Mode, 307

deregulation: across industries, 160; effects on college radio, 179, 311, 313, 316; hopes for diversity, 305, 309; media, 5, 137, 160–61, 171, 184, 196, 199–200, 247, 297, 302–4; problems for artists, 351

Diamandopolous, Peter, 325–26, 329–30, 334–36, 338–46. See also Adelphi University

Diamond, Mike, 74

Didjits, 143–44

Dischord Records, 92, 152–53, 257

disco music, 18, 28, 34–35, 38, 51, 59, 67, 96, 99, 123, 135, 155

diversity: elitism and, 263; failures of, 47–49, 106, 117, 179, 192, 228, 296, 300, 304, 321, 351; ideals, 37, 63, 68, 71, 123, 127–28, 194, 210, 217, 252, 271, 277–78, 284–86, 288, 316; musical genres, 35, 48; responsibility to, 179, 210, 274; threats to, 273

DJs: activism, 185–86, 189, 212, 287–88; advocacy for stations, 3, 23, 34, 75, 110, 172, 302–3; amateur (see amateur DJs); audience demands, 128, 136, 181; authenticity, 94, 200, 214, 247, 316; Black, 39, 208, 283, 337; censorship, 174–78, 183–84, 193, 206, 215, 239–40, 278, 283; college DJs (see student DJs); community (see community DJs); culture wars, 3–4, 15–16, 111, 168, 172, 183–84, 278, 282; educational roles, 260, 265, 267, 271; elitism, 9–10, 70, 109, 183, 192, 200, 247, 264, 312, 315; FCC regulations, 175–76, 242, 278, 303; freeform (see freeform); free speech, 175–76, 178, 186, 189, 212, 294; gatekeepers, 90,

DJs: activism (cont.)
147, 233, 275, 365; independent
music, 313, 322; internet, 296, 354,
362, 365; jazz, 264 (*see also* jazz);
local music, 263, 298, 320; marginalized communities, 29, 39, 163, 166,
189, 191, 208, 210, 233, 279, 287–88;
music curation, 365; networks, 102,
104–5, 142–43, 157–59, 228, 266, 271,
285, 355; payola, 254, 328; playing
Black artists, 128, 274, 278, 280, 283,
337; professional careers, 10, 19, 36,
83, 92, 148–50, 236, 251, 266, 269,
308, 316, 318; rap, 128, 274, 277–78,
281–82, 298; reggae, 334; relationships to artists, 1, 3, 32, 98, 139,
157–59, 279, 326–27, 336, 358;
relationships to labels, 78, 80–82, 86,
101, 150, 154, 254, 256–259, 261, 270,
277; relationship to zines, 102;
resistance to commercialization,
36–38, 51, 64, 70, 76, 99, 108–9,
130–37, 145–46, 229–43, 262–63,
295, 303–4, 321; sports, 352; student
(*see* student DJs); training, 24, 92,
150, 216, 236, 264, 266–68, 318, 328;
volunteer (*see* volunteer labor);
whiteness, 49, 271, 275, 277, 294;
women, 40, 42, 208, 210
do-it-yourself (DIY), 1–2, 29–30, 42, 44,
92, 94, 104–5, 166, 228, 253, 255, 272
Donohue, Tom, 7
Downs, Bertis, 66
Drayton, William, 114, 336, 339
Drew University. *See* WMNJ
drug use: artists, 53, 68, 96; culture
wars, 93, 161, 233, 288; DJs, 16, 69,
71, 111
Duke University. *See* WKDU

East Carolina University, 123
economic decline, 11, 26, 35, 116, 119
educational radio: class D license (*see*
class D license); culture wars, 165,
179; defense of programming, 136;

differences with public broadcasting,
58, 65, 71, 221; FCC regulations, 70,
133, 136, 354; nationalization of, 57;
new music promotion, 151; origins of,
6, 21; oversight of, 53, 71; purpose of,
35, 71, 133, 151, 179, 190, 203, 220,
278
Elektra/Asylum, 78, 85
Elektra Records, 147, 183
elitism: college education, 95, 129, 315;
college radio, 148, 179, 264, 304, 312,
315; corporate music industry, 92;
diverse programming, 263; DJs, 70,
129, 183, 306, 312; label reputation,
313; station reputation, 126, 271, 286,
352
Embarrassment, 154–58, 227
Emerson College. *See* WERS
engineering schools, 5, 36, 140, 187,
209, 284
Evergreen State College, 99–101, 103,
269, 296. *See also* KAOS

faculty: criticism of, 223–24, 229, 235,
237; educational goals, 225, 242, 326;
involvement in station governance,
57, 59, 61, 115, 201, 204, 207, 221,
227–31, 233, 240–43; opposition to
administration, 326, 334–36, 341,
345; opposition to student governance, 126, 223, 228–29, 232–33, 235,
237–42, 268; radio advisors, 31, 55,
223–26, 231, 233, 237, 239, 339;
support for student governance, 317
Fairness Doctrine, 111, 181, 185–86, 191
Farrell, Dwight, 297–98
Federal Communications Commission
(FCC): class D license (*see* class D
license); effect on college radio, 51,
55–56, 65, 136, 167–69, 176–77, 206,
278, 282, 303; emphasis on professionalization, 56, 59, 136, 164;
Fairness Doctrine, 111, 181, 185–86,
191; fines, 67, 167, 172, 184, 233, 242;
FM signals, 5, 21, 65; free speech, 171,

186; indecency guidelines, 171, 242; investigations, 3, 55, 113, 223, 337; licensing, 24, 53–55, 61, 85, 122, 165, 169, 174, 184, 231, 278, 290, 333, 339, 341, 344–46, 354; obscenity violations, 169–70, 354; petitions, 331, 344; public service requirements, 50, 56, 122, 125, 164, 199; regulations, 3, 56, 70, 122, 133, 163, 165, 167–69, 174–76, 219, 235, 345; resistance to, 164; rules, 57, 206, 283, 321, 332, 336; violations, 53, 111, 165, 167, 169–70, 172, 175, 230–31, 239, 333, 342; wattage allowance, 60, 62, 64, 66, 75, 231, 241

feminism, 7, 77, 89, 165, 210–11, 246

financing, 38, 115, 187, 198

First Amendment, 55, 70, 169, 171, 178, 216, 219, 295

Five Towns College, 343–44

FM: college radio on, 17, 21, 23–25, 36, 60–61, 75, 85, 110, 137, 149, 284, 297, 304, 317, 346; commercial, 18, 23, 49, 60, 63–64, 72, 76, 83, 87, 89–90, 100, 110, 112, 128, 143, 146, 150, 284–85, 294, 297, 304, 306, 309, 319, 321–22; corporatization of, 310; diversity on, 38, 85; freeform, 8, 16, 79, 87, 143; formatting (see radio formats); increased audience on, 23, 25, 220, 267, 318; investment in, 22–23, 53, 64, 122, 187, 319–20; licensing, 6, 16, 21, 24–25, 42, 59, 290; low-power, 58, 355, 357, 364; spectrum allocation, 5–7, 38, 53, 64–65, 146, 160, 175, 180, 194–95, 304, 317–18, 327; versus AM, 317, 321; versus carrier-current, 21–24, 226, 318–321; versus internet, 324, 361; wattage allowance, 38, 85, 285, 357

folk music: block scheduling, 208, 314; collegiate programming, 7, 22, 26, 37, 60, 64, 66, 73, 116, 146, 198, 219, 262, 264; educational, 278; fan base, 18; highbrow, 7, 179, 264

Foothill College. *See* KFJC

Forbes, Jim, 69–71

Fordham University. *See* WFUV

foreign-language programming, 60, 66, 191

Fowler, Mark, 161, 170, 172, 199

Framingham State University, 309

Frank, Thomas, 1–3

Freedman, Ken, 159

freeform: aesthetics, 359–60; commercial, 7–8, 143; community, 364; countercultural influences, 9, 16, 23, 27, 163; ethos, 266, 285, 312, 359–61; FM (*see* FM); Friends of Freeform, 219–20; influence on music, 86, 131, 151, 359, 361, 364; inspiring college radio, 60, 200, 346, 360; jazz, 121; protests to defend, 218–19; rejection of, 46, 217–18, 220, 251; resistance to commercialism, 7–8, 16, 146; scheduling, 26, 77, 79, 213–14, 217–18, 221, 346, 354; support for, 216–17, 219, 237, 251, 346, 364; versus album-oriented radio (AOR), 8, 37, 64, 78; versus public broadcasting, 59, 198–99, 218, 221; volunteer, 58, 216, 218, 251

free speech, 162, 164, 172, 176, 178–79, 182. *See also* First Amendment

Free Speech Movement, 162, 185

frequency change, 64–65

Friends of WBAU, 335, 337–39, 342–44. *See also* WBAU

Fugs, 15

fundraising: activism and, 287; conflict over use, 292, 294; declining donations, 295; DJ training, 239; increased audience and, 193, 265; pledge drives, 61, 359; regulations around, 122; standardized practices in, 217; station independence through, 133; strategies, 115, 319, 343; use against commercial competitors, 302

funk, 18, 35, 48, 150, 267, 274, 299

within Black culture, 114, 282, 284; promotion on college radio, 3, 42, 273–74, 278–81, 284–85, 298–300, 326, 339–40, 345, 355–56; versus rock, 29, 271–72, 274
Hofstra University, 332, 336, 343
Howard, Jerry, 231–32, 238

indecency: culture war battles (see culture wars); effect on professionalization, 56; FCC regulations, 55, 133, 170–71, 321; free speech and, 175, 278; Parents Music Resource Center (PMRC) (see Parents Music Resource Center); station policies, 176, 179, 242; threats to stations, 162
independent distribution, 1, 89, 105, 144, 152–53, 254, 256, 258, 262, 272
independent record labels: A&M (see A&M Records); acquisition by major labels, 242; alternative music, 251; challenges of distribution, 152; effects of deregulation, 351; growth of, 95; I.R.S. (see I.R.S. Records); mainstream breakthrough, 144, 242, 250, 269, 314; market share, 38; Mammoth Records, 266; Matador Records (see Matador Records); Merge Records (see Merge Records); network, 104–5; prioritized on college radio, 152–53, 200, 212, 276, 313; promotion on college radio, 85, 92, 105–7, 130–33, 139–44, 151–54, 251–58, 261–63, 266–72, 358; Rat Cage Records, 97, 104; Recording Industry Association of America (RIAA) membership, 350; record service, 75, 107, 293; relationship to music scenes, 127, 131, 253, 260; Rough Trade (see Rough Trade); Sire (see Sire Records); Sub Pop (see Sub Pop); tensions with major labels, 108, 260; Touch and Go Records (see Touch and Go Records); Twin Tone,

152, 229; value to stations, 75; versus major labels, 141, 253, 256
independent record stores, 85, 275; as alternative market, 94, 96–98, 158; Newbury Comics, 28; part of music scenes, 140, 297–98; radio's sales influence, 74, 77, 79, 86, 89, 142, 144–45, 147, 233, 272; source for records, 28, 30–31, 212, 256; Wuxtry Records, 81, 147
indie music, 18, 296
indie rock: aesthetics, 299; identification with college radio, 9, 271; influenced by college radio, 93–94; mainstream success, 300; part of diverse programming, 278, 298, 308; promotion on college radio, 3, 221, 347, 355; rejection of corporatization, 149; selling out, 273; support for stations, 360–61; versus hip hop, 272; whiteness, 9, 271, 347
inflation, 25, 38, 75, 113
Intercollegiate Broadcasting System, 44, 58, 136, 174
International Women's Day, 210–11
internet broadcasting, 296, 360
internships, 114, 252, 258, 306–7, 318–19, 341, 354
iPod, 302, 350
I.R.S. Records, 80–81, 84–86, 95, 107, 110, 144, 152–53, 250, 253, 258–59, 262
Isquith, Jack, 147, 154, 253

Jackson State University. See WJSU
jazz, 7–8, 22, 191–93
Jefferson Airplane, 16, 26, 163
Jello Biafra, 98, 104, 170, 182, 238
journalism: career goals, 143, 307, 341; curriculum, 189; faculty, 214, 225, 227–28, 240–41; majors, 36, 226, 235, 240; programs, 223–24, 226, 228, 236, 239–43; students, 184–85, 226, 233, 352
Joy Division, 142

KALX: activism, 185; budget cuts, 129; concerns over programming, 129–31; local music scene, 131–32; resistance to commercialization, 302, 304, 323

KANU, 226

KAOS: amateurism, 69, 100–101, 103; campus reputation, 99; programming, 102, 296; origins, 100; *Subterranean Pop*, 101–3

Kautsch, Mike, 228, 235, 240–1

KCMU: Censorship Undermines Radio Station Ethics (CURSE) (*see* CURSE (Censorship Undermines Radio Station Ethics)); funding, 294–95; governance, 213, 291–96; KUOW (*see* KUOW); labels, 294; local music promotion, 272; programming, 291–92, 294–95; obscenity, 206; signal strength, 272

KCR, 324

KCRW, 206

KCSB: campus support, 168, 170, 172, 174; censorship, 163, 168, 172; community relationships, 166, 179; conservative speech, 177–78, 180; confronting homophobia, 178; FCC investigation, 169–71; funding, 167; PMRC, 160, 167, 169, 174; obscenity, 161–62; student speech, 171, 174

KCSN, 317

KEDG, 320. *See also* KSSU

KEXP, 357, 365

KFJC, 50, 99, 363

KGRM, 283–84

KHPR, 57

KIPC, 215

KJHK: DJ training, 223, 227; educational goals, 226–28, 231, 236–37, 239–40, 242; FCC, 239, 242; format, 224, 228–30, 241, 243; funding, 226, 233, 239; internet broadcasting, 296; local music scene, 46, 155, 226–28, 230–231, 233, 238, 241; professionalism, 227, 232, 236, 240–41; relationship to commercial music, 46, 229,
233; signal strength, 226, 242; and struggle over station governance, 223, 230–32, 234–235, 237–38, 240, 242–44. *See also* KANU

KJZZ, 210

KLA: carrier-current, 21, 24; CMJ, 267; labels, 268–69; professional careers, 269; programming, 267–68; signal upgrade, 268

KLCC, 104

Klein, Howie, 135

Knab, Chris, 292–96

KNAC, 98

KOHL, 51, 78

KPFA, 98

KPFK, 170, 217

Kreitzer, Steve, 91, 103–5

KROQ: alternative radio, 23, 37, 146, 316–17; counterculture, 23–24; local music scene, 98; relationship to KUCI, 314; relationship to UCLA, 23–24; shifts in commercial radio, 112, 268

KSAN, 87

KSSU, 320, 324. *See also* KEDG

KTRU: censorship, 352; classical format, 109; decline, 362; elitism, 352; hip-hop, 274–75; independent music, 256–58; internet broadcasting, 351, 354; programming policies, 109–11, 175; relationship to mainstream music, 261; signal strength, 110; station governance, 352–54

KTUH, 56–57, 60

KUCI, 313–16

Ku Klux Klan, 186, 188–189, 223, 228, 282

KUNM: community relationships, 213–14, 216–17, 220; Friends of Freeform, 219; funding, 217, 219; NPR affiliation, 215–17; programming, 214, 218; station governance, 219–21

KUOW, 58, 213, 293. *See also* KCMU

KUSF, 36–37, 87, 111–12, 147, 158–59, 195, 362

mp3 sharing, 350–51, 358, 360–61
MTV: alternative music, 149; career path for college DJs, 141, 149, 151, 159; college radio resistance to, 95, 99, 261, 285; debut, 49; deviation from music, 299; hip-hop, 276; influenced by college radio, 149, 159, 259, 311, 313; marker of mainstream success, 136, 144, 155, 259, 261, 272, 310; new wave, 153; *120 Minutes*, 149; promotional potential, 112; punk, 246, 255, 258; relevance to college radio, 90, 245, 351; replaced by apps, 364; shutting out independent artists, 350; women artists, 211–12, 258; *Yo! MTV Raps*, 149, 327
multiculturalism, 11, 23, 35, 37, 194–95, 293, 326
musical discovery, perceptions, 271; process, 63, 93–94, 151, 351, 355–57, 364; programming decisions, 111–12, 124, 126, 139, 195, 266; record executives, 245, 251–52; zines, 96
music directors: advocacy for college radio, 84, 278, 303; advocacy as a fan, 65, 88, 258, 263–64, 310; creation of position, 77; defining mission and audience, 122–24, 154, 264–65, 267, 306, 313, 320; enforcing professionalism, 111, 148; emphasis on diversity, 263–64, 271, 277, 285; emphasis on independent music, 106–7, 146–48, 152–53, 212, 227, 253, 256, 258, 262–63, 269, 286, 310; encouragement for technical upgrades, 46; facilitating music networks, 77, 79, 88, 142, 148, 153, 227, 252–53, 259; managing FCC compliance, 175, 177; keeping records, 74, 268, 270–71; programming choices, 77, 110, 131, 141, 143, 154, 159, 212, 263, 268–69, 278, 308, 314, 320; relationships to labels, 80, 82, 86, 131, 159, 253–54, 258–59, 267, 270, 277

music festivals, 17, 25, 191, 310, 322
Mussel, Don, 60

Napster, 350–51
narrowcasting, 25, 184
Nash, Pete, 279–81
Nassau Community College, 328, 331–33, 337, 339, 341, 343–44. *See also* WBAU
National Association of Educational Broadcasters (NAEB), 54, 57
National Parent/Teacher Association, 161
National Political Congress of Black Women, 276
National Public Radio (NPR): *All Things Considered*, 215, 226; alternatives to, 84; associated with commercial radio, 294; CPB funding, 190, 215, 217; *Car Talk*, 106; demographic targeting, 208; emphasis on news, 198, 215; institutional relationships, 133, 199, 213, 221, 318; listener funding, 357, 359; *Morning Edition*, 215–16, 218, 319; origins, 8; podcasting, 357; *Prairie Home Companion*, 58, 217; pressure to professionalize, 53, 63, 199, 213, 216, 221; programming on college radio, 8, 60, 106, 146, 193, 198, 217–18, 221, 317, 320; resistance to, 213, 218, 293–94; station conversion to, 8, 57, 59, 72, 195, 213, 215, 354
Native American radio, 218
New Deal, 6, 11, 36
New Order, 49–50, 147, 154
news: alternative, 306; bias, 11; Black, 338; breaks, 227; campus, 71, 124, 184, 280; career path for college DJs, 2, 70, 148, 235, 294, 317; commercial appeal, 18; community, 113, 166, 227, 339, 364; demand for, 215, 218; gay, 287 (*see also* queer programming); local, 58, 60, 237–38, 278, 303, 311, 339; MTV programming, 261; music, 29, 43–44, 159; nationally syndicated,

8, 57–58, 133, 198–99, 207, 213, 215, 217, 221 (*see also* National Public Radio); prank, 223, 320; programming on college radio, 6, 21, 37, 71, 88, 106, 116–17, 123, 184–85, 187, 193, 215, 221, 226, 267, 317, 336, 339; programming versus music, 126; sensationalism, 246; training and experience in, 226, 235–36, 354

new wave: artists, 38, 41, 45, 182; audience, 35, 43, 46, 90, 115, 121, 123–24, 128, 131; creating college radio sound, 25, 34, 46, 61, 64, 73, 125–26, 135; commercial radio play, 112, 146, 149; definition of, 18; DJ advocacy for, 40–41, 80, 127; exposure on college radio, 45, 64, 80, 90, 105–6, 141, 147, 150, 157, 257, 261, 323; labels, 80–81, 88, 135, 254, 350; mainstream success, 31, 99, 105, 107, 131, 141, 145, 153, 159, 257, 261, 309; music scene, 42; resistance to, 37; selling out, 149; versus mainstream rock, 76–77, 106, 142; whiteness, 47, 182

New York University. *See* WNYU

Nirvana, 9, 101, 245–46, 265, 269–70, 285–286, 305, 309–12, 320, 323–24

noncommercial, educational (NCE) licenses, 6

Norian, Ken, 330–33, 336–37, 344

Northeastern University. *See* WNUR

Northwestern University, 63, 146–47, 262, 270. *See also* WNUR

Nowlan, Bob, 106–7

Nunnally, Jeff, 274–75

N.W.A., 278

Oatey, Sue, 331–33, 335, 337

Oberlin College. *See* WOBC

objectivity, 163, 181, 184–87, 189

obscenity: class D licensing and, 55; debates over, 3, 70, 163, 169–70, 276; definition of, 16, 163, 166, 168–70, 176; effects on college radio, 195, 206, 278, 321, 332; FCC investigations, 163, 170; FCC rules, 133, 165, 168–69, 244, 278, 321; FCC violations, 53, 67, 165; free speech and, 164; hardcore and, 111; hip-hop and, 276, 281, 283; legal cases, 70, 133, 162, 164, 166, 170; Parents Music Resource Center (PMRC) (*see* Parents Music Resource Center); policies, 170, 176–77; thrash, 231, 235; threat to morality, 167

Oedipus, 21, 27, 29, 120, 306

Offspring, 314–15

Ohlone College. *See* KOHL

oldies, 21, 77, 126–27, 130, 142, 145, 150, 219, 303

online streaming, 5, 296, 327, 357–58, 361, 364–65

Pacifica Foundation, 7, 16, 18, 56, 165, 175, 288

Pacifica v. FCC (1978), 55

Parents Music Resource Center (PMRC): disparagement of, 166 (*see also* Pork Dukes); framing of consumer information, 167, 276; hearings inspired by, 162, 276; motivations, 165, 172, 183, 276; political support for, 161, 169, 172; response to, 169–70, 178, 181, 195, 278; support for obscenity complaints, 161, 166, 168–69, 174 (*see also* KCSB)

Parker, Jackie, 340–43

passive consumers, 12, 88, 126, 206, 357

Pavitt, Bruce, 100–3, 105–6, 257

Phillips, Tazy, 313–14

playlist rules: affected by advertiser preferences, 154; commercial, 5, 83, 85–88; no-play, 123, 261; prioritizing local and regional music, 152; reflection on music directors, 131; resistance to, 37; tensions over women's music, 212; Top 40, 7; vagueness, 109; versus freeform programming, 199

pledge drives. *See* fundraising

pluralism, 6–7, 12, 23, 36, 48, 193
podcasting, 357–58, 365
Police (artist), 68, 80–81, 84, 93, 153, 228
polka music: community priority, 289, 291, 334; creating station value, 330, 339; DJs, 288–89, 334; tensions over broadcasting, 289, 291, 300. *See also* WHUS
PolyGram, 80, 84, 191, 242, 252–53
Pork Dukes, 166–67, 172, 177, 179
pornography laws, 161, 167
Post, Nathan, 161–62, 166, 168–69, 172, 174
postpunk, 1, 67, 73, 80, 211
power increase: administrator opposition to, 61; administrator support for, 59–60, 67; challenges to, 230, 241; complicated by class D license, 59, 67; considerations involved in, 51, 56–57, 61, 100, 241, 314; downsides of, 60; FCC approval for, 62; pressure to, 54, 87; professionalization and, 72, 110–11, 231; resistance to, 60, 235; student support for, 61, 226
Prince, 47, 107, 141
Princeton University. *See* WPRB American-Arab Anti-Discrimination Committee (ADC)
professionalism: aesthetics, 111; appealing to listeners, 42, 320; associated with commercialism, 100, 233, 304; associated with NPR affiliation, 53, 216, 226; college radio reputation for lacking, 85, 304, 319; emphasis on, 70, 72, 124, 260, 343; enforced on college stations, 15, 240; supporting educational goals, 316; relationship to FCC licensing, 72, 232–33; resistance to, 304; trends toward, 111, 227; versus educational goals, 135, 241
program director: audience management, 45, 115–16, 124, 289, 293; conflict with DJs, 117–18, 124, 176,

218–19; creating station policy, 176–77; defining station goals, 17–18, 26, 37, 46, 89, 110, 129, 131, 150, 153, 170, 202, 210, 217, 235, 260–62, 274, 286, 305, 315, 326; jazz programming, 191; supporting DJs, 27, 92, 116, 214, 296; relationship to music industry, 79, 106, 145, 285, 292, 305, 310, 326; reporting to charts, 45; role in professionalization, 76, 296; students as, 29, 40, 150, 231, 235, 307; versus music directors, 76; women as, 116, 118–19, 208, 307
progressive music, 15, 25, 32, 40–42, 46, 48, 89, 128, 226, 236
Progressive Music Journal. See CMJ
progressive politics, 180, 288
progressive radio, 7, 17–18, 152, 208, 305
progressive rock, 17–18, 23, 25, 28, 38–39, 46–47, 58, 66–67, 115, 122–23, 228
promotional swag, 75, 255, 328, 359
Prusslin, Norm, 177
public affairs programming, 60, 123–24, 126, 130, 166, 178, 187, 208, 215, 336
public broadcasting: Corporation for Public Broadcasting (*see* Corporation for Public Broadcasting); corporatization of, 196; culture wars, 136; divergence from college radio, 8, 58, 65; nationalized, 57; noncommercial radio, 9; professionalism, 9; relationship to college stations, 213, 319, 345; state support for, 216; supplemented by college radio programming, 66
Public Broadcasting Act of 1967, 8, 54, 57
Public Enemy, 114, 195, 275, 277, 280, 285, 326, 349–50
public relations: audience service and, 193; benefits of FM signal, 17, 55, 57; censorship and, 182; experts, 338;

related to NPR affiliation, 199; relationship to diverse programming, 47; university, 42, 184, 189, 192, 195, 203, 222, 247, 320

public service: atrophy of, 225; balance with educational roles, 273, 278, 284; college radio potential for, 11, 247; community, 18, 289; debates over indecency and, 55, 162; FCC requirements, 199, 279; obligations, 113, 115, 133, 189, 247; podcasting as, 358; programming, 38, 40, 88, 100, 322, 328–29; station role providing, 6, 117, 141, 162, 187, 225, 247, 271, 278–79, 330; university commitment to, 6, 22, 194, 322, 365; versus commercial radio, 139

public service announcements (PSA), 7, 39, 56, 111, 219

public sphere, 13, 213, 273, 300, 351, 365

punk: aesthetics, 27, 31, 227, 232, 358; artists, 43–45, 68, 90, 92, 98–99, 104, 166, 312, 352; audience requests, 123–24, 139; Black, 95; Boston scene, 26–27, 29, 157; British scene, 40–41, 68, 98, 104, 166; connections to hip-hop, 42; co-optation of, 2, 246; disruption of music industry, 35; divergences, 226; DIY ethos, 255; DJs, 37, 99, 139, 232, 352–53; educational value, 129; effects on rock, 18, 25, 32, 226–27, 323; emergence of, 26–27, 38; exposure on college radio, 23, 25, 29, 31–33, 37, 40, 45–46, 90, 103, 105, 142, 157, 227; fans, 26; gay, 144, 255; hardcore (see hardcore); Houston scene, 255, 353; indecency charges, 130, 166; New York scene, 29–31, 41, 97 (see also CBGB's); labels, 81, 95, 105, 107, 135, 253–54; late-night scheduling, 37, 92, 274; lesbian, 352; limiting, 177, 268; Los Angeles scene, 23, 41, 99, 314; Orange County scene, 314; politics, 92; popularity, 315; promotion on commercial radio, 24;

San Francisco scene, 135, 254; softening, 170; station identity with, 76, 88, 267, 293; *The Demi-Monde* (*see* WTBS/WMBR); *Turmoil Radio* (*see* WUSB); underground, 25; versus hip-hop, 29; versus mainstream music, 25, 30, 99, 128, 246; versus new wave, 34; wars, 323; Washington, D.C. scene, 231; women, 144, 246, 352

queer programming: activism, 7; DJs, 286–88; indecency charges, 288; lifeline for communities, 7, 287–88; *Out of the Closet*, 287; presenters, 287; *This Way Out*, 287

Rabid, Jack, 31–32, 92, 94–99, 135, 254

radio formats: album-oriented (*see* album-oriented radio); alternative, 323; classic rock, 306; commercial alternative, 9, 243, 297, 309, 364; conservative talk, 11; country, 38; diverse, 303; FM rock, 83; freeform, 16, 105, 146; modern rock, 306, 364; narrowing, 18, 83, 146, 346; repetitive, 61; R&B, 38; segmenting, 25; soft rock, 306

Ramones, 27, 62, 124, 139, 142–43, 155, 229, 352

Ranaldo, Lee, 361

ratings, 87–88, 118, 135, 171, 178, 220, 225, 260, 275, 310, 319, 361

RCA, 80, 146, 148, 258, 294

Reagan, Ronald, 84, 92, 115, 119, 122, 160–61, 167, 172, 180, 194, 198–99, 213

Recording Industry Association of America (RIAA), 167, 350, 360

record library: acquisition, 242; organization, 142, 209, 270, 296; personal DJ, 30, 267; show, 104; specialty, 209–10; station, 26, 120, 215, 274; transfer to university ownership, 333, 336 record rotations: adherence to, 26, 42; album-oriented (*see* album-oriented radio); AM radio, 27; Black artists in, 47–48, 128, 195, 274, 277, 285; classical, 52; college, 78; commercial, 78, 84, 285, 309; control over, 110–11, 126, 136, 142, 146, 150, 159, 190, 229, 266, 278, 296, 298, 310; disagreements over, 87, 159, 261; diversity in, 77, 256, 271, 277, 298, 310; FCC impact, 177; freedom from, 105, 136, 229, 311; hip-hop, 274–75; independent, 107; influence on CMJ, 42, 45; internet, 350; jazz, 78; major label influence, 75, 77, 79, 141, 146, 154, 159; popular artists on, 66–67; PSAs in, 219; rap, 251, 278; regular, 44–45; resistance to, 124; rock, 124, 166; standardization, 69, 72; stale, 286; tracking, 270

record service: disputes over fees, 81–82, 86, 88, 101, 254; free, 194; investment in college radio, 73; reduced, 78; relationship with labels, 77, 84–85, 145, 270, 293

reggae: college radio coverage, 18, 26, 60, 71, 100, 106, 208, 262, 267, 314; charts, 45, 278; defining alternative, 73, 77; freeform, 7; politics, 186; DJs, 334; programming cut, 355; punk influence, 97

religious broadcasting, 6, 113, 199, 361

R.E.M.: association with college radio, 9, 66, 72–73, 81, 90, 129, 133, 140; authenticity, 259; college DJs refusal to play, 229, 262–63; crossover to mainstream, 144, 147, 150–52, 157–58, 250, 256

Replacements, 90, 107, 144, 157, 229, 254

representation: balance, 128; Black, 3, 187; cultural, 10–11, 17, 115, 200, 208, 365; local, 5, 115, 184; media consolidation and, 160; musical, 143, 284;

questions of, 35, 174; student, 126, 216, 239; women, 208

requests: administrative, 68; college concert committees, 78; jazz, 63; new wave, 46; punk, 123, 139; responsiveness to, 77, 124, 139, 163, 237, 261, 310; student, 123; teenagers', 45; via fax, 296

Reznor, Trent, 139–40

Rheins, Carl, 329–37, 343–44, *See also* Adelphi University

Rice University, 108, 111, 175–76, 180, 186, 249, 256–57, 274–75, 352–54. *See also* KTRU

Ridenhour, Carlton D., 113–15

Rio Salado College. *See* KJZZ

Riot Grrrl, 93, 246, 286

Rockpool, 145, 230, 309

Rosenthal, Josh, 251–53

Rough Trade, 44, 80, 90, 105, 144, 256

royalties, 254, 296, 347, 351, 359–60

Run-D.M.C., 274, 326, 336

Sacramento State University, 317–18, 320, 324. *See also* KEDG

Salem State University, 307, 309

San Diego State University, 324. *See also* KCR

Santa Monica College. *See* KCRW

Santoro, Henry, 50, 306

Sarko, Anita, 37, 40–42

Schaap, Phil, 191

Schmidt, John, 328–29, 336–37, 339, 344–45

Scott, Sharon, 285–86, 364

Scott-Heron, Gil, 78, 79, 240

selling out, 13, 141, 149, 154, 212, 239, 245, 247, 272–73, 303, 307, 316, 321–22, 333

Seton Hall University. *See* WSOU

seven-inch albums, 1, 90, 104, 156, 212, 221, 265

Siemering, Bill, 193–95

Silber, John, 334, 345

WXYC: community service, 126–27; diverse programming, 125, 128, 263, 267, 271; DJs, 263–64, 267, 271; elitism, 264; freeform radio, 266; funding, 122–23; institutional relevance, 123–26, 265; local music scene, 263, 266; professionalism, 124; promotion of progressive rock, 123–24, 127, 265; station governance, 123, 125–27, 265; student audience, 123–25, 127–28, 263, 265; transfer to FM signal, 122

WZBC, 29, 147, 356

XTC, 111–12, 226

Yates, Don, 292–94

Yohannon, Tim, 98–99

Zappa, Frank, 49, 56, 58, 139, 167, 218, 223

zines: *Big Takeover, 96; Coast to Coast,* 97; *Damaged Goods,* 97; *Just Another Rag,* 97; *Maxmimum Rocknroll,* 93, 98, 104–5, 131, 136; *Sounds,* 97; *Trouser Press,* 97